COVERS ALL EXAM OBJECTIVES

100% CERTIFIED

Syngress knows what passing the exam means to you and to your career. And we know that you are often financing your own training and certification; therefore, you need a system that is comprehensive, affordable, and effective.

Boasting one-of-a-kind integration of text, DVD-quality instructor-led training, and Web-based exam simulation, the Syngress Study Guide & DVD Training System guarantees 100% coverage of exam objectives.

The Syngress Study Guide & DVD Training System includes:

- **Study Guide with 100% coverage of exam objectives** By reading this study guide and following the corresponding objective list, you can be sure that you have studied 100% of the exam objectives.
- **Instructor-led DVD** This DVD provides almost two hours of virtual classroom instruction.
- **Web-based practice exams** Just visit us at **www.syngress.com/certification** to access a complete exam simulation.

Thank you for giving us the opportunity to serve your certification needs. And be sure to let us know if there's anything else we can do to help you get the maximum value from your investment. We're listening.

www.syngress.com/certification

SYNGRESS®

SYNGRESS®

COVERS ALL 100% CERTIFIED EXAM OBJECTIVES

MCSE

Designing Security for a Windows Server 2003 Network: Exam 70-298

Elias N. Khnaser

Susan Snedaker

Chris Peiris

Rob Amini

Laura E. Hunter Technical Editor

KEY	SERIAL NUMBER
001	JFE498MVVF
002	PO98KLSSSY
003	JKRED279I9
004	PLGEPL9989
005	CVPL23GHBV
006	VBPLOP93346
007	JDDD43WD3E
008	2987JJGGMK
009	629DJTKK88
010	ITJLLKR45W

PUBLISHED BY
Syngress Publishing, Inc.
800 Hingham Street
Rockland, MA 02370

MCSE Designing Security for a Windows Server 2003 Network: Exam 70-298 Study Guide & DVD Training System

Printed in the United States of America
1 2 3 4 5 6 7 8 9 0
ISBN: 1-932266-55-0

Acquisitions Editor: Catherine B. Nolan
Technical Editor: Laura E. Hunter
Page Layout and Art: Patricia Lupien
Cover Designer: Michael Kavish
Copy Editor: Darlene Bordwell, Beth A. Roberts
Indexer: Nara Wood

Distributed by O'Reilly & Associates in the United States and Jaguar Book Group in Canada.

Acknowledgments

We would like to acknowledge the following people for their kindness and support in making this book possible.

Syngress books are now distributed in the United States by O'Reilly & Associates, Inc. The enthusiasm and work ethic at ORA is incredible and we would like to thank everyone there for their time and efforts to bring Syngress books to market: Tim O'Reilly, Laura Baldwin, Mark Brokering, Mike Leonard, Donna Selenko, Bonnie Sheehan, Cindy Davis, Grant Kikkert, Opol Matsutaro, Lynn Schwartz, Steve Hazelwood, Mark Wilson, Rick Brown, Leslie Becker, Jill Lothrop, Tim Hinton, Kyle Hart, Sara Winge, C. J. Rayhill, Peter Pardo, Leslie Crandell, Valerie Dow, Regina Aggio, Pascal Honscher, Preston Paull, Susan Thompson, Bruce Stewart, Laura Schmier, Sue Willing, Mark Jacobsen, Betsy Waliszewski, Dawn Mann, Kathryn Barrett, and to all the others who work with us.

The incredibly hard working team at Elsevier Science, including Jonathan Bunkell, AnnHelen Lindeholm, Duncan Enright, David Burton, Rosanna Ramacciotti, Robert Fairbrother, Miguel Sanchez, Klaus Beran, and Rosie Moss for making certain that our vision remains worldwide in scope.

David Buckland, Wendi Wong, Daniel Loh, Marie Chieng, Lucy Chong, Leslie Lim, Audrey Gan, and Joseph Chan of STP Distributors for the enthusiasm with which they receive our books.

Kwon Sung June at Acorn Publishing for his support.

Jackie Gross, Gayle Voycey, Alexia Penny, Anik Robitaille, Craig Siddall, Iolanda Miller, Jane Mackay, and Marie Skelly at Jackie Gross & Associates for all their help and enthusiasm representing our product in Canada.

Lois Fraser, Connie McMenemy, Shannon Russell, and the rest of the great folks at Jaguar Book Group for their help with distribution of Syngress books in Canada.

David Scott, Tricia Wilden, Marilla Burgess, Annette Scott, Geoff Ebbs, Hedley Partis, Bec Lowe, and Mark Langley of Woodslane for distributing our books throughout Australia, New Zealand, Papua New Guinea, Fiji Tonga, Solomon Islands, and the Cook Islands.

Winston Lim of Global Publishing for his help and support with distribution of Syngress books in the Philippines.

To all the folks at Malloy who have made things easy for us and especially to Beth Drake and Joe Upton.

Technical Editor & DVD Presenter

Laura E. Hunter (CISSP, MCSE, MCT, MCDBA, MCP, MCP+I, CCNA, A+, Network+, iNet+, CNE-4, CNE-5) is a Senior IT Specialist with the University of Pennsylvania, where she provides network planning, implementation, and troubleshooting services for various business units and schools within the university. Her specialties include Microsoft Windows NT and 2000 design and implementation, troubleshooting, and security topics. As an "MCSE Early Achiever" on Windows 2000, Laura was one of the first in the country to renew her Microsoft credentials under the Windows 2000 certification structure. Laura's previous experience includes a position as the Director of Computer Services for the Salvation Army and as the LAN administrator for a medical supply firm. She also operates as an independent consultant for small businesses in the Philadelphia metropolitan area and is a regular contributor to the TechTarget family of Web sites.

Laura has previously contributed to the Syngress Publishing's *Configuring Symantec Antivirus, Corporate Edition* (ISBN 1-931836-81-7). She has also contributed to several other exam guides in the Syngress Windows Server 2003 MCSE/MCSA DVD Guide & Training System series as a DVD presenter, contributing author, and technical reviewer. Laura was recently awarded the prestigious MVP award as a Microsoft "Most Valued Professional."

Laura holds a bachelor's degree from the University of Pennsylvania and is a member of the Network of Women in Computer Technology, the Information Systems Security Association, and InfraGard, a cooperative undertaking between the U.S. Government and other participants dedicated to increasing the security of United States critical infrastructures.

Contributors

Rob Amini (MCSE, MCDBA, MCT) is currently a systems manager for Marriott International in Salt Lake City, Utah. He has a bachelor's degree in computer science and has been breaking and fixing the darned machines since the Atari 800 was considered state of the art. In 1993 he began his professional career by fixing quirky IBM mainframes and various unix-flavored boxes. Then, after a long stint as a technician and systems admin, he gained fabled notoriety as a pun-wielding Microsoft trainer. Rob has continued as an instructor for more than three years and although teaching is his first love, he tends to enjoy technical writing more than a well-adjusted person should. When actually not working with and programming a variety of electronic gizmos, Rob enjoys spending every minute he can with his beautiful wife Amy and the rest of his supportive family. Finally, Rob would like to thank his dad, who has always been a wonderful father and great example to him.

Elias N. Khnaser (CCEA, MCSE, CCNA, CCA, MCP + I) is currently the Server Based Computing Architect for General Growth Properties. General Growth Properties is headquartered in Chicago, IL and is the second largest shopping mall owner and operator in the world, counting over 160 malls worldwide and growing. Elias provides senior-level network design, implementation, and troubleshooting of Citrix and Microsoft technologies for the company. Elias is also a contributing author at Techrepublic.com. Prior to working for General Growth Properties, Elias was a Senior Network Engineer at Solus in Skokie, IL, consulting for companies like Motorola, Prime Group Realty Trust, Black Entertainment Television (BET), Dominick's Corporate, and Total Living Network (TLN Channel 38).

Elias would like to acknowledge Steve Amidei and James Smith of General Growth Properties for their infinite support; to Stuart Gabel and Nial Keegan of Solus who opened the door of opportunity; to his friend Joseph K. Eshoo for all his help and encouragement, and to John Sheesley of Techrepublic.com for helping him write better articles. To his friends and family worldwide, this is for you! Finally, Elias would like to dedicate this work to his parents, especially his mother, and to the person that means everything in his life, Nadine Sawaya "Didi", for loving and supporting him.

Chris Peiris (MVP, MIT) works as an independent consultant for .NET and EAI implementations. His latest role is with the Department of Employment and Workplace Relations (Australia) as a Systems Architect. He also lectures on Distributed Component Architectures (.NET, J2EE & CORBA) at Monash University, Caulfield, Victoria, Australia. He has been awarded the title "Microsoft Most Valuable Professional" (MVP) for his contributions to .NET technologies. Chris is designing and developing Microsoft solutions since 1995. His expertise lies in developing scalable, high-performance solutions for financial institutions, G2G, B2B and media groups. Chris has written many articles, reviews and columns for various online publications including 15Seconds, Developer Exchange, and Wrox Press. He co-authored the book *C# Web Service with .NET Remoting and ASP.NET* by Wrox Press. It was followed by *C# for Java Programmers* (Syngress, ISBN: 1-931836-54-X), and *MCSA/MCSE Managing and Maintaining a Windows Server 2003 Environment: Exam 70-290* (Syngress, ISBN: 1-932266-60-7). Chris frequently presents at professional developer conferences on Microsoft technologies.

His core skills are C++, C#, XML Web Services, Java, .NET, DNA, MTS, Data Warehousing, WAP, and SQL Server. Chris has a Bachelor of Computing, Bachelor of Business (Accounting), and Masters of Information Technology degrees. He is currently under taking a PhD on "Web Service Management Framework". He lives with his family in Civic, Canberra, ACT, Australia.

Chris dedicates this book to Kushanthi. In his own words "thanks for the love, patience, advice, encouragement and your kindnes… and most of all, thanks for putting up with me and being a true friend"

Susan Snedaker (MCP, MCT, MCSE+I, MBA) is a strategic business consultant specializing in business planning, development, and operations. She has served as author, editor, curriculum designer, and instructor during her career in the computer industry. Susan holds a master of business administration and a bachelor of arts in management from the University of Phoenix. She has held key executive and technical positions at Microsoft, Honeywell, Keane, and Apta Software. Susan has contributed chapters to five books on Microsoft Windows 2000 and 2003. Susan currently provides strategic business, management and technology consulting services (www.virtualteam.com).

MCSE 70-298 Exam Objectives Map and Table of Contents

All of Microsoft's published objectives for the MCSE 70-298 Exam are covered in this book. To help you easily find the sections that directly support particular objectives, we've listed all of the exam objectives below, and mapped them to the Chapter number in which they are covered. We've also assigned numbers to each objective, which we use in the subsequent Table of Contents and again throughout the book to identify objective coverage. In some chapters, we've made the judgment that it is probably easier for the student to cover objectives in a slightly different sequence than the order of the published Microsoft objectives. By reading this study guide and following the corresponding objective list, you can be sure that you have studied 100% of Microsoft's MCSE 70-298 Exam objectives.

Objective Map

Objective Number	Objective	Chapter Number
1	**Creating the Conceptual Design for Network Infrastructure Security by Gathering and Analyzing Business and Technical Requirements**	1, 5
1.1	Analyze business requirement for designing security. Considerations include existing policies and procedures, sensitivity of data, cost, legal requirements, end-user impact, interoperability, maintainability, scalability, and risk.	1
1.1.1	Analyze existing security policies and procedures.	1
1.1.2	Analyze the organizational requirements for securing data.	1
1.1.3	Analyze the security requirements of different types of data.	1
1.1.4	Analyze risks to security	1
1.2	Design a framework for designing and implementing security. The framework should include prevention, detection, isolation, and recovery.	1

Objective Number	Objective	Chapter Number
1.2.1	Predict threats to your network from internal and external sources.	1
1.2.2	Design a process for responding to incidents.	1
1.2.3	Design segmented networks.	5
1.2.4	Design a process for recovering services.	1
1.3	Analyze technical constraints when designing security.	1
1.3.1	Identify capabilities of the existing infrastructure.	1
1.3.2	Identify technology limitations.	1
1.3.3	Analyze interoperability constraints.	1
2	**Creating the Logical Design for Network Infrastructure Security**	**3,4**
2.1	Design a public key infrastructure (PKI) that uses Certificate Services.	3
2.1.1	Design a certification authority (CA) hierarchy implementation. Types include geographical, organizational, and trusted.	3
2.1.2	Design enrollment and distribution processes.	3
2.1.3	Establish renewal, revocation and auditing processes.	3
2.1.4	Design security for CA servers.	3
2.2	Design a logical authentication strategy.	3
2.2.1	Design certificate distribution.	3
2.2.2	Design forest and domain trust models.	4
2.2.3	Design security that meets interoperability requirements.	4
2.2.4	Establish account and password requirements 8 for security.	
2.3	Design security for network management.	4
2.3.1	Manage the risk of managing networks.	4
2.3.2	Design the administration of severs by using common administration tools. Tools include Microsoft Management Console (MMC) Terminal Server, Remote Desktop for Administration, Remote Assistance, and Telnet.	4

Objective Number	Objective	Chapter Number
2.3.3	Design security for Emergency Management Services.	4
2.4	Design a security update infrastructure.	4
2.4.1	Design a Software Update Services (SUS) infrastructure.	4
2.4.2	Design Group Policy to deploy software updates.	4
2.4.3	Design a strategy for identifying computers that are not at the current patch level.	4
3	**Creating the Physical Design for Network Infrastructure Security**	**2,5,6,7**
3.1	Design network infrastructure security.	5
3.1.1	Specify the required protocols for a firewall configuration.	5
3.1.2	Design IP filtering.	5
3.1.3	Design an IPSec policy.	5
3.1.4	Secure a DNS implementation.	5
3.1.5	Design security for data transmissions.	5
3.2	Design security for wireless networks.	5
3.2.1	Design public and private wireless LANs.	5
3.2.2	Design 802.1x authentication for wireless networks.	5
3.3	Design user authentication for Internet Information Services (IIS).	5,6
3.3.1	Design user authentication for a Web site by using certificates.	6
3.3.2	Design user authentication for a Web site by using IIS authentication.	6
3.3.3	Design user authentication for a Web site by using RADIUS for IIS authentication.	6
3.4	Design security for Internet Information Services (IIS).	6
3.4.1	Design security for Web sites that have different technical requirements by enabling only the minimum required services.	6

Objective Number	Objective	Chapter Number
3.4.2	Design a monitoring strategy for IIS.	6
3.4.3	Design an IIS baseline that is based on business requirements.	6
3.4.4	Design a content management strategy for updating an IIS server.	6
3.5	Design security for communication between networks.	7
3.5.1	Select protocols for VPN access.	7
3.5.2	Design VPN connectivity.	7
3.5.3	Design demand-dial routing between internal networks.	7
3.6	Design security for communication with external organizations.	7
3.6.1	Design a extranet infrastructure.	7
3.6.2	Design a strategy for cross-certification of Certificate Services.	7
3.7	Design security for servers that have specific roles. Roles include domain controller, network infrastructure server, file server, IIS server, terminal server, and POP3 mail server.	2
3.7.1	Define a baseline security template for all systems.	2
3.7.2	Create a plan to modify baseline security templates according to role.	2
4	**Designing an Access Control Strategy for Data**	**8,9**
4.1	Design an access control strategy for directory services.	8
4.1.1	Create a delegation strategy.	8
4.1.2	Analyze auditing requirements.	8
4.1.3	Design the appropriate group strategy for accessing resources.	8
4.1.4	Design a permission structure for directory service objects	8
4.2	Design an access control strategy for files and folders.	9

Objective Number	Objective	Chapter Number
4.2.1	Design a strategy for the encryption and decryption of files and folders.	9
4.2.2	Design a permission structure for files and folders.	9
4.2.3	Design security for a backup and recovery strategy.	9
4.2.4	Analyze auditing requirements.	9
4.3	Design an access control strategy for the registry.	9
4.3.1	Design a permission structure for registry objects.	9
4.3.2	Analyze auditing requirements.	9
5	**Creating the Physical Design for Client Infrastructure Security**	**10**
5.1	Design a client authentication strategy	10
5.1.1	Analyze authentication requirements.	10
5.1.2	Establish account and password security requirements.	10
5.2	Design a security strategy for client remote access.	10
5.2.1	Design remote access policies.	10
5.2.2	Design access to internal resources.	10
5.2.3	Design an authentication provider and accounting strategy for remote network access by using Internet Authentication Service (IAS).	10
5.3	Design a strategy for security client computers. Considerations include desktop and portable computers.	10
5.3.1	Design a strategy for hardening client operating systems.	10
5.3.2	Design a strategy for restricting user access to operating system features.	10

Contents

Foreword **xxxi**

Chapter 1 Designing a Secure Network Framework **1**

Introduction 2

1.1 Analyzing Business Requirements for Security Design 3

1.1.1 Analyzing Existing Security Policies and Procedures 3

Acceptable Use Policies 4

Privacy versus Security 5

Security versus Usability 6

1.1.2 Determining Requirements for Securing Data 6

The CIA Triad 6

1.1.4 Analyzing Current Security Practices 8

Using Resultant Set of Policies 9

Recognizing Internal Security Threats 12

1.2 Designing a Framework for Implementing Security 13

1.2.1 Predicting Threats to Your Network 13

Recognizing External Threats 15

What Motivates External Attackers? 22

Implementing Risk Analysis 23

Addressing Risks to the Corporate Network 23

1.1.3 Analyzing Security Requirements for Different Types of Data 25

1.2.2 Responding to Security Incidents 26

Recognizing Attack Indicators 27

Creating an Incident Response Plan 28

1.2.4 Recovering Network Services After an Attack 31

1.3 Analyzing Technical Constraints when Designing Security 31

1.3.1 Recognizing Capabilities of the Existing Infrastructure 32
1.3.2 Identifying Technology Limitations 34
1.3.3 Analyzing Interoperability Constraints 34
Interoperability with MIT Kerberos 35
Integrating UNIX DNS with Windows Server 2003 37
Summary of Exam Objectives 39
Exam Objectives Fast Track 40
Exam Objectives Frequently Asked Questions 41
Self Test 42
Self Test Quick Answer Key 48

Chapter 2 Securing Servers Based on Function 49

Introduction 50
3.7.1 Defining a Baseline Security Template 50
Best Practices for Security Templates 52
Windows Server 2003 Predefined Security Templates 53
Default Security (setup security.inf) 55
Reapplying Default Security Settings 56
Domain Controller Default Security (DC security.inf) 56
Compatible (compat*.inf) 57
Secure (secure*.inf) 57
Highly Secure (hisec*.inf) 59
System Root Security (rootsec.inf) 62
No Terminal Server User SID (notssid.inf) 63
Configuring Security Templates 66
Account Policies 67
Local Policies 69
Event Log 71
Restricted Groups 72
System Services 72
Registry 73
File System 74
Configuring Security for Down-Level Clients 74
Deploying Security Templates 75
Using Group Policy to Deploy Security Settings 76
Reviewing the Result of Security Policy Settings 82

Using Security Configuration and Analysis to Review Security Settings 85
Using the secedit.exe Command-Line Tool 88
secedit configure 88
secedit analyze 90
secedit import 91
secedit export 92
secedit validate 93
secedit generaterollback 93
secedit refreshpolicy Replaced by gpupdate 94
Deploying Security Using Scripts 95
3.7 Design Security for Servers that Have Specific Roles 99
Common Server Roles 100
Server Security Best Practices 102
Configuring Security for Domain Controllers 106
Common Threats to Domain Controllers 107
Audit Backup and Restore Events 108
Restrict Access to Removable Media 108
Restricting Anonymous Access 109
Digitally Signing Authentication Traffic 110
Securing the Internet Information Server (IIS) Role 112
Using "Configure Your Server" to Set Up IIS 113
Basic Security for IIS 114
Using URLScan and IISLockdown 114
Configuring Security for POP3 Mail Servers 116
Security Levels 117
Authentication Methods 118
Securing Other Network Roles 118
Securing Network Infrastructure Servers 118
Securing DHCP Servers 120
Securing DNS Servers 120
WINS Servers 122
Securing File, Print, and Member Servers 123
Securing Terminal Servers 123
Securing Remote Access Servers 125
Streaming Media Server 128

3.7.2 Modifying Baseline Security Templates According to Role 129
Applying Security Across the Enterprise 132
Summary of Exam Objectives 138
Exam Objectives Fast Track 140
Exam Objectives Frequently Asked Questions 142
Self Test 143
Self Test Quick Answer Key 149

Chapter 3 Designing a Secure Public Key Infrastructure 151

Introduction 152
2.1 Designing a Public Key Infrastructure 152
Understanding PKI 155
2.1.1 Designing a Certification Authority Implementation 158
Geographical Hierarchy 162
Organizational Hierarchy 163
Network Trust Hierarchy 164
2.2 Designing a Logical Authentication Strategy 165
2.1.4 Designing Security for CA Servers 167
Common Threats Against Certificate Services 167
Securing an Enterprise Hierarchy 169
Securing a Stand-Alone CA 170
2.2.2 Designing Certificate Distribution 172
2.1.2 Designing Enrollment and Distribution 177
2.1.2 Approving Certificates by CA Administrators 179
2.1.3 Revoking Certificates by CA Administrators 180
2.1.3 Establishing Renewal and Auditing 181
Summary of Exam Objectives 185
Exam Objectives Fast Track 186
Exam Objectives Frequently Asked Questions 187
Self Test 188
Self Test Quick Answer Key 192

Chapter 4 Securing the Network Management Process 193

Introduction 194
2.3 Securing the Network Management Process 194

2.3.1 Managing the Risks of Network Administration 195
Security Policies for Administrators and IT Personnel 197
Delegating Authority Securely 197
2.3.2 Securing Common Administrative Tools 200
Microsoft Management Console 201
Terminal Server 201
Remote Desktop for Administration 205
Remote Assistance 207
Telnet 208
2.3.3 Designing Security for Emergency Management Services 208
2.4 Designing a Security Update Infrastructure 210
2.4.1 Designing a Software Update Service Infrastructure 211
2.4.2 Using Group Policy to Deploy Software Updates 213
2.4.3 Design a Strategy for Identifying Computers That Are Not at the Current Patch Level 215
2.2.2 Designing Trust Relationships Between Domains and Forests 217
Designing Forest and Domain Trust Models 221
Default Trust Relationships 222
External Trusts 222
Selecting the Scope of Authentication for Users 223
Realm Trusts 224
Shortcut Trusts 225
2.2.3 Designing Security for Interoperability 226
Summary of Exam Objectives 231
Exam Objectives Fast Track 232
Exam Objectives Frequently Asked Questions 233
Self Test 234
Self Test Quick Answer Key 239
Chapter 5 Securing Network Services and Protocols 241
Introduction 242
3.1 Designing Network Infrastructure Security 243
Common Types of Attacks 247
Assessing Risk for Network Services 249
IPSec Overview 251

Security Associations 252
Phase I Security Association 252
Phase II Security Association 256
IPSec Modes 256
IPSec Protocols 257
Authentication Header 260
Encapsulated Security Payload 261
The IPSec Process 263
IPSec Policies Overview 264
Default IPSec Policies 264
IPSec Rules 264
Predefined Filter Lists 269
Predefined Filter Actions 270
IP Packet Filtering 272
netsh Commands 272
How IPSec Policy Is Applied 273
Assigning Domain-Based IPSec Policy 275
Exporting and Importing IPSec Policy 276
Assigning OU-Based IPSec Policy 277
Assigning Local IPSec Policy 277
IPSec Driver Modes 278
IPSec Best Practices 282
3.1.3 Designing IPSec Policies 284
Configuring IPSec Policy 285
Assigning IPSec Policy 285
3.1.2 Designing IP Filtering 289
3.1.1 Configuring a Firewall Configuration 292
Securing DNS 293
Common Threats to DNS 294
DNS Namespace 295
Single Namespace 295
Delegated Namespace 295
Internal Namespace 295
Segmented Namespace 296
Securing the Namespace 296
DNS Server Service 297

DNS Zones 300
DNS Resource Records 302
DNS Clients 303
3.1.5 Designing Security for Data Transmission 303
SSL/TLS 303
S/MIME 309
SMB Signing 309
Port Authentication for Switches 312
1.2.3 Using Segmented Networks 313
3.2 Design Security for Wireless Networks 313
Types of Wireless Networks 314
Brief Wireless History 315
Threats to Wireless Networks 317
Quick Review of PKI and RADIUS/IAS 319
Public Key Infrastructure 319
Remote Authentication Dial-In User Service and Internet Authentication Service 320
Designing Wireless LANs 321
3.2.1 Designing WLAN Network Infrastructure 321
Active Directory 322
DHCP Configuration 326
DNS Configuration 327
Public Key Infrastructure 327
RADIUS/IAS 328
3.2.2 Designing Authentication for Wireless Networks 328
802.11 Identity Verification and Authentication 328
802.11 Wired Equivalency Privacy (WEP) Encryption 329
802.1X Authentication 329
802.1X and Extensible Authentication Protocol 329
IAS Support for 802.1X Authentication 331
802.1X Group Policy Settings 331
Selecting User or Computer-Based Authentication 334
Designing and Testing Wireless Access Infrastructure 336

Summary of Exam Objectives 339
Exam Objectives Fast Track 340
Exam Objectives Frequently Asked Questions 342
Self Test 344
Self Test Quick Answer Key 350

Chapter 6 Securing Internet Information Services 351

Introduction 352
3.3 Designing User Authentication for IIS 353
3.3.1 Designing Certificate Authentication 356
Directory Service Mapping 356
One-to-One Mapping 357
Many-to-One Mapping 359
3.3.2 Designing Windows Logon Authentication 362
Anonymous Authentication 362
Basic Authentication 364
Digest Authentication 366
Integrated Windows Authentication 367
3.3.3 Designing RADIUS Authentication 369
Using the Internet Authentication Server 370
Securing the RADIUS Implementation 373
3.4 Designing Security for IIS 375
3.4.1 Securing IIS Installations 376
Risks to IIS Servers and How to Harden IIS Against Them 381
Securing FTP 383
Securing NNTP 384
Securing SMTP 385
New Security Features in IIS 6.0 385
3.4.2 Designing a Monitoring Strategy for IIS 389
3.4.3 Creating a Monitoring Baseline 390
Identifying a Security Incident 398
3.4.4 Design a Content Management Strategy for Updating an IIS Server 399
Summary of Exam Objectives 401
Exam Objectives Fast Track 402
Exam Objectives Frequently Asked Questions 403

Self Test 405
Self Test Quick Answer Key 408

Chapter 7 Securing VPN and Extranet Communications 409

Introduction 410
3.5 Designing Security for Communication Between Networks 411
3.5.1 Using Windows Server 2003 as a Router 411
Static Routes 415
RIP 416
Open Shortest Path First 419
3.5.3 Designing Demand Dial Routing between Internal Networks 420
3.5.2 Designing VPN Connectivity 423
Selecting Protocols for VPN Access 425
PPTP 425
L2TP 433
New Windows Server 2003 VPN Features 438
Using Remote Access Policies 439
Designing Routing between Internal Networks 442
3.6/3.6.1 Designing an Extranet Infrastructure 443
3.6.2 Cross-Certification of Certificate Services 444
Summary of Exam Objectives 445
Exam Objectives Fast Track 446
Exam Objectives Frequently Asked Questions 447
Self Test 448
Self Test Quick Answer Key 452

Chapter 8 Securing Active Directory 453

Introduction 454
4.1 Designing an Access Control Strategy for Directory Services 454
Analyzing Risks to Directory Services 457
Assigning Rights and Permissions 458
Considerations for Using Administrative and Service Accounts 460
Designing Effective Password Policies 462

2.2.4 Establishing Account Security Policies 463
User Rights Assignments 463
Using Restricted Groups 470
Creating a Kerberos Policy 472
2.2.4 Establishing Password Security 474
Setting Password Complexity Requirements 477
Creating an Account Lockout Policy 478
Auditing User Account Activity 480
Creating an Auditing Policy 482
Auditing Logon Events 482
Auditing Object Access 484
4.1.2 Analyzing Auditing Data 485
4.1.1 Creating a Delegation Strategy 487
Service Administrators and Data Administrators 487
Isolation and Autonomy 487
Selecting a Delegation Structure 488
4.1.3 Designing the Appropriate Group Strategy for Accessing Resources 490
4.1.4 Designing a Permission Structure for Data 490
Using Global Groups 492
Using Domain Local Groups 492
Using Universal Groups 492
Combining and Nesting Groups 493
Domain and Forest Functional Levels 494
Summary of Exam Objectives 496
Exam Objectives Fast Track 499
Exam Objectives Frequently Asked Questions 500
Self Test 501
Self Test Quick Answer Key 506
Chapter 9 Securing Network Resources 507
Introduction 508
4.2 Designing an Access Control Strategy for Files and Folders 508
Analyzing Risks to Data 509
Physical Loss of Data 509
Data Corruption 510
Viruses, Worms, and Other Software Attacks 510

Security Breaches 511
Auditing Practices 511
Reviewing Access Control and Access Control Lists 511
Permissions 512
User Rights 513
Object Auditing 513
Access Control Lists 513
Access Control Entry 513
Groups 515
Security Groups 515
Access to Resources 516
User/ACL 516
Account Group/ACL (AG/ACL) 517
Account Group/Resource Group 518
Role-Based Authorization 519
Selecting Domain Local Groups or Local Groups as Resource Groups 519
Working with Security Groups 521
Defining Security Group Creation Policy 521
Defining a Security Group Request Process 522
Defining a Security Group Naming Policy 522
Defining a Security Group Nesting Policy 524
Defining a Security Group Retirement Policy 526
Delegating Security Group Maintenance 529
Delegating Account and Resource Group Maintenance 529
4.2.4/4.3.2 Analyzing Auditing Requirements 534
Logon Event 535
Account Logon Event 537
Directory Service Access Event 538
Privilege Use Event 538
Object Access Event 539
System Events 539
Process Tracking Events 540
Policy Change Events 540
4.3 Design an Access Control Strategy for the Registry 541

4.3.1 Design a Permission Structure for Registry Objects 552
Designing the Encrypted File System 553
EFS Behavior 555
EFS Best Practices 556
Certificate Storage 564
Certificate Enrollment and Renewal 565
Using *cipher.exe* 566
4.2.1 Creating a Strategy for the Encryption and Decryption of Files and Folders 571
Increasing User Awareness 571
Configuring File Recovery Agents 574
Removing Recovery Agent Policy 579
Recovering Files 580
Backing Up Keys 580
Disabling EFS 587
Third-Party Encryption Options 588
4.2.3 Designing Security for a Backup and Recovery Strategy 589
Securing the Backup and Restore Process 589
Designing a Secure Backup Process 592
Best Practices for Backups 594
Creating an Automated System Recovery Backup Set 596
Disaster Recovery Best Practices 598
Securing Emergency Management Services 601
Console Redirection 602
Special Administration Console Environment 605
!Special Administration Console Environment 606
Enabling Emergency Management Services 606
Headless Servers 607
Terminal Concentrators 607
Uninterruptible Power Supplies 607
Securing the Remote Management Process 608
Out-of-Band Security 608
Best Practices for Securing Emergency Management Services 609
Securing the Recovery Console 610
Specifying Startup Options for Computers 612

Summary of Exam Objectives 615
Exam Objectives Fast Track 617
Exam Objectives Frequently Asked Questions 619
Self Test 621
Self Test Quick Answer Key 626
Chapter 10 Securing Network Clients 627
Introduction 628
5.3 Securing Client Computers 628
5.3.1 Hardening Client Operating Systems 629
Minimizing Attack Vectors 629
Creating an Anti-Virus Protection Scheme 630
Enabling Patch Management 631
Securing Laptop Computers 634
5.3.2 Restricting User Access to Operating System Features 637
5.1 Designing a Client Authentication Strategy 639
5.1.1/5.1.2 Analyzing Authentication Requirements 640
Network Authentication 641
Securing User Accounts 645
Securing Account Naming Conventions 646
Choosing Authentication Protocols 646
Kerberos 647
NTLM Authentication 648
Digest Authentication 650
SSL/TLS 650
5.2 Designing a Secure Remote Access Plan 651
Choosing a Remote Access Method 652
Selecting a Remote Access Protocol 652
5.2.1 Designing Remote Access Policies 654
Understanding the Elements of a Remote Access Policy 655
5.2.2 Providing Access to Internal Network Resources 662
5.2.3 Using Internet Authentication Service 662
Authentication Protocols Supported by IAS 663
Using IAS for Dial-Up and VPN 665
Using IAS for Wireless Access 669

Using Network Access Quarantine Control 670
Remote Access Account Lockout 670
Summary of Exam Objectives 671
Exam Objectives Fast Track 672
Exam Objectives Frequently Asked Questions 673
Self Test 674
Self Test Quick Answer Key 681
Self Test Appendix 683
Index 759

Foreword

This book's primary goal is to help you prepare to take and pass Microsoft's exam number 70-298, *Designing Security for a Microsoft Windows Server 2003 Network*. Our secondary purpose in writing this book is to provide exam candidates with knowledge and skills that go beyond the minimum requirements for passing the exam, and help to prepare them to work in the real world of Microsoft computer networking.

What is Exam 70-298?

Exam 70-298 will fulfill the Design Exam requirement for the Microsoft Certified Systems Engineer (MCSE) certification, as well as for the new MCSE: Security specialization. Passing the 70-298 exam will also earn Microsoft Certified Professional (MCP) certification. Microsoft's stated target audience consists of IT professionals with at least one year of work experience on a medium or large company network. This means a multi-site network with at least three domain controllers, running typical network services such as file and print services, database, firewall services, proxy services, remote access services and Internet connectivity. In addition, an MCSE candidate should also have one year's experience in designing a network infrastructure and administering a desktop operating system.

However, not everyone who takes Exam 70-298 will have this ideal background. Many people will take this exam after classroom instruction or self-study to advance in the networking or security field. Many of those who do have job experience in IT will not have had the opportunity to work with all of the technologies covered by the exam. In this book, our goal is to provide background information that will help you to understand the concepts and procedures described even if you don't have the requisite experience, while keeping our focus on the exam objectives.

Exam 70-298 measures your ability to analyze business information for a secure network infrastructure, and to design a solution that meets those requirements. Objectives are case study-oriented, and include the following:

- **Creating the Conceptual Design for Network Infrastructure Security by Gathering and Analyzing Business and Technical Requirements** This requires you to analyze your organization's business requirements for designing security. Some possible considerations include existing policies and procedures, sensitivity of data, cost, legal requirements, end-user impact, interoperability, maintainability, scalability, and risk. You should also be familiar with design a framework for designing and implementing security, including tasks such as intrusion prevention, detection, isolation, and recovery. You will also need to be able to analyze technical constraints when designing security, including understanding the capabilities of existing hardware and addressing any interoperability constraints that may exist.
- **Creating the Logical Design for Network Infrastructure Security** This includes designing a public key infrastructure (PKI) using Certificate Services; designing a logical authentication strategy including domain and forest trust relationships; designing security for the network management process, and designing a security update infrastructure for your servers and workstations.
- **Creating the Physical Design for Network Infrastructure Security** This includes designing network infrastructure security such as IPSec and secure DNS implementations; designing security for wireless networks; and designing user authentication and overall security for Internet Information Services (IIS). You'll also need to understand how to design security for communication between networks, as well as designing security for communication with external organizations. Finally, you should be familiar with designing security for servers that have specific roles, such as domain controllers, network infrastructure servers, file servers, Terminal Servers, and POP3 mail servers.
- **Designing an Access Control Strategy for Data** This exam objectives covers the tasks necessary in designing an access control strategy for directory services, including designing appropriate group structures to assign permissions effectively, analyzing auditing requirements, and creating a strategy for delegating authority within Active Directory. You'll also need to be familiar with strategies for designing an access control strategy for files and folders, as well as the Registry. Some topics here include creating a secure backup and recovery strategy, and implementing the Encrypting File System (EFS).
- **Creating the Physical Design for Client Infrastructure Security** This includes designing a client authentication strategy; designing a security strategy for client remote access; and designing a strategy for securing client computers, including desktop and portable computers.

Path to MCSE 2003

Microsoft certification is recognized throughout the IT industry as a way to demonstrate mastery of basic concepts and skills required to perform the tasks involved in implementing and maintaining Windows-based networks. The certification program is constantly evaluated and improved; the nature of information technology is changing rapidly and this means requirements and specifications for certification can also change rapidly. This book is based on the exam objectives as stated by Microsoft at the time of writing; however, Microsoft reserves the right to make changes to the objectives and to the exam itself at any time. Exam candidates should regularly visit the Certification and Training Web site at www.microsoft.com/traincert/ for the most updated information on each Microsoft exam.

Microsoft presently offers three basic levels of certification:

- **Microsoft Certified Professional (MCP)** To obtain the MCP certification, you must pass one current Microsoft certification exam. For more information on exams that qualify, see www.microsoft.com/traincert/mcp/mcp/requirements.asp.
- **Microsoft Certified Systems Engineer (MCSE)** To obtain the MCSE certification on Windows Server 2003, you must pass six core exams (including four network operating system exams, one client operating system exam and one design exam) plus one additional elective. For more information, see www.microsoft.com/traincert/mcp/mcse/windows2003/.

Exam 70-298 applies towards these certifications.

NOTE

Those who already hold the the MCSE in Windows 2000 can upgrade their certifications to MCSE 2003 by passing two upgrade exams (70-292 and 70-296).

Microsoft also offers a number of specialty certifications for networking professionals and certifications for software developers, including the following:

- Microsoft Certified Database Administrator (MCDBA)
- Microsoft Certified Solution Developer (MCSD)
- Microsoft Certified Application Developer (MCAD)

Exam 70-298 does not apply to any of these specialty and developer certifications.

Prerequisites and Preparation

There are no mandatory prerequisites for taking Exam 70-298, although Microsoft recommends that you meet the target audience profile described earlier. Exam 70-298 is an in-depth exam, and one that you should undertake after you've already completed the core four requirements for the MCSE or MCSE: Security for Windows 2003.

Preparation for this exam should include the following:

- Visit the Web site at www.microsoft.com/traincert/exams/70-298.asp to review the updated exam objectives.
- Work your way through this book, studying the material thoroughly and marking any items you don't understand.
- Answer all practice exam questions at the end of each chapter.
- Complete all hands-on exercises in each chapter.
- Review any topics that you don't thoroughly understand
- Consult Microsoft online resources such as TechNet (www.microsoft.com/technet) and the Microsoft Security & Privacy center (www.microsoft.com/security), independent security resources such as SANS (www.sans.org), white papers on the Microsoft Web site and so forth, for better understanding of difficult topics.
- Participate in Microsoft's product-specific and training and certification newsgroups if you have specific questions that you still need answered.
- Take one or more practice exams, such as the one included with this book.

Exam Overview

In this book, we have tried to follow Microsoft's exam objectives as closely as possible. However, we have rearranged the order of some topics for a better flow, and included background material to help you understand the concepts and procedures that are included in the objectives. Following is a brief synopsis of the exam topics covered in each chapter:

- **Chapter 1 Designing a Secure Network Framework:** We begin the 70-298 exam with a look at analyzing a company's business requirements for securing its network and data. This includes examining existing security policies and procedures, includinh technical elements such as analyzing security requirements for different kinds of data. This chapter will also look at some of the common attacks that an enterprise network might face, and what motivates both internal and external attackers. Finally, we'll look at the some of the challenges created by interoperability concerns in a heterogeneous network, since real-world security planning will often require you to integrate earlier Microsoft operating systems into your design scheme, as well as non-Microsoft and third-party systems and services.

- **Chapter 2 Securing Servers Based on Function:** You'll learn how to secure servers in a consistent manner once you've configured one or more machines to fulfill a specific role on your network, as there are a number of security enhancements that can benefit domain controllers, Web servers, network infrastructure servers and file servers.. We'll talk about Security Templates as a way to apply consistent security settings to an entire network, or to a subset of computers or servers. We'll then talk about Group Policy Objects (GPOs) and scripting techniques as a way to quickly deploy common security settings and templates across an entire network.
- **Chapter 3 Designing a Secure Public Key Infrastructure:** This chapter discusses one of the biggest challenges in doing business on the Internet: how to verify someone's identity so that you can transmit confidential information to them. A popular solution to this challenge is the Public Key Infrastructure, or PKI. PKI provides a way for one to verify the identity of another, and for consumers to be sure that a company they're doing business with is really who it claims to be. We'll talk about common implementations of PKI, as well as its specific uses within Windows Server 2003, Certificate Services. This service provides the basis for IP Security (IPSec), Secure Sockets Layer (SSL) communication on a Web server, and the Encrypted File System (EFS) to secure files and folders stored on file shares.
- **Chapter 4 Securing the Network Management Process:** We begin with a discussion of how to secure the administrative process, including utilities such as Telnet, Remote Desktop and Emergency Management Services. We'll also look at strategies for applying security updates efficiently within an enterprise network, using tools like the Microsoft Baseline Security Analyzer (MBSA) and the Software Update Service (SUS). We'll finish with a discussion of designing a domain and forest trust model in Windows Server 2003 that will provide appropriate access for your network users without becoming a security risk or an administrative nightmare. We'll focus on how to design the domain and forest to provide the best possible security in a number of different scenarios, including enterprises that are supporting down-level or non-Microsoft clients and services.
- **Chapter 5 Securing Network Services and Protocols:** We discuss options within Windows Server 2003 for securing data as it traverses a network, especially the IPSec protocol. We'll take a look at the inner workings of IPSec, and how to implement it within an enterprise environment. We'll also look at ways to secure the Domain Naming System (DNS) service,

another common point of attack on a modern network. Last, we'll look at ways to secure wireless network traffic. We'll talk about at some common vulnerabilities of wireless transmissions, and ways to design a secure wireless LAN for your organization.

- **Chapter 6 Securing Internet Information Server (IIS):** We'll discuss user authentication within IIS to protect your users' and customers' privacy and personal information. We'll look at the various types of authentication offered by IIS 6.0, including Certificate Authentication, Integrated Windows logons, and RADIUS authentication using Internet Authentication Server, or IAS. After that, we focus on other aspects of securing Internet Information Services. We look at some common attack vulnerabilities for Web servers in general and IIS servers in particular, and then move on to finding ways to address these concerns for a single server or a large server farm. Some of these strategies include hardening the IIS installation and designing an effective monitoring plan so that you can respond to security incidents in a timely fashion. We'll close with a look at securing the process of actually updating Web content itself to secure against the public embarrassment of Web defacement or inadvertent information disclosure.
- **Chapter 7 Securing VPN and Extranet Communications:** We take a look at the the remote connectivity services and applications available in Windows Server 2003. Depending on your connectivity needs, Windows Server 2003 can actually function as a basic router, using either the Routing Information Protocol or the Open Shortest Path First algorithm. We then discuss in detail use of Windows Server 2003 as a Virtual Private Network, or VPN. Server 2003 to ensure that all traffic is sufficiently encrypted, and to control the use of company resources for VPN usage. Some topics include the use of Remote Access Policies to control aspects of the VPN connection process, accepting or rejecting connections based on user authentication, connection type, time of day, and the like. This chapter focuses on the best ways to design and deploy Windows Server 2003 VPN technologies to provide remote access without sacrificing the overall integrity of the corporate network data and resources.
- **Chapter 8 Securing Active Directory:** You'll learn to secure the directory that houses your user database information, to understand potential risks to Active Directory, and to design your user accounts in a secure fashion. In addition, we'll go over the use of security countermeasures such as Account and Password policies to keep the Active Directory database safe. We'll also discuss the use of auditing to ensure that no unauthorized user activity or other potential security incidents are taking place. We close

Chapter 8 with a discussion of the best ways to assign user permissions to network resources and data.

- **Chapter 9 Securing Network Resources:** We'll look some common risks that can affect file shares, such as data corruption caused by viruses or security breaches arising from incorrectly assigned permissions. Then we'll look at ways to design a permission structure for the files and folders in a large, multi-server environment, as well as best practices for securing the Windows Registry. Then we'll talk about the Encrypted File System, which combines public key cryptography with 3DES encryption to allow users and administrators to extend file security beyond NTFS permissions. The last topic we'll talk about here is designing a secure backup and recovery strategy for your network resources. We'll look at ways to secure the backup process itself, including physically securing backup media, and assigning rights and permissions to perform backups and restores in a secure manner.
- **Chapter 10 Securing Network Clients:** We'll spend some time examining the ways to maintain the overall security of the workstations on your network, including ways to secure the client operating system and maintain and enforce virus protection and patch management for all of your users. We'll also look at client authentication, ways to improve the security of your user accounts, and how to select the best authentication protocols to fit the needs of your enterprise. We'll also go over ways to enforce that choice throughout your network through tools such as Group Policy. Finally, we'll talk about creating a secure remote access plan for your end-users, and close with a discussion of Internet Authentication Service, Windows Server 2003's implementation of the RADIUS standard.

Exam Day Experience

Taking the exam is a relatively straightforward process. Both Vue and Prometric testing centers administer the Microsoft 70-298 exam. You can register for, reschedule or cancel an exam through the Vue Web site at www.vue.com or the Prometric Web site at www.2test.com/index.jsp. You'll find listings of testing center locations on these sites. Accommodations are made for those with disabilities; contact the individual testing center for more information.

Exam price varies depending on the country in which you take the exam.

Exam Format

Exams are timed. At the end of the exam, you will find out your score and whether you passed or failed. You will not be allowed to take any notes or other written materials with you into the exam room. You will be provided with a pencil and paper, however, for making notes during the exam or doing calculations.

The Windows 2003 Design exams are also based on a case-study or "testlet" format, rather than asking a series of unrelated questions. These case studies involve a fictitious company facing a particular situation regarding their current or planned IT infrastructure. You'll be presented with information such as interviews with the CEO/CIO of the company, IT goals, plans, needs, and infrastructure, physical and logical network diagrams, and various other pieces of information. Each exam will include three to five scenarios. Your job will be to read through the case study, distill the important information, and answer between eight and 12 questions about each scenario. In some cases, you will not be able to move back and forth between testlets; once you've completed one case study, it is gone forever – you cannot go back to either review or change your answers.

In addition to the traditional multiple choice questions and the select and drag, simulation and case study questions introduced in the Windows 2000 exams, Microsoft has developed a number of innovative question types for the Windows Server 2003 exams. You might see some or all of the following types of questions:

- *Hot area* questions, in which you are asked to select an element or elements in a graphic to indicate the correct answer. You click an element to select or deselect it.
- *Active screen* questions, in which you change elements in a dialog box (for example, by dragging the appropriate text element into a text box or selecting an option button or checkbox in a dialog box).
- *Drag and drop* questions, in which you arrange various elements in a target area.
- *Build list and reorder* questions, in which you build a list by dragging the appropriate source objects to the answer list, and then placing them in the correct order.
- *Create a tree questions*, which ask you to create a tree structure by dragging source nodes to the correct locations in the answer tree.

You can download a demo sampler of test question types from the Microsoft Web site at www.microsoft.com/traincert/mcpexams/faq/innovations.asp#H.

Test Taking Tips

Different people work best using different methods. However, there are some common methods of preparation and approach to the exam that are helpful to many test-takers. In this section, we provide some tips that other exam candidates have found useful in preparing for and actually taking the exam.

- Exam preparation begins before exam day. Ensure that you know the concepts and terms well and feel confident about each of the exam objectives. Many test-takers find it helpful to make flash cards or review notes to study on the way to the testing center. A sheet listing acronyms and abbreviations can be helpful, as the number of acronyms (and the similarity of different acronyms) when studying IT topics can be overwhelming. The process of writing the material down, rather than just reading it, will help to reinforce your knowledge.

- Many test-takers find it especially helpful to take practice exams that are available on the Internet and with books such as this one. Taking the practice exams not only gets you used to the computerized exam-taking experience, but also can be used as a learning tool. The best practice tests include detailed explanations of why the correct answer is correct and why the incorrect answers are wrong.
- When preparing and studying, you should try to identify the main points of each objective section. Set aside enough time to focus on the material and lodge it into your memory. On the day of the exam, you be at the point where you don't have to learn any new facts or concepts, but need simply to review the information already learned.
- The value of hands-on experience cannot be stressed enough. Exam questions are based on test-writers' experiences in the field. Working with the products on a regular basis, whether in your job environment or in a test network that you've set up at home, will make you much more comfortable with these questions.
- Know your own learning style and use study methods that take advantage of it. If you're primarily a visual learner, reading, making diagrams, watching video files on CD, etc. may be your best study methods. If you're primarily auditory, classroom lectures, audiotapes you can play in the car as you drive, and repeating key concepts to yourself aloud may be more effective. If you're a kinesthetic learner, you'll need to actually *do* the exercises, implement the security measures on your own systems, and otherwise perform hands-on tasks to best absorb the information. Most of us can learn from all of these methods, but have a primary style that works best for us.
- Although it may seem obvious, many exam-takers ignore the physical aspects of exam preparation. You are likely to score better if you've had sufficient sleep the night before the exam, and if you are not hungry, thirsty, hot/cold or otherwise distracted by physical discomfort. Eat prior to going to the testing center (but don't indulge in a huge meal that will leave you uncomfortable), stay away from alcohol for 24 hours prior to the test, and dress appropriately for the temperature in the testing center (if you don't know how hot/cold the testing environment tends to be, you may want to wear light clothes with a sweater or jacket that can be taken off).

- Before you go to the testing center to take the exam, be sure to allow time to arrive on time, take care of any physical needs, and step back to take a deep breath and relax. Try to arrive slightly early, but not so far in advance that you spend a lot of time worrying and getting nervous about the testing process. You may want to do a quick last minute review of notes, but don't try to "cram" everything the morning of the exam. Many test-takers find it helpful to take a short walk or do a few calisthenics shortly before the exam, as this gets oxygen flowing to the brain.
- Before beginning to answer questions, use the pencil and paper provided to you to write down terms, concepts and other items that you think you may have difficulty remembering as the exam goes on. Then you can refer back to these notes as you progress through the test. You won't have to worry about forgetting the concepts and terms you have trouble with later in the exam.
- Sometimes the information in a question will remind you of another concept or term that you might need in a later question. Use your pen and paper to make note of this in case it comes up later on the exam.
- It is often easier to discern the answer to scenario questions if you can visualize the situation. Use your pen and paper to draw a diagram of the network that is described to help you see the relationships between devices, IP addressing schemes, and so forth.
- When appropriate, review the answers you weren't sure of. However, you should only change your answer if you're sure that your original answer was incorrect. Experience has shown that more often than not, when test-takers start second-guessing their answers, they end up changing correct answers to the incorrect. Don't "read into" the question (that is, don't fill in or assume information that isn't there); this is a frequent cause of incorrect responses.
- As you go through this book, pay special attention to the Exam Warnings, as these highlight concepts that are likely to be tested. You may find it useful to go through and copy these into a notebook (remembering that writing something down reinforces your ability to remember it) and/or go through and review the Exam Warnings in each chapter just prior to taking the exam.
- Use as many little mnemonic tricks as possible to help you remember facts and concepts. For example, to remember which of the two IPSec protocols (AH and ESP) encrypts data for confidentiality, you can associate the "E" in encryption with the "E" in ESP.

Pedagogical Elements

In this book, you'll find a number of different types of sidebars and other elements designed to supplement the main text. These include the following:

- **Exam Warning** These focus on specific elements on which the reader needs to focus in order to pass the exam (for example, "Be sure you know the difference between symmetric and asymmetric encryption").
- **Test Day Tip** These are short tips that will help you in organizing and remembering information for the exam (for example, "When preparing for the exam on test day, it may be helpful to have a sheet with definitions of these abbreviations and acronyms handy for a quick last-minute review").
- **Designing & Planning** These sidebars explain how certain exam objectives are implemented or used in professional environments.
- **Configuring & Implementing** These are sidebars that point out the differences and details needed to properly configure your network environment in Windows 2003 Server.
- **Head of the Class** These are discussions of concepts and facts as they might be presented in the classroom, regarding issues and questions that most commonly are raised by students during study of a particular topic.

The book also includes, in each chapter, hands-on exercises in planning and configuring the features discussed. It is essential that you read through and, if possible, perform the steps of these exercises to familiarize yourself with the processes they cover.

You will find a number of helpful elements at the end of each chapter. For example, each chapter contains a *Summary of Exam Objectives* that ties the topics discussed in that chapter to the published objectives. Each chapter also contains an *Exam Objectives Fast Track,* which boils all exam objectives down to manageable summaries that are perfect for last minute review. *The Exam Objectives Frequently Asked Questions* answers those questions that most often arise from readers and students regarding the topics covered in the chapter. Finally, in the *Self Test* section, you will find a set of practice questions written in a multiple-choice form that will assist you in your exam preparation These questions are designed to assess your mastery of the exam objectives and provide thorough remediation, as opposed to simulating the variety of question formats you may encounter in the actual exam. You can use the *Self Test Quick Answer Key* that follows the *Self Test* questions to quickly determine what information you need to review again. The *Self Test Appendix* at the end of the book provides detailed explanations of both the correct and incorrect answers.

Additional Resources

There are two other important exam preparation tools included with this Study Guide. One is the DVD included in the back of this book. The other is the practice test available from our Web site.

- **Instructor-led training DVD provides you with almost two hours of virtual classroom instruction.** Sit back and watch as an author and trainer reviews all the key exam concepts from the perspective of someone taking the exam for the first time. Here, you'll cut through all of the noise to prepare you for exactly what to expect when you take the exam for the first time. You will want to watch this DVD just before you head out to the testing center!
- **Web based practice exams.** Just visit us at **www.syngress.com/certification** to access a complete Windows Server 2003 practice exam. These remediation tools are written to test you on all of the published certification objectives. The exam runs in both "live" and "practice" mode. Use "live" mode first to get an accurate gauge of your knowledge and skills, and then use practice mode to launch an extensive review of the questions that gave you trouble.

Chapter 1

MCSE 70-298

Designing a Secure Network Framework

Exam Objectives in this Chapter:

1.1	Analyze business requirements for designing security.
1.1.1	Analyzing existing security polices and procedures.
1.1.2	Analyze the organizational requirements for security data.
1.1.4	Analyze risks to security within the current IT administration structure and security practives
1.2	Design a framework for designing and implementing security.
1.2.1	Predict threats to your network from internal and external sources
1.1.3	Analyze the security requirements of different types of data.
1.2.2	Design a process for responding to incidents.
1.2.4	Design a process for recovering services.
1.3	Analyze technical constraints when designing security.
1.3.1	Identify capabilities of the existing infrastructure.
1.3.2	Identify technology limitations
1.3.3	Analyze interoperability constraints.

Introduction

Securing a Windows Server 2003 enterprise network is hardly a small undertaking, but it becomes quite manageable if you approach it in an organized and systematic way. Before we can get into the specifics of configuring software, services, and protocols to meet an organization's security needs, we first need to determine what those needs are. In the first chapter of this guide, we discuss the importance of understanding the "Why?" of the security design process before plunging headlong into the "What?" and "How."

In attempting to answer that all-important "Why?" we open this chapter with a look at analyzing a company's business requirements for securing its network and data. This includes examining any existing security policies and procedures with an eye toward how they might be incorporated into the new design, or how they might need to change to accommodate a new security framework. This step includes technical elements such as analyzing security requirements for different kinds of data—some financial or medical data might be subject to specific security or retention policies that a network administrator will need to address—and more human elements such as managing user expectations of security versus usability, and designing security awareness training to transform a user base from obstacle to ally.

Once you've determined your organization's security needs, your next questions is, "Whom are we securing our data *against*?" ("Knowing your enemy" is a mantra to live by, whether you're Sun Tzu or a network security administrator.) This chapter delves into the kinds of common attacks that an enterprise network might face, and what motivates both internal and external attackers. We also look at the steps needed to create a workable Incident Response Plan. After all, no matter how well you design your security system, you will almost certainly find yourself the victim of some type of security incident; it's how you respond to such an incident that can make or break a company's network.

As a final note, we discuss the challenges that interoperability presents to the creation of a security plan. In a perfect world, we'd certainly all like to be using nothing but the "latest and greatest" operating systems and hardware, but reality is often far different. Real-world security planning will often require you to integrate earlier Microsoft operating systems into your design scheme, as well as non-Microsoft and third-party systems and services. Because of this, understanding how Windows Server 2003 can enhance the security of both homogeneous and heterogeneous networks is a fundamental part of preparing for the 70-298 exam.

EXAM 70-298 OBJECTIVE 1.1

Analyzing Business Requirements for Security Design

While it might seem self-obvious, it's important to begin any security design process with one simple question: "Why?" Why has your organization hired or contracted with you to design their security infrastructure? What goals do they hope to achieve by implementing a security design framework? As you work through this chapter, always keep that fundamental "Why?" in the back of your mind, since a security design plan that does not meet an organization's requirements for securing its data and resources is hardly worth the paper it's written on.

Organizations will make an investment in network security to protect their data and resources, or *assets*, from anything that might damage those assets, or *threats*. A company's assets can include physical inventory such as server hardware and software, and intellectual property such as the source code to an application or a trade secret. Moving beyond that, most (if not all) companies would consider things such as their business reputation to be an asset as well. With so many choices in doing business today, many consumers base their business and purchases on their confidence level in a corporation, and a company's reputation being tarnished by a highly publicized security break-in can destroy that confidence and cost a company sales and customers.

It's relatively simple to assign a dollar value to a piece of equipment or real estate; any loss in this area is called a *quantitative* loss. Threats to things like intellectual property and reputation are far more difficult to nail down to a hard-and-fast number, so losses in this area are referred to as being *qualitative*. A network security design plan will use Risk Management (discussed later in this chapter) to assign priorities to different types of network threats, and use that prioritization to develop an effective and *cost*-effective security design for an organization. By combining an understanding of your company's current security procedures with knowledge of the types of network threats it might face, you can design a security framework that will meet your company's needs.

EXAM 70-298 OBJECTIVE 1.1.1

Analyzing Existing Security Policies and Procedures

Corporate security policies create a baseline for performing security-related duties in a systematic and consistent fashion based on your organization's information security requirements. In many cases, these policies will extend beyond the borders of the IT department and involve areas of Human Resources, Finance, and Legal departments attempting to address compliance and reporting issues specific to a given industry. Having well-developed security policies will also assist an organization in demonstrating its security consciousness to customers, stockholders, and the like. Security policies typically fall into one of three categories:

- **Physical policies** While physical security can often be overlooked by IT professionals, these policies discuss security measures that can be implemented using physical controls such as door locks, controlled room access, and procedures for adding or removing equipment from a machine room or office.
- **Technical policies** These are the kinds of policies that you will be most familiar with as a Windows administrator. Technical policies include security measures that protect data and resources at the operating system level, including security templates and NTFS permissions.
- **Administrative policies** These are typically procedural measures that control facets of information security that can't be enforced through technical measures, such as a nondisclosure agreement.

When designing a plan for securing a Windows environment, your first step should be analyzing any existing security policies and procedures with an eye to how they can be improved (or, if necessary, replaced) to meet the security needs of your organization. You should keep in mind some common reasons why security policies either fail or are not implemented properly within an organization. If users are unaware of security policies, the odds that they will comply with them are slim indeed—a policy that no one knows about is no better than not having any security policy at all. Security policies also run the risk of becoming outdated or too difficult for an end user to understand; try to keep the technical jargon to a minimum when explaining your users' rights and responsibilities within your security design plan. While creating and analyzing documentation might seem a tedious task, the existence of viable security policies can save both time and money when tracking down and addressing any security incidents that might occur on a corporate network.

Acceptable Use Policies

A common component of many enterprise security policies is an Acceptable Use Policy, often called an AUP. This means precisely what it sounds like—an AUP is a document that details the types of activity that are (and are not) permitted on a corporate network. Since many network security incidents arise from risks or situations created by internal employees, an AUP is crucial so that a corporation will know that a violation of network security has occurred, and what steps they should take to address the situation. (Consider the potential implications, for example, of an internal employee running a network scanner like Nmap to discover vulnerabilities on corporate machines, whether out of curiosity or maliciousness.) An AUP needs to address the rights and responsibilities of both employee and company in defining what type of network access is acceptable on a corporate network, and what steps the IT department will take to determine whether a violation of Acceptable Use has occurred.

The AUP is also an appropriate place to discuss what level of privacy an employee can expect on a corporate network. While many companies hold that "reasonable" personal use of resources like e-mail and Internet access are allowable, you need to specify whether things like network traffic and e-mail messages will be subject to monitoring. This is even more pertinent if your organization uses encryption to secure documents, since users need to understand what circumstances, if any, would require a member of management or IT to access their encrypted files or other personal encryption information. Consult a legal resource when creating or assessing an AUP, since privacy laws often vary from location to location. (We'll have more on privacy and its implications for network security in the next section.)

Privacy versus Security

According to the Microsoft Security Resource Kit, privacy can be best defined as "freedom from the intrusion of others in one's personal life or affairs." Privacy and security are related topics, but are not synonymous: information security is concerned with protecting sensitive information from anyone who doesn't have appropriate access to it, while privacy is more of a customer-centric concept concerned with meeting a person or organization's preferences for how information concerning them should be handled. Aside from the privacy concerns of employee information that we discussed in the last section, your company needs to be concerned about how it will handle and protect things like customer information and sales data. A common application of this is the disclaimer you'll see on many Web sites stating that lists of e-mail addresses will not be sold or distributed to other companies as marketing material, or options for consumers to opt out of receiving any directed marketing mailings. The terms under which your company will contact its customers need to be strictly defined and adhered to, if for no other reason than that it will improve your relation ship with your customers. (You'll do far less business with those people who decide that any e-mail from you is SPAM, after all.)

From a legal standpoint, privacy concerns are some of the most highly visible within information security today. Laws as old as the U.S. Federal Privacy Act of 1974 limit how the government can use peoples' personal data and information. More recently, industry-specific measures such as the Health Insurance Portability and Accountability Act (HIPAA) provide more stringent measures to control how your health and medical information can be processed, stored, or transmitted to prevent inadvertent or unauthorized disclosure or misuse.

Within private industry, organizations need to examine the privacy of their own information and assets, even if it's not mandated by legal regulations. Most companies, especially those that do business online, have created Privacy Statements that delineate what type of information a company will be collecting—are you tracking IP addresses? Referring sites? Machine data? All of these things should be specified in a Privacy Statement. Moreover, the Privacy Statement should clearly define how a customer's personal information will be used, and what other organizations, if any, will have access to this information. Your company's Privacy Statement should also detail how users or consumers can opt out of having their personal information shared or even stored at all if they change their minds at a later date. Finally, you should detail the information security measures that will be used to protect customer data, and be sure that the systems you implement will be able to measure up to the standards that you've laid out.

As a final note when considering your company's privacy policy, remember that IT and security professionals themselves can sometimes introduce risks to the privacy of information because of their nearly unlimited access to network data and resources. While we would like to think that all IT professionals have integrity, security professionals themselves should be aware of and subject to privacy measures to ensure the integrity of customer data.

Security versus Usability

Of primary concern when analyzing security policies is the need to balance security with usability—if your security policies are so stringent that your users are not able to access their data, then you haven't really designed a functional security scheme. While we all want to design the most secure network environment possible, mandating measures like a 20-character password will, in most cases, simply lead to administrative overhead and user frustration as they continually forget their passwords or need to have them reset. (And such a measure could actually *decrease* security by encouraging the dreaded "Password on a yellow sticky note next to the monitor" phenomenon.) When surveying existing documentation (or creating your own), always keep this balance between security and usability in mind.

EXAM 70-298 OBJECTIVE 1.1.2

Determining Requirements for Securing Data

No matter what kind of data you are dealing with, your task as a security professional is to ensure that it remains accessible, intact, and private. When securing data, a common phrase that you should be familiar with is *CIA*, which stands for *Confidentiality*, *Integrity*, and *Availability*. Taken as a whole, these are the three most important areas to consider when attempting to secure your network's assets and resources. The *CIA triad* makes up all of the principles of network security design. Depending on the nature of the information you're securing, some of the principles might have varying degrees of importance to you. However, all three will come into play at some point during the design process.

The CIA Triad

Confidentiality prevents any unauthorized disclosure of your data, and ensures that information will only be available to those people authorized to access it. Confidentiality is crucial when dealing with matters of privacy and protecting personal data such as credit card information, Social Security numbers, or other unique identifiers. It's also a critical matter when attempting to secure the kinds of intellectual property that we've already discussed: once a piece of "secret" information has been disclosed, there is no real way to *un*-disclose it. However, determining the confidentiality of data is not only a matter of determining whether a piece of information is secret. When considering confidentiality, you also need to control *how* data can be accessed. For example, a sales representative using a database query to generate a list of follow-up customer service calls would not be a breach of your data's confidentiality. However, that same sales representative querying the same database for a list of e-mail addresses to use in her own personal mass e-mailing would be another matter entirely. Therefore, the confidentiality of data depends not only on *who* can access it, but how they are doing so.

To prevent attackers from gaining access to you network's confidential data, you can use any number of technical, administrative, and physical countermeasures. Physical controls can include a secure safe-deposit box to house items like birth certificates or medical records. From a technical standpoint, users might only be allowed to access confidential data from a specific location, or by using a specific application. The use of cryptography and file encryption can ensure that only the owner of a file can access it, even if it is somehow transferred to a different location. In addition, end-user and administrative training can guard against an attacker using a so-called "social engineering" attack to obtain access to an employee's username and password. (More on social engineering in a minute.)

The next item in the CIA triad, *integrity*, refers to measures that preserve the accuracy and consistency of data against fraudulent or unauthorized alteration. Data integrity safeguards should ensure that only authorized persons are allowed to make changes to network data. Protecting data integrity also means making sure that authorized users cannot make *unauthorized* changes to corporate data—while a bank teller should be authorized to view your checking account information, he certainly shouldn't be able to transfer monies from your account into someone else's without your approval.

TEST DAY TIP

Confidentiality of data is concerned with who can *see* a piece of data. Integrity moves into the question of who can *modify* that data.

Mechanisms that are designed to ensure data integrity need to address both attacks on where data is stored, and while data is being transmitted across the network. If an attacker intercepts and changes data traveling from a server to a user's workstation, it is just as detrimental as if the attacker had altered the data on the server hard drive itself. It's important to note that not all attacks against data integrity are necessarily malicious; users can enter invalid data into an application, or an application error can cause an error in processing. (If anyone remembers the Monopoly game card that read "Bank Error in Your Favor, Collect $100," you have a good idea of this type of integrity failure.) Data integrity safeguards should protect against any type of integrity attack, whether intentional or innocuous. This can include administrative safeguards such as user training about the importance of accurate data entry, or technical controls in applications to ensure that 2+2 always equals 4, or to flag any unusual transactions for manual approval in case they were the result of an error. Some of the protections that can be used to prevent more malicious integrity attacks include the use of Intrusion Detection Systems (IDSs), data encryption, and the use of access control through the NTFS file system.

The final piece of the "Information Security Triad" is the *availability* of data. Just like the old question of whether a tree falling in the forest with no one around actually makes a sound, if your users cannot access their data when they need to, then any measures that protect that data's confidentiality and availability are hardly worthwhile. The recent spate of denial-of-service (DoS) attacks on the Internet have been designed to infringe on the availability of Internet-based Web services, sometimes affecting a company's network access altogether.

Data availability can be affected by more than just network attackers and can affect system and network availability. Environmental factors such as adverse weather conditions or electrical problems, and natural disasters like fires and floods can prevent systems and networks from functioning. This is why backup and restore and disaster recovery planning should be included in any network security design plan. (We'll talk about backup and restore processes in Chapter 4, "Securing the Network Management Process.")

EXAM 70-298 OBJECTIVE 1.1.4

Analyzing Current Security Practices

A step that is commonly overlooked in designing any network is examining where a company or network is at currently. Evaluating a company's existing security infrastructure will illustrate where any gaps or holes currently exist that need to be addressed by the new security design; it will help you determine how much actually needs to be changed or updated, rather than wholly reinventing the wheel. If the organization is already security-conscious, your security design might only require minimal updates to reflect new advances permitted by Windows Server 2003 security technologies. If there is no security infrastructure currently in place (or if the current security practices are not being enforced), however, you obviously have a whole different task ahead of you. This task includes securing the corporate network, and crafting procedures and policies that will be embraced by management and users alike.

Your evaluation of current security practices should extend not only to administrative policies issued by IT or Human Resources, but also any technical measures that are already in place or lacking. For example, do all users have administrative rights to their local workstations? This might require re-examining to better secure the workstation environment. Are there measures in place that prevent users from downloading or installing unauthorized software? Developing an awareness of the security practices of your organization will help you determine the best way to design a Windows Server 2003 infrastructure.

Using Resultant Set of Policies

If you are working with an existing Windows Server 2003 infrastructure, you might find that there are already technical policies in place that you need to analyze before designing a solution. Windows Server 2003 offers a new tool that will assist you in listing and troubleshooting any existing security settings on a network that have been applied through Group Policy Objects (GPOs). Resultant Set of Policies, or RSoP, is particularly useful in determining how existing GPOs have been applied, and determining which settings have or have not been applied to a specific user or group of users.

You'll use the RSoP Wizard to create a query that will list all GPO settings, security and otherwise, for a specific user or computer. You can access this wizard from a blank Microsoft Management Console (MMC), or from the Group Policy Management Console. When the wizard has completed, it will display its results in the MMC window. You can then save, change, or refresh the information used to generate the query. In Exercise 1.01, we'll examine the steps in running an RSoP query against a single computer.

TEST DAY TIP

If you need to create RSoP information for a number of different users, you can use the *gpresult.exe* command-line utility in a batch file or logon script. The gpresult utility was previously available under Windows 2000; however, RSoP is a new feature for Windows Server 2003.

EXERCISE 1.01

RUNNING AN RSOP QUERY

1. Open a blank MMC by clicking on **Start | Run**, typing **mmc**, and clicking **OK**.
2. Click on **File | Add/Remove Snap-in**. Select the **Standalone** tab, click on **Add**, then browse to Resultant Set of Policy. Click on **Add** again and then **Close**.

3. Click **OK** to return to the MMC.
4. Right-click on the **Resultant Set of Policy** node and select **Generate RSoP Data** as shown in Figure 1.1.

Figure 1.1 Generating RSoP Data

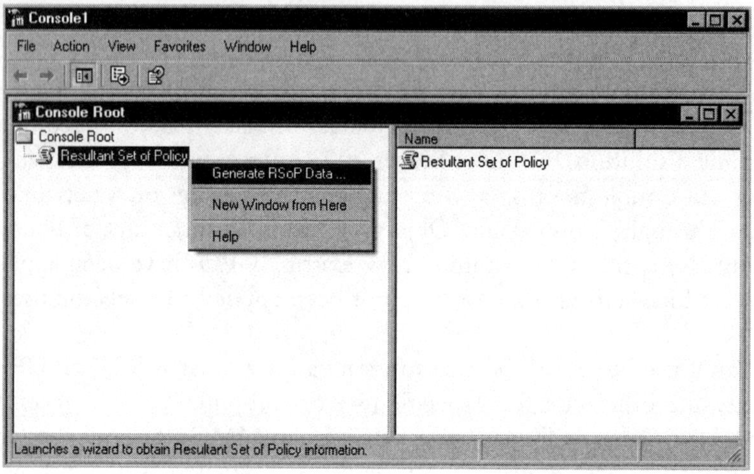

5. Click **Next** to bypass the initial Welcome screen.
6. On the **Mode Selection** page, click **Logging mode**, and then click **Next**.
7. The Computer Selection screen (shown in Figure 1.2) will give you the option to generate data about the computer where you're running the RSoP snap-in or to select another computer on the network. You can also place a check mark next to **Do not display policy settings for the selected computer in the results (display user policy settings only)** to restrict the output of the query. Click **Next** when you're ready to continue.

Figure 1.2 Computer Selection in the RSoP Query Wizard

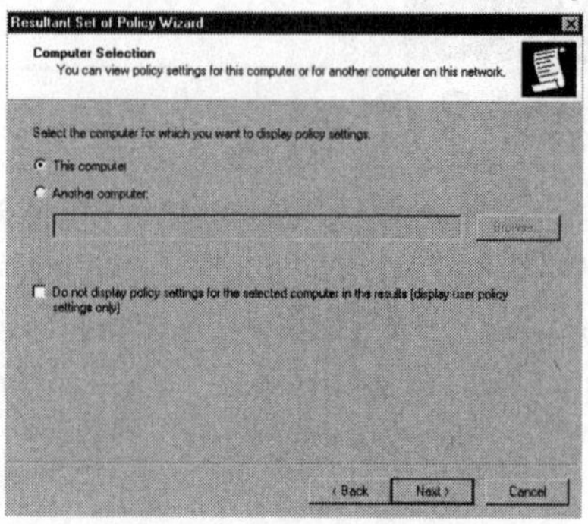

8. The next screen is the User Selection screen. Similar to the screen in the previous step, you can generate the RSoP query based on the currently logged-on user, or select another user in the Active Directory database. You can also restrict the results of the query by selecting **Do not display policy settings for the selected user in the results (display computer policy settings only)**.
9. The final screen will display a summary of the choices you've made. Click **Next** to begin the RSoP query. Click **Finish** when the query has completed.

After you run the Resultant Set of Policy Wizard, the RSoP console will be populated with data from the results of the query. The specific results for Software Settings, Windows Settings, and Extra Registry Settings will appear in the right-hand side of the MMC window.

Security Settings information will display each specific policy, the effective setting that has been applied to a given computer, and a "Source GPO column" indicating which GPO applied this setting. (This is particularly helpful if you have multiple GPOs on a network and are attempting to determine how GPO inheritance is structured.) The Source GPO column indicates which Group Policy objects affect a policy setting, as illustrated in Figure 1.3.

Figure 1.3 Results of RSoP Query

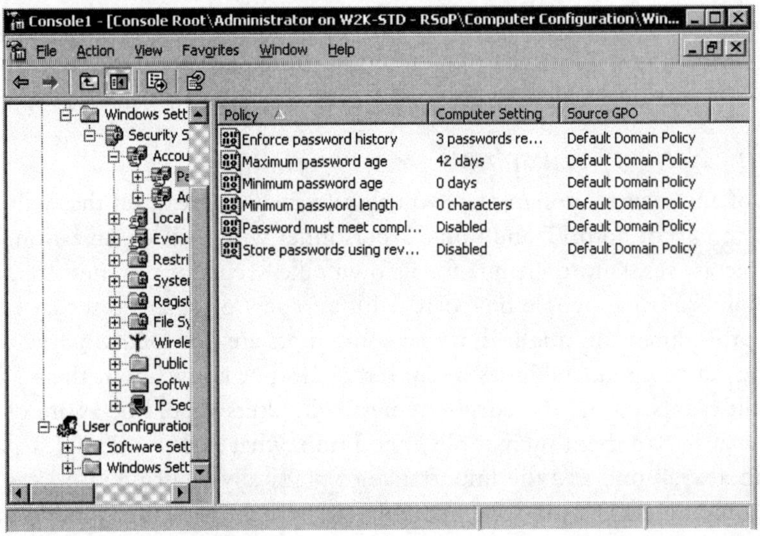

Using tools like RSoP will assist you in analyzing any technical security measures that an organization has already put in place, along with its existing administrative policies. Armed with this information, you will be able to assess the organization's current security policies, with an eye toward what might need to be changed to better protect against both internal and external attackers.

Recognizing Internal Security Threats

So, why is it so important to determine how an organization handles security for its internal users? Because in many ways, internal security threats from employees, contractors, or other sources can be even more damaging than external "hack attacks." This is because internal users have several factors working in their favor when they do damage against a network, whether unintentionally or maliciously. Internal users have far more opportunity to gain physical access to networking and computing equipment, even if it's just their personal workstation connected to the network LAN. Once an attacker gains physical access to a computer, most security safeguards become a simple matter to circumvent. If internal resources such as server rooms and wiring closets are not locked or secured in some way, the potential for damage increases exponentially. Additionally, if a company does not encrypt network traffic, it is a simple matter for an internal user to eavesdrop on network traffic to gain access to information that he should not actually have access to.

Moreover, internal users usually do not need to "break into" a network, *per se*, since they already have access via their username and password. This initial access to a corporate network gives any internal attackers a great advantage over their external counterparts, since the task of finding valid logon authentication to a network has already been handled for them by the network administrators. Especially if the attacker is someone with legitimate administrative privileges, it can be extremely difficult to determine if she is abusing her network credentials for illicit purposes.

Increasing Security Awareness

As a part of any security design plan, you should include measures that will provide security training for both IT and non-IT personnel within an organization. Since most people are resistant to change for its own sake, security awareness training is always helpful to bring people on-board with any new or changed security requirements or procedures. You might find that some users are not following security practices or introducing vulnerabilities because they do not know about their responsibilities in securing the corporate network. Users should be aware of security measures available to them such as file encryption, what makes a complex password better than a weak one, and the importance of physically securing resources like portable computers, PDAs, and the like. You should help your users understand when it is and is not appropriate to discuss their network logon information, and that they should under no circumstances share their password with anyone, even someone from (or claiming to be from) IT. Security Awareness Training is perhaps the *only* measure that will help to address nontechnical attacks like social engineering, which rely on cooperation from unsuspecting users to gain access to a network.

EXAM 70-298 OBJECTIVE 1.2

Designing a Framework for Implementing Security

Designing a secure network framework can be broken into four conceptual pieces:

- Attack prevention
- Attack detection
- Attack isolation
- Attack recovery

While the measures we'll be discussing in this guide are specific to different aspects of the Windows Server 2003 infrastructure, each topic will map back to one of these four key principles. This can include disabling unnecessary Windows services to prevent network attacks, installing an IDS to alert you of any suspicious network activity, or designing an Incident Response Plan to facilitate recovery from an attack. In this section, we'll take a broad look at topics relating to each of these four principles.

To adequately prevent attacks against your network, you'll first need to determine what form they might actually take. We'll look at the STRIDE model of classifying network attacks as a starting point for both attack prevention and detection. While the number of network attacks has grown exponentially in recent time, understanding how a specific threat is acting against your network will greatly assist you in acting to circumvent any damage. Another component of attack prevention that we'll discuss is Risk Management, where you prioritize your resources to create a secure yet cost-effective network structure. Finally, we'll look at Incident Response as a way to both detect and respond to any malicious activity on your network.

EXAM 70-298 OBJECTIVE 1.2.1

Predicting Threats to Your Network

Predicting network threats and analyzing the risks they present to your infrastructure is one of the cornerstones of the network security design process. Understanding the types of threats that your network will face will assist you in designing appropriate countermeasures, and in obtaining the necessary money and resources to create a secure network framework. Members of an organization's management structure will likely be resistant to spending money on a threat that they don't understand; this process will also help them understand the very real consequences of network threats, and to make informed decisions about what types of measures to implement. In this section we'll discuss some common network attacks that you will likely face when designing a secure Windows Server 2003 network, and how each of these attacks can adversely affect your network.

When classifying network threats, many developers and security analysts have taken to using a model called STRIDE, which is an acronym for:

- **Spoofing identity** These include attacks that involve illegally accessing and using account information that isn't yours, such as shoulder-surfing someone's password while he types it into his keyboard. This type of attack affects the *confidentiality* of data.
- **Tampering with data** These attacks involve a malicious modification of data, interfering with the *integrity* of an organization's data. The most common of these is a *man-in-the-middle* (MITM) attack, where a third party intercepts communications between two legitimate hosts and tampers with the information as it is sent back and forth. This is akin to sending an e-mail to Mary that says "The meeting is at 3 P.M.", but a malicious attacker intercepts and changes the message to "The meeting has been cancelled."
- **Repudiation** These threats occur when a user can perform a malicious action against a network resource and then deny that she did so, and the owners or administrators of the data have no way of proving otherwise. A Repudiation threat can attack any portion of the CIA triad.
- **Information disclosure** This occurs when information is made available to individuals who should not have access to it. Information disclosure can occur through improperly applied network permissions that allow a user the ability to read a confidential file, or an intruder's ability to read data being transmitted between two networked computers. Information disclosure affects the *confidentiality* of your company's data and resources.
- **Denial of service** So-called DoS attacks do not attempt to alter a company's data, but rather attack a network by denying access to valid users, by flooding a Web server with phony requests so that legitimate users cannot access it, for example. DoS attacks affect the *availability* of your organization's data and resources.
- **Elevation of privilege** This type of attack takes place when an unprivileged, nonadministrative user gains administrative or "root level" access to an entire system, usually through a flaw in the system software. When this occurs, an attacker has the ability to alter or even destroy any data that he finds, since he is acting with administrative privileges. This type of threat affects all portions of the CIA triad, since the attacker can access, change, and remove any data that he sees fit.

When you are analyzing a potential network threat, try to remember the STRIDE acronym as a means of classifying and reacting to the threat. You can use the STRIDE model, not only to assist you on the 70-298 exam, but also throughout the life of your corporate network when designing and maintaining security policies and procedures.

Recognizing External Threats

Now that we've discussed a model for classifying network threats, we can look at some of the more common attacks in more detail. While entire books can (and have been) be written solely discussing the kinds of threats that we'll be looking at in this section, we'll be giving you a "birds-eye" view of the kinds of attacks that your network security design will need to guard against.

TEST DAY TIP

For more detailed information on the attacks we'll discuss in this section, check out the Syngress Publishing Security+ Study guide, *Security+ Study Guide and DVD Training System* (ISBN 1-931836-72-8).

Denial-of-Service Attacks

As we've already mentioned, the DoS attack (and its first cousin, the *Distributed* DoS attack) works to disrupt services on a network so that legitimate users cannot access resources they need. Some examples include attempts to disrupt the connection between two specific machines, or more commonly, attempts to flood an entire network with traffic, thereby overloading the network and preventing legitimate traffic from being transmitted. There can also be instances where an illegitimate use of resources can result in denial of service. For example, if an intruder uses a vulnerability in your FTP server to upload and store illegal software, this can consume all available disk space on the FTP server and prevent legitimate users from storing their files. A DoS attack can effectively disable a single computer or an entire network.

A common venue of attack for DoS is against an organization's network bandwidth and connectivity; the goal of the attacker is to prevent other machines from communicating because of the traffic flood. An example of this type of attack is the "SYN flood" attack. In this type of attack, the attacker begins to establish a connection to the victim machine, but in such a way that the connection is never completed. Since even the most powerful server has only a certain amount of memory and processor cycles to devote to its workload, legitimate connection attempts can be denied while the victim machine is trying to complete these fake "half-open" connections. Another common DoS is the so-called "PING of Death," where an attacker sends so many PING requests to a target machine that it is again overloaded and unable to process legitimate network requests.

An intruder might also attempt to consume network resources in other ways, including generating a massive amount of e-mail messages, intentionally generating system errors that need to be included in Event Viewer logs, or misusing FTP directories or network shares to overload available disk space. Basically, anything that allows data, whether on a network cable or hard drive, to be written at will (without any type of control mechanism) can create a denial of service when a system's finite resources have been exhausted by the attacker.

Distributed Denial-of-Service Attacks

Distributed denial-of-service (DDoS) attacks are a relatively new development, made possible (and attractive to attackers) by the ever-expanding number of machines that are attached to the Internet. The first major wave of DDoS attacks on the Internet appeared in early 2000, and targeted such major e-commerce and news sites as Yahoo!, eBay, Amazon, Datek, and CNN. In each case, the Web sites belonging to these companies were unreachable for several hours at a time, causing a severe disruption to their online presence and effectiveness. Many more DDoS attacks have occurred since then, affecting networks and Web sites large and small.

EXAM WARNING

While most publicity surrounding DDoS attacks has focused on Web servers as a target, remember that any computer attached to the Internet can fall victim to the effects of a DDoS attack. This can include everything from file servers or e-mail servers to your users' desktop workstations.

The DDoS attack begins with a human *Attacker* using a small number of computers, called *Masters*. The Master computers use network scanners to find as many weakly secured computers as they can, and use system vulnerabilities (usually well-known ones) to install a small script or a service (referred to in the UNIX world as a *daemon*) onto the insecure computer. This machine has now become a *Zombie,* and can now be triggered by the Master computer to attack any computer or network attached to the Internet. Once the organizer of the DDoS attack has a sufficient number of Zombie machines under his control, he will use the Zombi-fied machines to send a stream of packets to a designated target computer or network, called the *Victim*. For most of the attacks, these packets are directed at the victim machine. Figure 1.4 provides a graphical illustration of the Master-Zombie-Victim relationship.

Figure 1.4 Illustration of a DDoS Attack

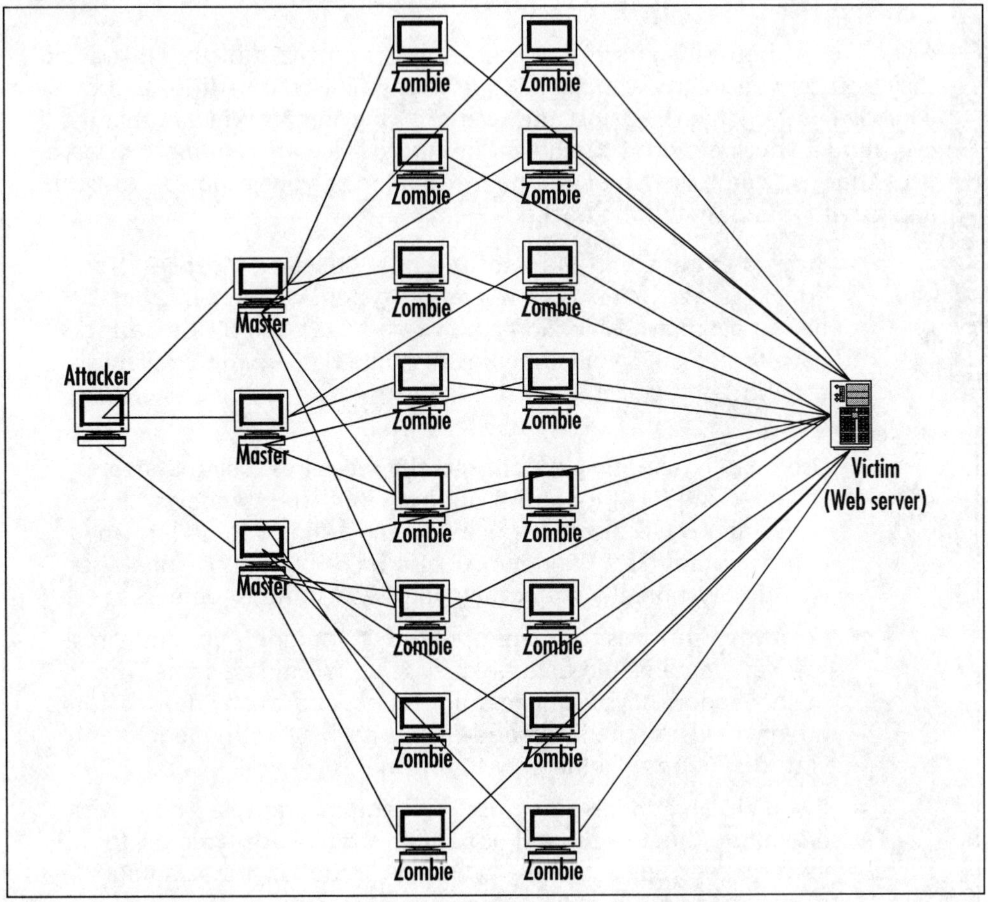

The distributed nature of the DDoS attack makes it extremely difficult to track down the person or persons who began it; the actual attacks are coming from Zombie machines, and the owners of these machines are often not even aware that their machines have been compromised. Making matters even more difficult, most network packets used in DDoS attacks use forged source addresses, which means that they are essentially lying about where the attack is coming from.

Head of the Class...

Combating Network Attacks

Given the widespread nature of DDoS attacks and the difficulty in tracing their source, you might wonder if there is anything you can do to protect your corporate network against this ever-growing threat. While nothing will ever render your network 100 percent immune, there are a number of practices that you can follow that will help to minimize your exposure to DDoS and other types of network attacks.

- Stay up to date with Microsoft Security Bulletins. Most DDoS attacks target well-known operating system vulnerabilities that have a patch available. Some particularly damaging DDoS attacks have targeted OS vulnerabilities that had had a patch available for two years, but that most administrators had not bothered to install.
- Use built-in operating system security measures. Using System File Checking (SFC) for your Windows 2000 and Windows XP workstations will alert your users to any attempt to update any critical system files. Windows XP also has a built-in personal firewall that will greatly strengthen your workstations' defenses.
- Keep your antivirus software updated. If you don't use anti-virus software, now would be a great time to investigate some. The major vendors have become quick to respond to any new threats, greatly reducing the likelihood that a machine with updated anti-virus definitions will fall prey to a DDoS or Trojan.
- If you are an administrator, use your administrative account with discretion. Create a second nonadministrative user account to perform everyday activities—a Trojan can do far more damage if it is allowed to run as an administrative account.

Viruses, Worms, and Trojan Horses

Viruses, Trojans, and worms are quite possibly the most disruptive of all of the security threats that we'll be discussing in this section. These three types of threats, working alone or in combination, can alter or delete data files and executable programs on your network shares, flood e-mail servers and network connections with malicious traffic, and even create a "back door" into your systems that can allow a remote attacker to take over control of a computer entirely. While you'll often hear these three terms used interchangeably, each one is slightly different. A *virus* is a piece of code that will alter an existing file, and then use that alteration to recreate itself many times over. A worm simply makes copies of itself over and over again for the purpose of exhausting available system resources. A worm can target both hard drive space and processor cycles.

EXAM WARNING

A computer virus typically targets the *integrity* of data by altering its contents. A worm primarily attacks data's *availability* by targeting system resources as a whole. Of course, a major virus attack will eventually affect the availability of your data as well, but its initial attack vector is concerned with attacking data integrity.

Trojan horses take their name from a Greek myth, in which attackers from Sparta infiltrated the Greek city of Troy by hiding inside a horse statue masquerading as a gift. When the Trojans brought the gift inside the city walls, they discovered too late that it was filled with Spartan soldiers who emerged from within the horse and took over the city. In similar fashion, a computer-based Trojan will disguise itself as a friendly file, usually an e-mail attachment. This file, when executed, can damage computer data or install a "back door" into the operating system that will allow a remote attacker to take over the system entirely.

NOTE

For more information about computer viruses and other similar threats, check out the Syngress Publishing book guide to *Configuring Symantec AntiVirus Corporate Edition* (ISBN: 1-931836-81-7).

Software Vulnerabilities

Some network attacks target vulnerabilities in the way that a software application or entire operating system has been programmed. For example, a *buffer overflow* attack occurs when a malicious user sends more data to a program than it knows how to handle. For example, you've all seen Web forms that ask you to fill in your personal information: first name, last name, telephone number, and so forth. A careless developer might program the "First Name" field to only be able to handle 10 characters; that is, a name that is 10 letters long. If the Web application does not check for buffer overflows, an attacker can input a long string of gibberish into the First Name field in an attempt to cause a buffer overflow error. At this point, the attacker could even embed the name of an executable file into that long string of text and actually pass commands to the system as if he or she were sitting at the server console itself. A similar software vulnerability is a *format string vulnerability* that would allow an attacker to insert random data into a file or database, once again including malicious code that can be executed against the server as if the attacker were sitting right in front of the keyboard.

Another attack that is specifically common to Web and FTP servers is a *directory traversal vulnerability*. This type of vulnerability allows a user to gain access to a directory on a server that he hasn't been specifically given permissions to, by virtue of having permissions to a parent or child directory. Say someone goes to the following URL: www.airplanes.com/biplanes/cessna/model1.html. He decides to manually change this URL (in other words, not following an <HREF> link on the site itself) to www.airplanes.com/biplanes/piper, to see if the directory structure holds any information there. If the Web site hasn't been properly patched and configured with the correct security settings, the user might find that he now has access to every single file in the piper/ directory. Even worse, he can once again execute a command from the Web browser by changing the URL to something like www.airplanes.com/biplanes/piper/del%20*.*. ("%20" is used in HTML to represent a space, so that command would read "del *.*" on a regular command line.) Another common attack also occurred in NetMeeting and Windows Media Player some time ago, where an attacker could insert special characters during a file transfer that would allow him to browse an unsuspecting user's hard drive directory structure.

Nontechnical Attacks

A final category of attacks that we'll discuss here are those that use less technical means to circumvent network security. So-called *social engineering* attacks rely on an unsuspecting user's lack of security consciousness. In some cases, the attacker will rely on someone's goodwill, using a tactic like "I've really got to get this done and I don't have access to these files, can you help me?" (Since at heart, most of us really want to be helpful to those around us.) Other social engineering attacks will use a more threat-based approach, insisting that the attacker is the secretary for Mr. Big-Shot VP who needs his password reset right away and heaven-help-you if you keep him waiting. This relies on the assumption that a show of authority will cause someone without adequate training to bypass security procedures to keep the "big-shot important user/client" happy. Since social engineering attacks are nontechnical in nature, the measures required to defend against them are more administrative than anything else is. It's critical to have well-understood security policies in place that apply to everyone, regardless of their position in your company. This will assist in preventing an attacker from circumventing security procedures because a help desk or other staff member is unaware of them.

Designing & Planning…

Blended Threats

As if it weren't hard enough to keep track of viruses, worms, and other similar attacks, the information security industry has coined a new term for a type of attack that blends the worst of both. *Blended threats* combine many of the characteristics of viruses, worms, Trojan horses, and attacks against software vulnerabilities to increase the rate at which they can spread and cause damage. If you've dealt with the fall-out of threats like Code Red (which began circulating in 2001), Klez, and the like, you've already seen how insidious a blended threat can be.

Blended threats spread using multiple methods, usually beginning with a malicious e-mail attachment. Once the unsuspecting user launches the attachment, the now-infected machine will use a network-based attack to scan for vulnerabilities in other systems, including embedding code in HTML files on a Web server, sending a deluge of virus-infected e-mail from a compromised e-mail server, or altering files on an internal server's network shares. Even worse, these attacks are able to spread without any human intervention—they continuously scan the local network or the Internet for new systems to attack and infect.

The Nimda worm presents a perfect example of how a blended threat operates and spreads. Machines were initially compromised by Nimda through an e-mail attachment that exploited a software vulnerability in Microsoft Outlook and Outlook Express. This software vulnerability allowed the infection to spread without the user's intervention, or even awareness. Once a desktop machine was infected, Nimda began to perform network scans to attack network shares and Web servers using a *yet another* software vulnerability in Internet Information Server.

The Internet Explorer vulnerability enabled Nimda to infect a Web server in such a way that any user who connected to the site would automatically have malicious code downloaded to his or her desktop, thus continuing the infection cycle. With so many venues to continue the spread of the virus, it's no wonder that Nimda caused worldwide havoc on many home and corporate networks.

The emergence of blended threats presents a huge challenge for Information Security professionals, since threats such as Nimda can now spread much more quickly than any of their nonblended predecessors. Without proper planning and monitoring, a network can become overloaded with a virus outbreak before an administrator is even aware of the problem. Moreover, since blended threats spread through methods other than just e-mail attachments, security professionals need to find new ways to secure other forms of network traffic such as Web server and file server traffic.

What Motivates External Attackers?

Just as you need to know "why?" a company is designing a security infrastructure, it's also helpful to know the reasons why total strangers seem compelled to make your life as a network administrator that much more difficult. Network attackers, usually referred to colloquially as *hackers*, attempt to break in to corporate networks for any number of reasons, and sometimes knowing the reason why they are doing so can assist you in defusing the threat and tracking down the perpetrator.

The most common, although perhaps not the most obvious, reason for attacking a company's network is to gain fame or notoriety. Whether it is someone seeking acceptance from an online hacker community, or someone who simply wants to see his or her name in the papers, attacks motivated in this manner tend to be extremely public in nature. A common attack in this category is Web site defacement, where an attacker will exploit a vulnerability in a company's Web server and change their default Web page to read something embarrassing or self-aggrandizing. Imagine if you went to the Web site of a company you were accustomed to dealing with and you were presented, not with the familiar home page, but a page containing offensive images or phrases like "The HAXOR Group 0WNS This Site!" Companies that are the victims of these attacks find themselves facing public embarrassment and financial loss, while the perpetrators often brag about the successful attack or laugh at the news reports of the company's dismay.

Another common phenomenon is the hacker who breaks into networks for fun; they enjoy the challenge of defeating an "undefeatable" security system. This can be anyone from a college student attempting to flex his computing muscles against Internet-connected machines, to an internal employee who just wants to see what she can get away with on the office PC. In many cases, these attackers do not consider their actions unethical or immoral, their thinking being that "if the vulnerability hadn't been there in the first place, I wouldn't have been able to exploit it."

The last category of attackers that we will discuss (although this list is by no means complete) are those who are motivated by personal gain, either hacking for pay or as a means of exacting revenge. In the case of the former, this can range from simple criminal actions to attackers performing industrial espionage (trying to steal the secret formula from the database server) or even information warfare between governments. The "revenge" attacker is typically a former employee of a company, who might plant a "logic bomb" to damage networking resources after he or she has been fired or laid off.

TEST DAY TIP

A *logic bomb* is a type of attack, whether a virus, worm, DDoS or Trojan, that lies dormant until triggered by a specific event. This event is usually associated with a date, such as the now-famous Michelangelo e-mail virus that was triggered to be released on the date of the artist's birthday.

Implementing Risk Analysis

A favorite Information Security lecturer of mine once commented that the only way to have a truly secure computer was to unplug the network cable from the wall, remove the keyboard, mouse, and monitor, and dump the CPU in the middle of the ocean. While this is a somewhat sarcastic statement, the message is clear: no computer network will ever be *completely* free from security risks. When designing security for your network, therefore, a large part of your job will actually be a matter of Risk Management—deciding how to use finite resources to provide your company with the best security measures possible. When creating a Risk Analysis strategy, you should involve staff from areas other than IT, including your company's Legal and Finance departments, to assist you in assigning values to various projects and assets. Anyone who plays a leadership role in any project or product that your company is working on should have a say in the Risk Analysis process.

The first step in implementing a Risk Analysis strategy is assessing the value of your assets and resources. Some assets, such as physical servers, networking hardware, and cabling, are relatively simple to assign a value to, based on their purchase price minus any depreciation from the accountants. Other items will need to be valued according to the cost of producing them—the salaries of programmers during the development of a new software application, for example—or the cost to the company if something were lost. Assigning a concrete monetary value to something like a lost sales lead caused by an e-mail server outage can be difficult, but the Risk Analysis process cannot be successful without having this information available.

Next, you need to identify the potential risks to each asset in turn, including (but not limited to) the kinds of attacks that we've already discussed in this chapter. For each potential attack, you'll define the potential damage that could be done to each asset, again in monetary terms. To use our example of a lost sales lead resulting from an e-mail server outage, let's say that the company Sales Manager does some research and determines that your company loses about $1,000 an hour when the e-mail server is unavailable. Last year, the e-mail server was unavailable for 20 hours when it became overloaded with messages created by the various viruses. You can use this to determine that virus threats cost your company $20,000 last year. You can use this sort of equation to assign a value to most types of security risks faced by your company, allowing you to prioritize your budget and resources where they will do the most good.

Addressing Risks to the Corporate Network

Once you have created a prioritized list of risks to your network, as well as their associated costs, your next step will be to determine a course of action in handling each risk. When deciding how to address risks to your network, you typically have one of four options:

- **Avoidance** You can avoid a risk by changing the scope of the project so that the risk in question no longer applies, or change the features of the software to do the same. In most cases, this is not a viable option, since eliminating a network service like e-mail to avoid risks from viruses would usually not be seen as an appropriate measure. (Network services exist for a reason; your job as a security professional is to make those services as secure as possible.) One potential example of how avoidance would be a useful Risk Management tactic would be a case where a company had a single server that acted as both a Web server and a database server housing confidential personnel records, when there is no interaction whatsoever between the Web site and personnel information. Purchasing a second server to house the employee database, removing the personnel database from the Web server entirely, and placing the employee database server on a private network segment with no contact to the Internet would be a way of avoiding Web-based attacks on personnel records, since this plan of action "removes" a feature of the Web server (the personnel files) entirely.
- **Transference** You can transfer a risk by moving the responsibility to a third party. The most well-known example of this is purchasing some type of insurance—let's say flood insurance—for the contents of your server room. While the purchase of this insurance does not diminish the likelihood that a flood will occur in your server room, by purchasing insurance you have ensured that the monetary cost of the damage will be borne by the insurance company in return for your policy premiums. It's important to note that transference is not a 100-percent solution—in the flood example, your company will likely still incur some financial loss or decreased productivity in the time it takes you to restore your server room to working order. Like most risk management tactics, bringing the risk exposure down to zero in this way is usually an unattainable goal.
- **Mitigation** This is what most IT professionals think of when implementing a Risk Management solution. Mitigation involves taking some positive action to reduce the likelihood that an attack will occur, or reduce the potential damage that would be caused by an attack, without removing the resource entirely as is the case with avoidance. Patching servers, disabling unneeded services, and installing a firewall would be some solutions that would fall under the heading of risk mitigation.
- **Acceptance** After you have delineated all of the risks to your infrastructure that can be avoided, transferred, or mitigated, you are still left with a certain amount of risk that you won't be able to reduce any further without seriously impacting your business (taking an e-mail server offline as a means to combat viruses, for example). Your final option is one of acceptance,

where you decide that the residual risks to your network have reached an acceptable level, and you choose to monitor the network for any signs of new or increased risks that might require more action later.

TEST DAY TIP

When determining the cost-effectiveness of a safeguard, remember this formula: The total savings to your organization is the amount of money that the safeguard will be saving you, minus the cost of the safeguard itself. Therefore, if you install a $25,000 firewall that you estimate will save you $100,000 from downtime due to hacker intrusions, the total cost savings provided by the firewall is:

$100,000 (savings) – $25,000 (cost of safeguard) = $75,000 net savings to the organization.

EXAM 70-298 OBJECTIVE 1.1.3

Analyzing Security Requirements for Different Types of Data

Once you've gone through the Risk Analysis process, you should have a good idea of what types of data are present on your network and how much the loss of each type of data will cost your organization, both in a quantitative and qualitative sense. At this point, it's often helpful to classify data into discrete categories to assist you in securing your information in an efficient manner. Many organizations use a four-tiered classification system that organizes data and resources into one of four categories:

- **Public** This might include informational items such as product listings on the corporate Web site and press releases issued by Marketing or Public Relations. There is probably little risk associated with someone attempting to steal this data, since it is assumed to be common knowledge among a company's customers and competitors. However, the integrity of this data still needs to be maintained to retain consumer confidence and potential sales. (Imagine the impact if a press release were altered to read that your company suffered a 10-percent loss in sales, rather than posting a 20-percent growth.)
- **Private** This will include information that might be widely known within your company, but perhaps sufficiently sensitive that you do not want to share it with the world at large. Data contained on a corporate intranet might be included in this category, since it often includes contact information for specific personnel, as well as information concerning internal systems that might not be appropriate for release to the public.

- **Confidential** This is the kind of information (along with Secret data) that most of us think of when we begin constructing a security plan. This can include information like customer financial records or corporate payroll information. The disclosure or alteration of data of this nature would almost certainly lead to real losses to the company, whether in terms of financial loss or reputation.
- **Secret** This is the most confidential classification of data, and most often extends to intellectual property such as trade secrets, patent information, or upcoming products and ventures. The loss or defacement of secret data would be almost irreparable, since a trade secret that has been disclosed to the public or to competitors cannot simply be made secret again with the wave of a wand. Data at this level must be afforded the most stringent protection levels within your corporate network.

After you have classified your organization's data and resources, you can use this information to assign different security templates or policies to the different categories. This will increase the efficiency of your network security design, since you will be able to more easily assign similar or identical security measures to data that has similar security requirements. It will also save you from wasting time or effort assigning the same level of protection to, say, your company's softball schedule that you assign to more critical information such as sales or payroll data.

EXAM 70-298 OBJECTIVE 1.2.2

Responding to Security Incidents

Despite the best security infrastructure design, an unfortunate reality of modern networks is that it's usually not a case of *if* you will need to address an attack against your network, but *when*. This is why it's crucial to formulate a security response plan *before* you need one, so that your company's personnel (both technical and nontechnical) will know how to respond to a network security breach. If left unchecked, a security breach can lead to stolen or corrupted data, identity theft, and embarrassing negative publicity for your company. An Incident Response plan details the actions that you take when a security incident occurs, allowing you to react to any security breaches in a rapid and efficient manner. It's also critical that your Incident Response plan has support throughout your organization and is tested on a regular basis to ensure that it addresses all necessary concerns. This includes creating detailed procedures and defining the roles and responsibilities of everyone on your staff so that everyone can act in concert. By staging "practice emergencies" and measuring how well and how quickly your staff can respond to them, you can minimize the impact that a security breach will have against your organization.

Recognizing Attack Indicators

When a network attack occurs, the key to minimizing any damage to your company's assets is rapid response. But how can you react to a network attack if you don't know that one is occurring? Recognizing the signs of an attack is the crucial first step in limiting the fallout of an incident such as a hack or virus attack. And you can only recognize when something is *wrong* on your network when you understand how things are supposed to look when they're *right*. Because of this, it's important to create a baseline of your network as early as possible. A network baseline will include such details as:

- Average %processor utilization on a specific server
- RAM usage and statistics such as average page faults/second
- Average %network utilization on a network segment

You should also be aware of specific times of the day, week, or month when your network baseline is predictably higher or lower—your network utilization might spike while transmitting sales figures at the end of each day. Alternately, a server's processor utilization might be extremely low at 2 A.M., so that 40 percent utilization might be a cause for alarm at this time when it wouldn't necessarily be so during the 9 A.M. to 5 P.M. day. A good network baseline should include data sampled at several points during the day over several weeks or a month, so that you can obtain a complete picture of the state of your network when it's operating under normal conditions.

Perhaps the most important tool in obtaining a network baseline and subsequently recognizing any adverse conditions is the use of *auditing*. Using the audit logs in the Windows Server 2003 Event Viewer will alert you to any errors or system events that might be occurring on your network. If you are running a Web server using IIS or using ISA or a third-party firewall solution, you will also have detailed information available through the separate audit logs for these applications or hardware components.

EXAM WARNING

For auditing to function correctly in an enterprise environment, you need to use *time synchronization* so that audit logs from multiple machines will all correctly reflect the time that events occurred.

Creating an Incident Response Plan

Incident Response refers to how your organization reacts to a network attack or any other type of security incident. Without an Incident Response plan, your company's reaction to such an attack will be unorganized at best, chaotic at worst. This lack of organization in and of itself can cause additional damage stemming from confusion in the wake of a security incident. Now that we've discussed how to recognize when an attack against your network is occurring, we'll move on to how to react to any breaches that occur. Whether you have a dedicated Incident Response Team, or include Incident Response with the duties of a network administrator or engineer, it's crucial to delineate exactly what those responsibilities are. You can separate the components of an Incident Response Plan into four logical steps:

1. Response
2. Investigation
3. Restoration
4. Reporting

The first step when drafting an Incident Response plan is deciding how you will *respond* to a network security incident. Your first instinct might be to power down the computer and immediately begin to work on resolving the incident. And while the restoration of network services is a crucial piece of Incident Response (and one we'll talk more about later), taking a few minutes to collect some information about the current state of the machine being attacked can assist immensely in determining how and why the attack occurred, and provide clues to better prevent a similar attack from happening in the future. At a minimum, you should record the following information before beginning to work on the machine:

- Machine name and IP address
- Operating system and service pack level
- Running services and processes
- Copies of all Event Viewer log files—Application, System, Security, and any machine-specific logs like File Replication or DNS.
- Evidence of intruder activity—any files that have been changed or removed, rogue processes listed in Task Manager, and so forth. At this point, you should be able to define the type of attack—is this a DoS attack? A software attack that has compromised your system integrity?
- Source of the attack—while you can't always be 100 percent accurate, you can use the Event Viewer and other access logs to determine where an attack is coming from. This can assist you in containing the attack, as we'll discuss in a moment.

- A list of who is dependent on this server and who will need to be notified of any downtime—developers, specific departments or offices, and so forth. Since a compromised system might need to be shut down or removed from the network rather quickly, any users who are dependent on this system need to be made aware of it so that they can plan their work accordingly.

Another critical step in responding to an incident is containing the intrusion so that no further damage is done to any additional network systems. Especially if the attack is ongoing, you need to prevent the intrusion from spreading. For example, if you are facing a DoS attack, you can set up filters at your firewall or border router to prevent any more packets coming from the attacker's IP address from reaching your network. In the case of a DDoS, there might be multiple points of attack, but measures such as these will at least minimize the effects of the attack on the rest of your network. And while you might not want to immediately power down the compromised computer so that you can collect information and evidence, you can certainly unplug the network cable to prevent the machine itself from further damaging any other resources, especially if the attack is one that has compromised the machine's operating system or other security functions.

TEST DAY TIP

No matter what your plans for Incident Response are, you should disconnect any compromised machine from your network to prevent other machines from becoming infected or compromised.

Analyzing a Security Incident

Once you've recognized that a security incident is taking place, you should gather as much information as possible about the attack, the attacker, and the system that's being targeted. Take a "snapshot" of the machine, preferably before rebooting it or removing it from the network, and record a list of all running processes, open network connections, and any files and directories that are being accessed or altered. As we mentioned in the last section, having a baseline to compare this to can be immensely helpful in discovering what has gone amiss on the system in question. You or your system administrators should know which processes and services should (and should not) be running on any production server, and you should also have an idea of what sort of network traffic is normal or acceptable in order to detect any anomalies.

Head of the Class...

Computer Forensics

Before you begin the recovery process, you'll need to decide whether your primary goal is restore the server to working order as quickly as possible, or to attempt to preserve the existing state of the machine in order to pursue (and potentially prosecute) the attackers. If your goal is to attempt to prosecute the attackers, it becomes critical not to tamper with any evidence that might be useful to law enforcement agencies. This begins to delve into the field of computer forensics.

Computer forensics is the application of computer skills and investigation techniques to aid law enforcement for the purposes of acquiring evidence relating to computer-based attacks. This primarily involves collecting, examining, preserving, and presenting evidence that is stored or transmitted in an electronic format, such as log entries and other files. Because the ultimate purpose of this evidence collection is that it might be used in court, you need to follow strict procedures in order for evidence to be usable in court or any internal action (like presenting information to Human Resources about an employee violating an AUP by using company resources to download unacceptable materials).

When a security breach has occurred, from a forensics standpoint you need to preserve the "scene of the crime" to the best extent possible. This means that any log files should not be changed in any way, and "Last Accessed" timestamps on files and folders must not be changed wherever possible. Additionally, you should make sure not to overwrite any data on the machine or transfer information to other systems without the use of encrypted transmission. This even extends to not powering down, rebooting, or changing any settings on the computer and photographing or otherwise documenting what is being displayed on the monitor in case power is lost while you are investigating. (Many computer-based attacks are only active as long as the machine is powered on; as soon as the machine reboots, all evidence of the attack and the attacker might be irretrievably lost.) There are now many specialized computer forensics tools that will allow you to make a complete copy of everything that is happening on a system so that the evidence of it can be preserved while you attempt to restore the compromised system to a working state. Finally, any evidence that is collected or removed from the scene needs to be stored in a detailed and systematic way. This *chain of evidence* documents who was in possession of the evidence at all times, and helps to prove that any information or data was not tampered with after the fact.

EXAM 70-298 OBJECTIVE 1.2.4

Recovering Network Services After an Attack

Once you've collected all of the incident tracking or forensics information you want, you can now turn to restoring a compromised machine to a healthy state. As with the rest of the Incident Recovery plan, you should document and test these steps beforehand as much as possible so that actual recovery times are as quick as possible, minimizing any downtime for your users. Unfortunately, once a system has been compromised, in many ways you can't trust *any* of the information that's stored on it because you don't know what the attacker has or has not changed. In most cases, for any system that has been breached, the best and most secure option is to reinstall the operating system from a clean copy of the installation media. Performing a full reinstallation will ensure that the affected system will be free of any Trojans, backdoors, or malicious processes that you might not even be aware of. Reinstallation also ensures that any data that's been restored from a known-good backup is also free of any unauthorized modifications. The obvious drawback to this is that rebuilding a system from scratch can be a time-consuming process. However, this downtime will be greatly lessened if you have redundant hardware that can be quickly brought online, as well as detailed system documentation. Your alternative to a full system recovery is to simply patch the affected system or run utilities designed to correct a specific attack. (Several major anti-virus vendors created utilities that were designed to remove the Nimda and Code Red worm infections from individual machines.) This method is less secure than a full reinstall and is only something you should do as a last resort. The danger with patching a system instead of reinstalling is that it's almost impossible to be sure if you've completely cleared the system of Trojans, holes, or corrupted data.

The last step in recovering your system services is to address and correct the vulnerability that caused the security breach in the first place. This might seem self-explanatory, but without a well defined Incident Response plan, many times you'll see an individual or organization simply place a machine back on the network only to have it attacked and breached again. This is where your initial analysis of the incident will become indispensable, since you need to determine the attacker's point of entry. Did the intruder enter your network through a buffer overflow attack? Be sure to patch the operating system and applications against this attack before returning the system to service. Were any passwords compromised? You should force any potentially compromised users to change their passwords, ensuring that they're using complex and hard-to-guess passwords for network access.

EXAM 70-298 OBJECTIVE 1.3

Analyzing Technical Constraints when Designing Security

While we'd all like to design a security system using all of the latest and greatest technology, budgetary constraints can often limit the scope of a network security design. Perhaps an organization supports satellite offices with down-level operating systems and they have not allocated funds to upgrade the hardware to be able to support the latest Windows operating system. Your design will need to provide the highest level of security possible, based on the technology that you have to work with. This might include designing a security structure that will interoperate with older Microsoft operating systems like Windows NT 4.0, or with third-party services such as UNIX DNS, MIT Kerberos, and other types of clients and servers. In preparing for the 70-298 exam as well as in dealing with real-world situations, you will achieve much success in understanding how Windows Server 2003 operates in a heterogeneous environment and not just a network that uses exclusively Windows Server 2003 software and services.

EXAM 70-298 OBJECTIVE 1.3.1

Recognizing Capabilities of the Existing Infrastructure

Before you can begin planning a Windows Server 2003 implementation, you need to determine if your existing computer and networking hardware will support this new technology. If an organization requires the security options offered by Windows Server 2003 but their current hardware will not support it, they will either need to allocate funds for upgrades or else obtain new hardware altogether. (On the other side of the equation, certain higher-end hardware and software functions will only run on the Advanced and Datacenter editions of 2003—the Standard Edition is not a one-size-fits-all option.) As you can see in the review in Table 1.1, there are many options for deploying Windows Server 2003, each with slightly different hardware requirements.

Table 1.1 Hardware Requirements for Windows Server 2003

Requirement	Standard Edition	Enterprise Edition	Datacenter Edition	Web Edition
Minimum CPU speed	133 MHz	133 MHz for x86-based computers; 733 MHz for Itanium-based computers	400 MHz for x86-based computers; 733 MHz for Itanium-based computers	133 MHz
Recommended CPU speed	550 MHz	733 MHz	733 MHz	550 MHz
Minimum RAM	128MB	128MB	512MB	128MB
Recommended minimum RAM	256MB	256MB	1GB	256MB

Continued

Table 1.1 Hardware Requirements for Windows Server 2003

Requirement	Standard Edition	Enterprise Edition	Datacenter Edition	Web Edition
Maximum RAM	4GB	32GB for x86-based computers; 64GB for Itanium-based computers	64GB for x86-based computers; 512GB for Itanium-based computers	2GB
Multiprocessor support	Up to 4	Up to 8	Minimum 8 required; Maximum 64	Up to 2
Disk space for setup	1.5GB	1.5GB for x86-based computers; 2.0GB for Itanium-based computers	1.5GB for x86-based omputers; 2.0GB for Itanium-based computers	1.5GB

Exam Warning

While some of the information in this section might seem like a review of earlier MCSE exams, any Windows Server 2003 topic is really fair game on the 70-298 exam. Don't be tripped up by thinking you can skip things you've already been tested on!

Bandwidth requirements are not quite as critical from a security standpoint, since security settings will be propagated to all clients and servers regardless of the speed of their connection. (Remember that Microsoft considers a slow link to be less than 500Kbps by default, and that certain nonsecurity elements of Group Policy like Folder Redirection and Software installation will not be deployed over slow links.) However, if a company has a satellite office that is connecting via a 56K dial-up connection, for example, you can use Windows Server 2003 security features to improve their performance by creating an Internet-based VPN. However, in a case like that, you would need to be aware of the operating systems in use at the branch office, and what type of security and encryption they would be able to support. (We'll discuss VPNs and remote access in Chapters 7 and 10.) Before creating a network security design that calls for specific technologies, be sure to ascertain that the client's infrastructure can support the specifics of that design. Otherwise, a plan that looks good on paper will not be one that you will be able to successfully implement for your client.

EXAM 70-298 OBJECTIVE 1.3.2

Identifying Technology Limitations

Windows Server 2003 maintains a high level of backward compatibility with Windows 2000 and Windows NT 4.0 computing environments, but it's important to keep in mind that these earlier versions (especially NT4) will not be able to take advantage of all of the security enhancements available to Windows Server 2003. For example, the default network protocol for Windows NT 4.0 is NTLM, or NTLMv2 if you've installed the NT4 Active Directory client. Using these protocols, your NT4 workstations and servers will be able to participate in a Windows Server 2003 domain. If your security design insists on Kerberos authentication as a security standard, however, NT4 machines will need to be upgraded or replaced, since NT cannot participate in Windows Kerberos authentication.

TEST DAY TIP

Remember that Windows 2000 Professional, Windows 2000 Server, and Windows XP Professional can all use Kerberos authentication to log onto a Windows Server 2003 network.

Windows NT 4 machines also require special consideration when securing network traffic. While NT4 natively supports the PPTP VPN protocol, a special add-on is required to use L2TP or IPSec in a VPN scenario. Further, NT4 cannot use IPSec or understand IPSec policies as they relate to securing LAN traffic—non-VPN network communications with NT4 machines will only be able to encrypt authentication traffic using NTLM or NTLMv2.

This is a critical piece to keep in mind if you are requiring IPSec-signed traffic with a specific server on your network, since NT4 machines will not be able to communicate under those conditions.

Finally, remember that Windows NT4 still relies heavily on NetBIOS and WINS to communicate between machines on a network, rather than using DNS as is becoming the Microsoft standard. The NetBIOS ports (TCP 135, 137, 138, 139 and 445) are a well-known point of attack, and should be protected by a firewall or router so that an external attacker cannot use them to damage NetBIOS-based systems. (We'll discuss securing network traffic and protocols further in Chapter 5.)

EXAM 70-298 OBJECTIVE 1.3.3

Analyzing Interoperability Constraints

In a large enterprise environment, Windows administrators often need to be able to integrate Microsoft technologies with server and client products from third-party vendors. The introduction of other operating systems and services, such as UNIX

DNS and MIT Kerberos, presents unique challenges when creating your security design. Finally, when supporting non-Microsoft clients such as Macintosh, you need to ensure that the clients have a common protocol installed so that they can communicate with the Windows network, and that that protocol meets your organization's security requirements.

Interoperability with MIT Kerberos

A Windows Server 2003 domain controller can function as the Key Distribution Center (KDC) for MIT Kerberos clients and hosts, allowing UNIX clients to use their own Kerberos utilities to authenticate to a Windows Server 2003 domain. Likewise, Microsoft clients can be configured to point to an MIT Kerberos KDC for authentication. A number of command-line utilities on the Windows Server 2003 CD help with configuring clients to authenticate against an MIT Kerberos KDC, including:

- **ksetup** Configures Kerberos realms, Key Distribution Centers, and Kerberos Password (Kpasswd) servers.
- **ktpass** Sets the password, account name mappings, and other information for Kerberos services that use the Windows 2000 Kerberos KDC.

These utilities and others are available in the Windows Server 2003 Support Tools. For UNIX hosts that are authenticating against a Windows Server 2003 KDC, you'll use these utilities, along with the familiar Windows MMCs to configure account and logon information. Table 1.2 illustrates the ksetup command-line options for both of these utilities, while Figure 1.5 illustrates the command-line options for the ktpass utility.

Table 1.2 ksetup Parameters for UNIX Kerberos Integration

Parameter	Description
/SetRealm <DnsDomainName>	Makes this computer a member of an RFC1510 Kerberos Realm.
/MapUser <Principal> [Account]	Maps a Kerberos Principal ('*' = any principal) to an account ('*' = an account by same name); If account name is omitted, mapping is deleted for the specified principal.
/AddKdc <RealmName> [KdcName]	Defines a KDC entry for the given realm. If KdcName omitted, DNS can be used to locate KDCs.
/DelKdc <RealmName> [KdcName]	Deletes a KDC entry for the realm. If KdcName omitted, the realm entry itself is deleted.

Continued

Table 1.2 ksetup Parameters for UNIX Kerberos Integration

Parameter	Description
/AddKpasswd <Realmname> <KpasswdName>	Add Kpasswd server address for a realm.
/DelKpasswd <Realmname> <KpasswdName>	Delete Kpasswd server address for a realm.
/Server <Servername>	Specify name of a Windows machine to target the changes.
/SetComputerPassword <Password>	Sets the password for the computer's domain account (or "host" principal).
/RemoveRealm <RealmName>	Delete all information for this realm from the Registry.
/Domain [DomainName]	Use this domain (if DomainName is unspecified, detect it).
/ChangePassword <OldPasswd> <NewPasswd>	Use Kpasswd to change the logged-on user's password. Use '*' to be prompted for passwords.
/ListRealmFlags (no args)	Lists the available Realm flags that ksetup knows.
/SetRealmFlags <realm> <flag> [flag] [flag] [...]	Sets RealmFlags for a specific realm.
/AddRealmFlags <realm> <flag> [flag] [flag] [...]	Adds additional RealmFlags to a realm.
/DelRealmFlags <realm> <flag> [flag] [flag] [...]	Deletes RealmFlags from a realm.
/DumpState (no args)	Analyze the Kerberos configuration on the given machine.

Figure 1.5 ktpass Command-Line Descriptions

```
----------------------most useful args
[- /]           out : Keytab to produce
[- /]         princ : Principal name (user@REALM)
[- /]          pass : password to use, use "*" to prompt for password.
----------------------less useful stuff
[- /]       mapuser : map princ (above) to this user account (default: don't)
[- /]         mapOp : how to set the mapping attribute (default: add it)
[- /]         mapOp :  is one of:
[- /]         mapOp :        add : add value (default)
[- /]         mapOp :        set : set value
```

Continued

Figure 1.5 ktpass Command-Line Descriptions

```
[- +]       DesOnly : Set account for des-only encryption (default:do)
[- /]            in : Keytab to read/digest options for key generation
[- /]        crypto : Cryptosystem to use
[- /]        crypto :  is one of:
[- /]        crypto : DES-CBC-CRC : for compatibility
[- /]        crypto : DES-CBC-MD5 : default
[- /]         ptype : principal type in question
[- /]         ptype :  is one of:
[- /]         ptype : KRB5_NT_PRINCIPAL : The general ptype-- recommended
[- /]         ptype : KRB5_NT_SRV_INST : user service instance
[- /]         ptype : KRB5_NT_SRV_HST : host service instance
[- /]          kvno : Override Key Version Number
                 Default: query DC for kvno.  Use /kvno 1 for Win2K compat.
[- +]        Answer : +Answer answers YES to prompts.  -Answer answers NO.
[- /]        Target : Which DC to use.  Default:detect
```

Integrating UNIX DNS with Windows Server 2003

The Microsoft DNS service has been designed in compliance with most industry standards for the DNS protocol. This means that you have the option to operate DNS using only Windows Server 2003, or integrating your name resolution services with any new or existing third-party DNS solutions. The most common of these is the UNIX Berkeley Internet Name Domain (BIND) DNS implementation. Windows Server 2003 DNS has been tested against the following versions of BIND with varying degrees of interoperability:

- BIND 4.9.7
- BIND 8.1.2
- BIND 8.2
- BIND 9.1.0

When dealing with a mixed DNS solution, your primary security concern is in the area of zone transfers and record updates. With Windows Server 2003 DNS, both of these tasks are controlled and regulated using built-in Windows security. If your DNS data will be transferred to a BIND server, you need to take precautions to ensure that the UNIX server has been secured against potential attacks against DNS name resolution. This can include restricting the servers that a BIND server is permitted to send a zone transfer to, and ensuring that the actual data transmission to and from the BIND server is encrypted. While the 70-298 exam won't expect you to be able to configure or secure a BIND DNS server, you should be aware that third-party DNS servers are subject to the same kinds of security risks as Microsoft DNS, and you need to take measures to secure them accordingly.

Summary of Exam Objectives

In this chapter, we took a bird's eye view of the process of securing a Windows Server 2003 enterprise network. As you can see, quite a bit of planning and preparation work needs to take place before you can dive right in and start recommending or configuring new technologies. Before you can get into these kinds of specifics, you should first analyze the organization that you're working with to determine what its security needs really *are*. Just as a house needs a proper foundation before it can support rooms, windows, and pretty colors on the walls and floors, designing a secure network requires you to start at the very beginning when working with any enterprise network.

When looking at an organization's security needs, you should begin with any existing security policies or procedures that the organization might already have in place. We started this chapter with an in-depth examination of how to analyze a company's business requirements for network and data security. This included looking at these existing security policies and procedures, either to incorporate them into a new security design, or to determine the kinds of changes they would need to work within a Windows Server 2003 network. Examining existing security policies extends to technical measures like analyzing security requirements for different types of data, since some kinds of data might be subject to specific security or retention policies, and some data is simply more mission-critical or sensitive than others. We also looked at administrative procedures such as being able to balance security and usability for users on a network, along with raising security awareness to better involve your user base in the security process. As a network administrator, you will need to balance the human and the technical in order to create the best security design for your organization.

After you've taken the crucial first step of determining your organization's security needs, the next thing you need to determine is what types of attacks your network will be subjected to. The bulk of this chapter dealt with many of the common attacks that an enterprise network will face, many of which you'll even hear about on the evening news as large Internet-based attacks spread quickly and multiply at an unbelievable rate. And since even the most secure network can never be 100-percent free from security risks, we looked at ways to organize an Incident Response plan, and how to prioritize a limited security budget to offer the best and most cost-effective security for your network even when working on a fixed budget.

We closed this chapter with a discussion of interoperability concerns, and the challenges created by the integration of down-level or third-party operating systems and services into a Windows Server 2003 network. Most real-world enterprise networks require some level of support for heterogeneous computing systems, whether it's NT4 client workstations that haven't been upgraded, or a pre-existing UNIX infrastructure. Knowing how to integrate these technologies into your security design scheme will be a critical task in preparing for the 70-298 exam, as well as in your real-world adventures as an MCSE.

Exam Objectives Fast Track

Analyze Business Requirements for Designing Security

☑ Administrative policies such as Acceptable Use Policies, Privacy Policies, and User Awareness Training can assist an organization in promoting a security-conscious environment.

☑ Understand how any network threats you come across can affect the confidentiality, integrity, and/or availability of your network data and resources in order to better defend against them.

☑ Internal network attacks can often be more damaging than external hack attacks, since internal users already have valid logon credentials and physical access to network resources.

Design a Framework for Designing and Implementing Security

☑ Use Risk Analysis to prioritize the relative importance of data on your network so that you will be able to secure data with different security requirements effectively and efficiently.

☑ Most (if not all) attacks will take one of the following forms when attempting to breach your network: spoofing, tampering, repudiation, information disclosure, denial-of-service, and elevation of privilege.

☑ Use auditing to create a baseline of network performance so that you will recognize anomalies that indicate an attack is taking place.

Analyze Technical Constraints when Designing Security

☑ When designing security, keep in mind security constraints imposed by the use of down-level operating systems like Windows NT4. This can affect your choice of LAN and VPN protocols, since Windows NT4 does not support Kerberos, or the use of IPSec for LAN-based encryption.

☑ Windows Server 2003 can serve as a KDC for non-Microsoft Kerberos clients, and Microsoft clients can also authenticate against an MIT Kerberos KDC using utilities contained in the Windows Server 2003 Support Tools.

☑ Zone transfers and resource record updates with UNIX or other third-party DNS servers need to be secured against malicious activities. Consult the BIND or other DNS server's documentation for information on how to secure the transfer of non-Microsoft DNS information.

Exam Objectives Frequently Asked Questions

The following Frequently Asked Questions, answered by the authors of this book, are designed to both measure your understanding of the Exam Objectives presented in this chapter, and to assist you with real-life implementation of these concepts. You will also gain access to thousands of other FAQs at ITFAQnet.com.

Q: My firewall logs are showing a number of network packets being processed by our external router that look as though they're originating from within my internal network. Can this be right?

A: The reason you're seeing this is that the packets are probably *spoofed*. This means that a malicious user has altered the packets so that their real source address has been removed, and in this case replaced with an address within your internal network. This is a common tactic to obscure the source of a network attack. You can put security measures in place on most modern routers that will filter this traffic, referred to as *ingress filtering* and *egress filtering*. Consult your router documentation for specific configuration details.

Q: Microsoft has just released a critical security update for one of the server products in my network. Should I skip the testing process and install the update right away to protect against the security vulnerability it is correcting?

A: Our best advice would be a resounding "No." While Microsoft Product Services does an outstanding job testing the patches they release, they cannot account for every possible hardware and software combination in existence in the world. Therefore, your best bet is to test the patch on a nonproduction server and check for any adverse effects before deploying it to your production servers. An untested patch can wreak as much havoc on a network as any security vulnerability.

Q: I am using Network Monitor from a Windows Server 2003 machine and am attempting to monitor traffic on my network. However, I am only seeing packets that are coming to or from this specific server; I'm not seeing any other traffic that's taking place. Am I doing something wrong?

A: No. The version of Network Monitor that comes with Windows Server 2003 will only record traffic that is coming to or from the network interface card (NIC) that it's running on. To monitor all traffic on your network, you will need a version of Network Monitor that is running in *promiscuous* mode to capture all packets regardless of source or destination. The version of Network Monitor that comes with Microsoft Systems Management Server (SMS) will perform this function for you.

Q: I need to search the Event logs for multiple Windows Server 2003 machines for any logon attempts by an employee who was recently terminated. Is there an easier way to do this other than opening each server's log file individually?

A: Yes. You can use the EventCombMT utility, a free utility available from the Microsoft Web site. This utility can perform a number of built-in searches, or you can create your own custom queries.

Self Test

A Quick Answer Key follows the Self Test questions. For complete questions, answers, and explanations to the Self Test questions in this chapter as well as the other chapters in this book, see the Self Test Appendix.

Analyzing Business Requirements for Designing Security

1. In performing a risk analysis of your network, you determine that your company lost approximately $100,000 last year from losses relating to laptops being stolen from unattended offices. Your company's CEO and CFO agree that they want to implement some type of safeguard that will reduce that number to a maximum of $50,000. You have been presented with three options to reduce losses. Option 1: A fully staffed reception desk that will sign visitors in and out of the building and examine all outgoing equipment to ensure that it is not leaving the premises illegally. It is expected that this will reduce losses due to equipment theft by 80 percent. The total annual cost for this measure, including equipment and personnel, will be $60,000. Option 2: A card-swipe system will be installed on all entrances

that will ensure that only employees carrying legitimate access cards will be able to enter company premises. It is expected that this measure will reduce losses due to equipment theft by 65 percent. The total annual cost for this measure, including equipment and installation, will be $15,000. Option 3: A user-awareness campaign will be launched to make users more cognizant of the risks inherent in leaving their laptops and other equipment unattended. Certain employees will be designated as "Loss Prevention Monitors" to keep an eye out for potentially hazardous situations such as laptops being left unattended, and inform management so that the offending employee can be reminded of the importance of securing his or her equipment. It is expected that this measure will reduce losses due to equipment theft by 25 percent. The total annual cost for this measure, including personnel time, will be $10,000. Which of these measures is the most cost-effective way to meet the request of your CEO and CFO?

A. Implement Option 1.

B. Implement Option 2.

C. Implement Option 3.

D. None of these solutions is cost-effective.

2. You are creating a security design for the Blue Sky LTD Corporation. The company CEO knows that many people on the network currently use information like their pets' or children's names for their network passwords; she is extremely concerned about hackers attempting to guess these passwords and gain access to corporate network resources. She has requested that password security be made more stringent in the new design, with a minimum of a 24-character password for all systems. What would you tell her is a potential drawback of requiring user passwords to be this long?

A. Users will be more likely to write down a password that is so difficult to remember.

B. User passwords should be at least 30 characters long to guard against brute-force password attacks.

C. There are no drawbacks; this creates network passwords that will be impossible for an unauthorized user to penetrate.

D. Windows 2003 will not allow a password of more than eight characters.

3. You are a security analyst for the Widgets Corporation, which uses Windows Server 2003 servers to store data regarding several patent-pending products that they are developing. Because of the sensitive nature of this information, both successful and failed attempts to access product-related data on the file server is logged to the Windows Security log, and the information can only be accessed

from within the Widgets headquarters—there is no current means of using VPN or other forms of remote access. While you are looking over the security logs one week, you notice that one of the Widgets product managers, Ethan Hopkins, accessed files for a number of different projects on a day when you know that he was out of the office for several days. When you question Ethan about it, he verifies that he was out of the office on that day and has no idea what could have happened. However, you discover in a passing conversation with your help desk manager that someone claiming to be Mr. Hopkins called the help desk that day demanding to have his password reset, since he had been called in for an important sales presentation and couldn't wait. What kind of attack has occurred here?

A. Password guessing

B. Spoofing

C. Network sniffing

D. Social engineering

Designing a Framework for Designing and Implementing Security

4. You are the network administrator for a large Windows Server 2003 network, supporting 40 servers and over 1000 Windows 2000 Professional and Windows XP Professional clients. You have received a call from a user who is complaining that his computer will no longer boot correctly. Upon investigating, you discover that the machine will only get halfway through the logon sequence before displaying the Blue Screen of Death. When you ask the user if he noticed anything unusual before the computer began misbehaving, he reports that he had just downloaded a game from a URL that a friend had sent him via e-mail. The machine seemed to run fine after the game was installed, but as soon as the user rebooted the machine, it no longer powered on correctly. What is the most likely reason why the user's machine is no longer booting correctly?

   A. The downloaded game is not compatible with Windows XP Professional.

   B. The workstation has suffered a hardware failure.

   C. The downloaded game was actually malicious code containing a Trojan horse.

   D. The workstation is undergoing a DoS attack.

5. You are performing a security audit of a Windows Server 2003 network for the branch office of a bank. You have detected an unauthorized computer that is capturing network traffic being sent between your head teller's workstation and the server used to settle account information at the end of the day. You suspect that this computer has changed some of the network data that has been transmitted between these two computers to alter the financial records coming from the teller workstation. What type of attack is most likely taking place in this scenario?

   A. DoS

   B. Man-in-the-middle

   C. Password guessing

   D. IP Spoofing

6. You are performing a Risk Analysis for Blue Sky, LTD., a charter plane service running a Windows Server 2003 network. Since Blue Sky receives a significant portion of its client referrals from the blueskyltd.com Web site, the CFO has decided that any losses due to a Web server outage would pose an extreme financial risk to the company. Because of this, you have decided to outsource the hosting of your Web site to a third party. You will pay this hosting service a monthly fee, in return for which they will guarantee 99.999-percent uptime and availability of the Blue Sky Web site for your customers. Which principle of Risk Management have you employed by taking this measure?

   A. Risk Avoidance

   B. Risk Mitigation

   C. Risk Transference

   D. Risk Acceptance

7. You are working as the network administrator responsible for monitoring and maintaining 25 Windows Server 2003 servers and 500 Windows XP Professional workstations. You are checking the Network Monitor that is running on your Web server and notice a sudden influx of TCP SYN (Synchronization) packet requests with no subsequent completion of the TCP handshake. What is this type of activity most likely an indicator of?

   A. Your network is beginning to sustain a DoS attack.

   B. Someone is attempting to guess passwords of user accounts on your network.

   C. This is normal activity and not something that you should worry about.

   D. Your company's Internet connection has failed and you should contact your Internet service provider (ISP).

Analyze Technical Constraints when Designing Security

8. You have been hired as a consultant by the Widgets, Inc. manufacturing company to design security for their company headquarters. The current network consists of several Windows NT4 application and file servers; users connect to the servers via NT4 workstations located throughout the floor of the manufacturing plant. Because of a specialized interface between the manufacturing equipment and the mission-critical software that controls it, user workstations cannot be upgraded away from NT4 until the Widgets developers are able to port the application to a new version of the desktop operating system. Because of a concern regarding the security of user passwords and logon information, the Widget's CTO wants all network communications to be encrypted. What is the highest level of encryption that you would recommend in this scenario?

   A. LM

   B. NTLM

   C. NTLMv2

   D. Kerberos

9. You have been contracted to create an Internet-based VPN solution for an organization with a large traveling sales force. The organization has standardized on Windows Server 2003 servers. Sixty percent of the sales force has been issued a new laptop running the Windows 2000 Professional operating system within the past year. As part of the VPN deployment, the remainder of the sales force will receive laptops that are running Windows XP Professional. The CEO and CTO both agree that the VPN solution should use the best security possible. Which protocol should you recommend when designing a VPN solution in this scenario?

   A. SPAP

   B. IPSEC/L2TP

   C. PPTP

   D. MS-CHAPv2

10. You are the network administrator for a network whose infrastructure is made up of a combination of Windows Server 2003 and UNIX servers. Currently, your company's DNS servers all exist on DNS servers using BIND version 8.1.2. You would like to transition the DNS service to Windows Server 2003 in order to take advantage of secure updates. Your CTO is concerned that the

transition needs to be seamless, and has asked you to bring a single Windows Server 2003 DNS server online and configure it to coexist with the existing BIND servers to ensure that client name resolution will not be interrupted. What should you be concerned with when configuring a Windows Server 2003 DNS server to coexist with a BIND DNS server? (Choose all that apply.)

A. Securing the zone transfer process.

B. Securing WINS lookups from the BIND DNS servers.

C. Configuring the BIND servers to use NTLMv2 authentication.

D. Securing the record update process.

Self Test Quick Answer Key

For complete questions, answers, and explanations to the Self Test questions in this chapter as well as the other chapters in this book, see the Self Test Appendix.

1. **B**
2. **A**
3. **D**
4. **C**
5. **B**
6. **C**
7. **A**
8. **C**
9. **B**
10. **A, D**

Chapter 2

MCSE 70-298

Securing Servers Based on Function

Exam Objectives in this Chapter:

- 3.7.1 Define a baseline security template for all systems.
- 3.7 Design security for servers that have specific roles.
- 3.7.2 Create a plan to modify baseline security templates according to role.

- ☑ Summary of Exam Objectives
- ☑ Exam Objectives Fast Track
- ☑ Exam Objectives Frequently Asked Questions
- ☑ Self Test
- ☑ Self Test Quick Answer Key

Introduction

When you're designing network security for a medium-to-large enterprise, it's often helpful to think of servers in terms of the *role* that they play on the network, rather than just as "Server1," "Server2," and "Server3." To assist in this process, Windows Server 2003 has introduced features such as the Configure Your Server Wizard that simplify the process of assigning a specific role to a given machine. Once you've configured a server (or group of servers) to fulfill a specific role on your network, you should then secure these different server roles in a consistent fashion to improve the overall security of your enterprise network.

In this chapter, we discuss the use of security templates as a way to apply consistent security settings to an entire network, or to a subset of computers or servers. You'll need to begin with a baseline security template that will define security settings common to your entire network. We'll start with a review of the use of security templates, which you should already be familiar with from preparing for the Windows Server 2003 Core Four exams. Once we've reviewed the use of security templates in Windows Server 2003, we'll focus on how to deploy these templates across an entire network in an efficient manner. (You certainly wouldn't want to individually configure security settings on a network with hundreds or thousands of machines, now, would you?) We'll focus on the use of Group Policy Objects (GPOs) and scripting techniques to quickly deploy common security settings across an entire network.

Once you've established your baseline security settings, you'll then need to modify those settings based on the function of a given server or group of servers on your network. A number of security enhancements can specifically benefit machines that are functioning as domain controllers (DCs), Web servers, network infrastructure servers, and file servers. Just as you used templates to create a common security configuration for your entire network, you can also modify that baseline to quickly configure a group of servers whose security requirements might differ from the common configuration. When designing a secure network infrastructure for a Windows Server 2003 network, the use and deployment of security templates will be of great use to you, both on the 70-298 exam and in real-world security deployments.

EXAM 70-297 OBJECTIVE 3.7.1

Defining a Baseline Security Template

Securing servers is critical in today's environment where corporations run their businesses via electronic networks. To assist in managing large networks, Windows Server 2003 includes predefined security templates. These templates allow the network administrator to use or modify predefined settings that can be applied to any number of similar computers in a network. The task of securing servers is both simplified *and* enhanced, since templates reduce the likelihood of error or omission when designing security for the enterprise.

Windows Server 2003 contains several administrative security tools that together form a comprehensive interface for managing a secure environment. Collectively, these tools are called the *Security Configuration Tool Set* or the *Security Configuration Manager,* and have the following elements:

- **Security Configuration and Analysis snap-in** The Security Configuration and Analysis snap-in works only on the local computer. It cannot be used to configure security on remote computers. However, network administrators often use it to design and test security configurations locally before rolling them out across the domain or organizational unit (OU).
- **Security Templates snap-in** Windows Server 2003 provides predefined security templates that can be applied, as is, in various situations. These temples can be modified and are used to configure and apply security settings on computers in similar roles across the network. These templates contain settings that allow the network administrator to review and configure security levels for account policies, local policies, event logs, restricted groups, file systems, Registry settings, and system services. These templates can be access and modified in the Security Templates snap-in to the Microsoft Management Console (MMC).
- **The command-line tool secedit.exe** The command line tool, secedit.exe, is used to analyze, configure, and export system security settings. There are a variety of command-line switches used with *secedit*, discussed in detail later in this chapter. This tool is often used in batch programs or scheduled tasks to apply security settings automatically. It is also the preferred tool for reapplying default security settings.
- **Security Extensions to Group Policy** The Security Extensions to Group Policy are used to define security configurations for various users, groups, or computers within a GPO. The Security Extensions are accessed via the Administrative Tools via the Active Directory Users and Computers console or via the Group Policy Object Editor snap-in via the MMC.
- **Hfnetchk.exe and Microsoft Baseline Security Analyzer (MBSA)** Windows Server 2003 also includes a command-line tool called Hfnetchk.exe, which stands for Hot Fix Network Checker, that analyzes Windows computers and reports any missing security updates. While this is not specifically a tool for setting security on servers, it is a useful tool for keeping your servers up to date with hotfixes and patches that can affect security after initial configuration and installation. Finally, there is a downloadable tool called Microsoft Baseline Security Analyzer (MBSA). As part of Microsoft's Strategic Technology Protection Program, the MBSA can perform local or remote scans of Windows systems. The tool runs on Windows 2000,

Windows XP, and Windows Server 2003 systems and is used to identify common system misconfigurations and missing security updates. It can be used to scan Windows NT, Windows 2000, Windows XP, Windows Server 2003, Internet Information Service (IIS) 4.0 and 5.0, SQL Server 7.0 and 2000, Internet Explorer (IE) 5.01 and later, as well as Office 2000 and 2002. MBSA will scan for missing security updates for the following products:

- Windows NT 4.0, Windows 2000, Windows XP, Windows Server 2003
- IIS 4.0 and 5.0
- SQL Server 7.0 and 2000
- IE 5.01 and later
- Exchange Server 5.5 and 2000
- Windows Media Player 6.4 and later

The MBSA tool uses the Hfnetchk.exe tool and creates an XML security report for each computer scanned. The MBSA tool provides a graphical user interface (GUI) for reviewing the reports via HTML. The current version, v1.1.1, can be downloaded from the Microsoft Web site.

To set baseline security for a network, you need to begin by analyzing the network and determining the security needs for numerous elements including servers (based on server role), client computers, applications, network communication, file systems, user accounts, and system services, to name just a few. In this chapter, we're focusing on setting baseline security for servers based on their roles.

Best Practices for Security Templates

Windows Server 2003 provides a number of predefined security templates. Before working with the templates, it's a good idea to review best practices as they relate to these security templates.

1. Always test security templates, whether predefined or customized, in a test environment before using them on a live or production system.
2. Never edit the Setup security.inf file. This is what establishes a minimum baseline security level for a Windows Server 2003 network. If you ever need to reapply security settings, you can use this file to reestablish a secure baseline. You'll also need to use this file if you remove a security template from a GPO. To avoid tattooing (discussed earlier), you should reapply the portion of the Setup security.inf file to restore all default settings changed by the removed template. If you want to define different baseline security components, you can create a copy of this file and edit the copy. However, be aware that the additional security templates build on *this* known baseline.

Your best bet is to modify the other templates and leave the Setup security.inf file unmodified.

3. Do not apply the Setup security.inf file via Group Policy. It should only be applied via the Security Configuration and Analysis snap-in or via the secedit command line. The best scenario is to apply specific parts of the Setup security.inf via the command line.
4. Never apply the Compatible template to DCs, as this will expose your DCs to serious security risks.
5. Always save modifications to templates as a different filename to preserve the original security template.
6. Thoroughly document all changes you make to each template. This way, you'll be able to assess the results of applying several templates, and it will greatly assist in troubleshooting.

Now that we've reviewed best practices related to security templates, let's look at the predefined templates provided in Windows Server 2003.

Windows Server 2003 Predefined Security Templates

Windows Server 2003 provides several different security templates, each of which applies a different group of security policy settings for distinct security needs. The release of Windows Server 2003 represents a departure from the way Microsoft has implemented security in the past. With this release, security is set to the fewest possible permissions. It is up to you, the network administrator, to modify settings as needed. However, before you make any changes, research and test the results to discover potential weaknesses and find out how intruders might exploit them to gain access to your network resources.

These predefined templates can be modified, although the default settings are more secure than were the default settings in previous Windows Server products. The templates can be accessed and modified via the Security Templates snap-in via the MMC. The security settings for a particular computer can be configured and analyzed via a related snap-in, the Security Configuration and Analysis snap-in, also accessed via the MMC, via the command-line tool *secedit*, or by importing the template into the local security policy. To configure a group of machines with a security template (either predefined or modified), you can import a template into security settings, an extension to Group Policy. The predefined templates are stored in the *systemroot*\Security\Templates location. The templates included in Windows Server 2003 are:

- Default security (setup security.inf)
- Domain controller default security (DC security.inf)

- Compatible (compat*.inf)
- Secure (secure*.inf)
- Highly secure (hisec*.inf)
- System root security (rootsec.inf)
- No Terminal Server user SID (notssid.inf)

The asterisk (*) in some of the filenames means that the characters will change based on application. For example, if applied to a DC, the secure*.inf file would be called securedc.inf. If applied to a workstation, the file would be called securews.inf. Each of these templates and their appropriate applications are discussed next. Using these templates provides baseline security for your network. Using these templates helps ensure you don't inadvertently omit or change a security setting that will leave your network vulnerable to both intentional and unintentional security breaches. Modifying these templates carefully will allow you to customize your network security to meet the needs of your organization.

Exam Warning

Windows 2000 used a template called Basic*.inf to apply default security settings. In Windows Server 2003, this template is called Setup security.inf. Windows Server 2000 also used a template for dedicated DCs called Dedica*.inf to optimize security for local users on DCs that did not run other server applications. Windows Server 2003 provides several templates related to DCs, including DC security.inf, securedc.inf, and hisecdc.inf. Be sure you're familiar with the templates used in Windows Server 2003 so you won't be confused between Windows Server 2000 and Windows Server 2003 security templates.

Each security template is designed with the assumption that it will be applied to computers that use the default security settings. This is why it's inadvisable to modify the Setup security.inf file—the file that provides the default security settings used in Windows Server 2003. These templates incrementally modify security settings, so it's important to understand what each security template does and how it's applied before modifying any of the templates. It's also critical to understand that if security settings have been modified from the default settings, it's recommended that you reapply default settings before applying these security templates. The security templates do not apply the default settings prior to making modifications, so you can end up with unspecified results if you apply these templates on top of nondefault security settings.

EXAM WARNING

When answering questions about security templates, try to determine if the security settings have been modified or if the settings are the defaults. On the exam, remember that these templates do not *apply* default settings; they work with existing settings, which are assumed to be default settings, and apply additional settings based on the template selected.

The security templates are text files and can be viewed using Notepad. To modify the templates, you should use either the snap-in or the *secedit* command-line tool. Figure 2.1 shows the Setup security.inf, the default security template, in Notepad.

Figure 2.1 Setup security.inf Viewed in Notepad

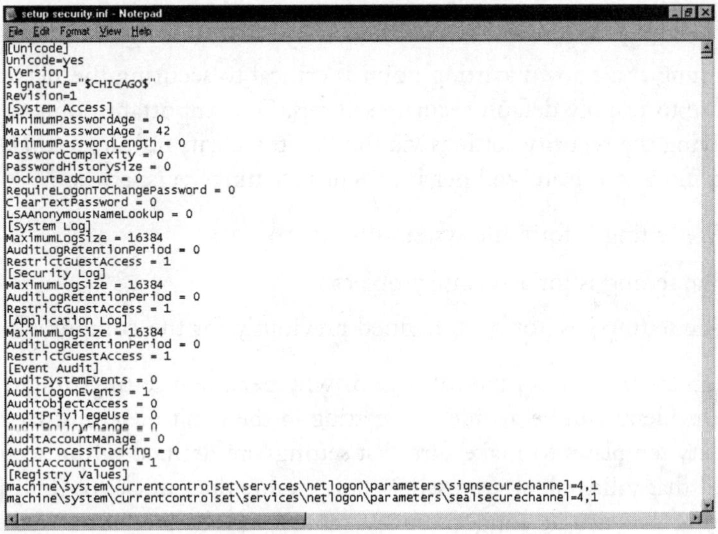

Default Security (setup security.inf)

The default security template is applied during initial installation of the operating system on each computer. Since installations can be clean or upgrades, the resulting settings can vary from computer to computer. This template establishes the default security settings applied to the system, including the file permissions for the primary system drive. It can be used on both client and server systems, but is not used on DCs. Baseline security for DCs is provided via the DC security.inf, discussed in the next section.

The Setup security.inf template should not be applied via Group Policy, because this baseline template contains a large amount of data (over 1000 security settings). Since Group Policy is refreshed from time to time, the large amount of data in the

Setup security.inf file can seriously degrade performance. Microsoft recommends applying the Setup security.inf template in sections, when needed, using the *secedit* command-line tool, discussed later in this chapter.

When you install Windows Server 2003, default security settings are installed via the Setup security.inf file. However, if you're upgrading from a previous Windows operating system or if you've previously modified settings, some of these security settings might not be set to the default values used in Windows Server 2003. To establish a sound baseline, it is sometimes best to reapply the default values, which does two things. First, it sets all security values to a known value so you don't have to guess where changes might have been made. Second, applying any of the other predefined security templates *does not* set default values. The templates modify certain security settings, but if the default values are not in place, there might still be settings that leave your network vulnerable.

Reapplying Default Security Settings

Since beginning at a known starting point is critical to securing the network, you might choose to reapply default security settings. One important point to note is that even reapplying the security settings via the Setup security.inf file, settings that are not defined in the template will persist. Security settings persist when:

- The setting is for a file system object.
- The setting is for a Registry object.
- The setting has not been defined previously for the computer.

Although there are a number of reasons why persistent settings might occur, many such incidents can be avoided by getting in the habit of setting security via the use of security templates to make sure that settings are defined in the security database and that valid values are used. When a value does not exist for a previously defined setting that also no longer exists, a value might be left "as is." This is sometimes referred to as "tattooing." Although you can reapply all default security settings via the Setup security.inf file, it is a significant step that should be avoided if possible. Rather than reapplying all default settings, you can use the *secedit* command to reapply default settings for just a portion of the database. We'll explore the *secedit* command and restoring default settings via the *secedit* command later in this chapter.

Domain Controller Default Security (DC security.inf)

This template is automatically generated any time a server is promoted to a DC. It contains default file, Registry, and system services settings appropriate to securing a DC. You should be aware that reapplying the Domain Controller Default security template will reset values to default values, which could cause problems on files,

Registry entries, or system services created by other applications. To determine if applications have modified any of the default settings, you can use the Security Configuration and Analysis snap-in to compare current settings to the default template. As with the other predefined templates, the DC security.inf template can be configured and applied using either the Security Configuration and Analysis snap-in or the *secedit* tool.

Compatible (compat*.inf)

The default security configuration (Setup security.inf) allows certified applications to run for members of the Users group. Noncertified applications—those applications not part of the Windows Logo Program for Software—will often only work when an end user has Power User permissions, because these applications require permissions that are typically only granted to the Power Users group, such as the ability to access the system's Registry. Rather than add all users to the Power Users group, the Compatible template modifies just those permissions needed by end users to run noncertified applications. This allows the network administrator to modify permissions for end users to run these noncertified applications, while maintaining tight overall security. Best security practices dictate that users be given the fewest possible permissions while still allowing them to access appropriate network resources. In the past, the only choices a network administrator had were to either add all users to the Power Users group or modify the User group permissions. Both scenarios create security holes by granting too many rights to end users who simply need to run a noncertified application. Using the Compatible security template, the network administrator can allow end users to have appropriate permissions to run noncertified applications and still not grant the full permissions granted to Power Users.

The Compatible template should not be applied to DCs. The template should not be imported to the Default Domain policy or the Default Domain Controller policy, as it will significantly compromise the security of the DC.

Secure (secure*.inf)

The Secure templates define security settings for all areas except those that are related to running noncertified applications. The Secure templates do not modify security settings for files, folders, and Registry keys, which are set by the Setup security.inf template. Secure templates are used to define stronger passwords, lockouts, and audit settings and to limit the use of LAN Manager and NTLM authentication protocols. The limiting of LAN Manager and NTLM authentication protocols is accomplished in two ways. First, servers are configured to refuse LAN Manager responses, and clients are configured to send only NTLM v2 responses. Computers running Windows NT must be Windows NT 4.0 SP4 or later to use NTLM v2. Windows 9*x* computers must have the Directory Service client installed in order to use NTLM v2. The Secure template has one additional effect that should be noted—it removes all members of the Power Users group.

It is also important to be aware of the compatibility constraints in using these security settings. These constraints can cause connectivity issues in a mixed environment and should be thoroughly tested before implementing them on your live network. Guidelines for using the secure*.inf template in a mixed environment include:

- If you want to apply the securews.inf security template to a client computer, you must ensure that all DCs that contain user accounts that might be accessed through the client computer are running Windows NT 4.0 Service Pack 4 or later (also referred to as NT4.0 SP4). If this is not the case, you cannot apply the securews.inf template to that client computer.
- If you want to apply the securews.inf security to client computers on domains with DCs running Windows NT 4.0, the DCs and client computers must have their time clocks set within 30 minutes of each other. If the clocks are more than 30 minutes off, the client will not be able to connect using a local account that is defined on the DC.
- The securews.inf template prevents the use of LAN Manager or NTLM authentication protocols. Therefore, if a client computer is configured to use the securews.inf template, it will not be able to connect to servers that use *only* LAN Manager authentication or that run Windows NT 4.0 prior to Service Pack 4.
- If servers are running Windows XP or later, a client computer configured to use securews.inf will not be able to connect using a local account on the target server unless the clocks on the client and server are within 20 hours of each other.

Test Day Tip

The secure*.inf security template prevents the use of LAN Manager Authentication protocol or the NTLM authentication protocol. For computers running Windows NT 4.0 Service Pack 4 or later, you can configure the system to send only NTLM v2 responses via the Registry. The setting is located in the **HKEY_LOCAL_MACHINE\SYSTEM\CurrentControlSet\ontrol\LSA\LMCompatibilityLevel** key. This should be set to 3, "Send NTLM v2 authentication only."

The secure*.inf template is also used to restrict anonymous user permissions. It prevents anonymous users from enumerating account names and shares. Clearly, access to account names and shares provides one half of the equation for gaining access to the network—the other half is the password. Gaining illicit access to a network is made far easier when account and/or share names are supplied. Thus, the secure*.inf template closes this door to anonymous users. It also prevents anonymous users from translating SID to names or names to SID. The SID, or security ID, is the data structure that identifies the user, group, and computer account. Every account is issued a SID when created. Preventing anonymous users from translating SID to name or name to SID also helps maintain a secure network.

The last notable feature of the secure*.inf template is that it enables (but does not require) server-side Server Message Block (SMB) packet signing. SMB is a file-sharing protocol, and packet signing secures packets shared between computers. SMB packet signing is disabled by default on servers but enabled by default on client computers. By enabling SMB packet signing on the server side, SMB packets will be negotiated when both sides are using the secure*.inf template. Enabling SMB signing requires that every packet in the stream be verified, which will have a noticeable impact on performance. If sensitive data is subject to attack, the reduced throughput might be an acceptable side effect for your organization.

EXAM WARNING

You're likely to see exam scenarios that involve authentication protocols in a mixed network environment. Keep in mind that the Secure template requires NTLM v2, so read the scenario carefully to see if it is referring to LAN Manager, NTLM, or NTLM v2. Microsoft Windows NT 4.0 requires Service Pack 4 (SP4) to support NTLMv2, and Windows 9x platforms need the Directory Service client installed in order to support NTLMv2. In addition, look for clues regarding clock times that are more than 30 minutes off, or, in the case of Windows XP, 20 hours off.

Highly Secure (hisec*.inf)

This security template is used for setting very high security between computers for network communications. It secures network traffic and protocols used to communicate between computers. Computers configured to use the hisec*.inf template cannot communicate with down-level computers, such as those running Windows 98 or Windows NT.

This template enhances the security settings of the secure*.inf template and adds further restrictions via encryption and signing requirements for authentication and data flow over secure channels. For example, while the secure template *enables* server-side SMB signing, the hisec*.inf template *requires* it. This template also requires strong encryption and signing for transmitting channel data related to trust relationships in the domain.

As you can see, applying the hisec*.inf template will increase your security for network communications, but it can also cause problems with down-level computers.

Let's look at a few of the configuration rules you should keep in mind when considering how to apply the hisec*.inf template.

- All DCs for the domain to which the client computer is joined must be running Windows 2000 or later. The client computer, in this instance, is the computer to which the hisec*.inf template is being applied.
- All DCs containing user accounts that will be accessed via the client computer must be running Windows NT 4.0 SP4 or later.
- If a client is configured with hisecws.inf and is using local accounts defined on the server, clocks of both the client and the target server running Windows 2000 or Windows NT 4.0 SP4 must be set to within 30 minutes of each other.
- If a client is configured to use the hisecws.inf template and is using local accounts defined on the target server, the clocks on the client and the target Windows XP server must be within 20 hours of each other.
- The client computer configured to use the highly secure template cannot connect to LAN Manager servers using share-level security.
- To apply the highly secure template to DCs, hisecdc.inf, all DCs in all trusted and trusting domains must run Windows 2000 or Windows Server 2003.

  If a server is using the highly secure template, clients that do not support NTLM v2 authentication protocol will be unable to connect. Windows 2000 or later clients can be configured to send only NTLM v2 responses by specifying this in the network security option on the local computer. This can be implemented via Group Policy in the Local Policies | Security Options | Network security settings. The variety of settings for both client and DCs is delineated in Table 2.1 and is set in the **Network security: LAN Manager authentication level** security settings policy shown in Figure 2.2.

Table 2.1 Comparison of Client and Server Authentication Settings in Group Policy

	Clients			Domain Controllers		
Settings	**LM**	**NTLM**	**NTLMv2**	**LM**	**NTLM**	**NTLMv2**
Send LM & NTLM responses	Yes	Yes	No	Accepted	Accepted	Accepted
Send LM & NTLM—use NTLMv2 session security if negotiated	Yes	Yes	Yes*	Accepted	Accepted	Accepted

Continued

Table 2.1 Comparison of Client and Server Authentication Settings in Group Policy

	Clients			Domain Controllers		
Settings	**LM**	**NTLM**	**NTLMv2**	**LM**	**NTLM**	**NTLMv2**
Send NTLM response only	No	Yes	Yes	Accepted	Accepted	Accepted
Send NTLMv2 response only	No	No	Yes	Accepted	Accepted	Accepted
Send NTLMv2 response only/ refuse LM	No	No	Yes	Refused	Accepted	Accepted
Send NTLMv2 response only/ refuse LM & NTLM	No	No	Yes	Refused	Refused	Accepted

*Yes, if supported by the server.

Figure 2.2 Network Security Settings: LAN Manager Authentication Level Security Settings Policy

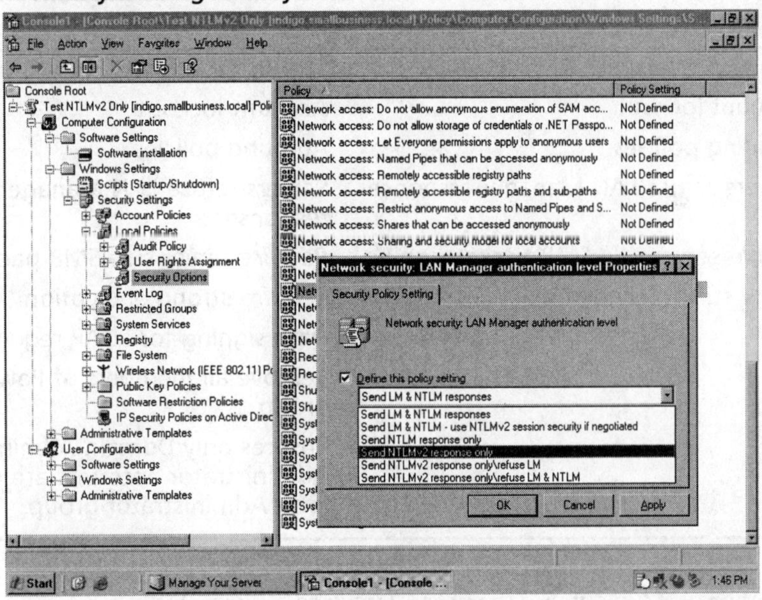

7. If a server is configured to use the hisec*.inf template, all clients must use SMB packet signing. Windows 2000 and Windows XP clients enable SMB packet signing by default, but other clients do not. These clients will require manual enabling of SMB packet signing, which is required in the hisec*.inf security mode.

The hisec*.inf template also limits the use of cached logon data, including data stored by Winlogon and Stored User Names and Passwords. This creates a more secure setting because logon data is not stored or cached on the system and cannot be retrieved by those attempting to gain illicit access to network resources. This security template also removes all users from the Power Users group and ensures that only Domain Admins and local Administrator accounts are members of the local Administrators group. Essentially, this template clears out the Power User and Administrator accounts to ensure that no inappropriate groups or users are included unless specifically added by a network administrator.

The hisec*.inf template assumes that all applications being run on the system are part of the Windows Logo Program for Software, which are considered "certified" programs. In this case, all users can run these applications without using the Compat*.inf security template and without modifying User permissions.

The secure*.inf and hisec*.inf templates are two of the most commonly used templates in setting security across the enterprise. Table 2.2 compares these two templates' security features.

Table 2.2 Comparison of the secure*.inf and hisec*.inf Predefined Security Templates

secure*.inf	hisec*.inf
Strong password	Strong password
Account lockout	Account lockout
Auditing policies	Auditing policies
Servers refuse LAN Manager responses	Servers refuse LAN Manager *and* NTLM responses
Enable server-side SMB packet signing	*Require* server-side SMB packet signing
Allow strong encryption	*Require* strong encryption
	Data signing for LDAP required
	Remove all members of Power Users group
	Ensures only Domain Admins and local Administrator accounts are members of local Administrator group

System Root Security (rootsec.inf)

When you initially install Windows Server 2003, all folder and file permissions are set using default values. The system root security template, rootsec.inf, resets these permissions on the system root folder, which then propagates to all subfolders and files. This template can be used to reset the root permissions of the system drive back to default values in the event they are inadvertently changed. This template can also be used to set the same root permissions on other volumes.

The permission entries of the root folder are replicated to all subfolders and files except in cases where a folder or file has permissions explicitly set. In this case, the explicitly set permissions will remain in effect. Only permissions inherited by the child object will be propagated; explicit permissions on the child object remain.

No Terminal Server User SID (notssid.inf)

Terminal server can be implemented using one of two security configurations:

- Full Security
- Relaxed Security

Relaxed security is used when legacy applications accessed through Terminal Server require access to the Registry, similar to using the compat*.inf template on non-Terminal Server servers. Full Security does not allow legacy applications access to the Registry. These are the only two actions that affect the security of Terminal Server itself. Using the No Terminal Server user SID template, Notssid.inf, does not increase the security on Terminal Server. It's only action is to remove the Terminal Server user SID from the access control lists (ACLs) on the server. Applying this template will not implement Full Security nor will it improve security on Terminal Server. When Terminal Server is not being used, this template can be used to remove the Terminal Server SIDs from the file system and registry locations. When running in Full Security mode, Terminal Server SIDs are not used.

We've looked at the security templates, so let's take a moment to review how to access the MMC and add both the Security Configuration and Analysis and the Security Templates snap-ins. Once you've done this, you can review any of the security templates in depth.

TEST DAY TIP

Review the predefined security templates so you'll remember the proper application of each, the settings each affects, and the limitations on using the templates in different settings. When you're comfortable with these templates and how they're used, the exam questions will be easier to answer because the obvious problems will pop right out at you, such as down-level clients, clocks out of sync, or authentication methods.

EXERCISE 2.01

ADDING THE SECURITY CONFIGURATION AND ANALYSIS AND SECURITY TEMPLATES SNAP-INS

To add the Security Configuration and Analysis and Security Templates snap-ins to the MMC, perform the following steps.

1. Click **Start**, then click **Run**.
2. In the Run dialog box, type in **mmc**, then click **OK**.
3. To create a new console, click on **File** and select **New**.
4. To open an existing console, click on **File** and select **Open**. Locate the console you want to open, click on it, and then click **OK**.
5. In the **File** menu, click **Add/Remove Snap-in**.
6. In the Add/Remove Snap-in dialog, click **Add**.
7. In the Add Standalone Snap-in dialog, locate then click **Security Configuration and Analysis**, and click **Add**. This step is shown in Figure 2.3.

Figure 2.3 Add/Remove Snap-In to the Microsoft Management Console

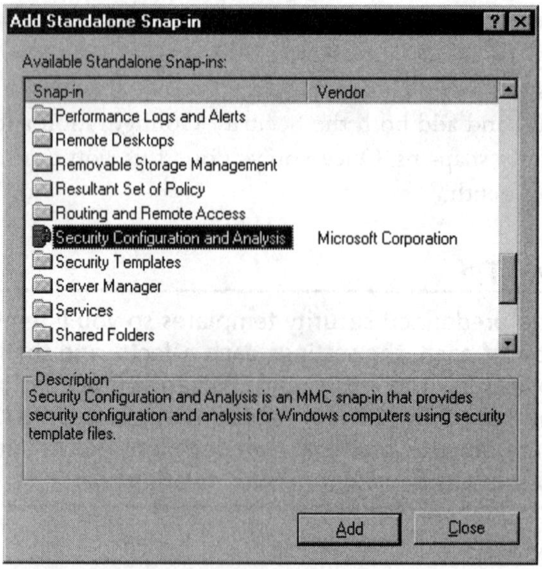

8. In the Add Standalone Snap-in dialog, locate then click **Security Templates**, click **Add**, click **Close**, and then click **OK** to add the snap-ins.

You are not required to have administrative credentials to perform these tasks. It is always recommended to perform tasks while signed in with the least permissions to maintain the highest possible security.

Notice that there are many snap-ins available to the management console, but in this case we're only interested in the Security Configuration and Analysis snap-in and the Security Templates snap-in. For more information on available snap-ins, consult the Windows Server help files or the Microsoft Windows Server 2003 Web site at www.microsoft.com/windowsserver2003/default.mspx.

Once you've added the Security Configuration and Analysis and the Security Template snap-ins, you can review the security templates in more detail. Figure 2.4 shows the security templates and how to review and modify any of the values in the templates. The template tree is shown in the left pane. You can see that the Setup Security template is open (indicated by the minus (–) sign to the left of the template name) and the Password Policy is selected (indicated by the gray bar across the words *Password Policy*). In the right pane, the security policies related to passwords in this template are shown. In this case, there are six policies listed. The second policy, Maximum password age, is selected. By double-clicking the policy name or by right-clicking on the policy name and selecting **Properties** from the menu, the Maximum password age Properties dialog box is displayed. The value for the Maximum password age policy is set in this dialog. In this example, it is set to 42 days. Notice the check box indicating that this value will be included in the template. After modifying a setting, click **OK** to accept changes or **Cancel** to exit without keeping changes. Remember, however, that it is recommended that you not make changes to the Setup security.inf template and that if you make changes to other templates, you should do so on a copy, not the original file.

Figure 2.4 Viewing and Modifying Predefined Template Settings

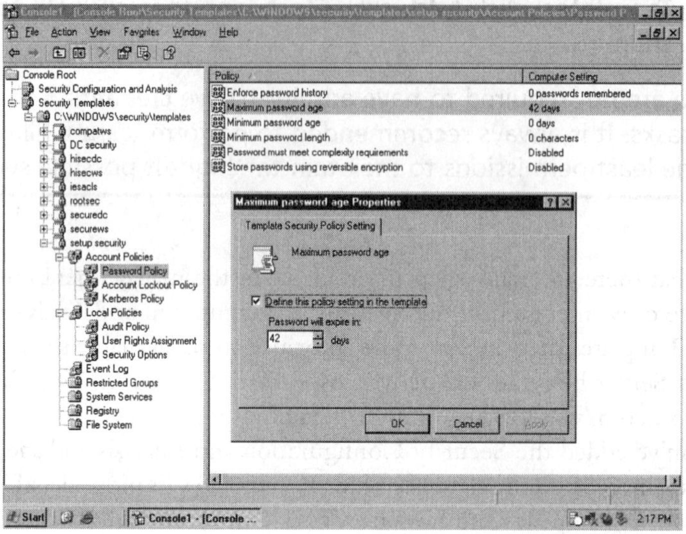

Take a moment to review the different security templates included in Windows Server 2003 in your MMC to see the various options and settings available in each template.

Configuring Security Templates

Now that we've examined the predefined security templates in Windows Server 2003, let's discuss how to configure these templates to set Registry and file system permissions, account and auditing policies, user rights, and more.

EXAM WARNING

Whenever a new feature is implemented or highlighted in a Microsoft product, it typically receives strong attention in the associated exam. In this case, expect to see many questions related to security templates and security policies on the exam. The preferred method of ensuring a consistent application of security policies is via security templates and the use of group policies, so make sure you're quite comfortable with these topics before sitting for the exam.

As discussed earlier, it's important not to modify the predefined templates provided in Windows Server 2003. Instead, select a template and save it with a different name to create a duplicate copy. Then, modify the copy of the template to ensure that the original file is always available both as a backup and as a method of comparing baselines to modified settings.

EXERCISE 2.02

SAVING A CONSOLE AND SECURITY TEMPLATES

In the last exercise, you added the Security Configuration and Analysis snap-in and the Security Templates snap-in to the MMC. In this exercise, you'll learn how to save the console for future use and to save the templates to preserve the original settings.

1. If you don't currently have the MMC open, click **Start**, then click **Run**. In the Run dialog box, type in **mmc**, then click **OK**.
2. To create a new console, click on **File** and select **New**. Add any snap-ins you want to save in this console. If you're working from the console in the previous exercise, you should have both the Security Configuration and Analysis snap-in and the Security Templates snap-in in the console.
3. In the **File** menu, click **Save**. The Save function will save the *console* with the snap-ins you've added. Select a name for the console, and then click **OK**.
4. To save the *security templates* with different names, click on the desired template in the left pane of the MMC. Right-click to display the menu and select **Save As**. Select a name different from the predefined template but one that will be descriptive of the template function. Click **OK**.
5. Once you've saved the predefined template with a new filename, you'll see that the MMC will update and show an additional template file. Make changes to this file to preserve the predefined settings in the Windows Server 2003 provided templates.

Each template has settings related to various areas of security. When you look at the security templates you opened in the MMC in Exercise 2.01, you saw that the template listing could be expanded. If you examined the tree, you saw that each template had the same elements, although the specific settings for each template differed. These areas are account policies, local policies, event log, restricted groups, system services, Registry, and file system. Let's review each of these areas.

Account Policies

Account policies define policy settings for password, account lockout, and Kerberos. The password policy contains settings for enforcing password history to prevent users from reusing the same password too frequently. It also sets the minimum and maximum password age parameters as well as the minimum password length. The password policy specifies whether a password must meet complexity requirements and whether passwords are stored using reversible encryption.

Strong passwords are defined as those that meet the criteria delineated in Table 2.3. When a strong password policy is set, user passwords must meet all of these criteria.

Table 2.3 Strong Password Requirements

Password Requirement	Example
At least seven characters	T4%v2(lm
Does not contain username, real name, company name	*Not* MicrosoftX2, martin$jones
Does not contain complete dictionary word	*Not* windows>n5s, icecream4U
Is different from previous passwords	*Not* studio1, studio2, studio3
Contains characters from four groups	
Uppercase	A, B, C
Lowercase	a, b, c
Numerals	1, 2, 3, 4,5
Symbols	~!@#$%^&*(){}|<>?[]\;',./

The Account lockout policies include the duration of the account lockout, the lockout threshold (how many invalid attempts are allowed before the account is locked), and how long before the account is reset. These settings are used to thwart attempts by individuals and automated programs from gaining unauthorized access to accounts. Keep in mind, however, that if these restrictions are too tight, your IT department will be dealing with excessive user complaints and requests for account access.

The Kerberos settings, which are used only on DCs, allow you to enforce user logon restrictions, set the maximum lifetime for a service ticket or a user ticket, set the maximum lifetime for user ticket renewal, and set the maximum tolerance for computer clock synchronization. You'll notice if you look at the Account Policies/Kerberos Policy settings in most of the templates that these settings are not included in the template. This brings up an important point. Each template contains the same defined areas. However, the settings in each template are not the same. When you review the list of policies in the right pane, any items not included in the template are listed as "Not Defined." Once the check box to "Define this policy setting in the template" is checked, the settings are applied to the template and the value of the setting will be displayed in place of the words "Not Defined."

Recall that for domain accounts, there is only one account policy, which is defined in the Default Domain policy and enforced by DCs in the domain. Local account policies can differ from domain account policies when the account is specifically for local accounts and not domain accounts.

Local Policies

Local policies are policies that, logically, affect the local computer. The three areas in local policies are audit policy, user rights assignment, and security options. Audit policy allows you to define what events to audit on the local computer. There is always a trade-off when auditing events. You want to audit events that are likely to be significant on your system. Auditing takes up computer resources, including disk space, and can impair system performance, so you'll need to find a balance between auditing and system performance that is acceptable in a given environment. Auditing can be used to log both successful and failed events.

Auditing logon events can be helpful in certain situations. Auditing successful logons makes sense only when you want to know who was able to gain access to the system. Since users often make typing errors, and unsuccessful logons do not allow a user onto the system, logging failed events can generate large log files. However, auditing failed logon attempts certainly makes sense as a security measure to detect and protect against brute-force attempts and dictionary attempts that continually try to log on. For servers that are exposed to the public network in any way to determine if someone is persistently trying to gain access and failing, auditing failed logon attempts is important.

Auditing account management success and failure can also be set in the Local Policies | Audit Policies section. This can be used to determine who successfully or unsuccessfully attempted to manage accounts on the local system. Remember, a majority of the security breaches in companies come from inside the company, not from anonymous outsiders.

The success or failure of attempts to access directory services, logon events, object access, policy change, privilege use, process tracking, and system events can all be set in the Local Policies section. Remember that these affect the local computer. If you set these in a template and apply the template via group policy, remember that all computers to which this template is applied will enable these auditing features. Since computers have different roles on the network, a "one size fits all" auditing scheme would not make sense. The local policies can be modified in the appropriate templates and rolled out to groups of computers in similar roles. We'll discuss this later in the chapter.

Also under Local Policies is the User Rights Assignment section. The policies in this section are all involved with what user rights users have on the local computer. A partial list of the policies is shown next. For a full list, view the Setup security.inf template in the console you saved in the earlier exercise.

- Access this computer from the network
- Add workstations to domain
- Allow log on locally
- Allow log on through Terminal Services
- Back up files and directories
- Change the system time
- Deny access to this computer from the network
- Deny log on locally
- Force shutdown from a remote system
- Manage auditing and security log
- Remove computer from docking station
- Restore files and directories
- Shut down the system
- Take ownership of files or other objects

Remember, when configuring these policies, you should always add users to groups and add groups to these policies. Computers can have more than one policy applied, and this can create conflicts. The order of precedence for policies is from highest to lowest precedence, or OU, domain, and then local computer. Group policy is passed down from parent to child object within the domain. If you assign a policy to a parent object, all the child objects will have that policy applied. For example, if you apply the strong password policy at the domain level, these settings will be passed down to the child objects, which in this case would be all computers in the domain. If you apply the policy to a child object, that policy will take precedence over the parent object's policies. Exceptions to this are when you block policy inheritance at the domain or OU level or you enforce policy inheritance by setting the No Override option. When you select No Override, the child policy containers are forced to inherit the parent's policy even if the child's policy conflicts with the parent's policy and even if Block Inheritance has been set on the child object.

It's also important to note that some settings are not compatible with down-level clients. In the dialog box for such policies, a note is included warning you of the incompatibility, as in the Impersonate a client after authentication Properties dialog shown in Figure 2.5.

Figure 2.5 Information Warning Regarding Down-Level Clients

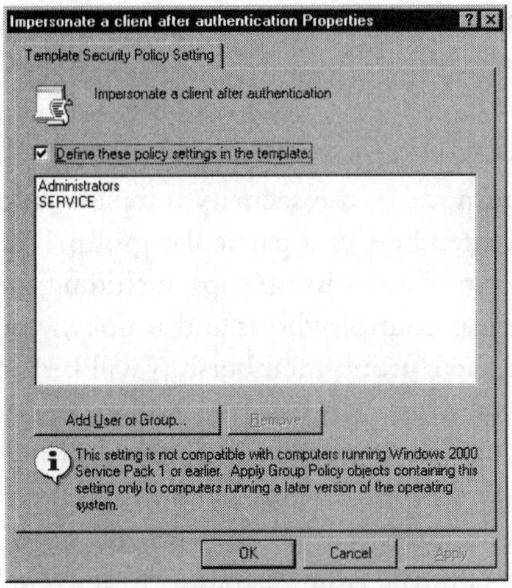

The third area covered in the Local Policies is Security Options. The Security Options section contains policies that affect accounts, auditing, devices, DCs, interactive logons, network clients, network access, network security recovery, shutdown, cryptography, and system settings and objects. In versions of Windows prior to Windows 2000, these types of security settings could only be modified via the Registry. In Windows 2000 and Windows Server 2003, these settings can be modified via the **Local Policies | Security Options** section of the template.

As with other areas of the Local Policies, these elements affect only the local computer. A number of security elements are not defined in the Setup secure.inf template, meaning that they are listed, but the check box that would include them in the template is cleared. If you want to understand more about any of the policies listed, you can right-click the policy and select Help to open the Microsoft Management Console Help dialog. You can browse to any of the individual policies to learn more about what the policy does and how it is used. It is advisable to read this information before applying a policy that you're not 100-percent clear on. As mentioned earlier, it's even more critical to test any templates, whether predefined or modified, on a test system to see how it impacts the computer, the users, and the network in terms of both security and usability.

Event Log

The Event Log node allows you to configure settings related to event logs, such as maximum log size, access rights for each log, and retention settings. There are three log types used: logs of *application* activity, logs of *security* activity, and logs of *system* activity. You can see in the Event Log Policy area that each setting has three entries. For example, there is a maximum log size policy for applications, security, and system.

To view events logged in the event logs, you can use the Event Viewer, which allows you to view and monitor logged events. The Event Viewer is accessed via Administrative Tools.

Restricted Groups

The Restricted Groups node of the security templates allows you to specify exactly who can or cannot be members of a particular group. Restricted groups can be used to configure membership of sensitive groups, including the Administrator group. By using this feature, you can control who is and is not included in a group, and every time the policy is refreshed, group membership will be modified to include only the members specified in the Members list. It has two properties: *Members* and *Member Of*. The Members list defines who belongs to the restricted group. The Member Of list specifies which other groups the restricted group belongs to.

For example, suppose there are five users on the local computer. You add Luke and Chantal as members of the Administrator group. When the policy is refreshed, only Luke and Chantal will remain in the Administrator group for the local computer, regardless of which users were in the group before the policy was applied.

Restricted Groups can be applied in one of two ways. It can be applied as a setting in the security template, which will then be applied during configuration of the local computer. It can also be applied by defining the setting in a GPO directly, which means the policy will be enforced each time the GPO is refreshed, about every 90 minutes on a workstation or member server and every 5 minutes on a DC.

The Restricted Groups setting should be used with care, because any account not on the Restricted Groups list will be removed when the settings are refreshed, even if that account is part of the Administrator group. However, using the Restricted Groups to limit membership to sensitive groups like the Administrator group can be quite useful in maintaining tight security.

System Services

The System Services Policies in the predefined security templates allows the administrator to modify settings related to system services such as startup, shutdown, indexing, license logging, and many more. There are three settings available—*automatic, manual* and *disabled*. If a service is set to automatic, check to make sure that it works properly before assuming no intervention is required. In addition, to optimize system performance and better security, set unused system services to manual so they do not automatically start up. This enhances system performance by starting up only those services that are needed. It also enhances system security because services that are not used are not running. Often, unused services that are left running create an opportunity for unauthorized access to the system or network.

Registry

The Registry Policy in any security template allows the administrator to define access permissions related to Registry keys and to set auditing on *system access control lists* (SACLs). To access the settings, double-click on the object name in the right pane of the MMC, or right-click and select **Properties** from the menu. Figure 2.4 shows the object named "user\.default" Properties dialog.

The Registry contains many different keys, and some keys have subkeys, much like the folder structure in Windows. In Registry Policy properties, you have two primary options:

- Configure this key then
- Do not allow permissions on this key to be replaced

When you configure a key via the Registry Policy properties by selecting **Configure this key then**, you have two additional choices for how that key should be configured:

- Propagate inheritable permissions to all subkeys
- Replace existing permissions on all subkeys with inheritable permissions

If you do not want to configure this key and do not want permissions on this key to be replaced, you can select the second radio button, as shown in Figure 2.6. **Do no allow permissions on this key to be replaced** will force permissions to remain as they are and not allow them to be modified. Selecting this choice disables the **Configure this key** options.

The final activity on in the Registry Policy Properties dialog is to edit security, if desired. By clicking **Edit Security**, you can add or remove groups or usernames, modify permissions, or use the Advanced button to fine-tune access.

Figure 2.6 Registry Policy Properties

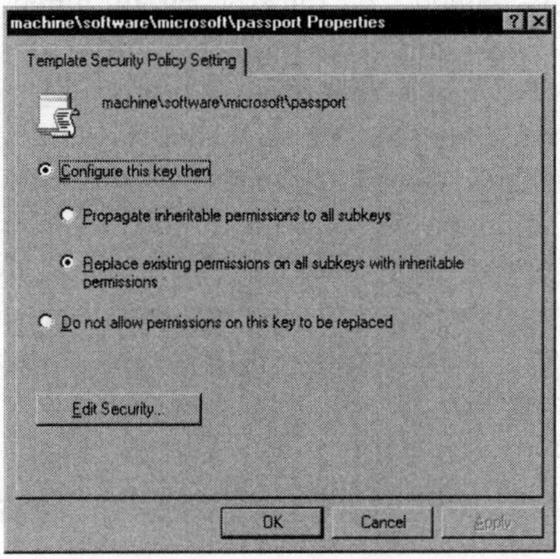

File System

The final node of the predefined security templates is the File System node. When you click on the File System node in the left pane of the MMC, the various file system object names will be displayed in the right pane of the MMC. As with the Registry node, these objects can be configured in the same manner—to propagate or replace permissions or to prevent permissions from being replaced on a file or folder object. This modifies both the *discretionary access control lists* (DACLs) and the SACLs.

TEST DAY TIP

Before the test, briefly review the seven areas that security templates configure. Being familiar with these areas will help you identify security settings that might be out of place.

Configuring Security for Down-Level Clients

We've touched on several considerations related to down-level clients throughout our discussion of the various security templates. Now, let's pull this information together to understand specifically how to deal with down-level clients. A down-level client is a computer that is running an operating system that was released prior to the current version—in this case, Windows Server 2003. Although a computer running Windows 2000 is now considered a "down-level client," Windows 2000 computers are closely compatible with Windows Server 2003, and for the purposes of this discussion are not considered down-level clients. Common down-level clients include computers running Windows NT 4.0 SP6a or other earlier versions of Windows NT, and computers running Windows 98, Windows Me, or Windows 95. Although there are compelling reasons to upgrade clients, including better security and management capabilities, you might be responsible for managing a network that includes down-level clients.

If you have down-level clients, you must be careful when using the secure*.inf and hisec*.inf templates. Depending on the operating system in use, the clients might not be able to use the NTLM v2 authentication protocol. If they cannot and there is an account on the secured server that the down-level client needs to access, it will be unable to do so. In some cases, you might be able to add in NTLM v2 to the client. In other cases, you will be unable to do so. In those cases, you'll need to determine whether to upgrade the client or not use the Secure or Highly Secure templates on the server to which these clients need to connect. Although there are steps you can take to improve security on the network with down-level clients, such a discussion is outside the scope of this chapter.

Microsoft released Active Directory Client Services extensions for Windows 95/98 and Windows NT 4.0 SP6a around the same time it released Windows 2000.

These extensions enable Active Directory interaction with these down-level clients. The extensions provide some, but not all, Active Directory services. The features are summarized in Table 2.4. You can download this for Windows NT-based computers at www.microsoft.com/ntworkstation/downloads/Other/adclient.asp.

Table 2.4 Active Directory Client Services Extensions Features

Active Directory Client Services Extensions Provide	Active Directory Client Services Extensions Do Not Provide
Site awareness enables client to log on to and change passwords on any DC rather than just the primary domain controller (PDC).	Kerberos support.
Active Directory Services Interface (ADSI) allows programmers to interface with Active Directory Services on down-level clients.	Group Policy or IntelliMirror capabilities.
Provides access to distributed file system (DFS) fault tolerance capabilities.	Internet Protocol Security (IPSec) or Layer 2 Tunneling Protocol (L2TP) protocols used for VPN.
Provides access to Active Directory Windows Address Book (WAB) to users on down-level client machines.	Service principal name (SPN) or mutual authentication.
Supports NTLM v2 authentication.	

In addition, down-level clients cannot use certain local security settings because they only support the File Allocation Table (FAT) file system format. To secure the system, the computer should be using the NT File System (NTFS), which allows the administrator to control access to files and folders.

If older applications that require access to the Registry are running, you might have to use the compat*.inf template to modify settings for users without adding all users to the Power Users group or without upgrading all Users group settings. However, using the compat*.inf template does allow applications to access the Registry, which can cause a security hole that can be exploited. This should be implemented with care and should never be applied to a DC.

Deploying Security Templates

We've discussed the various predefined security templates and you've become re-acquainted with the MMC. Now, let's look at how these security templates can be deployed across the network—from 1 computer to 10,000 computers.

Security settings can be analyzed and configured via the Security Configuration and Analysis snap-in, but as you learned earlier, this will only allow you to apply security settings to the local computer. If you configure security for a domain or OU using the Security Configuration and Analysis snap-in, you'd have to configure each client individually. This might not be a major problem in a 5- or 10-computer network, but it becomes unwieldy in a larger network. In this case, there are three options for applying security templates on a large number of computers. The first option is to use Secure Templates to create a template and then apply it to the appropriate GPO. You can also use the Security Extension to Group Policy to edit individual security settings on a GPO. You can also use scripting to apply these security template settings. Let's look at each of these options in more detail.

Using Group Policy to Deploy Security Settings

Group Policy allows you to configure many different options for computers within your organization, including desktop configurations, Internet Explorer settings, and security settings, to name just a few. Group policies are applied through Active Directory Sites and Services for sites within the organization, or via Active Directory Users and Computers for Domains and Organizational Units for domains and OUs.

Security settings accessed via group policy are the same as those found in Security Configuration and Analysis. Each area of policy is applied in a cumulative manner when applied via group policy. The order of application is local, site, domain, and OU. Policies are applied in this manner:

1. Policies related to the local computer are applied.
2. If site-level policies exist, they are applied next and will overwrite local policies.
3. Domain policies are applied, overwriting settings from the site and local computer.
4. Settings from the OU are applied.

The interval for refreshing group policy is a value that can be customized to your organization's needs, but the default setting is every 90 minutes for a workstation or server and every 5 minutes for a DC. The settings are also refreshed every 16 hours, regardless of whether there are changes. Group policy is also refreshed when a computer is restarted. Group policy can be manually refreshed by using the *gpupdate* command-line utility.

You can use group policy to deploy security settings set in one or more of the security templates we've discussed. The procedure for doing this differs slightly if you're on a workstation or server that is joined to a domain, or if you're on a DC and want to import a security template for a domain or OU. We delineate the steps in Exercise 2.03.

EXERCISE 2.03

USING GROUP POLICY EDITOR TO APPLY SECURITY TEMPLATES FOR A WORKSTATION OR SERVER JOINED TO A DOMAIN

In this exercise, you're going to apply a security template via the Group Policy Editor. Please make sure that you are working in a test environment and *not* on a live system or live network of any kind. If in doubt, check with your network administrator before taking the actions listed next. If you are unable to perform these tasks on a test system, be sure to cancel out of dialogs rather than click OK. This might prevent you from completing some of these tasks, but you should not risk applying these templates on a live system in any event.

To be able to import security templates, you must be a member of the Domain Admins group, the Enterprise Admins group, or you must have been delegated proper authority. As a security best practice, it's advisable to perform these actions using **Run As** rather than logging in to the Administrator account. For more information on using Run As, see the Help files in Windows Server 2003.

1. If you don't currently have the MMC open, click **Start**, then click **Run**. In the Run dialog box, type in **mmc**, then click **OK**.
2. To create a new console, click on **File** and select **New**.
3. Click **File** and select **Add/Remove Snap-in**.
4. In the **Add/Remove Snap-in** dialog on the Standalone tab (selected by default), click **Add**.
5. In the **Add Standalone Snap-in** dialog, scroll down until you locate **Group Policy Object Editor**. Click **Add.**
6. When you click **Add**, the **Select Group Policy Wizard** will open. In this wizard, you can select the GPO you want to work with.
7. When working on a workstation or server joined to a domain, the text box will be automatically populated with "Local Computer." This means that the GPO that will be edited is the Local Computer GPO. If this is not the GPO you want, you can browse to locate the GPO. Your browse options include domains/OUs, sites, computers, or all.
8. Click **Finish** in the Group Policy Wizard dialog to select the **Local Computer** GPO and close the wizard dialog. This screen is shown in Figure 2.7.

Figure 2.7 Group Policy Wizard

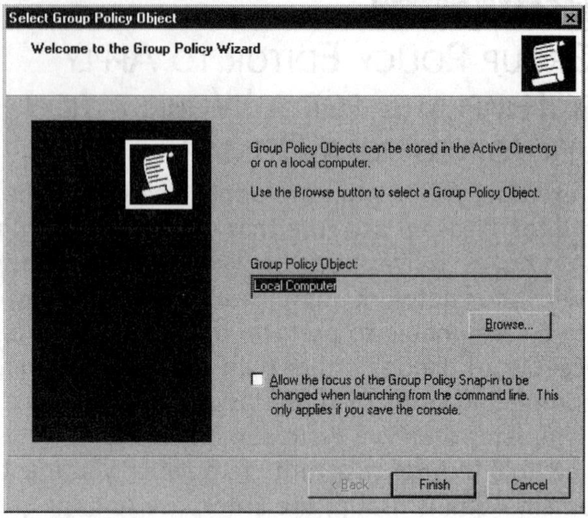

9. Click Close in the Add Standalone Snap-in dialog.
10. The **Add/Remove Snap-in** dialog should now contain *Local Computer Policy*. Click **OK** to close this dialog.
11. In the MMC, in the left pane, you should see *Local Computer Policy* under the Console Root. Click on the plus sign (+) to the left of Local Computer Policy, or simply double-click on Local Computer Policy to expand the tree. The Computer Configuration and User Configuration nodes are shown. These can also be expanded by clicking the + sign to the left of each.
12. Each listing has three nodes below, and the nodes are the same for each: **Software Settings**, **Windows Settings**, and **Administrative Templates.** If you want to edit GPOs related to the local computer, expand the **Computer Configuration** tree. If you want to edit GPOs related to local users, expand the **User Configuration** tree. The options underneath each node are different because some GPOs are specific to the computer and some are specific to the user configuration. For example, in Windows Settings, you'll notice that Scripts shows a description of (*Startup/Shutdown*) in the **Computer Configuration | Windows Settings | Scripts** node. In the **User Configuration | Windows Settings | Scripts** node, the option is (*Logon/Logoff*). This clearly makes sense since the computer is started up and shut down and the user logs on and off. For this exercise, expand **Computer Configuration**.

13. Expand the **Windows Settings** to locate the **Security Settings** node.
14. Right-click the **Security Settings** node and select **Import Policy** from the menu.
15. The **Import Policy From** dialog is displayed and defaults to the default security templates location (*%systemroot%\Windows\Security\Templates*). Select the template you want to import. Remember that if you have modified or will modify settings in the templates, you should work with a copy of one of the predefined templates. You can also import other policies by opening the Policies folder and opening any policies you have defined.
16. Do *not* import the Setup security.inf template. This method is used to import other security templates but should not be used with the Setup security.inf file. For this exercise, select the **securews.inf** template.
17. After you've the template to import, click **Open**.
18. Once you've imported the template, you can view or modify elements. The resulting screen is shown in Figure 2.8.

Figure 2.8 Imported Policy or Template in Group Policy Editor

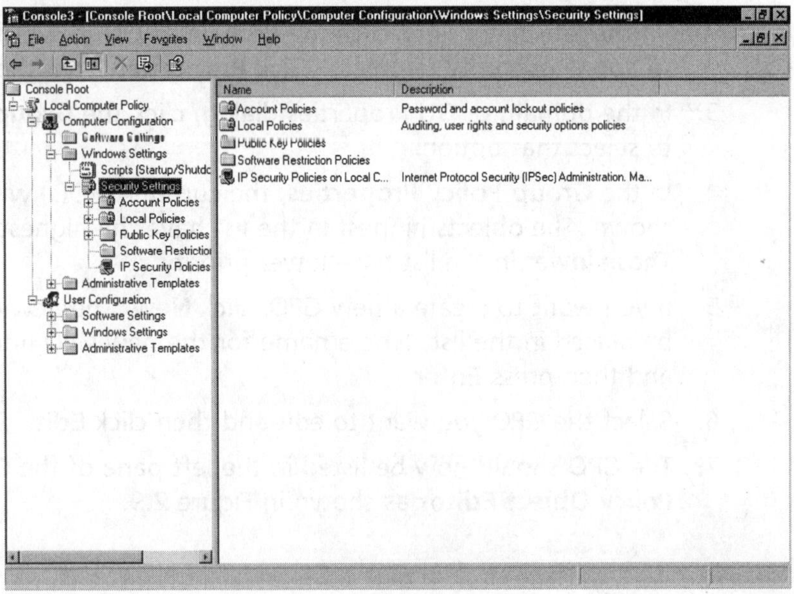

Remember that certain security settings from the domain or OU will override local settings, so not all of the settings you apply via the imported template might remain in effect on the computer. However, the settings you import will take effect for the local computer and local users. In addition, remember that the Setup security.inf file should not be applied via group policy in either exercise (2.03 or 2.04).

In the next exercise, you'll learn how to apply a security template on a DC. This process is very similar to that delineated in Exercise 2.03, but the starting point is different. Follow the steps in Exercise 2.04 closely.

EXERCISE 2.04

APPLY SECURITY TEMPLATES ON A DOMAIN CONTROLLER FOR A DOMAIN OR OU

To be able to import security templates, you must be a member of the Domain Admins group, the Enterprise Admins group, or you must have been delegated proper authority. As a security best practice, it's advisable to perform these actions using **Run As** rather than logging in to the Admin account. For more information on using Run As, see the Help files in Windows Server 2003.

1. Click **Start**, select **Administrative Tools**, and then select **Active Directory Users and Computers**.
2. In the left pane, right-click the domain or OU to which you want to apply a security template. Click **Properties** from the menu.
3. In the domain or OU Properties dialog, click the **Group Policy** tab to select that option.
4. In the **Group Policy Properties**, the current GPO(s) will be shown. The objects highest in the list have the highest priority. Those lower in the list have lower priority.
5. If you want to create a new GPO, click **New**. The new object will be placed in the list. Type a name for the new GPO into the box and then press **Enter**.
6. Select the GPO you want to edit and then click **Edit**.
7. The GPO should now be listed in the left pane of the **Group Policy Object Editor** as shown in Figure 2.9.

Figure 2.9 New Group Policy Object

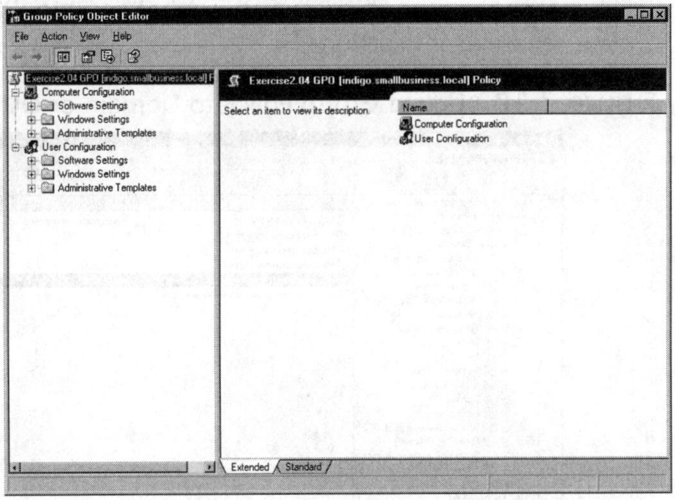

8. Each listing has three nodes below, and the nodes are the same for each: **Software Settings**, **Windows Settings**, and **Administrative Templates**.
9. Expand the **Windows Settings** to locate the **Security Settings** node.
10. Right-click the **Security Settings** node and select **Import Policy** from the menu.
11. The **Import Policy From** dialog is displayed and defaults to the default security templates location (%systemroot%\Windows\Security\Templates). Select the template you want to import. Remember that if you have modified or will modify settings in the templates, you should have created a copy of one of the predefined templates.
12. Do *not* import the Setup security.inf template. This method is used to import other templates and should not be used with the Setup security.inf file. For this exercise, select **securews.inf**.
13. After you've selected the template you want to import, click **Open**.
14. Figure 2.10 shows the resulting console. It looks similar to the earlier console, but the settings from securews.inf have now been incorporated. To verify this, expand the **Account Policies** node and then click on the **Password Policy** node once. In the right pane, notice that the elements of the securews.inf template are

visible. For example, the *Password must meet complexity requirements* policy is enabled, which is what you would expect to see in the securews.inf settings.

Figure 2.10 Applied Group Policy to Domain or OU

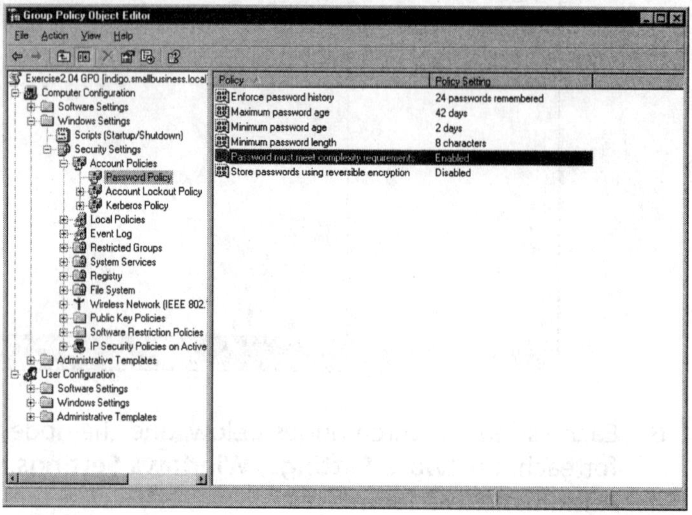

Reviewing the Result of Security Policy Settings

We've walked through two scenarios of importing security settings, via a template or group policy. You might be wondering how you can tell what the resulting security settings are. There are essentially three ways to accomplish this. First, you can use the Security Configuration and Analysis snap-in to analyze the local computer. You can also use the *secedit* command to analyze the local computer or any other computer or computer group (multiple computers can be analyzed via the *secedit* command). You can also use a snap-in called Resultant Set of Policy (RSoP). This allows you to see the results of the policies applied to a particular computer. In the next section, you'll learn more about the *secedit* command. Although the RSoP is often used to review other policies, it can be used to review the resulting security settings as well.

Exercise 2.05

Using the Resultant Set of Policy MMC Snap-in

The RSoP tool is very useful for seeing the result of group policy before it's applied across the enterprise. This exercise will help you become familiar with this tool.

1. Open the MMC via **Start | Run**, type in **mmc**, and then click **OK**.
2. Load the RSoP by clicking **File** and then **Add/Remove Snap-in**. In the Add/Remove Snap-in dialog, click **Add**.
3. In the Add Standalone Snap-in dialog, scroll down to locate **Resultant Set of Policy**. Click to select it and then click **Add**. Click **Close** to close this dialog.
4. In the Add/Remove Snap-in dialog, click **OK**.
5. If you click the snap-in in the left pane, you'll get a message alerting you that you must Generate RSoP Data. This is shown in Figure 2.11.

Figure 2.11 Action Alert in Resultant Set of Policy Snap-In

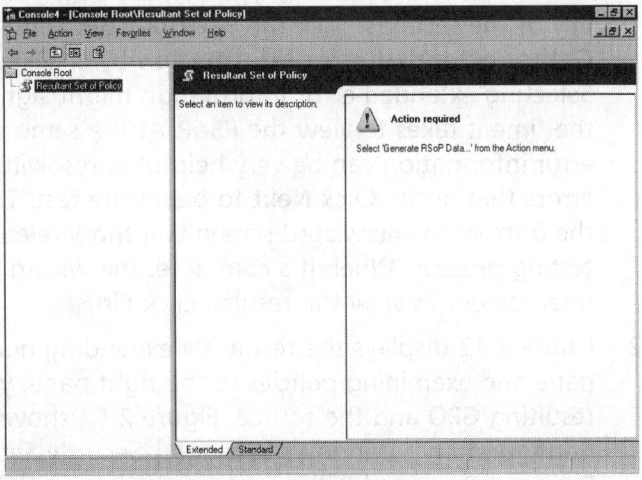

6. On the menu, click **Action** and then click **Generate RSoP Data**. This launches the **Resultant Set of Policy Wizard**. The wizard allows you to view policy settings applied to selected computers and users via logging mode, or simulate policy implementation to plan changes to your network via the planning mode. Click **Next**.

7. The Mode Selection screen allows you to choose **Logging mode** to review policy settings or **Planning mode** to simulate policy changes by using data from the Active Directory directory service.
8. Select **Logging mode**, and then click **Next**.
9. The Computer Selection screen in the wizard asks you to select which computer you want to check. If you select **Another computer**, you can use the **Browse** button to locate the computer. You also have the option of not displaying policy settings for the computer in the results, meaning that you will display only *user* policy settings by clicking in the check box. Select **This Computer** and click **Next**.
10. The next screen, User Selection, asks you to select the user for which you want to display results. Your choices are **Current user**, **Select a specific user**, or **Do not display user policy settings in the results**. This last choice is the inverse of the previous dialog that allowed you to display *only* user settings. Select **Current user** and click **Next.**
11. The next screen is the Summary of Selections screen. It shows a summary of the selections you've chosen. If you want to change any of the settings, click the **Back** button. You can choose to **Gather extended error information** by checking the check box. Selecting extended error information might significantly increase the time it takes to view the RSoP. At the same time, the extended error information can be very helpful in resolving any conflicts or errors that occur. Click **Next** to begin the test. The progress bar at the bottom of the wizard screen will show relative progress in the testing process. When it's complete, the wizard will display the final screen. To view the results, click **Finish**.
12. Figure 2.12 displays the result. By expanding nodes in the left pane and examining policies in the right pane, you can see the resulting GPO and the source. Figure 2.12 shows the Computer Configuration | Windows Settings | Security Settings | Account Policies | Password Policy node in the left pane. In the right pane, you can see that the *Enforce password history* policy shows the Computer Setting (actual value) and the Source GPO. In this case, it is the policy from the previous exercise. Other policies in this pane are the result of the Default Domain policy.

Figure 2.12 Resultant Set of Policy Results

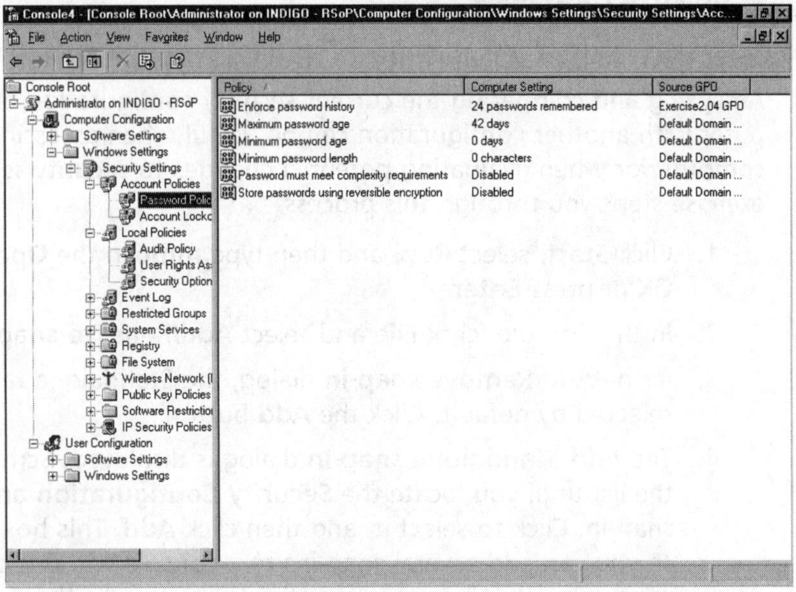

This process can be helpful whenever you want to see the effects of policies on users, groups, or computers, or whenever you want to see the effect of changes you'd like to make before you actually apply them.

Using Security Configuration and Analysis to Review Security Settings

Previously, we discussed using the MMC with the Security Configuration and Analysis snap-in to review security settings on a computer. The analysis compares settings in the database to the active configuration on the computer. This allows you to see what the effect of applying those settings would be on a particular computer. Although you cannot use the Security Configuration and Analysis snap-in to deploy security on anything but the local computer, you can and should use it to determine the effect on security before deploying to your network. For example, you can configure a DC running IIS and run the analysis. Depending on the results, you might modify the security database. Once completed, you could then deploy the modified security template via group policy or via the command-line tool secedit.exe.

Exercise 2.06 walks you through running an analysis on your computer and shows you some of the icons displayed based on the results of the analysis.

EXERCISE 2.06

ANALYZING AND COMPARING SECURITY CONFIGURATIONS

Analyzing and comparing the current security configuration on a computer with another configuration can be useful when assessing a specific computer or when evaluating potential changes to security settings. This exercise steps you through this process.

1. Click **Start**, select **Run**, and then type **mmc** in the **Open** box. Click **OK** or press **Enter**.
2. In the Console, click **File** and select **Add/Remove snap-in**.
3. In the **Add/Remove snap-in** dialog, the Standalone tab is selected by default. Click the **Add** button.
4. The **Add Standalone snap-in** dialog is displayed. Scroll through the list until you locate the **Security Configuration and Analysis** snap-in. Click to select it, and then click **Add**. This box stays open so you can add several snap-ins to a console without continually re-opening it. When you have finished selecting the desired snap-in(s), click **Close** to close the dialog box.
5. The **Add/Remove snap-in** dialog box now displays *Security Configuration and Analysis* in the dialog box. Click **OK** to close this dialog.
6. Click **Security Configuration and Analysis** in the left pane of the console for instructions on how to open or create a database for analysis.
7. Right-click **Security Configuration and Analysis** in the left pane and select **Open database** from the menu.
8. In the **Open database** dialog box, type **Exercise205** in the **File name:** box. Click **Open.** If you wanted to select an existing database, you can select one shown in the **Open database** dialog box listing. In this case, we are creating a new database named Exercise205.sdb.
9. The **Import Template** dialog is displayed. For this exercise, select the **hisecdc.inf** template by clicking to select it, and then click **Open**. Remember, this will not *apply* these settings to your computer; it will simply use them for comparison.
10. You are returned to the **Security Configuration and Analysis** console. Notice there are new instructions in the right pane describing how to configure or analyze your computer.

11. In the left pane, right-click **Security Configuration and Analysis** and select **Analyze Now**.
12. The Perform Analysis dialog opens prompting you for the location of the log file it will create. Accept the default by clicking **OK**.
13. The Analyzing System Security progress screen is displayed while security is being analyzed. Depending on the number of settings and the speed of your computer, this display might be shown for only a very brief time.
14. When the analysis is complete, there will be new items listed below the **Security Configuration and Analysis** node in the left pane of the MMC.
15. Browse through the various nodes in the left pane. Explore various policies in each grouping.
16. Select **Local Policies** and then select **Security Options**. The related policies are shown in the right pane. Table 2.5 lists and describes the various icons you might see after performing an analysis.
17. Review a number of settings in different nodes to become familiar with the results of the analysis.

Table 2.5 Security Analysis Results Icons

Icon	Description
Red circle with white X	The entry is defined in the database used for analysis and on the local system but the settings do not match.
Green check mark	The entry is defined in both the database and the local system and the settings match.
Question mark	The entry is not defined in the database used for analysis; therefore, the setting on the local computer was not analyzed. If an entry is not analyzed, it is possible the user running the analysis lacks sufficient permissions to perform the analysis on a specific object or area.
Exclamation point	The item is defined in the database used for analysis but does not exist on the local computer.
Standard icon (no flag)	The entry is not defined in the database or on the system.

TEST DAY TIP

Before the test, perform one or more security configuration analyses so you're very familiar with the results and what the different icons mean. You're likely to see at least one scenario question on the exam that includes this information. Be sure you are very clear about what each icon means so you can quickly assess what's going on in a scenario question that includes these icons.

Using the secedit.exe Command-Line Tool

Throughout this chapter, we've referred to the secedit.exe command-line tool. In this section, you'll learn more about the uses of the *secedit* command and you'll learn some of the common switches used with this tool. In a later section, you'll learn how you can use the *secedit* tool to automate security configuration tasks.

To run *secedit*, begin by clicking **Start** | **Accessories** | **Command Prompt**. Alternately, you can click **Start**, select **Run**, type in **cmd**, and then press **Enter** or click **OK**. A command prompt window will open. To view all switches for the *secedit* command, type **secedit ?** and press **Enter**. When the command is entered without any parameters, the help information is displayed. You can use the *secedit* command to configure, analyze, import, export, validate, or generate a rollback. If you type the *secedit* command with one of the switches and no parameters, the help information for that switch will be displayed. We'll look at each of these options so you understand how to use this handy command-line tool.

secedit configure

The first switch shown in the *secedit* help file is the *configure* switch. It is used to configure a system with security settings stored in a database. The parameters are described in Table 2.6.

Table 2.6 secedit.exe *configure* Switch Parameters

Parameter	Description
/db filename	This argument specifies which database file to use to perform the security configuration. It is a required argument.
/cfg filename	This argument specifies a security template to import into the database prior to configuring the system.

Continued

Table 2.6 secedit.exe *configure* Switch Parameters

Parameter	Description
/overwrite	This switch specifies whether the database should be emptied prior to importing the security template. If this parameter is not specified, the settings are accumulated in the database (if you import more than one security template, all settings will accumulate). If this parameter is not specified and there are conflicting security settings between the database and the imported template, the template settings win.
/areas area1 area2...	This argument specifies which security areas to apply to the system. If the parameter is not specified, all settings defined in the database are applied. To configure multiple areas, separate each with a space. See Table 2.7 for a description of the security areas that can be specified.
/log filename	This argument is used to specify the path to the log file. If no path is specified, the default log file will be used.
/quiet	This switch suppresses screen and log output. You can still review results of the analysis in the Security Configuration and Analysis snap-in in the MMC. This switch is commonly used when *secedit* is used in a batch or scheduled task.

Table 2.7 secedit Security Areas Descriptions

Security Area Name	Description
SECURITYPOLICY	Includes local and domain policy for the system, including account policies, audit policies, event log settings, and security options.
GROUP_MGMT	Includes Restricted Group settings for any groups specified in the Security template.
USER_RIGHTS	Includes User Rights assignment such as user logon right and granting of privileges.
REGKEYS	Includes Registry permissions on the local Registry keys.
FILESTORE	Includes file system permissions on the local file storage system.
SERVICES	Includes system service settings for all defined services.

An example of the command is shown here. Keep in mind that the command will assume the current directory unless another path is specified. The parameters are shown in bold only for clarity. This example assumes the database is stored in the path c:\windows\security\database and that the template is stored in the path c:\windows\templates. Your database and template locations might vary, and if not in the current directory, they should be specified. In addition, this example specifies two security areas, the SECURITYPOLICY area and the FILESTORE area. Each area is separated by a space.

```
secedit /configure /db c:\windows\security\database\hisecws.sdb /cfg
c:\windows\templates\hisecws.inf /overwrite /SECURITYPOLICY FILESTORE /log
hisecws.log
```

It's worth noting here that this is how you can reapply portions of predefined security templates and in particular, the setup security.inf. For example, suppose you've been working on creating a Security template for a particular group of computers on your network including the one you're working on. You imported the securews.inf template and made some modifications and saved the template as secure123.inf. However, you want this template to use default Registry settings from the setup security.inf. You can use the *secedit /configure* command with the */overwrite* switch and specify REGKEYS to configure just this set of policies in your custom template.

secedit analyze

The *analyze* switch causes secedit to analyze security for whichever element is selected. The parameters for the analyze switch are shown in Table 2.8. This switch allows you to analyze current database settings against other settings (typically baseline settings) and store the results in a log file. You can view the results in the Security Configuration and Analysis snap-in. The result will show you the difference between the current settings and the baseline settings, allowing you to see and address any potential security holes. This can be very useful when troubleshooting or for analyzing a system whose exact settings might be unknown as compared to a standard security template. You can also use this switch to analyze the difference between a baseline template and a custom security template you create.

Table 2.8 secedit.exe Analyze Switch Parameters

Parameter	Explanation
/db filename	This switch gives the path to the database that holds the stored configuration to be analyzed. This is a required argument. If the filename specifies a new database, the */cfg* filename switch must also be used.
/cfg filename	This argument is only used with the */db* parameter. It is the path to the security template to be imported into the database for analysis. If not specified, the analysis will be performed on the configuration already stored in the specified database.
/log logpath	This argument is used to specify the path to the log file. If no path is specified, the default log file will be used.

Continued

Table 2.8 secedit.exe Analyze Switch Parameters

Parameter	Explanation
/quiet	This switch suppresses screen and log output. You can still review results of the analysis in the Security Configuration and Analysis snap-in in the MMC. This switch is commonly used when secedit is used in a batch or scheduled task.

The */analyze* switches use the same parameters as the */configure* switch, although the area switch is not available for */analyze*. The */analyze* function analyzes the entire configuration, not sections of it.

secedit import

The secedit */import* switch allows you to import a security template into a database to apply the template settings to a system or to be analyzed against a system. As with the other commands, there are a set of required and optional switches that determine the type and scope of the import. These switches are delineated in Table 2.9.

Table 2.9 secedit.exe Import Switch Parameters

Parameter	Description
/db filename	This argument specifies which database file to be used to perform the security configuration. It is a required argument.
/cfg filename	This argument specifies a security template to import into the database prior to configuring the system.
/overwrite	This switch specifies whether the database should be emptied prior to importing the security template. If this parameter is not specified, the settings are accumulated in the database (if you import more than one security template, all settings will accumulate). If this parameter is not specified and there are conflicting security settings between the database and the imported template, the template settings win.
/areas area1 area2...	This argument specifies which security areas to be applied to the system. If the parameter is not specified, all settings defined in the database are applied. To configure multiple areas, separate each with a space. See Table 2.7 for a description of the security areas that can be specified.
/log filename	This argument is used to specify the path to the log file. If no path is specified, the default log file will be used.

Continued

Table 2.9 secedit.exe Import Switch Parameters

Parameter	Description
/quiet	This switch suppresses screen and log output. You can still review results of the analysis in the Security Configuration and Analysis snap-in in the MMC. This switch is commonly used when secedit is used in a batch or scheduled task.

secedit export

The *secedit* command also allows you to export security settings contained in a specified database. Table 2.10 shows the required and optional parameters for the */export* function. This function is typically used for two primary purposes. First, if you want to preserve the current settings on a system, you can export them. This can be useful if you want to experiment with various settings but want to bring the system back to its original known state. It's also commonly used to export customized settings that can be applied via GPO. For example, suppose you import the securews.inf template and make modifications to that template to address the particular needs of your organization. You save these settings as secureV1.inf. These are the settings you want to apply to all computers in your Finance department. Once you expert these settings, you can apply them via group policy to the computers in the Finance OU.

Table 2.10 secedit Export Switch Parameters

Parameter	Description
/db filename	This argument specifies which database file to be used to perform the security configuration. It is a required argument.
/cfg filename	This argument specifies a security template to import into the database prior to configuring the system.
/mergedpolicy	This switch specifies whether to merge domain and local policy security settings before exporting. If you include this argument, you are merging domain and local policies prior to exporting the security settings stored in the database.
/areas area1 area2...	This argument specifies which security areas to be exported. If the parameter is not specified, all settings defined in the database are exported. To export multiple areas, separate each with a space. See Table 2.7 for a description of the security areas that can be specified.
/log filename	This argument is used to specify the path to the log file. If no path is specified, the default log file will be used.

Continued

Table 2.10 secedit Export Switch Parameters

Parameter	Description
/quiet	This switch suppresses screen and log output. You can still review results of the analysis in the Security Configuration and Analysis snap-in in the MMC. This switch is commonly used when secedit is used in a batch or scheduled task.

An example of the */export* command is shown. Recall that when the no path is specified, the current directory is used. This is important to remember when using the *secedit* command, and it is especially important when using *secedit* in a script or scheduled task.

```
secedit /export /db hisecws.inf /cfg hisecws.inf /log hisecws.log
```

secedit validate

This command is used to validate security settings in a specific security template. There is only one argument for this command, the /cfg *filename* argument. An example of the *secedit validate* command is:

```
secedit /validate /cfg hisecws.inf
```

secedit generaterollback

The secedit command-line tool also has a *generaterollback* switch. This switch allows you to generate a rollback template with respect to a configuration template. When you apply a configuration template (/cfg *filename*) to a computer, the */generaterollback* option allows you to create a rollback template that will reset the security settings to the values in place before you applied the configuration template. If you generate a rollback template and decide you want to go back to your original values, you would have to apply the rollback template using the secedit command */import*. The *generaterollback* command simply takes a snapshot of current configuration values and creates a template that you can import to reset values. The syntax for this command is slightly different from other secedit commands, as shown by the parameters in Table 2.11.

Table 2.11 secedit generaterollback Switch Parameters

Parameter	Description
/cfg filename	This argument specifies a security template to import into the database prior to configuring the system.
/rbk filename	This switch specifies the name of the rollback template secedit will create. The file extension should be .inf.

Continued

Table 2.11 secedit generaterollback Switch Parameters

Parameter	Description
/log filename	This argument is used to specify the path to the log file. If no path is specified, the default log file will be used.
/quiet	This switch suppresses screen and log output. You can still review results of the analysis in the Security Configuration and Analysis snap-in in the MMC. This switch is commonly used when secedit is used in a batch or scheduled task.

An example of this command is:

```
secedit /cfg hisecws.inf /rbk hisecbk.inf /log /quiet
```

secedit refreshpolicy Replaced by gpupdate

In Windows 2000, the *secedit* command used the */refreshpolicy* switch to refresh local Group Policy settings and Group Policy settings stored in the Active Directory. This command is replaced in Windows Server 2003 by the command *gpupdate.exe*. This command-line tool does what the */refreshpolicy* switch in the *secedit* command did in Windows 2000. Table 2.12 shows the parameters for the *gpupdate* command. If you'd like to view help options for the *gpupdate* command, use the following command line string:

```
gpupdate ?
```

Without the question mark, the command will simply execute—meaning it will cause policy to be updated. This behavior is somewhat different from other command-line tools that will display help if you simply type in the name, such as *secedit*.

Table 2.12 gpupdate Switch Parameters

Parameter	Description
/Target: {computer | user}	This argument specifies that only a particular computer or a particular user policy settings should be refreshed. If not specified, both computer and user policy settings are refreshed.
/Force	This switch specifies that all settings should be refreshed. By default, only settings that have changed are refreshed. By using this switch, both changed and unchanged policy settings will be refreshed.

Continued

Table 2.12 gpupdate Switch Parameters

Parameter	Description
/Wait: {value}	This switch sets the number of seconds to wait for the policy processing to finish. The default value is 600 seconds or 10 minutes. The value "0" means do not wait. The value "-1" means wait indefinitely. If the time limit exceeds the set value, the command prompt returns but the policy processing continues.
/Logoff	This argument is used to specify whether the command will cause a logoff after Group Policy settings have been refreshed. This option has no effect if there are no extensions called that require a logoff. This switch is required for those Group Policy client-side extensions that do not process policy in the background but process policy when a user logs on. In order to process refreshed policy in these cases, it's mandatory that the logoff be forced. One example of this type of refresh is folder redirections, which are applied when the user logs on.
/Boot	This switch is used to force a reboot after Group Policy has been refreshed. Just as some policy is applied at user logon, other policies are applied at computer start up. In these cases, the system must be rebooted before the refreshed settings will be applied. This scenario is typical with software installation that requires a system reboot. If there are no extensions that call for a reboot, this switch has no effect.
/Sync	This switch causes the next foreground policy application to be done synchronously. A foreground policy application (when policy is applied) is done at computer boot and user logon. You can specify this for the user, computer, or both using the */Target* parameter. If this argument is used, the */Force* and */Wait* switches will be ignored if specified.

Using the *secedit* command-line tool is the preferred method for applying sections of security templates (/areas) and is the recommended way to restore portions of the Setup security.inf template to a system. The *gpupdate.exe* command replaces the *secedit* command switch */refreshpolicy* and is used to refresh Group Policy settings, including security settings.

Deploying Security Using Scripts

Now that you've learned about the *secedit* and *gpupdate* commands, let's look at how these can be used in scripts to automate the rollout of security settings across the domain or OU. By calling the *secedit.exe* tool at a command prompt from a batch file or automatic task scheduler, you can automatically create and apply templates and analyze system security. The *secedit* command is extremely helpful when you have multiple computers on which security must be analyzed or configured *and* you need to perform these tasks during off-peak hours.

Security can be implemented via group pOlicy, as you learned earlier in this chapter. Group policies are applied to two types of Active Directory objects—users and computers. Group policies can be used to assign and run scripts at particular times, such as when the user logs on or when the computer is booted. Scripts are stored in the Scripts subfolder in the Group Policy Template (GPT). The GPT is a structure consisting of the GPT folder and a set of subnodes that together contain all the Group Policy configuration settings for a particular GPO. Scripts assigned to run at logon or logoff are stored in the \USERS\SCRIPTS subfolder of the GPT. Scripts assigned to run at computer startup or shutdown are stored in the \MACHINES\SCRIPTS subfolder. The GPT is located in the system volume folder on the Windows Server 2003 DCs. The folder name is the GUID (which is a hexadecimal number) of the GPO to which it applies. For example:

```
%systemroot%\Sysvol\sysvol\test.net\Policies\[A234C8352-F089-44E8-38B9-
00C7EFD00C65]
```

TEST DAY TIP

Although most of the Microsoft literature recommends using the secedit.exe command-line tool, you're more likely to see scenarios that use the Security Configuration and Analysis snap-in. Therefore, be familiar with the *seced.exe* commands and options, but also spend time before the exam walking through several configuration and analysis scenarios using the snap-in.

Designing & Planning...

Working with Different Operating Systems and the Group Policy Management Console

As you've discovered, not all Windows operating systems support the same level of security. Each version of the operating system builds on the previous one to improve security and respond to common security threats. Even Windows 2000 and Windows XP, which are very similar, have slightly different features. In planning your security, you should consider maintaining separate security templates for each operating system. Clearly, applying a template that contains settings that are incompatible with the operating system's features will cause problems. So too, will relaxing security for *all* operating systems to accommodate varying degrees of security in each system. Test security templates on appropriate operating systems and within their roles (workstation, member server, Web server, and so forth). This will help maintain the tightest possible security while creating an organized and systematic approach to security.

As you know, OUs are virtual groupings based on whatever structure makes sense for your business. In some firms, OUs will be by business unit such as Finance, Sales, and Service. In other firms, it might be some other structure. If your firm uses a business unit model, you might decide to create child OUs in each business unit OU to deal with down-level clients. For example, in the Finance OU, you might create three child OUs: Windows 95, Windows 98, and Windows NT 4.0. You can populate each OU with the computers in the Finance department based on the operating system each is running. Once you've created these OUs, you can apply group policies related to the specific operating system without compromising security.

You can download and install the Group Policy Management Console (GPMC) from Microsoft to make working with Group Policy a bit easier. The GPMC is an MMC snap-in and can be accessed via Administrative Tools or via the MMC (added as a snap-in). As you can see in Figures 2.13 and 2.14, you can better visualize group policy via the GPMC. The GPMC allows you to better manage group policy because it centralizes and organizes information in a fairly intuitive manner.

Using the example of the OUs used to organize and manage down-level clients, Figure 2.13 shows what this looks like in the GPMC. In the left pane, you can see that Finance is an OU and there are three child OUs—Windows 95, Windows 98, and Windows NT. You could apply certain policies to the Finance OU and apply other policies to the child OUs.

Continued

By clicking on the OU in the left pane, you can see view Linked Group Policy Objects, Group Policy Inheritance, and Delegation for the OU. This makes managing down-level clients much easier and allows you to manage group policy in a more visual, intuitive manner.

You can also manage other aspects of your group policies. For example, both Figures 2.13 and 2.14 show WMI Filtering in the left pane. WMI Filtering is Windows Management Instrumentation, and the WMI filters allow you to dynamically determine the scope of GPOs based on the attributed of the target computer. When you link a GPO to a WMI filter, the filter is evaluated on the target computer. If the WMI filter evaluates to FALSE, the GPO is not applied. If the WMI filter evaluates to TRUE, the GPO is applied. The WMI filter is a separate object from the GPO, so to apply a WMI filter, you must link the filter to the GPO. Each GPO can only have one WMI filter, but that filter can be linked to multiple GPOs. It's important to note, however, that WMI filters are not supported in down-level clients—another good reason to group down-level clients into OUs. Windows XP and Windows Server 2003 support WMI filters, but Windows 2000 clients (and earlier) will ignore WMI filters and the GPO will be applied, regardless of the WMI filter.

Figure 2.13 Group Policy Management Console—Organizational Unit Management

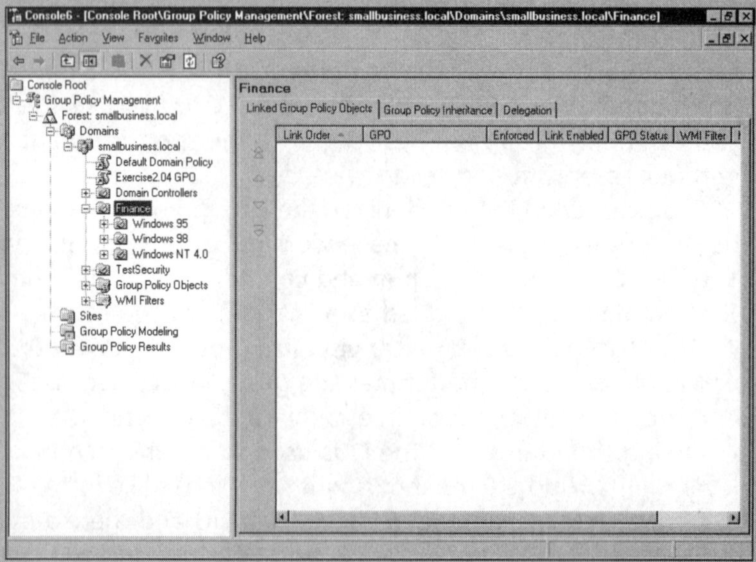

Continued

Figure 2.14 Group Policy Management Console—Management Options

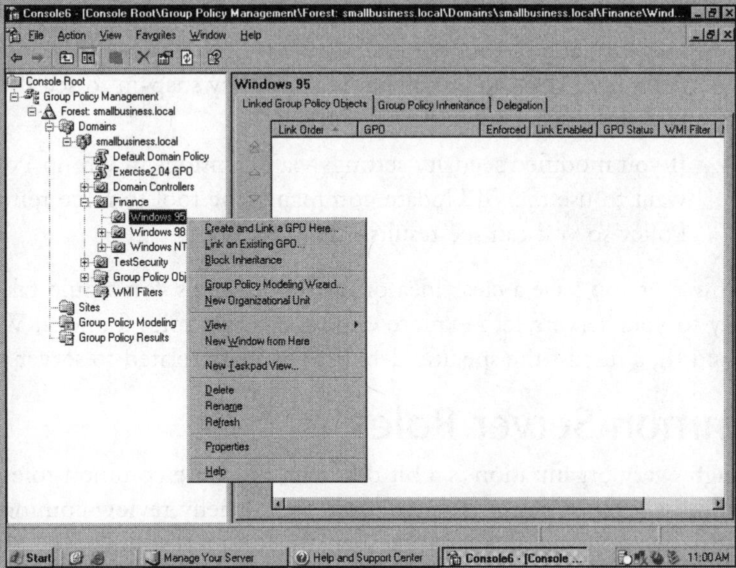

EXAM 70-297 OBJECTIVE 3.7

Design Security for Servers that Have Specific Roles

The baseline security established on a Windows Server 2003 system is generated from the Setup security.inf template. Although this sets a known starting point, it's important to apply additional security templates based on the role of the computer. Earlier, we reviewed the security templates and discussed their use. In this section, we're going to discuss the types of server roles and which predefined templates might be most appropriate. Your company's network configuration might vary as will your security needs, but these default settings will provide security and will certainly be the topic of several exam questions. Each of the predefined security templates provided by Microsoft covers a specific security need, but there will be cases where you will want to modify a template (remember, always a copy of the original template, never the original) to meet your organization's specific needs. It is recommended that you follow these steps in creating a secure environment for your network:

1. Begin with **Setup security.inf**. If needed, apply sections of the template to computers that might have been upgraded or modified (versus a clean install, which applies the Setup security.inf template during install). Specific sections can be applied via the *secedit* command-line tool.

2. Apply the predefined templates to servers based on roles (we'll discuss this in detail in a moment) in a test environment.
3. Test security on the network. Use the Security Configuration and Analysis snap-in or the *secedit* command-line tool to analyze security on a particular computer. Use the Resultant Set of Policy snap-in to see the results when you apply security via group policy.
4. If you modified security settings via extensions in Group Policy, you might want to use the GPUpdate command-line tool to force refresh of Group Policy so you can see results immediately.

Now that you have a clear idea of the logical steps you would take in applying security to your servers, let's explore common server roles found in Windows Server 2003 and then discuss the specific details of security related to server roles.

Common Server Roles

Although every organization is a bit different, there are common roles that servers play in most organizations. In this section, we'll briefly review common server roles and how these roles are impacted by security considerations.

Microsoft Windows Server 2003 identifies these types of servers:

- File server
- Print server
- Application server
- Mail server
- Terminal server
- Remote Access/VPN server
- Domain controller
- DHCP server
- DNS server
- WINS server
- Steaming Media server

In the next section, we'll review the security considerations for computers in these different roles. You'll learn how to assess the appropriate level of security for the server as well as how to apply security templates to multiple servers in similar roles across the domain or OU.

EXAM WARNING

Windows Server 2003 defines a number of different types of servers. Be familiar with these defined roles. You can be sure you'll see questions on the exam that refer to server roles, and knowing the specific differences can help you to understand the question more quickly and identify correct answers as well.

Designing & Planning...

Defining, Implementing and Securing Server Roles

Although Windows Server 2003 documentation identifies specific server roles, it's quite common in the real world to see server roles mixed and matched a bit more. Certainly, large organizations often have the resources and the need to separate server roles very clearly. However, small and medium-sized companies often have to find a compromise between the cost of having servers dedicated to one function and the security concerns that arise when various server roles are combined on one computer.

To find the best compromise, you should first begin by identifying current server roles and any server roles you'd like to add now or in the near future. Create a list of these server roles so you begin with a clear understand of what you have, what's needed immediately, and what will be needed in the future. Next, group these roles based on similarities in security needs. For example, you might need DCs, DNS servers, and DHCP servers. In a small firm, system performance and security considerations might allow you to place these services all on one computer. These services have similar security needs and they could logically be placed together. You could also group file, print, and application services (excluding IIS) on one server, again if performance permits. These types of services all have similar security needs and could be managed on one server.

Typically, any server that's going to connect to external resources, especially the Internet, needs very specific security. Keeping servers that face the public network safe is a challenge because these servers are common and highly visible targets for hackers and intruders. You might choose to group Internet-based services on one server if it is feasible and will maintain tight security.

Each of the servers should begin with a known security state, a baseline. This is applied via the predefined templates provided with Windows

Continued

Server 2003. Once you've defined the server roles for your organization, you can create incremental security templates for specific server roles—IIS, DCs, print servers, and so forth. These incremental policies build on the predefined baselines and are specific to the security needs of that server role and your organization. You can download samples from the Microsoft Web site at www.microsoft.com/downloads/details.aspx?FamilyID=8a2643c1-0685-4d89-b655-521ea6c7b4db&DisplayLang=en. This download is the *Windows Server 2003 Security Guide*, which includes tools, templates, and scripts that can be used to manage security in the enterprise.

Placing similar servers in OUs will allow you to create specific GPOs that can be linked to these OUs, providing a fairly easy way to apply security across the enterprise for all server roles. You can then import the incremental security template for that server role into the GPO and it will be applied to the OU when policy is refreshed (or you can force the update by using the gpudate.exe command line utility).

As you can see, there are few hard-and-fast rules on what services you can run on a server. It depends greatly on the company's particular needs, financial resources, and the similarity of security needs. Clearly, it would not be appropriate to put file, print, and application sharing on a DC, although there are no doubt some companies out there configured in exactly that manner. Keeping similar functions isolated improves performance on the network, and dramatically improves security. The cost of a security violation could far outweigh the cost of another server or two, so make sure your budgeting process takes this into account when deciding on how to configure server roles.

Server Security Best Practices

Although we've discussed best practices throughout this chapter, let's review best practices as it relates to server security here just so you're thoroughly familiar with these recommendations.

- Always control physical and network access to critical servers, especially DCs. Keep DCs in an access-controlled location.
- Always perform tasks on the servers with the least possible privileges. Do not perform tasks with Administrator privileges if possible. Use the *Run As* command when needed.

- Restrict user and machine access to groups that have loose security settings. Provide users and computers with the least possible permissions while still meeting their needs to access and use network resources.
- Secure the data on the computers using strong access control lists (ACLs) and, if needed, the syskey utility. The syskey utility provides protection against password-cracking software that targets the Security Access Management (SAM) database or directory services. It uses strong encryption that is much more difficult (if not close to impossible) and time consuming to crack.
- Require the use of strong passwords via the Password Policy settings.
- Restrict the downloading and installation of programs that do not come from known, trusted sources.
- Maintain up-to-date virus protection on all systems.
- Keep all software patches up to date. Patches often address newly discovered security holes. Applying patches in a timely manner on all affected machines can prevent problems that are easily avoided.

When you first install Windows Server 2003, you will choose what role or function it will play. If you want to add or change roles after the operating system has been installed, you can use the Configure Your Server Wizard. This wizard opens automatically the first time you log on to the server with administrative credentials. Later, you can use the Configure Your Server Wizard to modify the configuration. In Exercise 2.06, you'll learn how to use the Configure Your Server Wizard to configure your server for a particular role.

EXERCISE 2.07

USING THE CONFIGURE YOUR SERVER WIZARD

Select a test server to work with that will not disrupt normal operations. Log onto your system using the Administrative account.

1. Click **Start**, select **Administrative Tools**, and then select **Configure Your Server Wizard**.
2. The Welcome screen is displayed. If you are unclear about server roles, you can click the link provided to the Configure Your Server wizard help file on server roles.
3. Click **Next** to begin. Clicking **Help** on any screen will open the Configuring Roles for Your Server Help file.

4. The next screen, Preliminary Steps, provides a list of steps you should take before continuing the server configuration. This includes having your Windows Server 2003 CD or network share available. When you're ready to proceed, click **Next**.
5. The next screen in the wizard shows what server roles are already configured on the server. If a server role is not listed, you can add it via the **Add or Remove Programs** link. Figure 2.15 shows the Server Role selection screen. You can remove roles from a server via this wizard by selecting a configure server role and clicking **Next**.

Figure 2.15 Configure Your Server Wizard—Select Server Role

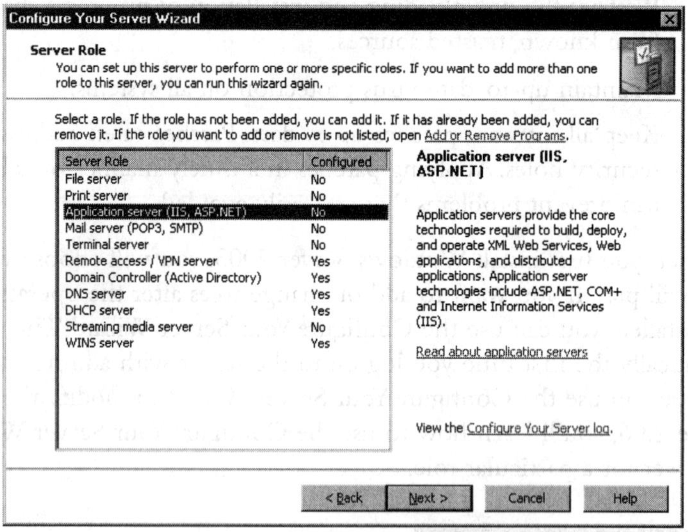

6. Select the desired server role. For this exercise, select **Application Server**. Click **Next**.
7. The Application Server Options screen provides the opportunity to install two additional tools, FrontPage Server Extensions and **ASP.NET**. Select ASP.NET and then click **Next**.
8. The next wizard screen confirms your selection and allows you to view the options chosen. In this case, the Summary list contains Install Internet Information Services (IIS), Enable COM+ for remote transactions, Enable Microsoft Distributed Transaction Coordinator (DTC) for remote access, and Enable ASP.NET If this is what you want to install, click **Next**. If not, click **Back** to go to the previous screen and make a different selection. This is shown in Figure 2.16. For this exercise, click **Next**.

Figure 2.16 Configure Your Server Summary of Selected Options

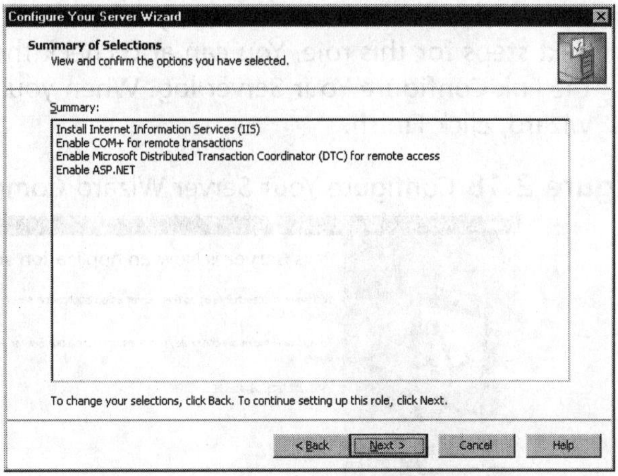

9. The next action the wizard takes is to apply the selections you've chosen. If needed, the Windows Components Wizard will automatically open to configure needed components. You might be prompted to insert your Windows Server 2003 CD or connect to a flat file or network share. The selected services and components are installed as shown in Figure 2.17.

Figure 2.17 Installing Components and Server Role

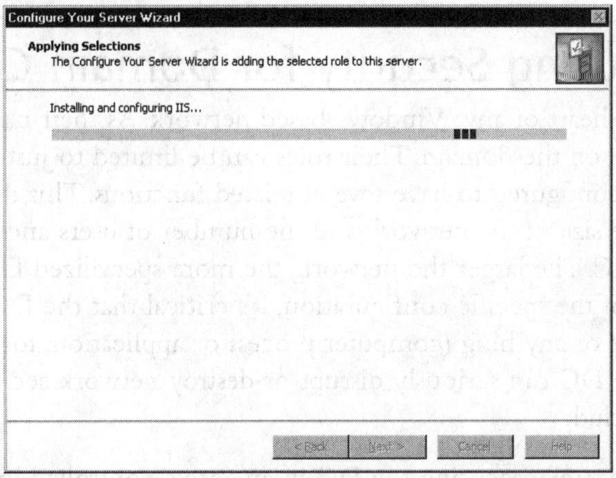

10. Once the needed Windows components have been installed, the wizard will display a final screen indicating that the server role installation was completed successfully, as shown in Figure 2.18. In this case, it states "This Server is Now an Application server." If

it fails, read the error message and follow the directions. If you want to know about next steps, you can click the link View the next steps for this role. You can also check the log file by clicking the link Configure Your Server log. When you're ready to close the wizard, click Finish.

Figure 2.18 Configure Your Server Wizard Complete

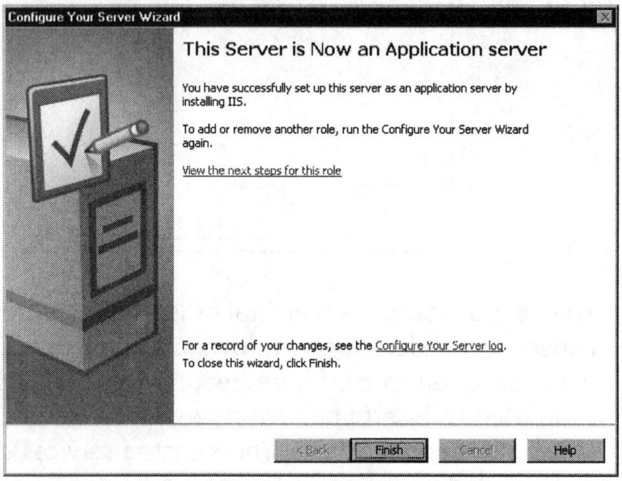

Configuring Security for Domain Controllers

DCs are the heart of any Windows-based network. As their name implies, they control activities on the domain. Their roles can be limited to just one function, or the DC can be configured to have several related functions. This decision is typically based on the size of the network and the number of users and processes that will access the DC. The larger the network, the more specialized DCs tend to become. Regardless of the specific configuration, it's critical that the DCs be well protected, since anyone or anything (computer process or application, for example) that can gain access to the DC can seriously disrupt or destroy network security. Basic security measures include:

- Physically securing the DC in an access-controlled location.
- Using the NTFS file system to protect data on the system volume(s).
- Requiring strong passwords on DCs to protect against unauthorized access.

- If possible, requiring smart card access on DCs. Using smart cards, passwords are generated randomly and encrypted using strong encryption methods.
- Removing all services that will not be used on the DC.

The DC typically authenticates domain logons and maintains the security policy as well as the master database for the domain. Although servers and DCs can validate user logons, only DCs manage changes to passwords or other changes to user and computer accounts. To configure security for the DCs in your network, you want to begin with a baseline—a known state. When you promote a server to a DC, the DC security.inf template is applied. This provides the baseline security for DCs that is equivalent to the Setup security.inf for all other types of servers. There are two other predefined security templates that can be used on DCs—the securedc.inf and the hisecdc.inf.

The securedc.inf template can be used if there are DCs or member servers in the domain that are not running Windows NT 4.0 SP4 or later. The securedc.inf file provides strong security but does not require SMB signing, strong encryption, or NTLM v2 authentication protocol use. This is not the most secure setting, but should provide a reasonable level of security in a mixed operating system environment. After applying and testing the securedc.inf template, you might find there are additional areas that can be secured without causing a disruption on the network. If so, make changes to a copy of the securedc.inf template and name the file something descriptive that will tell you what it does. For example, you might simply name it securedc2.inf.

If possible, consider applying the hisecdc.inf security template. Recall that the hisecdc.inf template requires strong passwords and SMB signing . Some down-level clients might not be able to connect to a DC with the hisecdc.inf template applied, so carefully test all scenarios before deploying this template on a DC in a mixed environment.

Common Threats to Domain Controllers

The most common threats to DCs are those that attempt to gain access to the security database on a DC. The DC contains all user accounts and passwords, so accessing this computer provides a hacker almost unlimited access to the network. Typical assaults include:

- Gaining physical access to the server to copy the security database onto removable media for later analysis.
- Gaining access to the security database to modify user rights to provide administrative access to unauthorized user(s).
- Gain access to the DC to modify computers on the domain to allow "rogue" computers to participate in the domain.

- Gain access to DC communications, via network connections, to monitor, capture, and exploit security information such as user accounts and passwords.

EXAM WARNING

Changes to default settings should be implemented by creating a new GPO and linking that new GPO to an OU that contains DCs. This new GPO should be added above the level of the Default Domain Controllers GPO so that the modified settings will take precedence over the default settings.

Audit Backup and Restore Events

The Active Directory database on a DC is a virtual gold mine for hackers. In addition to physically restricting access to the DC itself, auditing backup and restore events can help you monitor activities that could result in unauthorized copies of the database being created by those who legitimately or otherwise have Administrative privileges. Setting the **Local Policies | Security Options | Audit: Audit the use of Backup and Restore privilege** can be enabled to help you monitor potential abuses. By default, this option is not defined in the DC security.inf template. It is defined but disabled in the securedc.inf and hisecdc.inf templates.

Restrict Access to Removable Media

Another method intruders might use is to take removable media from a sensitive server to a computer on which they have full administrative rights. From there, they can modify permissions, take ownership, and access the data on the removable media. Again, the first line of defense is to physically protect the server in an access-controlled location. However, you can also restrict the ability to format and eject removable media via group policy by modifying the following GPO: **Devices: Allowed to format and eject removable media**. This GPO is accessed via the **Local Policies | Security Options** section of the DC security.inf, securedc.inf and hisecdc.inf templates.

This can be set to allow Administrators, Administrators and Power Users, Administrators and Interactive Users, or it can be left "Not defined." The recommended setting is to allow only members of the Administrators group to format and eject removable media. You can also audit this event if you suspect there are problems with members of the Administrators group.

Restricting Anonymous Access

In Windows Server 2003, access that was available to the anonymous user in Windows NT is now only available to the Everyone and Guest accounts. However, you might still need to provide anonymous access, because some services in earlier versions of Windows require anonymous access to request user accounts from DCs and to list network shares. You might also need to allow use of the Anonymous account across trusts in a forest if an administrator in a trusting domain needs to access a list of users of a trusted domain in another forest.

Windows Server 2003 restricts the Anonymous account by default. If you need to use this account, you should thoroughly document which systems require Anonymous access and why. Examine each situation to determine if there is an alternate way to accomplish the task—don't think that just because something has used Anonymous access in the past that it requires it. You can modify specific ACLs to include the Anonymous account, or you can make security policy changes that relax the default restrictions placed on the Anonymous account in Windows Server 2003. Once you've determined where the Anonymous account is needed, use the guidelines in Table 2.13 to apply it appropriately to avoid relaxing security unnecessarily.

Table 2.13 Managing Anonymous Access in Windows Server 2003

Action	Pros	Cons
Edit the ACLs of any resources that require it to allow the **Anonymous** logon.	Most secure approach.	Administratively intensive. You must identify, modify, and document each resource for which you modify the ACL to allow Anonymous logon.
Use the **Do not allow anonymous enumeration of SAM accounts and shares policy** GPO.	Prevents attackers from using Anonymous logon to enumerate accounts and shares on a computer.	Might prevent legitimate users from another domain from locating resources. Do not use this if you are running Windows versions prior to Windows 2000, or if you have an outbound one-way trust with a domain in another forest as these both use services that require the Anonymous logon to locate resources.

Continued

Table 2.13 Managing Anonymous Access in Windows Server 2003

Action	Pros	Cons
Use the **Let Everyone permissions apply to anonymous users** GPO.	Changes security back to Windows NT model, if needed.	*Do not apply this unless there is a very compelling reason to do so.* If you must use this method, you should edit the ACLs on sensitive resources to not allow the Everyone or Anonymous to access those resources. The Everyone access level does not require authentication, which leaves those resources completely unprotected from attack.
Add **Everyone** and **Anonymous** to pre-Windows 2000 compatible access group.	If you have clients running pre-Windows 2000 operating systems and you need to allow users to change their passwords, add the Everyone and Anonymous groups to the compatible access group, which enables anonymous access. Membership in this group is determined by a user option when installing the first domain. You can modify group membership as needed.	Not the most secure setting, but might be needed for down-level clients.

Digitally Signing Authentication Traffic

When a computer is joined to a domain, a computer account is established. In order to communicate with the DC, it must be authenticated. Three settings can be used to determine whether signed and encrypted authentication is used. The three GPO settings that deal specifically with digitally signing authentication traffic are:

- **Domain member** Digitally encrypt or sign secure channel data (always)
- **Domain member** Digitally encrypt secure channel data (when possible)
- **Domain member** Digitally sign secure channel data (when possible)

These can be accessed via the three DC security templates in the **Local Policies | Security Options** section of each template. If you enable **Domain member:**

Digitally encrypt or sign secure channel data (always), the member computer will only use secure channel data for communicating with the DC. If you have DCs in the domain that are running an operating system prior to Windows NT 4.0 SP6a, you cannot use this setting. Doing so will make the DC unable to communicate with the member computer, because earlier operating systems do not support this security feature. Upgrading all DCs to at least Windows NT 4.0 SP6a is a wise step in improving domain security. If possible, use this setting to thwart potential attacks including man-in-the middle, replay, and other types of attacks that use this communication data between member computers and DCs.

Consideration must be given to authenticating down-level clients. Any DC that is authenticating users on any version of Windows prior to Windows NT 4.0 SP6a cannot *require* (via the **always** setting) digital encryption and signing because it was not supported until NT 4.0 SP6a. Thus, the **when possible** setting will *request* digital encryption and signing whenever possible and will not *require* it on down-level clients or with down-level DCs that do not support these functions. For better security, begin migrating down-level clients and servers to Windows 2000 or later to take advantage of the improved security features.

If you are unable to use the **Domain member: Digitally encrypt or sign secure channel data (always)** setting because of down-level clients or DCs, you should enable the other two settings: **Domain member: Digitally encrypt secure channel data (when possible)** and **Domain member: Digitally sign secure channel data (when possible)**. The effect of these two settings is that a DC or member computer with these settings will request the best possible security and will negotiate a common security setting. Thus, if the member computer has these two settings enabled and it is communicating with a Windows NT 4.0 SP4 DC, it can negotiate to secure the channel using the highest security enabled on the Windows NT 4.0 SP4 DC.

A related setting is the **Domain controller: LDAP server signing requirements** GPO setting. This determines whether the Lightweight Directory Access Protocol (LDAP) server requires LDAP clients to use data signing. There are three possible values for this object: **none**, **require signature**, and **not defined**. The **none** setting allows signing to be used if the client supports it but does not require it. The **require signature** setting requires that data signing be negotiated unless Transport Layer Security/Secure Sockets Layer (TLS/SSL) is used. The **not defined** option does not apply any setting for this object. While the most secure setting is to **require signature**, there are problems with using this setting with down-level clients. Any clients that do not support LDAP signing will then be unable to perform LDAP queries against the LDAP server. The fix for this is that computers running Windows 2000 should have Service Pack 3 installed. Other computers require changes to the Registry discussed in Microsoft Knowledge Base article 325465. If you have down-level clients that require LDAP support, you should set this GPO to **none**, which will allow signing if the client supports it.

EXAM WARNING

DCs are likely to receive a lot of attention on the exam, so make sure you're comfortable with the role, risks, and security solutions available for Windows Server 2003 servers.

Securing the Internet Information Server (IIS) Role

The IIS role is one of the most vulnerable server roles due to its inherent exposure to the Internet. Whenever a server is connected to the public infrastructure, it is more visible and more vulnerable to external attacks. Windows Server 2003 includes significant changes to IIS that help protect it from attack. The most noticeable change is that IIS is no longer installed by default as it was in earlier Windows versions. When it is installed by the network administrator, the default permissions are "locked down" rather than left open. In earlier versions, the default settings were lax and administrators had to lock the server down. Failure to do this properly caused many security problems. The current model in Windows Server 2003 is to disable as many features and provide as few permissions as possible by default.

IIS was installed by default under Windows 2000 and, as a result, there were serious security flaws in most networks—especially those that weren't actively using IIS services. One way to improve security is to audit your pre-Windows Server 2003 servers to determine if any are running IIS but not actually employed as IIS servers. Removing all unused IIS installations will greatly improve security. One recent virus, the Code Red worm, attacked IIS directly. Other viruses in the future will certainly make IIS a prime target, so removing unused installations and closely monitoring active installations will greatly enhance network security.

As with all other critical servers, you should first implement basic security measures. These were discussed in the domain controller section and are repeated here for your reference.

- Physically secure the IIS server in an access-controlled location.
- Use the NTFS file system to protect data on the system volume(s).
- Require strong passwords on the IIS server to protect against unauthorized access.
- If possible, require smart cards to access IIS servers for local administration purposes. Using smart cards, passwords are generated randomly and encrypted using strong encryption methods.
- Remove all services that will not be used on the IIS server.

TEST DAY TIP

A new security feature in Windows Server 2003 is a new policy Prevent IIS from Installing, which allows administrators to control which servers running Windows Server 2003 can run IIS.

Using "Configure Your Server" to Set Up IIS

Since IIS is no longer installed by default, you must take steps to install it on a Windows Server 2003 computer. We've already gone through the Configure Your Server Wizard to set it up as an application server earlier in this chapter. The application server role includes IIS, so your computer should already be configured as with IIS. You can check this via the **Manage Your Server** in **Administrative Tools**. If you want to manage the server role, you can select **Manage this application server** from the **Manage Your Server** interface.

The Application Server interface is displayed and includes the IIS Manager. Expanding the tree in IIS Manager will show the computer as well as these three areas: Application Pools, Web Sites and Web Service Extensions. By default, IIS is locked down and dynamic content will not work unless specifically enabled. This is done in the Web Services Extensions area. Features such as ASP, ASP.NET, Server-Side includes, Web Distributing Authoring and Versioning (WebDAV) publishing, and FrontPage Server Extensions will not work until and unless enabled. In the Web Service Extensions dialog, you can allow or prohibit specific service extensions as well as add new service extensions. Figure 2.19 show the default list of Web Service Extensions.

Figure 2.19 IIS Default Web Service Extensions

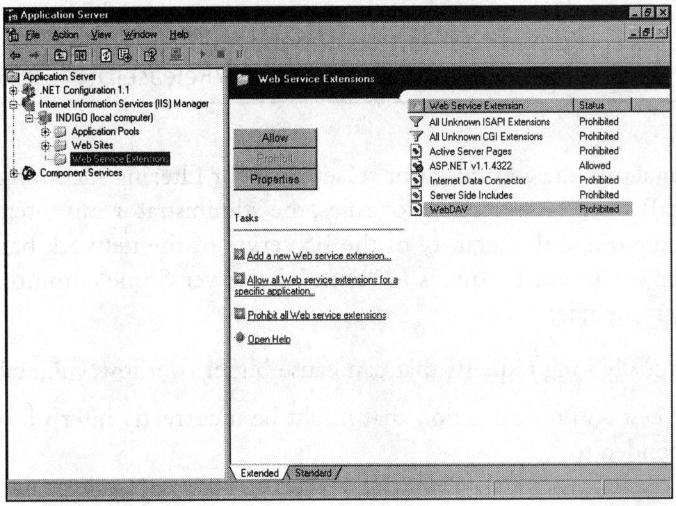

Basic Security for IIS

Once you've configured the server to run IIS, you should take the basic steps to secure the server. Placing all IIS servers (if your firm is running more than one) into an IIS OU will help you manage GPOs related to securing and managing IIS servers across the organization. Remember to only install the necessary IIS components, including Web Service Extensions, that you'll use. For example, if you don't use FrontPage technologies, you should not install FrontPage Extensions.

Another security measure you can take specific to IIS servers is to place content on a dedicated volume. This prevents an attacker from accessing system files and other critical files that would otherwise be on the same volume as content you are providing to the public via Web services. Providing a dedicated volume with NTFS permissions will limit a hacker's access to critical files and information that could be used to get further into the network.

IPSec filters can be applied to the IIS server to block or permit specific IP traffic and to secure sensitive IP traffic. IPSec filters are discussed in detail in Chapter 5.

Using URLScan and IISLockdown

The URLScan tool restricts the types of HTTP request that an IIS server will process. URLScan 2.5 is not included with IIS 6.0 because IIS 6.0 has built-in features that provide security functionality that is equal to or better than the features of URLScan 2.5. However, if you are not running IIS 6.0, you should consider using URLScan 2.5.

> **NOTE**
>
> You can download the URLScan utility from Microsoft's Web site at www.microsoft.com/technet/treeview/default.asp?url-/technet/security/default.asp.
>
> The IIS Lockdown tool can be downloaded from www.microsoft.com/downloads/release.asp?ReleaseID=43955.

URLScan allows the administrator to set rules for filtering incoming requests for the IIS server. By setting restrictions or rules, the administrator can filter out requests that might compromise the security of the IIS server or the network behind it. Intruders often use unusual requests to "trick" the server. Some common requests used by hackers include:

- Unusually long requests that can cause buffer overflow vulnerabilities
- Request an unusual action that might be incorrectly interpreted or responded to

- Be encoded by an unusual character set that might be incorrectly interpreted or responded to
- Include unusual character sequences that might cause unspecified results

Windows Server 2003 includes IIS 6.0, which include the features of URLScan, although they differ slightly. If you're using a version of IIS prior to 6.0, you can download URLScan from the Microsoft Web site. URLScan will create a configuration file that can be modified from time to time. If you're running URLScan 2.0, you can upgrade to URLScan 2.5 without losing your current configuration files. The upgrade simply adds new security features without modifying your current configuration files. URLScan is also incorporated into another downloadable tool, IISLockdown, which we'll discuss in a moment.

The latest version of URLScan has three significant changes from previous versions. It allows you to change the directory location of the log file, it can log longer URLs (previous versions truncated anything over 1024 bytes), and you can limit the size, in bytes, of a request. URLScan uses role-based templates to assist in setting up appropriate rules.

IISLockdown is another tool used with IIS. The latest version also includes the URLScan 2.5 tool that we just discussed. The IISLockdown tool is primarily intended for IIS installations prior to Windows Server 2003. As discussed, Windows Server 2003's IIS installation locks down IIS by default. The IISLockdown tool, now in version 2.1, removes services and lowers permissions to provide greater security for IIS. For example, IISLockdown removes or disables unused services such as FTP, HTTP, SMTP, and NNTP. Hackers often look for services that are enabled to exploit inherent properties of those services. When those services are not actively in use, they are often not being monitored or audited, leaving them vulnerable to attack. Disabling unused services improves security, and the IISLockdown tool can be used to do this.

Test Day Tip

Remember this for test day: IISLockdown is intended to accomplish the same things for IIS 5.0 that Windows Server 2003's default installation of IIS 6.0 does—it locks down unused services, ports, and protocols. URLScan is used to set rules for accepting and processing requests on IIS servers.

Before modifying IIS security, determine how the Web server is to be used. The Application Server role allows you to run application pools and to run IIS to provide Web services. Depending on the types of data used on this server, you might need strong security. For example, if you're setting up a Web server that will allow users to log in from any location to check on their 401(k) contributions and settings, you need to configure the server to reliably authenticate authorized users and restrict access to *only* those users. For strong security, you should also convert FAT partitions on the server's disk to NTFS formatted partitions.

There are also a variety of settings available for Web site authentication, including Anonymous, Basic, Digest, Advanced Digest, Integrated Windows, Certificate, and .NET Passport authentication. IIS is covered later in this book and these topics are discussed in detail. You can also implement encryption, Secure Sockets Layer (SSL), certificates, and auditing for additional security.

EXAM WARNING

You're not likely to run into a question about using URLScan or IISLockdown. You might run into questions that test your understanding of these tools and their use in an IIS 5.0 and IIS 6.0 environment. Be sure to be clear about the uses and features of each tool.

Configuring Security for POP3 Mail Servers

If you want to provide POP3 (Post Office Protocol) and SMTP (Simple Mail Transport Protocol) access to users and applications, you'll need to set your server up as a mail server. As with other server roles, this is done via the Configure Your Server Wizard located in Administrative Tools. POP3 provides e-mail *retrieval*, and SMTP provides e-mail *transfer*. POP3 accounts are used on the mail server to allow users to retrieve e-mail from the server using an e-mail client such as Microsoft Outlook.

As with IIS servers, POP3 servers are often targeted by hackers because these servers provide access to e-mail user accounts and passwords. There are two major considerations for POP3 servers: determine the proper level of security, and determine the authentication methods to be used.

Head of the Class...

Microsoft Exchange Server 2003

Windows Server 2003 includes the ability to run the server as a POP3 server. Many organizations elect to install and use Microsoft Exchange Server 2003. Although outside the scope of this exam and topic, let's take a moment to look at Microsoft Exchange Server 2003 to understand a bit more about it as it relates to e-mail and security.

By default, if you install Exchange Server 2003, the Microsoft Exchange POP3 service, Microsoft Exchange IMAP4 service, and the Network News Transfer Protocol (NNTP) services are *disabled*. If you upgrade from an earlier version of Exchange Server, your settings will be preserved. Recall that this is a similar behavior to when you install Windows Server 2003. The security settings are very tight, and applications and services are locked down by default. Settings after upgrades are different from settings from clean installations.

In Exchange Server 2003, the Built-in Users group does not have the right to log on locally. If you're setting up Exchange Server 2003 on a DC, the built-in users group has already been removed from the Log on Locally policy setting for the local computer. As with Windows Server 2003, the Anonymous access is disabled by default. An additional security setting in Exchange Server 2003 is that the Everyone group and the Anonymous Logon group are not assigned permission to create top-level folder permissions on public folders. If you're upgrading from an earlier version of Exchange Server, and the Everyone group or Anonymous Logon group had these permissions, *setup will remove them*.

Exchange Server 2003 also limits the maximum size of file to 10MB and sets the default size of public folders to 10MB as well.

For new installations of Exchange Server 2003, the default POP3 virtual server, the default IMAP4 virtual server, and the default NNTP virtual server are configured to use both basic authentication and Integrated Windows authentication.

As you can see, the default settings in Exchange Server 2003 mirror the default settings in Windows Server 2003. By installing with the fewest possible permissions and by removing access by the Built-in Users group, the Everyone group, and the Anonymous Logon group, Exchange Server 2003 is more secure in both design and deployment.

Security Levels

Since POP3 servers are highly visible targets for hackers, it's recommended that you install and configure a firewall and that you use the IP Security Protocol version 6 (IPSec v6). A firewall is a software and hardware interface that prevents unauthorized access to internal networks from external locations by means of filtering and routing. The mail server should not be connected directly to the Internet without a reliable firewall in front of it. If your organization already has a firewall in place, you can typically add the mail server so that it routes traffic through the firewall.

IPSec v6 is used to secure IP traffic in certain situations. Although it can be employed to secure all IP traffic all the time, the use of this secure IP protocol dramatically reduces throughput because IPSec packets must be encrypted and decrypted at each end. This can have an adverse effect on network performance. Therefore, although it *can* be implemented for all network traffic, it is neither recommended or needed. Most network traffic is innocuous and does not need to be secured. Some down-level clients will not support IPSec, so that must be taken into consideration as well. IPSec can be configured to block or allow specific types of traffic based on any combination of source and destination addresses, specific protocols, and specific ports.

Authentication Methods

The authentication method can be changed only when there are no other mail servers in the domain. If you are establishing the first mail server, you will need to determine the desired authentication method. If the server is either a DC or a member server, the authentication method is the default method used by Active Directory. Otherwise, the authentication method that will be used is determined by local Windows accounts settings.

Securing Other Network Roles

DCs and IIS are two of the most critical and visible server roles and are ones that hackers target because of the potential gold mine of sensitive data on these servers. However, there are other very critical server roles in an organization, all of which must be properly secured against intended and unintended security breaches. In this section, we'll look briefly at other server roles, likely attack points and countermeasures that can be taken to keep the network secure.

Securing Network Infrastructure Servers

Network infrastructure servers are those that control network services, including Dynamic Host Configuration Protocol (DHCP), Domain Naming System (DNS) and Windows Internet Naming Service (WINS). When installed via the Configure Your Server Wizard in Windows Server 2003, the default Windows Server 2003 settings are applied. By default, then, each of these services is installed with the hardest security configuration, and it is up to the network administrator to modify those settings if applications or services do not work properly in this tighter security framework.

We'll discuss DHCP, DNS, and WINS servers separately. However, there are best practices that apply to securing any server running a network infrastructure service. These are delineated in Table 2.14.

Table 2.14 Securing Infrastructure Servers Best Practices

Action	Comments
Place all infrastructure servers in an OU.	This allows you to apply group policy to infrastructure servers in a consistent manner.
Use NTFS on all drives.	NTFS provides file and folder security.
Install any service packs or updates for infrastructure services.	Keeping servers up to date on service packs and updates is critical, because service packs and updates often address critical security issues.
Install virus protection software.	Prevents malicious attacks via viruses, worms, and Trojan horse attacks.
Secure well-known accounts.	Rename the Administrator and Guest accounts, change their descriptions, and use complex passwords. Do not use the same name and password on all servers to prevent an attacker from gaining universal access if he or she can successfully crack one name/password set. The Guest account is disabled by default; ensure this setting is in place.
Secure service accounts.	Configure services to run outside the domain account realm. This prevents access to domain-level information such as domain passwords.
Implement IPSec filters.	Depending on the role of the server, you can apply IPSec filters to filter out unauthorized traffic, including source and destination ports and protocols.
Implement auditing of events related to infrastructure services.	Depending on the role of the server, you can enable auditing to monitor meaningful events and alert you to possible intrusion. Useful auditing might include auditing use of privileges, change events, and system events, among others.

In addition, a DC can be assigned the role of Infrastructure Operations Master in Active Directory. In this role, the DC updates the group-to-user reference any time group membership changes. It replicates these changes across the domain. It's important to note that the Infrastructure Operations Master role can be assigned only to one DC in a domain. As mentioned earlier, you can download additional security templates from the Microsoft Windows Server 2003 Web site, including incremental Infrastructure Server policies. Alternately, you can create incremental policies based on predefined security templates that are applied to servers in specific roles. Once you've defined the server roles and security needs, you can modify predefined templates or create additional templates that incrementally improve security provided by the predefined templates.

Securing DHCP Servers

DHCP servers manage a set of DHCP addresses, called a *scope*, and assigns addresses to computers in a dynamic fashion. This important role lacks many of the vulnerabilities compared to other server roles. However, in highly secure settings such as financial institutions, DHCP can be more securely configured. Doing so takes a fair amount of administrative work and almost reverts back to static IP addressing, so you would want to thoroughly assess the risk to your DHCP servers within your organization to decide what level of security is most appropriate.

To lock DHCP down, first require that all client computers use DHCP. Next, configure the DHCP server with a reservation for each client computer. By providing just enough IP addresses in the scope, via reservations, you ensure that no unidentified or unauthorized computers can gain an IP address from the DHCP server. This prevents a hacker from being assigned an IP address from the server or from "grabbing" all the IP addresses via one network interface on a computer to which the hacker has administrative rights. Although an intruder could try to identify an IP address that will work and that isn't currently in use, configuring the DHCP server in this manner will make that task more difficult for would-be intruders.

Another way to help prevent DoS attacks is to implement DHCP servers in pairs and divide their scopes between the two. Place 80 percent of the IP addresses for a scope on DHCP server 1, and the remaining 20 percent of the IP addresses from that scope on DHCP server 2. Split the scope on the DHCP server 2 in just the same way—80 percent on the server and 20 percent on the other server. This helps ensure that if one DHCP server is brought offline, either due to a malfunction or due to a malicious attack, users will still be able to acquire an IP address.

In general, the security provided by the DC security.inf template provides an excellent baseline. In some cases, the securedc.inf or hisecdc.inf templates can be implemented, depending on the clients using the DHCP servers. Certainly, DHCP servers should be behind the firewall, and unnecessary services should be disabled or uninstalled. Other basic security measures, including controlling access, using NTFS, removing unused services, securing critical accounts, and enabling auditing, should be employed as well.

Securing DNS Servers

The DNS Server service provides the means for computers, users, and applications to resolve names (fully qualified domain names, or FQDN) to IP addresses. Windows Server 2003's DNS Service, Dynamic DNS (DDNS), accepts dynamic DNS record registrations from computers that have dynamic IP addresses (via DHCP). DDNS provides the ability for all computers to be listed accurately in the DNS database.

There are four common threats to DNS servers:

- **Footprinting** Footprinting occurs when someone is essentially able to reverse engineer your DNS structure by capturing DNS zone data, including domain names, computer names, and IP addresses for network resources.
- **Denial-of-service** A denial-of-service (DoS) attack is one in which the server is hit with so many requests (legitimate or bogus) for service that it must deny service until it processes the requests in the queue. Often, hostile queries are unusually long or contain special characters in an attempt to jam the queue. This typically ends up denying service for legitimate users.
- **Data modification** Data modification is another method used by intruders. If footprinting is successful, the intruder can use legitimate IP addresses within a packet to attack the network. If successful, the packet appears to have originated on the internal network. This is known as *IP spoofing*.
- **Redirection** Redirection occurs when DNS data is redirected to an intruder after the intruder somehow gains control of DNS data. This can be done by polluting the DNS cache data with incorrect DNS data that will cause information to be redirected to the intruder. This is typically only possible when using nonsecure dynamic DNS updating. In Windows Server 2003, DNS cache pollution protection is enabled by default. This prevents DNS records in cache that originate from any place other than authoritative DNS servers. Although this setting might increase DNS queries, it will prevent redirection via DNS cache pollution.

As with other critical servers, basic security measures should be taken to eliminate common security holes. To secure DNS servers that are attached to the Internet, you can take several precautions to mitigate some of the risk:

- Place the DNS server in a perimeter network. A perimeter network is also known as a *screened subnet* or a *demilitarized zone* (DMZ) and is an IP segment that allows you to isolate services that are exposed to the external network without exposing internal resources.
- Add a second DNS server on another subnet to protect against DoS attacks.
- Encrypt zone replication traffic via IPSec or VPN tunnels to secure names and IP addresses during transmission.
- Configure firewalls to enforce packet filtering on UDP and TCP ports 53. UDP port 53 is used for the Domain Name Server, and TCP port 53 is used for the Domain Name.
- Restrict the number of DNS servers permitted to initiate a zone transfer.

- Monitor DNS logs and servers on a regular basis.

For DNS servers that are not exposed to the Internet, the following practices will help reduce security risks:

- Allow only *secure* dynamic updates and limit the list of DNS servers that are allowed to obtain a zone transfer.
- Implement Active Directory-Integrated zones with secure dynamic update.
- Monitor DNS logs and servers on a regular basis.

WINS Servers

The WINS Service is needed to resolve NetBIOS names to IP addresses for clients that cannot use Active Directory services. WINS servers are required unless all domains have been upgraded to Active Directory, all clients are running Windows 2000 or later, and there are no applications that rely on WINS for name resolution in order to run properly.

The biggest security risk to WINS is that information is sometimes replicated across public networks. Transmitting NetBIOS names and IP addresses across a public network creates a vulnerability that can be addressed by implementing IPSec v6 (discussed earlier) or by using Virtual Private Networks (VPN) tunnels for secure communications. Security measures are similar to other infrastructure servers and include the following recommendations.

- Use the strongest level of encryption possible to secure data transmissions.
- Configure Routing and Remote Access service (through which WINS can replicate across the Internet) to use IPSec (signing and/or encryption) with VPN tunnels to secure data communication.
- Use Kerberos v5 or other certificate-based authentication to ensure that identities are verified prior to establishing communication. Kerberos is used by default in Windows Server 2003, and IPSec can be configured to use the Kerberos authentication.

Another suggestion for securing WINS servers that need to replicate data across a public network is to place them on a perimeter network. In this case, placing a WINS server on a perimeter network will provide replication or resolution across the public network without exposing NetBIOS or IP information for internal network resources.

It's important to protect WINS-enabled networks to make sure that unauthorized users do not have physical or wireless access to the network. When a user connects to a network running WINS, user credentials are not required before requesting a name service from the WINS server. A malicious user with physical (or wireless) access can exploit this by launching a DoS attack, which can prevent other users from access the WINS Service.

Finally, you can reserve static IP addresses for mission-critical WINS servers (and other servers or machines whose name-address mapping on the network needs to remain stable). This prevents other computers from "grabbing" the WINS server's IP address and redirecting WINS traffic for the purposes of gaining access to computer names and IP addresses on the network. However, this adds to administrative overhead, so use this only for mission-critical servers.

Securing File, Print, and Member Servers

Securing file, print, and member servers is simplified in Windows Server 2003 because many IIS is no longer installed by default on these computers. This eliminates a number of potentially serious security holes. All other services not being used on a file, print, or member server should be removed or disabled. In addition, remember to implement the NTFS file system format on all system volumes, and secure well-known accounts (especially Guest and Administrator). Always keeps system updates and patches up to date to address known security issues, and, of course, install and maintain a strong virus protection program. Make sure you update the virus signature file on a regular basis. While this is true for every computer in your company, it's especially important for file, print, and member servers to which users often have greater access.

The security best practices described earlier in this chapter are the best set of security measures that can be taken to secure a file, print, or member server. If internal intrusion is a concern, these servers can be kept in a secure access-controlled location along with other more sensitive servers. Although these servers might not require controlled-access locations, they should be kept in locations that provide some security, as they hold all the information the company uses on a daily basis. It is acceptable to locate these servers outside controlled-access areas, but they should still be out of the path of heavy traffic to prevent intentional and unintentional mishaps. One of the best measures, which is part of security best practices, is to make sure that users have the fewest possible permissions. Members of the Power Users group usually have sufficient permissions to manage the day-to-day tasks of file, print, and member servers. However, you should monitor membership in the Power Users group, and audit any attempts by Power Users to use that authority inappropriately.

Securing Terminal Servers

Terminal Server is used for two primary functions—one is to allow remote users to connect to applications and files without running them on their own computers. The second use is remote administration of other computers. In Windows Server 2003, you no longer need to use Terminal Server for remote administration. Instead, you can use the Remote Desktop for Administration (RDA), formerly *Terminal Services in*

Remote Administration mode. RDA is installed by default on computers running Windows Server 2003.

Although outside the scope of this chapter, it's important to note that when you configure your server to run Terminal Server, you must properly configure licensing information, or unlicensed clients will be unable to connect after an initial evaluation period. However, once Terminal Server is properly installed and configured, you can activate Internet Explorer Enhanced Security Configuration settings. If activated, IE applies the following security settings to administrators: high security to Internet and Local intranet security zones, and medium security settings to Trusted sites zones. These settings disable scripts, ActiveX controls, and the Microsoft Virtual Machine (VM) that can be the source of security holes. The IE Enhanced Security Configuration settings can be modified via the Manage Your Server interface. Additionally, make sure the server is using NTFS so that you can set file permissions.

Terminal Server allows for two security modes: Full Security and Relaxed Security. Relaxed Security is compatible with legacy applications that require, for example, access to the Registry in order to run properly. Use Full Security whenever possible; otherwise, users will have access to Registry and file system locations. Although this might be required to run legacy applications, it also creates vulnerability. The security mode can be accessed via **Start | Administrative Tools | Terminal Services Configuration**.

Determining what level of encryption will be used is another critical step in securing Terminal servers. By default, Windows Server 2003 uses 128-bit encryption, which is considered High security. There are four levels of security available and they must be matched to the Terminal server clients' capabilities. These four levels are FIPS Compliant, High, Client Compatible, and Low. Table 2.15 describes each of these encryption levels.

Table 2.15 Encryption Levels in Terminal Services

Encryption Level (most secure to least secure)	Description
FIPS Compliant	The Federal Information Processing Standard (FIPS) describes cryptography requirements used by the U.S. government. This level of encryption uses only 3DES encryption and SHA1 for hashing requirements . If FIPS has been implemented by enabling the GPO **System cryptography: Use FIPS compliant algorithms for encryption, hashing and signing**, the Administrator for Terminal Services cannot change this in Terminal Services configuration or by using the Set client connection encryption level in Terminal Services.

Continued

Table 2.15 Encryption Levels in Terminal Services

Encryption Level (most secure to least secure)	Description
High (default)	This is the default setting and encrypts data sent from the client to server using 128-bit encryption, which is often referred to as strong encryption. With this setting, any client that cannot support 128-bit encryption will be unable to connect to the Terminal server.
Client Compatible	This setting is used to support down-level clients that do not support 128-bit encryption. This setting uses the strongest encryption the client is capable of supporting.
Low	This is the least secure method. Data sent from the client to the server is encrypted using 56-bit encryption. *Data sent from the server to the client is not encrypted.*

One new addition to Windows Server 2003 that helps mitigate this problem of legacy clients (which is one common reason for implementing Terminal Server) is to use the Remote Desktop Web Connection, which when installed uses an ActiveX control in Internet Explorer (5.0 or later). It's useful for roaming clients and works on a variety of platforms. However, it is an optional component of the World Wide Web service in IIS and must be installed and enabled via a Web server.

By default, members of the Administrators group and the Remote Desktop Users group can use Terminal Services connections to connect to a remote computer. The Remote Desktop Users group is empty by default, so you need to decide which groups or users should have permission to log on remotely. Users or groups must be members of the Remote Desktop Users group to have permissions to make Terminal Services connections to remote computers. Also be aware of the fact that membership in the Remote Desktop Users group does not also put the user in the local Users group. Determine which users or groups also need to be added to the local Users group.

Securing Remote Access Servers

Remote Access Servers (RAS) are used to provide access to the network for users who are not physically located in the same place as the network. The most typical scenario, as you can imagine, is with users who travel. Clearly, the first step in securing a RAS is to carefully determine who requires remote access. Granting remote access only to users who require it will greatly enhance security. If you're using the server as a router as well (often referred to as Routing and Remote Access Server, or RRAS), there are additional security considerations for securing the routing function.

There are essentially three elements to securing a RAS: the server, the network traffic, and the authentication. Each element is discussed in turn.

Securing the Server

Securing the server is clearly the first element in security. As you're read repeatedly, if there is any question at all about internal security, place the server in an access-controlled location. In any case, the server should be in a secure location within the building, even if access-control measures are not in place. The server's system volumes should be formatted with NTFS to protect files and folders on the system. Removing or disabling unused services and protocols is very important to prevent intruders from leveraging these to attack the system and gain access to network resources. Well-known accounts should be secured, especially the Guest and Administrator accounts. Requiring users to use strong and complex passwords will also help secure the RAS environment by eliminating easily guessed passwords.

Securing Network Traffic

You can secure network traffic, or in this case, traffic between the RRAS server and the remote user, via the use of signing, encryption, and tunneling. Users should be required to use the highest level of encryption supported as well. For Windows XP and Windows Server 2003 clients, 128-bit encryption keys can be used. This can be implemented via Remote Access policies. You can create a policy based on three different encryption levels: Basic, Strong, and Strongest, each described in Table 2.16.

Table 2.16 Remote Access Policy Encryption Options

Encryption Level	Description
Basic	Uses IPSec 56-bit DES or MPPE 40-bit encryption
Strong	Uses IPSec 56-bit DES or MPPE 4-bit encryption
Strongest	Uses IPSec 3DES or MPPE 128-bit encryption

IPSec can use different levels of encryption and is discussed in detail later in this book. Data Encryption Standard (DES) is used throughout Windows Server 2003. It employs a 56-bit key (the key is 64-bits, but 8 are used for error checking, resulting in 56 bits used for the encryption key). 3DES, or triple DES, uses the 56-bit key and processes each block three times, encrypting it with Key 1, decrypting it with Key 2, and encrypting it again with Key 3. The process is reversed on the receiving end. Microsoft Point-to-Point Encryption (MPPE) encrypts data in a Point-to-Point (PPP)-based connection. MPPE can use 128-bit, 56-bit, or 40-bit encryption. The 40-bit encryption is also called MPPE standard encryption.

Strong Authentication

If possible, you should require remote users to be running Windows 2000, Windows XP, or Windows Server 2003. These operating systems have security enhancements not found in earlier operating systems. If users are running these later operating systems, you can then require the use of stronger, more secure authentication methods such as Microsoft Challenge Handshake Authentication Protocol version 2 (MS-CHAP v2) or Extensible Authentication Protocol (EAP). Each of these is more secure than earlier authentication protocols used in operating systems prior to Windows 2000. These less secure protocols include Password Authentication Protocol (PAP), Shiva Password Authentication Protocol (SPAP), and Challenge Handshake Authentication Protocol (CHAP).

If you plan to run more than one RAS server, you should consider implementing Remote Authentication Dial-In Service (RADIUS) rather than Windows Authentication. RADIUS provides for centralized administration authentication, authorization, and auditing of remote access connections. For further security, RADIUS traffic can be secured via IPSec. In Windows Server 2003, RADIUS is implemented in a Microsoft framework called the Internet Authentication Service, or IAS. As a RADIUS server, IAS provides the centralized authentication, authorization, and auditing services. As a RADIUS proxy, IAS forwards authentication and accounting messages to other RADIUS servers.

By using Remote Access Policies, you can consistently and accurately apply security settings to remote access, including restricting users, user groups, times, or client configurations. To configure Remote Access policies, perform the following actions.

1. To configure Remote Access Policies, open **Routing and Remote Access** in **Administrative Tools**.
2. In the tree in the left pane, locate the desired server and locate the node **Remote Access Policies**.
3. To add a remote policy, right-click and choose **New Remote Access Policy**, or click **Action** on the menu and select **New Remote Access Policy**. The New Remote Access Policy Wizard will launch, stepping you through the process of creating a new Remote Access policy.
4. To modify existing policies, double-click the policy shown in the right pane, or right-click and select **Properties** from the menu.

Remote Access Policies only allow you to specifically allow or deny policies. Each policy is applied in order, and the order is also shown in the Routing and Remote Access console.

Streaming Media Server

The last specific server role we'll look at is the streaming media server. In the role of a streaming media server, Windows Server 2003 uses Windows Media Services to stream audio and video to internal (network) or external (Internet) clients. Windows Media servers proxy, cache, and redistribute content. Windows Media Services is not available on Windows Server 2003 64-bit versions, nor is it available in the Windows Server 2003 Web Edition.

As with all other server roles, examining default service settings will help determine if there are additional services you can disable to maintain higher security. In addition, using NTFS to secure the data storage is recommended on all servers. As with all servers, the Setup security.inf security template is applied when Windows Server 2003 is installed as a clean installation. If it's upgraded from a prior version, you should audit your security settings by using the Security Configuration and Analysis tool in Administrative Tools or the secedit.exe command-line tool.

In Windows Media servers, authentication and authorization plug-ins control access to content. The two options for authentication are anonymous and network. Anonymous authentication does not exchange challenge/response information with the media player. If you are streaming content to the general public, this authentication method is fine. Network authentication plug-ins authenticate users based on logon credentials and is used to secure access to streaming content to authorized users only.

After a user is authenticated, the user must be authorized to connect to the server. Windows Media Server can use the NTFS Access Control Lists (ACL) plug-in, IP Address Authorization plug-in, and the Publishing Points ACL Authorization plug-in. The Publishing Points ACL allows you to assign read, write, and create permissions for users and groups. By default, the Everyone group has read permissions, and the Builtin\Administrators group has full permissions. This type of plug-in is useful when you want to set restrictions on all content on a specific publishing point or server, or when the publishing point content is a live stream.

Exam Warning

Although Microsoft exams do tend to focus on new features in the operating system, the security-related exams tend to focus heavily on scenario questions involving a mix of operating systems, which mirrors real-world configurations. Make sure you're comfortable with the security considerations in Windows Server 2003 and with the security risks, configurations, and solutions for working with down-level computers in a networked environment. Your ability in this area will determine how well you do on the exam and on the job as well.

Windows Server 2003 can be configured to run in the server roles just listed. Table 2.17 summarizes the server roles and the services that are installed with each. Although these services can be installed without configuring the specific server role, administration is less complicated when services are installed via the Configure Your Server role. This also increases security by grouping services by role.

Table 2.17 Summary of Services for Server Roles

Server Role	Related Services
DC, DHCP, DNS, WINS	File system security, DHCP protocol, DNS, WINS (networking services), Certificate Services, TCP/IP
IIS	(Part of Application server role), Internet Authentication Service (networking services), Certificate Services, NNTP, FTP, SMTP
File server	Indexing Service, Remote Storage (network file and print services)
Print server	Fax Services (network file and print services)
Application server	IIS, Terminal Server, ASP.NET, Message queuing, UDDI Services
E-mail	POP3 (e-mail services), SMTP (e-mail services), RRAS (default Window Server 2003 component)
Terminal server	Terminal Server, Remote Desktop
Streaming media	Windows Media Services

EXAM 70-297 OBJECTIVE 3.7.2

Modifying Baseline Security Templates According to Role

In this chapter, we've looked at the predefined security templates provided in Windows Server 2003. You learned that this version of the operating system comes "locked down" by default and that modifications to the security templates often mean relaxing security a bit to allow users, services, or applications to function properly. In the past, security had to be tightened against the "out of the box" settings.

In this section, we're going to briefly recap server roles and discuss the templates that would most likely be used with them. Then, we'll discuss the specifics of how to roll these templates out to an enterprise that involves multiple domains and OUs in a manner that maintains tight security and reduces administrative overhead.

Table 2.18 shows a recap of server roles and security templates that can be applied to each role. As you plan your server security, you'll need to logically group your servers based on roles. Since each organization might implement server roles slightly differently, the data in the table is simply one model. Moreover, although Microsoft's predefined templates set security in a consistent and cumulative manner, you might still need to modify the predefined templates to meet your company's specific security needs. Remember that each template addresses seven specific security areas: account policies, local policies, event log, restricted groups, system services, Registry, and file system. Each server role in your organization might need specific settings in one (or more) of the seven security areas that are not part of the predefined templates' settings. In many cases, though, these predefined templates will meet a wide array of security needs for many different types of firms. Although you can modify security settings without using the templates, the templates (both predefined and those you create) provide an excellent tool for managing security settings by providing a consistent framework in which to work. The key is planning, testing, evaluating, and documenting changes before implementing them in the enterprise.

Table 2.18 Server Roles and Recommended Security Templates

Server Role	Security Template(s)	Comments
Domain controller	DC Security.inf (default), Securedc.inf, hisecdc.inf	When a server is promoted to a DC, the Default Domain Controller Security template is applied. Additional security can be applied via the securedc.inf template and the hisecdc.inf template. However, there might be connectivity issues with down-level clients, including Windows NT 4.0 and earlier. Establishing strong passwords, audit and account lockout policies increases security.
IIS 6.0	Setup security.inf (default), IIS Lockdown Wizard's customized templates for each IIS server role, secure*.inf	Unlike earlier versions, Windows Server 2003 does *not* install IIS by default, significantly reducing exposure to security threats. When installing IIS, download Microsoft's IIS Lockdown Wizard, which provides customized templates for IIS-specific security needs. Securing communication with IPSec, limiting the server role

Continued

Table 2.18 Server Roles and Recommended Security Templates

Server Role	Security Template(s)	Comments
		to IIS, and selecting appropriate authentication methods will increase security.
Application servers	Setup security.inf (default), secure*.inf, compat*.inf	The Application server role installs IIS. Some applications require the ability to modify Registry settings, and the compat*.inf template provides those settings.
Mail servers	Setup security.inf (default)	Mail servers should be evaluated in a manner similar to IIS, since they also interact with the public network infrastructure. Implement IPSec, close all unused ports, select appropriate authentication, and use firewall or perimeter network.
Infrastructure servers	Setup security.inf (default), secure*.inf, hisec*.inf	Infrastructure servers include those that provide DHCP, DNS, and WINS services to the domain. Each has specific security considerations. Logically group infrastructure servers by function and set security via GPOs. Using secure and hisec templates might impact down-level clients and applications.
File, Print and Member servers	Setup security.inf (default), secure*.inf, hisec*.inf, compat*.inf	File, print, and member servers should use NTFS to protect the file system (as should other server types). Auditing should be enabled to alert network admins to potential abuse of user rights, especially in groups to which administration has been delegated. Using secure and hisec templates might impact down-level clients and

Continued

Table 2.18 Server Roles and Recommended Security Templates

Server Role	Security Template(s)	Comments
		applications. The compat*.inf template might be needed to allow access to functionality for down-level clients.
Terminal server	Setup security.inf (default), secure*.inf	Review default settings for services, and disable any that are unused. Configure Internet Explorer Enhanced Security, and use group policy to manage users, applications, and local settings.
Remote Access server	Setup security.inf, secure*.inf, hisec*.inf	Begin with thorough planning for granting remote access permissions. Remove all services not in use. Consider requiring remote access users to upgrade to Windows 2000 or later. Use strong passwords, encryption. Implement IPSec or VPN tunneling. Enable appropriate auditing. Implement via group policy. Run on separate IP segment.
Streaming Media server	Setup security.inf (default), secure*.inf	Security via authentication and authorization based on logon credentials. User firewalls, perimeter networks, DMZs, and so forth. If providing external access, run on separate IP segment. Closely monitor permissions to place content on the server and audit-related events.

Applying Security Across the Enterprise

So far, you've learned about the default settings in Windows Server 2003 and the predefined security templates that are provided. You're seen how these templates can be applied to a variety of server roles. You've also learned that you can modify the security settings, but that you must also be cautious in making modifications and you should thoroughly document changes you make. You've seen that applying these security settings has a cumulative effect and that they can be analyzed prior to implementation using the *secedit.exe* command-line tool or the MMC snap-in Security Configuration and Analysis. In the last section, you saw that placing servers into logical groupings will allow you to configure security for each type of server. Again, you might be able to use the predefined templates, or you might need to modify these settings. When modifying settings, always work from a copy so you can preserve the original settings in the predefined templates.

So, now that you've evaluated server roles and created appropriate security templates, how can you roll these settings out across the enterprise without going to each and every machine? What's the best way to apply these settings to those servers that might be in many different locations? Let's look at how to best accomplish that.

As we've discussed, you can apply security to a single computer using the Security Configuration and Analysis snap-in, but that doesn't help with rolling it out to several or several hundred computers. Once you've analyzed settings in the Security Configuration and Analysis snap-in, you can export the database into a security template. This template can then be deployed automatically via one of two methods: via the *secedit.exe* command or via group policy. We've talked about both options throughout this chapter, but let's bring it all together now to figure out exactly when you would use each tool.

You can use the *secedit.exe* command-line tool to apply an entire template or sections of a template, as discussed earlier in this chapter. By using a batch program or script, you can apply security settings when the batch program or script runs. These can be logon scripts or batch programs set to run at computer startup, for example. The *secedit.exe* command-line tool itself does not have the capability to automatically run at a certain time or in certain circumstances. For that, you'll need to use a batch program or script. If you're not using an Active Directory domain, this is the only way to automatically roll out security settings across the enterprise.

However, the easiest way to apply security settings in an Active Directory domain is to use group policy. You can create a new GPO, import a security template, link the GPO to a site, OU, or domain, and the new settings will be applied the next time the GPO is replicated. When using this method, do keep in mind that GPOs are applied in a set order: site, domain, and then OU. In the last exercise of this chapter, you'll walk through the process of creating an OU and applying a template to that OU.

EXERCISE 2.08

APPLYING SECURITY TEMPLATES VIA CROUP POLICY

This exercise, like others in the chapter, should be done on a test computer in a lab environment and not on a live or production system. In this exercise, you'll create a new OU and apply a security template to that OU.

1. Click Start | Administrative Tools and select Active Directory Users and Computers.
2. Locate the domain name, right-click, and select **New** then select **Organizational Unit**.
3. In the New Object – Organizational Unit dialog box, type in **TestSecurity** in the Name: box. Click **OK** to accept.
4. The TestSecurity OU is displayed in the left pane. Locate that OU and right-click. Select **Properties**.
5. The TestSecurity Properties dialog box is displayed with four tabs: General, Managed By, COM+, and Group Policy. Select the **Group Policy** tab by clicking it.
6. Notice there are no GPO links because we created a new OU. To create a new group policy to link to the OU, click the **New** button.
7. If you have installed the **Group Policy Management** snap-in, the Group Policy tab is no longer used and the Group Policy tab button is labeled **Open**, as shown in Figure 2.20. Clicking the **Open** button will launch the Group Policy Management snap-in. The Group Policy Management snap-in is not installed in Windows Server 2003 by default. This snap-in is discussed in more detail in later in this book.

Figure 2.20 Creating a New Group Policy Link to OU

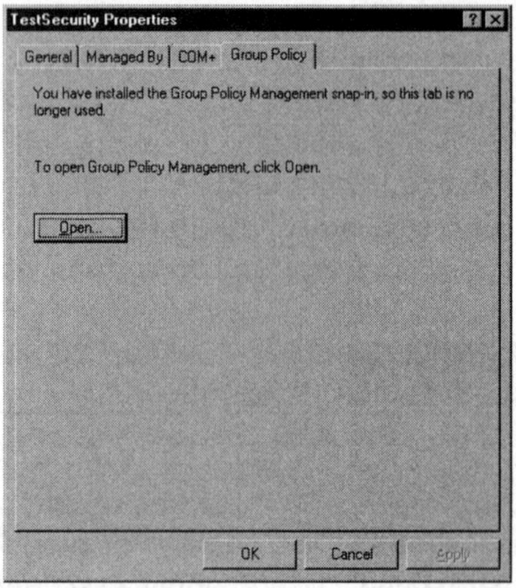

8. If you have not installed GPMC, the new GPO will be displayed. Replace the default name with the name **TestSecurity** and press **Enter** to accept the name.
9. If you have installed the GPMC, the GPMC will open. From this snap-in, you can perform the same tasks. In this case, click **Action** on the menu and select **Create and Link a GPO Here**. (If you wanted to link an existing GPO, you can select **Action | Link an Existing GPO** in the GPMC console.)
10. Now that we have a GPO link, we need to edit the properties. With **TestSecurity** still selected (in the dialog box), click **Edit**. If you're using GPMC, right-click **TestSecurity** and select **Edit**.
11. When you click **Edit**, you'll notice that the **Group Policy Editor** launches and your display changes to the GPE. In the left pane, you'll see **Computer Configuration** and **User Configuration**. Expand the **Computer Configuration** node by clicking the + sign to the left of the node, if it's not already expanded. Below the Computer Configuration node, three additional nodes are displayed: Software Settings, Windows Settings and Administrative Templates.
12. Expand the **Windows Settings** to display the **Security Settings** node. Although this node is expandable, at this point, do not expand it, but right-click on the node. Click **Import Policy** from the menu.
13. The Import Policy From dialog box will open and default to the default templates location on your computer. Figure 2.21 shows this step.

Figure 2.21 Import Policy Dialog

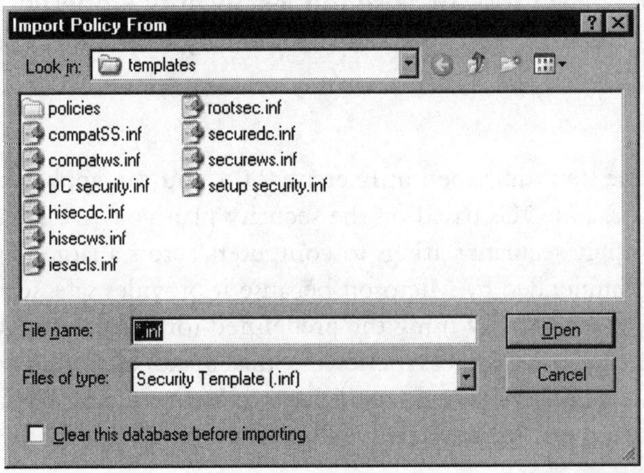

14. If you have a custom template you've created, you can select it at this time. Otherwise, you can choose from the predefined templates displayed. Remember, you should not apply the Setup security.inf template via Group Policy. Select any other template. For the purpose of this exercise, select the securews.inf template. Select the **Clear This Database before Importing** check box. This box clears out any remaining settings in the database so that the template settings will be applied properly in this database. After placing a check mark in the check box (by clicking on it), click **Open**.
15. The security settings have been imported into the **TestSecurity Group Policy** object.
16. In the left pane, expand the **Security Settings** node, locate and expand the **Account Policies** node, and then locate and expand the **Password Policies** node. Notice that the settings from the template have been applied.
17. Close the **Group Policy Editor** by clicking **File** and selecting **Exit**.
18. The Active Directory Users and Computers console is displayed with the **TestSecurity Properties** dialog box still open. Click the **Options** button.
19. If you wanted to examine the effects of the GPO, click the **Properties** button and then click the **Security** tab to review users and associated permissions. You can also review links via the **Links** tab to search for sites, domains, and other OUs that use this GPO. Since we just created this GPO, there will be no links. Click **Cancel** to exit. If you make changes that you want to preserve, click **OK**.
20. Click **Close** to close the TestSecurity Properties dialog. Click **File** | **Exit** to close the Active Directory Users and Computers console.

Using the steps described in Exercise 2.08, you can apply security templates to sites, domains, and OUs based on the security plan you've established. This is the easiest way to apply security settings to computers across a large network, and is the method recommended by Microsoft because it provides safe, secure, and consistent application of security. By using the predefined (or customized) templates, security management follows a logical framework that makes analyzing and troubleshooting security much easier. Although you'll have to be constantly vigilant in maintaining security, starting out with a clear baseline and a consistent method of applying security settings will give you a strong starting point in the never-ending task of maintaining secure network.

EXAM WARNING

If the Clear This Database check box is not selected prior to importing a security template, the settings will be merged with those already existing in the GPO. Watch for this on the exam, as security settings can differ radically depending on whether this check box is selected.

Summary of Exam Objectives

Windows Server 2003 provides new security tools and features that differ significantly from previous Windows Server products. Specifically, Windows Server 2003 is installed in a locked-down state, providing the fewest services and permissions possible while still providing standard functionality. The improved security tools make configuring, analyzing, troubleshooting, and maintaining security easier. These security tools, collectively called the Security Configuration Tool Set or Security Configuration Manager, include:

- Security Configuration and Analysis snap-in to Microsoft Management Console
- Security Templates snap-in to Microsoft Management Console
- Command-line tool secedit.exe
- Security Extensions to Group Policy
- Hfnetchk.exe and Microsoft Baseline Security Analyzer

Each of these tools is used to configure, analyze, and modify security settings in a Windows Server 2003 environment.

The Security Configuration and Analysis snap-in, accessed via the MMC, is used to compare current computer security settings to another set of security settings. By importing a security template containing a specific set of predefined settings, you can compare the settings and determine where security settings on the computer differ from a template. The template can be one of the predefined templates provided in Windows Server 2003, or it can be a custom template you create from scratch or by copying and then modifying one of the predefined templates. After analyzing the settings, you can configure the computer with the settings from the template or modify individual settings. The *configure* command only allows you to configure the local computer and cannot be used to configure other computers. However, once you've analyzed settings, you can apply those security settings to other computers by using the Security Extensions to Group Policy.

The MMC snap-in Security Templates provides access to all the predefined templates. You can copy, modify, and save security settings in this snap-in. The templates include the baseline template, Setup security.inf, as well as DC security.inf, Compat*.inf, Secure*.inf, Hisec*.inf, Rootsec.inf, and Notssid.inf. Each template configures a group of security settings commonly used in different scenarios such as DC, secure server, or file server.

An alternative to the Security Configuration and Analysis snap-in is the command-line tool *secedit.exe*. Using the various command-line parameters, including */import*, */export*, */analyze*, and */configure*, you can manage security on a local or remote computer. If the *secedit* command is included in a batch file or scheduled task, the security settings can be applied at any time across the network to any one or group of computers.

Using Security Extensions to Group Policy is the easiest way to apply a security template or any set of security policies to various GPOs. When applied in this manner, the application follows standard Group Policy rules, which apply group policies by local computer, domain, site, and OU. Account and password policies are applied only at the domain level. When applying security via GP, the settings will be updated when the GP is refreshed. The earlier command, *secedit /policyrefresh.* is replaced by the *gpupdate* command-line tool, which will force a policy refresh without waiting for the specified interval.

Each predefined security template provided in Windows Server 2003 is configured to provide the best overall security settings for each role. Although these templates can be modified, you should analyze the results of any changes prior to implementing them on a live system, as any changes can create unintended security holes. The templates are applied cumulatively, and other than the baseline template, *Setup security.inf*, will not establish default values. A template can have a security policy enabled, disabled, set to a particular value, or not defined. If it is not defined, it is not included in the template. It will not affect those settings in any manner and will leave whatever settings exist on the computer in place.

The Setup security.inf template establishes baseline security on a Windows Server 2003 system. It is used on a clean installation of Windows Server 2003. For systems that are upgraded from earlier versions, this template is not applied by default. However, to establish sound baseline security settings, it is recommended that you apply the Setup security.inf template to upgraded systems before applying other security templates. To reset portions of the security settings on a computer, you can use the *secedit.exe* command and specify a particular security area to configure, such as FILESTORE or USER_RIGHTS. Applying higher security templates, including the secure*.inf and hisec*.inf, can cause connectivity issues with down-level clients because these templates require the use of NTLM v2 or better authentication and SMB packet signing, for example. Down-level clients can install Directory Services (if available) to provide some additional functionality, but applying these templates should be tested thoroughly before implementation. The compat*.inf template is used to relax Registry and file security settings to allow legacy applications to run on the Windows Server 2003 platform. Using this template relaxes security and should be applied only if necessary, only in a limited manner and never on a DC.

Computers in Windows Server 2003 can be configured for various server roles. In some network situations, it is appropriate to configure a server with only one role where security and/or network demand is high. In other scenarios, it is appropriate to configure a server in multiple roles. Each server role installs and uses a set of services to enable that server function. Server functions (and related services) should not be enabled if not needed. In fact, one of the major changes in Windows Server 2003 is that IIS is no longer installed by default. This reduces the vulnerability of the server significantly.

Security best practices, especially with regard to servers, includes securing the computer in an access-controlled location to physically prevent unauthorized access. Additional security measures can be taken, depending on the role of the server. Applying security templates provides baseline security levels, and additional security can be implemented via Group Policy settings. These can include using the IPSec protocol to encrypt and secure network communications, using VPN tunneling to secure connections, SMB packet signing, among others.

Once security settings for various server roles have been analyzed and tested, these settings can be rolled out to computers via GPOs to servers in sites, domains, and OUs. Rolling out security settings in this way helps ensure consistent security application and management and can assist in troubleshooting security problems as well.

Exam Objectives Fast Track

Design Security for Servers that Have Specific Roles

- ☑ The Security Configuration Tool Set consists of five separate tools that are used to configure, analyze, and apply security settings.
- ☑ The Security Configuration and Analysis snap-in is used to configure and analyze security settings on a local computer.
- ☑ The predefined security templates can be accessed, modified, and saved via the Security Templates snap-in.
- ☑ The command-line tool, *secedit.exe*, is used to configure, analyze, and apply security settings via the command line. Entire templates or particular security areas can be applied to local or remote computers in real time, batch files, or scheduled tasks.
- ☑ Security Extensions to Group Policy provide a way to roll out security templates and custom settings via GPOs.
- ☑ The Microsoft Baseline Security Analyzer checks for security misconfigurations that might cause security problems.
- ☑ The MBSA also includes the command-line utility *Hfnetchk.exe*, which checks the system to ensure all available hotfixes, updates, and patches have been applied.
- ☑ The baseline security template provided in Windows Server 2003 is Setup security.inf. It is applied only to clean installations of Windows Server 2003.

- ☑ Other security templates include DC security.inf, compat*.inf, secure*.inf, hisec*.inf, rootsec.inf, and notssid.inf. Each is used in a particular setting to configure security accordingly.
- ☑ Predefined templates should be copied before being modified to preserve the settings in case default values need to be re-established.
- ☑ Configurable security areas include account policies, local policies, event log, restricted groups, system services, Registry, and file system.

Define a Baseline Security Template for All Systems

- ☑ Microsoft Windows Server 2003 identifies the following server roles: file, print, application, mail, terminal, remote access, DC, DNS, DHCP, WINS, and streaming media.
- ☑ Each server role can be configured via the Configure Your Server Wizard, which installs appropriate services for each server role selected. Each server role can be managed via the Manage Your Server tool.
- ☑ Server roles determine preset security configurations. Modifications can be made by editing a security template and applying that template to a group of servers in the same role.
- ☑ Reviewing the common threats to each server role helps determine the security measures that should be established as a baseline for each role.
- ☑ Best practices for servers include physically securing the server, implementing NTFS on the system volumes, securing well-known accounts, removing/disabling unused services and protocols, keeping updates and patches up to date, and installing and maintaining current signature files for virus protection.
- ☑ High-profile servers, such as DCs and computers running IIS, should use the highest level of security possible, while still accounting for network performance and down-level clients.
- ☑ Higher security typically slows response time, so finding a balance between security and usability is important.
- ☑ Once templates have been tested, they can be applied across sites, domains, and OUs via group policy. This helps ensure that all servers in a particular role are set with the same security settings. This helps establish and maintain baseline security for your network.

Exam Objectives Frequently Asked Questions

The following Frequently Asked Questions, answered by the authors of this book, are designed to both measure your understanding of the Exam Objectives presented in this chapter, and to assist you with real-life implementation of these concepts. You will also gain access to thousands of other FAQs at ITFAQnet.com.

Q: I can't find the Security Configuration Manager, where is it?

A: The Security Configuration Manager is also known as the Security Configuration Tool Set and consists of a set of tools available in Windows Server 2003 for managing security. These tools include the Security Configuration and Analysis snap-in to the MMC, the Security Templates snap-in to the MMC, the secedit tool, Security Extensions to Group Policy, the *secedit.exe* command, and the downloadable Microsoft Baseline Security Analyzer.

Q: Why can't I locate IIS on my newly installed Windows Server 2003?

A: IIS is no longer installed by default on Windows Server 2003. This provides much better baseline security. As a best practice, it is recommended you remove all unused installations of IIS on computers to reduce security risks.

Q: The settings in the secure*.inf template don't provide for certain settings we need to use on our network. What's the best way to deal with this?

A: In the Security Templates snap-in, you can open the secure*.inf template, save it with a different name (secure2.inf, for example), and make whatever modifications you need to the template. Make sure you thoroughly test the results, however, because the predefined templates are set to create the most secure environment possible, and modifications might expose your network to security problems.

Q: After I've analyzed security settings in the Security Configuration and Analysis snap-in, I want to apply these settings to 35 computers on our domain. How can I specify which computers to configure?

A: The Security Configuration and Analysis snap-in is used to analyze and configure settings, but it cannot be used to apply settings to remote computers. You can use the *secedit.exe* command in a batch file or schedule task to automate the process, or you can apply the template via Security Extensions to Group Policy. Using the *gpupdate* command-line utility will force a refresh of policies without waiting for the specified refresh interval to elapse.

Q: I want to check three servers that we recently upgraded from Windows NT 4.0 SP6a against our current security settings. What's the best way to do that?

A: Since the computers were upgraded to Windows Server 2003, you can run the Security Configuration and Analysis snap-in to check security. You can use the Setup security.inf template for analysis to check current settings against the baseline settings. You could also download and use the Microsoft Baseline Security Analyzer, which will identify security misconfigurations and identify any patches, updates, or hotfixes that are available but not applied to the system. You could also use the *secedit.exe* command with the */analyze* switch to analyze the servers in question. You could automate this task so it occurs during off-peak hours by running a scheduled task that calls the *secedit.exe* utility.

Q: What's the best way to secure a server that is running as both a DC and a DHCP server?

A: The DC security.inf template is applied to the server when it is promoted to a DC. You might also be able to apply the securedc.inf template to the server, depending on your down-level clients on the domain. In some cases, using the hisecdc.inf template might make sense in very sensitive network settings such as financial or medical, but again, down-level clients will determine the security settings you'll be able to implement.

Self Test

A Quick Answer Key follows the Self Test questions. For complete questions, answers, and explanations to the Self Test questions in this chapter as well as the other chapters in this book, see the Self Test Appendix.

Define a Baseline Security Template for All Systems

1. You are the network administrator for a small network that has 40 computers on a network. You have two Windows Server 2003 computers, one of which is a DC and the other is providing remote access to users who travel throughout the United States. The computer running the remote access services also runs DHCP, DNS, and WINS for your firm. There are two file and application servers running Windows 2000, and you have client computers running

Windows XP, Windows 2000, and Windows 98. Your applications are all the latest versions, although one was originally written for Windows 95 and another was developed in-house about six years ago. Based on this information, applying which predefined template might cause disruptions on the network?

A. Secure*.inf

B. Hisec*.inf

C. Compat*.inf

D. Setup security.inf

2. In the MMC snap-in Security Configuration and Analysis, you open a new database you call Test1. You select the securedc.inf template and click OK. At this point, what is the state of the security on the computer you're working on?

   A. The settings from the computer and the securedc.inf template have been merged.

   B. The settings from the securedc.inf template have been applied.

   C. The settings from the database, including the imported securedc.inf template, have been applied.

   D. The settings on the local computer have not changed.

3. You have opened the securedc.inf template via the MMC snap-in Security Templates. You expand the nodes in the left pane until you find the Account Policies. You select Kerberos Policy and notice that all the policies are "Not Defined." What step do you need to take in order to define any one of those policies?

   A. None. If a policy is not defined in a predefined security template, you cannot modify it.

   B. None. You should never modify the settings in a predefined security template.

   C. Double-click the policy, modify the settings, check the box to "Define this policy setting in the template," and click OK.

   D. Right-click the policy, check the box to "Define this policy setting in the template," and click OK.

4. After upgrading a computer from Windows 2000 to Windows Server 2003, you notice that some of the settings in the USER_RIGHTS area of security are not exactly as you'd like them. You'd like to use the settings for USER_RIGHTS found in the secure*.inf template. What is the best way to apply the settings for USER_RIGHTS from the secure*.inf template to the local computer?

A. Use the *secedit.exe /configure* command using the */cfg* switch to specify the securews.inf template, the */overwrite* switch to clear the existing database settings, and the */area* switch to specify USER_RIGHTS.

B. Use the *secedit.exe /analyze* command to analyze the difference between the USER_RIGHTS on the local computer and the USER_RIGHTS settings in the securews.inf template.

C. Use the *secedit.exe /cfg /USER_RIGHTS* command to configure the USER_RIGHTS area of the current security template.

D. Use the *secedit.exe /analyze* command with the */db* switch to specify which database should be analyzed. You do not need the */cfg* switch to analyze the settings in the configuration stored in the current database.

5. You've just completed a security audit and determined that you should tighten up password security settings on one of your Active Directory sites. Currently, the minimum password length is not defined, meaning that users could elect to use a blank password. To rectify this situation, you assign the task of modifying this to one of the junior network administrators. He implements the policy for the site through Active Directory Sites and Services, but the policy does not take effect. When he comes back to you to report the problem, what can you tell him about this problem?

   A. A local policy might be overwriting this new policy. Check local policy settings.

   B. Active Directory Sites and Services does not support applying security policies.

   C. You must use the *gpupdate* command-line tool to refresh the policy in order to see the policy in place.

   D. Password and account policies are applied at the domain level.

6. You've performed an analysis of your server's current security configuration as the first step in identifying the security settings you want to use for your application servers throughout the domain. The analysis results are as shown in Figure 2.22. (Results of the analysis that are typically listed under the Database Setting and Computer Setting have intentionally been removed.) Based on the data in this screenshot, what statements can you make about the results?

   A. The **Account lockout duration** and **Reset account lockout counter after** were not analyzed because they did not exist on the local system.

   B. The **Account lockout duration** and **Reset account lockout counter after** were not analyzed because they did not exist in the analysis database.

C. The **Account lockout duration** and **Reset account lockout counter after** were analyzed but the database settings did not match the local computer settings.

D. The **Account lockout duration** and **Reset account lockout counter after** were analyzed but the database did not contain definitions for these settings.

Figure 2.22 Security Analysis Results

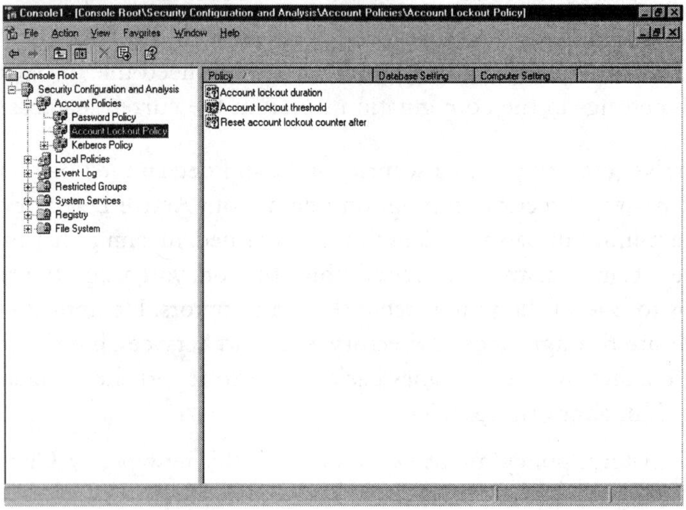

Design Security for Servers that Have Specific Roles

7. You've recently been tasked with upgrading several Windows 2000-based file and print servers to Windows Server 2003. You've already installed Windows Server 2003 on four other servers in the organization, two of which are located in another city connected by a high-speed Internet-based connection. What can you do to ensure that all Windows Server 2003-based file and print servers have exactly the same default settings on their drives?

   A. Apply the Setup security.inf template to all servers to set a baseline.

   B. Apply the DC secure.inf template to all servers to set a baseline.

   C. Apply the rootsec.inf template to all servers to set a baseline.

   D. Apply the securedc.inf template to all servers to set a baseline.

8. You work at a software company that sells an accounting software package to large institutions, including governmental organizations and school systems. The software package requires the use of SQL Server, and the company has found

over the course of several years that this requirement has made selling the product more difficult. In a recent meeting, you suggest running the SQL Server-based application on the company's servers and providing access to the software package to client via Terminal Server. In talking with clients, you've discovered that most of them are running Windows 95, Windows 98, or Windows XP clients. The VP of Client Services asks you about security, knowing that governmental agencies and school districts might be quite averse to transmitting financial data across the Internet to your company. You tell the VP you've devised a security plan to address just those questions. What elements does your plan include for the highest possible security?

A. The Terminal Server computer will run only the application for clients. It will use NTFS on the file system and will use Full Security. Clients will be able to access the application only via a secure connection. The computer will be in a controlled-access location and you'll disable drive redirection. You also require Client Compatible encryption and limit the number of user logon attempts and connection times.

B. The Terminal Server computer will run only the application for clients. It will use NTFS on the file system and will have the Notssid.inf template applied to remove unnecessary Terminal Server SIDs. Strong passwords will be required. The computer will be in a controlled-access location, and CD and floppy drive access will be restricted to the Remote Desktop Users group.

C. The Terminal Server computer will use NTFS on the file system, and additional security will be placed on the file system and Registry via the hisecws.inf template. Auditing the Remote Desktop Users group for unsuccessful logons will ensure only authorized users can make a connection. Strong passwords will be required. You will disable drive redirection and require encryption.

D. The Terminal Server computer will use NTFS on the file system. It will be placed in a secure location, and CD and floppy drive access will be restricted to Administrators. You limit the number of user logons and restrict connection times. You also set the encryption requirement to High so that data to and from the Terminal server is encrypted using 128-bit encryption.

9. Your network consists of four OUs located in three separate cities. Some clients require the use of WINS, so you've set up four WINS servers, two with static IP addresses. In two particular locations, computer names change frequently. Since replication takes place across a WAN and you're concerned with security, you've implemented the requirement to secure all replication data using IPSec. Based on this information, what is the most likely result?

A. Using IPSec will cause a significant problem with the WINS replication process, because IPSec cannot be used to secure WINS data across a WAN.

B. Name changes will be replicated across the WAN only during off-peak hours. Other WINS data will not be replicated unless there are changes made to the WINS database.

C. If you implement IPSec to encrypt the WINS replication data, logging of all WINS events is enabled by default, which can decrease network performance.

D. The replication time might be significantly increased and users might complain both of slower network connection times across the WAN and the inability to reach resources.

10. You have configured one of your servers to provide streaming media services to internal users. However, you want to make sure the data on the server is secure. You've formatted the server drive with NTFS to be able to manage file and folder permissions on the system. You also want to apply additional file system security to the server. You've previously created a security template based on the secure*.inf template, named securesv.inf, and you want to apply the permissions from that template to this server. The server's current security database is named winmedia.sdb. What is the easiest way to accomplish this task?

    A. *secedit.exe /import /db securesv.inf /cfg winmedia.sdb /FILESYSTEM /quiet*

    B. *secedit /db winmedia.sdb /cfg securesv.inf /overwrite /FILESYSTEM*

    C. *secedit /configure /db winmedia.sdb /cfg securesv.inf /overwrite /FILESTORE*

    D. *secedit /import /db winmedia.sdb /cfg securesv.inf /FILESTORE /quiet*

Self Test Quick Answer Key

For complete questions, answers, and explanations to the Self Test questions in this chapter as well as the other chapters in this book, see the Self Test Appendix.

1. **B**
2. **D**
3. **D**
4. **A**
5. **D**
6. **B**
7. **C**
8. **A**
9. **D**
10. **C**

Chapter 3

MCSE 70-298

Designing a Secure Public Key Infrastructure

Exam Objectives in This Chapter:

2.1	Designing a public key infrastructure (PKI) using Certificate Services.
2.1.1	Design a certification authority (CA) hierarchy implementation. Types include geographical,organizational, and trusted.
2.2	Design a logical authentication strategy.
2.1.4	Design security for CA servers.
2.2.1	Design certificate distribution.
2.1.2	Design enrollment and distribution processes.
2.1.3	Establish renewal, revocation, and auditing processes.

- ☑ Summary of Exam Objectives
- ☑ Exam Objectives Fast Track
- ☑ Exam Objectives Frequently Asked Questions
- ☑ Self Test
- ☑ Self Test Quick Answer Key

Introduction

One of the major challenges in our interconnected world is this: how can you verify the identity of people you've never seen before so that you can do business with them, and how can you transmit confidential information over a public network like the Internet? While there are any number of solutions to both of these problems, one that has become widely used due to its relatively low cost and ease of deployment is the public key infrastructure, or PKI. You'll see PKIs implemented for any number of reasons, but the most common application is for e-commerce transactions. PKI provides a way for a seller to verify the identity of a buyer, and for customers to be sure that the company they're transmitting their credit card information to is really who they think it is.

To accomplish this, you have a number of certificate authorities, or CAs, who act as impartial third parties to establish and verify the identities of organizations doing business on the Internet. You see, the entire PKI system is dependent on the concept of *trust*. The e-commerce vendor trusts a third-party CA (such as VeriSign) to issue a PKI certificate for its use. The consumer, in turn, trusts that the certificate issued by VeriSign is genuine; that is, that VeriSign has done some form of due diligence to verify that they are issuing a certificate to a legitimate company. Because consumers trust VeriSign and the PKI certificate issued to the e-commerce vendor *by* VeriSign, they then feel comfortable doing business with this e-commerce vendor.

PKI can also have a number of uses within a corporate enterprise. The Windows Server 2003 implementation of PKI, Certificate Services, allows for the use of IP Security (IPSec) to secure TCP/IP transmissions across a network, Secure Sockets Layer (SSL) communication on a Web server, and the Encrypted File System (EFS) to secure files and folders stored on file shares. While the mathematical concepts behind PKI can seem daunting, an understanding of this topic (both from a theoretical and practical level) is critical in enabling you to secure an enterprise network. To that end, this chapter begins with a detailed explanation of the concepts at work "under the hood" within PKI, and then discusses the practical implementations of PKI within Windows Server 2003. Be sure that you have a firm grasp of the topics presented in this chapter before moving on, since many other security topics within Windows Server 2003 rely on PKI and Certificate Services to function.

EXAM 70-298 OBJECTIVE 2.1

Designing a Public Key Infrastructure

We need to understand the PKI basic concepts before we dive into Windows Server 2003 CAs. There are millions of messages traveling through public networks like the Internet every day. How do we authenticate these messages? How do we know whether the messages are being tampered with before they get to the receiver? E-commerce would not be possible on the Internet if these questions could not be answered adequately. Every e-commerce transaction must satisfy three basic needs to be secure and complete:

- **The sender has the authority to send the required message.** The sender is authenticated to send the message to the receiver.
- **The message is authentic.** The message has not been altered on the way to the receiver. A hacker can obtain this message by tapping into the communication route. This hacker might change the content of the message and impersonate the original sender
- **The sender cannot falsely deny sending the message or the content of the message.** This is commonly referred to as *nonrepudiation.*

Therefore, we need to protect the data during the transmission process. We do that by encrypting the content of the message with mathematical algorithms. There are several ways to encrypt messages. All of them fall into two major categories: *symmetric* and *asymmetric* algorithms. The *symmetric* model works on a shared key that works well in a "protected" environment. The Automatic Teller Machine (ATM) activity at a bank is an example of a symmetric key exchange. The customer and the bank share the personal identification number (PIN) in a closed environment. The customer guards the key closely. He or she will not reveal it to others. The more people who know about the PIN number, the more the "scalability" of the security diminishes (more people can impersonate the customer). The bank and the customer know the same PIN number initially. However, this solution becomes increasingly insecure as soon as other people share the key—the PIN.

The second encryption technology is referred to as *asymmetric* or *public key cryptography*. It involves two asymmetric key pairs. There are not like the PIN number. The two keys for the bank and the customer are different. The two keys are referred to as the *private* and the *public* key. The public key can be shared with other users; however, the private key is unique for a user or a resource. The sender's authenticity and nonrepudiation is based on the private key signing of the digital documents. The private key and the public key are mathematically related to each other. However, it is impossible to calculate the private key by hacking the public key. The keys also perform inverse roles (what a one key encrypts can be decrypted by the other).

Digital certificates are based on public key cryptography. These certificates are made by applying two levels of cryptography to a message: *hashing* algorithms and *signing* algorithms. Here are the steps involved in creating a digital certificate:

1. A hashing algorithm is a very complex mathematical algorithm that is applied to the original message. The result will be a 160-bit string of digits that is unique to the original message. This is referred to as the *message digest.* There are several popular hashing algorithms used by the Microsoft platform: MD2, MD4, MD5, and SHA-1.

2. The signature algorithm is then applied to the message digest. The sender's private key is built into this signing process. This will result in a unique set of characters that we refer to as the *digital certificate*. The default signature algorithm in Windows Server 2003 is the *Microsoft strong cryptographic provider* algorithm.

Anyone can download digital certificate generation software and generate private and public keys. Tools to accomplish this are readily available on the Internet. Knowing this, how do we trust a document that is digitally signed? A malicious attacker can create digitally signed software just as easily as a well-known manufacturer, and the digital signature might mislead us to install malicious software on our network. Luckily, there is a solution to this problem: we only accept users who sign their documents with a certificate from a well-known vendor or trusted party. These trusted parties are commonly referred to as certificate authorities (CAs). Several major CAs issue certificates for e-commerce transactions; VeriSign and RSA are two of the well-known companies. In this case, a typical end user will be more confident that his or her transactions are protected by a reputable CA.

You might also need to use certificates internally within your organization. You can restrict access to valuable resources using certificates. PKI is used with technologies such as File Encrypted Security and IPSec to protect enterprise resources; these topics are discussed at more length in later chapters. We can use the Windows Server 2003 CA service to enable this functionality.

Let's try to put all this theory into practice. Figure 3.1 illustrates the complete PKI process in which we are trying to send an e-mail message to a recipient.

1. It begins with the sender requesting a certificate from the CA (1). We need to get a digital certificate to protect the e-mail message.
2. The CA will check the user credentials and issue a digital certificate. The CA can use the Active Directory and the Windows logon data to assist the certification generation. The CA will also publish the certificate in a public certificate repository (this way, when the receiver gets the message, he or she can authenticate the sender). This is represented by (2).
3. Then we try to sign the e-mail message with the key (3). The signing process is done in two phases.
4. The first phase is to apply the hashing algorithm (4). We obtain a message digest as the result of this.
5. Then we apply the signing algorithm with the private key on the message digest (5).

   The hashing algorithm and the signing data are contained in the certificate to assist step (4) and step (5). The result is the encrypted message.

Figure 3.1 PKI Overview

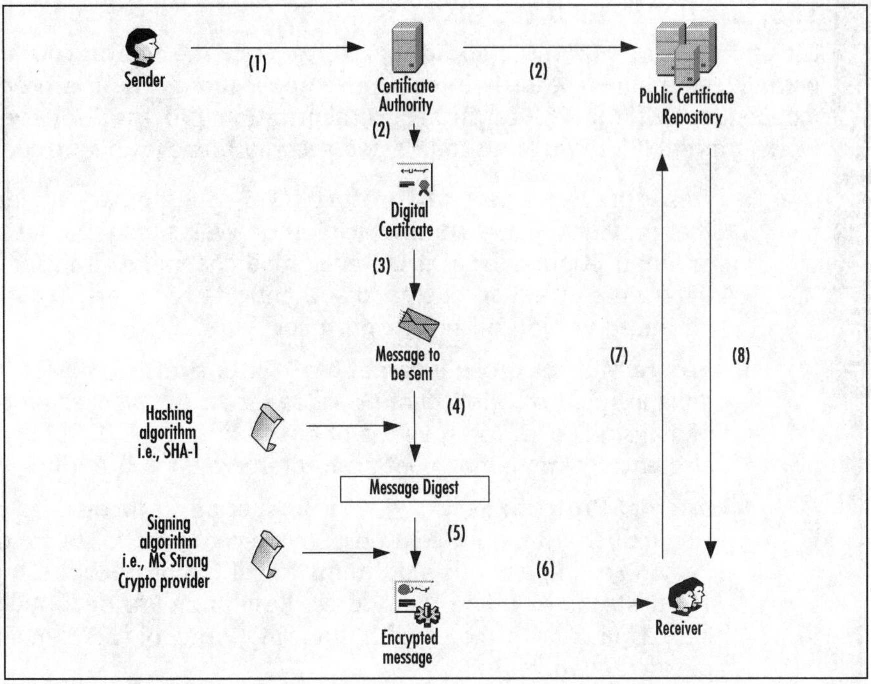

6. The encrypted message is sent to the receiver (6).
7. The receiver will communicate to the public certificate repository to validate the certificate details (7).
8. The public certificate repository will respond with a flag to indicate the authenticity of the message (8). The receiver will be able to decrypt the e-mail depending on this response.

This will complete the PKI implementation. Now let's try to understand the PKI process in more detail.

Understanding PKI

PKI could be described as a collection of standards, policies, laws, and procedures that will ensure security using public and private key pairs. PKI assists in electronic transactions with the help of digital certificates and CAs to verify and validate the potential users of our application.

The Windows Server 2003 PKI is based on the public key infrastructure X.509 (PKIX) standard and Internet Engineering Task Force (IETF) standards to ensure interoperability with other vendors. IETF also recommends some other security standards that work closely with the PKI architecture: Transport Layer Security (TLS), Secure Multipurpose Internet Mail Extensions (S/MIME), and IPSec.

Head of the Class...

TLS, S/MIME, and IPSec

Let's try to learn a bit more about these protocols. These protocols are used with PKI to enhance security in enterprise applications. These protocols are independent of the PKI certificate authentication process. However, they work with the PKI infrastructure to avoid security breaches by intruders.

- **Transport Layer Security protocol (TLS)** An industry standard that provides secure communication on Web sites (intranet and Internet). It provides a secure encrypted channel to transfer data between entities, and helps to authenticate the users. TLS is an advanced version of the SSL protocol.
- **Secure Multipurpose Internet Mail Extensions (S/MIME)** An enhancement of MIME that provides secure e-mail exchange with digital signatures to prove the origin of the e-mail. S/MIME will also encrypt the e-mail content to preserve data integrity.
- **Internet Protocol Security (IPSec)** A set of protocols that provide industry standard cryptography mechanisms to exchange data. IPSec implements algorithms for all the protocols in the TCP/IP stack, excluding the Address Resolution Protocol (ARP). IPSec is used with the Layer 2 Tunneling Protocol (L2TP) in virtual private networks (VPNs).

Let's look at the PKI architecture in detail. PKI is a combination of several key components. These components vary from actual certificates to lists that will authorize or revoke user access to the enterprise.

- **Digital certificates** This is the core of the PKI technology, and holds the public key to validate the user. The public key is an electronic signature that we use to sign and encrypt the data that the users exchange with the enterprise. The digital certificate contains the version, serial number, signature, issuer, validity, subject, and subject public key information, and issues a unique ID, subject's unique ID, and extension information. This will enable third parties to establish the user's identity and the issuer's identity.
- **Certificate authorities (CA)** CAs issue trusted certificates. The users need to obtain a certificate from a CA to own an electronic signature. There could be multiple CAs within an enterprise. These CAs will be arranged in a logical way to perform special tasks. Some might be configured to issue certificates to subordinate CAs, and others might be configured for internal or external issuing of certificates.

- **Certificate repositories** The certificates need to be stored after they are issued by the CA. A certificate repository is the "container" where the certificates are stored. The preferred location for a certificate repository in Windows Server 2003 is the Active Directory. The Active Directory will provide the certificates to the users on demand. The certificates are physically stored on the CA hard drives. The Active Directory will have references to locate the correct certificates on demand.
- **Key retrieval and recovery** This process recovers the private key portion of the public-private key pair in an emergency. (The user might have lost the key or the administrator needs to impersonate the user). This process does not recover any data or messages between the user and the enterprise server; it only recovers the private key credentials.

These are the major components of PKI. However, how do you administer the certificate issuing process? Can you prevent a malicious user from obtaining a certificate? We need to have some policies and technical controls in place to manage the certificate issue process. Here are some of the ways to dictate the structure of the PKI implementation:

- **Certificate policy and practice statements** These will document the use of certificates in the enterprise. The details of how the certificates are used, the trust relationship between the certificates and the resources, and the consequence when the trust is broken are detailed in these documents.
- **Certificate Revocation List (CRL)** This list specifies the certificates that should be revoked before the expiration date. Users on this list will no longer have access to resources secured by certificates.

EXAM WARNING

The CRL could be a long list that consumes a lot of bandwidth. The Windows Server 2003 Certificate Server introduces a new concept called the *Delta Certification Revoke List* (Delta CRL). The Delta CRL will publish the recently revoked certificates to consume less bandwidth. This will only display the partial revocation list, not the full CRLs.

- **Certificate Trust List (CTL)** The CTL documents the trusted certificates of the enterprise. This signed list is issued by the CAs. Management of a Windows Server 2003 CTL is done via Group Policy Objects (GPOs).

PKI could be used to perform many functions to secure the enterprise, including:

- Digitally signing e-mail, applications, and sensitive documents
- Secure remote access to computers over the Internet
- Use smart cards to enable authentication and single sign-on in the enterprise

Designing a CA is the first step of a PKI implementation. This will identify the certificate requirements for the enterprise. You can either upgrade from an existing Windows implementation (NT 4.0 or Windows 2000) or a third-party certificate service and take advantage of the new Windows Server 2003 features. When the design phase is completed, we can deploy a PKI solution for all internal security requirements and exchange of secure data communication with our business partners. Let's look at how to design the CA implementation.

EXAM 70-298 OBJECTIVE 2.1.1

Designing a Certification Authority Implementation

The design of the CA is very important. The correct CA design will provide reliable service to the users, and an organic structure to delete and add users. This will also reduce maintenance costs. You need to consider several factors when implementing a CA:

- **Designing the root CAs** An enterprise will have multiple CAs that will issue certificates to its users. These multiple CAs need to be controlled by a central figure, referred to as a *root CA*. The root CA will delegate the issuing of certificates to its subordinates. The root CA has to be implemented and correctly configured before we create a CA hierarchy. We need to consider some items before we design the root CA. The first item is the location of the CA. The ownership of the CA is also important. Who controls the CA and manages it (for example, the head office and its staff, or is it the responsibility of the IT department to host and manage)? Another important item is the "functionality" of the root CA? (Does the root CA just delegate to the CA hierarchy? Do we need to configure the root CA to issue certificates?) This will be discussed further in the next section.
- **Define CA types and roles** Windows Server 2003 has two types of CAs: *enterprise* or *stand-alone*. Both types can be configured as the root CA or a subordinate CA. A subordinate CA can further be configured as an intermediate CA or an issuing CA.

Designing & Planning…

Distinguishing Root CAs and Subordinate CAs

The root CA is the top of the CA hierarchy and should be trusted at all times. The certificate chain will ultimately end at the root CA. The enterprise can have a root CA as enterprise or a stand-alone CA (these topics are discussed later). The root CA is the only entity that can *self sign,* or issue self certificates in the enterprise. Windows Server 2003 only allows one machine to act as the root CA. The root CA is the most important CA. If the root CA is compromised, all the CAs in the enterprise will be compromised. Therefore, it is a good practice to disconnect the root CA from the network and use a subsidiary CA to issue certificates to users.

Any CAs that are not the root CA are classified as subordinate CAs. The first level of subordinate CAs will obtain their certificates from the root CA. These servers are commonly referred to as *intermediary* or *policy* CAs. They will pass on the certificate information to the issuing CAs down the chain. They are referred to as intermediary because they act as a "go-between" with the root CA and the issuing CAs.. The intermediary CA will instruct the issuing CAs with the certificates that are customized to the enterprise. This information is used by the issuing CAs to generate certificates for the end users. It is common in an enterprise to have an intermediary/policy CA that controls internal access, and then have another CA to control external access. A typical CA hierarchy of an enterprise is shown in Figure 3.2.

Figure 3.2 Common Arrangements of the CA Hierarchy of an Enterprise

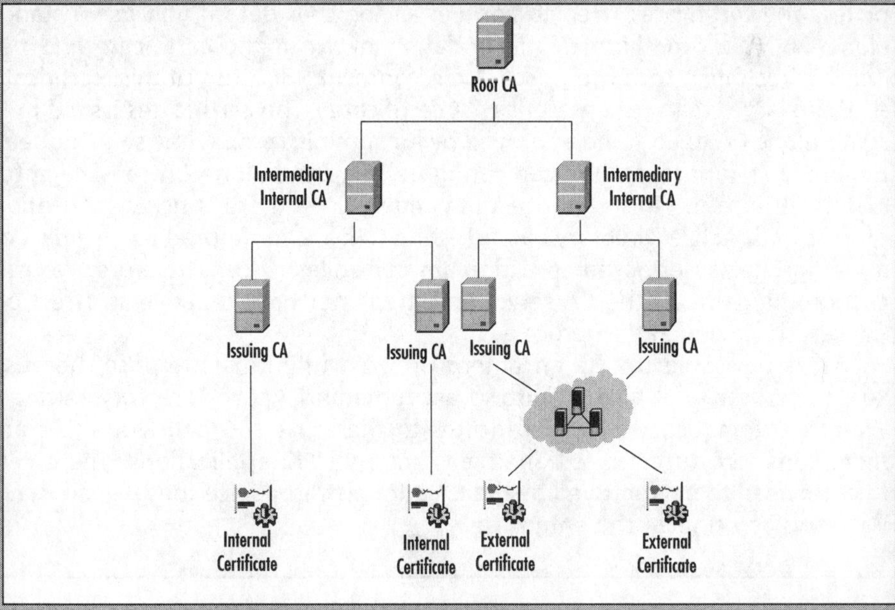

Head of the Class...

Enterprise and Stand-Alone CAs

Enterprise CAs publish certificates and CRLs to the Active Directory. The Active Directory will store information on the user accounts, the user, and the policy to approve or deny certificates. Enterprise CAs use certificate templates, which are used to generate certificates for the users. Therefore, we can use the Enterprise CA to issue automated certificates and approve them. Enterprise CAs also enable smart card logons. The smart card certificates are automatically mapped the to Active Directory settings, hence enabling smart card authentication via Active Directory.

Enterprise CAs are closely bound to the enterprise's Active Directory structure. Therefore, the enterprise CA can only issues certificates to the users of the Active Directory. We will not be able to change the name of the CA server after CA service has been installed on the machine. This will make the certificates invalid. The enterprise CA machine cannot be removed form the domain structure of the enterprise either. Therefore, we need to consider the Active Directory structure before we plan the PKI implementation. Multiple Active Directory forests in an enterprise can complicate things. We need to assign an enterprise CA for each of the multiple Active Directory forests to facilitate multiple Active Directory forests. Enterprise CAs also rely on the existence of the Active Directory schema. We might need to upgrade the Active Directory schema from Windows 2000 to Windows Server 2003 schema to optimize enterprise CA use (some features such as certificate template version 2 are only supported in Windows Server 2003 schema).

Stand-alone CAs do not use the Active Directory or the certificate templates. The certificates need to contain all the user data if you use a stand-alone CA. (We can share this information between the certificate and the Active Directory in the Enterprise CA environment.) Because of this, certificate sizes are larger than for enterprise CA certificates. The certificates issued by a stand-alone CA need to be approved by an administrator. (They sit in a queue until they are approved. We can configure the stand-alone CA to issue automated certificates. This is not recommended since there is no authorization process with Active Directory.) Stand-alone CAs are configured to be a part of a workgroup (as opposed to a domain controller (DC)). Therefore, we can change the name of the CA server and it will not have an adverse affect on the certificate generation process.

It is advisable to use an enterprise CA within an enterprise, because enterprise users will have Windows accounts and Active Directory settings. We can automatically issue certificates to these users. Stand-alone CAs are more commonly used in extranets and Internet PKI applications. These certificates need to be approved by the CA administrator since they will not have Windows accounts in the enterprise.

- **Are we going to have internal CAs or delegate to third-party CAs?** The answer to this question will depend on the structure and the budget of the PKI solution. It is advantageous to have an internal CA if the enterprise does a lot of internal business within the enterprise. If the enterprise conducts the majority of its business with external partners, an external CA would be better. The third-party CAs also add more confidence to the end user. Security audit experts will also feel more comfortable with an external third-party reputable vendor like VeriSign.
- **Evaluate the optimum level of capacity for the CAs.** The stakeholders of the enterprise should agree on the performance and the scalability of the CA servers. This is dependent on the number of certificates that a CA issues, the hardware that the CA servers run, and the size of the certificates themselves. You also need to consider the quality of the network resources and the number of clients you need to configure.

Designing & Planning...

Scalability of Windows Server 2003 PKI

A stand-alone Windows Server 2003 CA can host 35 million standard-sized certificates. The size of the certificates is a crucial factor. A Windows Server 2003 that runs on a dual processor with 512MB of memory can issue up to 2 million certificates per day. Network bandwidth and the quality of the network resources are the major concern for many CA implementations, and will dictate the number of CAs in the organization. The bandwidth for 2 million certificates exchanging information on the network can generate a considerable amount of traffic. While we can easily attach or disconnect CA servers from the network, a network upgrade is quite expensive and time consuming. Some other important factors to consider on CA servers include:

- **Number of CPUs** The more CPUs, the greater the throughput.
- **Disk performance** This depends on the number of certificates enrolled and the size of the certificates. A higher performing disk controller will be needed if the certificates are larger or the numbers of certificates exceeds 2 million a day.
- **Hard disk capacity** The general size of a certificate is about 17k. The log entries for the certificate will be around 15K. The size of the certificate database increases with the number of certificate enrollments; therefore, we need to provide for this.
- **Number of CA administrators** Some organizations have a distributed CA administrative model that spans multiple offices and IT departments. It is usually a good practice to centralize the control to a small team to save network bandwidth and administration costs.

These are the factors we need to consider when we design a CA. Now we need to understand how we arrange these CAs to issue certificates to the end users. There are several models to group *or* organize CAs to facilitate a PKI implementation. These are commonly referred to as *trust hierarchies*.

The Windows Server 2003 PKI model consists of well-defined parent-child relationships between CA servers. The child CA is certified by the parent CA and is trusted to issue certificates to the next layer of CA servers. A best practice is to organize the CA servers in a three-tier model, commonly referred to as the *three-tier CA model*. The three tiers are the root CA, intermediary CAs, and issuing CAs. Let's learn a bit more about these trust hierarchies with an example. We will be referring to a fictitious company, IronCladSecurity, for demonstration purposes. The company has subsidiaries in the United States, Germany, and Singapore. It is a large company with many business partners. IronCladSecurity employs 10,000 employees in these subsidiaries, and has a combination of employees and contractors as its workforce.

Geographical Hierarchy

The CAs in a geographical hierarchy are organized according to the geographical location of the subsidiaries of the enterprise. This model allows the regional CA administrators to manage their domains more efficiently. IronCladSecurity has offices in the United States, Germany, and Singapore. Therefore, the three-tier CA trust hierarchy for this company based on geography could be similar to Figure 3.3.

Figure 3.3 Example of Geographical Hierarchy

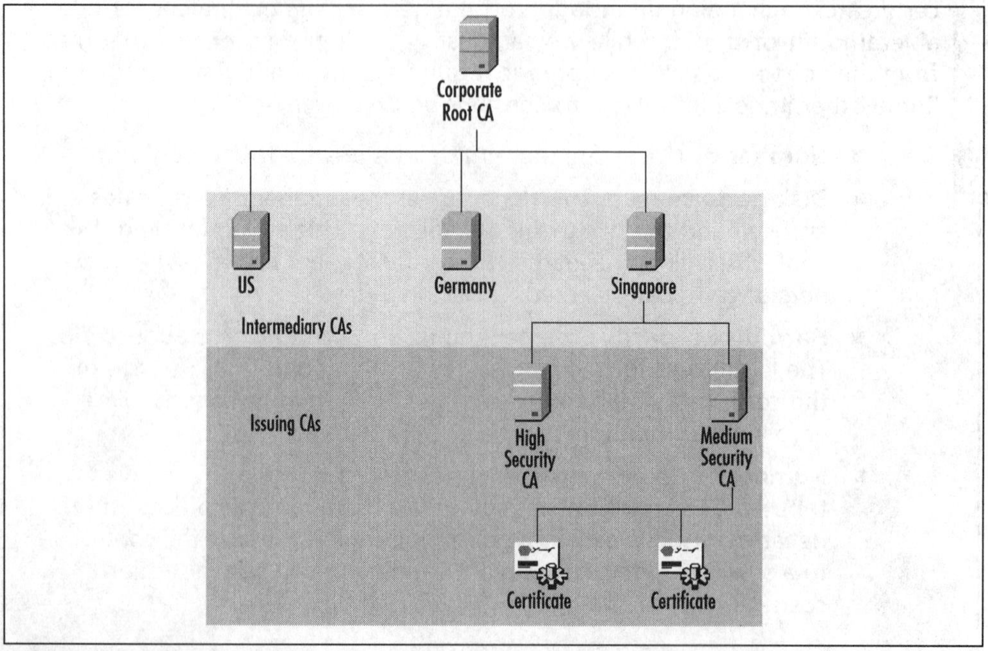

There is one corporate root CA. This could be based in the United States, Germany, or Singapore. This is the first tier of the CA hierarchy. The second tier is the intermediary CAs. These CAs are based on location. Therefore, the United States, Germany, and Singapore will have CAs to manage their subsidiaries. The third tier is the issuing CAs. Figure 3.3 illustrates the issuing CA's hierarchy of the Singapore subsidiary. Two types of certificates need to be issued from the Singapore CA: high security certificates (which are for sensitive information and will be very detailed and expensive) and medium security certificates (which do not have the same sensitivity as high security). Medium security certificates are less verbose and less expensive than the high security certificates. We have designed a CA server each to facilitate the *high* and *medium* level security users.

Organizational Hierarchy

The trust hierarchy can also be designed to accommodate the organizational structure of an enterprise. IronCladSecurity employs both permanent employees and contractors. It could be risky to issue the permanent employee certificates to the contractors. IronCladSecurity also has multiple business partners. One partner might not want to share a common certificate with other partners. The issue of certificates for internal employees is another matter. These issues will justify a trust hierarchy based on organizational structure. The trust hierarchy for IronCladCompany might look similar to Figure 3.4.

Figure 3.4 Example of Organizational Trust Hierarchy

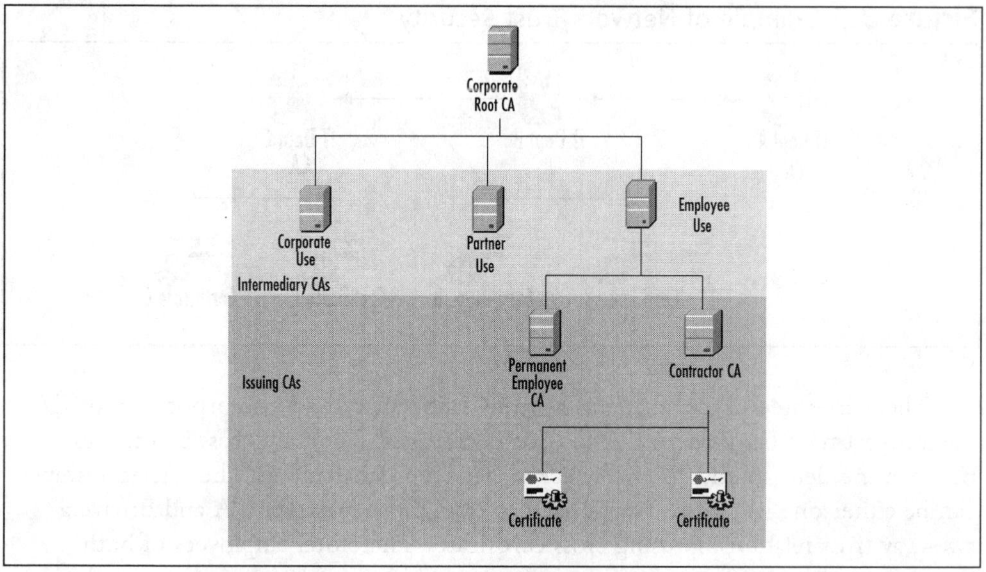

The organization-based trust hierarchy of IronCladSecurity is also based on the three-tier CA model. There is one corporate root CA. The intermediary CAs are assigned to facilitate the organizational structure. There is one CA assigned for corporate certificate usage. The second CA is assigned to issue certificates to business partners. The third CA is used to issue certificates to the employees. IronCladSecurity has contractors and permanent employees; therefore, it is a better design to assign an issuing CA to both the contractors and permanent employees.

Network Trust Hierarchy

Some organizations have distributed and independent IT departments. It could be difficult to identify and implement a single entity as a root CA, and there might be little communication between these subsidiaries since they operate independently within their domain. A single root CA design would not be appropriate for this scenario.

We can overcome this issue by designing a network trust model. There is no single root CA in this model; instead, there are multiple CAs taking the role of the root CA. There are "trust relationships" between these CAs, which is achieved by each CA issuing the other a *cross certificate*. These cross certificates can be bidirectional or unidirectional. Let's try to explain this scenario with IronCladSecurity. IronCladSecurity has given permission to its various IT departments to implement a network trust model. Each IT department will have a CA server. The IT department will trust the other IT department with the help of a cross certificate. Figure 3.5 illustrates this model.

Figure 3.5 Example of Network Trust Security

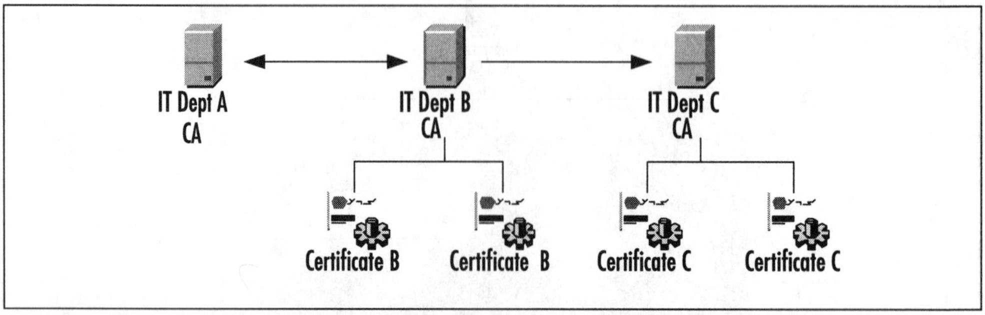

There are three IT departments at IronCladSecurity, and no corporate root CA. Each department has its own CA to issue certificates. There are cross certificates between the departments to enable access between departments. These relationships can be either one way or bidirectional. For example, departments A and B have a two-way trust relationship using cross certificates. Therefore, employees of both departments A and B can use resources of the two departments (in other words, a department A user can request a department B certificate and use a department B resource, and vice versa). However, there is only a one-way trust between departments B and C. Therefore, department C will not be able to obtain any certificates from department B. Hence, a department C user will not gain access to department B resources. Department B has one-way access to department C; therefore, department B user can gain access to department C resources.

TEST DAY TIP

The network trust model is harder to maintain than the root CA model. It becomes more difficult to manage as the number of CAs in the enterprise increases. There can also be a negative impact on network bandwidth in this model. This is recommended when there is minimum communication between the departments.

The network trust model also presents a challenge in that there is no root CA. Therefore, a global directory (such as Active Directory) must be installed in this enterprise. The only way we can find/ locate other department's CAs is using a mechanism like Active Directory.

EXAM 70-298 OBJECTIVE 2.2

Designing a Logical Authentication Strategy

A logical authentication strategy for an enterprise could be very complex. We need to provide a secure environment to communicate with our business partners. The enterprise might consist of many employees situated in many locations. Those employees might work at company premises and external locations (using remote services from their homes). These employees could also travel for their work purposes. The most important feature of the authentication strategy is to prevent intruders from accessing sensitive data. We need to consider all these features to build a logical authentication strategy for the enterprise.

Windows Server 2003 provides a secure framework for users, computers, and services of the enterprise. This is achieved by creating Active Directory accounts for each resource that needs to be accessed in the enterprise. The first step of the strategy is to review the existing authentication strategy. We should take note of the resources that are not supported in the old authentication regime. Then, we need to create the users in Active Directory that can access these resources. These users need to be created with the assistance of a *user account management plan*. This plan will document the users, their access, and the reason for them to have access to the resources. Then, we have to configure the computer accounts for the resources. This computer information should be documented in the *computer account management plan*. These accounts will be individual user accounts or service accounts. (service accounts are common accounts that can be used by multiple users). The next step is to secure the authentication process of the enterprise. This can be done in many ways:

- **Create a strong password policy for users and service accounts in the enterprise.** We should have an alphanumeric combination that should exceed at least eight characters.
- **Configure an account lockout policy.** Intruders automate sophisticated algorithms to discover passwords for user accounts. Therefore, we have to configure Windows Server 2003 to deal with repeated failures of password authentication. The account should be locked out if the user is unable to submit the correct password in a specified amount of attempts (t is common to lock the account after three invalid password submissions).
- **Limit the usage according to time.** Accounts can be configured to operate on a time table (for example, the accounts can be configured only to work from 9:00 A.M. to 9:00 P.M. Monday through Friday). This will deter the hackers who are trying to penetrate the system on other time slots.
- **Monitor the expiration time frames of the PKI certificates.** We need to set the expiration dates on all certificates issued by the enterprise. The time frame that a certificate is valid changes from organization to organization. We need to revisit this time frame regularly to analyze the best certificate life span for an enterprise. This will prevent disgruntled former employees from trying to compromise the system.

We can use PKI certificates to authenticate many users and resources. We can implement the Web Enrollment Support System (discussed later) to issue certificates to Web pages. These Web pages can easily authenticate onto other enterprise resources with the help of these certificates. We can use role-based security with the help of a PKI architecture. The certificate has all the details about the users and their access. Therefore, we can import the security information to any resource of the enterprise. The resource can accept or deny access according to the certificate information. We can put the necessary roles for a user in the Active Directory. The CA server will examine the Active Directory entries (using Windows' logon API) in order to generate a certificate for this user. The roles information will be embedded into the user's certificate. The roles will be examined by the resources (with the help of Active Directory) each time the user tries to gain access to the resource. We will issue a new certificate to the user when the roles are modified.

We can also use smart cards to extend the PKI security infrastructure. The employees need to enter the smart card to every device they want to access. The smart cards "force" the employee to use the asymmetric key and a PIN to authenticate (this is discussed later in the chapter). We will also discuss using 802.1x certificates to authenticate into wireless devices in a later chapter.

We also need to take steps to protect enterprise and stand-alone CAs . The enterprise CAs communicate to Active Directory regularly. Therefore, it is advised to have the enterprise CA in the same subnet as the Active Directory servers. This will minimize the network traffic and latency. (Most enterprises will have a "high security" server farm with sophisticated security; for example, armed guards, secure doors, and technical security such as smart cards authentication. Therefore, the enterprise CA server will plug in to this special high security farm.) The enterprise CA needs to authenticate to a DC to access Active Directory. Therefore, it is difficult to take the enterprise CAs offline. Hence, we need to carefully plan the enterprise CA addition to the network (once the name of the enterprise CA is set, it will be difficult to alter the machine name without compromising the existing certificates). The stand-alone CA implementation is discussed in the section *Securing a Stand-Alone CA*.

EXAM 70-298 OBJECTIVE 2.1.4

Designing Security for CA Servers

Securing enterprise CA servers is a very important step in a PKI implementation. Hackers can inflict a myriad of attacks on sensitive data if the CA servers are compromised. They can modify the certificates or alter the configuration of the CA servers, thus impacting all systems within the enterprise IT systems. We should take steps to protect the CA servers. Let's discuss this topic in more detail. We will first investigate the common threats against CAs.

Common Threats Against Certificate Services

The root CA is the most important CA in the enterprise. The entire PKI implementation will be in jeopardy if the root CA is compromised, because the root CA provides all certificate information through policy CAs to issuing CAs within an organization. If the root CA is compromised, intruders can tamper with certificate information or issue fraudulent certificates by misusing the issuing CAs. The issuing CAs will be helpless since they will merely follow the root CA's lead.

How do we protect the root CA from being compromised? The most common way for an intruder to hack into the CA is via a network attack. Networks in a large enterprise can be very complex; therefore, they are very difficult to maintain and audit. This can enable intelligent hackers to penetrate systems through unpatched or undetected loopholes. These loopholes could be simple as a stolen access card belonging to a system administrator, or a sophisticated software algorithm that scans the open ports on an enterprise firewall. A successful attacker could retrieve the private key of the root CA and manipulate or destroy enterprise resources. The important fact is to protect the CA *before* an intruder strikes.

The best way to protect the root CA is to disconnect it from the network. That way, even if the network is compromised, the intruder will not gain access to the root CA. The same steps can also be applied to intermediate or policy CAs; they should be disconnected from the network in a high-security environment. Doing so will prevent the private key from being compromised by intruders. We can make the CA servers offline using any of the following steps:

- **Install a stand-alone Windows Server 2003 as the root CA.** Configure it to be physically disconnected from the network.

Test Day Tip

The best practice is not to install the CA server as a member of a domain. This will be an issue when the CA administrators bring the server online for maintenance or backup. The password for domain accounts expires every 30 days by default. Therefore, the CA's server passwords will be invalid after the 30-day period. The solution for this is to make the offline CA a member of a workgroup.

We should not configure an enterprise CA as the root CA. The enterprise CAs communicate with a global directory (in other words, the Active Directory). The Active Directory updates will have issues when the root CA is offline; therefore, the root CA should be a stand-alone CA.

- **Shut down the CA service.** The CA server can be online; however, we can disable or stop the CA service of the computer. This step will restrict the certification generation process and disable the activities of the certificate generation. It will stop the CA from issuing, denying, updating, or viewing certificate data and will disable the auto-enrollment of certificates. However, the CA server is still vulnerable to a hacker who scans the file system to obtain certificate data.
- **Physically shut down the CA server.** This is commonly practiced on high-security root CA servers. The root CA servers are physically shut down until they are needed to issue new certificates to policy/intermediary CAs. However, this will prevent CA auditing on the CA server.

Exam Warning

The offline CAs can still publish certificates and certificate revocation lists (CRLs) in Active Directory. They need to be online to communicate with the Active Directory to publish CRLs. You should take steps to coordinate the CRL updates so that the CA server is online to interact with Active Directory. It is a good practice to bring the CA online on an agreed time schedule to populate the new CRL. (This could be done by making the CA server "'visible" to the network; in other words, starting the CA service or powering up the CA machine.) The parent CAs should also be online to instruct the subordinate CAs to process certificate update information.

The Authority Information Access (AIA) is the endpoint to obtain the certificate data. This is usually the local HTTP server. The CRL default location is a directory on the local machine. These local file paths and HTTP virtual directories are invalid when the CA is offline. Therefore, they have to be modified to point at online resources when we take the parent CA offline.

Head of the Class...

Impact of Offline CAs

There is no impact on the client-side certification because the CA is offline. The client needs the CRL and AIA data to verify the certificate credentials. The client will check the certificate chain and make sure that the entry is not in the CRL. These CRLs and AIA information are obtained from other online subordinates issuing CAs. These online CAs issue information according to the instructions given by the offline parent CAs. The offline CAs process a very small number of requests from subordinates issuing CAs. Therefore, administrative costs on offline CAs are negligible. Let's try to explain this with our IronCladSecurity example form the previous section.

IronCladSecurity follows a geographical hierarchy CA structure. It has a root CA in the U.S. office. There are policy CAs in the United States, Germany, and Singapore. There are issuing CAs at each geographical location. The root CA in the United States will be disconnected from the corporate network. The root CA will only be available to update or issue new certificates to policy CAs in the United States, Germany, or Singapore. The policy CAs are also offline most of the time. They are only online to issue certificates to issuing CAs. The issuing CA servers on the corporate LAN will be the only "visible" CA servers most of the time. The root CA and policy CA will be online for predefined time periods for maintenance (for example, to update Active Directory information) and certificate updates.

Let's try to put all this information into practice. We will be designing a sample best-practice Windows Server 2003 PKI solution for a fictitious company. We will initially look at the enterprise hierarchy of the CA server. Then, we will discuss the steps to secure the stand-alone CA server.

Securing an Enterprise Hierarchy

An enterprise hierarchy can consist of many CAs. We need to organize them in a logical structure. The enterprise can only have one root CA. The root CA should not depend on any other resources of the enterprise (for example, Active Directory). Therefore, we should not use an enterprise CA as the root CA. The interaction with Active Directory might cause some issues. (The updates will not be reflected in realtime since the CA is offline.) The solution is to implement the root CA as a standalone CA.

We will apply the three-tiered CA model to this enterprise. There will be a single offline root CA at the top. The root CA will delegate to policy CAs. The distribution of policy CAs depends on the organizational structure or the business model. We recognize three main areas of certificate distribution in this fictitious company. There is an external need to issue certificates to business partners. The internal security needs to dictate two types of certificates. Certificates issued by an internal high-security CA server protect the sensitive data. The medium security certificates are issued by an internal medium security CA. Figure 3.6 illustrates this CA architecture.

Figure 3.6 Example of a Three-Tiered CA Enterprise Hierarchy

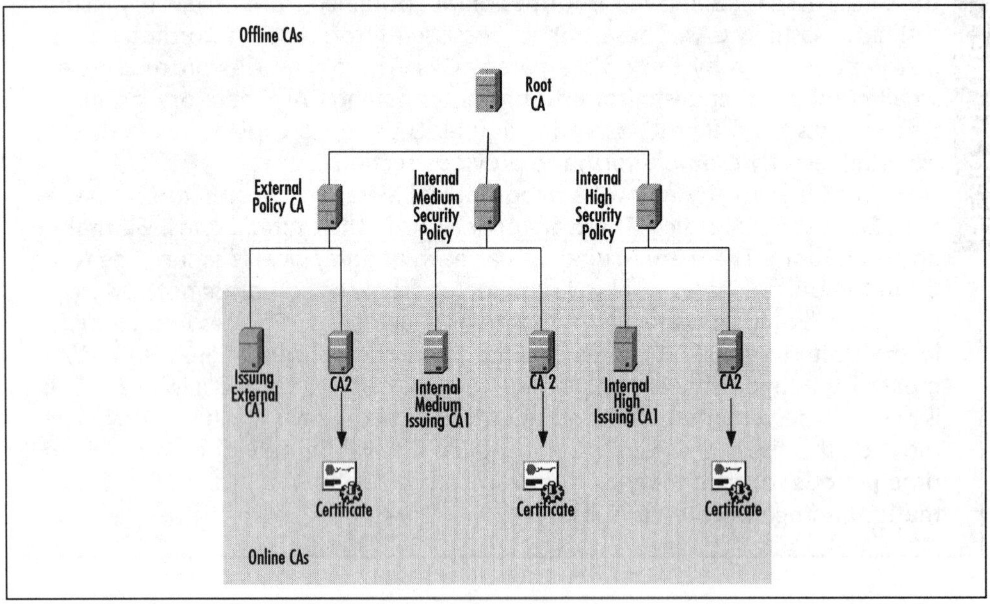

This structure will enable a secure and flexible mechanism to issue certificates for the enterprise. The architecture will also scale to add or delete any CA servers. We can add or delete policy and issuing CAs at our discretion. Let's investigate how to secure stand-alone CAs and cryptographic service providers (CSPs).

Securing a Stand-Alone CA

Securing a stand-alone CA can be done in several ways. It is best practice to implement the root CAs and the intermediary CAs as stand-alone CAs. We can make these servers offline and disconnect them form the network. These steps were discussed in the section *Common Threats Against Certificate Services*. The certificates issued by the CAs need to be stored in a secure environment, commonly referred to as a CSP. Here are some of the other ways to secure them:

- **Using hardware CSPs** There are hardware CSPs that can handle complex cryptography and key storage. Hardware CSP key storage is more secure than software CSP. They cannot be easily tampered as opposed to software CSPs where the keys can be stored on local hard disks. This will enable CA administrators to enable more life time on certificates on hardware CSPs.

Exam Warning

Some hackers are sophisticated enough to obtain memory dumps of a software CSP. This can lead to compromising the private keys of the organization. Hardware CSP does not have this issue. The hardware CSPs do not store the key information in memory; they are kept in hardware devices. This will restrict the hackers from obtaining sensitive private key information.

You also need to take into account the physical access to the hardware CSP. The hardware should be stored in a secure area of the building with limited access. You must also take necessary steps to back up the access accounts information and private key data.

- **Hardware CSPs can be expensive to purchase and maintain.** An alternative is to use smart cards to store the keys.

Exam Warning

The smart card implementation adds another level of security to the enterprise. Smart cards store a cryptographic key on the card. These cards are only accessible with the correct PIN); therefore, you need both the smart card and the PIN number to access or revoke certificate information. This will eliminate the risk of theft of a smart card and it being used for fraudulent purposes. It could be an expensive exercise to issue every employee a smart card. However, it is recommended that at least the CA administrators are equipped with smart cards to manage the CA servers. The smart cards will also enable a Single Sign On regime in the enterprise (since the user carries his own certificate from one location/machine to another).

- You also need to take into account the physical access to the CAs and CSPs. These should be physically stored in a secure environment and accessed only by a small administrator team. Auditing on these servers is highly recommended to track any intruders or misuse by malicious employees. It is also recommend to back up this information on a regular basis.

EXAM 70-298 OBJECTIVE 2.2.2

Designing Certificate Distribution

We have learned about PKI design in detail. Now, we put the theory to practice. We will learn how to implement a PKI implementation from scratch. The first step is to install the certificate server on Windows Server 2003. This not installed by default.

TEST DAY TIP

You should not install a CA on a FAT file system The FAT system will not support domain-based security. The best practice is to install CA on an NTFS system. The NTFS system will enable seamless interaction with Active Directory and share user account information.

EXERCISE 3.01

INSTALLING A CA ON WINDOWS SERVER 2003

1. Navigate to **Start | Control Panel | Add Remove Programs**.
2. Select **Add Remove Windows Components** from the left pane.
3. You will be presented with a **Windows Components Wizard** window. Choose **Certificate Services** from the options available. Your screen should be similar to Figure 3.7.

Figure 3.7 Selecting Certificate Service to Install

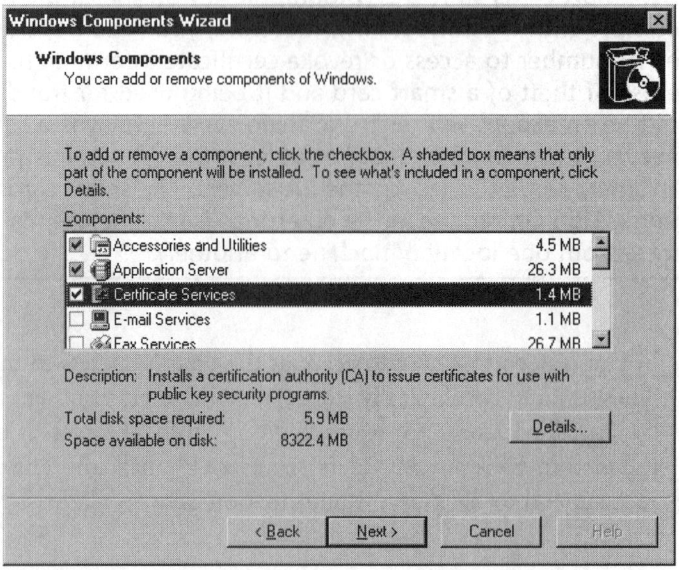

You will get a message box as soon as you click the **Certificate Services** option box. This is a warning sign to make the user aware of the consequences of changing the machine name and the domain of the server. The certificates will be invalid if we change the machine name. (The certificates generated form this server will have a binding to server-specific information, the server name.) Active Directory will also lose track of the server if the machine name or domain is reconfigured. The Warning looks similar to Figure 3.8. Click **Yes** to navigate to the next screen.

Figure 3.8 Warning Screen before Installing Certificate Services

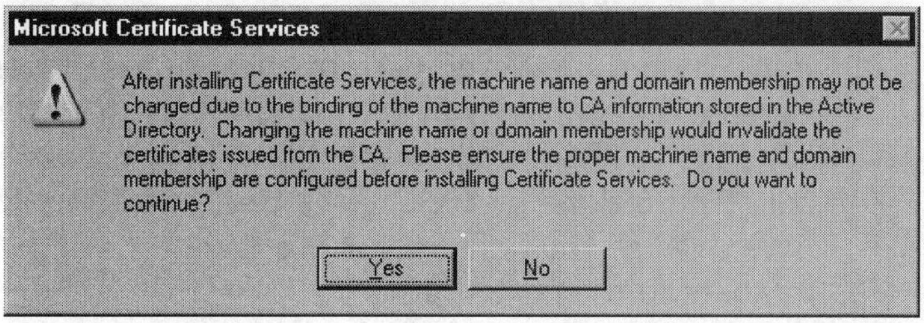

4. The next screen will let you select a CA type. There are several types of CA servers: enterprise root, enterprise subordinate, stand-alone root, and stand-alone subordinate. The server will also do a quick check to see whether Active Directory is present in the network. You can install an enterprise root or an enterprise subordinate if Active Directory is present in the network. You will only be able to install a stand-alone CA if Active Directory is not present. The enterprise option will be grayed out in this case. This scenario is illustrated in Figure 3.9. We are trying to create a root CA for demonstration purposes. Select **Stand-alone root CA** and click **Next**.

Figure 3.9 Selecting a CA Type

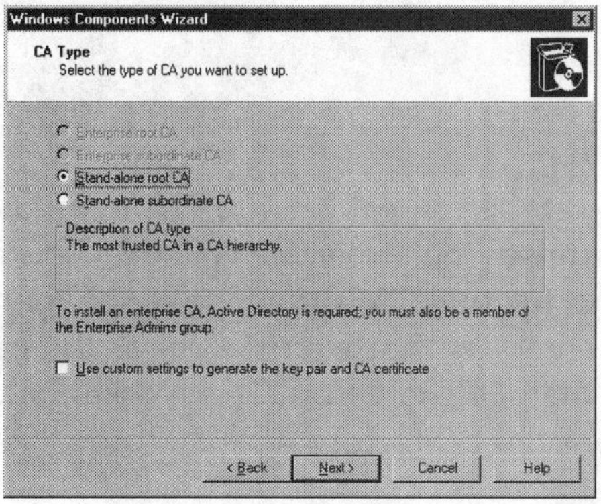

5. The next screen will let you choose the private and public key pair. Figure 3.10 shows the options available. You can choose a CSP from the **CSP** menu and associate a hashing algorithm to it. Several CSPs are included in Windows Server 2003: MS Base DSS Cryptographic Provider, MS Enhanced Cryptographic Provider, and MS Strong Cryptographic Provider. The default is MS Strong Cryptographic Provider. There are several built-in hashing algorithms available in Windows Server 2003: MD2, MD3, MD5, and SHA-1. The default is SHA-1. (These are sophisticated hashing algorithms that are used to encrypt data.) We can also select the key length. The key length can be 512, 1024, 2048, or 4096. The default is 2048. The longer the key length, the more secure the transaction is. However, performance can be hindered due to the increase of complexity in key manipulation. You can also import key pairs by clicking the **Import** button or use an existing key pair. (This is done by clicking the **Use an exiting key** option.) We have selected the defaults for this demonstration. Click **Next** to navigate to the next screen.

Figure 3.10 Selecting Public and Private Key Pairs

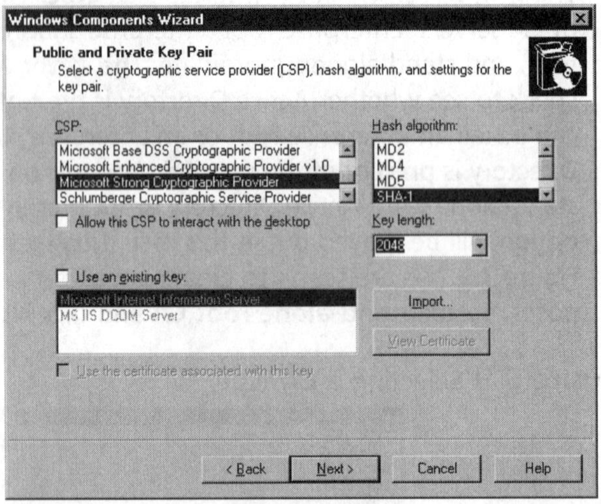

6. The next screen will let you configure the CA naming for the enterprise. The screen is similar to Figure 3.11. The **Common name for this CA** is the identity of your CA on the network. We will enter CertificateRootServer as the name. The name should be less than 64 characters. This is a limitation imposed by the Lightweight Directory Access Protocol (LDAP) used by Active

Directory. The name will be truncated if it exceeds 64 characters. We also need to enter the distinguished name suffix. This is also an LDAP requirement to populate the Active Directory. This entry will identify our root CA object from the rest of the Active Directory objects. Then, we finally choose the life span of a certificate. We have chosen one month as the preferred life span for a certificate generated by this root CA (the default industry standard is one year). Click **Next** to navigate to the next screen.

Figure 3.11 CA Identity Information

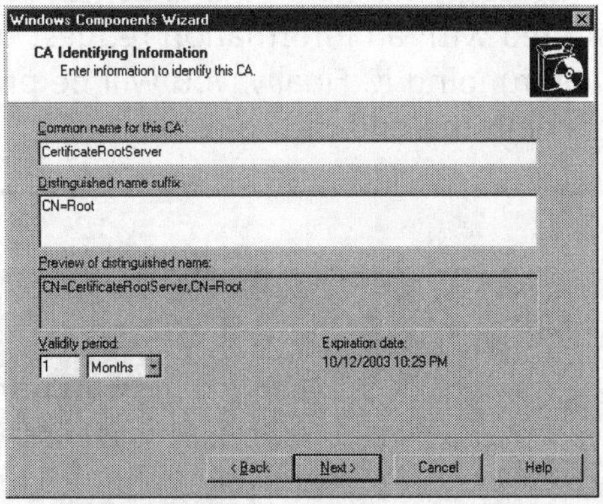

7. The next screen is to configure the certificate database locations and logs. The certificates are stored locally on the CA server. The default location for the certificates is %SystemRoot% \ System 32\certlog. The best practice is to store the certificate on a different physical disk. This will maximize the CA throughput of the server. Your screen should be similar to Figure 3.12. Click **Next** to proceed to the next screen.

Figure 3.12 Configuring Database Settings

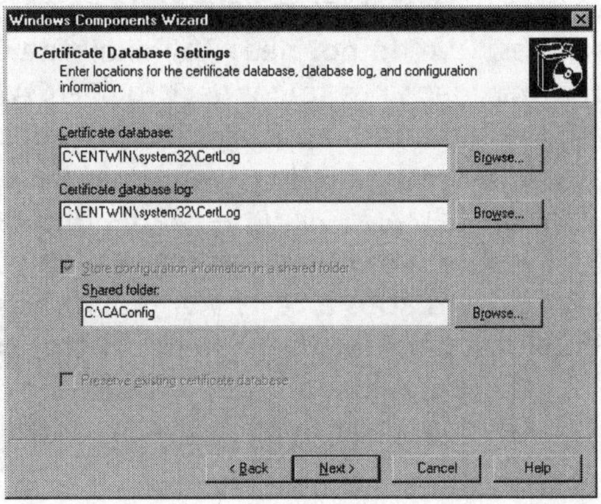

Exam Warning

The Active Directory does not act as a database for the stand-alone CA server. The installation will automatically populate the CA information in the Active Directory if an Active Directory is present on the network. The certificates are stored locally on the CA server and the Active Directory will be informed of the location. The certificates will be stored in user object containers in an enterprise CA implementation.

8. The next step will install the CA on the server. You will also be presented with an information request to stop IIS if you are already running it. Finally, you will be presented with a screen confirming the end of the setup.

Head of the Class...

CA Web Enrollment Support System

The Windows Server 2003 CA installation will provide an ASP Web front to request and manage certificates. This is installed by default during installation and is referred to as CA Web Enrollment support. You can also uninstall or reinstall this using the **Start | Control Panel | Add Remove Programs | Add Remove Windows Components** utility. We need to select **Certificate Authority** and click the **Details** button. We can select the **Certificate Service Web Enrollment Support** from the options. We can select or deselect the option to install or uninstall, respectively. This can be used as an alternative to the Microsoft Management Console (CA) window. However, some options are not available in the Web Enrollment Support system (for example, we cannot enable CA server auditing though this interface). This interface will add value to CA administrators to manage the certificates from multiple secure machines. (We do not need to install the CA MMC administration console on other machines to connect to the CA.)

The Web Enrollment Support system provides many services to CA administrators; for example, they can request a certificate using this tool. CA administrators can also view the status of a pending certificate and download a certificate or CRL using these Web pages. The Web enrollment support system adds a certsrv virtual directory to the hosting IIS machine. The local path for this system is **http://<Server Name>/certsrv/**. The Web Enrollment Support system is commonly used to issue certificates to Web browser applications to authenticate the users.

Let's look into some administrate tasks associated with Windows Server 2003 CA server. We will be looking into enrollment, renewal, revocation, and enable auditing on CA servers. We will use the CA Web Enrollment system to request a certificate and use the CA MMC to navigate through the certificate life cycle.

EXAM 70-298 OBJECTIVE 2.1.2

Designing Enrollment and Distribution

The first step is to request a certificate from the CA. This could be achieved using the Web Enrollment Support system. This interface will generate a certificate and add it to the pending queue of the CA. The CA administrator needs to open the MMC console and grant access to use the certificate.

EXERCISE 3.02

REQUEST A CERTIFICATE FROM THE WEB ENROLLMENT INTERFACE

1. Open an Internet Explorer window and navigate to **URL http://<Server Name>/certsrv/** (this will be http://devsvr01/certsrv/ for demonstration purposes).
2. Click the **Request a Certificate** link. You will be presented with a view similar to Figure 3.13. We are trying to create a certificate for Web browsers. Therefore, we will click the **Web Browser Certificate** link. You can also generate a certificate to authenticate your e-mails using this interface by selecting the **E-Mail Protection Certificate** link. The advance certificate request will present you with more options to create sophisticated certificates, including modifying hash algorithms and key lengths of key pairs to the default settings of the CA server.

Figure 3.13 Select a Certificate Type

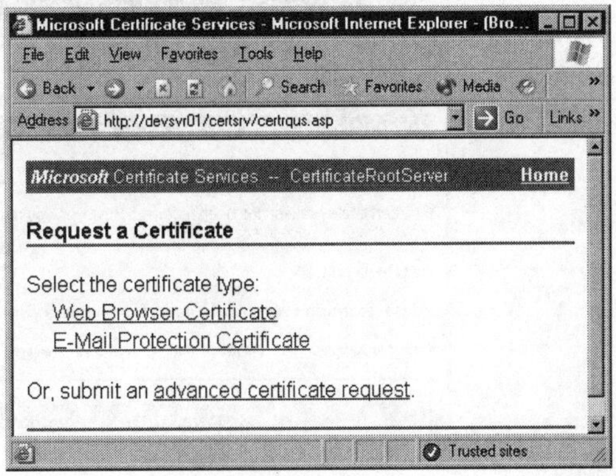

3. Figure 3.14 shows the next screen you will be presented with. Enter the user details for the certificate. You can also change the default CSP by selecting the **More Options** link.

Figure 3.14 Enter the User's Details to Issue a Certificate

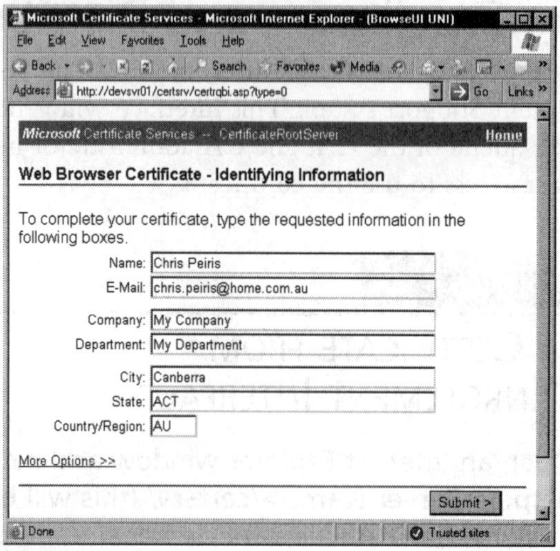

4. Click **Submit** to send the request to the CA server. This will enter the certificate details onto a CA pending queue. The CA administrator will approve or deny the request according to the organization policies. The confirmation screen looks similar to Figure 3.15. We need to keep track of the **Request ID**. We might need to refer to this when we approve the certificate from the pending queue. This ID is automatically generated by the CA server; therefore, your ID number will differ from the one in the exercises.

Figure 3.15 Confirmation Screen for a Certificate Request

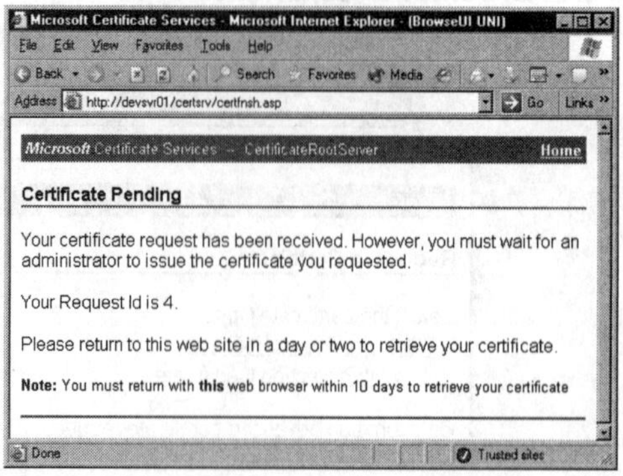

Any user in the enterprise can log on to this public Web site and request a certificate using these Web pages.

EXAM 70-298 OBJECTIVE 2.1.2

Approving Certificates by CA Administrators

Let's investigate the CA administrator's role that will approve or revoke these certificates. Note that we are switching roles from an enterprise user to a CA administrator to perform these tasks.

Exercise 3.03

Approve or Deny a Certificate from the CA Pending Queue

1. Navigate to **Start | Administration Tools | Certification Authority**.
2. The Certification Authority management console will appear. Navigate to and select **Certification Authority | <CA Server name> | Pending Requests**. This will be **Certification Authority (Local) | CertificateRootServer | Pending Requests** in our demonstration. Your screen should be similar to Figure 3.16.

Figure 3.16 Pending Queue of the CA

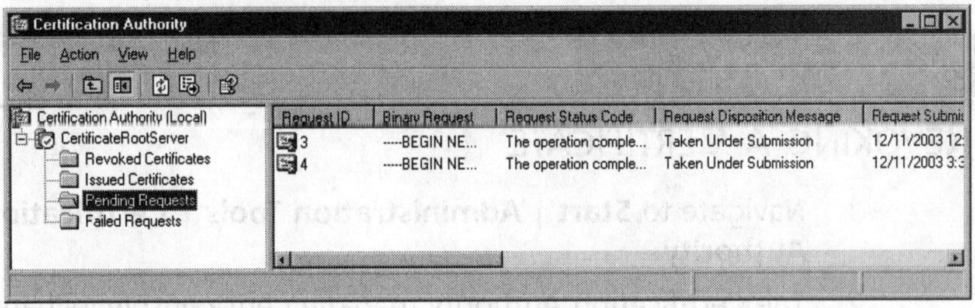

3. Right-click on the interested certificate. This will be the certificate with the **Request ID** 4 (refer to the previous exercise). You will get a context menu. Select **All tasks** from it and then select **Issue**. You can also deny the request by clicking the **Deny** option. Your screen will be similar to Figure 3.17. The certificate will be deleted form the **Pending Requests** and will be added to the **Issued Certificates** on approval by the CA administrators.

Figure 3.17 Approve a Certificate from Pending Queue

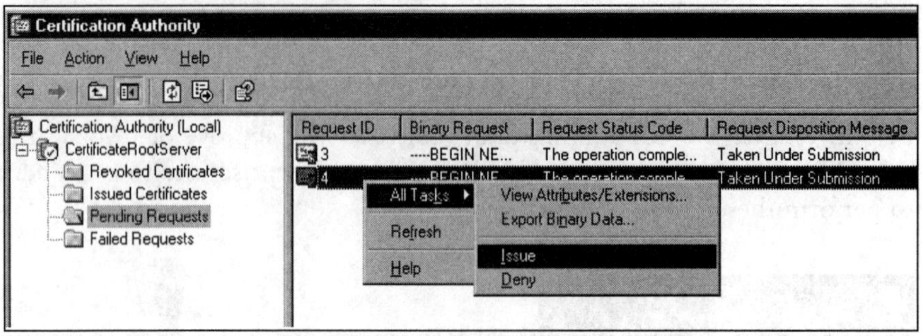

4. Navigate to the **Issued Certificate** folder. You should see the newly issued certificate (Request ID 4). You can view the certificate by double-clicking on the certificate.

EXAM 70-298 OBJECTIVE 2.1.3

Revoking Certificates by CA Administrators

The CA administrator can revoke a certificate before it expires. This is also done through the Certification Authority MMC snap-in. Exercise 3.04 lists the steps to revoke a certificate.

EXERCISE 3.04

REVOKING A CERTIFICATE

1. Navigate to **Start | Administration Tools | Certification Authority**.
2. The Certification Authority management console will appear. Navigate to and select **Certification Authority | <CA Server name>**. This will be **Certification Authority (Local) | CertificateRootServer** in our demonstration.
3. Navigate to the **Issued Certificates** and right-click on the certificate you want to revoke.
4. Select **All Tasks | Revoke Certificate**. The certificate will be moved from the **Issued Certificates** folder to the **Revoked Certificates** folder.

EXAM WARNING

Auto-enrollment will automatically issue certificates without a CA administrator. This feature was available in Windows 2000 Server. We could auto-enroll computer certificates in Windows 2000; however, we could not auto-enroll user certificates. The user details could be verified to a higher level of detail. Windows Server 2003 has a better model of integrating with Active Directory. Therefore, auto-enrollment for users is available under Windows Server 2003.

Auto-enrollment features are set by CA administrators in the certificate templates. A user who is authorized to use these Certificate templates will be auto-enrolled. Auto-renewal is also a new feature in Windows Server 2003. This capability will enable CA servers to renew certificates when they expire automatically without any human interaction.

EXAM 70-298 OBJECTIVE 2.1.3

Establishing Renewal and Auditing

We need to protect the public key and private key pairs of the enterprise. If these keys are compromised, the security of the enterprise is in serious jeopardy. Intruders can cause malicious harm to the resources by getting unauthorized access. A disgruntled employee could act as an intruder to sabotage the IT system. This intruder can log on to the CA server and issue fraudulent certificates to unauthorized users. What will you do as the CA administrator to avoid this scenario?

TEST DAY TIP

It is best practice to enable auditing on the CA server activity. This will allow us to see any attempts of hacking in to the CA server. Auditing is a new feature in Windows Server 2003. We can enable auditing on multiple activities that are related to issue certificates.

We can enable auditing on Windows Server 2003 with ease. Let's learn how to do this. Auditing will enable us to monitor activities to identify the issue.

EXERCISE 3.05

ENABLE AUDITING ON A CA SERVER

1. Navigate to **Start | Administration Tools | Certification Authority.**
2. The CA MMC will appear. Navigate to and select **Certification Authority | <CA Server name>**. This will be **Certification Authority (Local) | CertificateRootServer** in our demonstration.
3. Right-click and select **Properties** from the context menu. You will see the **<CA Server Name> Properties** window. Navigate to the **Auditing** tab. Your screen should be similar to Figure 3.18. We might need to track the CA activities. The intruder is changing the CA configuration and issuing fraudulent certificates to others. Therefore, we select the options shown in Figure 3.18.

Figure 3.18 Auditing Tab of the CA Properties

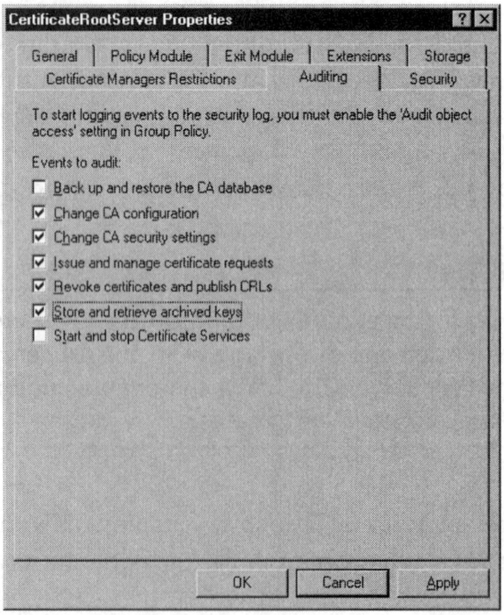

4. Click **Apply** to apply the new audit policy on the CA. The audit trial will be added to the **Security Log** in the **Event Viewer**.
5. Now we can monitor the Security Log in the Event Viewer and track down the disgruntled employee. (Every CA configuration, every CA server setting change, and so forth will be documented

in the security log in our demonstration.) The Event Viewer can be found at **Start | Administrative Tools | Event Viewer**.

After we track down the intruder, we might need to take some extra steps. The intruder was able to get into the CA server and issue certificates. Therefore, the public and private key pairs have been compromised on the CA server. Consequently, we need to reset the key pairs so that the old keys will not grant access to the system. This process is commonly referred as the *renewal of keys*. You will also need to renew the keys when they expire. Let's learn how to renew keys.

EXERCISE 3.06

RENEWAL OF CA KEYS

1. Navigate to **Start | Administration Tools | Certification Authority**.
2. The CA MMC will appear. Navigate to and **select Certification Authority | <CA Server name>**. This will be **Certification Authority (Local) | CertificateRootServer** in our demonstration.
3. Click on the **Action** menu item. Select **All tasks | Renew CA Certificates**.
4. The dialog box in Figure 3.19 will appear, asking you to stop the certificate server. Select **Yes**.

Figure 3.19 Confirmation to Stop the Certificate Service

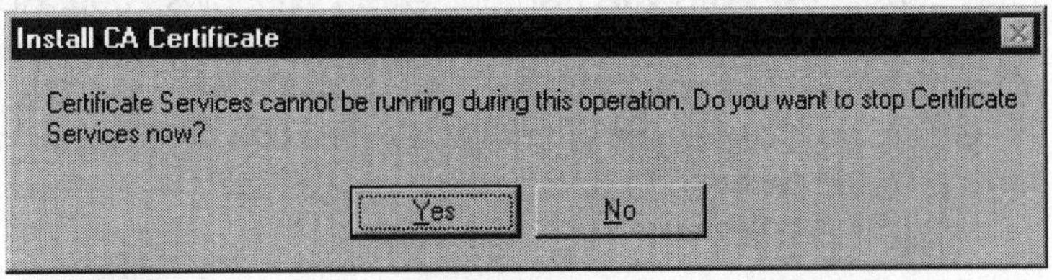

5. You can obtain a new certificate with the old key pairs. Unfortunately, this is not safe because the keys were compromised by the disgruntled employee. Therefore, we need to generate both the certificate and key pairs. You will be presented with a message screen that will confirm to change the keys. It will be similar to Figure 3.20. Click **Yes** to generate a new key pair. This will generate a new key pair and restart the certificate server.

This scenario could be an expensive exercise for the enterprise. It is easy to generate the public key on the server. However, distributing the private key to each employee or business partner will cost money and time. Therefore, we should take strict measures to protect the CA certificate information.

Figure 3.20 Confirmation to Generate New Keys

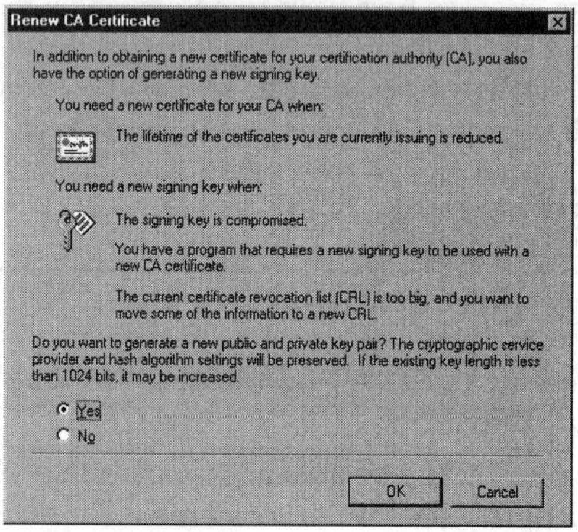

Test Day Tip

We can do all of these MMC console functions using the command-line utility *certutil.exe*. This was also present in Windows 2000. However, there are some new options available in Windows Server 2003 to mainly interact with the Active Directory. We can publish certificates and CRL lists directly to the Active Directory under Windows Server 2003 CA Server. This could be done with the following syntax.

certutil -dspublish [cert|crl]

Summary of Exam Objectives

This chapter concentrated on public key infrastructure (PKI) concepts on Windows Server 2003. We initially discussed the basics of PKI implementation. PKI is an asymmetric cryptography mechanism to secure information. We have two sets of keys under PKI, the public and the private key. The sender signs digital documents with the public key and sends to the receiver. This signing process has two steps. The first is to apply a hashing algorithm on top of the message. The hashed message is commonly referred to as the "digest message." The digest message is then mixed with the sender's key information to obtain the "message to be sent." The receiver will authenticate the sender's key with the help of an external CA authority (for example, VeriSign).

There are two types of certificate authorities (CAs): an enterprise CA and a stand-alone CA. An enterprise CA will communicate to the Active Directory to issue certificates. The stand-alone CA will not communicate with the Active Directory. The best practice is to use a three-tiered CA model in an enterprise. The first tier is a single root CA. The root CA will manage all the CAs in the enterprise. The root CA will directly manage the second tier. We refer to them as the *policy* or *intermediate* CAs. The number of policy CAs can change from organization to organization. The policy CAs will give instructions to issuing CAs. The issuing CAs will "issue" the certificates to clients.

The root CA and the policy CAs should be offline (disconnected from the network hierarchy). The issuing CAs are online to issue certificates. This is an important security measure to protect the CAs. The enterprise should have clear time windows to bring the root CAs and policy CAs online for updates (we need to update the CRL list to reflect new security measures).

The three-tier CA can be organized in many ways. They can be organized in a geographical structure to suit multinational companies. They can also be organized to reflect the organizational structure. In some cases, we need to have CAs that are independent of the governing CA (in this case, the CAs are not controlled by a root CA). A network CA structure is available to accommodate this scenario.

There are several threats against CA servers. We should be very careful with the root CA. The entire enterprise's security could be in jeopardy if the root CA is compromised. We should take measures to increase physical security and use smart cards for authentication. The smart cards will enhance security with a personal identification number (PIN) in addition to the private key. We can also use hardware CSP to enhance security.

Finally, we investigated the CA server setup in Windows Server 2003. Windows Server 2003 implements a Web Enrollment Support system to request certificates. It also supports auto-enrollments and auto-renewals. Windows Server 2003 also supports delta CRL lists. We can manage the CA server using the CA MMC snap-in or the *certutil.exe* command-line tool.

Exam Objectives Fast Track

Design a Public Key Infrastructure (PKI) that Uses Certificate Services

- ☑ The first step of a PKI implementation is to design the root CA. The root CA has a self-signed certificate that must not be compromised. There is only one root CA in a Windows Server 2003 environment.
- ☑ The root CA should communicate with at least two intermediary CAs (one for issuing internal certificates and one for external). The intermediary or policy CAs should control multiple issuing CAs who will submit the certificate to users.
- ☑ There are two types of CAs. The enterprise CAs will communicate to an Active Directory and issue automatic certificates. The certificate information can be obtained by the Windows account information and the Active Directory settings.
- ☑ The stand-alone CAs do not communicate with an Active Directory. They issue certificates with the approval of a CA administrator. They can be configured to issue automatic certificates; however, it is not recommended.
- ☑ An enterprise can design its CA structure according to the location or the organization structure. These will be based on the three-tiered CA model. You can also adapt a network trust model where the cross certificates will enable access to independent CAs across multiple independent IT departments.
- ☑ The root and the intermediary CAs should be offline. They can be made offline by shutting down the computer, CA service, or configuring as a Windows Server 2003 stand-alone server that is disconnected form the domain.
- ☑ You can also use hardware CSPs and smart cards to enhance CA security in the enterprise. Smart cards will force the user to have the key in the smart card and to provide a PIN number to confirm authenticity.

Design a Logical Authentication Strategy

- ☑ Install the Windows Server 2003 Service on an NTFS system. Do not use a FAT file system. This will use Windows authentication details and smooth access to Active Directory.

- ☑ Windows Server 2003 introduces a Web Enrollment Support system. This system will enable you to issue certificates to Web pages and manage them.
- ☑ You can issue, deny, revoke, and reissue certificates using the CA MMC. You can also use the command-line utility *certutil.exe*.
- ☑ Any user can request a certificate through the Web Enrollment Support system. The request will sit in a pending queue until the CA administrator approves it. The CA administrator will issue or deny the certificate using the MMC console. The pending certificate is moved to **issued certificates** or **denied certificate** folders depending on the action.
- ☑ It is recommended to enable auditing on the CA server. This will monitor the activity on the server. The audit trail can be viewed in the **Security log** of the **Event log**.
- ☑ You might need to revoke the certificates and renew the key pair if you detect any unauthorized activities. These activities can be monitored using the audit trail.
- ☑ Windows Server 2003 also supports a new auto-enrollment and auto-renewal features.

Exam Objectives Frequently Asked Questions

The following Frequently Asked Questions, answered by the authors of this book, are designed to both measure your understanding of the Exam Objectives presented in this chapter, and to assist you with real-life implementation of these concepts. You will also gain access to thousands of other FAQs at ITFAQnet.com.

Q: How many root CAs can an enterprise have?

A: You can only have one root CA. This root CA will manage one or many other CAs.

Q: Can the root CAs issue certificates?

A: Yes; however, it is not recommended. The root CA should be protected by the intermediary CAs and should be disconnected from the network.

Q: Are we only supposed to have two intermediary CAs? Can we have multiple CAs?

A: Yes. The best practice is to have an internal and external intermediary CA (minimal requirement). You can design the PKI architecture to have multiple CAs for other purposes. (You might have a large client that accumulates 60 percent of your business. You can dedicate a special external CA just for this client.)

Q: Can an enterprise PKI architecture exist without a root CA?

A: Yes. A network trust hierarchy model does not have a root CA. However, a global directory (such as Active Directory) must be populated to find the other "fellow" CAs of the enterprise.

Q: Can we have certificate template in stand-alone CAs?

A: Yes. Certificate templates are available in both enterprise and stand-alone servers.

Q: Do we need Active Directory support to create certificate templates in the organization?

A: Yes. Certificate templates will not be available if no Active Directory is present.

Self Test

A Quick Answer Key follows the Self Test questions. For complete questions, answers, and explanations to the Self Test questions in this chapter as well as the other chapters in this book, see the Self Test Appendix.

Designing a Public Key Infrastructure

1. NoMoreHackers Inc. is implementing a PKI implementation. You have been asked to work as a consultant to design the PKI blueprint for the company. You have met with the CIO and the senior management to gather the requirements. You are confident of creating a sophisticated PKI architecture for the company. What will be your first step in the process?

   A. Determine the location of the CAs.

   B. Design the root CA.

   C. Determine which CA trust hierarchy we will use.

   D. Design the head office CA first, and then proceed to the regional offices.

2. IronCladSecurity Ltd's organization structure has several components. The majority of IT needs of the enterprise are met by the IronCladSecurity staff. This includes manufacturing, accounting, and sales divisions of the company. They also subcontract to other IT companies to provide IT services. The proposed PKI security structure should support all these business activities. What do you recommend to implement at IronCladSecurity under Windows Server 2003?

A. Have one root CA and one intermediary CA.

B. Have one root CA for internal use and one intermediary for external use.

C. Have one root CA and two intermediaries for internal and external use.

D. Have two root CAs for internal and external use.

3. You are contemplating the hierarchy of the CA servers at IronCladSecurity. IronCladSecurity has 40 offices in the United States, Germany, and Singapore. They have both contractors and permanent employees working for them, and have multiple IT departments. However, there is no Active Directory implementation for the enterprise. IronCladSecurity prefers to have independent entries as subsidiaries. Therefore, they do not prefer to link the three IT systems to accommodate a global IT system. What trust hierarchies can IronCladSecurity support?

   A. Geographical and network

   B. Network and organizational structure

   C. Geographical and organizational structure

   D. Organizational structure and network

4. You are reviewing a previous PKI implementation of a company called NoMoreHackers. It has come to your attention that all of the CA servers are connected to the network. The root CA, intermediary, and issuing CAs are connected to the same domain. You believe this a severe security risk and have instructed the company to take the servers offline. What step will not assist you to make the CA servers offline?

   A. Shut down the CA computer.

   B. Shut down the CA service.

   C. Shut down the CSP service.

   D. Configure CA as a Windows Server 2003 stand-alone server that is not connected to the domain.

5. You are proposing a new PKI implementation for NoMoreHackers to replace the existing security structure. You have proposed a three-tier CA server structure with online and offline CAs to protect the CAs from intruders. You will have root CA, policy CAs, and issuing CAs in your implementation. Which CAs will be set as offline CAs?

   A. Only the root CA; the issuing and policy CAs can be online.

   B. The root CAs and policy CAs; the issuing CAs will be online.

C. Only the policy CAs; the root CA and issuing CAs can be online.

D. The policy and issuing CAs will be offline; the root CA will be online.

Designing Certificate Distribution

6. You are about to install a CA on Windows Server 2003. You have a choice of two machines. One is a single processor machine with 1GB of memory with an existing Windows Server 2003 on a FAT file system. The other system is a twin processor with 512MB of memory on an NTFS file system. Which one would you choose to host the CA?

   A. Use the first CA with 1GB of memory. The CA needs a lot of memory.

   B. Use the first option because of the FAT file system.

   C. Use the second option because Windows Server 2003 works best on a single-server system.

   D. Use the second system because of the NTFS system.

7. We are going through the wizards to install a CA on a Windows Server 2003 server. We have selected the type as a stand-alone root CA. We have also selected the MS Strong Cryptographic Provider as the CSP. Now we need to select a hashing algorithm for the private and public key pair. What is a Windows 2003 hashing algorithm that comes with default CA installation?

   A. Asymmetric

   B. .NET Crypto API

   C. Triple DES

   D. SHA-1

8. Our management has asked us to install a CA to issue certificates to the employees and the business partners of our company. We are contemplating either Windows 2000 Server or Windows Server 2003 as our CA implementation. You have read that there are several new features in the Windows Server 2003 CA architecture that support a better implementation for the company. What are the new features?

   A. Certificate templates

   B. Auto-enrollment and Active Directory support

   C. Web enrollment support interface and Active Directory support

   D. Auto-enrollment and Web enrollment support interface

9. You are been appointed as the new CA administrator of one of the subordinate CA servers. You will administer the CA through the MMC Certification Authority application. You are experimenting with the different functionalities of the CA console. What is not available to you modify in the CA MMC console?
   A. Revoke certificates
   B. Issue certificates from the pending queue
   C. View certificate details
   D. Change certificate's hash algorithm

10. Several of your company resources are behaving strangely. You have noticed that some of the printer queues were deleted using an administrator account. All of these printers are protected using the PKI certificates of the company. You suspect that someone has obtained the CA keys and is impersonating the administrator account to delete the print queue. How will you solve this puzzle?
    A. Monitor the CA auditing logs and renew the CA keys.
    B. Disable auditing to save space for larger new key pairs.
    C. Monitor the CA auditing logs; however, stick with the old key pairs.
    D. Disable auditing and generate a new public key; however, use the same private key.

Self Test Quick Answer Key

For complete questions, answers, and explanations to the Self Test questions in this chapter as well as the other chapters in this book, see the Self Test Appendix.

1. **B**
2. **C**
3. **C**
4. **C**
5. **B**
6. **D**
7. **D**
8. **D**
9. **D**
10. **A**

Chapter 4

MCSE 70-298

Securing the Network Management Process

Exam Objectives in this Chapter:

- 2.3 Designing security for network management
- 2.3.1 Managing the risk of managing networks.
- 2.3.2 Design the administration of servers by using common administration tools. Tools include Microsoft Management Console (MMC), Terminal Server, Remote Desktop for Adminstrations, Remote Assistance, and Telnet.
- 2.3.3 Design security for Emergency Management Services.
- 2.4 Designing a security update infrastructure
- 2.4.1 Designing a Software Update Services (SUS) infrastructure.
- 2.4.2 Design Group Policy to deploy software updates.
- 2.2.2 Design forest and domain trust models.
- 2.2.3 Design security that meets interoperability requirements.

- ☑ Summary of Exam Objectives
- ☑ Exam Objectives Fast Track
- ☑ Exam Objectives Frequently Asked Questions
- ☑ Self Test
- ☑ Self Test Quick Answer Key

Introduction

Most security recommendations focus on ways to protect your end users' data, resources, and network traffic, but the network management process itself can quickly become an avenue for an attacker to gain a foothold on your network if it is not handled properly. Improper use of administrative tools can introduce security vulnerabilities just as easily as user behavior—perhaps even *more* easily, since the very nature of the administrator is that he or she can perform high-level tasks that, when done improperly, can have catastrophic effects on the stability of a network or server. To address this topic, we begin this chapter with a discussion of ways to secure the administrative process. As with most security measures, this effort consists of both technical measures to secure the use of specific administrative utilities (such as Telnet, Remote Desktop, and Emergency Management Services) and human measures to institute security policies concerning the way a network should and should not be administered.

Once we've discussed the necessary steps in securing the administrative process, we'll look at two common tasks for security administrators: creating a patch management strategy and designing trust relationships for large-scale networks. Although Windows Server 2003 includes major improvements in the security of Microsoft operating systems, the need to apply security updates to computers in an enterprise network is an inescapable reality. To address this need, Microsoft has made many tools and utilities freely available to network administrators, such as the Microsoft Baseline Security Analyzer (MBSA) and the Software Update Service (SUS). Understanding how to implement these tools will greatly improve the overall security process when you're designing and implementing a secure Windows Server 2003 network.

We'll wrap up this chapter with a look at the domain and forest trust model in Windows Server 2003. The notion of trusts goes back as far as the introduction of Windows NT, but the more recent server operating systems have made many more options available for administrators to grant access across an enterprise without sacrificing security or ease of administration. The trust process itself should be familiar to you from your studies for the MCSE 2003 Core Four Exams, so we'll focus on how to design the domain and forest to provide the best possible security in a number of scenarios, including enterprises that are supporting down-level or non-Microsoft clients and services.

EXAM 70-298 OBJECTIVE 2.3

Securing the Network Management Process

The problem of implementing security in networks lies in the fact that you are always defending against attacks and you are defending against an enemy you don't know, don't see, and can't predict. As an administrator, you need to protect every aspect of your network to prevent an attack, whereas an attacker only needs to find a single opening to gain malicious access to your resources.

On the physical network, your first priority is to restrict access to the network perimeter with a firewall or through some kind of secure communications, such as a virtual private network. Once you're within the network itself, you'll use administrative tools to create a file-and-folder permission structure that will restrict unauthorized access to your data by any internal users. You'll also secure your user accounts by creating strong password policies and auditing user access and actions through the Group Policy Editor.

But what about the actual tools that you're using to perform these tasks? The very tools and utilities that you use to administer your network can create a huge potential for misuse, allowing malicious attackers to gain administrative access to a machine or an entire network. Imagine what could happen if an attacker gained access to the DNS Management MMC snap-in: They could create, delete, or modify host entries to redirect your clients to malicious or compromised Web hosts, and they could view your DNS registrations to obtain a complete picture of your network to use for further attack. Or think about a malicious user finding a way to use DHCP Manager to change scope information, removing or changing address assignment information and rendering your clients incapable of accessing network resources. In perhaps the worst-case scenario, consider the potential damage if an attacker obtained administrative access to the Active Directory Users and Computers utility; at this point they would have *carte blanche* to create and delete user and computer accounts, change group information, and otherwise entirely compromise your user account database.

Because of this potential for misuse, you should always set security guidelines and policies on how your network should be administered. Windows Server 2003 allows you to implement role-based administration and enforce many security guidelines and policies using Group Policy and Delegation of Administration, as we will see in the upcoming sections of this chapter.

EXAM 70-298 OBJECTIVE 2.3.1

Managing the Risks of Network Administration

When a company experiences period of growth and expansion, it often adds more IT staff in addition to infrastructure such as servers and networking equipment. There will probably be situations in which administrators are hired to do specific tasks, or they could be less experienced administrators who aren't strong in all aspects of the network management process. For this reason, you don't want to grant all your administrators the same level of administrative rights, because if an administrator or engineer is unfamiliar with a particular technology, he or she may introduce a security risk to your network by either exploring the network out of curiosity or by failing to ask for help performing a particular task. For example, if you hired a new network administrator who has never worked with DNS before, but you place no restrictions on that person's authority to administer your company's DNS server, he or she may cause as much damage to your DNS records due to a lack of knowledge as any malicious attacker. However, if you have delegated administration and management policies in place, you will be able to better control the authority held by various members of your administrative staff. Another reason that you want to implement this kind of security is to protect your network against actively malicious administrators seeking to harm a network. Having a network management policy in place will also help you secure your network against your own IT staff, if such protection becomes necessary.

As you can see, the network administration process itself can become a threat to the security of your enterprise network if you do not take steps to design a secure model for network management. If this model is weak or nonexistent, you can introduce vulnerabilities stemming from user accounts that possess excessive administrative rights (as in the scenario just mentioned), or the lack of a framework or stated policy can cause your organization to make poor decisions regarding information security, such as failing to run any kind of background or reference check on someone beginning work as a network administrator.

Network administrators can also be vulnerable to social engineering attacks because of the elevated privileges and permissions that they hold on a network. Say that an attacker obtains the telephone number to your help desk and calls pretending to be the personal assistant to the vice president of sales. The caller says that this VP is going into a meeting and needs his password reset right away, or it's going to cost the company a large account because he won't be able to give his sales presentation at the meeting with the big client. If your help desk has no policies in place to verify this caller's identity, the help desk staff may reset the password as requested, since most people really want to be helpful and don't want to get themselves in trouble with a VP. Using this kind of social engineering, the attacker has now obtained a valid password for the VP's user account, which he or she can now use to infiltrate your network. Having policies in place will not only inform administrators about what actions they should take in situations like this—it also lets your users know what is expected of *them*—in other words, no matter what their position in the company, they will be required to go to the help desk in person to have a password reset, or whatever is the appropriate policy for your organization.

Test Day Tip

Remember that a *social engineering* attack is one that uses nontechnical means to obtain information about or access to your network. This can take the form of an attacker trying to impersonate someone over the phone, posing as a contractor to gain entry to a server room, or otherwise deceiving technical or nontechnical personnel into revealing information, running malicious applications, and the like.

Security Policies for Administrators and IT Personnel

You'll use a network management policy to specify ways to manage your enterprise network in a secure manner. As we've just mentioned, improper use of management tools can create just as many security vulnerabilities as the behavior of any misbehaving user or malicious attacker. Because your organization needs to trust its administrators to use their authority in a responsible fashion, you'll need some type of policy in place to regulate the people who can possess administrative rights and be able to manage network resources such as file resources and infrastructure services. A security policy will also ensure that administrators manage your network resources securely and are themselves protected against attackers when they use their administrative privileges. A properly defined network management policy includes a detailed explanation of the tools for managing a network, a list of users or user groups who can manage the network, and appropriate procedures for managing network resources.

An example of a technical means of controlling the administration process would be implementing Group Policy on an OU where user accounts reside. This Group Policy Object (GPO) might prevent certain administrators creating their own MMC consoles and force them to use only the tools to which you have given them access through a customized MMC console. To further tighten and harden this security model, you can even explicitly allow or deny access to MMC snap-ins through Group Policy so that if the administrator were able to access an MMC console in author mode, the only tools he or she would be able to add would be those that you have explicitly given them access to.

Another piece of the security policy puzzle is less amenable to technical controls and revolves instead around administrative policies for the way your network should be administered. This includes a certain amount of due diligence and care in how administrative credentials are used, creating a second "everyday" account and performing administrative tasks using the *RunAs* function. This diligence also extends to performing security functions in a timely manner, including disabling accounts of former employees and changing administrative and service account passwords on a regular basis. Finally, your administrators should be aware of the tools that are acceptable for use in managing a network, and they should be aware of the most secure way to use each of them. We'll discuss several of these utilities in upcoming sections.

Delegating Authority Securely

Because any organization needs to place as much trust in its network administrators as it does in its financial, human resources, or legal personnel, when securing your network management model it's important that you take the greatest care in selecting those individuals. This becomes even more critical for individuals who possess far-reaching administrative rights, such as those assigned to the Domain Admins or Enterprise Admins groups. At a minimum, you should perform some type of background or reference check on any new IT personnel you interview. Once they are in place, they need to be educated—not only on the technical aspects of the tasks that they'll be performing, but in how to comply with any company or industry policies and regulations to maintain security.

When you get down to the technical aspects of delegating authority over portions of the Active Directory tree, remember that best practices suggest that you divide administrative duties among your IT staff so that they have enough permission to do the task they were hired to do, but not an excessive amount beyond that. This is another application—the "least privilege" concept, which refers to granting users (in this case, administrators) the least amount of rights and permissions possible and then relaxing the permission structure only as a specific need arises. Once you begin to delegate administrative rights to other staff members, you should also create and maintain an audit policy that includes monitoring network administration activities so that you can be sure that administrative tasks are being performed correctly and appropriately.

Within Active Directory itself, you can structure your delegation strategy based on roles. For example, let's say that you have both Web and application servers in your organization, and each of these server types has its own team of administrators. You can group your Web servers into a single OU and then delegate administration of this OU to the Web servers administrators. You can then do the same for an Application Servers OU. The result would be that the Web servers and application servers administrators would be able to perform administrative tasks only within the scope of their respective OUs. You can lock this down even further using predefined MMC consoles that will restrict the tasks administrators can perform, even within the OUs over which they have authority. By implementing a model like this, you create additional layers of security for your network (sometimes referred to as *defense in depth*), so if an administrative account in one OU is compromised or if an administrator were to decide to wreck havoc on the network, the scope of any damage would be isolated to the OU that the specific administrative account has been delegated to manage.

In Exercise 4.01, we'll create a new OU within a Windows Server 2003 domain, then delegate the ability to manage user accounts to a user within the OU.

EXERCISE 4.01

CREATING AN ORGANIZATIONAL UNIT AND DELEGATING CONTROL TO A LOCAL ADMINISTRATOR

1. Open **Active Directory Users and Computers**.
2. Right-click the domain, then select **New | Organizational Unit**. Enter a descriptive name for the OU and click **OK**.

3. From the MMC console, right-click the OU that you just created. (Press **F5** to refresh the console if you don't see the new OU listed.)
4. Click **Delegate control** to start the Delegation of Control Wizard.
5. Click **Next** to bypass the introduction screen.
6. On the Users or Groups screen, click **Add** to specify the users who should have the administrative rights you specify for this OU. Click **Next** when you're ready to continue.
7. In the **Tasks to Delegate** screen shown in Figure 4.1, you can either select one or more preconfigured tasks to delegate or create a custom task. In this example, we're going to delegate the ability to **Create, delete and manage user accounts**. Make that selection and click **Next** to continue.

Figure 4.1 Using the Delegation of Control Wizard

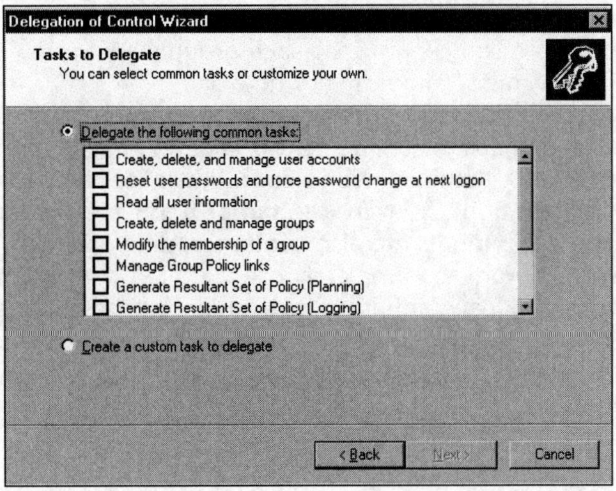

8. On the Summary screen, review the selections you've made, and click **Finish** to complete the delegation process.

Designing & Planning...

Putting It All Together: Designing the Network Management Policy

So you've taken on the administration of a network for which the management policy is ad hoc at best, nonexistent at worst. Where do you start when you have to start from scratch? Understanding the steps in creating a network management design will be a useful tool, both for the 70-298 exam as well as in the real world.

Your first step should be to determine *how* your network is (or is going to be) managed. This management model could be a centralized one, where administration is performed by a small group of administrators, usually at a single location. This type of network management provides a great deal of security at the expense of a certain amount of flexibility. (Think of the groans from remote sales offices when they need to "call corporate" to get a password reset or set up a user ID for a temporary employee.) At the opposite end of the spectrum is a *decentralized* management model, in which different management tasks are performed by smaller, often geographically distant administrative groups. This provides more flexibility than a centralized model, but you need to be careful that each group's autonomy doesn't negatively impact the overall security of your network.

Another option for network management is *outsourcing*, whereby a third party (perhaps a management firm or an individual consultant) handles all your network administration needs. You'll see this most often in smaller companies that don't need (or can't afford) to have IT administration on site full time, but this model has also begun cropping up even in large-scale organizations that want to completely concentrate on their company's products or services and leave administrative tasks to "the experts." Obviously, the model you choose is unlikely to fit neatly into one of these categories and will be a combination that best suits your needs.

EXAM 70-298 OBJECTIVE 2.3.2

Securing Common Administrative Tools

All the security in the world can't help if the tools at the administrator's disposal are not properly secured. These tools are designed to allow you to make major modifications to and troubleshoot your network; if these tools fall into the wrong hands, they can be used to damage and interrupt business productivity in your organization. Inappropriate use of network management tools (either by administrator themselves or by attackers gaining access to them) can reveal administrative credentials and other sensitive information about your network. Securing the network management process involves a delicate combination of managing people, technology, and policy; a well-designed plan takes each of these areas into account to ensure that the network remains secure.

Microsoft Management Console

The Microsoft management Console (MMC) is not an administrative tool itself, but it provides a framework for various utilities called *snap-ins* to manage various pieces of the Windows Server 2003 network. You can load a single snap-in into an MMC console or create custom consoles containing multiple management utilities. Some organizations allow administrators to load and use any snap-in that they want. This can create security issues, however, in that any attacker who was able to gain administrative access to the MMC would be able to launch any available utility and wreak havoc on the entire network as a result. Security best practices call for creating custom MMC consoles for administrators that contain only the utilities they need and restricting access to those utilities that they *don't* need. You can do this by building custom consoles and locking them down by removing the Author Mode option, which allows users to add and remove snap-ins. You can enforce these types of restrictions using Group Policy in the \User Configuration\Administrative Templates\Windows Components\Microsoft Management Console node. The MMC-specific settings you can configure are:

- **Restricted/Permitted snap-ins** This container contains a list of all the snap-ins that are available to add through an MMC console. You can permit or restrict access to every snap-in based on the people for whom you are configuring this policy.
- **Restrict the user form entering author mode** By enabling this setting, you prevent the user from entering author mode in the MMC, which means that the user will not be able to modify the MMC console you created for them. Without this policy, an administrator would be able to get around your permission, enter author mode, and add more snap-ins you didn't intend to allow that person to use.
- **Restrict users to the explicitly permitted list of snap-ins** This setting is used in conjunction with the Restricted/Permitted snap-ins. If you enable this setting, all the snap-ins are disabled except those that you explicitly allowed in the Restricted/Permitted snap-ins. If you disable or do not configure this setting, all snap-ins are enabled except those that you explicitly restricted in the Restricted/Permitted snap-ins.

Terminal Server

Since its integration into Windows 2000, Terminal Services has proved to be an invaluable remote administration tool as well as a great application server platform. With Terminal Services, you can log in to your Windows Server 2003 machines and perform administrative tasks from virtually any type of device, including Pocket PC devices and Windows CE devices. The power and convenience of Terminal Services is obvious; however, this power comes with the potential to introduce security vulnerabilities into your network if the use of this technology isn't carefully managed. This risk is especially great because Terminal Services is such a well-known application that it provides a tempting target for malicious users or hackers to attempt to gain access to your network. All that any attacker needs to know is the server's IP address, DNS, or NetBIOS name and he or she can try to access the Windows logon screen and attempt to log on to the server.

EXAM WARNING

Another term you might hear when people discuss the Windows logon screen is the *GINA*, which is short for *graphical identification and authentication*.

Like Windows 2000, Windows Server 2003 has two operating modes for Terminal Server, in:

- **Remote Desktop for Administration** We discuss this section a little later in this chapter. This is the mode you would put your Terminal Server in if you only needed the feature for administrative purposes. Two simultaneous connections are allowed when the server is in this mode. This remains unchanged from Windows 2000.
- **Terminal Services (formerly Application server mode in Windows 2000)** This mode enables the Terminal Server to accept multiple simultaneous client connections that can run applications on the Terminal Server. However, for the purposes of this book, we only discuss how to secure the Remote Desktop for Administration feature of Terminal Server.

So, what kinds of countermeasures can you take to protect yourself against attacks targeting your Terminal Servers? Before we answer that, it's good to note that no significant vulnerabilities or security breaches have been recorded against the Terminal Services function. Although this is certainly a good thing, it can change quickly, and you should be proactive in securing your Terminal Services installation. The following sections describe some things you can do to protect yourself and your network against attacks directed at your Terminal Servers.

Changing the Terminal Services Port

By default, Terminal Services listens for incoming connections on TCP port 3389. This means that all a hacker would require in order to launch a session, access the GINA, and start a brute-force password attack would be the Terminal Services Client, which is a free downloadable tool. By changing the TCP port the server listens on, you greatly increase the difficulty for an attacker to access the Ctrl + Alt + Del screen—the attacker would need to know not only the IP address or DNS name of the Terminal Server but also the new port that Terminal Services is listening on. The new Terminal Services Client in Windows XP and Windows Server 2003 (also called Remote Desktop) will allow you to specify the port you want to use to connect to the Terminal Server, a feature that was previously unavailable with earlier versions of the client. To change the TCP port that the Terminal Server listens on, follow these steps:

1. Click **Start | Run | Regedt32**.
2. Drill down to the following registry key: **HKEY_LOCAL_MACHINE\System\CurrentControlSet\Control\TerminalServer\WinStations\RDP-Tcp**.
3. Find the Sub key PortNumber (you will notice it is set to the default, 3389).
4. Change it in hex to whatever port number you decide you want the protocol to listen on.
5. Reboot the Terminal Server.

Once the port on the Terminal Server is changed, users who need to access Terminal Services will need to know the port the server is configured to listen on and need to make some configuration changes before they can access the server. In Exercise 4.02, we'll walk through the steps involved in changing the Terminal Services port from the client connection.

EXERCISE 4.02

CHANGING THE DEFAULT TERMINAL SERVICES CLIENT PORT

1. From your Windows XP client, launch **Remote Desktop Connection**, usually by clicking **Start | All Programs | Communications | Remote Desktop Connection**.
2. Type in the server name or IP address in the Computer: text box, and append that with the port number (in the form **server-name:port number**), as shown in Figure 4.2.

Figure 4.2 Creating a Remote Desktop Connection

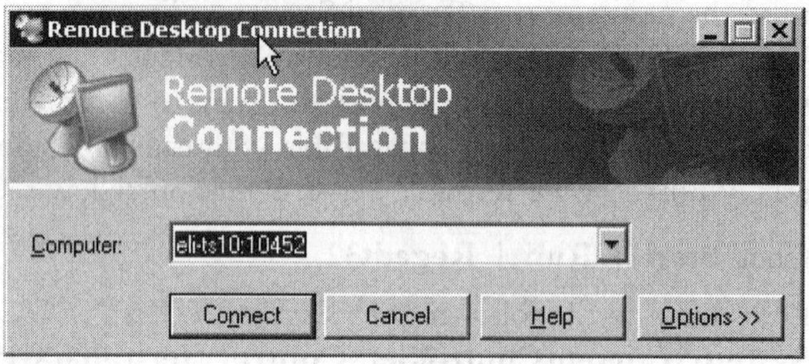

3. From the Remote Desktop Connection window, click **Options**.
4. You will see a window to configure any other necessary connection settings, as shown in Figure 4.3.
5. Click **Save As** and save the connection, making sure you preserver the **.RDP** extension.

Figure 4.3 Configuring the Remote Desktop Connection

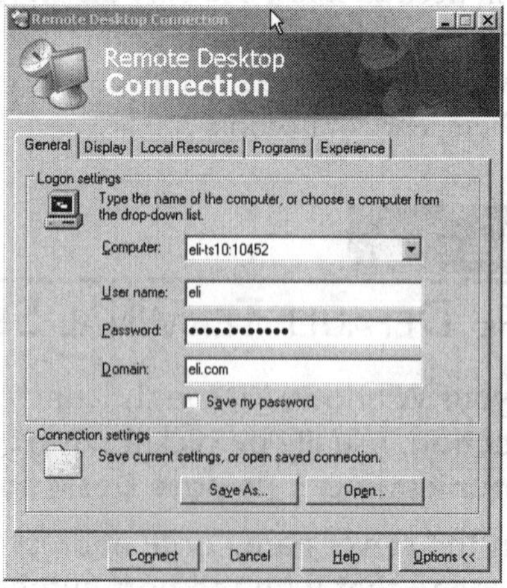

If you don't want to modify the server port for every connection you make, you could modify the Default.rdp file from the client machine you are using to connect to a Terminal Server and set the server port within the Default.rdp. Doing this ensures that every connection you create will have the new port configured in it automatically. However, be careful with this tactic, since you have just written down the server port in a well-known file location, which means that any knowledgeable attacker can check it to see if you have exposed the new port number in this manner.

Remote Desktop for Administration

In Windows 2000, to enable Remote Administration for administrators, you had to open Add/Remove Programs in Control Panel and actually install Terminal Services and, during that process, select this mode. With Windows Server 2003, this process has been modified. All you have to do to enable Remote Administration mode is to enable it through the Remote tab in the Control Panel's System, as follows:

1. Click **Start | Control Panel | System**.
2. Tab to **Remote** (see Figure 4.4).
3. Check the box next to **Turn on Remote Assistance and allow invitations to be sent from this computer**.

Figure 4.4 Activating Remote Assistance

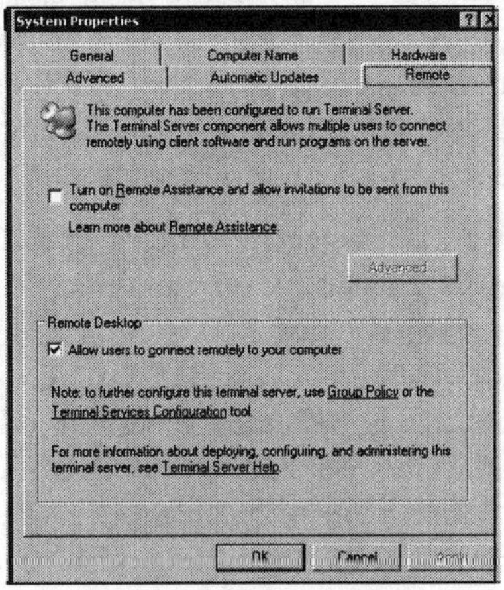

Windows Server 2003 has made several security enhancements to the Terminal Services and Remote Desktop for Administration software pieces that greatly increase your ability to secure this portion of your network management model. Some of these security improvements are as follows:

- **Security Policy Editor** You can assign user rights to Terminal Services user using the Security Policy Editor utility. This will give the specified users the ability to log on to a Terminal Server if they are not members of the Remote Desktop Users group (described elsewhere in this section).

Exam Warning

If you have a multihomed Terminal Server and you need to set permissions to the server that are specific to each NIC, you'll need to use the Terminal Services Connection Configuration utility that was common in previous versions of TS.

- **128-bit encryption** By default, all incoming Terminal Server connections will be secured using 128-bit RC4 encryption. You can specify that only 128-bit connections be allowed; however, bear in mind that older client operating systems may only be capable of encryption that's lower than 128 bit, which would render them unable to connect.
- **FIPS compliance** FIPS is an additional level of encryption included with Terminal Server in Windows Server 2003. This level of security refers to the Federal Information Processing Standard (FIPS) encryption algorithm. It is designed to provide compliance for organizations that require this level of encryption for server-to-client communications.
- **Remote Desktop Users group** Instead of adding individual users to the Terminal Services Connection Configuration (TSCC) program used in previous TS versions, with Windows 2003 you can simply make them members of the Remote Desktop Users (RDU) group. You can use this as part of a group nesting strategy whereby you add the Domain Users group to the RDU group, which would allow anyone with a valid user account on your network to gain access to the Terminal Server, or you can restrict group membership in RDU to filter who has access to Terminal Services.
- **Software restriction policies** Just as with a regular workstation connection, you can use software restriction policies in Windows Server 2003 to simplify the process of locking down your Terminal Servers by only allowing certain programs to be run by specified users. For Terminal Services, this feature is now built directly into the operating system, replacing the Application Security tool used by administrators to lock down earlier versions of TS.
- **Single-session policy** For an extremely high-security environment, you can limit your users to a single Terminal Server session, regardless of whether it is active or idle. You can even enforce this setting across multiple Terminal Servers if you are using a TS "farm" to support a large number of connections.

Remote Assistance

Remote Assistance is a great help-desk and troubleshooting tool offered with Windows XP and Windows Server 2003, but just like everything else, it can create a security hole if it's not properly configured. This tool essentially grants another user the ability to remotely control another computer's keyboard and mouse, allowing that person to assist in troubleshooting a particular problem. As you can imagine, allowing this capability to fall into the wrong hands can have a devastating effect on your network clients and servers. The largest risk associated with Remote Assistance is that the remote user has access to the exact same resources as the local user who has requested help. The benefit of this tool, obviously, is that the remote user can see exactly what's going on and help the user accordingly. Unfortunately, if a malicious user is able to create a Remote Assistance session, he or she will potentially have access to confidential system files and data on your network.

To limit your vulnerability to security issues caused by Remote Assistance, don't rely on your users to use their best judgment on how to control access to their machines. Rather, set up Group Policy to only allow IT support personnel to take advantage of Remote Assistance. Windows Server 2003 Group Policy has settings specially dedicated to Remote Assistance, which are located in \Computer Configuration\Administrative Templates\System\Remote Assistance. These Remote Assistance-specific settings are:

- **Solicited Remote Assistance** If enabled, this setting allows users to ask for assistance from other users who can help resolve an issue they are facing. You can configure this setting to allow helpers in one of two ways: Helpers can actively take control of the requester's mouse and keyboard, or they can be limited to simply viewing the requester's screen and then offering help using the telephone or a chat application. You can also configure how long a request for assistance is valid. So, for example, after one hour, the help request will be withdrawn if it has not been answered. You can further configure the method by which invitations are sent.

Test Day Tip

Remember that Remote Assistance requests can be made via e-mail, by Windows Messenger, or through a file.

- **Offer Remote Assistance** This setting acts in conjunction with the previous one by dictating *which* users or groups can offer assistance, either actively or in a view-only capacity.

To configure Remote Assistance Group Policy, follow these steps:

1. Launch an MMC console by clicking **Start | Run** and typing **MMC**, then pressing **Enter**.
2. Add the **Active Directory Users and Computers Snap-in** by clicking **File | Add/Remove Snap-in**.
3. Click **Add**, select **ADUC**, and click **Add**.
4. Expand **ADUC** and right-click at the root of the domain. (Configuring the policy at the root of the domain ensures it is applied to all your domain computers.)
5. Click **Properties**. Select the **Group Policy** tab, then select the **Default Domain Policy**, and click **Edit**.
6. Click your way through **Computer Configuration | Administrative Templates | System | Remote Assistance**.
7. Enable **Solicited Remote Assistance,** which in essence allows users to enlist the help of other users to troubleshoot a problem.
8. Enable **Offer Remote Assistance** and then select the users who can respond to users' help requests by clicking the **Show** button and then adding the Active Directory groups that are responsible for such tasks (such as Helpdesk, IT Support, and so on).
9. Click **Apply**, and then **OK**.

Telnet

Telnet is a very powerful remote administration tool that allows an administrator (or potentially a hacker) to use command-line utilities from a text-based command-line window. Because it is infrequently used as an administrative tool and typically passes credentials using clear text, Telnet is disabled by default on all Windows Server 2003 machines. You should enable the Telnet service only if you see a real need for it, especially since the other administrative tools at your disposal offer more features and far better security. The Telnet service should remain disabled unless a need arises that requires it.

EXAM 70-298 OBJECTIVE 2.3.3

Designing Security for Emergency Management Services

A long-awaited (and perhaps overdue) feature in the Windows family is the ability to manage a server via an out-of-band connection such as a COM or serial port. *Out-of-band management* refers to the ability to connect to a server using nontraditional methods for remote server management such as a telephone line or a serial port and then having the ability to troubleshoot the server through a Terminal emulator window similar to a Telnet session. Emergency Management Services (EMS) allows you to manage or troubleshoot a server when it is not fully functional or when the operating system has not fully loaded. It also allows you to manage the server in a "headless" configuration, meaning without having a mouse, keyboard, or video device attached to it. You connect to EMS through Terminal Emulators connecting through a COM or a serial port. Once you've determined that your server hardware will support it, you can enable EMS using the bootcfg.exe utility. You can use this tool to create an entry in the Boot.ini file to enable Windows console redirection.

EXAM WARNING

Remember that the opposite of out-of-band management is *in-band management*, which is the term used to describe management of a server that is fully functional using traditional tools such as Remote Desktop for Administrators or Terminal Services.

EMS requires a server to be equipped with special firmware that will allow the server to take advantage of all its features. Furthermore, although EMS was designed to allow you to troubleshoot severs that have not booted or are not working properly, you will need to configure EMS and set it up properly while the system is up and running—you cannot install EMS after a server is already experiencing difficulties. When the system is up and running, you can configure the hardware and install the required firmware to allow EMS to function properly when the time comes. EMS allows you to perform the following tasks:

- Start up or shut down a server
- Install the Windows operating system if the server can communicate with Remote Installation Services (RIS)
- Manage a Windows Server 2003 system when you are unable to access it the traditional way, over the network using standard tools
- View system STOP (Blue Screen of Death) errors
- Change the BIOS settings
- Select which operating system to start
- View Power On Self-Test (POST) results

EMS security measures rely in large part on your choice of terminal concentrator, since that is the device that you'll use to connect to the server. Be careful making this selection, since Telnet security features such as passwords and encryption are not standard on all terminal concentrators. If your device does not include security features, consider using a direct-dial remote access or VPN connection, or use a router to secure network traffic to the terminal concentrator. Here are some other security considerations in configuring EMS on your network:

- **Secure access to the physical servers** This is the first step in securing *any* server implementation, whether it's running EMS or not. Your servers should live in a secured area where only authorized personnel have access to them. If for whatever reason you do not have a server room at your location, you should secure the servers in some other way, using locking cabinets or racks.
- **Choose service processors** These are built onto the system's motherboard and provide a medium that allows EMS to run when the operating system is not functioning properly. When the server's kernel or loader is not even partially loaded, service processors can give you access to the server because they run independently from the regular processors that run the usual operating system.
- **Create a separate network for administration** For additional security, you can create a second network dedicated solely to network management traffic from EMS. You can use filter lists on your routers to allow only specified computers to access this second network, making sure it is not connected to the Internet in any way. This will almost completely negate the possibility of an outside attacker gaining access to your EMS-enabled devices. However, it reduces your network management flexibility, since you will not be able to use EMS from a location that doesn't have access to this second network.

EXAM 70-298 OBJECTIVE 2.4

Designing a Security Update Infrastructure

Patching a large enterprise full of server and client systems has become something of an administrative nightmare in most IT shops because of the importance of staying on top of security patches that Microsoft releases on a not-infrequent basis. Although Microsoft makes every effort to release patches in a timely manner, sometimes attackers themselves use security bulletins that inform them of a vulnerability to gain the ability to exploit it. With this awareness, an attacker can scan for companies whose machines have not been patched against the vulnerability, often severely damaging their systems. As the security specialist in your organization, you should have as part of your overall strategy a plan to analyze and quickly deploy the security patches that Microsoft releases.

To include new features and more functionality in newer versions of an OS, programmers have to write more lines of code. More lines of code mean more room for security holes, which leads to more patch releases. Not only do you need antivirus software to protect your system against malicious programs, you also need to worry about security patches so that hackers don't take advantage of a security hole. This was the case with the Blaster worm, which recently exploited the RPC/DCOM service and caused servers that didn't have the proper security patches to constantly reboot themselves, thus disrupting productivity by creating an unstable environment.

To help organizations and security specialists with this huge burden of securing networks against security vulnerabilities, Microsoft has made available a free product known as Software Update Service, or SUS. SUS essentially works as an internally controlled Windows Update site that allows you to analyze and approve security patches and then apply them to your networked computers in a consistent manner.

EXAM 70-298 OBJECTIVE 2.4.1

Designing a Software Update Service Infrastructure

When deploying SUS, it's important to be aware of not only its capabilities but also its limitations. SUS certainly isn't a one-size-fits-all solution, and you should be certain that SUS will meet your needs before you deploy it.

SUS allows you to control which patches are visible to your users and automates the download and installation process so that no user intervention is required. Another important feature that is often overlooked is its ability to optimize bandwidth, especially for a large organization. Rather than having 5,000 clients each download a 3MB update (that's 15 *gigabytes* of information being pushed down your expensive Internet connection), you will be able to host the update locally and have clients download their information over an internal LAN connection.

In short, SUS allows you to maintain what is effectively an internal Windows Update Web site, where your SUS server contacts the actual Windows Update Web site and downloads updates that an administrator can review and approve for deployment. SUS has many advantages over Windows Update, the most obvious of which is that with SUS, you can control and approve the patches that are installed, as shown in Figure 4.5. As hard as Microsoft tries to build a software update package that will not break anything, sometimes patches that are not tested can damage a specific environment, rendering your computers unusable rather than tightening security on them.

Figure 4.5 Approving Critical Updates in SUS

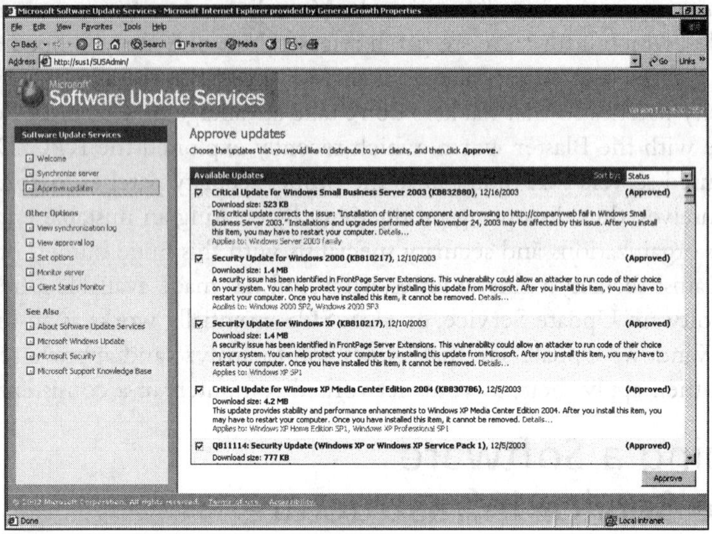

However, SUS is far from a panacea, and it's important to remember its limitations. SUS only allows you to deploy critical updates and service packs that you download from Microsoft. You cannot deploy other Windows Update files, including software updates and updated device drivers, using SUS. Nor can you create your own .EXE or .MSI files and have SUS deploy them for you; anything that SUS deploys needs to be a critical update downloaded directly from Microsoft.

If you are working in an environment that supports many down-level or legacy clients, it's absolutely key to remember that SUS will only deploy patches for "modern" Microsoft operating systems, a definition that extends to the following:

- Windows 2000 Professional
- Windows 2000 Server, all versions
- Windows XP Home
- Windows XP Professional
- Windows Server 2003, all versions

If you are still supporting Windows NT or 9*x* clients, you will not be able to deploy patches for these operating systems using SUS. On the server side, you can't automate the installation of updates for back-end applications such as SQL or Exchange Server. Finally, there's no good way to "push" installations to your clients, since SUS is designed to operate in the background with no user intervention. So, if there is a newly released patch that you need to install on your client workstations right away, SUS doesn't offer an intuitive way to force an update for your clients.

When your environment is spread over geographically distant sites or remote offices, you need to accommodate these sites with SUS as well. You can configure secondary SUS servers for your remote offices that poll the main SUS server, download the updates from it, and in turn make them available to their local users. With SUS, you have the ability to configure these child SUS servers to synchronize with the main server on a time interval of your choosing, as shown in Figure 4.6. Whenever possible, you should configure this schedule so that this polling takes place during off-peak hours when network traffic is low so that SUS doesn't hog bandwidth, especially over expensive WAN links. This is especially important when you are dealing with remote sites that are connected using slower links, such as 56K ISDN lines; you want to ensure that the synchronization occurs after hours, when users have left for the day. Otherwise your SUS design might actually create a DoS for these remote users, since they won't have the bandwidth that they need to do their jobs. However, if your WAN topology can handle the traffic (if your sites are connected via multiple T1 lines, for example), you can configure synchronization to occur as soon as one hour after the master SUS server has downloaded its patches.

Figure 4.6 Synchronizing Child SUS Servers

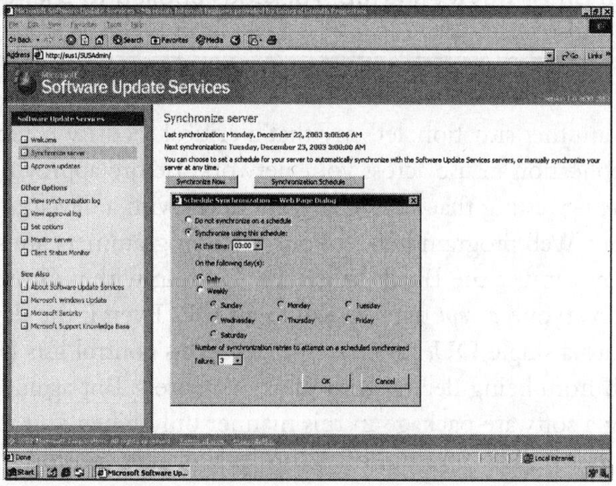

EXAM 70-298 OBJECTIVE 2.4.2

Using Group Policy to Deploy Software Updates

Group Policy is another great way you can deploy software in general and patches and updates in particular. Using GPOs, you can even customize who gets which updates and can thereby exert more granular control over the software distribution process, allowing you to prioritize updates based on importance. (As we discussed in the last section, this is something that SUS will not allow you to do.)

For example, let's say that a security patch has just been released that addresses a particularly dangerous security vulnerability in IIS. Instead of simply approving the patch and making it available for everyone via SUS and then crossing your fingers until it's deployed, you can create a GPO to forcibly update the OU, site, or domain that contains all your IIS Web servers. Especially if you have grouped your Web servers into a single discrete container such as an OU, this is quite an efficient way to deliver an update, since only the machines that need the update are the ones that receive it, and they receive the critical update as soon as Group Policy refreshes. This creates an even greater advantage over SUS if you have remote offices and child SUS servers to contend with. In this scenario, you would first need to wait until the child SUS server in the Web servers' site synchronizes with the master server before that patch is even available to them. Using Group Policy, you are pushing the package to all the necessary servers regardless of geographic location.

TEST DAY TIP

Software installations in Group Policy can be applied to either computer or user configurations. Software packages applied to Computer Configurations are installed on computer startup. Packages applied to user configurations are installed at user logon.

Let's explore another situation; let's say that a critical security patch has been released for an application in use across your network. Before approving the update in SUS, you find during testing that the update interferes with a development application that is used by your Web programmers. If your Web programmers are separated into their own OU, you can use the Block Inheritance setting within Group Policy to push this patch out to everyone *except* the Development OU. Even if the development users aren't separated into a single OU, you can still use access control lists (ACLs) to prevent the harmful patch from being deployed to their computers. But again, you have the option of pushing a software package in this manner only when you use Group Policy, as shown in Figure 4.7. SUS does not offer this level of fine control.

Figure 4.7 Configuring Software Installation Policies

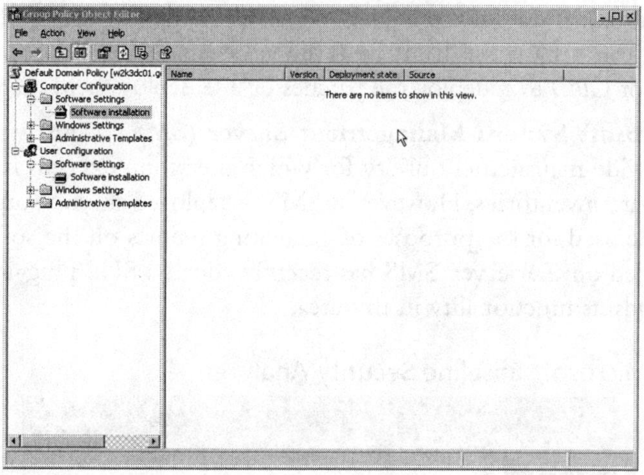

TEST DAY TIP

Remember that a user needs Read and Apply Group Policy permissions to a GPO to be able to have that GPO applied to that user. You can alter the ACL on a GPO to control which users or groups will and will not have a GPO applied to them.

EXAM 70-298 OBJECTIVE 2.4.3

Design a Strategy for Identifying Computers That Are Not at the Current Patch Level

Now that you have configured your preferred method of pushing security patches to workstations and servers, how do you audit to make sure that your strategy is actually working? You'll need to perform some kind of audit to ensure that your machines are receiving the patches that they should receive and to identify machines on your network that do not possess the most up-to-date patch information. This audit is necessary because you never know when a machine may be experiencing some issues whereby it is not getting the updates and is therefore susceptible to attack. Many tools are available to help you scan your network and generate reports of the current security patch level on machines. Microsoft offers several tools to assist with this task, including:

- **Microsoft Baseline Security Analyzer (MBSA)** This is a free utility that provides you with the ability to scan your domain or subnet periodically to check whether computers have failed to install patches or updates. MBSA can also report on a computer's compliance with some security best practices, such as strong password requirements. It can also check a computer to make sure that it is not open to any known security vulnerabilities (see Figure 4.8). What MBSA does not offer, however, is the ability to deploy the missing or failed patches. Once MBSA finds the vulnerability, you'll need to go back to SUS or GPO to redeploy the patches or else deploy them manually.

- **Microsoft System Management Server (SMS)** This is an enterprisewide management utility for which the scope exceeds hardware and software inventories. However, if SMS is deployed in your organization, it can be used for the purposes of generating reports on the software that is installed on the server. SMS has recently added a SUS plug-in that further extends its functionality in this area.

Figure 4.8 Microsoft Baseline Security Analyzer

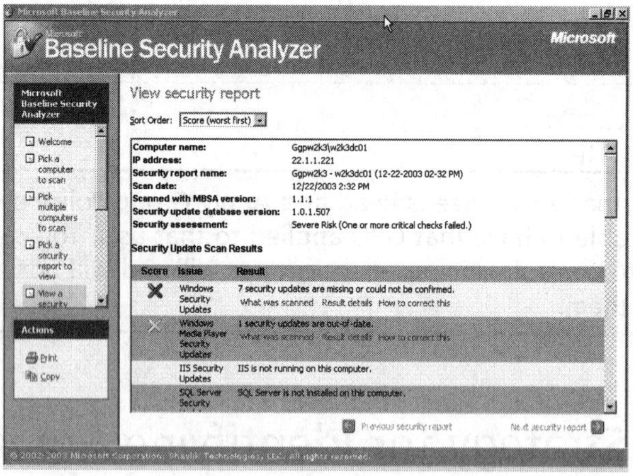

A number of third-party tools and applications can also address this issue. Here are some of the more popular ones:

- **HP OpenView: www.openview.hp.com** OpenView is infamous for its enterprisewide management capabilities. It operates at the same level as SMS and should be implemented as part of a larger management strategy, not just for patch management.
- **NetIQ Security Manager: www.netiq.com** Security Manager by NetIQ offers a product designed for patch management. Everything from analysis and reporting to deployment of patches is included.
- **Gravity Storm Software Service Pack Manager 2000: www.securitybastion.com** This product, like NetIQ, also offers a well-rounded method of gathering information about current computer patch levels and can even poll the corresponding Microsoft article if you are unsure what

the missing or failed patch does. This product also offers the ability to deploy the missing patches and offers scheduling so that deployments do not adversely affect network traffic.

TEST DAY TIP

You will not need to be familiar with specific third-party utilities for the 70-298 exam. However, you should be familiar with the abilities and limitations of the free and built-in Microsoft utilities so that you can recognize a scenario in which a third-party utility might be appropriate.

EXAM 70-298 OBJECTIVE 2.2.2

Designing Trust Relationships Between Domains and Forests

A trust creates the framework that governs domain-to-domain or forest-to-forest relationships. A trust allows users in different domains or forests to access resources in other domains or forests based on the trust that is established. Just as in previous versions of the Windows Server operating system, Windows Server 2003 trusts allow network administrators to establish relationships between domains and forests so that, for example, users from Domain A can access resources in Domain B. Unlike previous releases of Windows, however, Windows 2000 and Server 2003 allow for the creation of two-way, transitive trusts. This means that if Domain A trusts Domain B, and if Domain B trusts Domain C, then Domain A automatically trusts Domain C. (You may remember the days of Windows NT 4.0, when the number of trust relationships you needed to create in a large environment became staggeringly large: A network with 10 domains would require the administrator to manually create *90* trust relationships to allow for the kind of trust relationships that Windows 2000 and Windows Server 2003 create automatically.) In this section, we'll cover the various types of trust relationships that you can create to allow your users to quickly and easily access the resources they require.

Let's review some of the terminology that you'll encounter when you're dealing with designing trust relationships:

- One-way trust
- Two-way trust
- Transitive trust
- Nontransitive trust

In a one-way trust, Domain A trusts Domain B. What this means is that Domain A is trusting Domain B's users and granting them access to its resources. As you can see in Figure 4.9, Domain A is the *trusting domain,* and Domain B is the *trusted domain.* With a one-way trust, the trusted domain contains the user resources that require access, and the trusting domain contains the resources that are being accessed. Diagrammatically, this concept is represented using an arrow pointing toward the trusted domain, as you can see in the figure. If you have a hard time remembering which domain is the trusted domain and which is the trusting domain as well as which way the arrow is supposed to point, it might help to try to remember it this way: Think of the last two letters in *trust-ED* as talking about a guy named Ed. The *trust-ED* domain is the one that contains users, since that's where *ED* is. The trusting domain, on the other hand, contains the thing that your users are trying to access. It's the *trust-ING* domain because that's where the *THINGS* are. Using this mnemonic device when you're looking at a diagram of a one-way trust relationship on the 70-298 exam, you can remember that the direction-of-trust arrow is pointing to *ED.*

Figure 4.9 The One-Way Trust Relationship

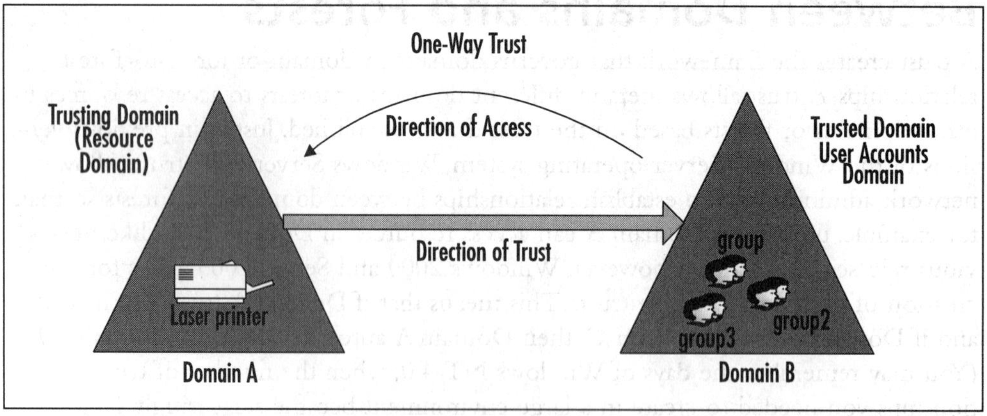

When setting up one-way trusts from a Windows Server 2003 domain or forest, you have two possible options:

- **One-way: incoming** Users in your Windows Server 2003 domain or forest will be able to access resources in the external realm, but external users will not be able to access any resources in your Windows Server 2003 domain. In this case, the Windows 2003 domain will be the trusted domain (since that's where *Ed* and all the other users are), and the external domain or forest will be the trusting domain, since that will be where the resources (or *things*) are.
- **One-way: outgoing** This is the reverse of one-way: incoming. Here, users in the external domain or forest will be able to access resources within your domain, but your Windows Server 2003 users will not be able to access any

resources in the external realm. Likewise, the Windows Server 2003 domain will be the trusting domain, since it contains the resources being accessed, and the external domain or forest will be the trusted domain, since it contains the users who will be accessing the resources.

Unlike a one-way trust, a two-way trust means that both Domain A and Domain B are simultaneously trusting and trusted domains, respectively, which means that users in both domains can access resources in either domain. Figure 4.10 will help you visualize this trust relationship.

Figure 4.10 The Two-Way Trust Relationship

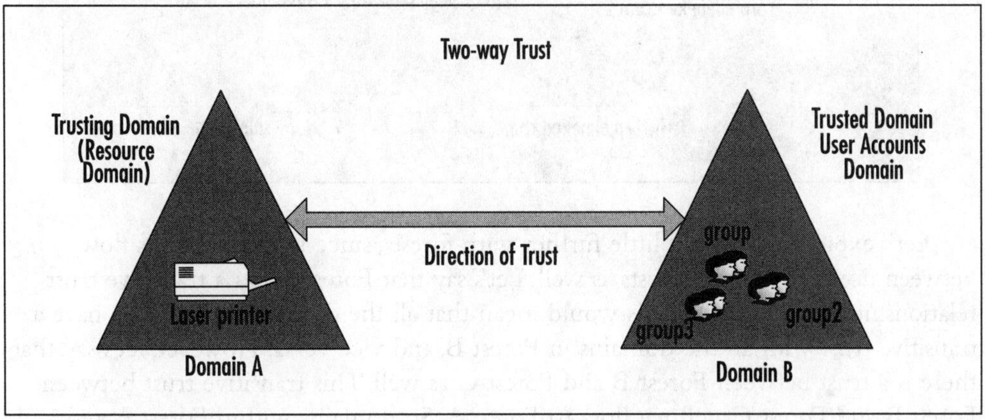

All Windows 2000 and Windows Server 2003 domains are designed with transitive trusts by default. Remember the transitive property from your high school mathematics class: If A equals B and B equals C, then A must therefore equal C. It works the same way in a transitive trust relationship: If Domain A trusts Domain B and Domain B trusts Domain C, then Domain A automatically trusts Domain C. (This is different from the NT 4.0 trust environment in which you needed to manually create another trust between Domain A and Domain C.) For example, when you create a child domain, a two-way transitive trust is automatically created between the parent and child domains. You can see this illustrated in Figure 4.11. In plain English, this means that using *transitivity of trust*, a user in any domain can access any resource in any other domain in the same forest.

Figure 4.11 Trust Transitivity in Domains

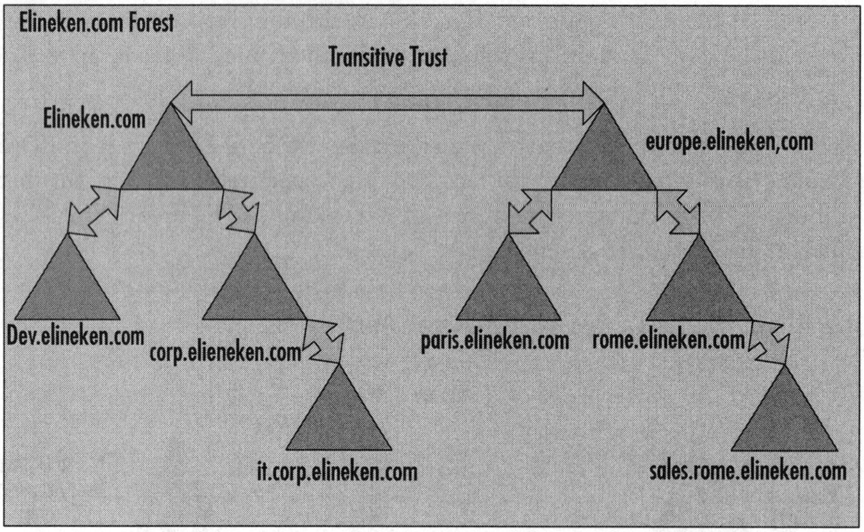

Let's explore this idea a little further with forests, since transitive trusts flow between domains in two forests as well. Let's say that Forest A has a transitive trust relationship with Forest B. This would mean that all the domains in Forest A have a transitive trust with all the domains in Forest B, and vice versa. However, let's say that there is a trust between Forest B and Forest C as well. This transitive trust between Forest B and Forest C will *not* flow to Forest A. So domains within Forest A and Forest C will not have any trust relationships between them unless you manually configure a trust between Forest A and Forest C. See Figure 4.12 for an illustration of this concept.

Exam Warning

Two-way transitive trust relationships are possible only if your forest is operating in the Windows Server 2003 forest functional level. We'll be talking about domain and forest functional levels later in this section.

Figure 4.12 Transitivity of Forest Trusts

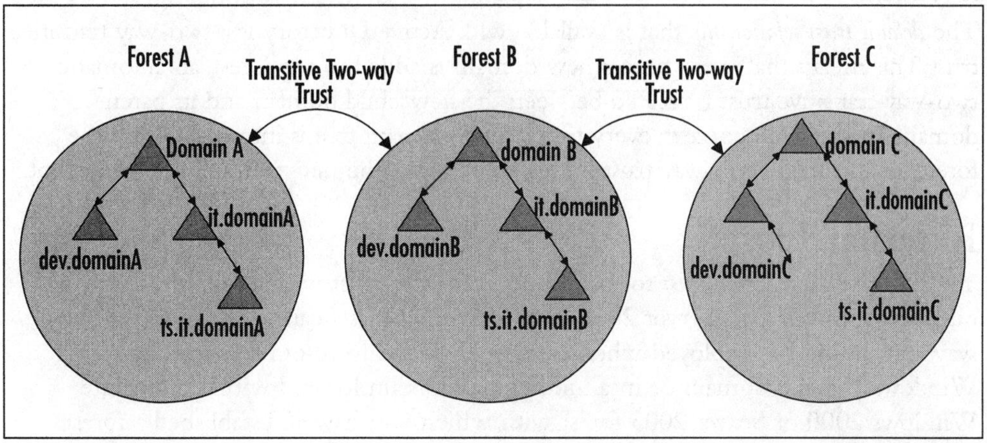

A nontransitive trust is similar to the way that trust relationships functioned in Windows NT4.0: The trust is limited to the domains where it was explicitly configured. As we've already discussed, a number of transitive trust relationships are created by default in Windows Server 2003. This level of transitivity can be a deciding factor in your security design, since if you need a domain to have absolutely no default trust relationships with any other domains in your organization, you should consider creating a separate forest. (You'll often hear this referred to as a *security boundary*. To completely isolate resources, you should use the forest as the security boundary, rather than the domain.) A number of trust relationships in Windows Server 2003 are non-transitive by default; we'll be talking more about each one in the next section.

Designing Forest and Domain Trust Models

Trust relationships will be an integral part of your security design when you need to create user access for separate businesses or departments with differing security requirements. There may also come a time when you will be adding or removing domains from your Active Directory structure because of an event such as a company merger or branch closure. These and other business-oriented events can trigger a need to reconfigure your domain and security structure to accommodate these types of changes. The use of domain and forest trusts will be a great asset in designing your environment for both security and ease of management. You should also be familiar with the different types of trusts that are available to you and when to use each type or model to best accomplish the task at hand. In the following sections we will discuss the various types of trust.

Default Trust Relationships

The *default trust relationship* that is available with Active Directory is a two-way transitive trust. This means that every time a new domain is added to the forest, an automatic two-way transitive trust is created between the new child domain and its parent domain. In the same context, every time a new domain tree is introduced into the forest, an automatic two-way trust is created between the new tree and the forest root.

External Trusts

You'll create an *external trust* to form a nontransitive trust with a domain that exists outside your Windows Server 2003 forest. External trusts can be one-way or two-way and should be employed when users need access to resources located in a Windows NT 4.0 domain or in an individual domain located within a separate Windows 2000 or Server 2003 forest with which you haven't established a forest trust. You'll use an external trust instead of a forest trust if the trusting domain is running Windows NT 4.0 or if you want to restrict access to another forest simply to resources within a single domain. You can create external trusts using either the GUI interface or the command line. As with most of the functions discussed in this chapter, to perform these procedures you must be a member of the Domain Admins or Enterprise Admins group or you must have been delegated the appropriate authority by a member of one of these groups.

Creating an External Trust With the Windows Interface

1. Click **Start | Programs | Administrative Tools | Active Directory Domains and Trusts**. Enter the appropriate username and password to run the utility if you've configured the shortcut to use *RunAs*.
2. Right-click the domain that you want to create a trust for, and click **Properties**.
3. From the **Trusts** tab, click **New Trust** and then **Next**.
4. On the Trust Name screen, enter the DNS or NetBIOS name of the domain that you want to establish a trust with, then click **Next**.
5. The next screen allows you to establish the Trust Type. Click **External Trust**, then click **Next** to continue.
6. From the Direction of Trust screen, select one of the following:
   - **Two-way** will establish a two-way external trust. Users in your domain and the users in the specified domain will be able to access resources in either domain.
   - **One-way incoming** allows users in your Windows Server 2003 domain to access resources in the trusting domain that you specify, but

the trusting domain will not be able to access any resources in the 2003 domain.

- **One-way outgoing** is the reverse of one-way incoming, allows users in the external domain to access resources in your domain, but your users will not be able to connect to resources in the external domain.

7. Click **Next** when you've determined the direction of the trust you're creating. On the Outgoing Trust Properties sheet, you can choose one of the following options:

   - To allow users from the external domain to access to all resources in your Windows Server 2003 domain, select **Allow authentication for all resources in the local domain**. (You'll most commonly select this option if both domains are part of the same company or organization.)
   - To restrict users in the external domain from obtaining access to any of the resources in your domain, click **Allow authentication only for selected resources in the local domain.** This option should be used when each domain belongs to a separate organization. Once you've made your selection, click **Next** to continue.

8. If you have Domain Admin or Enterprise Admin access to each domain involved in the trust relationship, you can create both sides of an external trust at the same time. Click **Both this domain and the specified domain** on the Sides of Trust page.

EXAM WARNING

As a best practice, Microsoft recommends using the *RunAs* function to perform most trust procedures. You can configure Active Directory Domains and Trusts to use the *RunAs* function by right-clicking the shortcut and selecting RunAs. You'll be prompted for the username and password that you want to use to access the administrative utility. If you leave the logon information blank, you'll be prompted to enter it every time you launch the utility.

Selecting the Scope of Authentication for Users

Once you've created a trust relationship between two separate forests, you'll need to indicate the scope of authentication for users from the trusted domain. You can either allow users in the trusted forest to be treated as members of the Authenticated Users group in the local forest, or you can specify that users from the other forest must be granted explicit permission to authenticate to local resources. (You'll hear the latter option referred to as an *authentication firewall.*) If users from the trusted domain are not treated as members of the Authenticated Users group in the trusting domain, they will only be able to access any resources for which they have been granted specific permissions. This is a more restrictive means of granting access and should be used when the trusting domain contains extremely sensitive or compartmentalized data. Specify the scope of authentication for any trusts you've created using the following steps:

1. Click **Start | Programs | Administrative Tools | Active Directory Domains and Trusts**.
2. Right-click the domain that you want to administer, and select **Properties**.
3. On the **Trusts** tab, select the trust that you want to administer under **Domains trusted by this domain (outgoing trusts)** or **Domains that trust this domain (incoming trusts)** and do one of the following:

   - To select the scope of authentication for users who authenticate through an *external* trust, select the external trust that you want to administer, and then click **Properties**. On the **Authentication** tab, click either **Domain-wide** or **Selective authentication**. If you select **Selective authentication**, you need to manually enable permissions on the local domain and on the resource to which you want users in the external domain to have access. Otherwise, the users from the trusted domain will automatically be added to the Authenticated Users group in the trusting domain.
   - To select the scope of authentication for users authenticating through a *forest* trust, click the forest trust that you want to administer, and then click **Properties**. On the **Authentication** tab, click either **Forest-wide** or **Selective authentication**. If you select **Selective authentication**, you need to manually enable permissions on each domain and resource in the local forest that users in the second forest should be able to access.

EXAM WARNING

Selective authentication is available only with external and forest trusts. It cannot be used with a realm trust.

Realm Trusts

Windows Server 2003 allows you to create a trust relationship with an external Kerberos realm, allowing cross-platform interoperability with other Kerberos services such as UNIX and MIT-based implementations. You can establish a *realm trust* between your Windows Server 2003 domain and any non-Windows Kerberos V5 realm as shown in Figure 4.13. This trust relationship will allow pass-through authentication, in which a trusting domain (the domain containing the resources to be accessed) honors the logon authentications of a trusted domain (the domain containing the user accounts). You can grant rights and permissions in the trusting domain to user accounts and global groups in the trusted domain, even though the accounts or groups don't exist in the trusting domain's directory. Realm trusts can also be either one-way or two-way.

You can create a realm trust using the Active Directory Domains and Trusts GUI or the *netdom* command-line utility. To perform this procedure, you must be a member of the Domain Admins or Enterprise Admins group or you must have been delegated the appropriate authority by a member of one of these groups.

Figure 4.13 Realm Trusts

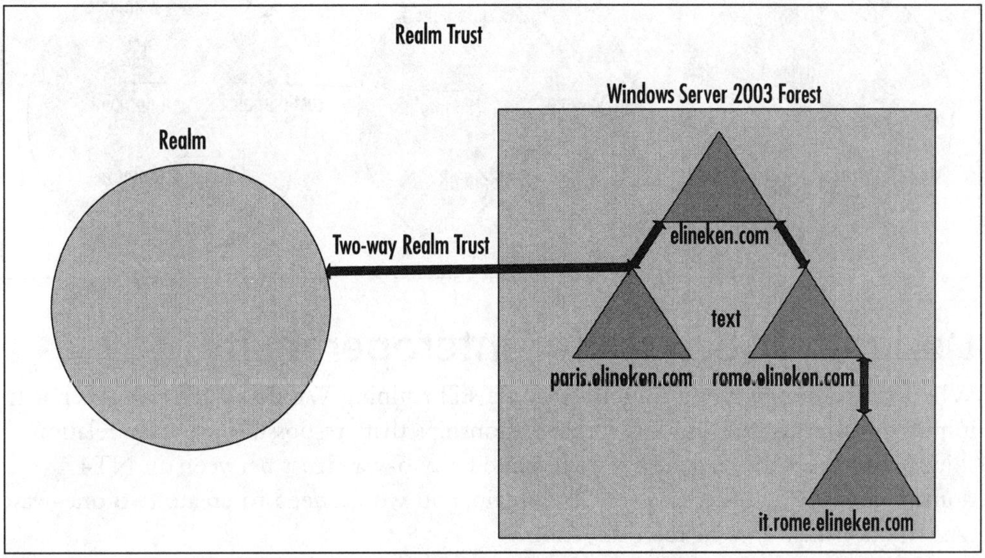

Shortcut Trusts

Authentication requests between two domains in different domain trees must travel a *trust path*—that is, a series of individual relationships between the two domains. This can be a somewhat lengthy process within a complex forest structure, but you can reduce this process through the use of *shortcut trusts*. Shortcut trusts are one-way or two-way transitive trusts that you can use to optimize the authentication process if many of your users from one domain need to log on to another domain in the forest structure.

As illustrated in Figure 4.14, the shortcut trust between Domain A and Domain F will shorten the path traveled for User1's login request between the two domains. In the figure, UserA must access the printer in Domain F by referring to the trust relationships between Domain A and Domain B, then between Domain B and Domain C, and so forth until reaching Domain F.The shortcut trust creates a trust relationship directly between Domain A and Domain F, greatly shortening the authentication process in an enterprise domain with a large series of forest trust relationships.

Figure 4.14 Using a Shortcut Trust

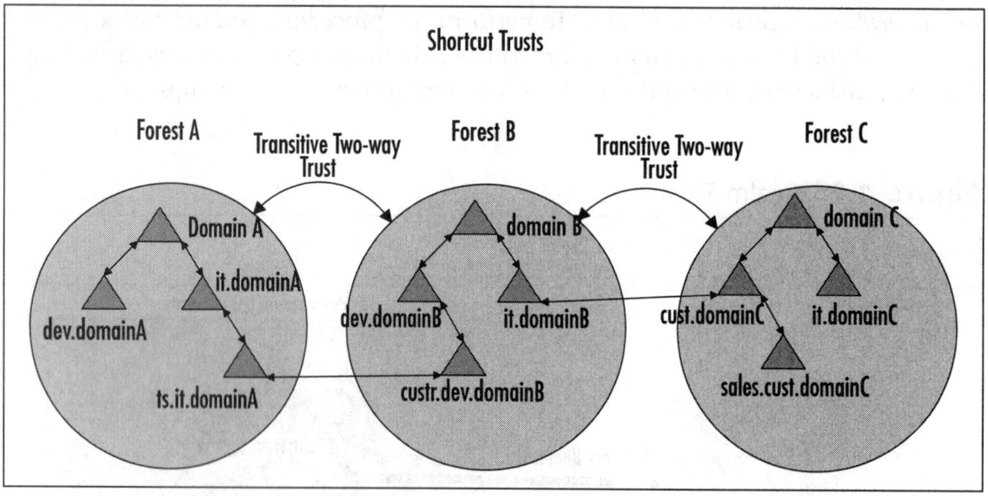

EXAM 70-298 OBJECTIVE 2.2.3

Designing Security for Interoperability

When you're dealing with domains that are still running Windows NT or earlier, it is important to note that the only trust relationships that are possible are trust relationships that you set up manually. If you wanted a two-way trust between an NT4 domain and a Windows Server 2003 domain, you would need to create two one-way trust relationships, one in each direction.

Whenever you are supporting down-level domains and controllers with Windows Server 2003, you need to be aware of the concept of domain and forest functional levels on your network. You probably recall that in Windows 2000, you were able to configure your Active Directory domains in either mixed mode or native mode. Mixed-mode operation provided backward compatibility for any remaining NT4 backup domain controllers (BDCs) still existing on your network. Mixed-mode domains could contain Windows NT 4.0 backup domain controllers and were unable to take advantage of such advanced Windows 2000 features as universal security groups, group nesting, and security ID (SID) history capabilities, as well as other Microsoft packages such as Exchange 2000. When you set your domain to native mode, these advanced functions became available for your use.

Windows Server 2003 takes this concept of domain functionality to a new level, allowing you to establish four different levels of *domain functionality,* with differing feature sets available, depending on your network environment. The four domain functional levels available in the new release of Windows Server are as follows:

- Windows 2000 mixed
- Windows 2000 native
- Windows Server 2003 interim
- Windows Server 2003

The default domain functional level is still Windows 2000 mixed mode, to allow you time to upgrade your domain controllers from Windows NT 4.0 and Windows 2000 to Windows Server 2003. Just as in the previous release of Windows, however, when you raise the functional level, advanced domainwide Active Directory features become available. Just as NT4 controllers were not able to take advantage of the features available in Windows 2000 native mode, Windows 2000 controllers will not be aware of the features provided by the Windows Server 2003 level of domain and forest functionality.

In Table 4.1, you can see the four levels of domain functionality available in Windows Server 2003 and the types of domain controllers that are supported by each.

Table 4.1 Domain Functional Levels Within Windows Server 2003

Domain Functional Level	Domain Controllers Supported
Windows 2000 mixed (default)	Windows Server 2003 family
	Windows 2000
	Windows NT4
Windows 2000 native	Windows Server 2003 family
	Windows 2000
Windows Server 2003 interim	Windows Server 2003 family
	Windows NT4
Windows Server 2003	Windows Server 2003

Test Day Tip

The Windows Server 2003 interim domain functional level is a special level that's available if you're upgrading a Windows NT 4.0 PDC to become the first domain controller in a new Windows Server 2003 domain.

When you upgrade the domain functional level of your Windows Server 2003 domain, new administrative and security features will be available for your use. Just as when you set Windows 2000 to either mixed or native mode, specifying the domain functional level is a one-way operation; it cannot be undone. Therefore, if you still have domain controllers that are running Windows NT 4.0 or earlier, you shouldn't raise the domain functional level to Windows 2000 native. Likewise, if you haven't finished migrating your Windows 2000 controllers to Windows Server 2003, you should leave the domain functional level lower than Windows Server 2003.

Similar to the domain functional level, Windows Server 2003 has created different *forest* functional levels that can enable new Active Directory features that will apply to every domain within an Active Directory forest. When you first create a Windows Server 2003 Active Directory forest, its forest functional level is set to Windows 2000. Depending on your environment, you can consider raising the forest functional level to Windows Server 2003; however, just as with the domain functional level, changing the forest functional level is a one-way operation that cannot be undone. Therefore, if any of your domain controllers are still running Windows NT 4.0 or Windows 2000, you shouldn't raise your forest functional level to Windows Server 2003 until your existing controllers have been upgraded.

Table 4.2 details the types of domain controllers that are supported by each of the forest functional levels.

Table 4.2 Controllers Supported by Different Forest Functional Levels

Forest Functional Level	Domain Controllers Supported
Windows 2000 (default)	Windows NT 4.0 Windows 2000 Windows Server 2003 family
Windows Server 2003 interim	Windows NT 4.0 Windows Server 2003 family
Windows Server 2003	Windows Server 2003 family

Head of the Class...

Windows Server 2003 Domain and Forest Functionality

When you raise the domain and/or forest functional level within your Active Directory environment, certain advanced features will be available for your use. At the domain level, the Windows Server 2003 functional level provides the following advantages that are not available in either Windows 2000 mixed or native mode. You can enable these features on a domain-by-domain basis:

- **Domain controller rename tool** This Resource Kit utility allows you to rename a domain controller if your business or organizational structure changes.
- **SID history** Allows you to migrate security principals from one domain to another.
- **Converting groups** This enables you to convert a security group to a distribution group, and vice versa.
- **InetOrg Person** These objects ease the migration from other LDAP-enabled directory applications to Active Directory.
- **lastLogonTimestamp attribute** Keeps track of the last logon time for either a user or computer account, providing the administrator with the ability to track the history of the account.

Raising the forest functional level creates the following features that you can implement throughout your Windows Server 2003 forest:

- **Domain rename** Allows you to rename an entire Active Directory domain.
- **Forest trusts** Enable two-way transitive trusts between separate Windows Server 2003 forests. In Windows 2000, trusts between forests were one-way and intransitive.
- **InetOrg Person** These objects can now be made available throughout your entire Windows Server 2003 forest.
- **Defunct schema object** You can now reuse the object identifier, the ldapDisplayName, and the schemaIdGUID that are associated with a defunct schema object, whether a class or an attribute.
- **Linked value replication** This feature allows individual values of a schema attribute to be replicated separately. In Windows 2000, if an administrator or application made a change to a member of a group, for example, the entire group needed to be replicated. With linked value replication, only the group member that has changed is replicated, greatly improving replication efficiency and speed in larger environments.

Continued

- **Dynamic auxiliary classes** These allow you to link auxiliary schema classes to an individual object rather than entire classes of objects. They also serve to improve replication under Windows Server 2003.
- **Global catalog replication** This has also been improved by propagating only partial changes when possible.

Summary of Exam Objectives

In this chapter, we took a step back from looking at how to secure the various components of the Windows Server 2003 infrastructure and asked the question: How do we secure the tools we're *using* to secure the network? As we've seen, the network management process itself can quickly provide an attacker a means of infiltrating your network if you do not set up administrative and technical controls to prevent it. Any well-designed network security plan should take both of these types of measures into account to control things such as how administrative credentials are used on a network, how to secure the utilities that are used (and which of those utilities should be permitted in the first place), and how to defend against vulnerabilities arising from improper behavior on the part of network administrators. As with most security topics we've discussed, this effort will only be complete if it includes both technical measures to secure the use of specific administrative utilities and the creation of administrative policies, such as mandating the use of *RunAs* or policies regarding the necessary information to obtain before resetting a user's password over the phone.

After looking at the overall importance of creating a secure network management policy, we also examined two other critical pieces of the network management puzzle. Although Microsoft has made great strides in improving the security of the Windows Server 2003 operating system, it's simply unavoidable that, as time goes on, new security vulnerabilities will be discovered and new patches will be released to correct them. Deploying security patches, especially in a large enterprise environment, has always been a problematic situation for network administrators. In an effort to make this process simpler and improve the overall security of its operating systems, Microsoft has made a number of utilities freely available to network administrators to assist in the patch management process. In Chapter 4 we looked at two in particular—the Microsoft Baseline Security Analyzer (MBSA) and the Software Update Service (SUS)—and how they can be incorporated into a network security design.

We wrapped up this chapter with a review of the domain and forest trust model and how it has been updated for Windows Server 2003. In preparation for the 70-298 exam, we focused on ways to create your domain and forest designs to provide the most secure environment possible in an enterprise environment, including the need to incorporate dissimilar operating systems and corporate cultures to create a secure, unified whole.

Exam Objectives Fast Track

Designing Security for Network Management

- ☑ The network management process itself needs to be secured as part of your security design to prevent malicious users from employing administrative tools to gain access to your network.
- ☑ Restrict use of administrative credentials on your network as much as possible through workstation restrictions, mandating the use of the *RunAs* function, and creating a second "everyday use" account for your administrative staff.
- ☑ Be sure that any administrative tools that are not authorized for use on your network are disabled, especially the Telnet service and the ability for lower-level administrators to create their own MMC consoles.

Designing a Security Update Infrastructure

- ☑ Software Update Service (SUS) can act as an internal Windows Update solution for your Windows 2000, Windows XP, and Windows Server 2003 family computers.
- ☑ Use the Microsoft Baseline Security Analyzer (MBSA) to identify any machines on your network that are not at the most current patch level.
- ☑ Use Group Policy Software Installation settings to create more granular control over who receives software patches and updates and to manually update machines quickly if a critical patch is released.

Designing Trust Relationships Between Domains and Forests

- ☑ Base your decision to create multiple domains within a single forest on whether you need to maintain a separate security boundary or Active Directory schema for either organization or business units. Use multiple domains or OUs to delegate some administrative responsibility while still maintaining a centrally administered network. If you need to maintain two discrete entities in terms of security and network management, multiple forests are the way to go.

- ☑ Raising the domain or forest functional level allows you to implement security and administrative improvements, but it will not allow any Windows NT 4.0 or 2000 controllers to participate in the domain. You'll need to either upgrade all down-level controllers on your network or else demote them to standalone server status.
- ☑ By default, Windows Server 2003 creates a two-way transitive trust relationship between all domains within a domain and between all domains in two forests that are linked by a two-way forest trust.

Exam Objectives Frequently Asked Questions

The following Frequently Asked Questions, answered by the authors of this book, are designed to both measure your understanding of the Exam Objectives presented in this chapter, and to assist you with real-life implementation of these concepts. You will also gain access to thousands of other FAQs at ITFAQnet.com.

Q: I am setting up a multiforest Windows Server 2003 network for two law firms that are in the process of merging. The first firm is located in Baltimore, Maryland, the second in Raleigh-Durham, North Carolina. I want to create a two-way forest trust between these networks, but each firm's servers are located behind a stringent firewall. Which ports do I need to enable on the firewall to allow the trust relationship to exist?

A: For a two-way trust, you need to enable LDAP (TCP and UDP ports 389). You also need to enable Microsoft's SMB protocol (UDP Port 445), the endpoint resolution portmapper (TCP port 135), and Kerberos, which operates on UDP port 88. If you were creating only a one-way outgoing trust, you would not need to enable the Kerberos port.

Q: I have a department within my organization that requires access to resources on a third-party vendor's Windows 2000 network. This department would like to make its internal resources available to the vendor as well. This is a single department within a large organization. Do I have any way to prevent this vendor from having access to my entire forest?

A: Use Selective Authentication to restrict the resources to which the external vendor has access. You will then need to manually enable permissions on the local domain and on the resources that you want users in the external domain to have access to.

Q: What are some best practices to protect my network and staff against social engineering attacks?

A: Make sure that your users and administrators are aware of some of the indicators of social engineering attacks, such as requests to do something that would be in violation of your company's security policy, or someone using a friendship or a personal relationship to get someone to do something that violates security policies. Your staff should also be wary of any unusual network requests, especially if they supposedly need to be carried out "right away."

Q: What happens to Windows NT trust relationships when you upgrade to Windows Server 2003?

A: When you upgrade a Windows NT domain to a Windows Server 2003 domain, all your existing Windows NT trusts are preserved as is. Remember that trust relationships between Windows Server 2003 domains and Windows NT domains are nontransitive.

Self Test

A Quick Answer Key follows the Self Test questions. For complete questions, answers, and explanations to the Self Test questions in this chapter as well as the other chapters in this book, see the Self Test Appendix.

1. Your forest is structured according to the illustration in Figure 4.15. You have a group of developers in the east.fixed-wing.airplanes.com domain who need to access files in the development.central.biplanes.airplanes.com domain on a regular basis. The users are complaining that accessing the files in the development domain is taking an unacceptably long time. What can you do to improve their response time?

Figure 4.15 Figure for Question 1

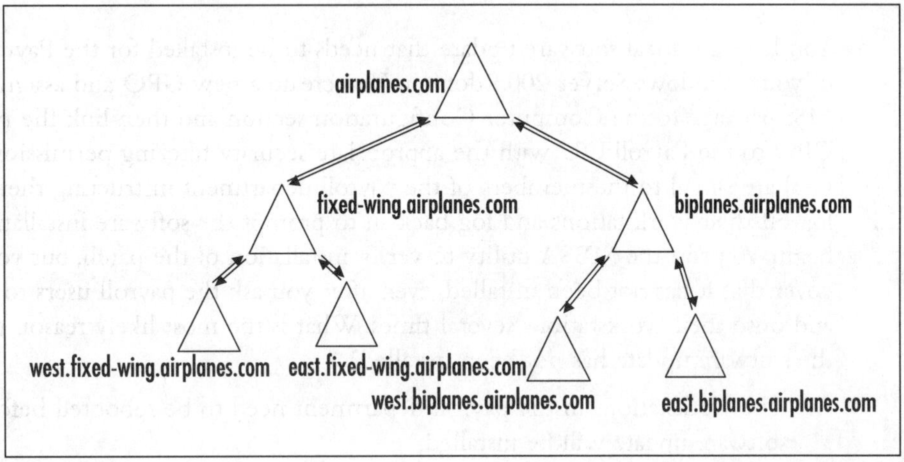

A. Create a domain local group in the development domain and add the developers' user accounts to it.

B. Create a shortcut trust between the east.fixed-wing.airplanes.com domain and the development.central.biplanes.airplanes.com domain.

C. Place the resources in the development domain into an OU. Use the Delegation of Control Wizard to grant the users in the east.fixed-wing.airplanes.com domain the appropriate permissions.

D. Create an external trust between the fixed-wing.airplanes.com domain and the biplanes.airplanes.com domain.

2. You are the network administrator for a medical research facility running Windows Server 2003. Your firm is beginning a joint research operation with a major university, and many of your users will need to access files and folders on the university's network. The university that you are partnering with uses a UNIX Kerberos environment. Your company's resources should not be accessible by the university staff. How can you accomplish this using the least administrative effort?

   A. Create a two-way realm trust between your network and the UNIX network.

   B. Create a one-way: outgoing external trust between your network and the UNIX network.

   C. Create a one-way: incoming realm trust between your network and the UNIX network.

D. Create a one-way: outgoing realm trust between your network and the UNIX network.

3. You have a critical software update that needs to be installed for the Payroll OU of your Windows Server 2003 domain. You create a new GPO and assign the MSI package to the Computer Configuration section and then link the new GPO to the Payroll OU with the appropriate security filtering permissions. You send an e-mail to the members of the payroll department instructing them to log off their workstations and log back in to prompt the software installation to begin. You run the MBSA utility to verify installation of the patch, but you discover that it has not been installed, even after you ask the payroll users to log off and onto their workstations several times. What is the most likely reason that the software update has not been installed?

   A. The workstations in the payroll department need to be rebooted before the software update will be installed.

   B. Software installation packages can only be assigned at the domain level.

   C. The software can be installed using the Add New Programs section of the Add/Remove Programs Control Panel applet.

   D. Logon scripts are running asynchronously; they must be reconfigured to run synchronously.

4. Hope Pharmaceuticals is a large organization that is headquartered in Chicago, Illinois. The company has six other locations in North America and Europe. In North America, the company has locations in Chicago, New York, and Arizona. In Europe, it has locations in Paris, London, and Rome. The Active Directory infrastructure consists of two forests: one for North America and one for Europe. Recently, the Chicago location and the Paris location have been working together closely on deals and possible mergers. Users have started to complain of slow response times in authenticating and accessing resources in either domain. What would be the best way to improve authentication performance between Chicago and Paris?

   A. Create a shortcut trust between the Chicago office and the Paris office.

   B. Create a realm trust between the Chicago and Paris offices.

   C. There is nothing you can do to improve performance.

   D. Move the Paris domain into the North America forest.

5. You are the IT manager for an organization with three locations in Fresno, San Francisco, and La Jolla, running Windows Server 2003 on the server side and Windows XP Professional on the client side. To cut down on Internet band-

width usage from the Windows Update client, you have installed an SUS server in each of the three locations. The SUS server is configured as the master SUS server, and Fresno and La Jolla's servers are configured as child servers. Microsoft releases a critical security update, and a few hours later you learn that a hacker group from Eastern Europe has already released an Internet worm to take advantage of any unpatched machines. You quickly download the new patch to your SUS server in San Francisco and approve the patch for distribution. Your CEO asks if your network is protected from this new threat, and you assure him that your patch management solution is up to the task. Unfortunately, you receive several calls toward the end of the day from users in Fresno who report that their machines are rebooting without warning and that network response time is almost nonexistent. On further investigation, you discover that the machines in Fresno and La Jolla were not updated with the new Microsoft patch and became victims of this new Internet worm. Your workstations and servers in the San Francisco office have received the patch. Why did SUS fail to update the machines in your two remote locations?

A. You did not install the SUS client on your client workstations.

B. The Internet connection between the Fresno and La Jolla offices did not permit the SUS traffic to pass.

C. The SUS servers in Fresno and La Jolla had not received the new update yet.

D. The security update was incompatible with your client workstations.

6. Your network is experiencing massive Internet bandwidth consumption from external sources. On investigating, you discover that a new Internet worm has been created that exploits a newly discovered vulnerability in Microsoft's Internet Information Service. You have seven IIS servers in your organization that are colocated in various cities across the United States to provide load balancing for your Web applications. Within Active Directory, all your Web servers are contained within a single OU. What is the quickest way to efficiently patch all your company's IIS servers against this new vulnerability while minimizing downtime for your Web server applications?

   A. Force the SUS server to immediately update all machines in the domain.

   B. Manually install the patch on each Web server.

   C. Create a GPO within the Computer Configuration | Software Installation settings. Link it to the Web Server OU. Reboot each Web server in turn so that the update can be applied.

   D. Create a GPO within the User Configuration | Software Installation settings. Link it to the Web Server OU. Perform a logout/login on each Web server so that the update can be applied.

7. You have 12 servers at various locations that you want to manage remotely. You have read about Emergency Management Services and believe this is a good solution for your environment. You review the hardware for each of the servers in question and determine that the firmware on all of them supports console redirection. Your servers are already running Windows Server 2003 and are x86-based systems. What is your next step in implementing EMS for these servers?

   A. Use the EMS Special Administration Console to install EMS for the remote computer. Configure console redirection via the server firmware after EMS is installed.

   B. Reinstall Windows Server 2003 from the installation CD. EMS configures itself during a bootable CD installation if the computer supports firmware console redirection and the Serial Port Console Redirection (SPCR) table.

   C. Reboot the computer into Safe mode. Install EMS from the Run line, and then reboot to enable EMS.

   D. Use Bootcfg.exe to edit the Boot.ini file located on the system partition root to enable Windows loader console redirection and the SAC.

8. You are the network administrator for a large, multinational corporation. Your Active Directory tree is configured with one domain for North America, one for Europe, and one for Asia. Each office on each continent has been configured with its own OU, and an administrative assistant in each office has been delegated the authority to reset user passwords within each OU. You have a single global group in each domain that contains the user accounts for the central help desk for each domain. To assist the local administrators with troubleshooting issues, you have distributed instructions concerning the use of the Remote Assistance feature in Windows XP and Windows Server 2003. After a server outage in the Dresden office, you discover that a local administrator was having a network issue and sent a Remote Assistance request to a friend of hers, who uploaded a virus-infected executable to the Dresden network, thinking that it was a diagnostic utility. What is the most efficient way to prevent this situation from recurring on your network? (Choose all that apply.)

   A. Use Group Policy to restrict to whom your users can send Remote Assistance requests.

   B. Use PGP encryption to encrypt the Remote Assistance e-mail request.

   C. Disable Remote Assistance on all client workstations. Manually re-enable it as needed.

   D. Create a network security policy forbidding Remote Assistance requests to any users other than central IT staff.

Self Test Quick Answer Key

For complete questions, answers, and explanations to the Self Test questions in this chapter as well as the other chapters in this book, see the Self Test Appendix.

1. **B**
2. **C**
3. **A**
4. **A**
5. **C**
6. **D**
7. **D**
8. **A, D**

Chapter 5

MCSE 70-298

Securing Network Services and Protocols

Exam Objectives in this Chapter:

3.1	Design network infrastructure security.
3.1.3	Design an IPSec policy.
3.1.2	Design IP filtering.
3.1.1	Specify the required protocols for a firewall configuration.
3.1.4	Secure a DNS Implementation.
3.1.5	Design security for data transmission.
1.2.3	Using segmented networks.
3.2	Design security for wireless networks.
3.2.1	Design public and private wireless LANs.
3.3.2	Design 802.11x authenication for wireless networks.
3.3	Design user authentication for Internet Information Services (IIS).

Introduction

In the early days of computer networks, when users and resources were situated in a single location with no connections to the outside world, protecting a company's data was simply a matter of securing the files and folders that resided on the network servers and client computers. It was a simple matter of ensuring that your internal users had access to the resources they required to do their jobs, without being able to get into areas that they shouldn't. However, as networks have grown in complexity and connectivity, the need to protect network information as it traverses the network has become an increasingly critical issue. Security administrators quickly discovered that data traveling from one location to another (especially if it traveled over a public medium like the Internet) was at risk of being stolen, altered, or intercepted by a third party. We quickly realized that we needed a way to secure data as it traveled over a network in order to protect its confidentiality and integrity. Windows Server 2003 provides a number of options for securing data as it traverses a network; we'll discuss the most prevalent of these technologies here.

The most exciting advance in Windows Server security in recent years has doubtless been the introduction of IP Security, or IPSec, support within Windows 2000 and Windows Server 2003. IPSec can be implemented at both the server and client level to encrypt data as it traverses even public networks like the Internet, allowing business in multiple locations to transmit data in a secure fashion. We'll take a look at the inner workings of IPSec, and how to implement it within the enterprise using policies that can be applied to an entire Windows Server 2003 domain. We'll also look at how IPSec can effectively function as a firewall within the Windows operating system to perform port filtering or enforce packet signing across a network. We'll also look at ways to secure the Domain Naming System (DNS) service, another common attack vector that needs to be secured on a modern network.

Finally, we'll discuss ways to secure wireless network traffic. Wireless technologies are growing in popularity for both private and public networks, and present their own unique challenges to network security. We'll look at some common vulnerabilities of wireless transmissions, and ways to design a secure wireless LAN for your organization. True, we're covering a lot of material here, but it will certainly illustrate some exciting ways to secure your enterprise network using Windows Server 2003. Developing a firm grasp on the technologies discussed in this chapter will make you a better security administrator, and will be invaluable as you prepare for the 70-298 exam.

EXAM 70-298 OBJECTIVE 3.1

Designing Network Infrastructure Security

Designing a secure TCP/IP-based network begins with thorough planning. Whether you're designing a new network or upgrading an existing network, the first step is to clearly map out the existing or desired network structure. By knowing where resources are located and what services they require, you'll be able to develop a more secure network infrastructure.

The network infrastructure is comprised of hardware and software elements and has both a physical and logical structure. Hardware clearly includes servers, hosts, and gateways, as well as printers, mobile devices, and even the network cabling specifications (grade, length, connection points). The software side includes operating systems, applications, and services such as Dynamic Host Configuration Protocol (DHCP) and other network protocols, and the NTFS file format, to name a few. The physical structure includes where servers are located in a building or at different locations, how locations are connected, cabling diagrams and the overall physical organization of network resources. The logical groupings include domains, organizational units (OUs), user and computer groups. Although this list is not exhaustive, it gives you an idea of the scope of the elements that should be clearly delineated, listed, inventoried, and mapped out. Once you understand how your network infrastructure is organized, you can begin the task of developing security policies and practices.

The high-level elements involved with designing a secure network infrastructure are:

- Plan network security.
- Create secure boundaries.
- Deploy network security technologies.
- Deploy server, application, and user security technologies.
- Deploy network monitoring and auditing.

This chapter focuses specifically on how to design network security technologies, and in particular, the Internet Protocol Security protocol (IPSec) to create a secure network from end to end.

Your overall network security plan should include several elements. The first step is to create secure boundaries. This includes both internal and external boundaries in both physical and virtual groupings. Internally, you can place sensitive servers or users with higher security needs on isolated network segments. You can place vulnerable servers in access-controlled locations and strictly limit access to those servers. Externally, you must configure firewalls, perimeter networks, or demilitarized zones (DMZ) to protect your network from external threats. We'll discuss this in more detail when we look at securing wireless networks later in this chapter. The use of firewalls and proxy servers protects the network by physically isolating the corporate network resources from the external network. Through the use of filtering and security policies, access through the firewall is controlled and the chance of intrusion is much lower than without these precautions. With proxy servers, internal network addresses and configuration information is hidden from external view because all authorized traffic in to and out of the company flows through the proxy server. Proxy servers and firewalls serve different but related functions, so in some cases, one server can be configured to serve both functions. External access must be controlled, and monitoring and auditing should be used to keep watch over network security at all times. In addition to these strategies, securing the network includes these best practices:

- Physically securing critical network servers, including access-controlled locations, using the NTFS file system format.
- Using Encrypting File System (EFS) where appropriate.
- Requiring user authentication, strong passwords, and other strong account policies.
- Securing network service data traveling on the network.
- Securing application and user data traveling on the network.
- Securing network access points and network access.

After developing your overall security plan, you need to drill down to design the security for the network infrastructure. Network infrastructure includes those services and protocols used to run network services. This includes DHCP, Domain Naming System (DNS), Windows Internet Naming System (WINS), authentication traffic, and IP traffic, to name just a few. As you know, the Windows operating system uses the TCP/IP suite as the networking protocol. The introduction in Windows 2000 of the IPSec framework made a significant contribution toward securing the network infrastructure. IPSec can be used to secure data and network services traffic across the intranet and across the extranet, including across the Internet. It uses signing, encryption, or both to secure IP packets in a manner that prevents common security problems. Remote access can be secured through creating a virtual private network (VPN) using Layer 2 Tunneling Protocol (L2TP), which uses IPSec to provide secure data transmission across external connections such as the Internet. We'll look at IPSec in detail in this chapter.

As with any security model, you must find a workable balance between security and usability. Typically, the higher the security, the lower the usability. A network that is so secure that users cannot access resources is not particularly useful. By the same token, a network that is so accessible that it's constantly attached is not useful either. An unsecured network creates a significant liability for the firm in terms of exposing corporate or trade secrets, private corporate data, and even user privacy. Finding this balance requires that you take several logical steps to implement the best solution for your firm. These steps include:

1. **Assess the risk to your network and system data and determine the appropriate level of security.** Assessing risk means looking at your physical building and network location. Can anyone just walk into the office, or is access controlled? Do visitors have to sign in, or do they roam freely about? Are exterior doors kept locked, or is there a lot of traffic in and out? These are the kinds of assessments you'll need to make about the physical security of your network infrastructure. Another part of the risk assessment is to identify the risk or downside of your company's data being compromised. For example, if you deal with individual health records, compromising that data could have serious legal consequences. The same is true if you're dealing with financial data, human resources data, personal user data such as social security numbers, or even sensitive proprietary or confidential corporate data.
2. **Identify valuable information.** Even if your firm deals with sensitive data, it's likely that not all the data is critical and must be secured. It's important to assess what is valuable information and what is not. Certainly, usernames, passwords, and social security numbers would rank high on the list of valuable information that should be protected. Identifying valuable data is key to avoiding over- or under-protecting the network. To determine the need for security, consider the consequences of particular data being stolen by a hacker and published on the Internet. If it would have serious consequences (legal, financial, ethical, organizational), that data needs to be secured. In addition to a balance between security and usability, there is also a balance between securing data and network performance. Every time you choose to secure a particular class of network traffic, you add layers of overhead to the IP packet transmission process that can, in some cases, cause serious degradation of system performance.
3. **Define security policies based on risk.** Once you've assessed risk and identified valuable data, you can define security policies based on that information. Typically, there are three levels of security defined for Windows Server 2003 and the IPSec framework:
    - **Minimal security** There is no sensitive data exchanged and the risks to the system are low. IPSec is not implemented (default setting).
    - **Standard security** Certain computers, including servers, store valuable data and should be secured. Windows XP and Windows Server 2003 use security policies that provide for data security but do not require the highest level of security. Two examples of secure policies

that involve standard security are Client (Respond Only) and Server (Request Security). Each of these settings uses the highest security *available* between the two computers without *requiring* the highest security. These policies will be discussed in more detail later in this chapter.

- **High security** If servers store highly sensitive data such as financial data, medical records, or other highly sensitive information, high security should be implemented. This is especially true of data that is transmitted via remote access or via the Internet. The security policy Secure Server (Require Security), a default policy in the high security model, requires IPSec for all traffic being sent or received. Unsecured communication with any computer that cannot use IPSec is not allowed.

4. **Determine how security policies can best be implemented in the enterprise**. You can implement security in a number of ways in Windows Server 2003. The preferred method is via IPSec policies that consist of one or more IPSec rules. These rules include:

   - Selected filter list
   - Selected filter action
   - Selected authentication method
   - Selected connection type
   - Selected tunnel setting

   There are essentially two ways to configure IPSec policies. You can create a new policy and define rules for the policy, or you can create a set of filter lists and actions and then create policies. In either case, these policies must then be assigned to a computer, user group, domain, or OU, to name a few. We'll discuss this in more detail later in this chapter.

5. **Ensure security management and technology requirements are available and in place.** To create the most secure network infrastructure possible, you should implement Active Directory, which was first introduced in Windows 2000. In addition, you should upgrade as many servers and clients as possible to Windows 2000, at the very minimum, and Windows XP or Windows Server 2003 optimally. This will allow you to use the very latest technologies for implementing and managing security in your environment. In addition, your security management should include organizing computers in similar roles into OUs for better security and ease of administration. OUs are virtual groupings of computers for ease of management and appear as objects within a folder. For example, you can place all application servers into an OU. When designing and implementing security solutions such as security templates and IPSec policies, you can apply these

to all computers in an OU, a much easier and more secure method than managing each computer individually.

6. **Provide users with an easy and secure method of accessing the appropriate resources.** As mentioned earlier, security is always a fine balance between keeping data secure and allowing legitimate users access to needed data. By implementing security methods such as smart cards, VPN, and IPSec, the security becomes almost entirely transparent to users and still maintains tight security where needed. Higher security almost always means slower response times, because security services require CPU cycles to be processed. Testing and evaluating security measures with realistic loads is an important part of security management. Automating tasks, such as enforcing security policies via group policies, will also reduce problems.

Common Types of Attacks

So far, we've talked in general terms about what you should consider when reviewing securing network infrastructure. Let's take a moment here to review the common types of attacks. Understanding attacks clearly is the key to implementing needed security technologies for your network.

Many types of attacks can occur, and it seems someone is figuring out another way to attack a secure computer system almost every day. Some of the common methods are eavesdropping, data modification, IP address spoofing, password-based attacks, denial-of-service (DoS) attacks, man-in-the-middle attacks, compromised key attacks, sniffer attacks, and application-layer attacks.

- **Eavesdropping** Eavesdropping occurs when an intruder is monitoring network data and can read any unprotected data that travels across the network.
- **Data modification** An intruder can modify data in a packet without the sender or the receiver ever knowing it.
- **Identity spoofing (IP address spoofing)** IP addresses are used to identify computers on a network. Attackers can assume another computer's IP address and the packet appears to originate from a valid address on the network. This is known as identity spoofing, IP address spoofing, or IP spoofing.
- **Password-based attack** Gaining access to one or more legitimate passwords is like payday for a hacker. Older applications don't always protect password information, and it is sometimes transmitted in clear text.
- **Brute force attack** Hackers can also run programs against user accounts in attempt to derive the password. This is called a brute force attack since

the hacker will have to run through every conceivable combination of alpha, numeric, and special characters to find a combination that works with a given user account. One form of brute force attack is a *dictionary attack* where words from the dictionary are used as the basis for trying to guess legitimate passwords. This is one reason why policies requiring complex passwords prohibit the use of any contiguous combination of letters found in a dictionary.

- **Denial-of-service attack** These attacks don't typically generate data for the hacker, but instead are intended to disrupt the services provided to legitimate users. DoS attacks can cause abnormal application behavior or termination. A DoS attack is sometimes used as a smoke screen to keep IT staff busy while a hacker gets into the network in some other way. Some DoS attacks can cause peculiar computer behavior that results in exposing protected data.
- **Man-in-the-middle attack** This occurs when someone is monitoring, capturing, and controlling data between the sender and receiver. The danger is that each side assumes the other party is the intended party, and data can be exchanged with an interloper without either side's knowledge.
- **Compromised key attack** A key is a secret code or number used to encrypt or decrypt information. If a hacker is able to obtain a key, the hacker can then use that key to compromise other data or network areas. A key that is obtained by a hacker is considered a compromised key.
- **Sniffer attack** A sniffer is a device that can read, monitor, and capture network data as it crosses the wire. When packets are unencrypted, anyone who can monitor data on the network can compromise security.
- **Application-layer attack** This attack targets application servers by deliberately causing the application or server to fail. When this occurs, the attacker might be able to bypass normal security or controls. Once compromised, the application server can be used to spread viruses, introduce a sniffer program to gain further data, disable other security controls for future attacks, or simply delete or modify data on the server, including the operating system, the applications, and data files that reside on the server.
- **Social engineering** Ironically, one of the most common security breaches is caused by social engineering, which occurs when a legitimate user is duped into revealing usernames, passwords, IP addresses, credit card information, or other sensitive data. In recent years, almost everyone with an Internet e-mail account has received at least one e-mail that appears to be from a legitimate source asking for username and password, credit card information, and so forth. This is social engineering and poses one of the

greatest security risks. However, in this chapter, we'll focus on the technology-based risks discussed. The best defense against social engineering is really not technology based. Educating users about the risks and the tricks they're likely to encounter is the very best way to protect the network from social engineering threats.

Assessing Risk for Network Services

Now that we've reviewed the overall security practices and some of the common risks, let's look at some of the common network services that should be assessed for risk and the need for additional security. These are:

- Dynamic Host Configuration Protocol (DHCP)
- Domain Name Service (DNS)
- Windows Internet Naming Service (WINS)
- Internet Information Server (IIS)
- Routing and Remote Access (RRAS)
- Application and file sharing

Each of these services uses the Transmission Control Protocol/Internet Protocol (TCP/IP) suite of protocols for sending and receiving data across the network. It is this data moving along the medium (wire or wireless) that becomes an additional threat to network security, as intruders who gain access to this infrastructure data can compromise the network in a number of ways. When we think of data, we typically think of files or user data. However, network data such as usernames or IP addresses are more common targets of attack because gaining this information is ultimately far more useful in gaining further access to or control of the network. Thus, this data must be evaluated for risk and secured appropriately.

As we discussed earlier, by grouping servers that have similar functions or roles together into OUs, you can more effectively manage common threats. If all DNS servers are placed in an OU, you can apply security measures such as security templates or group policies on all of them. This reduces administration, error, and troubleshooting time. Since an OU is simply a logical grouping, using OUs is the easiest method for managing security for computers. Of course, the flip side is also true—if you make an error in setting up security, it will affect *all* computers in that OU. Testing, monitoring, and auditing are the best ways to mitigate that risk.

DHCP is the method used in Windows Server 2003 to dynamically assign IP addresses for legitimate domain member computers. Malicious users conceivably could attempt to lease all the IP addresses from a DHCP server, which would result in the inability of legitimate computers to obtain an IP address. Without an IP address, those computers would be unable to join to the domain. In smaller companies, this is not usually a major threat, but in larger companies, this threat must be addressed. In Chapter 2, "Securing Servers Based on Function," we discussed how to secure a DHCP server against these threats.

DNS is a very popular target for hackers, because access to this data provides the hacker with very valuable information about computer names, IP addresses, and the network structure. Protecting DNS data has become increasingly important, especially as contact with the Internet has increased. Using IPSec to secure DNS traffic is one part of the security solution for DNS, which we'll examine in detail later in this chapter.

WINS is still required for any computers running operating systems prior to Windows 2000. Computers running Windows 2000, Windows XP, or Windows Server 2003 use DNS for name resolution instead of the Microsoft proprietary WINS method. If your network has older clients, you will still need to provide WINS for NetBIOS name resolution services. The threat to WINS, however, is typically when WINS traffic is replicated across a wide area network (WAN). In these cases, replication can be set up to use IPSec or VPN tunnels to protect this traffic during replication. We'll discuss how to secure WINS traffic with IPSec.

IIS provides Web-related services, including File Transmission Protocol (FTP), HyperText Transport Protocol (HTTP), and Network News Transport Protocol (NNTP), among others. IIS is probably the most vulnerable and the most hacked application because of its exposure to the Internet. An entire chapter in this book is dedicated to securing IIS, so we won't go into too much detail here. However, there are a number of ways IIS can be secured, and some of the new features in Windows Server 2003 help address vulnerabilities of IIS. In Windows Server 2003, IIS is no longer installed by default, which improves security right out of the box. In addition, when IIS is installed, it is locked down by default. There are also several tools that can further analyze and lock down security to help mitigate risk.

RRAS is also a very vulnerable point in the network. It's become increasingly common in today's networking environment to have users working from locations other than the office. Remote access increases the user's range in terms of data access, but it certainly opens the door to intruders. RRAS must employ strong user authentication to ensure that only authenticated users gain access to network resources. In addition, the data that flows back and forth from a remote user to the corporate network must be secured, because in most cases, that data is traveling over a public network. This makes the data far more susceptible to capture, monitoring, modification, and attack. IPSec is an excellent part of the security solution for remote access, and we'll explore IPSec in just a moment.

Finally, application and file data is transmitted across the network via application servers (including Terminal Server) and file and print servers. Data can be secured via securing physical access to computers, using the NTFS file format to protect files and folders on system volumes, and using IPSec to secure sensitive data as it travels the network.

As you know, each of these server roles implements many different types of network and system protocols. Applications all use different methods to communicate with the user and with other network resources. The most effective security solution is one that:

- Is transparent to the application and the user.
- Will protect only sensitive data on the internal and external network.
- Will be easy to administer and hard to crack.

The IPSec framework is just such a solution, so let's review IPSec now.

IPSec Overview

This book assumes you're already familiar with both Active Directory and IPSec. However, we will review IPSec here to refresh your memory, and then we'll look at how to use IPSec policies to secure the network infrastructure.

IPSec is a suite of protocols that provides protection of data integrity, and authentication. It can also provide optional privacy and replay protection. The IPSec protocols are defined by the Internet Engineering Task Force (IETF) Request for Comments (RFCs) 2401 through 2409 (or IETF RFCs 2401–2409). This specification defines security protocols, security associations, key management, and algorithms for authentication and encryption.

IPSec provides security services at the transport layer of the TCP/IP stack . The IPSec driver interfaces with the TCP/UDP transport layer and the Internet layer, making it transparent to users and applications. It can receive network communication and, through the use of filters and rules, it can:

- Select required security protocols.
- Determine algorithms to use for a particular service.
- Use cryptographic keys required by any of the services.

IPSec is used to secure the communication channel between computers and to secure the data flowing across that channel. IPSec can secure any path between a pair of computers, whether it's client to client, server to server, client to server, or between a security gateway and any host.

IPSec secures data by signing the packet and encrypting data. You can choose to use one or the other or both. Signing the packet involves using a hash value to make sure the packet has not been tampered with. Encrypting the data involves an encryption algorithm as well as keys for encrypting and decrypting the data.

Security Associations

IPSec begins creating a secure environment by securing the channel between two computers. Essentially, a security association is an agreement between two computers that includes how they will exchange and protect data that flows between them. This agreement is called a security association (SA), which is defined by IETF RFC 2408. This specification defines the Internet Security Association and Key Management Protocol (ISAKMP)/Oakley. There are two parts of this—creating a security association and managing keys for data encryption. Oakley is a key generation protocol. Within Microsoft, the ISAKMP process is often referred to as the Internet Key Exchange (IKE). IKE specifies:

- How security associations are created (Phase I).
- How keys are exchanged (Phase II) once the SA is established.

Once a security association is formed and keys are exchanged, data can be sent back and forth in one of several secure states.

The first SA (Phase I SA) specifies *how* the two computers trust each other and it protects their security negotiation. IKE operates in main mode during this phase. The second SA (Phase II SA) specifies the actual security methods and keys for each direction of communication. IKE operates in quick mode in this phase and automatically creates and refreshes a shared, secret key for each SA. The secret key is then independently created by both computers so the key is not transmitted across the network. Both main mode and quick mode statistics can be viewed in the IP Security Monitor snap-in to the Microsoft Management Console (MMC).

Phase I Security Association

Both phases of establishing a security connection require policy negotiation. In Phase I, four mandatory parameters must be established via negotiation:

- Encryption algorithm
- Hash algorithm
- Authentication method
- The Diffie-Hellman (DH) group to be used for the base keying material

IPSec Encryption Algorithms

IPSec can be used to ensure data confidentiality via encryption. The encryption method used by IPSec is based on one of the algorithms shown in Table 5.1.

Table 5.1 IPSec Encryption Algorithms

Encryption Algorithm	Description
Data Encryption Standard (DES)	Standard DES uses 56-bit encryption. This is the default value used in Windows Server 2003.
Triple DEC (3DES)	3DES uses 56 bits times 3 making it far more difficult to "crack" than DES. With 3DEC, the data is encrypted with the first key, decrypted with the second key, and encrypted again with a third key, hence the term "triple" DES.
40-bit DES	As its name implies, a less secure encryption algorithm is 40-bit DES. This is sometimes used for down-level client support because earlier versions of Windows operating systems do not support DES or 3DES.
None	You can choose not to encrypt data at all. This might make sense in scenarios where either the down-level client cannot support any encryption (in which case you probably want to consider upgrading that client) or in situations where the data itself is not particularly sensitive.

Encryption is one of several components of Public Key Infrastructure (PKI), covered in detail elsewhere in this book.

To encrypt and decrypt, you need keys. Public cryptographic systems use two keys—a public key known to anyone and a private or secret key known only to the sender and receiver. This system was originally devised in 1976 by Whitman Diffie and Martin Hellman. For this reason, public key cryptography is sometimes referred to as *Diffie-Hillman encryption* or *asymmetric encryption*, because it requires two keys instead of one (which is called symmetric encryption).

IPSec Hash Algorithms

You can choose between two hash functions when implementing IPSec policy: Message Digest (MD5) and Secure Hash Algorithm 1 (SHA1). The hash function is also used by other security protocols, including the Challenge Handshake Authentication Protocol (CHAP) and the Extensible Authentication Protocol (EAP). Table 5.2 compares the two hash algorithm methods.

Table 5.2 IPSec Hash Algorithms

Hash Algorithm	Description
Message Digest (MD5)	MD5 is based on IETF RFC 1321 and completes four passes over the data blocks, using a different numeric constant for each word in the message on each pass. This process creates a message digest, which is the message converted into a fixed string of digits. It is a one-way hash function, meaning that it is virtually impossible to reverse engineer the string to derive the original text. The result of this process is a 128-bit hash that is used for the integrity check.
Secure Hash Algorithm 1 (SHA1)	The SHA1 was developed by the National Institute of Standards and Technology described in the Federal Information Processing Standard (FIPS) Publication 180-1. The computational process is similar to that used in the MD5 hash, but SHA1 results in a 160-bit hash being used instead of a 128-bit hash. The longer hash generated by SHA1 provides greater security than the MD5 hash.

Authentication Methods

The authentication methods that can be used by a security association include certificates, Kerberos v5, and pre-shared keys. Table 5.3 compares the three authentication methods that can be used and are discussed in order of most-to-least secure.

Table 5.3 IPSec Authentication Methods

Authentication Methods	Description
Certificates	Certificates are issued by certificate authorities (CAs). Some well-known organizations that provide certificates (act as CAs) are Microsoft, Entrust, VeriSign, and Netscape. An encrypted digital certificate contains the applicant's public key and other identification information. Certificates are the most secure form of authentication and are the most viable choice in environments that require high security.

Continued

Table 5.3 IPSec Authentication Methods

Authentication Methods	Description
Kerberos v5	Kerberos v5 is an authentication protocol and was established as the default authentication protocol in Windows 2000. If Kerberos v5 is used, the computer identity is *unencrypted* until encryption of the entire payload takes place during authentication. This creates a security hole that can be exploited. Authentication via Kerberos should not be implemented in highly secure settings. In those cases, use certificates.
Pre-shared keys	Pre-shared keys are fast and easy to use because they use a shared, secret key that is previously agreed upon by two users. It does not require the use of a public key certificate or the Kerberos v5 protocol. This key is used for authentication only and does not encrypt the data. Typically, pre-shared keys should be used only when certificates or Kerberos v5 cannot be used. Pre-shared keys store the authentication key in clear text in the IPSec policy, which means this method is not very secure.

Diffie-Hellman (DH) Groups

The fourth element in Phase I SA negotiations is the negotiation of the Diffie-Hellman (DH) group to be used for the base prime numbers, which are called the *keying material*. Each DH group defines the length of the keying material. These are summarized in Table 5.4.

Table 5.4 Diffie-Hellman Groups

Diffie-Hellman Group	Description
DH Group 2048 (high)	The highest setting, Group 2048, uses 2048 bits of keying material as the basis for encryption. This is a highly secure setting.
DH Group 2 (medium)	DH Group 2 (medium) is the default setting in Windows Server 2003 and provides medium protection by using 1024 bits of keying material.

Continued

Table 5.4 Diffie-Hellman Groups

Diffie-Hellman Group	Description
DH Group 1 (low)	DH Group 1 (low) is defined by the use of 768 bits of keying material for encryption. This is considered the least secure and in most cases where security is a concern, it should not be used. This is sometimes used with down-level clients that do not support the use of more bits for encryption.

The strength of the DH group is directly proportional to the strength of the key. Clearly, the longer the key length, the more difficult it is to crack—both in terms of the time and level of sophistication needed to do so.

Phase II Security Association

Phase II of the security association negotiation determines how data will be secured via:

- The IPSec protocol to be used
- The hash algorithm
- The encryption algorithm

Remember, the hash and encryption algorithms in Phase I are used to negotiate communication *between the two computers*. The hash and encryption algorithms in Phase II are used *on the data* itself. Like Phase I, Phase II also uses hashing and keying algorithms for packet integrity (hashing) and data security (keying and encrypting). The third element is the IPSec protocol to be used. The IPSec protocols are the *Authentication Header (AH)* and the *Encapsulating Security Payload (ESP)*. Before we discuss the details of these two protocols, it's important to review the two modes for IPSec.

IPSec Modes

AH and ESP can be used in transport mode or tunnel mode. Essentially, transport mode secures only the IP payload while it's in transit. Tunnel mode secures the entire packet, including the original IP header, by signing (and/or encrypting) the entire contents of the packet, including the IP header.

Transport mode is the default mode in IPSec and is used for end-to-end communications between two computers. When transport mode is used, only the IP payload is encrypted via the use of AH or ESP.

In tunnel mode, IPSec encrypts the IP header *and* the IP payload. This contrasts with transport mode that encrypts only the IP payload. In tunnel mode, the entire IP packet is encapsulated with an AH or ESP header and with an additional IP header.

The IP addresses in the *outer* IP header are the tunnel endpoints (source and destination), such as a proxy server or gateway. The IP addresses *in* the encapsulated IP header are the *ultimate* source and destination for the packet. By encapsulating the ultimate source and destination, IP addresses are protected while the data travels from one tunnel endpoint to another. These endpoints typically connect via an unsecured medium such as the Internet. Now let's look at the protocols used in these two modes.

IPSec Protocols

IPSec uses either AH or ESP to protect packets from modification or viewing. The AH protocol, IP protocol 50, is used to sign a packet to ensure it is not modified in any way. AH protects the IP header from modification as well as the IP payload. ESP can sign and encrypt data in an IP packet. When using ESP, the original IP header is only protected when ESP is used in tunnel mode.

IPSec protects an IP packet using one of two methods (or both methods, if desired). The AH protocol uses various methods to protect the integrity of the packet. It is sometimes referred to as IP protocol 50 since that is the port is uses. IPSec using AH will attach an AH header to the IP packet. This AH header contains information about the packet that guarantees the packet will arrive at its destination without alteration. If the receiving computer receives an IPSec protected packet with the AH header information intact, it can be sure the packet is unaltered. If the packet has been altered, the receiving computer will reject the packet. The packet structure IPSec uses when protecting a packet with AH is shown in Figures 5.1 and 5.2. Two modes can be used with each protocol, transport mode or tunnel mode. Thus, there are two packet structures possible when using AH (and ESP). The shaded area is the original IP packet data, the area in white indicates the AH segment(s).

Figure 5.1 IPSec Transport Mode with Authentication Header

Figure 5.2 IPSec Tunnel Mode with Authentication Header

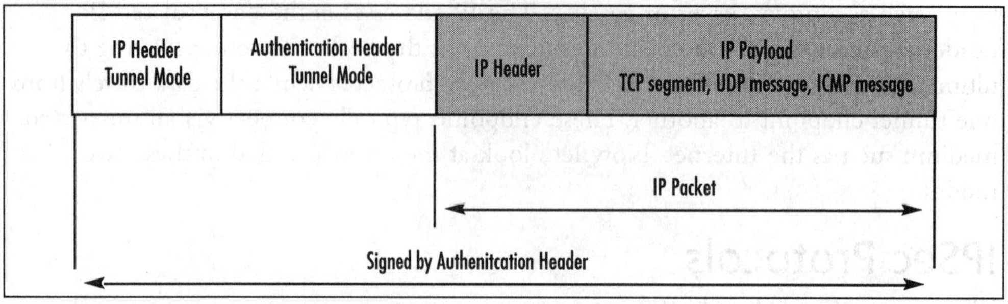

The second IPSec protocol is *ESP,* IP protocol 51, which is used to ensure not only that the packet will arrive intact but that the data within it is secure. Securing data is often referred to as *data confidentiality* or *data privacy.* ESP signs and encrypts data to make the packet and its payload secure. In the default mode (transport), ESP does not protect the IP header because it only signs the IP payload. Therefore, ESP can be used in conjunction with AH to protect the entire packet, although for practical purposes, this is used only where there is a very strong need for security. The additional overhead required to formulate a packet with both AH and ESP protection is generally more than most firms need, but can be implemented if the computers using it can handle the load generated. In tunnel mode, ESP encapsulates and secures the original packet, including the IP header, but does not secure the outer IP header. ESP uses an ESP header, ESP trailer, and an ESP authentication trailer to protect the data. Figures 5.3 and 5.4 show the two packet formats with ESP, again in *transport* or *tunnel* mode. Again, the gray areas show the original IP packet contents, and the areas shown in white are the ESP segments.

Figure 5.3 IPSec Transport Mode with ESP

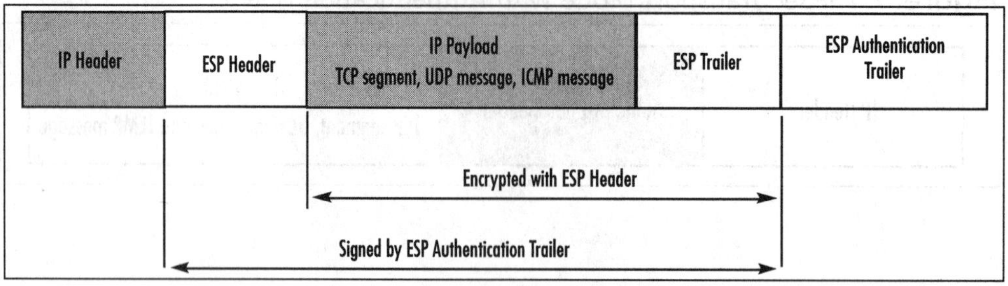

Figure 5.4 IPSec Tunnel Mode with ESP

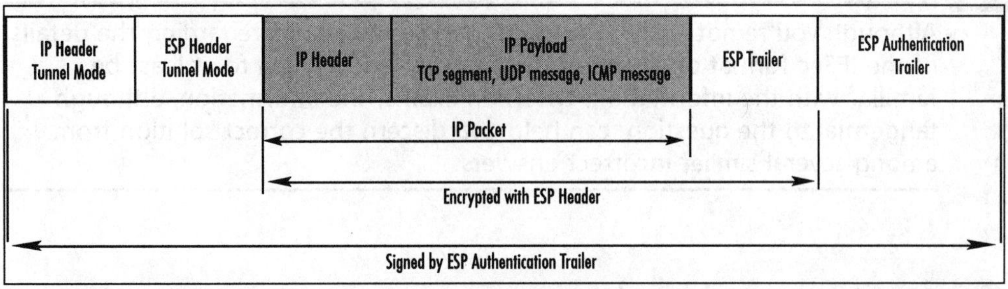

Now that you've looked at the two protocols and how they protect the packet, let's compare the two to see how they're similar and different. Understanding these concepts will be important when you implement IPSec and on the exam. Table 5.5 delineates the similarities and differences between AH and ESP.

Table 5.5 Comparison of Authentication Header and Encapsulated Security Payload Protocols

Requirement	Protocol	Description
Data and header must be protected from modification and replay, data remains readable.	AH	Use in situations where data does not need to be secret but must be authenticated. One common use of AH is where firewall filtering requires packet inspection; the packet must be authenticated but must remain readable.
Data must be protected but IP addressing does not require protection.	ESP	Use in situations where data must be kept secret such as database traffic or protocol data.
Both the IP header and the IP payload need to be protected.	Both AH and ESP	Use in situations that require the highest security. Typically, ESP is implemented alone for security because implementing AH and ESP creates tremendous overhead.

Typically, ESP provides adequate protection for secure situations because it protects everything except the IP header. The IP addresses for ESP-protected packets cannot be spoofed because ESP guarantees authentication of the data's origin. Therefore, the additional overhead required to protect an ESP packet with additional AH protection is generally not worthwhile.

EXAM WARNING

Although you're not likely to run into *specific* questions regarding the details of the IPSec format on the exam, it's always a good idea to at least be familiar with the information. Often on exams, the information, although tangential to the question, can help you discern the correct solution from among several similar incorrect answers.

Authentication Header

Using a hash function, the data in the authentication header is protected from tampering and in turn, it protects the data by signing the entire packet. Some data in the packet might not be included in this protection because data in some fields might legitimately change during transportation, such as the *Time To Live* (TTL) field. The packet format for AH in *transport* mode is shown in Figure 5.1.

Let's compare that to the IP packet using AH in *tunnel* mode, as shown in Figure 5.2. A new IP header and the AH header are placed in front of the original IP header. The new IP header is the address of the intermediary such as a gateway or router. The AH signs the entire packet, including the new IP header. Notice that the IP header in the middle is the IP header of the original packet and contains the ultimate source and destination addresses. The outer IP addresses are used to route the packet to intermediaries and to protect the ultimate source and destination addresses. An important note is that the intermediaries, such as gateways or proxy servers, need not be configured with IPSec because the packet appears to be a normal packet to these computers.

Clearly, using IPSec in tunnel mode makes sense when you want to protect traffic that has to pass through an unprotected area such as the Internet or some other untrusted source. Tunnel mode is often used for remote access and typically not used for local connections where transport mode is generally more appropriate. Keep in mind that if the data is being sent between two *host* computers using IPSec tunneling, the IP header on the outside of the encapsulated data is the same as the IP header on the inside.

A few notes of caution here. Tunnel mode secures IP traffic; it can't be used to secure non-IP traffic. Windows Server 2003 does not support protocol-specific or port-specific tunnels.

Tunnels can be configured via IP Security Policy Management and Group Policy to specify rules for inbound and outbound tunnel traffic. We'll explore IP Security Policy in depth later in this chapter.

Before we leave AH, it's helpful to understand what's actually *in* the AH segment. Without going into tremendous detail, let's look at the elements of the AH. Table 5.6 describes each element and its use.

Table 5.6 AH Header Description

Name of AH Header Field	Description of Field
Next Header	This field is used to describe the IP payload that follows the AH header by using the IP protocol ID.
Length	This field indicates the length of the AH header.
Security Parameters Index (SPI)	This field is used in combination with AH (or ESP) and the destination address to identify the correct security association to which the packet belongs.
Sequence Number	The sequence number is what provides anti-replay protection. This number is a 32-bit, incrementally increasing number that begins with the number 1. It indicates the packet number sent over the security association. The sequence number cannot repeat for the life of the quick mode security association, which is what protects the packet from replay. The receiver checks the sequence number against packets received from this security association. If it is a duplicate number, the packet is rejected.
Authentication Data	The authentication data is called the integrity check value (ICV), also known as the *message authentication code*. This value is used to verify the message integrity and authentication. The ICV is calculated over the packet. The receiver calculates the ICV and checks it against the one sent by the sender.

Encapsulated Security Payload

AH is fine to use for authentication and integrity, but it does not provide privacy. To keep the data in a packet confidential, it must be encrypted. That's where the second IPSec protocol comes in, Encapsulated Security Payload (ESP). Like AH, ESP works in transport or tunnel mode, and like AH, ESP provides authentication, integrity, and anti-replay protection. Where ESP differs is that it provides data encryption, which AH does not. In the default transport mode, only AH will protect the IP header, so you can see why you might want to use both AH and ESP to fully protect a packet. Figure 5.3 shows the format of a packet using ESP in transport mode.

The difference between AH and ESP becomes immediately apparent when you look at the packet format because ESP *appends* data to the IP packet itself. The signed portion of the packet is signed for integrity and authentication. The encrypted portion provides confidentiality of the payload. ESP is used in tunnel mode when packets will be sent over an unsecured link. The packet format for ESP in tunnel mode is shown in Figure 5.4.

Notice that a new header for tunneling is added to the packet. Everything that follows, then, is signed, except for the ESP authentication trailer. The entire packet is appended with an ESP authentication trailer and then the packet is encrypted. Thus, the original IP header is encrypted as part of the encapsulated data. The new tunnel header is only used to route the packet between endpoints. Both AH and ESP can be used singly or together in tunneling mode to provide integrity, authentication, and confidentiality.

As with AH, the fields used in the ESP header have specific functions that help understand how the packet is protected. Table 5.7 describes the elements found in the ESP header, ESP trailer, and ESP authentication trailer.

Table 5.7 Encapsulated Security Payload Header Descriptions

Name of ESP Field	Description of Field
Security Parameter Index (SPI) *Used in ESP header*	This field is used in combination with ESP (or AH) and the destination address to identify the correct security association to which the packet belongs.
Sequence Number *Used in ESP Header*	The sequence number is what provides anti-replay protection. The sequence number cannot repeat for the life of the quick mode security association, which is what protects the packet from replay. The receiver checks the sequence number against packets received from this security association. If it is a duplicate number, the packet is rejected.
Padding *Used in ESP trailer*	Padding of 0 to 255 bytes is used to make sure the encrypted payload's data falls on *byte* boundaries required by encryption algorithms.
Padding Length *Used in ESP trailer*	Indicates the length of the padding used in the padding field. The receiver uses this information to remove the padding after the data has been decrypted.
Next Header *Used in ESP trailer*	Identifies the type of data in the payload.

Continued

Table 5.7 Encapsulated Security Payload Header Descriptions

Name of ESP Field	Description of Field
Authentication Data *Used in ESP authentication trailer*	The authentication data is called the integrity check value (ICV) or message authentication code. This value is used to verify the message integrity and authentication. The receiver calculates the ICV and checks it against the one sent by the sender.

Although you might not see specific questions on the format of the AH or ESP protected packets, you might see questions that ask you to assess what type of IPSec formatting is best in a given environment. Understanding how AH and ESP work alone and in combination in transport and tunnel modes will certainly give you a great understanding of IPSec and how to best implement it in your organization.

TEST DAY TIP

An important differentiation between AH and ESP is that ESP provides confidentiality. When you are assessing questions and answers on the exam, pay particular attention to this detail. If confidentiality is required, you must use ESP either by itself or in combination with AH. Keep this in mind when assessing proposed answers or solutions on the exam.

The IPSec Process

The *IPSec Policy Agent* resides between the transport layer and the Internet in the TCP/IP stack. Its job is to monitor all inbound and outbound IP traffic and to "grab" any IP traffic that meets the requirements of the IPSec policies applied to that computer. When an IP packet that matches an IPSec policy is captured, it is secured in the manner specified by that policy. This security is performed by the *IPSec driver*. Once the packet is secured by the IPSec driver, it is sent up (transport layer) or down (Internet or network layer) the TCP/IP stack for delivery. At the receiving end, the computer's IPSec works in reverse to identify IPSec packets, verify packet integrity, and decrypt data (if needed). If the packet has been compromised, the receiving computer rejects the packet.

Note that when a secured packet reaches an intermediary computer such as a gateway, proxy, or firewall, the packet is simply passed along as any other packet would be. These intermediary computers do not have to have IPSec implemented for them to properly handle a secure packet.

IPSec can use several different methods for protecting data integrity and confidentiality. The protocols and methods that can be used are specified by IPSec policies on the computers. For example, although two computers will negotiate various security options, the negotiation is limited to the filters applied by both computers' IPSec policies. If they have vastly different policies specified, they might not be able to create an SA at all. That's why it's important to understand your network configuration and test your security configurations thoroughly before rolling them out to your organization.

IPSec Policies Overview

Now that we've reviewed IPSec, let's take a look at how IPSec is implemented in Windows Server 2003. IPSec policy consists of several elements: filter lists, filter actions, and rules. It's critical to understand how these work together to enforce security across the enterprise. It's important for you on the job and will certainly be one of the key topics on the exam.

Default IPSec Policies

In Chapter 2, you learned about predefined security templates provided in Windows Server 2003. Windows Server 2003 also provides predefined IPSec rules, filter lists, filter actions, and default policies. Unlike the predefined security templates, though, these predefined IPSec rules, filter lists, actions, and policies are intended to provide *examples* of how to implement IPSec policies. They *cannot* be used in organizations without modification. There are three default policies that each use a number of predefined rules, filter lists, and filter actions. We'll review these policies and the different elements here so you can become familiar with how IPSec policies work. The three default policies are Client (Respond Only), Server (Request Security), and Server (Require Security). Table 5.8 shows the description and the rules, filter lists, and filter actions used for each predefined IPSec policy.

IPSec Rules

IPSec policies are applied based on rules. A rule provides the ability to create secure communication based on the source, destination, and type of IP traffic. Each rule contains a list of IP filters and a set of security actions to take. Each policy can contain one or more rules, all of which can be active simultaneously. The <Dynamic> Default Response rule is discussed later in this section, as it is present in all IPSec policies and cannot be deleted, although it can be deactivated. Each IPSec rule consists of these elements:

- A selected filter list
- A selected filter action
- Selected authentication methods
- A selected connection type
- A selected tunnel settings

Table 5.8 Predefined IPSec Policies

Policy Name	Description	Rules, Filter Lists, Filter Actions
Client (Respond Only)	This policy can be used (once modified) to allow client computers to respond to security requests but not to initiate them. For example, you might have a DHCP server or Application server set to *require* security, and the client can respond to these requests. The policy contains the *default response rule*, which creates dynamic IPSec filters for inbound and outbound traffic based on the requested port and protocol being secured. If a server is locked down (discussed later in this section), the default response rule will not allow the client to communicate with that locked-down server. The default response rule is present in all IPSec policies by default. It cannot be removed, but it can be deactivated.	**Rule 1** (default response rule) - IP Filter list <Dynamic> - Filter Action: Default Response - Authentication: Kerberos - Tunnel Setting: None - Connection Type: All
Server (Request Security	This predefined policy is an example of a policy that could be used on computers that would prefer secure communication but would allow fallback to unsecured communication. For servers dealing with mixed clients (including down-level clients), this option provides the best balance between security and connectivity for down-level clients. There are three rules in place. The first looks at all IP traffic and requests security negotiations. If the client computer supports IPSec, a negotiation will take place. Rule 2 allows all Internet Control Message Protocol (ICMP), used	**Rule 1** – IP Filter List : All IP Traffic – Filter Action: Request Security (Optional) – Authentication: Kerberos – Tunnel Setting: None – Connection Type: All **Rule 2** – IP Filter List: All ICMP Traffic – Filter Action: Permit – Authentication: N/A – Tunnel Setting: None – Connection Type: All **Rule 3** Default Response Rule – IP Filter List: <Dynamic>

Continued

Table 5.8 Predefined IPSec Policies

Policy Name	Description	Rules, Filter Lists, Filter Actions
	to report errors and exchange limited control and status information for IP-based communications on the network. Rule 3 is the default response rule and is used to ensure a computer responds to security requests.	– Filter Action: Default Response – Authentication: Kerberos – Tunnel Setting: None – Connection Type: All
Server (Require Security)	Servers that transmit highly sensitive data should require secure communications. This predefined policy is an example of how such a policy can be designed. It contains three rules: Rule 1 requires secure communication, Rule 2 allows ICMP traffic, and Rule 3 is the default response rule. Computers running Windows 2000 require the High Encryption Pack or Service Pack 2 (or higher) to be installed in order to communicate using the 3DES algorithm. If the Windows 2000 computer does not have the High Encryption Pack or SP2 installed, it will fall back to the less secure DES. Windows XP and Windows Server 2003 support 3DES, and no modification or additional configuration is required.	**Rule 1** – IP Filter List: All IP Traffic – Filter Action: Require Security – Authentication: N/A – Tunnel Setting: None – Connection Type: All **Rule 2** – IP Filter List: All ICMP Traffic – Filter Action: Permit – Authentication: Kerberos – Tunnel Setting: None – Connection Type: All **Rule 3** Default Response Rule – IP Filter List: <Dynamic> – Filter Action: Default Response – Authentication: Kerberos – Tunnel Setting: None – Connection Type: All

To get a better feel for how these IPSec policies are constructed, we'll step through one of the predefined IPSec policies in the next exercise so you can examine the various elements and graphically see how IPSec policies work.

EXERCISE 5.01

VIEW PREDEFINED IPSEC POLICY – SERVER (REQUEST SECURITY)

1. Click **Start**, select **Run**, type **mmc** in the Open text box, click **OK** or press **Enter**.
2. The Microsoft Management Console opens a new console. Click **File**, select **Add/Remove Snap-in**.
3. In the Add/Remove snap-in dialog with the **Standalone** tab selected (default setting), click **Add**.
4. In the Add Standalone Snap-in, scroll down and select **Group Policy Object Editor**. Click **Add** and then accept the default select of "Local Computer" for the *Group Policy Object*. Click **Finish** and then click **Close**.
5. *Local Computer Policy* should be displayed in the box in the Add/Remove snap-in dialog. Click **OK** to close the dialog.
6. In the left pane of the MMC console, click the + to expand the **Local Computer Policy** node.
7. Click the + to expand the **Computer Configuration** node.
8. Click the + to expand the **Windows Settings** node.
9. Click the + to expand the **Security Settings** node.
10. Click **the IP Security Policies** on the **Local Computer node**.
11. In the right pane, the three default IPSec policies are displayed. In the right pane, click the **Server (Request Security)**, which should be the first policy listed.
12. On the menu, click **Action** and then select **Properties**. Alternately, you can right-click the policy and select **Properties** from the menu, or simply double-click the policy name to display the **Properties**.
13. The **Rules** tab is selected by default. Click the **General** tab to select it.
14. The **General** tab shows the policy name and description as well as the setting for how often it should check for policy changes.
15. Click the **Settings** button to display **Key Exchange Settings**. You can change settings for the authentication and generation of new keys based on time length or sessions. You can also specify

methods. If you want to use **Master Key Perfect Forward Secrecy** (PFS), click the check box to select that setting. If you enable this setting, the session key limit is not used. If both a master key lifetime and a session limit are specified, whichever limit comes first causes a new main mode negotiation to take place. By default, IPSec policy does not specify a session limit. Clicking this box will disable the Sessions option.

16. Click the **Methods** button. Figure 5.5 show the Key Exchange Security Methods dialog that is displayed. Notice that the settings are for IKE and specify the security method preferences, in order. To modify a setting, click the setting and then click **Edit**. To add a new setting, click **Add**. To remove a setting, click **Remove**. You can also use the **Move up** or **Move down** buttons to change the order of preference. Notice as you use the horizontal scrollbar that you can modify encryption, integrity (hash), and Diffie-Hellman Group settings here.

Figure 5.5 Key Exchange Security Methods Dialog

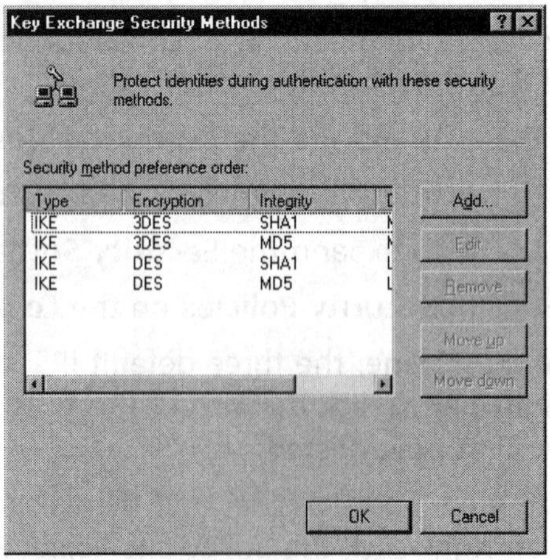

17. Click **Cancel** to exit the **Key Exchange Security Methods** dialog without accepting changes.
18. Click **Cancel** to exit **the Key Exchange Settings** dialog without accepting changes.
19. You should now be back to the **Server (Request Security) Properties** dialog. Click the **Rules** tab.
20. With the Rules tab selected, you can see the three IP Security rules defined. These match the information in Table 5.8.

21. Select the first IP Security rule, **All IP Traffic**, and use the horizontal scroll bar to view the various settings: **IP Filter list, Filter Action, Authentication, Tunnel Endpoint,** and **Connection Type.**
22. Click **Edit** to view the options on this first rule.
23. The Edit Rule Properties dialog gives you access to all the modifiable parameters. The tabs in this dialog are **IP Filter List, Filter Action, Authentication Methods, Tunnel Setting**, and **Connection Type**. If desired, look at the various options on the tabs to become familiar with the options on each.
24. Click **Cancel** to exit without saving changes.
25. Click **Cancel** to exit the Server (Request Security) Properties dialog without saving changes.
26. Close the MMC console by clicking **File**, then selecting **Exit** and clicking **No** when prompted to save the console.

As you can see, you can create intricate IPSec policies using the parameters and options we just explored in Exercise 5.01. Later, we'll create a policy so you can get some hands-on experience with creating IPSec policies.

The IPSec policy we just reviewed, Server (Request Security), contains three predefined rules, shown previously in Table 5.8. The first is to filter All IP Traffic and request security, the second is to filter All ICMP Traffic and to permit it, and the third is the <Dynamic> Default Response Rule. Let's discuss these rules in more detail.

Predefined Filter Lists

There are two predefined filter lists—one that looks for All IP Traffic and one that look for All Internet Control Message Protocol (ICMP) Traffic.

The All IP Traffic filter list looks for all IP traffic sent or received by the computer on which the filter list (via the IPSec policy) is applied. By default, the Internet Key Exchange (IKE) traffic is excluded. Other traffic types are matched against IPSec filters. IPSec does not negotiate security associations for multicasts and broadcasts, although you can configure, block, or permit filter actions specifically for these.

The All ICMP Traffic filter list looks for all ICMP traffic (IP protocol 1) sent and received by the computer. Since this traffic is used for low-level IP communication and error reporting, it is permitted in even the most secure predefined IPSec policy.

The <Dynamic> Default Response is created automatically every time a new IPSec policy is created. It cannot be created manually. It is called the default response rule because it is used to respond to security requests when no other rules apply. You can disable this rule in the Rules tab (see Exercise 5.01 step 19). You can also modify the authentication method or the security method used by the default response rule, if needed. The <Dynamic> tag indicates that the filter list is generated automatically based on the receipt of IKE negotiation packets. The filter action of Default Response cannot be configured with the typical filter actions (*Permit*, *Block*, or *Negotiate*). Unlike the other predefined rules, when you select a rule and click **Edit** (Exercise 5.01, step 23), you will only have two tabs (not five): Security Methods and Authentication Methods. To deactivate the default response, click the check box to the left of <Dynamic> to clear the check box, as shown in Figure 5.6.

Figure 5.6 Disabling Default Response Rule

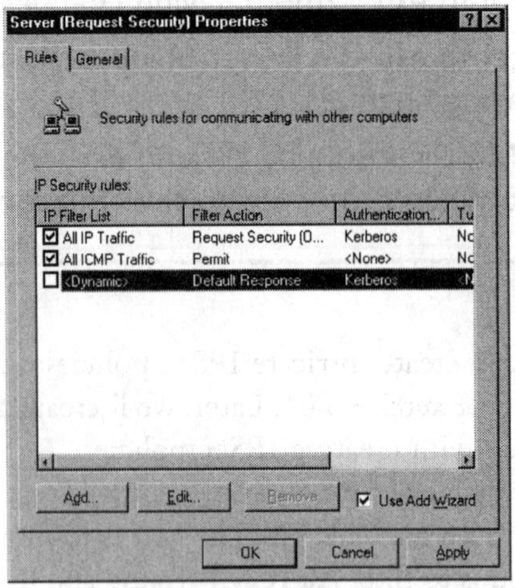

Predefined Filter Actions

Microsoft provides three predefined filter actions as examples: **Permit**, **Request Security (Optional)**, and **Require Security**.

- **Permit** When the filter action is set to permit, traffic is permitted.
- **Request Security (Optional)** This filter action requests security when it can be negotiated and is set to **Negotiate Security**. There are two exceptions to negotiated security when using this setting.
  - Incoming initial traffic is allowed, and if negotiation fails after three seconds, communication is allowed with a non-IPSec-aware computer. This is also known as *inbound passthrough*.
  - If security negotiation fails after three seconds, negotiation is halted and unsecured communication with a non-IPSec computer is allowed. This

secures traffic to all IPSec-aware computers but allows unsecured communication for non-IPSec-aware computers. This is known as *fallback to clear.*

This filter action should not be used for traffic that goes through the Internet. Using this filter on Internet traffic could result in a DoS attack. If you request security and spend three seconds per negotiation, an attacker could send repeated requests that would virtually halt all other traffic.

This setting uses a preset list of security methods during the negotiation process. The first method uses the highest security and the last uses the lowest security, as shown in Table 5.9

Table 5.9 Security Negotiation Order of Preference

Type	AH	ESP Encryption	ESP Integrity	Key Lifetimes (KB/sec)
Custom	None	3DES	SHA1	100000/900
Custom	None	DES	SHA1	100000/900
Custom	SHA1	None	None	100000/300
Custom	MD5	None	None	100000/300

- **Require Security** This filter action applies to all IP traffic and requires security using Kerberos trust. It does allow initial incoming unsecured communication *(inbound passthrough)*. The *fallback to clear* function is disabled so that no unsecured communication with untrusted clients is allowed. Traffic is secured via the Negotiate security mode in which both computers negotiate the most secure communication possible. However, if negotiation fails, a connection will not be established. This filter action should not be used on the Internet as it is vulnerable to DoS attacks since it will attempt negotiation with all incoming traffic. Table 5.10 shows the security methods used with this setting, in order of preference from highest to lowest. To create the most secure setting possible, known as *lockdown*, you can disable the inbound passthrough, thus disabling the ability of any unsecured traffic from being accepted. In this state, the client computer must be forced to negotiate security with the server to initiate communication. The client computers must be configured with an IPSec policy that will do this. If the client computer is configured to only use the default response rule, it will not be able to communicate with the locked-down server.

Table 5.10 Security Methods for the Require Security Setting

Type	AH	ESP Encryption	ESP Integrity	Key Lifetimes (KB/sec)
Custom	None	3DES	SHA1	100000/900
Custom	None	3DES	MD5	100000/900
Custom	None	DES	SHA1	100000/900
Custom	None	DES	MD5	100000/900

IP Packet Filtering

IP addresses are either local or remote addresses, meaning they originated on your network or they came from elsewhere. As you know, each IP address contains two sections—the network ID and the host ID. IP packet filtering is used to provide a way to define exactly what IP traffic is passed through (not secured), secured, or blocked.

Each filter within the filter list describes a particular set of network traffic to be secured. The list identifies both inbound and outbound filters. Rules must always have filters to cover the traffic to which it applies. For example, if you have two computers, Black and White, and Black always wants to exchange data in a secure manner with White, the following must be set up:

- Black's IPSec policy has a filter for any outbound packets going to White.
- White's IPSec policy has a filter for any inbound packets coming from Black.

A filter contains the source and destination address of the IP packet. This setting can be set wide or narrow—you can filter an entire network, subnet, or just a single IP address. A filter also contains the protocol being used to send the packet. The default is TCP/IP, but the filter can be modified to specify other protocols within the TCP/IP suite such as ICMP and UDP. A filter also contains the source and destination port of the protocol for TCP and UDP. The default covers all ports, but this can be modified to suit your organization's needs.

netsh Commands

The *netsh.exe* command can be used to work with IPSec policies and it is referred to throughout this chapter. Let's take a minute to review the *netsh.exe* command. *netsh.exe* is a command-line utility that can be used instead of the console-based management provided by the IP Security Policy Management and IP Security Monitor snap-ins in the MMC.

The *netsh* command has many different uses in Windows Server 2003. Each type of use is called a *context*. For example, you can use the DHCP context to manage

DHCP, or you can use the IPSec context to manage IPSec. For more information on using the various contexts with the *netsh.exe* command, you can refer to the Windows Server 2003 help files. We're going to limit our discussion to the IPSec context. Support for this context was added to Windows Server 2003, providing another method of managing IPSec policy for admins more familiar or comfortable using the command-line utility. Using *netsh.exe*, you can configure and view dynamic or static IPSec main mode settings, quick mode settings, rules, and configuration parameters. This command-line utility is particularly useful when you want to use scripts to configure IPSec or to extend features not available via the snap-ins. These features include IKE (Oakley) logging, logging intervals, computer startup security, computer startup traffic exemptions, IPSec diagnostics, default traffic exemptions, and strong certificate revocation list (CRL) checking. To use the *netsh.exe* command, open a command prompt (**Start | Run |** type in **cmd | OK**) and type **netsh ipsec**. This establishes the context for the *netsh.exe* command.

The command structure begins with static or dynamic mode, meaning that the syntax of the command begins in this way: *netsh ipsec static* or *netsh ipsec dynamic*. Both modes have many options. For example, in the static mode, you can add, delete, or modify a filter; add, delete, or modify a filter list; or add, delete, or modify a policy. Dynamic mode also has a long list of options you can set.

You can use the *netsh ipsec static* mode to create, modify, and assign IPSec policies without immediately affecting the configuration of the active IPSec policy. Using the *netsh ipsec dynamic* mode, you can display the active state of IPSec and immediately affect the configuration of the active IPSec policy. Dynamic commands immediately configure the security policy database (SPD) but take effect only when the IPSec service is running. If the IPSec service is stopped, the dynamic settings are discarded. A few of the dynamic commands do not take effect immediately and require that the computer or the IPSec service be restarted. It's important to note that the IPSec policy agent does not interpret *netsh ipsec dynamic* commands, so you need to understand the IKE main and quick mode policies to use these commands effectively. Another caution is that because almost all of these commands are executed immediately, you can create invalid IPSec policy configurations "on the fly."

One important note here is that the *netsh.exe* commands for IPSec can only be used to work with IPSec policies on computers running Windows Server 2003. The command line to configure IPSec policies for computers running Windows XP is *ipseccmd.exe*. Windows 2000 computers use the command-line *ipsecpol.exe*

How IPSec Policy Is Applied

IPSec policies are retrieved at the time the computer starts up (system start time) and at a specified interval in the IPSec policy, if the computer is joined to a domain. IPSec policy is stored in Active Directory and cached in the local Registry of the computer to which a policy is applied. This occurs for all computers joined to the domain. If the computer is temporarily not connected to the domain, the cached policy information will be used. When the computer reconnects to the domain, new policy is applied that overrides the cached policy data. If a computer is a stand-alone computer or is part of a domain that is not using Active Directory, the policy data is stored in the local Registry.

Policy is applied to a computer because the IPSec Policy Agent Service starts automatically every time the computer starts. The IPSec Policy Agent is a service that resides on each Windows 2000, Windows XP, and Windows Server 2003 computer. Its function is to retrieve the appropriate IPSec policies from Active Directory (or the Registry if the computer is not connected to or not a member of a domain) and to send the IPSec policy information to the *IPSec driver.*

The IPSec driver uses the IP Filter List from the active IPSec policy to determine which outbound packets match the criteria set in the policy. Any packet that meets those criteria must be secured via IPSec as defined by the policy. For example, if a policy requires that all data from the Finance department be authenticated but not encrypted, the IPSec driver will make sure all finance packets use the authentication method listed in the IPSec policy. Figure 5.7 shows the interaction of Active Directory, IPSec policy, the policy agent, and the IPSec driver.

Figure 5.7 Interaction of IPSec Components

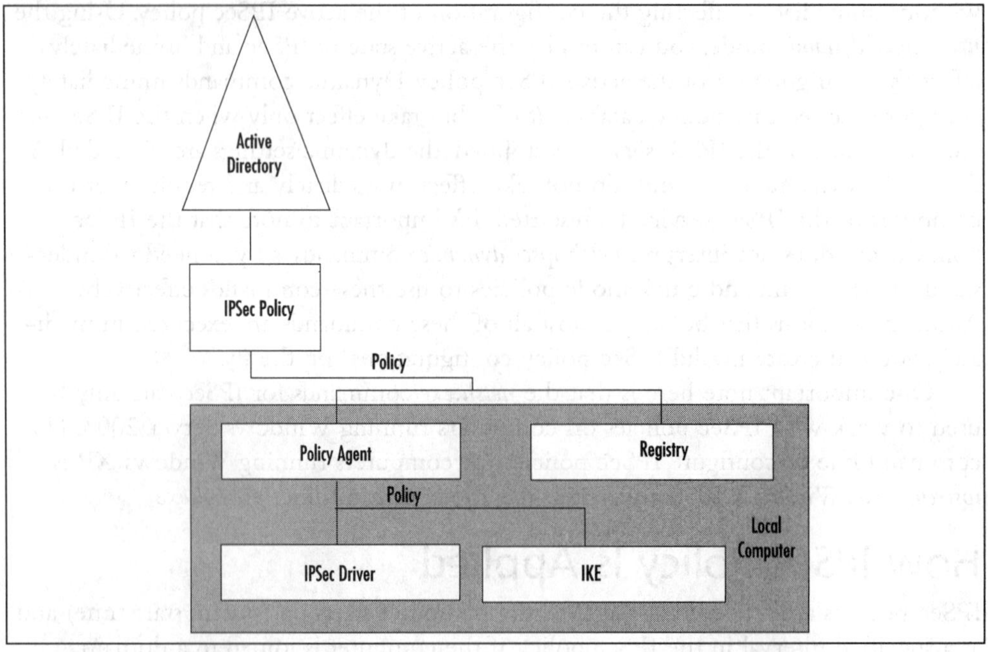

The IKE negotiates security between the computers as well as the methods to be used to secure the data. The IPSec driver monitors inbound and outbound traffic and compares it to the IPSec rules within the applied policies. When they match, the IPSec driver determines the proper action to take based on the filter list and filter actions. The packet is secured in the manner specified by the policy and sent to the receiving computer. On the other end, the receiving computer's IPSec driver receives the session key, SA, and SPI from the IKE. (Recall that the SPI is the *Security Parameters Index* (discussed in the *Head of the Class* sidebar earlier), which indicates to which SA the packet belongs.) The IPSec driver checks the signature, ensures the packet is intact, and decrypts it, if necessary. It sends the original IP packet up the stack to the appropriate application. Figure 5.8 depicts this process.

Figure 5.8 IPSec Process

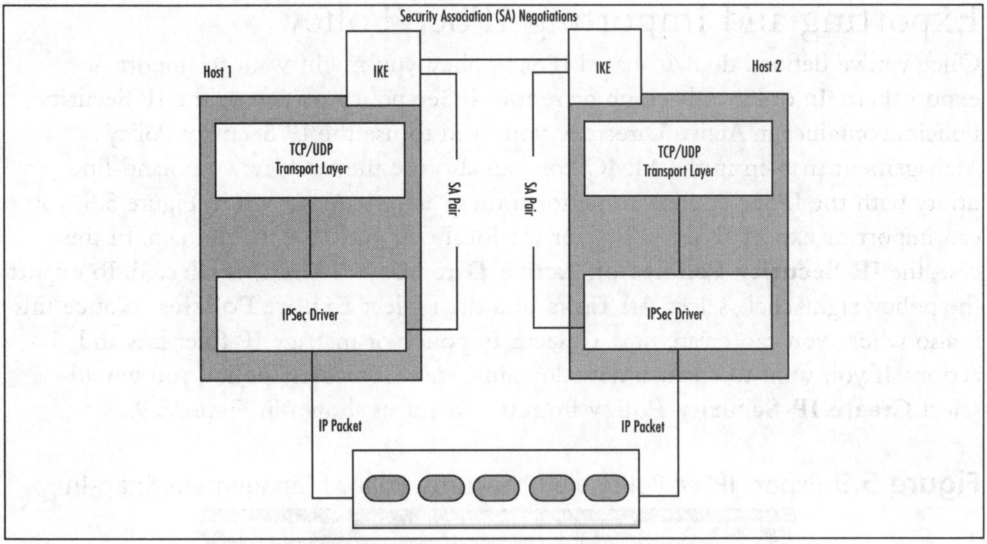

Assigning Domain-Based IPSec Policy

After you've created your overall security plan and created IPSec policies to protect the data you want to secure, you'll need to apply the policies. In this section and the following two sections, we'll discuss, at a high level, how to apply these policies to three specific objects: domains, OUs, and local computers.

When you define IPSec via Group Policy and link the Group Policy Object (GPO) to the domain, the IPSec policy will propagate throughout the domain when the GPO is propagated. Like GPO, IPSec policy is applied from lowest to highest priority: local, site, domain, OU, persistent policy (if used). Unlike GPOs, IPSec policies from different OUs are never merged. Domain-based IPSec policies are limited to 10 rules, although Windows Server 2003 supports over 1500 rules per policy. It is recommended that you set broad IPSec policies at the domain level to reduce configuration issues and administrative overhead required to manage IPSec policy.

During the rollout phase of IPSec security, you should set your domain-based IPSec policy to Negotiate security, which allows unsecured communication with untrusted computers. This way, no computer will be blocked as you're rolling out policy. Once you're sure that all IPSec policies are being applied as expected, you can modify the security to require only secured communications. Of course, testing the policy on a single computer and monitoring results is recommended before rolling out any policies.

IPSec policies should first be applied to the domain to provide baseline security settings. Tighter IPSec filtering can be done on specific OUs that might require additional security.

Exporting and Importing IPSec Policy

Once you've defined domain-based IPSec policy, you might want to import or export them. In order to back up or restore IPSec policy objects in the IP Security Policies container in Active Directory, you need to use the IP Security Policy Management snap-in in the MMC. You can also use the *netsh.exe* command-line utility with the IPSec context to perform these actions. As shown in Figure 5.9, you can import or export IPSec policy for the local computer for the domain. In this case, the **IP Security Policies on Active Directory** (domain) is selected. To export the policy, right-click, select **All Tasks**, and then select **Export Policies**. Notice this is also where you can create new IP security policy or manage IP filter lists and actions. If you want to create a new domain-based IP security policy, you would select **Create IP Security Policy** from the menu, as shown in Figure 5.9.

Figure 5.9 Export IPSec Policy via IP Security Policy Management Snap-In

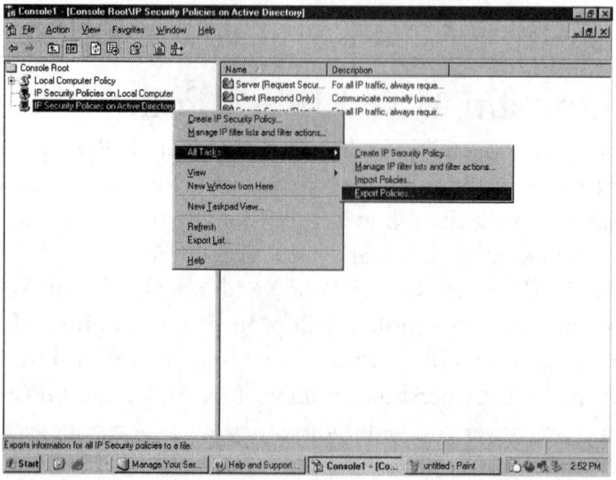

When you use the *Export Policies* command, all IPSec policy objects are stored in one file given an extension of .ipsec. When you import policies, you can import .ipsec files into the destination policy stores. If you import IPSec policy into Active Directory (as you would do if you were to have the Active Directory level open, as is the case in Figure 5.9), you would overwrite existing IPSec policy objects. This can be good if you believe your Active Directory IPSec policy is corrupted or incorrect and you want to restore from a known good file. However, if you do not want to overwrite existing values, do not import into Active Directory. If you suspect your IPSec policies in Active Directory are corrupted, you can import the .ipsec file via the snap-in or via the *netsh ipsec static importpolicy* command. It's important that you leave either the snap-in or the command-line utility (depending on your method) open long enough to complete the import or export. Closing either before all IPSec policy data has been written could result in corruption.

EXAM WARNING

If IPSec policy is corrupted, you must delete IPSec policy objects so new IPSec policy can be successfully imported. If you are managing IPSec over slow WAN links, transfer the IPSec policies in *.ipsec* export files by copying the file to the remote computer first. Then, use Remote Desktop Connection to connect to the remote computer and perform the operation.

Assigning OU-Based IPSec Policy

By default, the policies applied at the OU level override the baseline domain policies. For example, you can group all client computers into one OU and apply appropriate client-type IPSec policies to the OU. You can keep sensitive servers in another OU and apply more secure IPSec policies to this OU. You could also place sensitive client computers, such as those in Finance, Research, or Human Resources, into separate OUs and apply varying degrees of security to those OUs.

When you assign an IPSec policy within a GPO such as an OU, a pointer is recorded that points to the IPSec policy within the GPO. If you make changes to the IPSec policy, the GPO is not aware of those changes. The GPO is only aware of changes to the IPSec policy itself. The IPSec service detects changes related to the IPSec policy, and this detection interval can be specified in the General tab of the properties of the policy via the IP Security Policy Management snap-in. This interval is known as the *IPSec polling interval*.

Assigning Local IPSec Policy

Local GPOs can be overridden by GPOs assigned to sites, domains, and OUs when operating in an Active Directory framework. On a network without Active Directory, you can use the local policy to apply IPSec policies (and group policies) to individual computers. Every computer running Windows Server 2003 has one local GPO called *local computer policy*. When this is used, Group Policy settings can be stored on the local computer regardless of whether they are joined to an Active Directory domain. However, if they are joined to an Active Directory domain, local policy will be overridden by any policies with higher precedence.

Persistent policies are used on local computers as a way to secure the computer during the startup process. This policy adds or overrides the local or Active Directory policy and remains in effect regardless of whether other policies have been applied. Persistent IPSec policies provide a more secure framework because they provide a secure transition from computer startup to the application of IPSec policy. Persistent policy can also be used as a failsafe mechanism in case of corruption or errors during the application of higher precedence IPSec policy. Persistent policy can cause problems if it is the only policy applied and you are trying to diagnose a problem remotely, as the diagnostic traffic might be blocked. Persistent policies can be configured via the *netsh* commands. Persistent policies are stored in the computer's local Registry and are loaded by the IPSec policy agent during computer startup. The IPSec driver is set to *secure mode* (discussed later in this chapter) if the persistent policy is successfully applied. Although you can make changes to persistent policy at any time, changes are not implemented until the IPSec service is restarted.

TEST DAY TIP

To provide maximum protection for a computer during startup, you should configure and apply a persistent policy. For many systems, this might not be needed, but if you're applying IPSec security, you most likely want to also apply persistent policy to prevent security holes during startup. Be sure to review policies before the exam and look for this type of question on the exam.

IPSec Driver Modes

In understanding how policies work, it's important to understand that the IPSec driver operates in three modes: *computer startup*, *operational*, and *diagnostic*. Computer startup mode is used when the computer is starting up. Operational mode is used when the computer is up and running in normal operational mode. Diagnostic mode is used for troubleshooting.

Computer Startup Mode

The IPSec driver is loaded at startup along with other system services and drivers. Computer startup mode is used until the IPSec Policy Agent put the driver into operational mode. At startup, the IPSec driver can perform any one of the following actions:

- **Permit** In permit mode, no IP packets are filtered (all are permitted) and no IPSec security is used. Permit mode is the default state of the IPSec driver if no IPSec policy has been applied to the computer.
- **Stateful** In stateful mode, all outbound traffic is allowed and it creates inbound traffic filters based on the outgoing traffic. Inbound unicast, broadcast, and multicast packets are dropped. The stateful mode is the default mode of the IPSec driver if an IPSec policy has been assigned to the computer.
- **Block** In block mode, all packets are discarded except for those that match specific filters configured to be used in block mode. All inbound and outbound DHCP traffic is permitted by default, to allow the computer to obtain an IP address.

The default state of the driver can be modified using the command-line utility *netsh.exe*. To modify the state, use the *netsh ipsec static set config bootmode* command.

Depending on the startup type of the IPSec service, the IPSec driver will start in one of three modes: *disabled*, *manual*, or *automatic*. In disabled mode, the IPSec driver loads in permit mode, no IPSec security is applied, and the IPSec driver does not filter any packets. In manual mode, the IPSec driver also starts in permit mode and no packet security filtering occurs. Automatic mode starts the IPSec driver in a startup mode specified by the IPSec policy agent. If no IPSec policy is applied, the IPSec driver will start in permit mode. If IPSec policy is applied, the IPSec driver will load in the stateful mode.

Once the IPSec service starts, persistent policy (if any) is applied and the IPSec driver is set to secure mode, which is the default configuration.

Operational Mode

Once the IPSec service starts on a computer, the IPSec policy agent sets the IPSec driver to one of three operational modes: *secure*, *permit*, or *block*.

- **Secure** In secure mode, the IPSec policy filters are enforced for standard IPSec operations. The IPSec policy agent puts the driver into secure mode after it applies any persistent policies present (persistent policies are discussed in the next section) and before it applies the Active Directory policies or local policies. If no persistent policies are defined, IPSec security does not begin until either the Active Directory or local policy has been applied. If no IPSec policy is assigned, no IPSec protection is provided in this mode.
- **Permit** When the IPSec driver is set to permit in the operational mode, it does not filter IP packets, and no IPSec security is enforced or applied. If the IPSec service is manually stopped on a computer, the operational mode will be set to permit.

- **Block** In block mode, any exemptions that might apply at startup are not applied and all inbound and outbound traffic is blocked. This mode is used to increase security in case the IPSec policy agent fails to apply persistent policy. Persistent policy, as the name implies, remains on the computer. It is applied via *netsh.exe* commands. We'll explore persistent policies in just a moment.

It's important to note here that you cannot set these modes via the *netsh* command. The operational mode can only be configured by the IPSec policy agent.

Diagnostic Mode

You can use the diagnostic mode for troubleshooting to log events and errors. The IPSec driver logs can record inbound and outbound drop events on a per-packet basis during both startup mode and operational mode. Logging is disabled by default, and care should be used when enabling logging. It should not be used for extended periods of time. Depending on the level of logging you configure, your System log file can fill very quickly.

TEST DAY TIP

A few days before the test, review the overall process of how all the IPSec components interact, and pay special attention to the startup and operational modes of the IPSec driver. Also remember that the *netsh* commands for IPSec can only be used to configure IPSec policies for computers running Windows Server 2003.

Designing & Planning…

What's New in IP Security in Windows Server 2003

There are changes to the implementation of IP Security in Windows Server 2003 that can impact how IPSec works with computers running earlier versions of Windows, including Windows 2000 and Windows XP. Since you're likely to see this kind of information included in questions on the exam and run into these issues on the job, it's important to review the changes related to deploying IPSec in Windows Server 2003. These are summarized in Table 5.11.

Continued

Table 5.11 New IPSec Features in Windows Server 2003

New IPSec Feature	Description and Use Guidelines
Default exemptions have been removed.	Windows 2000 and Windows XP contained default exemptions for IPSec filtering. Specifically, these operating systems exempted broadcast, multicast ISAKMP, Kerberos, and Resource Reservation Protocol (RSVP) traffic. In Windows Server 2003, only ISAKMP traffic is exempt by default.
netsh enables command-line support for IPSec.	The *netsh.exe* command-line utility now has an IPSec context, which allows you to run IPSec-related commands from within this utility. Previous versions of Windows used different commands, *Ipsecpol.exe* and *Ipseccmd.exe*.
IPSec filters update IP configurations of partners.	The source or destination address fields that a computer interprets as the DHCP server, DNS server, WINS server, or default gateway can be configured using the IP Security Policy Management snap-in or the *netsh.exe* command. IPSec policies can now automatically manage changes in the IP configuration of the source or the destination by using DHCP or static IP configurations.
Network Address Translation traversal (NAT-T) support added.	IPSec in Windows Server 2003 now supports ESP-protected IPSec traffic passing through a NAT. Some applications might not work if their traffic is protected with IPSec ESP and passed through a NAT. IKE detects NATs and uses EDP ESP encapsulation to send all user data via UDP port 4500. The use of the AH protocol through a NAT is not supported.
Resultant Set of Policy (RSoP) now supported for IPSec.	The RSoP snap-in is used to view the results of various policies applied to a computer to address unanticipated results. Support of IPSec policies has been added in Windows Server 2003.
Support for Diffie-Hellman Group 2048.	The DH Group 2048 provides high security via the use of 2048-bit keying material to create security algorithms. Previous operating systems only supported DH Groups 1 and 2.

Continued

Continued

Table 5.11 New IPSec Features in Windows Server 2003

New IPSec Feature	Description and Use Guidelines
Persistent IPSec policy is supported.	Persistent IPSec policy is policy that is present during computer startup, before other policies are applied. Persistent IPSec policy can be used to protect the computer during the startup process. Admins can also force local IPSec policy to be applied when Active Directory policy is applied. Typically, Active Directory policy would override any local policy.
Stateful filtering of network traffic during startup.	IPSec in Windows Server 2003 now supports stateful filtering during startup. It permits only outbound traffic the computer initiates during startup and the inbound traffic sent as a response.
IP Security Monitor snap-in added.	This provides more detail about IPSec than the previous utility *Ipsecmon.exe*.

IPSec Best Practices

Microsoft outlines several best practices related to implementing IPSec.

- **Establish an IPSec deployment plan** As we discussed earlier, planning is a critical part of the process in developing security plans.
- **Create and test IPSec policies for each deployment scenario** Before deploying IPSec, all scenarios should be tested in a lab environment.
- **Do not use pre-shared keys** These are stored in plain text and provide relatively weak authentication. Pre-shared keys should be used only for testing. In a live environment, certificates or Kerberos v5 should be used.
- **Do not use Diffie-Hellman Group 1 (low)** DH Group 1 only provides 768 bits of keying strength. In today's demanding environment, use Group 2 (medium) for interoperability with Windows 2000 and Windows XP, or Group 2048 (high) for strong security using 2048 bits of keying strength. DH Group 2048 is only provided in Windows Server 2003.
- **Use Triple Data Encryption Standard (3DES)** This uses a stronger encryption algorithm than does DES. Use 3DES for enhanced security.

Windows 2000 computers must have the High Encryption Pack or Service Pack 2 installed in order to use 3DES. If the High Encryption Pack or Service Pack 2 is not installed, the security is set to the weaker DES. If not all computers support 3DES, use DES. Windows XP and Windows Server 2003 computers support 3DES by default.

- **For computers connected to the Internet, do not send the name of the Certification Authority (CA) along with the certificate request** For computers connected to the Internet, enable the option to exclude the name of the CA from the certificate request to protect sensitive information about trust relationships from intruders.
- **For computers connected to the Internet, do not Kerberos v5 as an authentication method** The computer identity is sent unencrypted until encryption of the entire payload occurs. This leaves the computer identity exposed during the authentication process. To secure computers connected to the Internet, use certificate authentication instead.
- **For computers connected to the Internet, do not allow unsecured communication** You should disable the option to *accept unsecured communication but respond with IPSec.* Disabling this will prevent DoS attacks. Also disable the option to *allow unsecured communication with non-IPSec-aware computers*. If this option is not disabled, you are allowing unsecured communication. This is appropriate only in environments where IPSec is not needed.
- **Restrict the use of administrative credentials** Administrative credentials can be used to attack the system, so these credentials should be restricted and monitored.
- **Test IPSec policy thoroughly when working with different versions of the Windows operating system** Not all IPSec features are supported in all versions of Windows; thorough testing will prevent problems for users and problems with security.
- **Use the IPSec Policy Management console in Windows Server 2003 to manage IPSec policies** This console provides for streamlined IPSec policy management. Be sure to use the console in Windows Server 2003, since earlier consoles lack features found in Windows Server 2003 and will not support newer IPSec features.
- **Use Terminal Server to remotely manage and monitor IPSec on computers running different versions of Windows** Remote management and monitoring of IPSec is only supported on computers running the same versions of the Windows operating system. To remotely manage IPSec on computers running a different operating system, use Terminal Server.

EXAM WARNING

As with other details of IPSec, the exam won't test you directly on your knowledge of these individual elements. However, whenever Microsoft publishes best practices, you can be sure you'll see questions on the exam that test your understanding of these best practices in scenario questions. Make sure you're familiar with these recommendations and keep them in mind when answering exam questions.

EXAM 70-298 OBJECTIVE 3.1.3

Designing IPSec Policies

We've reviewed IPSec, how it works, how it's implemented and when. Now, let's delve into the actual design and implementation of IPSec policies. Remember, the policies you apply on your systems should reflect the security plan you've delineated for your network infrastructure.

Earlier, we discussed placing computers with similar security needs into OUs to simplify the application and management of IPSec policy. These can be placed in three general security groups—*minimal*, *standard*, and *high*. *Minimal* security should be used with computers that do not exchange sensitive data. This group could include client computers and perhaps some file or print servers. IPSec is not active by default so no action is required to disable IPSec on these computers. *Standard* security should be applied to computers that store valuable data. This could include file servers and perhaps some application servers. Both Windows XP and Windows Server 2003 provide examples of standard security policies that secure data but do not require the highest level of security. Remember, there's always a balance between security and usability, so you don't want to lock down servers with IPSec policies when there's no clear need. The standard security settings typically provide this balance. These predefined standard security policies include *Client (Respond Only)* and *Server (Request Security)*. These should be used as the basis for your standard security to balance the need for security with the need to optimize usability and system efficiency. *High* security should be applied to computers that contain highly sensitive data that puts them at risk for attack, data theft, or system disruption. Any computer on the public network that provides remote access or vital system services should be secured with the high security level. The high security default policy *Server (Require Security)* requires IPSec protection for all traffic being sent and received except for initial inbound communication. Unsecured communication with a non-IPSec-aware computer is not allowed at all. Figure 5.10 shows these default policies for the domain.

Figure 5.10 Default Policies in Active Directory

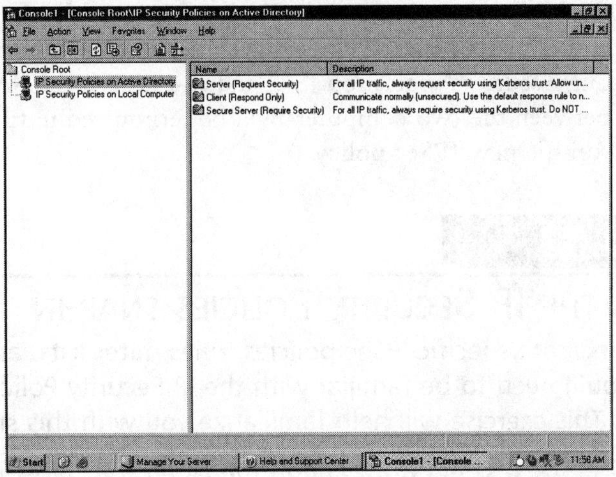

Configuring IPSec Policy

You can configure IPSec policy in one of two ways. You can create a new policy, define rules, and then add filter lists and filter actions. You can also create filter lists and filter actions and then create policies and add rules that combine the filter lists and actions. Use whatever method makes the most sense for your particular needs. Using the first method, you'll add filter lists and filter actions during the rule creation. Using the second method, IPSec policies are created and rules are added that combine the desired filter list with desired filter action. Once IPSec policies are configured, they must be assigned.

IPSec policies can be configured via the IP Security Policy Management snap-in in the MMC or via the *netsh* command-line.

Assigning IPSec Policy

Once IPSec policies have been created, the list is available to assign to any level of the Active Directory hierarchy, but only one policy can be assigned at any given level in Active Directory. IPSec policy applied to an OU takes precedence over domain-level policy for members of the OU, which is why servers should be placed into OUs. You should also apply IPSec policy to the highest OU possible to avoid dealing with potential IPSec policy conflict and to ease security administration. A child OU will inherit the IPSec policies from its parent OU unless policy inheritance is explicitly blocked or explicitly assigned. Before assigning an IPSec policy to a GPO, make sure the GPO meets the requirements of the IPSec policy. For example, if your IPSec policy requires the use of a computer certificate, make sure the computer has a certificate. Finally, since an IPSec policy might remain active even after a GPO to which it is assigned is deleted, you should get in the habit of unassigning the IPSec policy first and then delete the GPO. Typically, you should wait 24 hours before removing the GPO to make sure changes have been propagated successfully.

Keep in mind that when policies are changed, the IPSec service might be forced to delete an existing Security Association (SA) and re-establish the SA. In this case, communication between the two computers will be terminated until a new SA is negotiated based on the new IPSec policy.

Exercise 5.02

Exploring the IP Security Policies Snap-in

Before you create specific IPSec policies, rules, filter lists, and filter actions, you'll need to be familiar with the IP Security Policies snap-in in the MMC. This exercise will help familiarize you with this snap-in.

1. Click **Start**, select **Run**, and in the Open box, type in **mmc**, and then press **Enter** or click **OK** to open the MMC.
2. A new console is opened by default. Click **File** and then select **Add/Remove Snap-in**.
3. In the **Add/Remove Snap-in** dialog, click the **Add** button.
4. In the **Add Standalone Snap-in** dialog, scroll down to locate and select the **IP Security Policy Management** snap-in. Click **Add** to add the snap-in.
5. The **Select Computer or Domain** dialog will open. This allows you to select which computer or domain the snap-in will manage. You can manage policies on the local computer (the default setting) or you can select the Active Directory domain the computer belongs to, a different Active Directory, domain or another computer. Accept the default (**Local computer**) and click **Finish.** The Select Computer or Domain dialog closes, returning you to the **Add Standalone Snap-in** dialog.
6. The active dialog is the **Add Standalone Snap-in** dialog. Click **Close** to return to the Add/Remove Snap-in dialog. Click **OK** to close this dialog and return to the MMC.
7. Click **IP Security Policies on Local Computer** in the left pane to select this snap-in. By clicking it, you cause the default policies to be displayed in the right pane. You should see **Server (Request Security)**, **Client (Respond Only)**, and **Secure Server (Require Security)**. Following each is a description. You can adjust column widths by positioning your mouse over the vertical line separating

labels in the gray header area (Name, Description, Policy Assigned, etc.) and left-clicking and pulling to the left or right.

8. Locate **Server (Request Security)** and double-click that policy to display the properties. Alternately, you can select the policy, right-click, and then select **Properties** from the menu.
9. The tab selected by default is the **Rules** tab, which displays the IP Security rules that are part of this policy. Each rule contains several elements: IP Filter List, Filter Action, Authentication, Tunnel Endpoint, and Connection Type.
10. Select the **General** tab by clicking it. This tab displays the policy name, description, and how often it will check for policy changes. The default value is 180 minutes, or every three hours.
11. You can configure additional settings for the key exchange by clicking the **Settings** button. Click the **Settings** button to display **Key Exchange Settings**.
12. You can change settings for the Key Exchange in this dialog. Click the **Methods** button to display the IKE security methods options.
13. In the Key Exchange Security Methods dialog, you can set the preference order for key exchange. The default settings are shown in Figure 5.11.

Figure 5.11 Default Settings for Key Exchange Security Methods for Default IPSec Policy

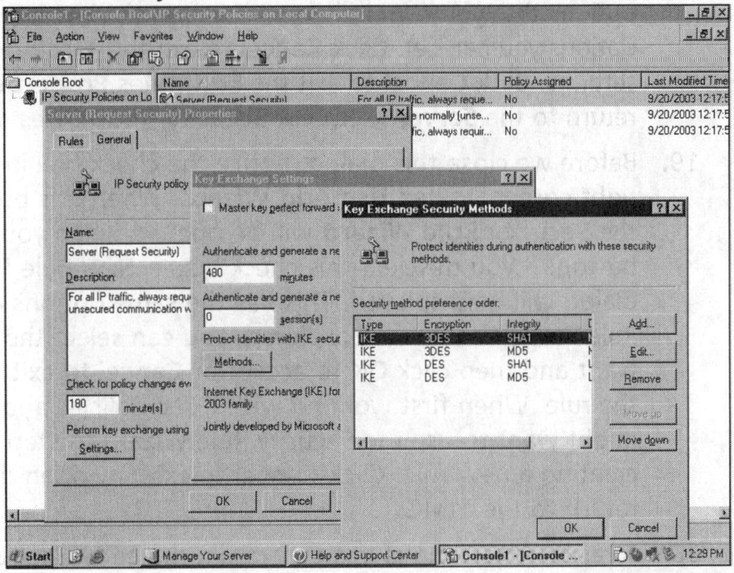

14. Use the horizontal scroll bar to view all the fields, which include Type, Encryption, Integrity, and Diffie-Hellman Group. Individual algorithms can be modified by double-clicking the desired algorithm or by clicking the **Edit** button. Each drop-down list shows choices we've discussed earlier in this chapter. Take a moment to click each drop-down arrow and view the choices. Test your recall of each of these elements by reciting to yourself the definition and use of each element. The choices you should see are Integrity Algorithm – MD5 or SHA1, Encryption Algorithm – 3DES or DES, Diffie-Hellman group – Low (1), Medium (2), or High (2048).
15. To avoid making any changes, click **Cancel** to exit. Click **Cancel** to exit the Key Exchange Security Methods dialog. Also click **Cancel** to exit the Key Exchange Settings dialog.
16. You should now have just the **Server (Request Security) Properties** dialog open. Click the **Rules** tab to select that tab.
17. The IP Security rules list contains three rules. Double-click the first rule **All IP Traffic** to display the properties for editing. Alternately, you can click the first rule then click the **Edit** button below.
18. The **Edit Rule Properties** dialog is displayed. There are five tabs in this dialog: IP Filter List is selected by default. The other tabs are Filter Action, Authentication Methods, Tunnel Setting and Connection Type, all the fields shown in the Rules dialog. The IP Filter List, Filter Action, and Authentication Methods tabs have options that you can drill down through to view the many different options you can set. Click **Cancel** to exit these without changing settings. Click **Cancel** to exit the **Edit Rules Properties** dialog and return to the **Server (Request Security) Properties** dialog.
19. Before we close this dialog, notice the check box in the lower-right corner labeled **Use Add Wizard**. When this box is selected, the **Security Rule Wizard** will be opened when you click the **Add** button. If you deselect this check box, a New Rule Properties dialog will be displayed. This has the same options as the Edit Rule Properties we just explored. You can select the options you want and then click **OK** to accept or **Cancel** to exit without saving the rule. When first working with IPSec policies and rules, you might want to use the Security Rule Wizard to step you through creating a new rule. Click **Cancel** to exit any open dialogs and return to the MMC.
20. To access the various options within the console related to the IP Security Policies on the Local Computer, right-click the selection

(IP Security Policies on Local Computer) or click **Action** from the menu.

21. Click **Action** and select **All Tasks**.
22. Notice the actions you can take—you can create a policy, manage filter lists and actions, restore defaults, and import and export policies.
23. Exit the MMC by clicking **File** and then selecting **Exit**. Click **No** when prompted to save the console.

As you can see, many levels of options can be configured within the IPSec policies. To keep things simple and make configuring, managing, and troubleshooting IPSec policy easier, make sure you define the fewest possible number of IPSec policies to meet your security needs, apply them at the highest possible level, and apply them to computers in similar roles via the use of OUs. Now you're ready to begin configuring IPSec policy for computers.

EXAM 70-298 OBJECTIVE 3.1.2

Designing IP Filtering

When designing IP filtering, there are a few design suggestions that will make your task easier. These are delineated in Table 5.12 and describe recommendations for both filter lists and filter actions.

Table 5.12 Filter List and Filter Actions Recommendations

IP Filter Lists	IP Filter Actions
Use general filters if you want to cover many computers with one list. Use Any IP Address or a subnet IP rather than using specific computers' IP addresses.	For remote communications, consider using high security levels including 3DES, short key lifetimes, and Perfect Forward Secrecy (PFS) to prevent attacks based on known keys.
Segment your network and define filters that allow you to group and secure traffic by segment.	When using custom security methods, only set ESP confidentiality to **None** when a higher layer protocol will encrypt the data. Using None can create security holes.

Continued

Table 5.12 Filter List and Filter Actions Recommendations

IP Filter Lists	IP Filter Actions
The order in which filters is applied is from most specific to least specific. The order is not indicated by the order in which they are displayed when viewing IPSec policy. As a result, you might see odd communication behavior during computer startup that should clear up after all filters have been processed.	Do not enable security for nonessential data or when computers are not IPSec aware. To prevent communication with rogue computers, use Filter Actions including blocking or pass-through policies.

For configuring secure servers, including firewalls and computers in perimeter networks, you can review the common list of TCP and UDP ports and ensure you block or permit traffic as needed for the correct function of the computer(s) in question. The Internet Assigned Numbers Authority (IANA) provides a full list of TCP and UDP ports from 0 through 65535. The current version of the list is available at www.iana.org/assignments/port-numbers, and some of the more common TCP and UDP ports are listed in Table 5.13.

Table 5.13 Commonly Used TCP and UDP Ports

Port Number (TCP or UDP)	TCP Description	UDP Description
20	File Transfer [default data]	File Transfer [default data]
21	File Transfer [control]	File Transfer [control]
22	SSH Remote Login Protocol	SSH Remote Login Protocol
23	Telnet	Telnet
25	Simple Mail Transfer Protocol	Simple Mail Transfer Protocol
38	Route Access Protocol	Route Access Protocol
42	Host Name Server	Host Name Server
53	Domain Name Server	Domain Name Server
80	World Wide Web HTTP	World Wide Web HTTP
88	Kerberos	Kerberos
101	NIC Host Name Server	NIC Host Name Server
109	Post Office Protocol—Version 2	Post Office Protocol—Version 2
110	Post Office Protocol—Version 3	Post Office Protocol—Version 3

Continued

Table 5.13 Commonly Used TCP and UDP Ports

Port Number (TCP or UDP)	TCP Description	UDP Description
113	Authentication Service	Authentication Service
115	Simple File Transfer Protocol	Simple File Transfer Protocol
118	SQL Services	SQL Services
119	Network News Transfer Protocol	Network News Transfer Protocol
137	NetBIOS Name Service	NetBIOS Name Service
138	NetBIOS Datagram Service	NetBIOS Datagram Service
139	NetBIOS Session Service	NetBIOS Session Service
143	Internet Message Access Protocol	Internet Message Access Protocol
156	SQL Service	SQL Service
161	SNMP	SNMP
162	SNMPTRAP	SNMPTRAP
179	Border Gateway Protocol	Border Gateway Protocol
389	Lightweight Directory Access Protocol	Lightweight Directory Access Protocol
443	HTTP protocol over TLS/SSL	HTTP protocol over TLS/SSL
989	FTP protocol, data, over TLS/SSL	FTP protocol, data, over TLS/SSL
990	FTP protocol, control, over TLS/SSL	FTP protocol, control, over TLS/SSL
995	POP3 protocol over TLS/SSL (was SPOP3)	POP3 protocol over TLS/SSL (was SPOP3)

As you can see, there are many TCP and UDP ports defined. The list in Table 5.13 is just a small portion of the entire list maintained by IANA. However, it's helpful to know what TCP and UDP ports are used for which common network functions so you can properly block or permit that traffic. It's also important to understand that TCP and UDP ports can be reserved (port numbers above 1000), and the highest number defined is 65535. Individual companies such as Cisco, Microsoft, and Hewlett-Packard (and hundreds of others) can reserve TCP and UDP port numbers for specific applications. This is also important to know as a network administrator. For example, suppose the director of the Research department comes to you and asks to install an instant messaging (IM) program for the researchers to use in her department. You do some research and find this program uses UDP port 334 for communicating. You could permit UDP port 334 traffic on the research segment but could block it at the gateway or router to keep IM local to that segment. This is an example of a UDP port being used for a particular application and one that might not be one of the more well-known ports.

EXAM 70-298 OBJECTIVE 3.1.1

Configuring a Firewall Configuration

Firewalls can be used between segments of a network or, more commonly, to protect the corporate network from the Internet. Since the firewall by definition provides a security boundary, configuring IPSec for a firewall makes sense. First, let's look at the firewall function in Windows Server 2003.

Windows 2000, Windows XP, and Windows Server 2003 all included a host-based firewall, often referred to as *distributed firewall software* or *personal firewalls*, called Internet Connection Firewall (ICF). Originally designed for home users, businesses found it useful to employ the ICF to provide an additional layer of protection against attack. ICF is a basic firewall program designed to prevent basic intrusion, but it does not include the robust features of full firewall applications. Most third-party firewall applications protect computers from software that could violate user privacy (including spyware, Trojan horses, etc.) or allow an attacker to misuse the target computer. ICF does not provide these features.

Most businesses separate their internal network from the Internet as a common sense security measure. This is typically done using firewalls that block traffic sent to specific ports or protocols. However, corporate networks have gained a level of complexity that often makes it difficult to protect sensitive data at all times. This is especially true because it's difficult, if not impossible, to know every single port that is carrying important information or that needs to be secured. IPSec allows you to provide broader coverage than a firewall might by allowing you to permit, block, or negotiate security for unicast IP traffic.

The difference between IPSec and ICF is that IPSec provides complex *static* filtering based on IP addresses, and ICF provides *stateful* filtering for all addresses on a network interface. IPSec is often used in intranets to secure communication between two trusted computers using the Kerberos service or for specific paths across the Internet where PKI can be used. To secure communication via remote access, you would more likely use L2TP/IPSec for VPN connections. This configuration does not require the creation and deployment of IPSec policies. We'll discuss this to some extent later in this chapter when you learn about securing a wireless network.

Exam Warning

It's important to understand the difference between ICF and IPSec in terms of securing the perimeter. Use ICF when you want to implement a firewall for a network interface that can be accessed via the Internet. Use IPSec when you want to secure traffic on the network or when you need to allow access only to a group of trusted computers.

By default, Windows Server 2003 only exempts IKE traffic from filtering. IKE traffic is needed to establish secure communication channels between two computers so secure data can be exchanged. However, you can modify this to remove the exemption and require all traffic to be secured. If you do this, you must configure a IPSec policy on client computers in order for secure communications to be successfully negotiated. The *<Dynamic> Default Response* rule will not allow a successful negotiation when the server is "locked down." For firewalls and servers sitting on the Internet, removing this exemption is the most secure configuration. Leaving this setting "as is" can expose the server to a DoS attack. For servers not on the Internet or not acting as firewalls, it is acceptable to allow IKE traffic to be unsecured but to require all other data be secured by IPSec.

To configure a firewall between IPSec computers, it must be configured to:

- Forward inbound and outbound IPSec traffic on UDP source and destination port 500. This allows ISAKMP traffic to be forwarded.
- Forward inbound and outbound IP protocol 50 (ESP).
- Forward inbound and outbound IP protocol 51 (AH).
- Forward inbound and outbound UDP source and destination port 4500.

  Although we're not specifically discussing NAT in this section, it should be noted that if you're using NAT-Traversal (NAT-T), you must also configure forwarding on UDP source and destination port 4500.

IPSec can be routed as normal IP traffic, although the forwarders do not have the ability to examine the packet if it is encrypted with ESP. When there is a firewall or gateway in the path of the IPSec traffic, IP forwarding must be enabled at the firewall as described. L2TP/IPSec traffic looks like IPSec traffic. The firewall forwarding L2TP/IPSec traffic should be configured to allow IKE (UDP port 500) traffic as well as IP protocol 50 (ESP).

In some cases, it might be necessary to allow Kerberos traffic through the firewall as well. In this case, permitting forwarding of UDP and TCP port 88 should also be configured.

EXAM 70-298 OBJECTIVE 3.1.4

Securing DNS

DNS is the method of resolving IP addresses to domain names or domain names to IP addresses. This vital network service is a target of interest to hackers because access to this data provides valuable data for attacking the network and gaining unauthorized access. Let's review the common threats to a DNS server and then we'll discuss ways to harden security for DNS traffic on the network.

Common Threats to DNS

There are a number of common threats to DNS that must be considered and mitigated when planning security for the enterprise. Table 5.14 shows the common threats and how hackers can exploit these threats. We'll look at ways to mitigate these threats in a moment.

Table 5.14 Common Threats to DNS

Common DNS Threats	Description of Threat
Footprinting	Footprinting is a process where DNS zone information is obtained by a hacker. Once the hacker has the zone data, that person can gather DNS domain names, computer names, and IP addresses for any resource. The hacker can then target servers with sensitive network functions or data. The attacker typically begins the attack by mapping out, or footprinting, the network structure based on captured DNS data. From this information, the attacker can use the structure to determine sensitive servers.
Denial-of-service (DoS)	A DoS attack occurs when an attacker attempts to deny availability of network services to legitimate users by flooding the DNS server(s) with recursive queries. As the server is flooded with queries, CPU processing will spike and eventually users will be unable to get DNS services because the server(s) will be busy trying to respond to this flood of queries.
Data modification or IP spoofing	Once an attacker has successfully footprinted the domain structure, he or she will likely then attempt data modification using valid IP addresses in packets the attacker created in an attempt to pass these packets off as legitimate. This is also called IP spoofing. With a valid IP address and an address that is within the address range of a desired subnet, the attacker can then access network resources including sensitive data.
Redirection	Redirection is an attack that occurs when the hacker is able to redirect DNS name queries to servers under the attacker's control. Redirection can be accomplished in several ways. One common way is to pollute the DNS cache with erroneous data that will cause the DNS server to forward DNS queries and data to the attacker's computer. Redirection can occur anytime a hacker has write access to the DNS server records, which can occur during unsecured dynamic updates.

To properly protect the DNS server service on your network, you must address security at these levels: DNS namespace, DNS server service, DNS zones, DNS resource records (RR), and DNS clients. Let's look at each of these in more detail.

DNS Namespace

The DNS namespace is a hierarchical naming structure that identifies network resources and that resource's place within the space. In contrast, WINS is a flat naming structure that identifies resources but does not indicate that resource's place within that structure. The DNS namespace at the top level is regulated by the Internet naming authority, ICANN (Internet Corporation for Assigned Names and Numbers). If your company does not and will not ever connect to the Internet, you can choose whatever namespace you choose. However, most companies do connect to the Internet and must register a unique namespace via the ICANN process.

The namespace is typically designated by a name followed by an extension, somecompany.com, thiscompany.biz, bigcompany.us, and so forth. The namespace can be divided for administration and security purposed. Let's look at how namespaces can be divided.

Single Namespace

A single domain namespace is what you are assigned if your company registered for a domain name. Even in a small company, if you are connected to the Internet, you should separate your namespace into one or more namespaces to designate internal and external names.

Delegated Namespace

You can divide the namespace into one or more zones, which can then be stored, distributed, and replicated to other DNS servers. The decision to delegate the namespace is typically dependent on whether you need to delegate management of part of the namespace for administrative ease, whether you need to divide a large zone for better DNS service (response time, replication time, etc.), or whether you want to extend your namespace with subdomains to accommodate organizational needs.

Internal Namespace

An internal namespace is the namespace you define for your private corporate network. Companies configure these differently, but one common example is to create separate namespaces for separate segments of the business. This can be a fairly flat system or a deeper hierarchy, depending on your organization's needs. For example, your external namespace, as regulated by ICANN, might be somecompany.com. You might choose to create a subdomain (internal namespace) for each division: Finance, Sales, Human Resources, Service, and Manufacturing. Within each of those subdomain namespaces, you can create additional namespaces. For example, you might have na.sales.somecompany.com for North American sales, eu.sales.somecompany.com for European sales, and so forth. All of these are internal namespaces and must be protected. This is exactly the kind of information a hacker would seek to learn via footprinting.

Segmented Namespace

You can split your namespace between internal and external DNS servers. Your external DNS is the root domain, and your internal space is a subdomain of the external space. For example, if your external namespace is somecompany.com, your internal namespace can be defined as corp.somecompany.com. The internal namespace is managed by internal DNS servers behind a firewall, and resolution from external DNS servers to a corporate address occurs from the external DNS server to the internal DNS server via queries.

Securing the Namespace

To secure the DNS namespace, you should separate DNS servers that must resolve names on the Internet from those that do not. By separating internal and external DNS servers, you can restrict external contact to the internal DNS servers. Hosting your internal name space on internal servers and your external name space on external servers will create a first line of defense. To resolve queries for external names made internally, you configure internal DNS servers to forward external queries to external DNS servers for resolution. External hosts use only external DNS servers for name resolution.

For example, by using a segmented namespace, you can create these namespaces: somecompany.com, corporate.somecompany.com, and operations.somecompany.com. The somecompany.com namespace could be on an external DNS server and could resolve external Internet queries. The corporate and operations subdomains would be hosted on internal DNS servers. One DNS server would be the primary master for corporate.somecompany.com, and another would be the secondary server for the subdomain namespace. A second DNS server (perhaps the secondary just described) would be the primary master for the operations.somecompany.com, and the other DNS server would be the secondary for this subdomain. However, in no case does either DNS server resolve Internet name queries—these are all forwarded to the external DNS server.

For external queries for internal namespace resolution, you should configure the external DNS server to send those queries to only one internal DNS server designated for this role. Configure a packet-filtering firewall to allow only UDP and TCP port 53 communications between your external DNS server and a single internal DNS server. This allows external queries for internal resources but prevents other external computers from gaining access to the DNS namespace.

DNS Server Service

There are a number of ways the DNS Server Service can be configured to reduce the risk of and exposure to attack. The first step is to examine the configuration of the DNS Server Service to review settings that affect security. The second step is to manage the discretionary access lists (DACLs) on DNS servers that are running on domain controllers (DCs). Finally, implementing the NTFS file system on DNS servers running any operating system that supports NTFS protects the files on the server. Let's look at these steps in more detail.

1. **Examine DNS server configuration to review security settings** There are four primary areas to examine and configure for security. Table 5.15 shows these four areas along with recommendations for securing these settings.

Table 5.15 Securing the DNS Server Service

DNS Security Area	Recommendation	Comments
Interfaces	Some DNS servers are multi-homed computers (multiple network interface cards). The default setting is for each interface to listen for DNS queries using all its IP addresses (all IP addresses assigned to all network interfaces). Limit the IP addresses that the DNS Server Service listens on. The only IP address it should be configured to listen on is the IP address used by its DNS clients—those clients that use it as their preferred DNS server.	This can be configured via the DNS console by selecting **Action | Properties | Interfaces** and select **Only the following IP addresses.** This will create a static setting that will need to be managed manually in case of change to the IP configuration information. This is an effective security measure because only hosts on the same network or network segment will have access to the DNS server, reducing the exposure to attack.

Continued

Table 5.15 Securing the DNS Server Service

DNS Security Area	Recommendation	Comments
Secure cache against pollution	We discussed briefly that cache on a DNS server might be corrupted, allowing the attacker to redirect DNS traffic to a computer the attacker controls. By default, the DNS Server Service is secured from cache pollution via the **Secure cache against pollution** option, which is enabled by default. This prevents cache from being corrupted with records that were not requested by the DNS server, which is typically the only way DNS records get into cache.	In the DNS console, click **Action | Properties | Advanced** tab. In **Server options**, select **Secure cache against pollution**, and then click **OK**. This is set by default but can be verified. This prevents entries in cache the DNS server did not specifically request.
Disable recursion	Recursion can be used to attack a DNS server by causing a DoS attack. By default, recursion is **enabled.** A DNS server may perform recursive queries on behalf of DNS clients and DNS servers that have forwarded DNS client queries to it. If your network does not need this functionality, it should be disabled.	In the DNS console, choose the DNS server, and select the **Action | Properties | Advanced** tab. In **Server options**, place a check mark in the **Disable recursion** check box and then click **OK.** If you disable recursion on a particular server, you will be unable to use forwarders on that server.
Root hints	Root hints are stored in the file cache.dns in the **systemroot\System32\Dns** folder and contains the DNS data stored on the server that identifies the authoritative DNS servers for the root zone of the namespace. The root hints file for internal servers should point only to DNS servers hosting the root domain and NOT to DNS servers hosting the Internet root domain.	To update the root hints on the DNS server, open the DNS console. Select the desired DNS server and select the **Action | Properties | Root hints** tab. Select **Add**, **Edit**, or **Remove** as appropriate to modify your root hints file. This prevents internal DNS servers from sending private DNS information over the Internet when responding to name resolution requests.

The first step in securing the DNS Server Service is to review security settings related to the service, as we've just done. The next step is to manage access.

2. **Manage DACLs on DNS servers running as DCs** DNS servers configured as DCs use DACLs. The DACL allows you to control permissions for Active Directory users and groups that control the DNS Server Service. Table 5.16 lists the default users and groups as well as the permissions for the DNS Server Service when running on a DC. When a DNS server is running as a DC, its DACL can be managed using the Active Directory object or via the DNS console. It's important that administrators don't inadvertently undo each other's security settings via Active Directory and the DNS console, which operate independently but ultimately set the same settings. Although these default settings might be acceptable, best practices for assigning permissions suggests that removing and reducing rights that are not needed and restricting membership to groups with wide power (Administrators, Enterprise Administrators, etc.) will reduce the risk of abuse of credentials.

Table 5.16 Default Users, Groups, and Permissions for the DNS Server Service on a Domain Controller

User or Group	Default Permissions
Administrators	Read, Write, Create All Child objects, Special Permissions
Authenticated Users	Read, Special Permissions
Creator Owner	Special Permissions
DnsAdmins	Full Control. Read, Write, Create All Child objects, Delete Child objects
Domain Admins	Full Control, Read, Write, Create All Child objects, Delete Child objects
Enterprise Admins	Full Control, Read, Write, Create All Child objects, Delete Child objects
Enterprise Domain Controllers	Special Permissions
Pre-Windows 2000 Compatible Access	Special Permissions
System	Full Control, Read, Write, Create All Child objects, Delete Child objects

3. **Implement NTFS file system on all DNS servers** The third step in securing the DNS Server Service is implementing the NTFS file system format on all system volumes. NTFS allows you to control access to files and folders on a very granular level and integrates with Active Directory, which provides security features not available on volumes running FAT or FAT32.

DNS Zones

DNS zone data can be secured by using secure dynamic updates and security features found in Active Directory when DNS is integrated with Active Directory. There are four major components to securing DNS zones: configure secure dynamic updates, manage DACLs on DNS zones stored in Active Directory, restrict zone transfers, and understand the pros and cons of zone delegation.

- **Configure secure dynamic updates** DNS in Windows Server 2003 is configured not to use dynamic updates, by default. While this is the most secure setting, it also prevents you from using the dynamic update feature that provides significant benefit to administration of zones data. For security, you can implement dynamic updates by storing DNS zones in Active Directory. This is called Active Directory-Integrated zones and allows you to use the secure dynamic update feature in Active Directory to provide both secure and dynamic updates to DNS zone data. Secure dynamic update restricts DNS zone updates to those computers that are authenticated and joined to the Active Directory domain where the DNS server is located. It also forces the secure dynamic update to adhere to the security settings defined in the ACLs for the DNS zone.
- **Manage DACLs on DNS zones stored in Active Directory** Just as the DACLs in the DNS Server Service must be reviewed and modified, as needed, so too must the DACLs for the DNS zones stored in Active Directory. Table 5.17 summarizes the users, groups, and permissions set by default.

Table 5.17 Default Users, Groups, and Permissions for DACLs in Active Directory-Integrated Zones

Default Users and Groups	Default Permissions
Administrators	Read, Write, Create All Child objects, Special Permissions
Authenticated Users	Create All Child objects
Creator Owner	Special Permissions

Continued

Table 5.17 Default Users, Groups, and Permissions for DACLs in Active Directory-Integrated Zones

Default Users and Groups	Default Permissions
DnsAdmins	Full Control, Read, Write, Create All Child objects, Delete Child objects
Domain Admins	Full Control, Read, Write, Create All Child objects, Delete Child objects
Enterprise Admins	Full Control, Read, Write, Create All Child objects, Delete Child objects
Enterprise Domain Controllers	Full Control, Read, Write, Create All Child objects, Delete Child objects, Special Permissions
Everyone	Read, Special Permissions
Pre-Windows 2000 Compatible Access	Special Permissions
System	Full Control, Read, Write, Create All Child objects, Delete Child objects

- **Restrict zone transfers.** Typically, zones are transferred only to DNS servers listed in the name server (NS) resource records of a zone. This is the default behavior of DNS in Windows Server 2003. However, to increase security, this setting can be changed to allow zone transfers to specified IP addresses of the DNS servers. This can help prevent redirection attacks by allowing zone transfers to occur only between specific computers with specific IP addresses.

  To modify DNS zone transfer settings, open the DNS console, select the DNS zone and select **Action | Properties | Zone Transfer** tab. To disable zone transfers, clear the check box labeled **Allow zone transfers**. To allow zone transfers, select the check box labeled **Allow zone transfers**. If you allow zone transfers, you can specify one of the following:

  - Allow zone transfer **To any server**. This is not a recommended setting, as it exposes your DNS data to attack. This setting provides virtually no security.
  - Allow zone transfer to servers listed on the Name Servers tab. Select **Only to servers listed on the Name Servers tab**. This is the default setting, which provides medium security.
  - Allow zone transfer **Only to the following servers**. If you select this option, you can enter the IP address of any DNS servers to which you want to transfer zones. This is the most secure setting because it specifies the exact IP address.

- **Understand the pros and cons of zone delegation.** Zone delegation is the process whereby zone administration is separated for ease of administration. The downside to this is that you have more people involved with securing your vital network resources. The more people with the ability to administer your data, the less secure your overall network is. There is a tradeoff between delegation and security, and you must assess the risk for your organization. DNS zones are more secure when there is a single authoritative DNS server but are more difficult to administer. Conversely, delegating zones for various namespaces to different administrators eases administration but reduces security. This is an especially important consideration for the company's top-level domain namespace or any namespace that contains very sensitive data.

DNS Resource Records

A DNS RR contains information about resources in the domain. There are different types of RRs that provide names, IP addresses, and other information related to hostnames. Default settings for DNS RR might be adequate for your organization. To harden security, DNS can be integrated with Active Directory to use Active Directory security features when hosted on a DC. If DNS is integrated with Active Directory, managing the DACLs on the DNS RRs will provide additional security. Again, work with user and group permissions set to the minimum to allow proper functioning. Table 5.18 lists the default permissions for DNS RRs in Active Directory.

Table 5.18 Default DNS Resource Record Permissions for Users and Groups in Active Directory

Default Users and Groups	Default Permissions
Administrators	Read, Write, Create All Child objects, Special Permissions
Authenticated Users	Create All Child Objects
Creator Owner	Special Permissions
DnsAdmins	Full Control, Read, Write, Create All Child objects, Delete Child objects
Domain Admins	Full Control, Read, Write, Create All Child objects, Delete Child objects
Enterprise Admins	Full Control, Read, Write, Create All Child objects, Delete Child objects
Enterprise Domain Controllers	Full Control, Read, Write, Create All Child objects, Delete Child objects, Special Permissions

Continued

Table 5.18 Default DNS Resource Record Permissions for Users and Groups in Active Directory

Default Users and Groups	Default Permissions
Everyone	Read, Special Permissions
Pre-Windows 2000 Compatible Access	Special Permissions
System	Full Control, Read, Write, Create All Child objects, Delete Child objects

DNS Clients

The last of the five areas for securing DNS data is controlling the DNS server IP addresses used by DNS clients. When possible, use static IP addresses for the preferred and alternate DNS servers used by the client. By default, DNS server data is included in dynamic DHCP configuration data, which is fairly secure. However, if the DHCP server is compromised, the DNS server IP address can be modified in DHCP (by an attacker), and DNS clients could be redirected to a bogus DNS server controlled by the attacker. After assessing your organization's risk, you might choose to statically assign the IP address of the preferred and alternate DNS server on DNS clients. In addition, you can control which DNS clients have access to a DNS server. As discussed earlier, you can configure a DNS server to only listen on specific IP addresses. If DNS servers are configured in this way, only DNS clients configured with the IP addresses as preferred or alternate DNS servers will contact the DNS server.

EXAM 70-298 OBJECTIVE 3.1.5

Designing Security for Data Transmission

Thus far, we've reviewed IPSec to understand how IP traffic can be secured. We've also looked at securing DNS, a vital service on most networks today. Now, let's look at the specifics of designing security for the transmission of data. After that, we'll look at the specific needs of securing data for wireless networks.

There are a number of other methods for securing data being transmitted in a number of different scenarios. IPSec works well in some instances, but other options are more viable and appropriate in other instances. In this section, we'll review these options and discuss what they are, how they're used, and how they protect data and privacy on the network.

SSL/TLS

The Secure Sockets Layer/Transport Layer Security (SSL/TLS) protocol is typically used to secure HTTP/HTTPS traffic on Web sites. However, SSL/TLS works below the application layer in the TCP/IP stack and can be used transparently by applications that require security for application layer protocols such as FTP, LDAP, or SMTP. SSL/TLS provides server authentication, optional client authentication, data encryption, and data integrity. SSL/TLS can be used to protect against masquerade attacks, man-in-the-middle attacks (sometimes called bucket brigade attacks), and rollback and replay attacks.

SSL was originally developed by Netscape Communications Corporation to secure transaction over the Web. The current version is SSL 3.0. An earlier version, SSL 2.0, is still in use. After SSL was devised, the IETF created a standard for similar functionality called the Transport Layer Security protocol. Although there are subtle differences between SSL 3.0 and TLS 1.0, they are often referred to as SSL/TSL. TLS uses a keyed-hashing for Message Authentication Code, referred to as HMAC. SSL 3.0 uses the Message Authenticate Code (MAC) algorithm. The HMAC's keyed hashing makes it harder to break because the hash algorithm is used in combination with a shared secret key, and both parties must have the same shared secret key to prove the data is authentic.

SSL/TLS works between the application layer and the transport layer and includes two layers of its own: the handshake layer and the record layer. The handshake layer is responsible for setting up the secure connection, and the record layer contains the data. The handshake layer manages the authentication, encryption, and hash algorithms.

Authentication via SSL/TLS is accomplished using an X.509 certificate issued by a CA. Both symmetric and asymmetric keys are used for encryption in SSL/TLS. Symmetric keys, known also as shared secret keys, use the same key to encrypt and decrypt the message. Asymmetric keys use different keys to encrypt and decrypt the message. Typically, one of the keys is a public key and the other key is known only to the owner of that key (private key).

The hash algorithm used is either Message Digest 5 (MD5) or the Standard Hash Algorithm 1 (SHA1). MD5, as you recall, generates a 128-bit hash value, and SHA1 generates the stronger 160-bit hash value. In addition, the SSL/TLS hash algorithm includes a value that checks integrity of the data. TLS uses HMAC and SSL uses MAC. Although HMAC is stronger, both are acceptable hash algorithms to use. Windows Server 2003 supports using SSL and MAC.

Test Day Tip

Although they are similar, SSL and TLS do not interoperate. Both parties must use either SSL or TLS. If the other party cannot use the same protocol, communication will not occur. SSL uses MAC and TLS uses HMAC. Don't be fooled by the common use of SSL/TLS—they are two separate but similar protocols that cannot be used interchangeably.

Using SSL/TSL provides several important benefits that might make it an appropriate security technology in your organization.

- **Strong authentication, message integrity, and privacy** SSL/TLS provides the ability to transmit secure data using encryption. It also provides server authentication and optional client authentication to prove that the parties involved in the communication are who they say they are. This is accomplished through the use of digital certificates. Data integrity is provides through an integrity check function, similar to that used in the IPSec AH or ESP protocols.
- **Algorithm flexibility** SSL/TLS provides the ability to select authentication methods, encryption algorithms, and hashing algorithms to be used during the secure session.
- **Easy to deploy and use** Deploying SSL for secure browsing in Windows Server 2003 requires that you check a check box to enable this security feature via IIS. Since SSL/TLS resides below the application layer, it is transparent to applications and users and requires no user interaction to enable the secure communication. Although it can be used with various applications and application layer protocols, those applications must be written to use SSL/TLS.

However, there are two notable drawbacks to using SSL/TLS:

- **Increased CPU utilization** As with any encryption system using public keys, the use of SSL/TLS requires additional CPU processor cycles creating overhead that must be anticipated and managed. The increased processor time to manage SSL/TLS is greatest when connections are being set up.
- **Administrative overhead** SSL/TLS uses certificates and certificate-based systems require regular maintenance to configure the system and manage certificates.

Configuring SSL/TLS

You can configure SSL on your Web server but must first obtain a valid certificate. You can use the Web Server Certificate Wizard in Windows Server 2003, or use a third-party company to obtain a certificate. After you've obtained and installed your certificate, you can enable SSL in IIS.

EXAM 70-298 OBJECTIVE 3.3

EXERCISE 5.03

CONFIGURING IIS TO USE SSL

Follow these steps to configure your Web server to use SSL in IIS. If you do not have your server configured as an IIS server or if you do not have a valid certificate, you will be unable to perform all of these steps. Review them even if you cannot perform them on your system, as you will likely need to know this information for the exam.

1. Click **Start | Administrative Tools | Internet Information Services (IIS) Manager**.
2. Expand the IIS node in the left pane to display the three subnodes: **Application Pools, Web Sites**, and **Default Web Site**.
3. Click the + to expand Web Sites, and select the Web site to which you want to add SSL. Right-click on that Web site and select **Properties**.
4. The **[Name] Web Site Properties** dialog is displayed. In the **Web site identification** section on the **Web Site** tab, click **Advanced**, as shown in Figure 5.12.

Figure 5.12 Web Site Properties Dialog

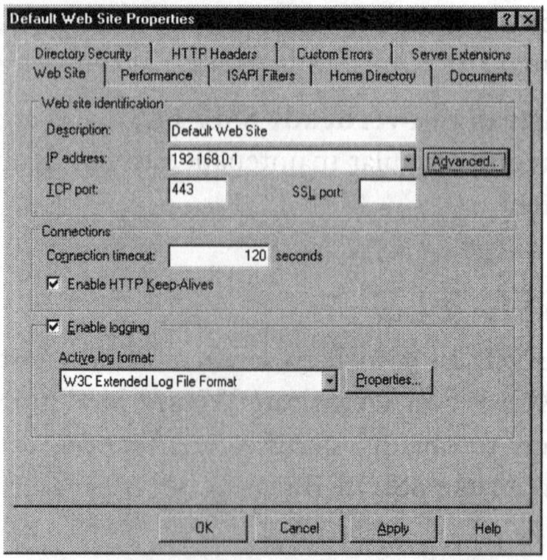

5. In the **Advanced Web site identification** box, under **Multiple identities for this Web site**, verify the address for the IP address is assigned to port 443, the default port for secure communications. Click **OK**.

6. To configure additional SSL ports for this Web site, click **Add** under **Multiple Identities of this Web site**. Configure additional ports, and then click **OK**.
7. On **Directory Security**, under **Secure Communications**, click **Edit**.
8. Click to select the check box labeled **Require secure channel (SSL)** in the **Secure Communications** box, as shown in Figure 5.13.

Figure 5.13 Require Secure Channel (SSL) Configuration

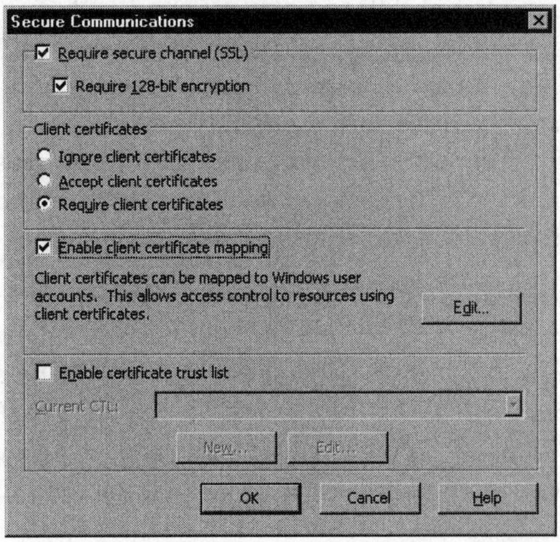

9. To enable SSL client Certificate authentication and mapping, click the check box for **Enable client certificate mapping** and click **Edit**.
10. If you click the check box labeled **Required 128-bit encryption**, the browser must support 12-bit encryption.
11. On **the Secure Communications** dialog, you can also specify how to handle client certificates: **ignore**, **accept**, or **require**. Requiring client certificates provides the most secure solution and is appropriate for limiting access to the site.
12. You can enable client certificate mapping, which allows access control to resources using client certificates that can be mapped to user accounts.
13. You can enable a trust certificate list by clicking the check box labeled **Enable certificate trust list**. A certificate trust list is a signed list of root certificate authorities that have been deemed reputable by the administrator.

14. Click **OK** to accept changes or **Cancel** to discard changes in the **Secure Communications** dialog.
15. Click **OK** to accept or **Cancel** to discard changes to the **[Name] Web Site Properties** dialog.
16. Click **File | Exit** to close the IIS Manager console.

There are a number of different scenarios in which you might elect to implement SSL/TLS. For example, it's fairly common to see SSL/TLS implemented on Web sites (HTTPS) to provide secure communications with a Web site, particularly when securing an e-commerce transaction. Today, almost all e-commerce servers use SSL/TLS to secure username, password, and credit card transaction information. Although e-commerce is the most predominant and visible application of SSL/TLS, there are other scenarios in which using this security protocol makes sense.

- **Authenticated client access to a secure site** You can provide access to authenticated clients to a secure site by requiring both client and server certificates and by mapping those certificates. Client certificates can be mapped on a one-to-one basis or a many-to-one basis via Active Directory Users and Computers. You can create a group of designated users, map the users' certificates to the group, and give the group permission to access the secure site.
- **Remote access** SSL/TLS provides authentication and data protection for remote users logged in to Windows-based systems. E-mail and other applications that use SSL/TLS provide security by requiring authentication and data encryption.
- **SQL access** SQL Server administrators can require client authentication when clients attempt to connect to SQL Server. Either the client or the server can also be configured to require encryption of the data transferred. This is an important feature for SQL databases that contain sensitive information such as payroll, financial, or medical records.
- **E-mail** Microsoft Exchange servers can use SSL/TLS to protect data between servers on the Internet or on the internal intranet. End-to-end security is best accomplished with **Secure/Multipurpose Internet Mail Extensions (S/MIME)**, discussed in the next section. However, data between servers can be secured via SSL/TSL regardless of whether S/MIME is implemented.

Firewalls and SSL/TLS

If you're using firewalls, SSL/TLS provides an interesting challenge. You have essentially two options. You can open the firewall to allow HTTPS traffic on port 443, which is the typical port for secured HTTP traffic with SSL. However, this means the firewall must allow the traffic based on the *apparent* source and destination of the packet because the packet is encrypted.

The alternative is to configure the firewall as a proxy server. The problem is that the proxy server must transmit the authenticated identity of the original user to the internal system, which might or might not be secured, exposing this information. You'll have to choose which is the better solution for your firm and monitor it carefully.

S/MIME

S/MIME is used to secure e-mail traffic from one end to the other. As mentioned earlier, SSL can be used to secure server-to-server traffic, but S/MIME is best suited for end-to-end security.

S/MIME is an extension of MIME that supports secure e-mail by enabling the e-mail originator to digitally sign an e-mail to provide proof of both origin and message integrity. It also enables e-mail to be encrypted to provide confidential communication via the Internet. Microsoft Exchange Server 2000 and Exchange Server 2003 both support S/MIME. However, one notable change from Exchange Server 2000 to Exchange Server 2003 is that Key Management is replaced by Certificate Services. Another significant change in Exchange Server 2003 is that it extends the scope of client support by the Microsoft Office Outlook Web Access S/MIME ActiveX Control. This enables Internet Explorer 6 SP1 and later Web clients to send and receive secure S/MIME e-mail. Discussing Exchange Server is outside the scope of this chapter, but it's important that you understand what S/MIME is and in what scenarios it makes sense to use it since you will undoubtedly run into questions related to or involving S/MIME on the exam.

SMB Signing

The Server Message Block (SMB) protocol provides the basis for file and print sharing and remote Windows administration. SMB signing can be implemented to prevent man-in-the-middle attacks because the data in transit is protected. SMB support the digital signing of SMB packets to prevent modification while SMB packets are in transit. As with most security measures, there is a balance between requiring SMB security and system performance.

If you think back to Chapter 2, you'll recall that Server Message Block Signing is *negotiated* in the secure*.inf predefined security template and is *required* in the hisec*.inf predefined security template. These settings can be implemented via the predefined security templates, security templates you create, or via Group Policy. It is recommended that you configure these settings inside a security template or group policy to make managing security more streamlined and consistent. To configure these settings via security templates, use the **Security Template** snap-in in the MMC. To configure these settings via group policy, open the appropriate policy via the **Group Policy Editor** snap-in in the MMC and expand the console tree in this manner: **Computer Configuration | Windows Settings | Security Settings | Local Policies | Security Options**.

There are four settings related to Server Message Block Signing, as shown in Figure 5.14. By viewing these settings within the predefined security template, securews.inf, you can see exactly how these settings relate. Each of these policy settings can be Enabled, Disabled, or Not Defined. When Enabled, the setting is enforced via the template or group policy. When Disabled, the setting is not enforced. When Not Defined, the check box for that policy has been cleared and that policy is no longer defined in the security database.

- **Microsoft network client** Digitally sign communications (always)
- **Microsoft network client** Digitally sign communications (if server agrees)
- **Microsoft network server** Digitally sign communications (always)
- **Microsoft network server** Digitally sign communications (if client agrees)

Figure 5.14 Server Message Block Signing Options

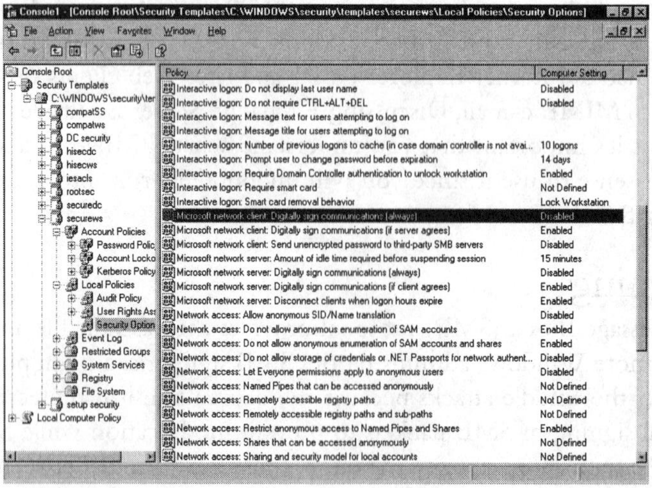

These settings must be used in certain combinations for communication to be successful. Table 5.19 outlines these combinations and the results. The *if server agrees* or *if client agrees* option essentially enables SMB signing on that computer. If this setting for either the client or server is disabled, SMB signing is disabled on the computer. This is the default setting (SMB disabled) for member servers.

Table 5.19 Server Message Block Signing Options

Server Setting*	Client Setting**	Result
Always	Always	SMB signing is required by both client and server. Communication without SMB signing is not allowed.
Always	If server agrees	SMB signing will occur because the client will use SMB signing if the server agrees to it. Since the server requires it, SMB signing will be required and used.
Always	Not defined	The client will not be able to communicate with that server because the server requires SMB signing, which the client is not configured to use.
If client agrees	Always	SMB signing will occur because the server side supports it and the client side requires it.
If client agrees	If server agrees	Both the client and server are able to negotiate the use of SMB signing; therefore, SMB signing will occur.
If client agrees	Not defined.	SMB signing will not occur. The server side will request SMB signing but the client is not configured to support SMB signing. None used.
Not defined	Always	SMB signing will not be implemented because the server is not configured to support it and the client requires it.
Not defined	If server agrees	SMB signing will not be implemented because the server does not support it. The client will attempt to use SMB signing until it finds that the server does not support SMB.
Not defined	None	SMB signing will not occur because neither the client nor the server is configured to use it.

** The Microsoft network server: Digitally sign communications node is implied.*
*** The Microsoft network client: Digitally sign communications node is implied.*

By default, client-side SMB signing is enabled on workstations, servers, and DCs. This means the default setting for the client side is *Microsoft network client: Digitally sign communications (if server agrees)*. By default, server-side SMB signing is only enabled on DCs, and is disabled by default for member servers. This means the default setting for DCs is *Microsoft network server: Digitally sign communications (if client agrees)* is enabled and the default setting for member servers *is Microsoft network server: Digitally sign communications (if client agrees)* is *disabled*.

What this means is that essentially, all computers (running Windows NT or later) can sign SMB packets, if requested, without further configuration. DCs, by default, are the only servers that are configured to use (enabled) SMB signing. Other computers can be configured to use SMB signing, either as an option or as a requirement. An example of a use for this is a member server that stores sensitive research data. You can configure this server to always require SMB signing. You can either use the default client-side setting, which will use SMB because SMB signing is enabled by default, or you can require SMB signing on the client side as well.

Port Authentication for Switches

Network switches are commonly used to filter network traffic, reducing traffic to segments by filtering or blocking traffic that is not addressed for a particular network segment attached to the switch. Switches effectively segment a network. However, most switches send and received packets to and from any node (computer) attached to the switch. In less secure locations within a corporation, unauthorized users could gain access to the network via a switch. For example, conference rooms, lobbies, or shipping/receiving docks are all places a switch might be located to which outsiders have easy, often unchecked access. In these cases, securing the switch traffic can help secure the network.

Newer switches can be configured to require switch node authentication and authorization before data is transmitted from the network to the node attached to the switch. To accomplish this, each switch is required to have a user account database, but this becomes an administrative nightmare pretty quickly. Newer switches can now be RADIUS clients (in Microsoft, those are IAS clients), using the RADIUS protocol to send connection requests and accounting messages to the RADIUS server. RADIUS servers have access to user account databases and can better manage this data. The RADIUS server can then receive and process the switch's request for a connection and accept or reject it based on stored credentials.

IAS supports switch access authentication via Extensible Authentication Protocol-Transport Layer Security (EAP-TLS), Ethernet port type, or virtual local area network (VLAN).

- **EAP-TLS** is used to provide certificate-based authentication for either the computer or the user.
- **Ethernet port type** is typically used when configuring remote access policies. Using this port type, you can create various remote access policies that contain connection parameters specifically designed for switch nodes.

The use of VLAN switching is determined by whether or not the switch access client is authenticated.

EXAM 70-298 OBJECTIVE 1.2.3

Using Segmented Networks

One of the most common methods of securing network data is to segment the network into smaller sections. Switches, routers, gateways, or firewalls can be configured in between these network segments to manage traffic between and among various network segments. This can be especially helpful for computers in a particular department that require additional security. By placing these computers on a network segment, traffic to and from that segment can be filtered via the gateway.

When traffic for a host on another network or network segment is sent from a host, the packet goes to the host's default gateway. The IP address of a packet is compared to the host's IP address and subnet mask. If the network ID matches, the packet is destined for a computer on the local segment and is not passed on to the gateway. If the network ID does not match, the packet is forwarded to the default gateway for routing to the intended host.

Segmenting a network also improves the efficiency of the network because multicast and broadcast traffic is kept on the local segment, preventing it from being transmitted across the entire network. By segmenting a network, local traffic stays local and remote traffic is forwarded to the gateway. The gateway can be configured to block or permit different types of traffic to protect network segments from either receiving or sending data to unauthorized networks, segments, or hosts.

EXAM 70-298 OBJECTIVE 3.2

Design Security for Wireless Networks

We've covered a lot of ground so far in this chapter. We've covered different ways to protect data across the network. However, we haven't discussed how to protect the wireless network. As you know, wireless technologies are proliferating, and as standards and technologies continue to mature, wireless will no doubt continue to grow in popularity.

Critics of wireless networks point to inherent weaknesses in wireless technologies that create security holes. However, with recent improvements in wireless standards and technologies incorporated into Windows Server 2003 (and Windows XP), many of these issues are adequately addressed. Every networking method has some inherent weaknesses. As with all security planning, you must find an acceptable balance between the need for security and the need for the network to be a useful business tool accessible to and for the people that use its resources. In this section, we'll describe the *most* secure implementation of wireless networking within the Windows Server 2003 framework as well as touch on some of the less secure methods that you might have seen or read about. Although this chapter assumes your understanding of PKI and RADIUS, we'll review these briefly to refresh your understanding of these technologies.

Types of Wireless Networks

There are essentially four types of wireless networks, based on their range or scope:

- Wireless personal area networks (WPANs)
- Wireless local area networks (WLANs)
- Wireless metropolitan area networks (WMANs)
- Wireless wide area networks (WWANs)

A WPAN connects wireless personal devices such as cellular phones, personal digital assistants (PDAs), laptops, or wireless printers. WPANs operate using either infrared or radio frequency (RF). Bluetooth is one example of a radio-frequency-based WPAN and is defined by the IEEE 802.15 specification. Most WPANs provide connectivity up to about 30 feet and, because it uses RF, it can penetrate walls, pockets, and briefcases. Infrared WPANs are limited to line-of-sight and at a distance generally not greater than about three feet. Wireless keyboards and mice often use infrared.

WLANs are designed to provide connectivity to a local area, typically defined as a building or office. WLANs are based on the 802.11 standard. IEEE 802.11 WLANs original throughput was about 1–2Mbps. Current throughput via the802.11g standard is about 54 Mbps and the range is about 300 feet. Special antennae can be used that boost the range up to five kilometers. A WLAN is implemented by attaching wireless access points (WAPs) to the wired LAN. Wireless users connect via a WAP to the LAN. Some implementations can be peer-to-peer WLANs. Wireless bridges can also be used to connect devices to the wireless network or to connect two wireless networks together.

WMANs connect buildings within a campus or city through infrared or radio frequency. The infrared implementation has limitations due to the requirement to have line-of-site for connectivity. RF is subject to interference from other devices that might operate at the same or nearby frequencies. RF WMANs include multichannel multipoint distribution services (MMDS) and local multipoint distribution services (LMDS), although a standard for this has not yet been finalized.

WWANs have existed for a while and are most commonly implemented via cell phones. The current technology is not standardized and there are several companies and/or technologies vying for their place in the standard. These technologies are all referred to as second generation (2G), and the International Telecommunication Union is working on a third generation standard known as 3G. Current technologies include Cellular Digital Packet Data (CDPD and Code Division Multiple Access (CDMA).

Brief Wireless History

It will be helpful to begin with a brief history of wireless networking to help you understand the challenges inherent in this type of solution as well as the growing need to implement this type of solution in many organizations.

The Institute of Electrical and Electronic Engineers (IEEE) devised the wireless standard, 802.11, when wireless technology was in its infancy. As you know, the 802.X standards define various standards related to Ethernet networking. At the time of the development of 802.11 standards, there were significant governmental restrictions (U.S. government) on the use of high-strength encryption. Network security was also not a high priority at the time. Thus, the 802.11 standard was developed with relatively weak security by today's security standards (and facing today's security threats).

In today's environment, commonly available network "audit" tools are available that make breaking into an unsecured wireless network quite simple. The word "audit" is in quotes because some of these programs are very legitimate network tools and others are nothing more than ill-disguised hacker tools. One such tool describes itself as a tool that cracks encryption keys on 802.11b WEP networks.

You've probably heard stories of people driving around cities trying to gain access to wireless networks. This practice, called *wardriving*, brought to the forefront the inherent weakness of some of the wireless networking technologies and also served to point out how many wireless networks were implemented with no security at all.

The IEEE 802.11 standard allows for two wireless network types: *ad hoc* and *infrastructure*. In the ad hoc type of wireless network, computers are brought together "on the fly" and each computer can communicate with all other computers in this ad hoc network. Several different algorithms can be used to control data flow on this network. One such algorithm is called the Spokesman Election Algorithm (SEA), which assigns the "master" role to one computer to manages this network. Another algorithm uses a broadcast and flooding method to establish order on the ad hoc network. This can be selected via Wireless Network (IEEE 802.11) Policies via the Group Policy Editor snap-in in Windows Server 2003.

An *infrastructure-based wireless network* is just as the name implies—it relies on network infrastructure to establish and maintain order. This type of network uses fixed wireless access points (AP or WAP) with which mobile devices can communicate. These WAPs access the LAN and provide a variety of services to the mobile client. These services can (and should) include authentication, access control, and data encryption.

The 802.11 standard for wireless networks has evolved. The progression has been 802.11b, 802.11a, and 802.11g. The 802.11 standard supports operation in the 2.4 through 2.5 GHz range (radio frequency) and has a maximum bit rate of 2 megabits per second (Mbps). The next standard to be implemented was 802.11b (often referred to simply as Wi-Fi), which supports two additional speeds—5.5 Mbps and 11 Mbps, still within the 2.4 to 2.5 GHz range. The next standard to emerge was the 802.11a standard, which operates in a different frequency range than does 802.11 or 802.11b. The range for 802.11a is 5.725 through 5.875 GHz and the maximum throughput is 54 Mbps. Finally, the 802.11g specification was announced in June 2003 and essentially doubles the throughput for 802.11b from 11 Mbps to 54 Mbps. Thus, 802.11g uses the 2.4 to 2.5 GHz range with maximum throughput of 54 Mbps. 802.11g is essentially an extension of 802.11b and is therefore backward compatible. Devices that use 802.11g can co-exist with 802.11b devices, and if needed, 802.11g devices can fall back to the slower 11 Mbps throughput speed. 802.11b devices are not forward compatible, meaning they cannot be "boosted" to run 54 Mbps throughput, although they can co-exist with the faster 802.11g devices.

You might wonder why the frequency (GHz) specification is given or specified, but this is an important element in understanding wireless networks. This range is within the radio frequency range, and as the wireless network range expands, there might be cases where the wireless network range overlaps with other commercial uses of radio frequency, causing interference for both uses. Radio frequency can also be used as an attack method by using the wireless frequency to disrupt communication between a wireless network and wireless device.

The 802.11 standard includes a protocol called Wired Equivalent Privacy (WEP). WEP provides some level of security, but, as the previous paragraph points out, there are tools readily available that can crack WEP encryption. An extension of WEP is called Wi-Fi Protected Access (WPA) and is just beginning to be available on the market. Both WEP and WPA provide methods for encrypting wireless traffic between wireless clients and wireless access points (APs or WAPs).

WEP and WPA provide secure communication, but some method must be used to authenticate users. Different 802.1X-based WLANs offer different solutions to this need. The preferred solution within the Windows Server 2003 environment is the use of the IETF standard called Extensible Authentication Protocol (EAP). EAP can use various authentication methods that are based on passwords, public key certificates, or other credentials.

The IEEE has also defined standards for authenticating access to a network and, optionally, for managing keys to protect traffic. Although this framework, called 802.1X, can be implemented in wired LANs, its applicability to wireless access is clear.

Although there is a wealth of information available on these standards and many more, our focus will be on these technologies.

NOTE

For more information on the IEEE, visit their Web site at www.ieee.org. Additional information on the IETF can be found at www.ietf.org. Understanding standards and reading about changes to standards is a good way to keep up to date on changing technologies that might become important to your network and your organization.

Threats to Wireless Networks

Before going into the technologies any further, let's look at some of the threats to wireless networks. Clearly, some of the threats are the same as on a wired network, but there are threats that are specific to wireless networks. We'll look at each threat and point out the best current solution for mitigating that threat. Table 5.20 lists the threats and descriptions and defines whether the threat is a wired/wireless threat or just a wireless threat.

Table 5.20 Common Threats to Wireless Networks

Threat	Description	Type of Threat
Eavesdropping	The unauthorized capturing of transmitted data for malicious purposes.	Both (wired and wireless)
Data modification	The interception and modification of data transmitted between to parties by a third party.	Both
Spoofing	The modification of data to appear as though data came from the sender or receiver when it was from a third party.	Both
Free-loading	When an unauthorized party uses your network bandwidth.	Wireless
Denial of service (DoS)	When a server is flooded with service requests that cause legitimate users to be denied use of that service because it is busy or overloaded.	Both, although different on wireless
Accidental network access	When a user with a wireless connection on his or her device accesses the network accidentally.	Wireless
Rogue wireless networks	When legitimate users within a company establish an unauthorized wireless LAN that is connected to the corporate network.	Both

As you can see, many of the threats to wireless networks are the same as for wired networks, although the methods of attack and mitigation might be slightly different. An interesting note about DoS attacks is that a wireless DoS can be caused by something as innocuous as a nearby microwave oven. More sophisticated DoS attacks target the wireless protocols, and less sophisticated attacks typically generate a DoS attack by flooding the WLAN with random traffic.

In addition to these threats, there are widely reported problems with WLAN technologies that are leveraged by attackers. Some of these problems that cause companies to delay or reject wireless networking include:

- Confusion over wireless security standards
- Management concern about the ability to control and manage wireless networks
- Regulatory concerns about privacy, including finance and health care (HIPAA)

Early adopters of wireless technologies discovered that the security measures outlined in the 802.11 specification were flawed. There have been a number of attempts to address these flaws, which might have caused further confusion. Emerging standards provide better security, but there are still companies that are resistant to adopting a wireless model of any kind because of these concerns, both real and perceived.

Another major concern for some companies is the perceived inability to manage wireless LANs effectively. When someone actually taps into a wired network, intrusion can be detected and the intruder must find a way to physically connect to the network. With wireless networking, intrusion is virtually undetectable so it's difficult (or impossible) to determine who's connected to your wireless network. According to Les Vadasz, retired executive vice president of Intel, who spoke at the Wi-Fi Planet Conference & Expo (December 2003), over two-thirds of network architects at large enterprises fear that adding wireless will compromise their network security, and more than half of executives see rogue access points as a serious problem. There are methods for mitigating this, which we'll discuss in this section.

There is a growing body of legislation, both at the U.S. national and state level, to protect electronic data in cases where that data is sensitive. Two examples are data from the finance sector, whether it's a record of your online brokerage account or a record of corporate finances, and health care data. In 1996, the U.S. government established the Health Insurance Portability and Accountability Act of 1996 (HIPAA), which among other things, requires specific and secure handling of personal health care data.

These concerns are quite legitimate and, coupled with the growing list of attacks discussed earlier, are rational reasons why companies might elect to wait on implementing wireless networks. However, as we'll discuss shortly, there are effective technologies available today to eliminate or mitigate many of the risks, much as there are with wired networks. It might take a bit more planning on the front end to design and implement a secure wireless network. However, the cost savings and other tangible and intangible benefits will offset that additional work in many instances.

Quick Review of PKI and RADIUS/IAS

There are several considerations when designing and implementing a wireless network. You must:

- Design a secure wireless network strategy as part of your overall security strategy.
- Design a secure wireless architecture to implement the most secure technologies and architectures.
- Evaluate (and/or implement) PKI.
- Evaluate (and/or implement) RADIUS/IAS.
- Design securing around the 802.1X standard.

Before we go into the design of the wireless network, let's take few minutes to review both PKI and RADIUS, which is implemented as Internet Authentication Service (IAS) in the Windows platform. Although familiarity with PKI and RADIUS/IAS is assumed, both topics are covered in detail in this book, so our review here will be brief.

Public Key Infrastructure

A PKI consists of certificates, CAs, and other registration authorities (RAs). Together, these verify and authenticate the identity of each party. Standards for PKI are evolving, but support for PKI is implemented in Windows Server 2003 and Windows XP. Although earlier versions of Windows supported elements of PKI, Windows Server 2003 and Windows XP use the latest features in PKI technology.

PKI is used in a number of different ways in Windows Server 2003. For example, it can be used to secure a wireless network, as we're discussing. It is also used to implement secure e-mail via S/MIME and to secure Web traffic via SSL and TLS, all discussed earlier. You can use PKI to implement smart cards for strong authentication as well as to implement EFS and IPSec.

Certificate

A certificate is a digital statement issued by a CA verifying and vouching for the identity of the certificate holder. The certificate binds a public key to the identity of the certificate holder, who holds the corresponding private key. Windows Server 2003 certificate-based processes use the X.509v3 format, which includes information about the certificate holder (person or entity), information about the certificate, and optional information about the CA.

Certificate Authority

A CA is an entity responsible for establishing and vouching for authenticity of the public keys issued to the certificate holder or other CAs. CA activities including binding the public key to the identity of the certificate holder, managing certificate serial numbers, and certificate revocation.

Certificate Revocation List

A CRL is used by both CAs and certificate verifiers to verify that a certificate is still good. In cases where a certificate is stolen or is otherwise considered invalid, a certificate can be revoked by the CA. When a certificate holder uses a certificate for authentication, that certificate is verified against the CRL. If it matches, the authentication is denied and the user is denied access. If it does not match (meaning it is not on the CRL), the user is authenticated and the authentication process continues.

Certificate Services

Windows Server 2003 (Standard, Enterprise, and Datacenter Editions only) includes functionality to set up and maintain your own CA via Certificate Services. You can issue, manage, and revoke certificates using Certificate Services.

Remote Authentication Dial-In User Service and Internet Authentication Service

RADIUS is a protocol defined by IETF RFCs 3865 and 2866. RADIUS is implemented in Windows Server 2003 as IAS, which is why you often seem them referred to together. RADIUS is used to provide centralized authentication, authorization, and accounting for dial-up access, VPNs, authenticating Ethernet switches, Digital Subscriber Line (DSL) access, wireless network access, and other network access methods.

RADIUS is implemented in a client/server model. The RADIUS server provides the authentication, authorization, and accounting services to RADIUS clients. RADIUS clients are typically remote access servers (RAS), VPN servers, or wireless access points (WAP). When a user wants to access the network, the user connects to the RADIUS client (again, RAS, VPN, WAP, etc.) and the authentication credentials and connection information are sent to the RADIUS server for verification. The RADIUS server authenticates and authorizes the user and sends a RADIUS message back to the RADIUS client. The user is then permitted access as defined by access policies and user permissions. The RADIUS messages from the client to the server and from the server to the client are never transmitted back to the user or user machine.

For point-to-point (PPP) authentication protocols, the results of authentication between the access server/RADIUS client (RAS, VPN server, WAP) and the user's computer are then forwarded to the RADIUS server for verification. PPP protocols include:

- Password Authentication Protocol (PAP)
- Challenge Handshake Authentication Protocol (CHAP)
- Microsoft Challenge Handshake Authentication Protocol (MS-CHAP)
- MS-CHAP version 2 (MS-CHAP v2)

RADIUS supports the use of RADIUS proxies, which forward traffic back and forth between RADIUS clients, RADIUS servers, and other RADIUS proxies. RADIUS traffic between RADIUS clients, servers, and proxies is secured using a common shared secret, commonly configured as a text string at both ends.

Designing Wireless LANs

Designing a secure wireless network takes planning and integration with existing infrastructure. Some industry analysts believe that wireless networking will become the de facto standard, so understanding how to design a wireless network will help you both on the job and on the exam.

EXAM WARNING

You should expect to see strong emphasis on wireless networking on this exam. Wireless networking is a hot topic these days, and the improvements to the Windows Server 2003 wireless networking capabilities will certainly warrant several questions on the topic. Make sure you're very comfortable with PKI, RADIUS/IAS, and wireless topics for this exam.

The elements of designing a wireless network include:

- Designing WLAN network infrastructure
- Designing wireless authentication
- Designing wireless access infrastructure

EXAM 70-298 OBJECTIVE 3.2.1

Designing WLAN Network Infrastructure

Although there are many ways to design and implement a wireless network, we're only going to consider methods that provide a secure wireless solution using technologies in Windows Server 2003. The following network infrastructure elements must be in place in order to implement a secure WLAN. These are summarized in Table 5.21.

Table 5.21 WLAN Network Infrastructure Requirements

Infrastructure Requirement	Function
Active Directory	Stores user and computer accounts, validates credentials.
DHCP	Provides automatic IP configuration for wireless devices.
DNS	Provides name resolution.
PKI	Provides certificates for authentication and authorization. Used by EAP-TLS, PEAP-TLS. TLS can use smart cards or Registry-based certificates.
RADIUS/IAS	Provides centralized authentication, authorization, and accounting for remote connections, including WLAN.

Let's take a look at each of these in more detail.

Active Directory

You'll need to determine which users and groups should have wireless access. Then, via groups and group policy, you can enforce those selections. With Active Directory, these settings are enforced across the domain to ensure consistent application of access and security policies for all users, including wireless users.

Several group policy settings are related to wireless connections, including data installed on wireless clients regarding user and computer certificate auto-enrollment, Wireless Network Policy settings that specify the preferred networks, 802.1X settings, and WEP settings. These can be specified in group policy.

EXERCISE 5.04

CREATE A WIRELESS NETWORK POLICY

To create a wireless network policy via group policy, use the following steps.

1. Open the **Microsoft Management Console** by clicking **Start | Run** and then typing **mmc** in the Open: box. Click **OK** or press **Enter**.
2. Click **File | Add/Remove Snap-in**. In the Add/Remove Snap-in dialog, click **Add**.

3. In the Add Standalone Snap-in dialog, scroll down to select the **Group Policy Editor** snap-in. Click **Add**. When prompted to select the *Group Policy Object*:, click **Browse**.
4. Locate the *Default Domain Policy* in the **Browse for a Group Policy Object**, click to select it, and then click **OK**.
5. Click **Finish** to select the Default Domain Policy as the GPO.
6. Click **Close** on the Add Standalone Snap-in dialog to return to the Add/Remove Snap-in dialog. Click **OK** to return to the MMC.
7. In the MMC's left pane, click the + to expand the Default Domain Policy.
8. Click + to expand the **Computer Configuration** node.
9. Click + to expand the **Windows Settings** node.
10. Click + to expand the **Security Settings** node.
11. Click + to expand the Wireless Network (IEEE 802.11) Policies node. If there is nothing beneath the node, the + will not be displayed and the tree will not expand.
12. Right-click **Wireless Network (IEEE 802.11) Policies** or click **Action** on the menu and select **Create Wireless Network Policy**. This launches the Wireless Network Policy Wizard. Click **Next** to continue.
13. Type a name for the wireless policy in the *Name:* box. Type a description for the policy that will help you identify this policy and describe what it does. Click **Next**.
14. The next screen is the completion screen. Leave the check box labeled *Edit Properties* selected and click **Finish**.
15. The policy properties will be displayed, as shown in Figure 5.15.

Figure 5.15 Sample Domain Wireless Policy Properties Dialog

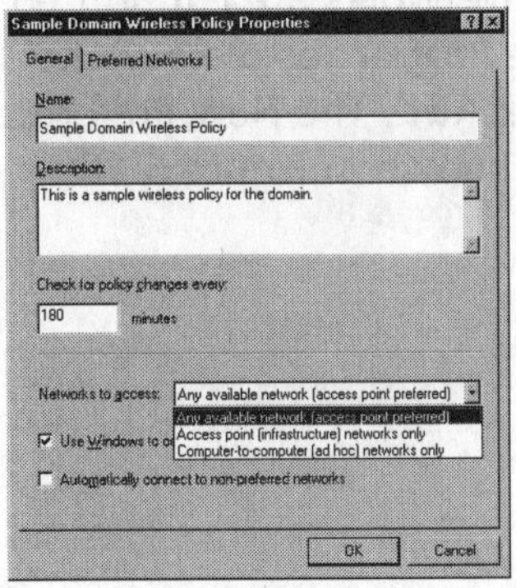

16. If you want to modify how often Active Directory polls for changes, you can change the value in the **Check for policy changes every:** setting, which defaults to 180 minutes.
17. Specify the type of wireless network the clients can access by selecting a network type in the **Networks to access** drop-down box as shown in Figure 5.15. For this exercise, select the default **Any available network (access point preferred)**. This setting allows the wireless user to connect to any available network but will attempt to connect to the Preferred Network first. Using this setting does allow users to participate in an ad hoc network and, depending on your corporate environment, this might pose a security problem. If it does, select the second choice, **Access point (infrastructure) networks only**. There might be reasons to only allow the computers to connect to only via an ad hoc network. If so, select the third option, **Computer-to-computer (ad hoc) networks only**.
18. To allow clients to configure their own wireless settings, leave the **Use Windows to configure wireless network settings for clients** check box selected. To prevent users from doing this, clear the check box.
19. To allow users to connect to networks that do not appear in the **Preferred Networks** tab, check this box. To ensure clients connect only to networks that appear on the **Preferred Networks** tab, clear the check box for **Automatically connect to non-preferred networks**. This option is cleared by default for security. When this is not selected, Windows XP users will be notified of available wireless networks but will not be automatically connected. If the user chooses to connect to the nonpreferred network, they must take an action to do so. This choice strikes a balance between security and usability.
20. Preferred Networks are configured on the **Preferred Networks** tab of the **Properties** dialog. Click to select this tab. To add a network, click **Add**. The New Preferred Settings Properties dialog opens, as shown in Figure 5.16.

Figure 5.16 Adding a New Preferred Network

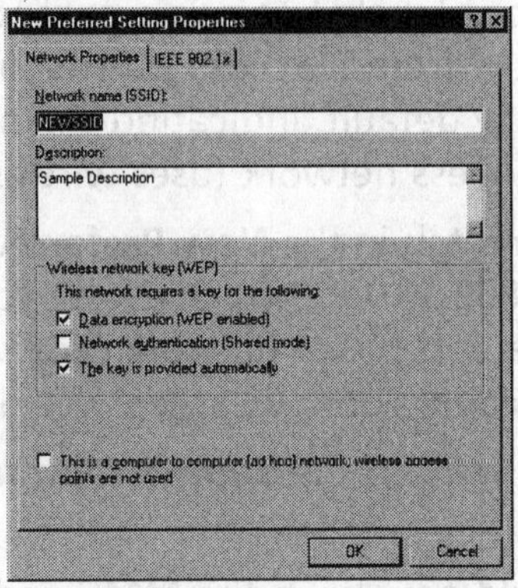

21. Enter a unique name for the new preferred network and enter a description in the description box that will help you to identify this network.
22. In the Wireless network key (WEP) section, there are three check boxes: **Data encryption (WEP enabled), Network authentication (Shared mode)**, and **The key is provided automatically**.
    - Selecting the **Data encryption (WEP enabled)** setting will require a network key to be used for encryption. Select this to ensure encryption is used to provide security on the wireless network. This is selected by default.
    - Selecting the **Network authentication (Shared mode)** setting will require that a network key be used for authentication. If this is not selected, the network will operate in open system authentication mode, which is more secure. This setting should be cleared. A shared key strategy uses a static WEP key, which can be easily cracked and requires a fair amount of administrative work to change or update. Due to the administrative burden, shared keys are rarely changed, which leads to security holes. This is not selected by default.
    - Selecting **The key is provided automatically** setting determines whether a network key is automatically provided for clients. This option should be selected so that the policy uses 802.1X to provide dynamic WEP session keys for encryption traffic. This is a more secure solution than using static WEP keys. This is selected by default.

23. The last option in the **New Preferred Setting Properties** dialog is a check box labeled **This is a computer-to-computer (ad hoc) network; wireless access points are not used**. This box is not selected by default, indicating the network is an infrastructure-based wireless network (uses wireless access points).
24. The second tab in the **New Preferred Setting Properties** dialog is the IEEE 802.1X tab, which allows you to set parameters for 802.1X, a port-based network access control. We'll discuss this later in this section. For now, accept the default options and click **OK**.
25. Click **OK** to close the **Sample Domain Wireless Policy Properties** dialog.
26. You should now be in the MMC and should have a Wireless Network (IEEE 802.11) Policies policy, as shown in Figure 5.17.

Figure 5.17 Wireless Policy Defined in Default Domain

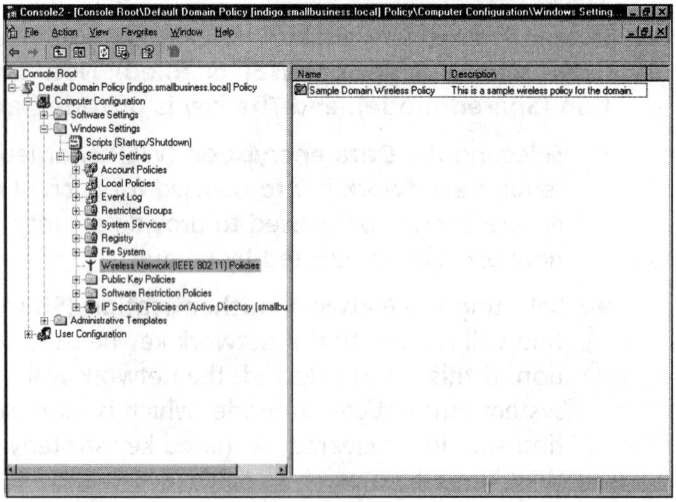

DHCP Configuration

DHCP scopes and leases are configured differently for wireless networks than they are for wired networks. Typically, scopes are defined by network segments, a collection of related IP addresses. To configure a secure wireless solution, create a separate scope for wireless clients. By using a separate scope, you can configure lease requirements differently for wired and wireless clients.

Wireless users connect and disconnect from the network far more often than do computers that are connected to a wired network. The default lease period for an IP address is eight days. Your organization might use a slightly different default, but typically, leases are not renewed more often than every few days to once a week. Wireless users do not release their IP address when they disconnect from the network. This means that if you use the default (or standard) lease period, the unused IP addresses held by the disconnected wireless users will be unavailable for long periods of time. For the scope that contains the wireless users, reduce the lease time significantly. The preferred setting will depend on a number of factors, most notably the typical behavior of wireless users on your network and the tolerance to the additional load on the DHCP server(s). For example, if most of your wireless users connect and disconnect throughout the day but remain at one location, you might use a lease period of 18 hours. However,, if you have a lot of wireless users connecting, disconnecting, and leaving the network for several weeks at a time, you might elect to create shorter lease periods of several hours. You might also choose to create more than one scope for wireless users if your users' wireless connection behaviors are dramatically different.

DNS Configuration

To configure DNS for secure wireless networking, it's recommended that you integrate DNS with Active Directory to support secure dynamic updates. This is a recommended configuration for wired and wireless networks. In DNS, you should identify the DNS zones in which wireless computers will register DNS address records. If you're not using Active Directory-Integrated zones, then you should ensure that DNS zones are configured for dynamic updates, since wireless computers' DNS settings might change more often than computers connected via the wired LAN. As discussed in the DHCP section, if you set your IP lease time to a lower value, your DNS records might change more often. Using secure dynamic updates provides the most secure configuration and reduces administrative overhead.

Public Key Infrastructure

PKI is discussed at length elsewhere in this book. As we discussed earlier, PKI relies on certificates to provide strong authentication credentials. You will need to set up a CA in Windows Server 2003 to create certificates for PKI, or obtain your certificates from a third-party provider. Once the certificates are created, they must be properly installed on the servers and clients that will use them.

Although it is possible to implement a wireless network without the use of PKI and RADIUS/IAS (discussed next), it is highly recommended that you use the Windows Server 2003 features to design and build a *secure* wireless network.

RADIUS/IAS

A discussion of how to design and implement RADIUS/IAS is outside the scope of this chapter. However, you should use RADIUS/IAS to manage remote connection authentication for better security and ease of administration. You should verify that the Internet Authentication Server (IAS), Microsoft's implementation of the RADIUS standard, can use the Extensible Authentication Protocol—Transport Layer Security (EAP-TLS). This requires the installation of a certificate on the IAS server. This topic is covered in additional detail in various other chapters in the book.

If you use Active Directory as the directory service and IAS as the RADIUS server, you can provide a single logon solution for users. This way, users can log on the same way whether they're connecting to the wired network or the wireless network. If you implement certificates, you can use smart cards for user logon authentication. The IAS server must also support Protected Extensible Authentication Protocol (PEAP)-Microsoft Handshake Challenge Authentication Protocol version 2 (MS-CHAPv2). This is used for password-based security environments.

EXAM 70-298 OBJECTIVE 3.2.2

Designing Authentication for Wireless Networks

The security mechanisms available for securing a wireless network are:

- 802.11 identity verification and authentication
- 802.11 Wired Equivalency Privacy (WEP) encryption
- 802.1X authentication
- IAS support for 802.1X authentication

We'll discuss each of these in detail so you can see how security differs among these security solutions.

802.11 Identity Verification and Authentication

This is the least secure method because it uses *open system authentication* and *shared key authentication*. Open system authentication is not true authentication because it performs only identity verification between the wireless client and the wireless access point. Shared key authentication is even less secure than open system authentication. Shared key authentication provides authentication by verifying that the wireless client has the shared key. Under the 802.11 standard, it is assumed the shared key was provided to the wireless client via a secured method such as over a secure wired network or via floppy disk.

For better security, do not use the shared key authentication method because it requires the exchange of a secret key that is shared by all wireless access points and wireless clients, making it more vulnerable to attack.

802.11 Wired Equivalency Privacy (WEP) Encryption

The 802.11 specification also defines an encryption algorithm, Wired Equivalency Privacy (WEP). It provides data confidentiality by encrypting data sent between the wireless access point and wireless clients. The encryption used by WEP is the RC4 stream cipher that uses either 40-bit or 104-bit encryption key. The integrity of the data frame itself is provided by an integrity check value (ICV) in the encrypted portion of the frame so it cannot be tampered with or viewed.

Recent studies have shown that there are flaws within the WEP encryption method, and there are now several software products available that can easily crack WEP encryption, so this method is less secure that it was even three or five years ago.

Although there are known issues with this method, it is widely used in wireless networks that are configured today. It might be appropriate for smaller organizations that do not have the infrastructure or IT capabilities to implement and manage a more complex solution requiring certificates and other encryption methods, as described next. The balance between security and ease of implementation and management might make sense for some organizations where the risk of intrusion is low or where the cost of recovering from intrusion is low. However, in organizations where security of network data is critical, this is no longer a viable solution.

802.1X Authentication

802.1X is the IEEE standard for authenticated access to Ethernet-based networks and wireless 802.11 networks. This standard supports centralized user identification, authentication, dynamic key management, and accounting, all features that can be provided by a RADIUS server. The 802.1X standard improves security because both the wireless client and the network authenticate to each other. A unique per-user/per-session key is used to encrypt data over the wireless connection and keys are dynamically generated, reducing administrative overhead and eliminating the ability to crack a key because the key is generally not used long enough for a hacker to capture enough data to then determine the key and crack it.

The 802.1X authentication method is supported in Windows XP (requires Service Pack 1) and Windows Server 2003. 802.1X authentication is only available for the access point (infrastructure) network type that requires the use of a network key (WEP). The most secure solution uses 802.1X, and connecting to a wireless network using anything less secure exposes your data to potential capture, modification, and malicious packet injection.

802.1X and Extensible Authentication Protocol

The 802.1X standard uses EAP for message exchange during the authentication process, to protect the contents of the authentication process. Remember that EAP is an extension of the PPP protocol that provides arbitrary authentication mechanisms to be used for the validation of a connection. Thus, with EAP, arbitrary authentication mechanisms such as certificates, smart cards, or passwords can be used to authenticate the wireless connection.

There are three authentication methods available using EAP, and you can use any of the following:

- **EAP-TLS** EAP-TLS uses certificates for server authentication. Client and computer authentication is provided by either certificates or smart cards.
- **PEAP with EAP-MS-CHAPv2** Protected EAP (PEAP) with EAP-MS-CHAPv2 uses certificates for server authentication. User authentication is via username and password (also called password-based authentication).
- **PEAP with EAP-TLS** PEAP with EAP-TLS uses certificates for server authentication and either certificates or smart cards for user and computer authentication. PEAP is supported for wireless user and computer authentication, but is not supported for VPN or remote access clients. PEAP with EAP-TLS provides an encrypted channel for EAP-TLS authentication traffic.

EXAM WARNING

If you deploy both *PEAP* and *EAP unprotected by PEAP*, don't use the same EAP authentication type for both. For example, if you deploy PEAP with EAP-TLS, don't use EAP-TLS without PEAP. Using authentication methods with the same type (in this case, EAP-TLS), one with PEAP and the other without PEAP, creates a security vulnerability. If you see exam scenarios or solutions that use the same authentication method with and without PEAP, you'll know that solution causes a security hole (which might be the right answer, depending on how the question is presented).

To use EAP-TLS, you'll need to verify that the certificate infrastructure is in place. Windows Server 2003 supports Certificate Servers, so you can issue certificates to the users, computers, and IAS servers involved in wireless networking. EAP-TL is not supported if the IAS or remote access server is not a member of the domain.

To use PEAP-MS-CHAPv2, you'll need to verify your IAS servers have computer certificates installed. On the other end, you'll need to verify that all wireless computers have the root CA certificates of the issuer of the computer certificates that the IAS servers have installed. You can use third-party CAs to issue certificates as long as the certificates meet the requirements for TLS authentication.

IAS Support for 802.1X Authentication

As stated earlier in this chapter, IAS is the Microsoft implementation of RADIUS, another IEEE standard. Thus, a Microsoft IAS server is a RADIUS server. As such, it can be used to enhance security and deployment of wireless networks. Although configuration of an IAS is outside the scope of this chapter, you should be familiar with configuring IAS on Windows Server 2003 computers.

When you use RADIUS/IAS, wireless access points are configured as RADIUS clients and use the RADIUS protocol to send connection requests to the RADIUS/IAS server. The RADIUS server uses a user account database to verify the user against the database (authentication) and then verifies that user has appropriate permissions to connect to the LAN via the wireless access point (access). Once the RADIUS server compares the request with the user database information, it either issues permission for the user to connect or rejects the request. This information is passed back to the wireless access point using the RADIUS protocol.

This configuration, using IAS with wireless access points, is the most secure solution for wireless networking in the Windows Server 2003 environment.

802.1X Group Policy Settings

Now that we've discussed 802.1X and earlier stepped through creating a wireless network policy, let's look the range of settings available on the IEEE 802.1X tab.

Briefly, this is accessed with the Group Policy Object Editor snap-in in the MMC.

1. Right-click the **Wireless Access Policy** (or whatever name you gave it).
2. Click the **Preferred Networks** tab, click the **Network Name** shown in the Networks: box, then click **Edit**.
3. In the **Edit [Network Name] properties**, click the **IEEE 802.1X** tab.
4. Figure 5.18 shows this dialog with the associated options. We'll walk through each of them now.

Figure 5.18 IEEE 802.1X Properties in the Selected Preferred Network

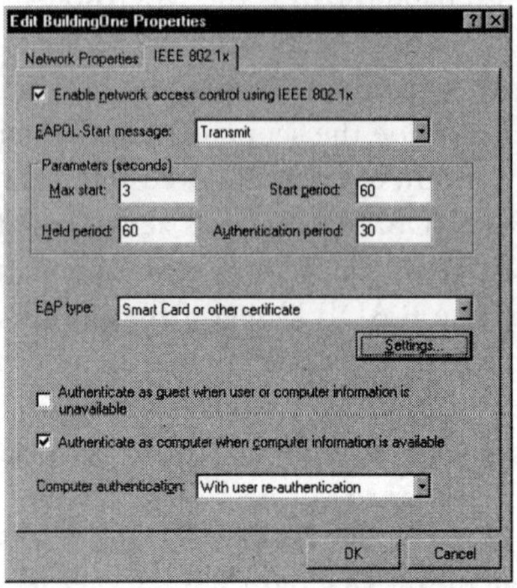

- **Enable network access control using IEEE 802.1X** This check box must be selected to use 802.1X capabilities on this wireless network.
- **EAPOL-Start message** Your three options are: Do not transmit, Transmit, and Transmit per IEEE 802.1x. This message tells the client to begin the authentication process. It specifies whether to transmit EAP over LAN (EAPOL)-Start message packets and if so, how to transmit them. The default setting of **Transmit** is typically acceptable.
  - **Parameters (seconds)** These parameters are used to define the EAPOL-Start message packet. The default settings are usually the best settings unless you have clear reasons for changing them.
  - **Max Start (default 3)** Determines the number of successive EAP over LAN-Start messages the client will transmit when not receiving a response.
  - **Held Period (default 60)** Determines the amount of time the client will wait before re-attempting a failed 802.1X authentication.
  - **Start Period (default 60)** Determines the amount of time between EAPOL-Start messages when resending.
  - **Authentication Period (default 30)** Determines the amount of time between 802.1X request messages resent upon *not* receiving a response.

- EAP type
  - **Smart card or other certificate** Smart card or other certificate is the default option for EAP type. This specifies EAP-TLS as the EAP type.
  - **Protected EAP (PEAP)** You can select this option as your EAP type to use Protected EAP.
- **EAP type Settings** Both EAP types have various options that can be configured via the Settings button. Figure 5.19 shows the Smart Card or other Certificate Properties, and Figure 5.20 shows the PEAP settings available.

Figure 5.19 Smart Card or Other Certificate Properties Options

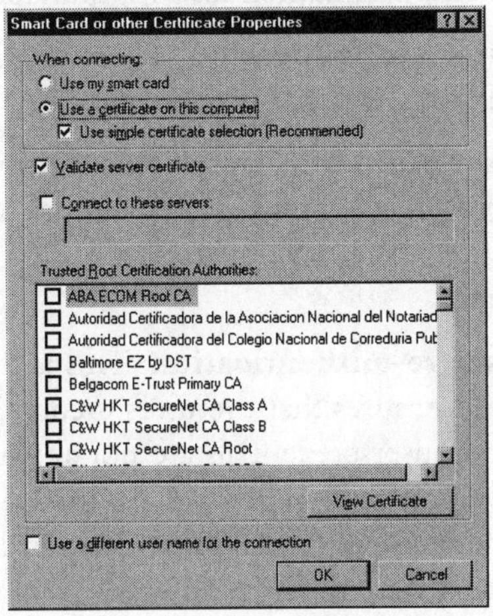

Figure 5.20 Protected EAP Properties Options

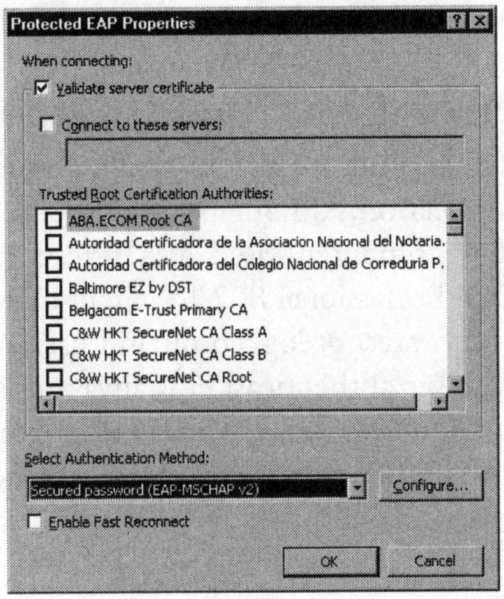

- **Authenticate as guest when user or computer information is unavailable** This check box is cleared by default. If you want to provide public wireless access for visitors to connect to the Internet, for example, you can check this box to allow guest authentication. Unless the wireless network is for public use and is not connected to the internal corporate network, do not use this setting.
- **Authenticate as computer when computer information is available** This setting uses computer-based authentication, discussed in more detail in the next section. It is recommended that you check this box, which is checked by default, for the best security and most convenient network configuration. If this box is not checked, the next option, computer authentication, is disabled.
- **Computer authentication** There are three options to choose from in this final IEEE 802.1X parameter.
- **With user authentication** If this setting is selected, when users are not logged on, the computer credentials are used. However, when a user logs on, the authentication established by the computer credentials is maintained.
- **With user re-authentication** This is the default (and recommended) option and ensures that the users credentials are used whenever possible. When user credentials are not available, computer credentials will be used. Computer credentials are used until a user logs on. Then, the user credentials are used. When the user logs off, the computer credentials are again used.
- **Computer only** This options specifies that user credentials will not be used and that only computer credentials will be used. User credentials are never checked with this option selected.

Selecting User or Computer-Based Authentication

For the most secure wireless network, you should consider using both user- and computer-based authentication. Although user authentication is a natural choice, there are instances when computer-based authentication also makes sense. The default choices in Windows XP Professional 802.1X client allow for computer-based authentication when users are not logged on and user authentication when users are logged on. This ensures user authentication is always used when a user is connected but also allows various Windows features to work properly when the user is logged off. Table 5.22 delineates the computer-based authentication scenarios.

Table 5.22 Computer-Based Authentication Scenarios

Windows Feature	Scenario
Active Directory Computer Group |Policy	Recall that computer group policy is applied during computer startup and at regularly scheduled intervals. Computer-based authentication provides this capability because no user is logged on during startup.
Remote Desktop Connection	A computer that is on but not logged in to by a user can be accessed via the RDC if computer-based authentication is used.
Systems management agents	Microsoft System Management Server and other system agents can access the computer without user intervention with computer-based authentication.
Network logon scripts	Network logon scripts are run during user logon. Computer-based authentication is required because the user is not yet logged on and has not yet received user authentication.
Shared folders	If the computer is on but not logged in to, shared files and folders on the wireless device are still available if computer-based authentication is used.

Head of the Class...

Understanding WEP Flaws, Threats, and Countermeasures

There are ever-evolving threats to WEP encryption. As mentioned earlier, there are programs available today that will crack WEP encryption. However, WEP can still be used effectively, and the emerging WPA standard will address some of the security flaws in WEP. It is anticipated that throughout 2004, WPA-based hardware and software solutions will become more widely available. However, let's take a look at the WEP encryption vulnerability.

Even with 802.1X dynamic key management *and* WEP, a determined hacker could still leverage flaws within the WEP encryption scheme. This flaw is well documented and if you want to understand the mathematical basis for this flaw, you can read about it in great detail in a draft document located at www.isaac.cs.berkeley.edu/isaac/wep-draft.pdf entitled "Intercepting Mobile Communications: The Insecurity of 802.11 DRAFT." Suffice it to say that the flaw can be leveraged but it requires two things: a certain amount of network

Continued

traffic to be captured by the attacker, and a sufficient amount of time (or computer power) for the hacker to perform the crack.

The primary strategy, then, for keeping WEP secure, is to limit the amount of time a key is used. This prevents adequate network data from being captured before the key is changed and prevents the hacker from having time to crack the code before a new key is used. This is accomplished via the key refresh functionality present in wireless access points or by setting IAS RADIUS options to enforce automatic client-re-authentication including WEP key refresh. By forcing the re-authentication every 10 minutes, the hacker does not have time to both capture sufficient data and crack the key. Let's look at the math.

We know the theoretical maximum throughput rate for 802.11a is 54 Mbps. We also know that the actual throughput is about 60 percent of that, or 32Mbps. This is the equivalent of 4MB/second (a byte is eight bits, so 32 megabits divided by 8 bits is 4 megabytes). WEP only encrypts data packets, and data packets average 80 bytes. 4MB divided by 80 bytes equals 50,000 packets per second. Based on attacks known at this time, a maximum of 10 minutes (or the rough equivalent of 30,000,000 packets) is the recommended time for using a single WEP key.

It's important to understand several things, though. First, computing power continues to increase as do the sophistication of cracking programs. Second, there is additional network overhead used every time a key is re-established. When users frequently have to be re-authenticated, it can cause increased loads on IAS servers, WAPs, and client computers, which could have a negative impact on usability.

Look closely at your business model, your corporate computing needs, and your infrastructure to determine the threat level of wireless attack. Moreover, although it's hard to do at times, you'll have to assess the cost of prevention versus the cost of remediation. It's difficult to assess the cost of stolen data, but it must be assessed in order to understand the cost/benefit of implementing the security solutions for both your wired and wireless network.

Designing and Testing Wireless Access Infrastructure

The third major step is to design and test the wireless access infrastructure. Now that you've either created or prepared your network infrastructure for wireless network access and defined authentication and access, you must put it all together.

The recommended configuration is to have:

- Two IAS servers for fault tolerance of the RADIUS-based authentication.
- Active Directory integration for better security and a single logon for wireless users.

- Certificate infrastructure for strong authentication to protect wireless access.
- Wireless access policies to protect the network by controlling who can access the wireless network and in what manner.
- Sufficient WAPs so enabled wireless clients can obtain network connectivity throughout the approved wireless area.
- WAPs configured as RADIUS clients in order to manage secure connections and data with the IAS/RADIUS server.

The functional diagram shown in Figure 5.21 delineates these components and the process of secure wireless client authentication and authorization. How this is implemented in your organization will differ based on different variables, including building layout and configuration, desired/required wireless network availability, and more. However, if you configure your wireless network access to use these components, you will have the most secure wireless network configuration currently available.

Figure 5.21 Functional Diagram of Wireless Access Infrastructure

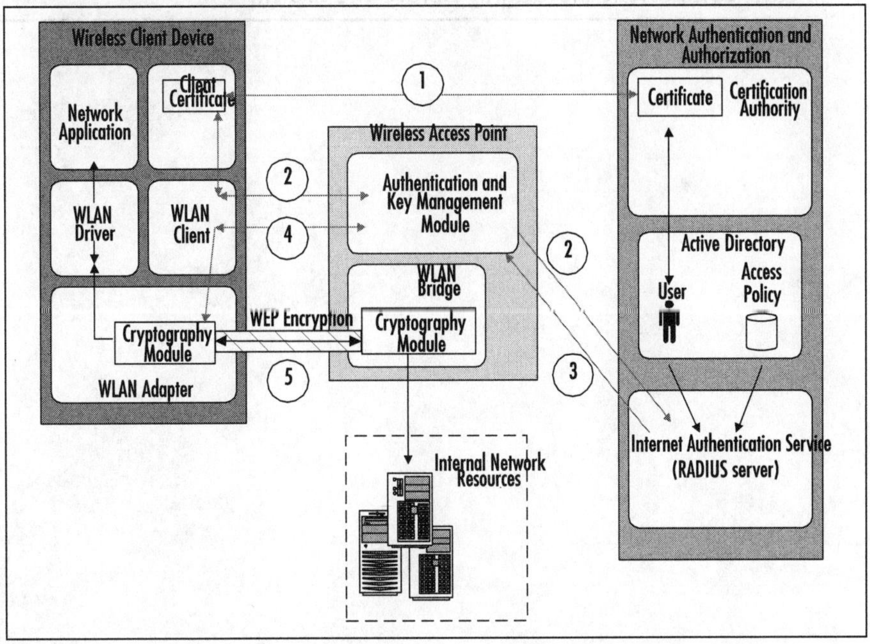

1. The wireless client establishes credentials with the CA before wireless access is attempted. Often, this is done on a secure wired network or via removable media (floppy disk, CD-ROM, etc.).
2. The wireless client initiates contact with the wireless network by passing its credentials to the wireless access point. The WAP passes these credentials on

to the IAS (RADIUS server) for verification. The IAS is integrated with Active Directory and can verify the legitimacy of the credentials as well as the access policies for the user.

3. Based on the IAS results, access to the network is either granted or denied. If access is granted, encryption keys are generated and exchanged over a secure channel with the WAP.
4. The encryption keys are exchanged securely between the WAP and the wireless client.
5. The wireless client and WAP create a secure connection and the wireless client begins exchanging data with the internal network.

TEST DAY TIP

You are practically guaranteed to get questions on designing a secure wireless network, so be sure to review the functional diagram and understand each component thoroughly before the exam.

Summary of Exam Objectives

Window Server 2003 contains a number of significant improvements to network security, which has become a greater concern over the past several years as hackers become more sophisticated. The threats to network infrastructure represent the largest threats to network security because compromising vital network infrastructure services can seriously disrupt corporate networks, destroy data, and breach confidentiality. As a result, Windows Server 2003 provides numerous ways to protect the infrastructure.

Network infrastructure consists of physical assets such as cabling, hubs, routers, and servers, and the software aspects such as DHCP, DNS, and WINS—services that define, create, and manage the elements that provide network functionality. Each of the critical services can be configured to be more secure, reducing or eliminating the threat of attack.

Ethernet-based networks, the majority of networks implemented today, use the Internet Protocol (IP) as the basis of network activity. The implementation of the IP Security protocol by Windows 2000 and Windows Server 2003 provides significant opportunities to secure network infrastructure. IPSec consists of several elements, including the IPSec Policy Agent that looks for IPSec policy and applies it to the computer, the IPSec driver that implements the filter lists and filter actions specified by the IPSec policies, and the IPSec protocols that provide data integrity, anti-replay, and optional confidentiality services.

The IPSec protocols are the Authentication Header (AH) and Encapsulated Security Payload (ESP). AH provides data integrity by signing the IP packet header, which prevents the packet from being tampered with in any way. However, it does not provide data encryption, which would provide confidentiality. Encryption is implemented via ESP, which encapsulates the data and encrypts it. AH and ESP are typically not used together. AH is used where packet integrity is important but confidentiality is not. ESP is used where confidentiality is important because it also provides some level of packet integrity although it does not protect the original IP header.

IPSec policies can be implemented via group policy and can be defined via the IP Security Policy Management snap-in or via the Group Policy Object Editor snap-in in Windows Server 2003. Three predefined example IPSec policies are provided, including Server (Request Security), Secure Server (Require Security), and Client (Respond Only). These can be used as the basis for custom IPSec policies but should not be implemented "as is."

Other methods of securing the network infrastructure include using Secure Sockets Layer (SSL), which is widely implemented for secure Web sites. S/MIME can be used to secure end-to-end e-mail security, and Server Message Block signing provides secure communication between computers.

Wireless networking has become increasingly popular in the corporate environment. Standards are based on the 802.11 IEEE specification. Early standards did not provide significant security because, at the time, security was not as great a concern, wireless network technology was just emerging and there were government regulations regarding the use of encryption technologies. The standards have evolved from 802.11 to today's most secure implementation to date, 802.1X, which is the IEEE standard the defines authenticated access to wireless networks.

Authenticated access can be accomplished in a number of ways, depending on the existing or desired network infrastructure. Wired Equivalent Privacy (WEP) defines an encryption algorithm for data security, but recent flaws discovered in the WEP algorithm make it vulnerable to cracking. Eliminating the use of static keys and shared keys can help reduce the risk, as can reducing the required time interval between re-authentication, which would generate new keys and reduce or eliminate the change of someone being able to crack the encryption.

Within the Windows Server 2003 framework, implementing wireless networking using Active Directory, DNS integrated with Active Directory, and RADIUS servers (implemented as IAS) provides the most secure configuration. When wireless access points (WAPs) are configured as RADIUS clients, user or computer credentials are passed from the client to the WAP and the WAP requests authentication from IAS. IAS checks the database for credential authentication and checks policies to see if the computer or user is authorized for wireless access. IAS then notifies the WAP that credentials were accepted or rejected. If accepted, the computer or user is then granted access via the wireless access point. A combination of strong authentication and data encryption provides the strongest security currently available for wireless networks in Windows Server 2003.

Exam Objectives Fast Track

Securing the Network Infrastructure

- ☑ A secure network begins with a thorough assessment of current and future network infrastructure considerations.
- ☑ Understanding current and emerging threats and risk mitigation is essential for managing a secure network.
- ☑ The following infrastructure components should each be assessed and secured:
  - Dynamic Host Configuration Protocol (DHCP)
  - Domain Name Service (DNS)
  - Windows Internet Naming Service (WINS)
  - Internet Information Server (IIS)

- Routing and Remote Access (RRAS)
- Application and file sharing

☑ Internet Protocol Security (IPSec) provides for security via transport and tunnel mode via the use of two protocols: Authentication Header (AH), which verifies the integrity of the packet, and Encapsulated Security Payload (ESP), which encrypts the data and signs the packet for both privacy and integrity.

☑ Windows Server 2003 provides three default IPSec policies that can be used as examples on how to create, modify, and implement IPSec policies.

☑ IPSec in Windows Server 2003 now supports ESP-protected IPSec traffic passing through a NAT-T.

☑ DNS is a highly desirable target for hackers. You can segment your DNS namespace and use the top-level namespace for public/Internet connection and a separate, internal namespace for the corporate network. Separating the internal and external DNS servers and namespaces by firewalls and perimeter networks protects the internal namespace.

☑ Integrating DNS with Active Directory gives you the capability to perform secure dynamic DNS updates, which reduces the risk to DNS.

☑ The Secure Sockets Layer/Transport Layer Security (SSL/TLS) protocol is typically used to secure Hypertext Transport Protocol (HTTP/HTTPS), but can also be used by other applications that require security for application layer protocols such as FTP, LDAP, or SMTP.

☑ Secure/Multipurpose Internet Mail Extensions (S/MIME) is used to secure e-mail traffic from one end to the other. SSL is often used to secure server-to-server traffic, but S/MIME is best suited for end-to-end e-mail security.

☑ SMB signing can be implemented to prevent man-in-the-middle attacks because the data in transit is protected. SMB supports the digital signing of SMB packets to prevent modification while SMB packets are in transit.

Designing Security for Wireless Networks

☑ Threats to wireless networks are very similar to threats to wired networks. Rogue WLANs, the inability to know who's connected, accidental access, and free-loading are problems associated only with WLANs.

☑ A secure design for a wireless network includes designing WLAN network infrastructure, designing wireless authentication, and designing wireless access infrastructure

- ☑ You can create Wireless Network (IEEE 802.1X) Policies via the Group Policy Editor to control wireless networks and access.
- ☑ The use of PKI and RADIUS/IAS integrated with Active Directory provides the most secure wireless network solution.
- ☑ 802.1X is the IEEE standard for authenticated access to Ethernet-based networks and wireless 802.11 networks. This standard supports centralized user identification, authentication, dynamic key management, and accounting, all features that can be provided by a RADIUS server.
- ☑ The use of strong authentication methods including EAP-TLS, PEAP with EAP-TLS, and PEAP with EAP-MS-CHAPv2 ensures authentication and encryption are used to create a secure wireless network connection.
- ☑ The fairly recent discovery of flaws in the WEP encryption technology means that additional authentication and encryption methods should be employed whenever practical.
- ☑ Understanding the authentication and encryption functional process helps to both design and implement the most secure wireless network possible in a Windows Server 2003 environment.

Exam Objectives Frequently Asked Questions

The following Frequently Asked Questions, answered by the authors of this book, are designed to both measure your understanding of the Exam Objectives presented in this chapter, and to assist you with real-life implementation of these concepts. You will also gain access to thousands of other FAQs at ITFAQnet.com.

Q: Doesn't network infrastructure refer to a lot more than just DHCP and DNS?

A: Yes, typically it does. However, when we're dealing with a wired network, the physical security of the infrastructure is typically discussed separately from the network-based (electronic) security elements. Ensuring network cabling isn't jacked into or that unauthorized computers are not on the network are certainly parts of securing the infrastructure, but these threats are typically easier to spot and easier to manage.

Q: How do IPSec policies and group policies relate to one another?

A: Group policies are policies that include many different elements, including user configuration, software configuration settings, event logs, startup or logon scripts, and more. IP Security policies can be implemented as part of a Group Policy Object (GPO) and applied to domains, OUs, or groups.

Q: Why don't you typically use the AH and ESP IPSec protocols together?

A: The AH protocol signs the packet to ensure the integrity of the data and header. It prevents someone from modifying the packet in any way, but doesn't do anything to prevent someone from reading the data in the packet. ESP, however, encrypts the data, including the original IP header. Typically, if you use both AH and ESP, the CPU cycles it takes to perform both actions is relatively large and you'll bog down the computers at both end of the process (sending/receiving). Typically, if data privacy is important, ESP can be used to protect the packet. If privacy is not a concern, AH is used.

Q: How can someone "accidentally" connect to a wireless network?

A: If someone has a wireless device, such as a Windows XP-based laptop, that is configured to look for a network connection automatically, when it finds a wireless access point, it might connect to the network. This can be a problem in companies that have frequent vendor, partner, or sales visitors who rely on their laptops while away from their own companies. Inadvertent connection to your corporate wireless network creates a significant security breach, even if the user doesn't intend it. It's also vulnerable to viruses, worms, and other harmful code that can spread through the unknown user's computer to the corporate network.

Q: When is ad hoc wireless networking used?

A: It occurs without the use of wireless access points when computers configured for wireless networking negotiate a communication strategy and communicate among themselves in a peer-to-peer fashion. This might be an appropriate configuration for users in a meeting who do not need access to the corporate network but do need access to shared files, for instance. It might also be useful in locations that are not configured with wireless access points or where wireless access points fail (out of range).

Q: If WEP is so flawed, why is it used at all?

A: WEP can still be used in wireless networks where other security measures do not exist. It might surprise you to know that many wireless network installations are not configured with any security at all. Therefore, in that case, using WEP would be better than nothing. Moreover, if configured properly, WEP can still be secured if keys are not static and if keys are re-negotiated frequently. This prevents a hacker from having sufficient time and data to crack the encryption with today's tools and technologies. That will certainly change in the future, but additional security methods are emerging in both hardware and software to address the continuing security threats.

Q: Is using PKI and RADIUS servers really a viable option for most companies?

A: The answer depends on two things. First, how much of a risk is there to the corporate network, how well can it be segmented and protected, and how much security is enough security for your firm? There is always a cost/benefit analysis that must be assessed to determine the cost of implementing security solutions like PKI and RADIUS/IAS versus the benefits provided by the more secure solution. There is no hard-and-fast answer, but as technologies continue to emerge and improve and the cost of wiring buildings and stations increases, the balance will likely tip in favor of implementing highly secure wireless networks.

Self Test

A Quick Answer Key follows the Self Test questions. For complete questions, answers, and explanations to the Self Test questions in this chapter as well as the other chapters in this book, see the Self Test Appendix.

Securing the Network Infrastructure

1. A recent task force in your company defined several threats to the network that need to be addressed. As the head of that task force, you have been assigned the job of mitigating these threats with the least restriction to users and network availability. The top threat was identified as password attacks. Which solution would best address this threat while still meeting the criteria set forth?

   A. Implement strong password policies on all OUs and monitor network traffic to determine if data modification is taking place.

   B. Implement strong password policies at the domain level, and apply account lockout policies.

   C. Implement IPSec for all communication between clients and domain infrastructure servers.

   D. Limit user logon hours to normal working hours and implement account lockout policies. Monitor all logons attempted outside of specified logon hours.

2. Your firm has 12 Windows XP Professional SP1 computers used in a manufacturing environment that are located on the shop floor where about 200 employees work. These computers are used by a variety of staff, and in any given work day, there might be 20 or 30 people that log on to the various computers. Recently, you've noticed some odd IP traffic on the computers early in the morning, just before the start of the first shift. You had previously applied IPSec policy to the computers in this group via an OU that contains these 12 computers. What else could you do that might protect these computers and the network based on this information?

   A. Apply persistent policies to the 12 computers in the OU so that the computer is protected during startup and shutdown.

   B. Use smart cards for user authentication to prevent unauthorized access before and after working hours.

   C. Modify the IPSec policy to filter all IP traffic prior to start of shift.

   D. Check to see if the odd IP traffic is related to power fluctuations that might occur as other equipment on the shop floor is powered up at start of shift.

3. You're checking the configuration of several computers that are connected directly to the Internet. One of the computers recently suffered a denial-of-service (DoS) attack, but the other three were fine. You notice that the computers that were not attacked had IPSec policies applied as shown in Figure 5.22. These settings are not the same as on the computer that was attacked. Which setting(s) are the most likely reason why these computers were not attacked or not successfully attacked?

Figure 5.22 IPSec Settings

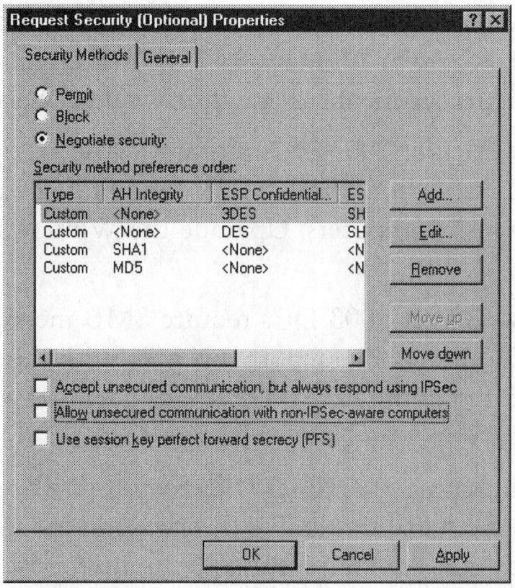

A. The computers that were not successfully attacked did not have the check box selected for **Accept unsecured communication, but always respond using IPSec**.

B. The computer that was successfully attacked did not have the check box **Allow unsecured communication with non-IPSec-aware computers** selected..

C. The computers that were not attacked did not have the **Use session key perfect forward secrecy (PFS)** selected.

D. The computers that were not successfully attacked had the check box **Allow unsecured communication with non-IPSec-aware computers** selected.

4. Your network consists of three servers running Windows NT 4.0 SP6a, two servers running Windows 2000, and one server configured as a domain controller (DC) running Windows 2000. The client computers are a mix of Windows 95, Windows 98, and Windows XP. You decide to upgrade the network to improve security. You retire two of the computers running Windows NT 4.0 and replace them with two computers on which you will configure Windows Server 2003. You install Windows Server 2003 on the first computer and configure it as a DC and DHCP server. You install Windows Server 2003 on the second computer and configure it as a DC and DNS server. You configure secondary DHCP and DNS server services on one of the Windows 2000 computers, which is configured as a member server. After you complete this, you find that none of the Windows 95 computers can connect to the domain and only some of the Windows 98 computers can. What is the most likely cause of this problem?

   A. The Windows 95 and Windows 98 computers are still trying to be authenticated by the two Windows NT 4.0 servers that were replaced. Reconfigure all clients to use the Windows Server 2003 computers instead.

   B. Windows Server 2003 DCs require SMB message block signing and cannot communicate with Windows 95 computers in a domain. Upgrade the Windows 95 computers. Upgrade the Windows 98 computers to Windows XP.

   C. Windows Server 2003 DCs require SMB message block signing. Windows 95 and Windows 98 support this only with the Active Directory client installed. Install the Active Directory client service or upgrade the operating system to Windows XP.

   D. The Windows Server 2003 DCs require SMB message block signing and as a result, the remaining NT 4.0 server and the Windows Server 2003 computers are not communicating. Upgrade the Windows NT 4.0 server to Windows 2000 or Windows Server 2003.

Designing Security for Wireless Networks

5. You've just been hired as the IT manager for a small company. The company's IT infrastructure consists of one domain, three segments, a handful of servers, and about 95 client computers, most of which are running Windows XP. Internet access is provided through a firewall and proxy server via an Internet service provider (ISP). The corporate Web site is hosted externally by a third party, and employees connect to the Web site just as they would to any other Web site. The company has recently expanded and there are two groups of employees who regularly share files among themselves using Windows XP-based laptops. You've been tasked with finding a solution that will provide these two groups with connectivity in two different areas to enable file sharing. As always, the company is on a tight budget and wants this done quickly on a small budget. What's the best solution?

   A. Configure the two groups that require file sharing to use ad hoc wireless networking.

   B. Configure the two groups to use shorter DHCP IP lease times by applying wireless policies to them.

   C. Install wireless access points. Determine if PKI and RADIUS are implemented, and if not, implement them to provide security.

   D. Issue smart cards to the members of the two groups to provide strong authentication for the wireless users and provide wireless access via WAPs throughout the building.

6. Your firm has three wireless network defined via Wireless Network (IEEE 802.1X) Policies. One network is configured to use *Network authentication (Shared mode)*. The two other wireless networks use *Data encryption (WEP enabled)*. Based on this information, what steps can you take immediately to improve security across the board?

   A. Enable *Network authentication (Shared mode)* on the two wireless networks currently using *Data encryption (WEP enabled)*.

   B. Edit the properties for the one network configured to use *Network authentication (Shared mode)* and set it to use WEP or, preferably, 802.1X. In addition, on the RADIUS server or wireless access points, force re-authentication every 10 minutes by changing the WEP key refresh option.

   C. Edit the WEP properties on the wireless network and configure the *Data encryption (WEP enabled)* setting to use both PEAP with EAP-TLS and EAP-TLS.

D. Delete the network that is using *Network authentication (Shared mode)* and create a new network using the *Data encryption (WEP enabled)* setting.

7. You are implementing a wireless network in portions of your large warehouse facility. There are a number of computers used by different users throughout the day for pulling or verifying orders. Users log on with smart cards to verify their identity so that orders are tied to user logon for verifying inventory, order accuracy, and other business metrics. You implement PEAP with EAP-TLS for strong authentication since users have smart cards. Throughout the day, some of these computers are used and some are idle and the pattern of usage varies depending on the day, time, and volume of business. You typically manage these computers remotely so that you can do things like update virus definition files or install software upgrades. You configure the settings as shown in Figure 5.23. Based on this information, what is the most likely result?

Figure 5.23 Network Configuration

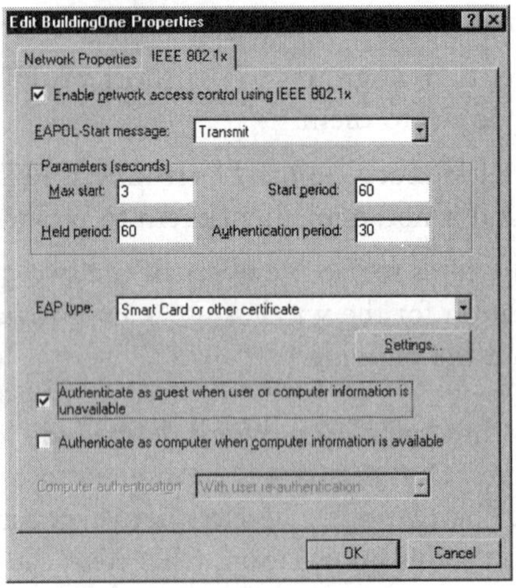

A. You will improve security by requiring authentication as guest when user or computer information is unavailable.

B. You will have to provide smart cards for any Guest users who need to access the network.

C. You will not be able to authenticate users via smart cards.

D. You will be unable to remotely manage the computers on the wireless network.

8. Your network infrastructure already makes use of PKI technologies to create a secure network environment. The infrastructure included a remote access server, and most servers are running Windows Server 2003, although there are still a handful running Windows 2000. All clients have been upgraded over the past 18 months to Windows XP. You recently added IAS to your infrastructure and configured the remote access server as a RADIUS client. You have implemented several wireless networks in your building. You've installed numerous wireless access points throughout the building and coverage is quite good throughout the building where wireless users roam. There is an area of the building that is not configured with WAPs because the area is a secure area that requires strong authentication just to physically access the area. You have not implemented wireless security in this area but are concerned about rogue WLANs being installed by employees in this highly secure area. What is the best solution to this situation?

   A. Implement a WLAN in the highly secure area using 802.1X using PEAP with EAP-TLS. Establish the WAPs as RADIUS clients and use the RADIUS server to authenticate computers and users.

   B. Regularly inspect user computers in the highly secure area for signs of wireless components. Set up a filter to prevent any IP packets with the IP address of the highly secure network segment to get into the rest of the network.

   C. Implement a WLAN with limited range in the highly secure area. This way, users outside of the highly secure area cannot freeload.

   D. Implement a WLAN in the highly secure area that is not connected to the wired network. Require strong authentication and data encryption using PEAP-EAP-MS-CHAPv2 since some of the servers are running Windows 2000.

Self Test Quick Answer Key

For complete questions, answers, and explanations to the Self Test questions in this chapter as well as the other chapters in this book, see the Self Test Appendix.

1. **B**
2. **A**
3. **A**
4. **C**
5. **A**
6. **B**
7. **D**
8. **A**

Chapter 6

MCSE 70-298

Securing Internet Information Services

Exam Objectives in this Chapter:

- 3.3 Designing user authentication for Internet Information Services (IIS).
- 3.3.1 Design user authentication for a Web site by using certificates.
- 3.3.2 Design user authentication for a Web site by using IIS authentication.
- 3.3.3 Design user authentication for a Web site by using RADIUS for IIS authentication.
- 3.4 Designing security for Internet Information Services (IIS).
- 3.4.1 Design security for Web sites that have different technical requirements by enabling only the minimum required services.
- 3.4.2 Design a monitoring strategy for IIS.
- 3.4.3 Design an IIS baseline based on business requirements.
- 3.4.4 Design a content management strategy for updating an IIS server.

Introduction

Internet Information Services (IIS) is one of the most popular solutions for private and commercial Web servers on the Internet today. Because of its popularity, and the overall prevalence of Windows-based machines on the Internet, IIS has become a favorite target of hackers and virus/worm authors. One of the major goals of Microsoft's Secure Computing Initiative was to improve the security of Microsoft software in three areas: by default, by design, and by deployment. IIS 6.0, the version of the Web server software that's bundled with Windows Server 2003, is one of the first major services to reflect this initiative. As opposed to previous releases of the server operating system where IIS was turned on by default, an administrator now needs to install and enable IIS on a Windows Server 2003 machine, and manually enable support for technologies such as Active Server Pages (ASP) and the Network News Transfer Protocol (NNTP). In this chapter, we'll look at the steps needed to create a secure IIS deployment for your enterprise network.

The first major topic that we'll discuss is user authentication within IIS. Gone are the days when the majority of Web servers provided nothing but static content where users were content to browse information anonymously and go merrily on their way. Improvements in e-commerce, customized Web content and the like have increased expectations for an interactive Web experience, and this kind of expectation requires some level of user authentication to protect users' privacy and personal information. We'll look at the various types of authentication offered by IIS 6.0, including certificate authentication, integrated Windows logons, and RADIUS authentication using Internet Authentication Server, or IAS.

Once you've decided on a user authentication scheme, you can focus on other aspects of securing IIS. We'll finish this chapter with a discussion of some common attack vulnerabilities for Web servers in general and IIS servers in particular, and then move on to finding ways to address these concerns for a single server or a large server farm. Some of these steps include ways to harden the IIS installation itself, as well as designing an effective monitoring scheme so that any potential security incidents will be noticed and responded to in a timely fashion. We'll close with some thoughts on securing the process of actually updating Web content itself to secure against the public embarrassment of Web defacement or inadvertent information disclosure. Windows Server 2003 offers an array of options for securing its Web server software; your job as a security administrator and MCSE candidate is to use these options to design a secure IIS deployment for your enterprise network.

EXAM 70-298 OBJECTIVE 3.3

Designing User Authentication for IIS

Microsoft has done a great job of redesigning IIS to be more reliable and robust. Perhaps the most significant modification is the emphasis on the *worker process model*. This concept was initially embedded into IIS 4.0 as "Running an application in a separate memory space." Let's investigate these modifications in detail.

IIS separates all user code from its WWW service. The user application (different Web sites) functions as a separate Internet Server Application Programming Interface (ISAPI) application. The separate ISAPI workspace is referred as a *worker process*. IIS 5.0 used to run each Web site within its own *inetinfo.exe* memory space (inetinfo.exe is the application that implements IIS 5.0). IIS 6.0 worker process Web sites do not run within the inetinfo.exe (WWW services) memory space. Since the worker process runs in an isolated environment from the WWW service, an error in the Web site application code (or malicious attack) will not cause the Web server to shut down. The worker process can also be configured to run on a specified CPU. The worker process model can store application-specific data in its own memory space. IIS 5.0 stored all the application data within the inetinfo.exe memory space. Therefore, we can assign a Web site to run on specific CPUs. This mechanism will enable us to dedicate more resources to popular Web sites. (These resources for a Web site can be bundled as an *application pool*.) The IIS Web request process is illustrated in Figure 6.1.

Figure 6.1 IIS 6.0 Worker Process Model

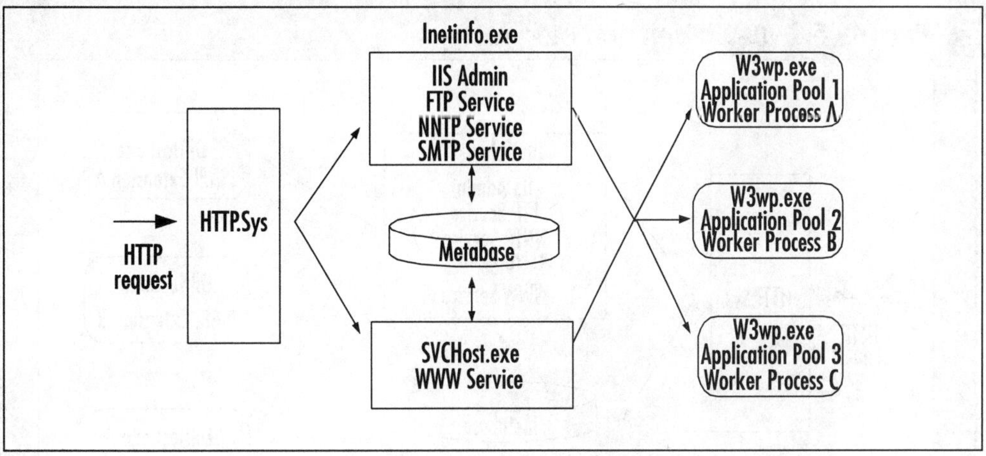

The Web request from the user is met by the HTTP listener. This HTTP request listener is referred to as HTTP.Sys. HTTP.Sys analyzes the request and validates authentication on it. An error message will be sent to the user if the request is invalid by HTTP.Sys. The request is passed to Inetinfo.exe or SVCHost.exe if the request is valid. Inetinfo.exe will handle all FTP, NNTP, SMTP, and IIS Admin requests. The

SVCHost.exe will handle all the WWW requests. Both InetInfo.exe and SVCHost.exe will communicate with the metabase to process requests. (The metabase is an XML repository that will hold the configuration settings for the IIS 6.0 server.) All the requests are queued to be processed by a Web site. There are different queues for each worker process. IIS 6.0 will create a new W3wp.exe instance as a worker process if the request refers to new data. All the existing Web sites will have worker processes assign to them. Each worker process will have an application pool for resource management. The request will be processed by one of the worker process models. The response will be channeled by the worker process through either Intetinfo.exe or SVCHost.exe to the user.

Head of the Class...

Is the Worker Process Model the Same as IIS 5.0 Isolation Mode?

IIS 6.0 runs the worker process model by default. You can also configure IIS 6.0 to run in *IIS 5.0 isolation mode*. The worker process model is more flexible than the IIS 5.0 isolation model. The worker process can isolate individual sites, which will minimize the risk of a malicious attack on the WWW service. IIS 5.0 isolation mode still runs *within* the inetinfo.exe memory space, so an error in the application can bring down the whole server (WWW, NNTP, FTP, and SMTP services). The IIS 5.0 architecture is illustrated in Figure 6.2.

Figure 6.2 IIS 5.0 Isolation Model

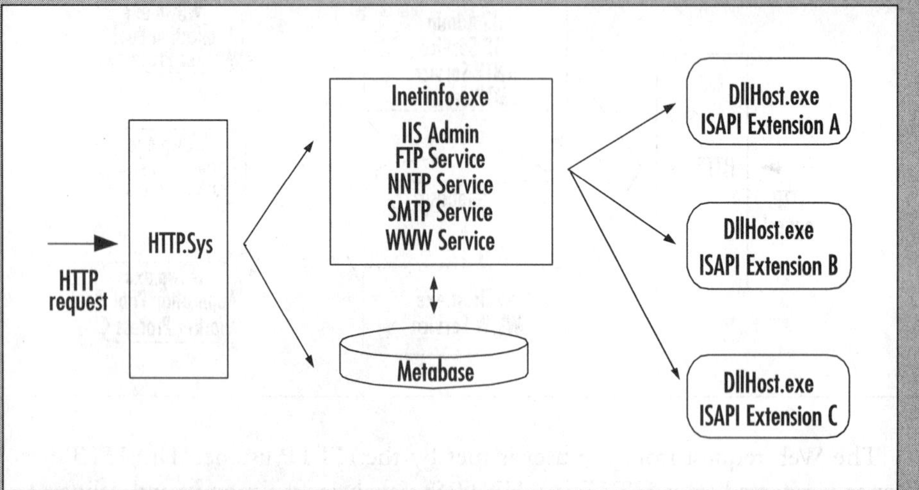

Continued

This model is similar to the IIS 6.0 model, but less scalable. The incoming requests are met by HTTP.Sys. (HTTP.Sys is a user mode element in IIS 5.0. It is a kernel mode element in IIS 6.0.) HTTP.Sys will forward the request to Inetinfoe.exe. Inetinfo.exe will handle all WWW, FTP, NNTP, and SMTP calls in IIS 5.0. Inetinfo.exe will communicate with the metabase to facilitate the execution of the Web request. (The metabase in IIS 5.0 is implemented as a binary executable. The IIS 6.0 metabase is XML driven.) This will forward all the requests to a single queue. (This is a notable difference in IIS 6.0. IIS 6.0 will have multiple queues for multiple Web sites.) Each Web site will run as an ISAPI extension under DllHost.exe. The generic queue will forward the correct request to the appropriate ISAPI application to process the contents.

IIS 5.0 used ASP as the default scripting mechanism; IIS 6.0 uses ASP.NET. IIS 6.0 can run ASP, and all the code should run smoothly in an upgrade from IIS 5.0 to IIS 6.0. If the ASP code is not compatible, you might have to revert to IIS 5.0 isolation mode.

In Windows Server 2003, the HTTP stack is implemented as a kernel mode device driver called HTTP.Sys. All incoming HTTP traffic goes through this kernel process. This kernel process is independent of an application process. IIS 6.0 is an application process and external to HTTP.Sys (application processes run in *user mode*, and the operating system functions are run in *kernel mode*). HTTP.Sys is responsible for the following: connection management (managing the database connections from the ASP.NET pages to databases), caching (reading from a static cache as opposed to recompiling the ASP.NET page), bandwidth throttling (limiting the size of the Web requests to a Web site), and text-based logging (writing IIS information into a text log file).

In IIS 5.0, the HTTP request was consumed by the IIS inetinfo.exe (the incoming HTTP requests were first analyzed by inetinfo.exe process). HTTP.Sys in IIS 6.0 relieves IIS of this responsibility. In doing so, it enhances IIS performance in the following ways:

- HTTP.Sys enables caching (referred as *flexible caching*) at the kernel level so that static data can be cached for faster response time (independent of the user mode caching). This will be faster than user mode caching. We need to be careful with flexible caching. Since HTTP.Sys is separate from IIS, we can still cache old data after an IIS restart.
- HTTP.Sys introduces a mapping concept called *application pooling*. Application pooling allows Web sites to run together in one or more processes, as long as they share the same pool designation. Web sites that are assigned different application pools never run in the same process. A central

Web site (credit card verification Web site) can be accessed by all the other miscellaneous sites (shopping cart e-commerce sites) by using this method. By using the correct application pool information, HTTP.Sys can route the HTTP traffic to the correct Web site.

- HTTP.Sys increases the number of Web sites you can host using the application pool concept. This architecture also increases performance and more controlled access to valuable IIS resources.

EXAM 70-298 OBJECTIVE 3.3.1

Designing Certificate Authentication

Certificates are a proven mechanism to authenticate users in IIS 6.0. A certificate is a digital fingerprint for a user or for a number of users. This digital fingerprint will provide access information of the user to IIS 6.0. The certificate management is a part of the Secure Sockets Layer (SSL) in IIS. SSL will manage the encrypted communication between the client and the server. The certificate information need to be "verified" by a Windows user account, a process is referred to as *mapping*. There are three ways to map a certificate to a Windows user account: Directory Service mapping, one-to-one mapping, and many-to-one mapping. These three mechanisms provide a very flexible certificate mapping mechanism in Windows Server 2003. We are able to map multiple users to single certificate information (using wildcards), and a number of certificates to the same user by using the mapping mechanisms. Let's look at them in more detail.

Directory Service Mapping

Directory Service (DS) mapping uses native Windows Active Directory Service to authenticate users. This is the least popular of the three mapping methods, because of the necessity of an Active Directory and this mechanism does not bring the "third-party security vendor support" that comes with other certificate mappings. The user will feel more comfortable with VeriSign-issued certificates as opposed to an internal Active Directory user account of the enterprise. (VeriSign is a reputed certificate vendor. Their certificates are used on multiple platforms in various e-commerce implementations. The general public will feel secure dealing with a trusted third party like VeriSign.) DS mapping information is shared across all IIS servers; therefore, we do not need to replicate them in each server. However, it is not as flexible as other methods to perform wildcard matching. We need to be a member of a Windows domain to apply DS mapping. This mapping will suit us best if we want to integrate our Web sites as an intranet within the enterprise. We will not be able to implement one-to-one or many-to-one mapping if we proceed with a DS mapping. This mapping is used in large-scale implementations for internal data sharing.

One-to-One Mapping

One-to-one mapping compares the user certificate to the one stored on the server. The client browser sends the user certificate to the IIS 6.0. The certificate details need to match exactly to proceed with authentication. The server needs to be updated with the new certificate information if the user decides to get a new certificate. This mechanism suits smaller implementations or a small set of users who will have access to sensitive data. One-to-one mapping provides higher security than the other two mappings do. Certificate revocation and usage can be closely monitored in this mapping mechanism. Exercise 6.01 shows us how to implement one-to-one mapping in IIS 6.0.

EXERCISE 6.01

IMPLEMENTING ONE-TO-ONE MAPPING

1. Navigate to **Start | Administrative Tools | IIS Manager**.
2. Select **Web Sites** and then **Default Web site**. We will use this Web site for demonstration purposes.
3. Right-click on the **Default Web site** and select **Properties**. Navigate to the **Directory Security** tab. Your screen should be similar to Figure 6.3.

Figure 6.3 Directory Security Tab of IIS 6.0

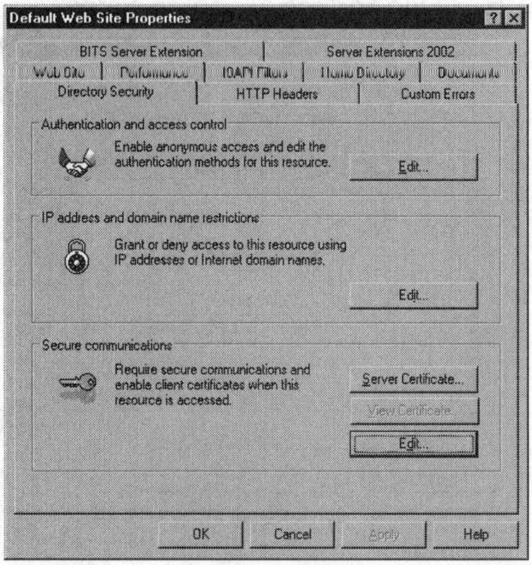

4. Click the **Edit** button in the **Secure communications** box. Your screen should be similar to Figure 6.4.

Figure 6.4 Enable Secure Communication

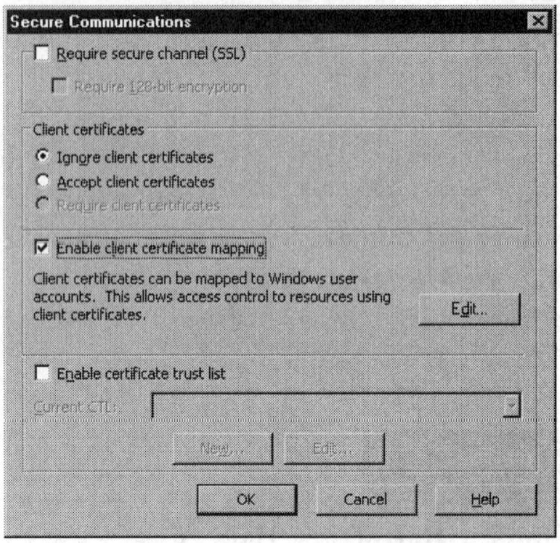

5. Click the **Enable client certificate mapping** option box and click the **Edit** button. You should be presented with the **Account Mapping** screen (see Figure 6.5). Select the **1-to-1** tab. You can view the existing certificate mappings (it is not a good practice to map a certificate using the Administrator account). You can select these existing mappings and the details will appear in the **Subject** and **Issuer** group boxes.

Figure 6.5 One-to-One Mapping Screen

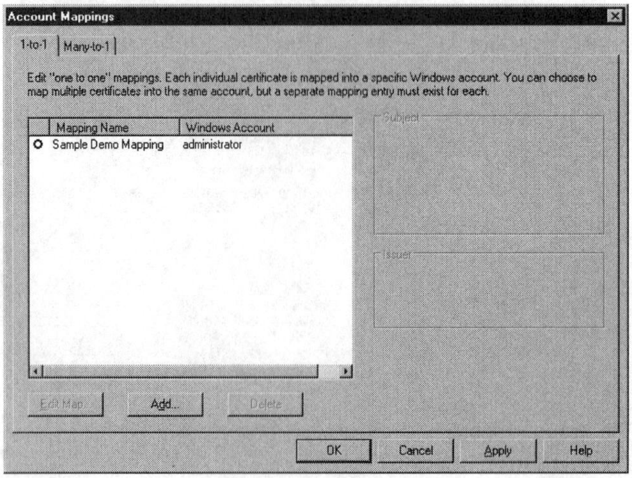

6. Click the **Add** button and you will be presented with the dialog box to navigate to the certificate. Select the certificate and click

the **Open** button. You will be asked to enter the credentials to add the mapping. It is good practice to use an account with fewer privileges. We are trying to create a mapping to the IIS 6.0 server; therefore, we will use the IUSR_ComputerName account in this case. (The machine name is DEVSRV2; therefore, the account will be IUSR_DEVSVR2.) Your screen should be similar to Figure 6.6. Click **OK** to return to the **Account Mapping** screen.

Figure 6.6 Select Credentials for Mapping

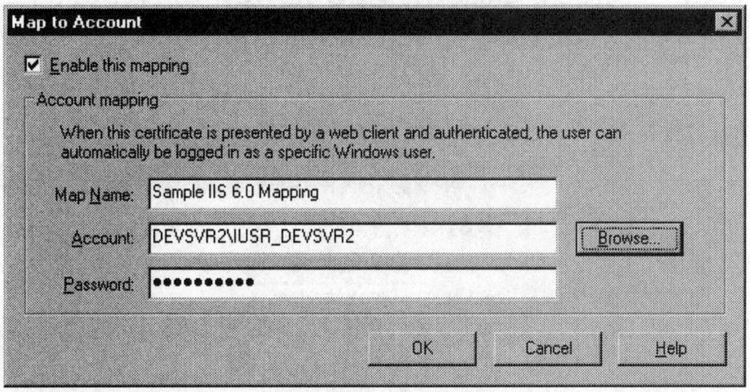

7. Click **Apply** button to apply the certificate mappings.

Many-to-One Mapping

Many-to-many matching does not compare the complete certificate information; it only compares specific information (for example, the issuer or the subject) using wildcards. Therefore, the user certificate information does not need to match exactly to proceed with authentication. It only needs to adhere to certain criteria set by the enterprise domain administrators. The users will be able to authenticate even if they update their certificates (provided that they do not alter the wildcard criteria). Many-to-one mapping is popular with large-scale implementations. We can create one or more matching rules to correspond to one or more Windows accounts. Administration of the mapping process is also easier compared to the other two.

Many-to-many implementations can also be used to leverage the IIS 6.0 anonymous IUSR_ComputerName account. The entire pool of certificates can be matched with wildcards to the IUSR_ComputerName account to be authenticated. This mechanism can also be used on certificates issued by certificate authorities (CAs). We can define rules that will seamlessly map the certificate information to user accounts in this way. Let's look at the many-to-many mapping process in Windows Server 2003 IIS 6.0.

EXERCISE 6.02

IMPLEMENT MANY-TO-ONE MAPPING

1. Follow steps 1 through 5 in Exercise 6.01.
2. Select the **Many-to-1** tab from the **Account Mapping** screen. Make sure the **Enable wildcard client certificate matching** option box is checked. You can also see the existing mapping in this screen. Click the **Add** button to create a new many-to-one mapping. Your screen should be similar to Figure 6.7.

Figure 6.7 Add a Wildcard Rule

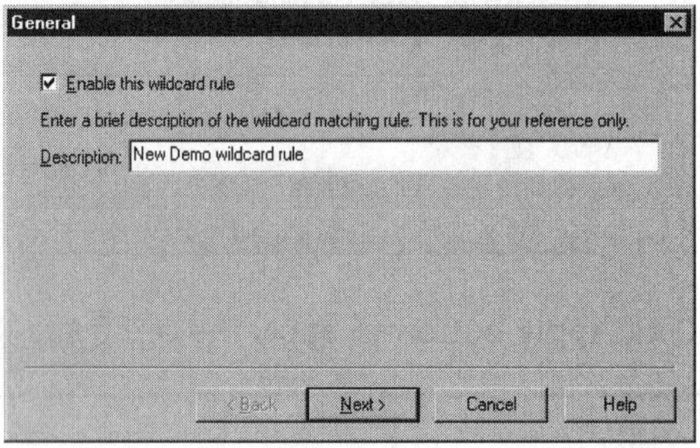

3. Enter a name for the new rule in the text box. We will enter **New Demo wildcard rule** for demonstration purposes. Click the **Next** button to navigate to Figure 6.8.

Figure 6.8 The Rules Window

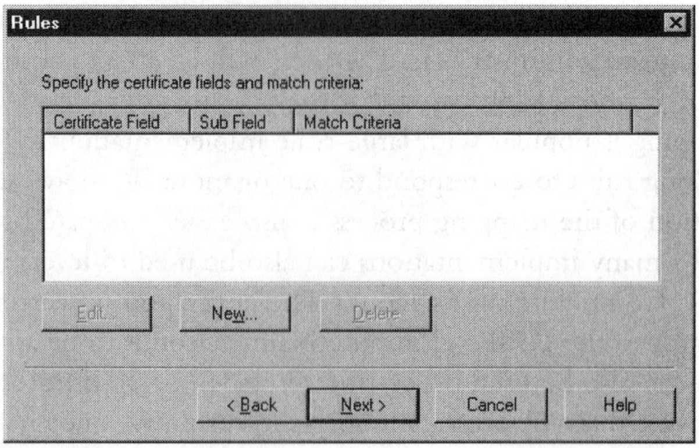

4. Click the **New** button to create a new rule. You will be presented with Figure 6.9 to configure the rule.

Figure 6.9 Enter Rule Information

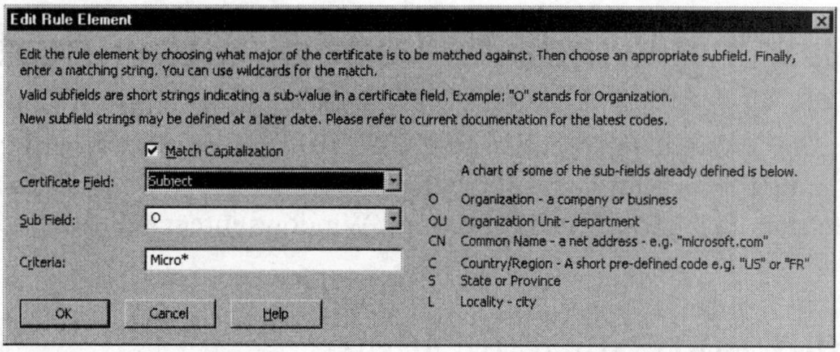

5. This screen will let you define the rule. We will try to define a rule that will inspect the *Subject* field of the certificate to inspect the contents of the *organization sub* field. We will enter the wildcard **Micro*** as the filter. Therefore, any Microsoft certificate will be able to authenticate using this setting. Click the **OK** button when finished. You will be asked to enter the credentials for the mapping. We will use the same IUSR_DEVSVR2 account in this exercise. Your screen should be similar to Figure 6.10.

Figure 6.10 Enter Credentials for Many-to-One Mapping

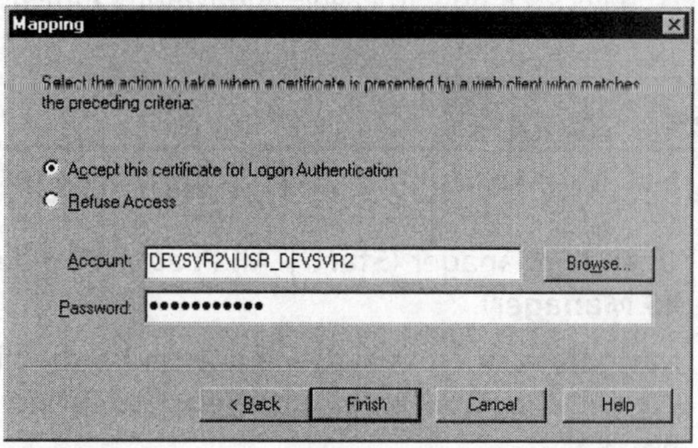

6. Click the **Finish** button to end the wizard and apply the changes.

This process will implement an IIS 6.0 certificate authorization on IIS 6.0 server. The client browser will be equipped to handle this authorization mechanism. (All the major browsers are capable of handling certificates and they are built in to the browser functionalities.) This client browser will communicate with the server to provide the certificate information to be validated by the IIS 6.0 server. This process is detailed in Chapter 10 "Securing Network Clients."

EXAM 70-298 OBJECTIVE 3.3.2

Designing Windows Logon Authentication

There are several Windows logon authentication mechanisms available in Windows Server 2003. Windows accounts can be used to authenticate users to gain access to Web and FTP content. These authentication methods are anonymous access, basic authentication, digest authentication, and Windows integrated authentication. Let's look at each in detail.

Anonymous Authentication

The anonymous authentication method is the least secure of the Windows Server 2003 authentication options, and is used on Web content that does not require any security (the content is available for public consumption). We do not need to provide credentials to view Web content using this authentication. Therefore, IIS 6.0 will provide public access to Web and FTP sites without prompting for a username or a password.

IIS 6.0 impersonates a user account to assign a connection. This user account is automatically created at the installation. The name format for this account is IUSR_Computer*Name* (for example, if the server name is devsvr01, the account will be IUSR_devsvr01). The account is added to the *Guest* user group at installation. Therefore, NTFS account permissions can be configured on the Guest group to protect the IIS server. Let's see how to enable anonymous authentication on IIS 6.0.

EXERCISE 6.03

CONFIGURE ANONYMOUS AUTHENTICATION

1. Open IIS Manager (**Start | All Programs | Administrative Tools | IIS Manager**).
2. Navigate to the correct Web site and right-click on **Properties**. We will choose the **Default Web Site** for demonstration purposes.
3. Select the **Directory Security** tab.
4. Click the **Edit** button of the **Authentication and access control** group box.
5. Select the **Enable anonymous access** option from the **Authentication Methods** window. We can also change the

anonymous account by clicking the **Browse** button. The screen should be similar to Figure 6.11.

Figure 6.11 Enable Anonymous Access

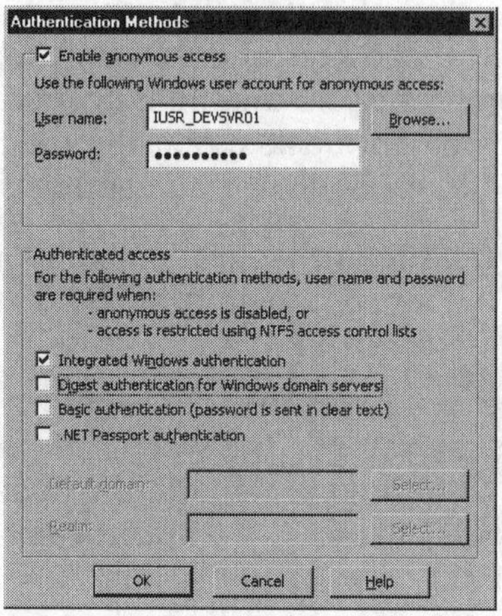

We are using a machine called devsvr01; therefore, the default anonymous account is IUSR_DEVSVR01.

IIS 6.0 will impersonate the IUSR_ComputerName account when a request is received. IIS 6.0 is aware of this account and its password (since it was automatically generated during installation). IIS will inquire about the NTFS permissions on the IUSR_ComputerName account before any code is executed. The code will be exe cuted if the permissions are granted. IIS will prompt the user to try another authentication method if the permissions are denied. If no other authentication method is configured, IIS will return an "HTTP 403 Access Denied" error.

Test Day Tip

You can enable multiple authentication options on a Web site. However, anonymous access will be executed before the other authentication methods. We can alter the account for anonymous access at the Web server level or at the virtual directory level. (The default account is IUSR_ComputerName. This can be changed to any account you prefer.) We do not need to have "logon locally" access in Windows Server 2003. The default logon type in IIS 6.0 is clear text. (We need to have "logon locally" access in previous IIS versions.) Therefore, the username and password will be communicated using clear text. You can also change the permissions of the IUSR_ComputerName account using the *Group Policy Manager* Microsoft Management Console (MMC).

Head of the Class...

Sub-Authentication Component

The sub-authentication component was used in IIS 5.0 to manage the passwords of anonymous accounts. This was a security risk in IIS 5.0. An intruder can gain access to the sub-authentication component and modify the passwords. This will have an adverse effect on the Web servers. IIS 6.0 on Windows Server 2003 does not configure the sub-authentication account by default. This will protect IIS 6.0 from intruders modifying the passwords. We need to apply the following steps to configure the sub-authentication component.

1. Register the sub-authentication component (use a command prompt window and type **rundll32 %windir%\system32\iis-suba.dll,RegisterIISSUBA**).
2. All worker processes that uses anonymous authentication should run as **LocalSystem**. (The worker process uses the LocalSystem account to communicate with the operating system. The user impersonates the IUSR_ComputerName account to communicate with IIS 6.0.)
3. The Metabase property **AnonymousPasswordSyn** should be set to **true**. This could be done by editing the metabase XML file.

Basic Authentication

Basic authentication is widely used by all Web servers. The browser will request the user's username and password. The user will enter the details into the Web browser. The collection of username and password details is referred to as *credentials*. The Web browser will send the credentials to the Web server to authenticate. The credentials will be *base-64 encoded* before they are sent to the Web servers, and are not encrypted. Therefore, anyone "snooping" into the network can obtain these details.

The credentials should match to a Windows account on the Web server. A connection will be established if the credentials are authenticated. The user will be allowed three attempts to connect. An error message will be displayed if the user exceeds three attempts.

Basic authentication is included in the HTTP specification; therefore, it is supported by most browsers. This has a wider appeal than integrated and digest authentication. The only issue is the "insecure" transmission of the credentials. An intruder can easily intercept the communication and obtain the username and password. The remedy for this is the application of SSL; therefore, the Web browser and the Web server should exchange the basic authentication credentials over an SSL connection. Exercise 6.04 shows us how to configure basic authentication.

EXERCISE 6.04

CONFIGURE BASIC AUTHENTICATION

1. Open IIS Manager and navigate to the **Authentication Methods** window (refer to steps 1 through 4 in Exercise 6.03).
2. Select the **Basic authentication (password is sent in clear text)** option. You will get a warning to illustrate the limitations of basic authentication. The screen will be similar to Figure 6.12. Click **Yes** to proceed.

Figure 6.12 Basic Authentication Warning

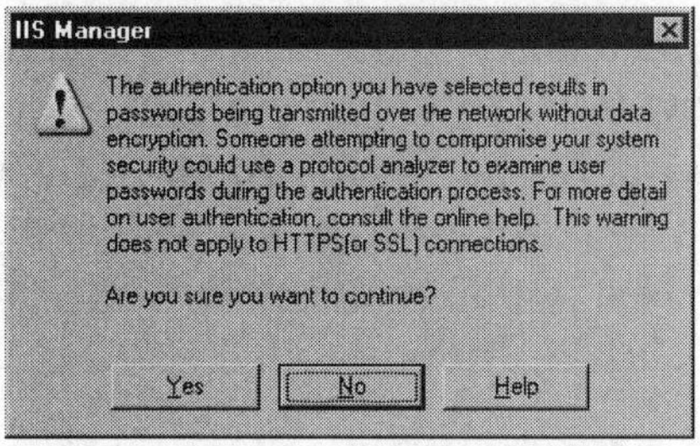

3. Type the domain name of the network to which you are attached. We can also select the domain by clicking the **Select** button. The current IIS domain name will be taken if the field is kept empty. We will use **MyDomain** for demonstration purposes.
4. You can also configure an optional **Realm** property. This will appear in the browser window when the user tries to authenticate. We will enter **test Realm** for demonstration purposes. The screen should be similar to Figure 6.13.

Figure 6.13 Basic Authentication Settings

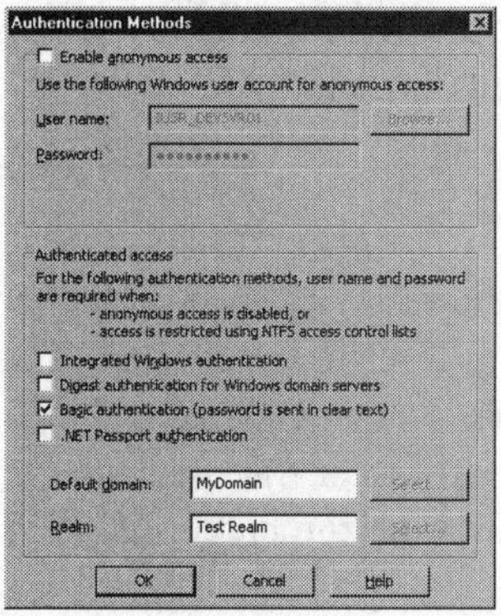

Digest Authentication

Digest authentication is similar to basic authentication. The limitation of basic authentication is that the transportation of the credentials as clear text. Digest authentication overcomes this issue by having MD5 hashed encrypted credentials. This MD5 hash or *Message Digest* cannot be deciphered from the hash. Digest authentication is only available on directories that support WebDAV (Web Distributed Authoring and Versioning). Exercise 6.05 illustrates how to enable digest authentication on IIS 6.0.

Exercise 6.05

Configure Digest Authentication

1. Open IIS Manager and navigate to the **Authentication Methods** window (refer to steps 1 through 4 in Exercise 6.03).
2. Select the **Digest Authentication for Windows domain servers** option. You will be informed about the Active Directory involvement in digest authentication. The screen will be similar to Figure 6.14. Click **Yes** to proceed.

Figure 6.14 Digest Authentication Warning

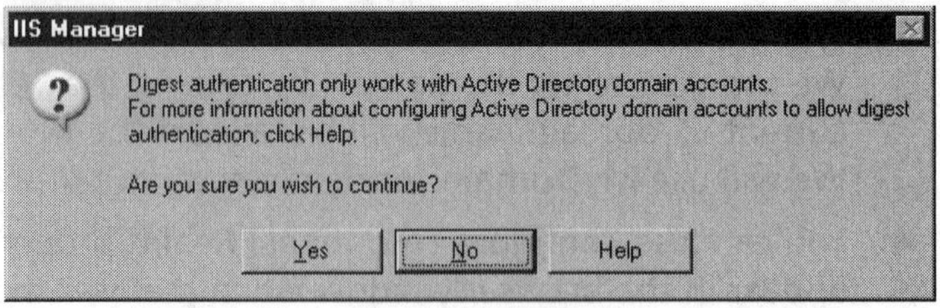

3. You can also configure an optional **Realm** property. This will appear in the browser window when the user tries to authenticate. We will enter **test Realm** for demonstration purposes. The screen should be similar to Figure 6.13 with the digest authentication option turned on.

Let's look at the digest authentication process. The user will issue a Web request to the IIS 6.0 server using Internet Explorer 5.0 or later. The IIS 6.0 server will inform the user that digest security is enabled and provide realm details. Internet Explorer will ask the user to enter the username and password details (credentials). Internet Explorer will combine the credentials and realm to create the MD5 hash.

This MD5 hash will be sent to the IIS 6.0 server. IIS 6.0 will send the MD5 hash to the domain controller (DC) for verification. The DC will refer to the Active Directory to compare the credentials and authenticate the user.

EXAM WARNING

There are several requirements to implement digest security. Digest security is only supported on Internet Explorer 5.0 and later. Therefore, all the client browsers in the enterprise should meet these criteria. The users also must have a valid Active Directory account to compare the credentials when we authenticate. We do not need any additional software to support digest authentication. However, digest authentication uses HTTP 1.1. Not all browsers support HTTP 1.1; therefore, non-HTTP 1.1 browsers will not be able to use digest security in Windows Server 2003.

TEST DAY TIP

The user and the Web server should have two trust relationships to implement digest security. (The server and the client might belong to two different networks. Therefore, the two networks need to trust each other in order for them to communicate. A "two-way" trust will enable both "server trusting the client" and "client trusting the server." Therefore, information can flow both ways.) The DC should be Windows 2000 or later. We need to use the sub-authentication component of IIS 6.0 to communicate with a Windows 2000 DC. We also need to use the *LocalSystem* account if the IIS 6.0 server operates in worker process isolation mode.

Integrated Windows Authentication

Integrated Windows authentication is the default authentication mechanism in IIS 6.0. This was formerly called NTLM or Windows NT Challenge/Response method. Integrated Windows authentication uses a hashed algorithm to encrypt the credentials; therefore, it is a safe authentication method. It uses Kerberos V5 and NTLM authentication to implement integrated Windows authentication.

EXAM WARNING

NTLM and Kerberos have different features. Kerberos can pass through proxy servers; however, it is terminated by firewalls. Most corporate firewalls will stop Kerberos from entering their system. These corporate firewalls will let NTLM pass through to the system. However, NTLM is stopped at the proxy servers of the enterprise. Enterprise Web applications will not be able to use either Kerberos or NTLM. A combination of both can deliver a secure authentication mechanism, which we refer to as *integrated Windows authentication*. However, both the client and server need to have a trusted connection to the Key Distribution Center (KDC) and Active Directory to implement Kerberos v5.

Let's see how this authentication is implemented. The client browser does not request the username and password from the user (however, Internet Explorer 4.0 and later can be configured to request the username and password in integrated Windows authentication). The client *logged on user credentials* (on the client computer) are used initially. This information is passed to the IIS 6.0 server. The user is prompted to supply the credentials if the information is invalid. The user can retry the credentials until he or she is authenticated.

This authentication mechanism has its limitations. Integrated Windows authentication will not work over HTTP proxies. We also need to have Internet Explorer 2.0 or later to implement this authentication method. Therefore, it is more suited to an intranet environment that can be tightly controlled by the system administrators. Exercise 6.06 shows us how to configure IIS 6.0 to implement integrated Windows authentication.

EXERCISE 6.06

CONFIGURE INTEGRATED WINDOWS AUTHENTICATION

1. Open IIS Manager (**Start | All Programs | Administrative Tools | IIS Manager**).
2. Navigate to the correct Web site and right-click on **Properties**. We will choose the **Default Web Site** for demonstration purposes.
3. Select **Directory Security** tab.
4. Click the **Edit** button of the **Authentication and access control** group box.
5. Select **Integrated Windows Authentication**.

TEST DAY TIP

The Kerberos service needs to be registered before we use integrated Windows authentication. (Kerberos runs as a service that can be turned on and off from Control Panel of Windows Server 2003.) We should be careful with the user account under which this service runs. We need to alter the settings of the service account if the account is modified. The service must be referring to one service account object. Each application pool will use this account to implement Kerberos in IIS 6.0. Since an IIS 6.0 application pool will facilitate multiple Web sites and virtual directories, it will be difficult to isolate Web sites form each other. However, we can isolate each site at the domain name level; for example, www.stiA.com, www.siteB.com, and so forth.

EXAM 70-298 OBJECTIVE 3.3.3

Designing RADIUS Authentication

There are multiple network options for organizations. Technical advances enable us to use Internet, virtual private networks (VPNs), and wireless access to the same resources. These multiple implementations add another level of complexity to our enterprise. We do not want to have different authorization and authentication mechanisms to access different resources (for example, we should be able to log on to our wireless devices using our VPN credentials). The Remote Authentication Dial-In User Service (RADIUS) is a protocol that defines "single sign-on" access to multiple network resources. The implementation of RADIUS in Windows Server 2003 is referred to as Internet Authentication Server (IAS).

IAS in Windows Server 2003 implements a RADIUS server and a RADIUS proxy. The RADIUS server will provide centralized connection for authentication, authorization, and accounting functions for networks that include wireless access, VPN remote access, Internet access, extranet business partner access, and router-to-router connections. IAS proxy functions are different from these server functions, and includes forwarding IAS authorization and accounting information to other IAS servers. The Microsoft IAS is built on the standard RADIUS protocol specification that is published by the Internet Engineering Task Force (IETF). The RADIUS authentication as a server and a proxy is illustrated in Figure 6.15.

Figure 6.15 RADIUS Architecture in Windows Server 2003

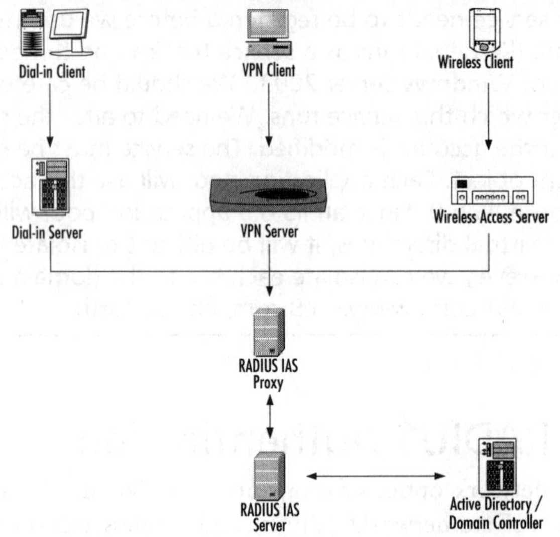

There are several remote access methods in an enterprise: dial-in client desktops, VPN clients, and wireless devices in our demonstration. The dial-in clients will connect to a dial-in server. The VPN clients will connect to a VPN server. The wireless devices will access the network through a wireless access server. All three servers will connect to a Windows Server 2003 RADIUS IAS proxy machine. This proxy will channel the requests to the IAS server. The IAS server will communicate with the DC and the Active Directory to perform authentication duties. Let's look more closely at using the IAS server.

Using the Internet Authentication Server

IAS is installed as an optional server in Windows Server 2003, and is not installed by default. Therefore, we need to add IAS manually to our Windows Server 2003. Exercise 6.07 shows the steps to install IAS to implement RADIUS authentication on IIS 6.0.

Exercise 6.07

Install Internet Authentication Server

1. Navigate to **Start | Control Panel | Add Remove Programs**.
2. Click the **Add /Remove Windows Component** button.

3. Navigate to **Network Services** and click the **Details** button. Your screen should be similar to Figure 6.16.

Figure 6.16 Select Network Services

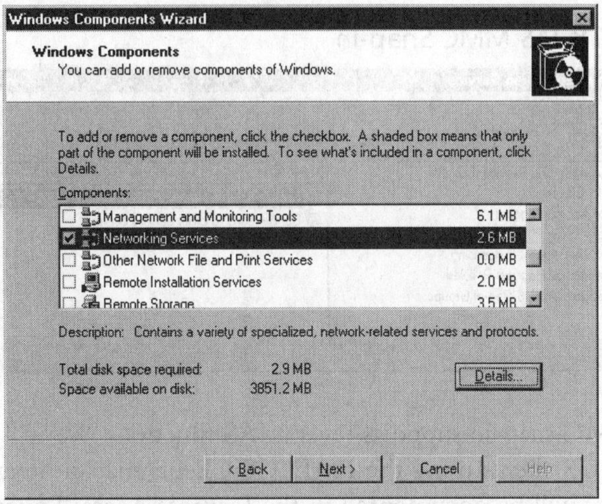

4. Select Internet **Authentication Service** and click **OK**. This screen should be similar to Figure 6.17.

Figure 6.17 Select Internet Authentication Service

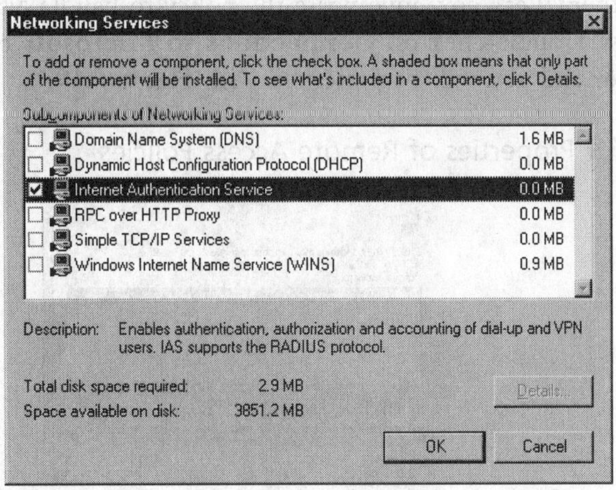

5. The installation will start and you will be notified with an information message at the end of the setup.

These steps will install IAS on your server. The installation will add the **Internet Authentication Service** program item under **Start | Administrative Tools** to navigate to the service. The service can be managed by an MMC snap-in. The IAS MMC snap-in will be similar to Figure 6.18.

Figure 6.18 IAS MMC Snap-In

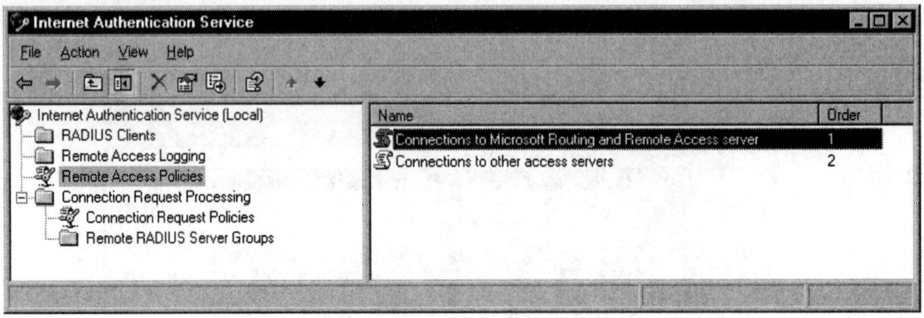

The MMC snap-in supports several IAS functions. We will be able to keep track of all RADIUS clients using the RADIUS Clients snap-in item. All the logging for remote access will be documented in the Remote Access Logging snap-in item. We can also define policies under the Remote Access Policies item. These policies for remote access can be different form one enterprise to another. There are two default policies created by the installation: *Connections to Microsoft routing and remote servers* and *Connection to other servers*. We can change these policies by selecting them and double-clicking on them. Let's now investigate the policy to handle Microsoft routers and remote access. Double-click on **Connections to Microsoft routing and remote access server** and you will be presented with Figure 6.19.

Figure 6.19 Properties of Remote Access Policies

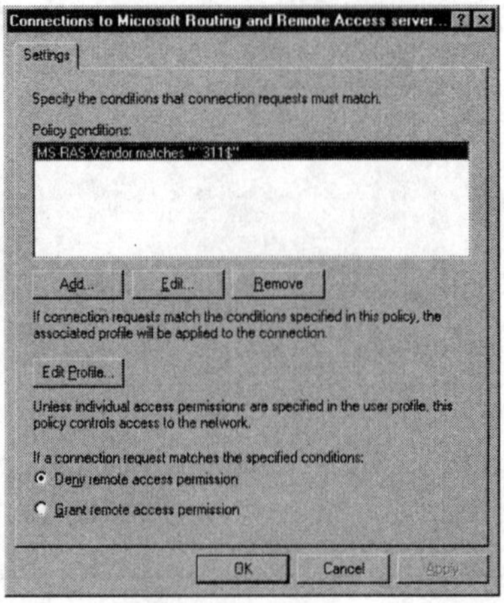

This screen will specify the protocol to communicate to other Microsoft servers in the enterprise. The connection to enterprise is enabled if this policy is met. We can also edit the policy by clicking the **Edit Profile** button. The screen should be similar to Figure 6.20.

Figure 6.20 Edit the Default Policy Settings

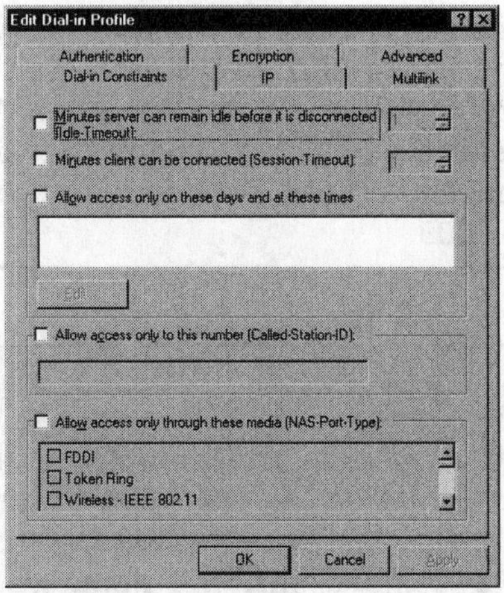

Windows Server 2003's IAS server is highly configurable for remote access policy. We can configure the policy on dial-in connection properties. We can restrict access according to time and session length. We can also restrict the port times that remote access is granted (for example, Token Ring or wireless access). We can use the **IP** tab of the **Dial-in Profile** window to restrict machine access by IP address. We can also grant or deny encryption algorithms by using the **Encryption** tab. The **Authentication** tab will enable to you to configure the appropriate authentication algorithms for remote access to the enterprise. Let's investigate the security measures that will enable us to secure the IAS server on the enterprise.

Securing the RADIUS Implementation

RADIUS servers will be hosted in a server room with other enterprise software servers. These servers need to be physically protected from intruders. This will include locked doors, security alarm systems and dedicated server space for the IAS servers. We can also make some configuration changes to protect the servers from intruders.

EXAM WARNING

We should test all RADIUS clients using local authentication methods before we make them enterprise RADIUS clients. This will enable us to troubleshoot problems more efficiently. We should not install a Windows Server 2003 IAS server on the same partition as a Windows 2000 IAS server. Both IAS servers use the same Program Files directory to store remote policies and logging details of each IAS implementation. Consequently, Windows Server 2003 IAS data will override the Windows 2000 IAS data. We should also avoid adding a Windows Server 2003 IAS implementation into a Windows NT 4.0 domain that will read the user accounts on a Windows Server 2003 DC. This situation will restrict the Lightweight Directory Access Protocol (LDAP) to query the IAS on Windows Server 2003.

Head of the Class...

Security Issues with IAS Access

We should not send sensitive information (for example, passwords and shared secrets of the enterprise) as plain text on the enterprise network. Intruders might use packet snooping software to listen to the communication between the servers and the clients. Therefore, we should take steps to encrypt the data communication. The data encryption mechanisms will protect the data if the intruders get hold of it. Intruders need to decrypt the data to obtain the information. There are two ways to combat this problem:

- **Use Terminal Services to access the IAS server** Terminal Services offers 128-bit encrypted communication between the client and the server. This mechanism will encrypt the sensitive information in the network. Terminal servers send the desktop image to the Terminal Services clients. The clients will collect the mouseclicks and screen information and send it to the server. There will be no processing of information at the client end. The server will process the mouseclicks and the screen data to determine the user action at the client end. Therefore, all the processing is done at the terminal server end (the client will only provide the mouseclick information). This is an additional security measure on top of the encryption process.
- **Use IPSec to encrypt communication between the RADIUS server and the client** IPSec can be used to encrypt the communication between the two machines. We need to install the Windows Server 2003 Administration Tool Pack on the client machine to enable this.

It is also a good practice to enable logging at the IAS server. This will enable an audit trial if the servers are compromised. There are two logging facilities that we can use to enable logging on IAS:

- **Event log entries in the event log** This is used primarily for connection attempts to the IAS servers for auditing and troubleshooting purposes. The entries will be logged in the System log.
- **Log user authentication and accounting requests** This is primarily used for billing purposes and connection analysis. The entries could be written to a text file or SQL Server database for reference on demand.

We need to make sure that we have sufficient storage capacity to accommodate logging on the server. We also need to back up the log files regularly, because they cannot be duplicated if they are damaged. It is also advisable to accommodate a failover server should the SQL Server log machine fails. This could be achieved by creating a duplicate SQL Server machine on the different subnet of the network.

We should also consider some good practices to implement IAS in a large enterprise. It is a good practice to add the users to logical groups in the enterprise. These groups should be small in number, and the only groups allowed access to the IAS server. This mechanism is preferred over adding every user to gain access to the IAS server.

TEST DAY TIP

You can also make some Registry modification to increase the performance of the IAS server. If the IAS server is not a DC and it is receiving a large number of requests, we can change the HKEY_LOCAL_MACHINE\SYSTEM\CurrentControlSet\Services\Netlogon\Parameters. We need to add a new attribute called MaxConcurrentApi. We can modify the value from 2 to 5 in this new entry. We need to be little cautious about this attribute; a higher number can impose more burdens on the DC of the network.

EXAM 70-298 OBJECTIVE 3.4

Designing Security for IIS

IIS provides many services in Windows Server 2003. It supports Web, FTP, SMTP, and NNTP services. Web sites can be configured as Internet sites, intranet sites, or extranet sites. Some contents of intranet sites need to be available as content for extranet sites. Therefore, it is a tedious task to design security to address every one of these implementations. Let's detail some of the most common security implementations.

The most common Web sites are public Internet sites. These have to be enabled for public access by default. Therefore, we need to enable anonymous login for all the public Web sites. We need to take extra caution to ensure the IUSR_ComputerName account is not mishandled. The IUSR_ComputerName account should only belong to the Guests Windows group; it should never be a part of the Administrators or Power User groups. These groups' access will severely compromise IIS security. The IUSR_ComputerName account should not have any write access either, only read access. We should also enable IIS logging on all public Web sites.

Intranet sites are internal to an enterprise. Therefore, we can leverage the existing security architectures for an intranet site. We can use integrated Windows authentication, digest authentication, or basic authentication as our authentication mechanisms. The user should already have a Windows account to log on to desktops and servers of the enterprise. We can use this account for basic authentication to integrated Windows authentication. Integrated Windows authentication is the preferred option. However, we need to enable Kerberos to implement integrated Windows authentication. Most large organizations have Active Directory implementations. We can leverage this Active Directory implementations to use digest security for our intranet sites. The enterprise DCs will oversee the intranet site communications. Therefore, the best place to start troubleshooting the intranet security breaches is the event log of the IIS servers and DC machines.

Extranet sites are similar to intranet sites, except that they are for an "external" audience. This is a mechanism of sharing business information with business partners. We will not have the luxury of enterprisewide Active Directory or network implementations of intranet sites under extranet implementations. The two organizations will have different IT systems on different IT platforms in most cases. Therefore, integrated Windows authentication or digest authentication will be difficult to implement. (It will be a tedious task even if both organizations are on Windows platforms. We need to create "two-way trust bridges" to communicate from one organization to another.) The best authentication technique will be basic authentication. However, we need to implement an SSL encryption to secure the clear text credential communication between the two organizations. We should also enable IIS logging on every extranet site to facilitate debugging of IIS security breaches. Let's look at how to secure IIS 6.0 installations.

EXAM 70-298 OBJECTIVE 3.4.1

Securing IIS Installations

IIS is not installed by default in the Windows Server 2003 setup, except in the Web Server Edition. There are three different ways to install IIS:

- Use the Configure Your Server Wizard
- Use the Add or Remove option from the Control Panel
- Use the Unattended Setup

Head of the Class...

Default IIS Access Options

All of the installation methods described here will install IIS in "locked" mode. That means you only get access to static Web material. All the ASP.NET scripts, Server Side Includes, WebDAV access and Front Page Extensions will be disabled by default. If you try to access any of these facilities, you will get a 404 (Page not found) error. You must enable these features through Web Services Extensions node in IIS Manager if you want to use them.

If you enable these features, you can disable them later to increase security. This involves using the Web Service Extensions node in the IIS MMC. Any Web service extension can be enabled or disabled individually as long as it's registered in the Web Service Extensions node, or you can prohibit all extensions from running. You can also add new extensions, and you can figure IIS so that a specific application will be able to use the Web Service Extensions.

Web Service Extensions is a new feature in IIS 6.0. This utility will give a Control Panel-like functionality to your IIS components. We will be able to allow, prohibit, or change the properties using this tool. This will also let you add new IIS extensions (ISAPI applications and third-party IIS tools) to the IIS 6.0 server. You can also enable or disable all Web Service Extensions by using this MMC. Here is a list of components the Web Service Extensions can enable or disable:

- ASP.NET executions
- ASP executions
- CGI and ISAPI applications
- Front Page Server Extensions 2000 and 2002
- WebDAV support for IIS directories

We can get to the Web service extensions by using **Start | Administrative Tools | IIS Manager** and clicking on the **Web Server Extensions** node on a selected server name. Figure 6.21 is similar to a default view of the Web Service Extensions window.

Figure 6.21 Web Service Extensions View

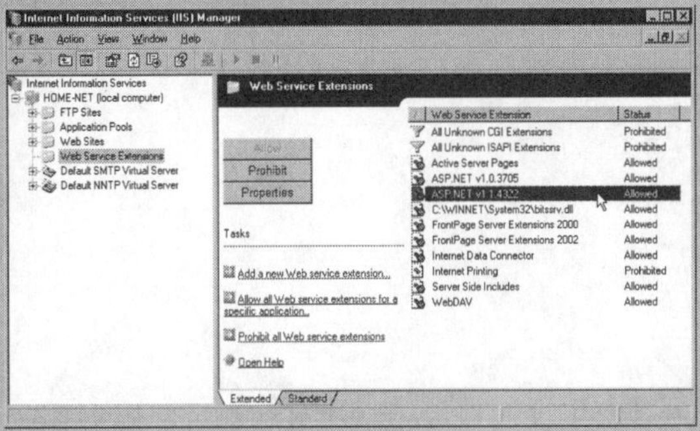

Installation best practices will ensure the optimum scalability and performance of IIS 6.0. Here are some of the important steps to ensure maximum security with IIS:

- The file system onto which you install IIS should be NTFS. If the partition is not already formatted as NTFS, upgrade the FAT32 file system to NTFS prior to installation or during the upgrade process.
- The Configure Your Server Wizard will let you install multiple application server components (DNS, file server, and so forth). Therefore, you can install other components parallel to IIS 6.0 setup.
- Use **unattended setup** to install IIS on multiple machines. (This mechanism will use a script file to install IIS. We do not need to run the installation wizard manually.)
- Make sure the Internet Connection Firewall (ICF) is enabled and configured properly unless you will be relying on a separate firewall product. Let's spend some more time on this new topic in Windows Server 2003.

Internet Connection Firewall

Windows Server 2003 comes with a very basic internal software firewall called the Internet Connection Firewall (ICF). This facility is disabled by default. If you enable it, the firewall can be configured to enable or disable protocol access through IIS. (The protocols in question that relate to IIS are HTTP, HTTPS, FTP, and SMTP.) IIS 6.0 will *not* function correctly if the ICF is *enabled* and the relevant protocols are *disabled* (for example, the IIS 6.0 Web server will not function if the HTTP and HTTPS protocols are disabled). You basically have two options when it comes to the ICF:

- Disable the firewall and use an existing firewall mechanism.
- Enable the firewall and filter the correct protocols.

Designing & Planning...

Firewall Protection for Web Servers

Microsoft recommends that you use the ICF for small to medium-sized Web project developments if you do not have a more sophisticated firewall solution (such as Internet Security and Acceleration Server) deployed. ICF is adequate to protect Internet traffic on most Web sites. However, large organizations should consider ISA or another heavy-duty firewall product. You do not need to enable the ICF if you have a corporate firewall to protect your Web servers.

It is common to place Web servers that are to be accessed from the Internet in a demilitarized zone (DMZ) or perimeter network (also called a screened subnet). This can be done in one of several ways. You can configure a tri-homed DMZ in which you have a firewall server (such as ISA) with three interfaces (an internal network interface to the LAN, a public interface with a public IP address, and a DMZ interface with a public address). Alternatively, you can configure a back-to-back DMZ, where you have both an external and internal firewall server.

The most cost-effective method is to use the second option and maximize Windows Server 2003's built-in functionality. Exercise 6.08 shows you how to configure the protocols.

Exercise 6.08

Configure Protocols in Internet Connection Firewall

1. Open **Start | Control Panel | Network Connections | Local Area Connection.**
2. Navigate to the **Advanced** tab and select the **Protect my computer and network by limiting or preventing access to this computer** option from the internet check box (see Figure 6.22).

Figure 6.22 Enabling the Internet Connection Firewall

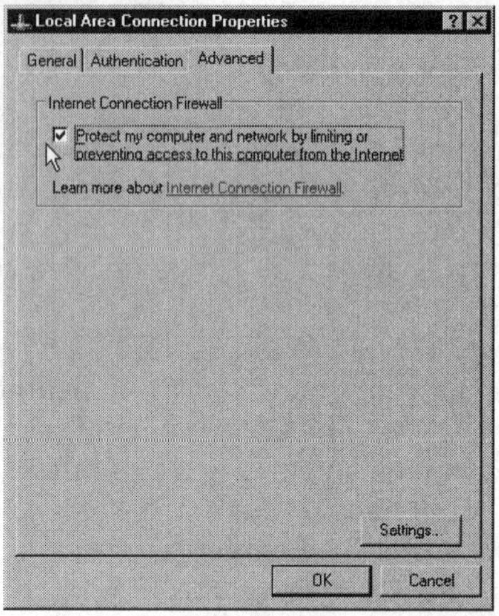

3. Click the **Settings** button and navigate to the **Services** tab. This will bring up a window to select or deselect the access protocols to your server. This is the list of protocols the IIS server will understand to process user requests. Select the correct check box next to the protocol name to enable requests using the particular protocol. You can disable the protocol access by clearing the check box. Your screen should be similar to Figure 6.23.

Figure 6.23 Available Protocol Configuration Window

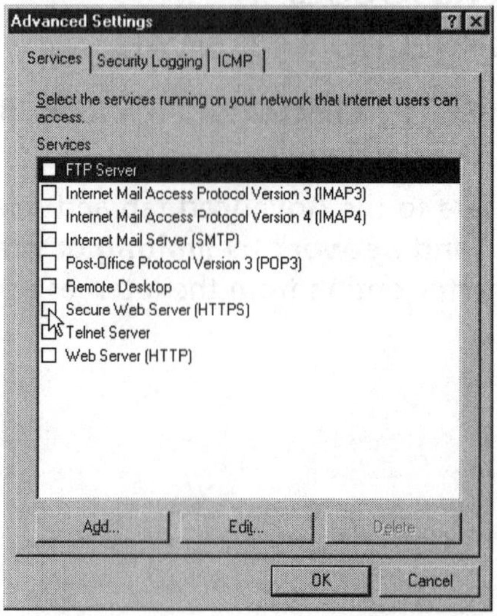

4. Select the appropriate protocols for your organization. Most organizations will enable HTTP, HTTPS, SMTP, and FTP access through the firewall. Each time you select a protocol, a small window will appear, prompting you to enter the machine name or IP address of the server that hosts the service. Figure 6.24 shows the entry to enable HTTPS access to a machine called home-net.

Figure 6.24 Entering Machine Name or IP Address to Configure the Firewall

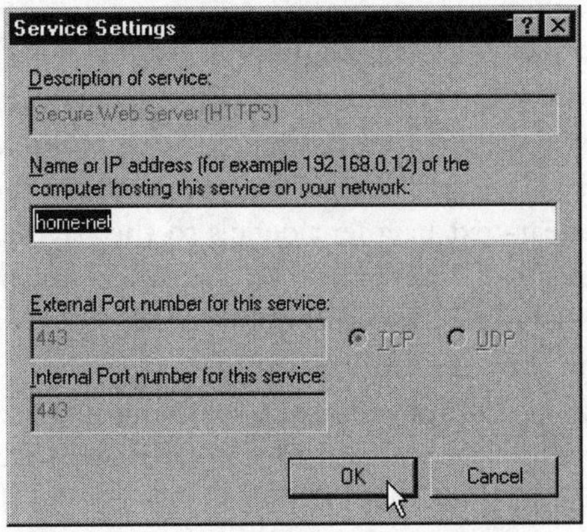

5. Click **OK** and repeat the process for all other protocols.

When you complete these steps, you have enabled the correct access to your organization through the ICF.

Risks to IIS Servers and How to Harden IIS Against Them

We have discussed the IIS installation risks and their remedies in the pervious section. Let's now discuss some security risks to the IIS servers. We will concentrate on an operational IIS Web server and its challenges. We will use a fictitious AllWebRequest online shopping site as an example to illustrate the scenarios.

The AllWebRequest online shopping site sells bicycles and bicycle accessories. This Web site is hosted on a Windows Server 2003 IIS 6.0 implementation. The scripting is done using ASP.NET pages that are written in C# language. The users will use a third-party e-commerce gateway for checkout facilities. We have used basic authentication as our preferred authentication method to implement the e-commerce shopping site.

The first risk is the non-HTTP requests that are directed to the IIS server. We need to disable all non-HTTP and HTTPS data. We do not need to open any ports other than port 80 and 443 for this public Web site. (Intruders can penetrate the system if other ports are open. For example, intruders can mimic sales orders or purchase orders if we open port 21, which is used for e-mail access. If an intruder writes an e-mail from port 21, it can be forwarded to the third-party e-commerce gateway to transfer funds to bogus accounts. The third-party e-commerce gateway will authorize the transaction since it arrived from our servers. The remedy for this is to enable The ICF or use the corporate firewall to filter all non-HTTP and non-HTTPS data to the server.)

The next risk to the AllWebRequest IIS server is the authentication mechanism. The Web site is hosted internally within the enterprise. However, the payment e-commerce gateway is an external entity. Therefore, there are two risks here. The online user will use clear text to transfer credentials to the IIS server. The IIS server will also transmit clear-text payment details to the payment gateway. Both of these transactions are risks to the enterprise. An intruder can intercept either of these transmissions with the help of packet-snooping software. Therefore, we need to encrypt both these communication lines with SSL.

We should also be careful of the file structure of the AllWebRequest online shopping site. The third-party e-commerce gateway broker will be an executable or a DLL. Therefore, we need to assign *execute* permission at the Web site level to proceed to the payment gateway. We need to assign execute permission to the entire root directory if we mount this DLL or .EXE on the root directory. This is not a recommended practice. The complete root directory will have execute access, which is not a healthy scenario for the IIS server. We should minimize write and execute access as much as possible on IIS servers. The best way to get around this problem is to copy the DLL or exe to a new directory and only assign execute access to that new directory (and leave the root directory with read access).

We also need to factor the ASP.NET scripting manipulations (ASP.NET code can be scripted in a malicious way to harm the IIS 6.0 servers). This is another risk to the enterprise. We should not use any HTTP GET methods to post data to the server in our client-side scripting. This will display the form tag information on the URL box of the browser. A clever intruder can piece together some malicious request by observing these requests. Therefore, we should use the HTTP POST form method to direct HTTP requests to the IIS server. The Intruders can also pass in JavaScript <script> code </script> tags in the URL string. This is picked up by the URLScan algorithm in IIS 6.0. We should also be careful of the SQL injection issues with IIS. This is similar to the previous JavaScript mechanism. The key difference is that the code fragments are SQL database commands. These commands are generated by the hackers by observing HTTP GET entries to the Web site. (HTTP GET posts are appended to the URL query string and are displayed to the user. The user can change the URL query string and re-post the data to observe a different outcome of the same Web page.) Therefore, we should never display database table names in the query string. We can stop these SQL injections with URLScan and configuring the SQL database to best practices. (URLScan is can algorithm that every oncoming request is subject to in IIS 6.0. This will scan the URL query string for invalid characters and <Script> tags and filter them from the query string.) We can also minimize the query string manipulations by assigning execute permissions to a small number of directories. Some other IIS best practices are:

- **Log on with the least credentials** Do not log on as Administrator to the IIS servers. This will enable the servers to configure software with fewer credentials. Use the *RunAs* command if you want to run IIS Manager as an administrator.
- **Disable the unwanted services in IIS 6.0** Disable the FTP, NNTP, or SMTP services that are not used on the server. This will save valuable resources to be dedicated to the WWW service.
- **Keep virus scanners up to date** A virus scanner compares its virus signature database with file system folders. This signature database needs to be updated regularly, since new viruses are introduced frequently. Therefore, we need to make sure these signature databases are up to date to protect our IIS and Web site files from viruses.
- **Keep all software patches up to date** Windows Server 2003 comes with Auto Update version 1.0. This will inform server administrators when new patches become available.

Now let's investigate how to secure other IIS 6.0 components; specifically, FTP, NNTP, and FTP.

Securing FTP

The File Transfer Protocol (FTP) is a valuable component of IIS 6.0. FTP is used to "swap" or "share" files between servers and clients. This could be dangerous practice for businesses with sensitive information. Most large organization firewalls will block FTP access. (It is unhealthy for the organization; for example, a disgruntled employee could FTP out sensitive data to its competitors.)

We can create individual accounts for each FTP user using IIS Manager. We also need to provide a username and password to initiate the FTP transfer. These credentials are passed as clear text from the client to the FTP server, which is not secure for the enterprise. An intruder can "sniff" these packets and obtain the credentials. The intruder can use these credentials to download sensitive information or upload malicious content to the server.

Therefore, how do we secure FTP communication? We need to implement FTP communication over a secure channel like VPN. VPNs use the Point-to-Point

Tunneling Protocol (PPTP) or Secure Internet Protocol (IPSec) to encrypt data and facilitate secure FTP communication. We can also use SSL encryption on WebDAV supported directories for the same purpose.

Securing NNTP

The Network News Transfer Protocol (NNTP) is another important component of IIS 6.0. The default settings will enable any user to connect to the newsgroups without any authentication process. The users can request to view all newsgroups and subsequently subscribe to them anonymously. In some cases, we need to restrict access to the newsgroups to protect sensitive information. We can increase security on our NNTP implementation by:

- **Enabling basic authentication or integrated Windows authentication on the NNTP Service** We need to create user accounts and add them to appropriate groups initially. Then we need to grant access to the correct News folder directories to enable authentication. We need to be careful regarding the local service account that NNTP uses. This account needs to be granted access to the complete NNTP directories to manage the NNTP implementation correctly.
- **Restricting NNTP access by IP address** All IP addresses have access to NNTP by default. We can configure NNTP to grant or deny according to a specific IP address in IIS 6.0. We can also use wildcard characters to specify a subnet mask to deny or grant access. We can use domain names also. However, domain name wildcards will need to do an additional Domain Name Service (DNS) lookup. Therefore, it will be slower than the previous method.
- **Restricting the number of NNTP operators** Operators are the administrators of the NNTP service. Windows Server 2003 enables all the users in the Administrator group as NNTP operators. We need to configure this setting to prevent all Administrator group access. We should only let a small number of operators manage the NNTP service.
- **Using SSL to encrypt the communication** We can also use SSL at the server and the client. The SSL certificate needs to be installed at the server. The client newsgroup reader (for example, Outlook Express) should support SSL communication to facilitate this.

Securing SMTP

The Simple Mail Transfer Protocol (SMTP) service is responsible for e-mail communication between IIS 6.0 and its clients. Most e-commerce sites use the SMTP service to send and receive purchase orders. Therefore, we need to protect our SMTP service from malicious attacks. Here are some ways to secure the SMTP service in IIS 6.0:

- **Minimize the number of operators that can manage the SMTP service** This is similar to NNTP service operators. We need to enable a small team or a designated Windows account group to manage the SMTP operator access.
- **Use Transport Layer Security (TLS)** We can configure SMTP to use TLS on all incoming mail connections. TLS is similar to SSL. It will secure the connection between the SMTP server and the mail client. However, it will not authenticate users to the SMTP services. We need to generate key pairs at the SMTP servers to implement TLS and share them with the incoming mail clients.
- **Restrict IP and network access** This is similar to NNTP service IP restrictions. We can grant or deny access on an IP address or a subnet mask.
- **Set basic authentication or Windows integrated authentication on outbound messages** This is also similar to the NNTP implementation.

The preceding are some ways to secure all IIS 6.0 components. Let's now investigate the new security features in IIS 6.0.

New Security Features in IIS 6.0

IIS 5.0 and earlier versions were constantly patched by hotfixes from Microsoft. IIS was once considered one of the main security holes in the Windows architecture. This was a major deterrent to using IIS as a commercial Web server. IIS 6.0 comes with an impressive list of new security features designed to win back commercial users. You will learn about these new features in the next sections.

Advanced Digest Authentication

Advanced digest authentication is an extension of *Digest Security*. Digest Security uses MD5 hashing to encrypt user credentials.(username, password, and user roles). So, what's the purpose of MD5 hashing? *Basic authentication* sends the username and password details over the network medium in base-64 encoded format. These details can be easily "sniffed" (captured with a protocol analyzer) and decoded by an intruder, who could then use the credentials for nefarious purposes. The MD5 hash enhances security by applying more sophisticated, more difficult to crack cipher algorithms to deter these intruders. An MD5 hash is made up of binary data consisting of the username, password, and *realm*. The realm is the name of the domain that authenticates the user. All of this means that Digest Security is more secure than basic authentication.

EXAM WARNING

An MD5 hash is embedded into an HTTP 1.1 header. This is only supported by HTTP 1.1-enabled browsers. Digest or advanced digest authentication mechanisms cannot be enabled if the target browsers do not support HTTP 1.1. Internet Explorer 5.0 and later support HTTP 1.1, as well as recent versions of Netscape, Opera, Mozilla, and other popular browsers.

Advanced Digest Security takes the digest authentication model a bit further by storing the user credentials on a DC as an MD5 hash. The Active Directory database on the DC is used to store the user credentials. Thus, intruders would need to get access to the Active Directory to steal the credentials. This adds another layer of security to protect access to Windows Server 2003 Web sites, and you do not need to modify the application code to accommodate this security feature.

TEST DAY TIP

Both digest and advanced digest authentication only work on Web Distributed Authoring and Versioning (WebDAV) enabled directories. WebDAV is a file sharing protocol that is commonly used in Windows Internet-related applications. WebDAV was previously referred to as Web Folders. It is a *secure* file transfer protocol over intranets and the Internet. You can download, upload, and manage files on remote computers across the Internet and intranets using WebDAV. WebDAV is similar to FTP. WebDAV always uses password security and data encryption on file transfers (FTP does not support these tasks).

Server-Gated Cryptography

Communication between an IIS Web server and the Web client is done using the HyperText Transfer Protocol (HTTP). These HTTP network transmissions can be easily compromised due to their text-based messaging formats. Therefore, we need to encrypt these HTTP calls between the client and the server. Secure Sockets Layer (SSL) and Transport Layer Security (TLS) are the most common encryption mechanism used on Web sites. SSL/TLS enables secure communication by encrypting the communication channel with a cipher algorithm. TLS is the later version of the SSL protocol.

IIS 5.0 and earlier versions included SSL/TLS for secure communication between the Web client and the server. Server Gated Cryptography (SGC) is an extension of SSL/ TLS. It uses a strong 128-bit encryption mechanism to encode the data. SGC does not require an application to run on a client's machine. It was available since IIS 4.0. SCG needs a valid certificate at the client Web browser, which can be encoded and decoded. A special SGC certificate is needed to enable SGC support built in to IIS 6.0. We can obtain a certificate by contacting a CA. This certificate can be added to IIS as any other certificate. IIS 6.0 supports both 40-bit and 128-bit encryption sessions. This means your old 40-bit SGC certificates are still valid in IIS 6.0. SGC is commonly used for financial sector applications (banking and financial institutions) to protect data.

TEST DAY TIP

Forty-bit SGC certificates in IIS 6.0: If you try to open an existing 40-bit SGC certificate, you might get a "The certificate has failed to verify for all of its intended purposes" warning. These certificates are targeted to Windows 2000 servers. Thus, you can have a valid certificate and can be misled by this warning. Windows 2000 only supports 40-bit encryption, and Windows Server 2003 supports both 40-bit and 128-bit encryption.

Selectable Cryptographic Service Provider

SSL/TLS offer a secure environment in which to exchange data. The downside is performance. SSL/TLS are very CPU intensive. IIS 6.0 comes with a new feature called the *Selectable Cryptographic Service Provider* (CSP) that lets the user select from an optimized list of cryptography providers. A cryptographic provider will provide you with an interface to encrypt communication between the server and the client. CSP is not specific to IIS and can be used to handle cryptography and certificate management. Microsoft implements two default security providers: the Microsoft DH SChannel Cryptographic provider and the Microsoft RSA SChannel Cryptographic provider. The Microsoft implementations are optimized to IIS 6.0 for faster communications. The private keys for these Microsoft implementations are stored in the Registry. The Microsoft Cryptographic API (Crypto API) for every provider contains identical interfaces for all providers. This will enable developers to switch between providers without modifying the code. Each provider will create a public and a private key to enable data communication. The private key is stored on hardware devices (such as PCI cards, smart cards, and so forth) or in the Registry. The other CSP keys can also be stored in the Registry. It makes more sense to store private keys as Registry settings for computer access to the server. The private key will be stored on smart cards and other portable devices if we have a mobile distribution environment. (This is similar to Plug and Play support for devices in Windows 2000 and Windows Server 2003 environments.) The CSP can be configured using the **Welcome to the Web Server Certificate Wizard** (click **Properties** of a Web site, select the **Directory Security** tab, and then click the **Server Certificate** button).

Configurable Worker Process Identity

One of the most serious problems with previous IIS versions was the instability of the World Wide Web Publishing Service (WWW). The failure of this service could result in the shutdown of the machine. IIS 6.0 runs each Web site in an isolated process environment. This isolated process environment is called a *worker process*. Therefore, a Web site malfunction could be limited to its process environment (and hence will not lead to a Web server shutdown). IIS 5.0 did not implement a worker process model. IIS 6.0 can also run an IIS 5.0 isolated environment. The IIS system administrator can choose between the worker process model or the IIS 5.0 isolation model by selecting the correct option from **Services** tab by right-clicking on **Web Sites**. You can click the **Run WWW service in IIS 5.0 isolation mode** option box to run IIS in IIS 5.0 isolation mode. IIS will run on the worker process model if you do not check the box. IIS can run only at one mode at a time. Therefore, we will not be able to run worker process model Web sites and IIS 5.0 isolation mode Web sites simultaneously.

The worker process can be run with a lower level of permission than the system account. The worker process will shut down the application if the IIS server is targeted with malicious code. IIS 6.0 can detect malicious code by observing the rapid fail-over mechanism. This process will be explained later in the chapter. The rapid fail-over program will restart IIS 6.0 when the system has generated a specified number of errors in a specified amount of time. IIS 6.0 (which is by default run by the local system account) is not affected since the worker process can be configured to run under a less privileged account.

Default Locked Down Status

The default installation of IIS 6.0 will result in a "lightweight" Web server. The only default feature available will be the access to static content. This is to deter any malicious access by intruders. This *restricted* functionality is referred as **Default Locked down** status. This feature will force the system administrators to manually enable and disable the features that are necessary for the applications. They can do this through the Web Services Extensions node of the IIS Manager.

New Authorization Framework

Authorization refers to the concept of confirming a user's access for a given resource. (Authentication refers to obtaining access to the resource. When a user is authenticated, we need to make sure whether he or she is authorized to perform any tasks on the resource. This is the basis of authorization.) There are two types of ASP.NET authorization options available for IIS 6.0:

- **File authorization** The *FileAuthorizationModule* class is responsible for file authorization on Windows Server 2003 systems. The module is activated by enabling Windows authentication on a Web site. This module does access control list (ACL) checks on the authorization access on an ASP.NET file for a given user (it could be either ".asmx" file for ASP.NET application, or a ".asmx" file for a Web service) . The file is available for the user if the ACL confirms the user access to the file.
- **URL authorization** The *URLAuthorizationModule* class is responsible for URL authorization on Windows Server 2003. This mechanism uses the URL namespace to store user details and access roles. The URL authorization is available to use at any time. The authorization information is stored in a text file on a directory. The text file will have an <authorization> tag to allow or deny access to the directory (this will apply to the subdirectories if not specified). Here is a sample authorization file:

```
<authorization>
     <allow users="Chris"/>
     <allow roles="Admins"/>
     <deny users="Gayan"/>
     <deny users="?"/>
</authorization>
```

This file will enable *Chris* to access its content. It will also allow anyone with an *Admins* user role. The user *Gayan* is denied access. Anyone else will not be able to gain access to this directory (indicated by the "?" wild card).

EXAM 70-298 OBJECTIVE 3.4.2

Designing a Monitoring Strategy for IIS

We have learned to implement security measures to protect IIS 6.0 from intruders. These security measures need to be monitored frequently to detect any compromise of these mechanisms. Therefore, we should also spend some time designing a monitoring strategy for IIS 6.0

There are several ways of monitoring IIS 6.0 security measures. All Windows Server 2003 service calls can be monitored through the event logs. We can also use the Network monitor for this purpose. We should also enable logging on all of the IIS activities. This will enable us to backtrack to the original intrusion using the chronological entries. All these measures should be implemented as baseline requirements to facilitate all IIS 6.0 servers in the enterprise. Let's discuss how to implement a monitoring baseline now. We will first detail all the baseline requirements and then discuss how they help to identify the intruders in the section *Identifying a Security Incident*.

EXAM 70-298 OBJECTIVE 3.4.3

Creating a Monitoring Baseline

Implementing a monitoring baseline is an important element of enterprise architecture. This will set security standards for the organization and act as the minimum security requirements for the enterprise. We can do the following to create a monitoring baseline. All these tools are available in Windows Server 2003 or native in IIS 6.0. We will discuss each item in detail in subsequent sections.

- Configure IIS logs
- Enable Security Auditing
- Monitor Event log activities
- Enable Heath Detection
- Monitor Network Monitor and System Monitor activities

Configure IIS Logs

We can enable logging on Web sites and FTP sites. This will record user and server activity. These log files will enable system administrators to regulate access to content, evaluate the popularity of different Web sites, plan security requirements, and troubleshoot potential security breaches. We can use several log formats to record data. IIS logging can be enabled or disabled with IIS Manager on demand. Although logs can be read by a text editor, there are specialized third-party software tools to analyze these logs. We can also use Object Database Connectivity (ODBC) connections to log the IIS entries to SQL server databases.

TEST DAY TIP

IIS 5.0 logs record the encrypted requests when we log SSL connections. IIS 6.0 logs the decrypted amount of bytes (which reflect the actual request size, not the SSL encryption additions). IIS 5.0 only logs entries in ASCII format, while IIS 6.0 logs entries in both ASCII and UTF-8. The time taken for the Web request is measured by HTTP.Sys. It will activate the time mechanism when the first byte of the request arrives. It will calculate the time span when the last byte is sent to the client.

We can record logs in many formats: W3C log file, IIS log file, and NSCA log file. W3C log file format is an ASCII format that can be customized. The other log file formats are not customizable. Here is a sample W3C log file entry:

```
#Software: Internet Information Services 6.0
#Version: 1.0
#Date: 2003-12-26 17:42:15
```

```
#Fields: time c-ip cs-method cs-uri-stem sc-status cs-version
17:42:15 172.11.255.255 GET /test.htm 200 HTTP/1.0
```

The first three lines define the IIS server settings and time stamp. The fourth line describes the log file captions (the description of the fields that we are logging information on). The last line is the actual log entry. The log entry was made at 17.42.15 from the machine 172.11.255.255. The client sends a GET HTTP request to the server to the *test.htm* page. This call is successful and returns a 200 response (200 means success). The communication was done using HTTP 1.0. Now let's learn how to enable logging in IIS 6.0 and customize log fields.

Exercise 6.09

Configure IIS Logging

1. Open IIS Manager (**Start | Administrative Tools | IIS Manager**).
2. Navigate to the Web site or the FTP site. Select **Web Sites** and then **Default Web site** for this demonstration.
3. Right-click on the **Default Web site** and select **Properties**.
4. Select the **Web Site** tab. Click the **Enable logging** option box. Your screen should be similar to Figure 6.25.

Figure 6.25 Enable Logging for Default Web Site

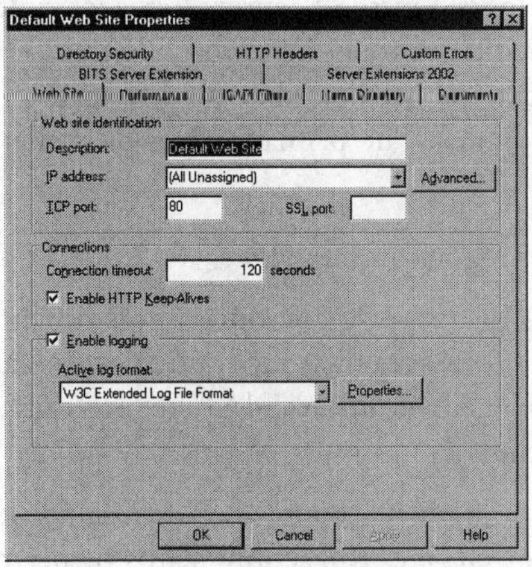

5. Click the **Properties** button to customize log entries. The **Logging Properties** window will appear. The **General** tab will enable you to modify the log filename and the frequency that the log is written (for example, hourly, daily, monthly, and so forth).

6. Click the **Advanced** tab and you can select the fields you want to log in the IIS logs. It is good practice to log the date, time, server IP, host, URI query, username, and client IP address as minimum requirements to investigate security breaches. Your screen should be similar to Figure 6.26. Click **OK** when finished customizing the log fields.

Figure 6.26 Customizing Log Fields

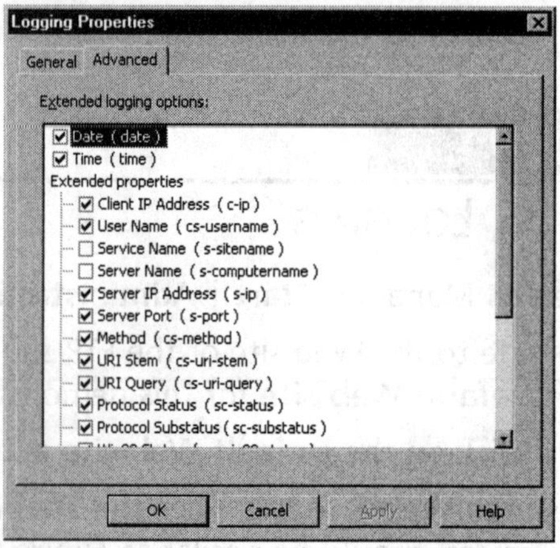

Enable Security Auditing

Security events are logged in the Security log, accessible by administrators via the Event Viewer. An audit entry can be either a *Success* or a *Failure* event in the Security log. A list of audit entries that describes the life span of an object, file, or a folder is referred to as an *audit trail*. The primary types of events that you can choose to audit include:

- Computer logons and logoffs.
- System events (when a computer shuts down or reboots, or something happens that affects system security, such as the audit log being cleared, system time is changed, or an invalid procedure call port is used to try to impersonate a client).
- User and computer account management tasks (such as the creation of accounts or changes to account status or permissions).
- Access to files, folders, and objects.

Configuring security auditing will help you track potential security issues and provide evidence in relation to security breaches. It is best practice to create an audit plan before you enable auditing on your system. The audit plan will detail the purpose and objectives of the audit. The audit plan should contain the following:

- The type of information you want to audit
- How much time you have to review audit logs
- The resources you have for collecting and storing audit logs (disk space, memory, and processor usage)
- The intended scope of the audit

You'll need to ask yourself some questions as you prepare the audit plan. Is the purpose of the audit plan to prevent security breaches from unauthorized sources? If so, you need to enable the audit failure events on logons and collect information on it. Is the objective of the auditing to get a snapshot of the organization's activities for forensic purposes? In that case, you need to enable both success and failure events to collect data on all applications.

It is important to remember that the audit trail information can result in a very large amount of data if both the success and failure audits are enabled. Too wide a scope for the audit can also make it difficult for you to find the information you're looking for within a huge file that records thousands of events.

Head of the Class...

Periodically Back Up Audit Information

The administrative account or administrative privileges are a prime target for hackers so there is always the possibility of intruders gaining administrator access to your system. With these privileges, an intruder can do malicious damage to your system and delete the audit events from the event log. If this happens, there will not be an audit trail to determine the cause and the damage to the system. To minimize the damage that would be caused by such an attack, you need to duplicate the audit information periodically. You can use the Microsoft Operations Manager (MOM) to copy audit events periodically and store them in a secure network drive; this provides a backup of the audit trail information.

MOM is a monitoring and management tool released by Microsoft in 2000 and used for a variety of enterprise-level management tasks. You can download a trial version from Microsoft's Web site at www.microsoft.com/MOM/default.asp.

The Audit Account Logon Events and Audit Logon Events items are enabled for auditing by default in Windows Server 2003. By default, object access auditing is not enabled. You can view the security audit entries under the **Security** section of the **Event Viewer**.

Let's learn how to define an audit policy on a local computer. The local audit policy dictates the audit procedures on the local machine. It does not dictate the audit policy for the rest of the network computers. Exercise 6.09 walks you through the steps required to enable the auditing policy on the local computer. You need to have administrator access to perform any of the auditing policy changes.

Exercise 6.09

Enabling Audit Policy on a Local Machine

1. Click **Start | Programs | Administrative Tools | Local Security Policy.**
2. In the left pane of the console, expand **Local Policies** and click **Audit Policy**. Your screen should look similar to Figure 6.27.

Figure 6.27 Local Audit Policy Settings

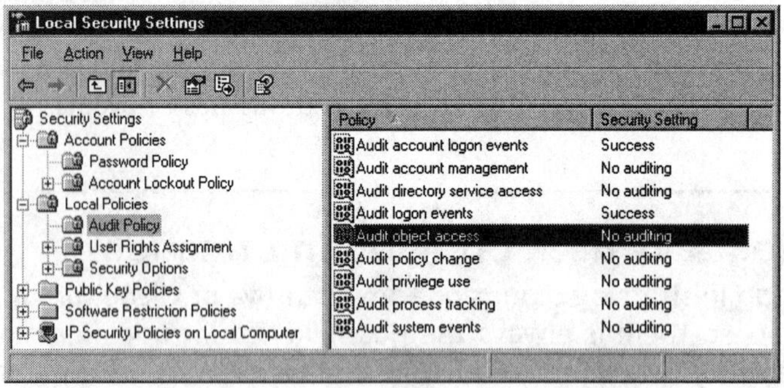

3. In the right details pane, select and double-click the option for which you want to define audit policy. For this exercise, select the **Audit object access** option. You see a dialog box similar to Figure 6.28. Here you can choose to enable success and/or failure audits by checking the option box(es).

Figure 6.28 Enable Success or Failure Audit Options

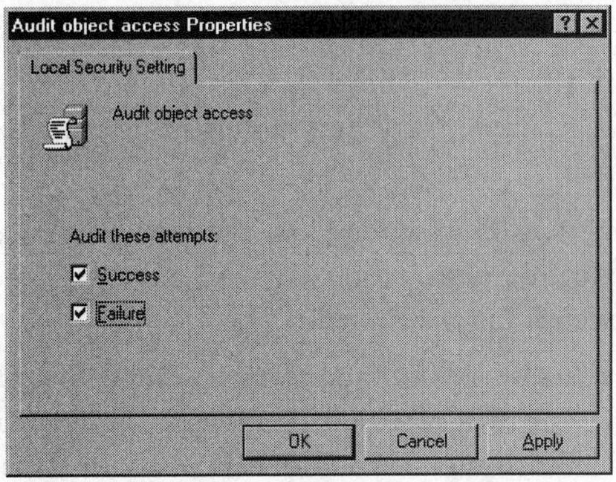

4. Click **OK** or the **Apply** button. Now we can enable auditing on objects, files, and folders on the local computers.

Monitor Event Log Activities

The Event Viewer is used to monitor many different aspects of server activity. To access this tool, click **Start | Programs | Administrative Tools | Event Viewer**. The Event Viewer is displayed as an MMC that is stored at SystemRoot\System32\eventvwr.mmc. The Everyone user group has read and execute access to manipulate the Event Viewer. The Administrator group and the System account have *full control* (full control consists of read, write, modify, and execute permissions).

Event log data is displayed in the Event Viewer. There are at least three different event log files: the Application, Security, and System logs. Your Event Viewer can display additional logs, depending on applications and services you have installed on the server. For example, if the computer is configured as a DNS server, it will have a DNS log in addition to the three default logs. There are five major event types. The *error, warning*, and *information* types occur in the Application and System logs. The *Success Audit* or *Failure Audit* types occur in the Security log. Following are descriptions of each event type and its function:

- **Error** Indicates a significant problem in the system. This can have adverse effects on the application or operating system if ignored (for example, the DHCP service not starting at reboot can lead to the lack of IP assignment for the network computers).
- **Warning** Indicates the possibility of future errors to come, but conditions do not pose an immediate threat to the system (for example, e.g., *low disk*

space is a warning that can lead to various errors if ignored, but does not indicate an immediate threat).

- **Information** Describes a successful operation of the system or an application (for example, SQL Server logs an information event when the SQL server starts up correctly).
- **Success Audit** All audited security events that are completed successfully will be logged in this category, (for example, a successful user logon when security auditing is enabled).
- **Failure Audit** All audited security events that fail will be logged here (for example, you will receive an authorization error if you try to log on to a shared drive to which you don't have access. This will result in a failure audit entry in the Security event log).

The event log service is automatically started when the Windows Server 2003 system starts. There are three default log files available in Windows Server 2003. These same logs were also available in Windows NT, 2000, and XP. The default logs are:

- **Application log** This log is available for application developers and system administrators. The developers can monitor their application activities in this log. The system administrator can trace and monitor the applications and how they interact with each other using this utility. It can be used to record application errors, warnings, and information events. Scripting languages (such as C#, C++, VB 6.0, and so forth) include Application Programming Interface (API) calls to log entries in the Application log. This log can be used to display a myriad of application errors (for example, the application can record a "Source file not found" error when files needed to complete a transaction are missing).
- **Security log** Events that affect system security are logged in this event log. These events include failed or successful logon attempts, creating, opening or deleting files, changing properties or permissions on user accounts and groups, and so forth. We will be using this log to monitor IIS security closely.
- **System log** Events related to Windows system components are stored in this log file. This includes entries regarding failure of drivers and other system components during startup and shutdown.

Enable Health Detection

Health detection simplifies IIS Web site management. Health detection is performed by IIS over all its worker processes. This adds another level of reliability to the Web applications. The inetinfo.exe process (IIS) will check the availability of each worker process (different Web sites) periodically. This time limit can be configured by IIS Manager (240 seconds by default). Therefore, IIS will maintain a "heart beat" between its worker processes. (Heart beat is similar to the *ping* facility. The IIS server will try to communicate with worker processes to make sure they are alive.)

Health detection enables IIS to monitor its worker process functionality. We can enable pinging and configure rapid application fail-over (discussed later in the chapter). You can also set the startup and shutdown time for a worker process using the option.

EXERCISE 6.10

ENABLE HEALTH DETECTION

You can enable health detection by following this process. This process only works if you're running in worker process isolation mode.

1. Start IIS Manager (**Start | Administrative Tools | IIS Manager**).
2. Select **Application Pools.**
3. Navigate to the correct Web site.
4. Right-click on the site and click **Properties**.
5. Select the **Health** tab and enter your proffered settings. Your screen should be similar to Figure 6.29.

Figure 6.29 Enable Health Detection

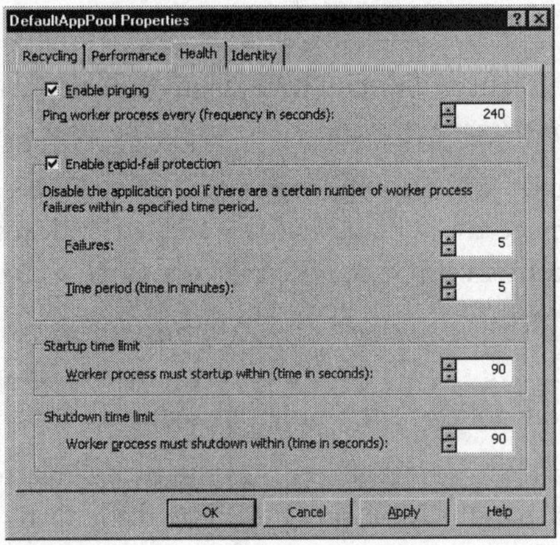

7. You can configure the *ping* interval using the *Enable Pinging* group box. This interval describes the timeframe to contact a worker process to make sure it functions accordingly. The default

setting is 240 seconds. *(Rapid-fail protection* is initiated by IIS when too many application pool errors are generated for specified timeframe. The default is five errors occurring in five minutes. This scenario will trigger the IIS to restart and issue a *503 error* to the client.) You can also configure the worker process a startup time (if the worker process restarts) and a shutdown time (if the worker process gets into a deadlock position) using this screen.

8. Click **OK** or the **Apply** button to apply the changes.

We can also use the Network Monitor and System Monitor to analyze abnormal activity in your network and system, respectively. Let's discuss how we identify these security breaches.

Identifying a Security Incident

Most intruders will not have a valid username or a password to hack in to the enterprise systems. They will use sophisticated *random password generators* to find the correct password. (The username may be compromised earlier. Most enterprises will have a policy that will force employees to change their passwords monthly. Therefore, obtaining the password is harder than obtaining the username.) IIS 6.0 authentication can be configured to stop any user if he or she is not able to provide the correct password in three attempts. If the user is unsuccessful after three attempts, the logon details will be written to the Security log. Therefore, we can use the following mechanisms to identify the security breach:

- Analyze Security log and investigate the user access. We can investigate the user's abnormal activities and disable the user account.
- The entries will also be logged at IIS logs. We can analyze the IIS logs and obtain more user details and the client IP address data. Then, we can restrict access to them using our *Restrict user on IP address* mechanisms.
- We can also use the Security Auditing information as evidence against the intrusion. We should have a security trail of all objects since we changed the local audit policy in the previous section.
- Some of these security breaches might be able to corrupt the worker process and stop the Web site. It will be difficult to pinpoint the exact server that is affected by this in a large Web farm. We can use health detection in IIS 6.0 to recover from this scenario. It will be able to inform the IIS administrators very quickly since there is a *heart beat* between all the servers.

- Most of these intrusions are carried out during nonbusiness hours. Therefore, we can use Network Monitor to analyze network traffic and suspicious client IP activities during these hours.
- Most organizations will build a custom authentication DLL to facilitate application access. This DLL can integrate into System Monitor to analyze the authentication calls and network traffic that is generated by the incoming clients. We can measure the activity with the help of performance counters and analyze the results.

EXAM 70-298 OBJECTIVE 3.4.4

Design a Content Management Strategy for Updating an IIS Server

Content is the greatest driver for a successful Web site. The Web site content needs to update very frequently in the current Web sites. Most Web sites are operated as Web farms. (A Web farm is a collection of multiple IIS servers that are load balanced to facilitate higher throughput of Web requests simultaneously.) Therefore, we need to deploy content to these multiple IIS servers quickly and efficiently. We also need to manage the content and its deployment (for example, roll back or schedule content deployment on a specific timeframe).

There are several tools available to deploy content to Web farms. Microsoft Content Management Server (CMS) is a dedicated server that manages Web content. We can specify the source content directories and destination directories in a GUI interface. CMS will manage the deployment or the rollback of the content. We will also have a GUI interface to view the logging details of the job. Microsoft Site Server 4.0 also came with a content management project. This is also similar to CMS functionality. There are also several third-party content management tools (for example, Vignette) available that will plug in to IIS 6.0. Sharepoint Portal Server can also be configured to take a role as content management server if necessary.

We can also use the "virtual directory" concept to centralize important information and minimize deployment. We will be able to "point" all the Web farm machines to a single machine to avoid content deployment to all servers. This method will consume valuable network resources since all the servers need to obtain data form this single point. We might also need to provide for a backup server if this single content point goes offline.

Summary of Exam Objectives

IIS 6.0 implements a worker process model to handle Web requests. This is different from the IIS 5.0 isolation model. Each worker process is handled by an instance of W3wp.exe and uses an application pool. The application pool will manage the resources of the Web site. HTTP.Sys is the new kernel mode driver to consume the incoming Web requests.

Certificate authentication is supported by the IIS 6.0 SSL implementation. The certificate details need to be verified against a Windows account. This verification process is referred to as "mapping." There are three mapping mechanisms available in IIS 6.0: Directory Service, one-to-one, and many-to-one. The *Directory Service* is a native Active Directory mapping that supports internal authentication for a large enterprise. The *one-to-one* mapping will match the exact certificate details from the client browser to the server certificate. They need to match precisely to authenticate. This will only suit a small set of users. The *many-to-one* implementation is more flexible. We match partial criteria using custom rules in *many-to-many*. This implementation is more popular than the previous two.

There are several Windows logon authentication mechanisms supported by IIS 6.0: anonymous authentication, basic authentication, digest authentication, and Windows integrated authentication. The default is Windows integrated authentication. Anonymous authentication will impersonate each user with an IUSR_ComputerName account to direct Web requests to IIS 6.0. Basic authentication needs to be wrapped in SSL since it transmits credentials as clear text. Digest authentication will be implemented with the help of an Active Directory in the enterprise.

An enterprise implements several remote networks in the current climate. They need to support remote dial-up Internet, VPN, and wireless access to the employees and their business partners. The Remote Authentication Dial-In User Service (RADIUS) protocol defines a "single sign- on" mechanism to authenticate users to the enterprise. The RADIUS implementation in Windows Server 2003 is refereed to as Internet Authentication Service (IAS). IAS can act either as a proxy or an authentication server to facilitate the enterprise remote access needs.

Designing security for IIS servers can be a complex and tedious task due to the flexibility of the Internet, intranet, and extranet sites. Windows Server 2003 comes with Internet Connection Firewall (ICF) to facilitate small to medium-sized organizations. It also installs IIS 6.0 in a *locked-down state*. We need to enable Web Services Extensions to enhance the appropriate settings for the enterprise. We can also implement SSL, TLS, and Point-to-Point Tunneling protocols to secure FTP, NNTP, and SMTP virtual servers.

We need to design a monitoring strategy to support IIS 6.0 authentication options. We will facilitate event logs, IIS logs, security auditing, and network monitor software to achieve this. IIS logs can be configured to support all Web sites and FTP sites. We can identify security breaches by analyzing the Security event logs and IIS server logs. IIS server logs can be configured to record all the environmental variables of a Web request.

Microsoft Content Management Server (CMS) can be used to replicate content to multiple IIS servers in a Web farm. CMS will create projects to manage the deployment and provide GUI interface to troubleshoot the projects. We also need to take into account the content deployment strategy when we initiate an IIS 6.0 implementation on Windows Server 2003.

Exam Objectives Fast Track

Designing User Authentication for IIS

- ☑ HTTP.Sys is the new kernel process that accepts all incoming IIS traffic. It uses application pools to assign resources to Web sites.
- ☑ IIS 6.0 runs on a separate worker process model. This means every Web site is a separate ISAPI application memory space and is detached from IIS. This mechanism is different from the IIS 5.0 isolation model.
- ☑ We can use certificates to authenticate a user to IIS 6.0. These certificates can be mapped to Windows user accounts in many ways. They are Directory Service, one-to-one, or many-to-one mechanisms.
- ☑ The most flexible method is many-to-one certificate mapping. This has less overhead in administration and less maintenance compared to the others. It will also support large organizations and third- party certificate authorities (CAs).
- ☑ There are several authentication methods available in IIS 6.0: anonymous, basic, digest, and integrated Windows authentication.
- ☑ The IIS 6.0 default authentication method is integrated Windows authentication. This is enabled by default by the installation process.
- ☑ IIS 6.0 will impersonate the IUSR_ComputerName account to enable anonymous access. This access should only be available on the public nonsensitive Web sites of the enterprise.
- ☑ Basic authentication is supported by most browsers. This authentication is specified in the W3C HTTP specification. However, this mechanism is not the safest—it will transfer the username and the password as clear text to the IIS server.

- ☑ Digest authentication is similar to basic authentication. However, the credentials are encrypted as an MD5 hash message digest. This authentication is only available on WebDAV directories.
- ☑ Integrated Windows authentication also uses a hash algorithm to encrypt the data communication between the client and the IIS server. It also implements the Kerberos V5 protocol to assist the Windows operating system to authenticate users.
- ☑ The Remote Authentication Dial-In User Service (RADIUS) protocol defines a "single sign-on" mechanism for multiple remote connections to the enterprise (for example, VPN, Internet, and wireless access).
- ☑ RADIUS implementation in Windows Server 2003 is referred to Internet Authentication Service (IAS). The IAS acts as both a proxy server and authentication server for enterprise users.

Designing Security for IIS

- ☑ There are several risks to IIS installations. Windows 2003 delivers Internet Connection Firewall and Web Service Extensions to combat some of them.
- ☑ IIS 6.0 is installed in a locked-down stage in Windows 2003. We need to use Web Services Extensions to configure the correct settings after the installation.
- ☑ FTP username password credentials are passed as clear text. Therefore, use SSL on WebDAV or Point-to-Point Tunneling Protocol on VPN to encrypt the FTP credentials.
- ☑ There are several ways to secure Web, FTP, NNTP, and SMTP implementation of IIS 6.0. Most of them will include encryption mechanisms like SSL, Transport Layer Security (TLS), or Point-to-Point Tunneling Protocol.
- ☑ There are several new security features in IIS 6.0: advance digest authentication, server-side cryptography, selectable cryptography provider, and new authorization framework.
- ☑ There is a Heath Detection system between IIS and the separate worker processes.
- ☑ ASP.NET is the default scripting mechanism available in IIS 6.0. It will still support the old ASP applications.
- ☑ 503 errors are due to the influx of HTTP requests to HTTP.Sys. This could lead to rapid-fail protection to restart the worker process.

☑ Create a monitoring base line by using IIS logs, Security event logs, Security auditing, and Health Monitor in IIS 6.0.

☑ We can also use Network Monitor and System Monitor to track abnormal behavior (due to security breach) of the network and the system, respectively.

☑ Content Management servers can be used to deploy content to multiple IIS servers in a Web farm. We can also use other third-party content management servers for the same purpose (for example, Vignette).

Exam Objectives Frequently Asked Questions

The following Frequently Asked Questions, answered by the authors of this book, are designed to both measure your understanding of the Exam Objectives presented in this chapter, and to assist you with real-life implementation of these concepts. You will also gain access to thousands of other FAQs at ITFAQnet.com.

Q: Can we use anonymous access for FTP sites, or is it restricted to Web sites only?

A: Anonymous access is available on both FTP sites and Web sites.

Q: What default Windows access group is the anonymous Web account part of?

A: The anonymous Web account (IUSR_ComputerName account) is part of the Guest Windows group.

Q: What authentication mechanism in IIS 6.0 is supported by most browser types (with the exception of anonymous authentication)?

A: Basic authentication is supported by most of the browsers. It is also specified in the HTTP W3C specification.

Q: Does digest authentication use clear-text usernames and passwords to authenticate?

A: No it does not. It uses MD5 hash message digest that cannot be deciphered by an intruder.

Q: Can we apply basic authentication on all Web site directories?

A: Yes.

Q: Can we apply digest authentication on all Web site directories?

A: No. Digest authentication only works on WebDAV directories.

Q: Is the sub-authentication component available by default in IIS 6.0?

A: No. The sub-authentication component needs to be installed manually in IIS 6.0.

Q: Can the Windows 2000 IAS server co-exist with the Windows Server 2003 IAS on the same partition?

A: No. The Windows Server 2003 IAS will overwrite the policy and login database of the Windows 2000 IAS implementation.

Q: Can we use certificate mapping without Windows login accounts?

A: No. We need to map a certificate to a Windows account to implement certificate mapping.

Q: Can we use certificate authentication in FTP transfers?

A: No. Certificate authentication is not enabled in FTP service.

Q: How do I replicate Web content on multiple servers?

A: IIS 6.0 does not have a built-in content replication tool. Content replication is a major issue to manage large Web farms. Use the Microsoft Content Management Server (CMS) or Site Server tools for content replication.

Q: How do I obtain SSL security access information?

A: This could be achieved through **IIS Manager**. Click on the Web site and select **Properties**. Then, select the **Directory Security** tab. Click the **View Certificate** button under the **Secure Communications** group box. The certificate will have information on the version, serial number, signature algorithm (for example, sha1RSA), Issuer, Valid From, Valid To, Subject, and Public key information.

Q: Can we have multiple SSL security certificates for a single Web site?

A: Unfortunately, no. Only one security certificate is permitted for a single Web site.

Q: Can I reuse the same server certificate for multiple Web sites?

A: Yes. You can use the same SSL security certificate in multiple Web sites. Multiple sites have to be configured separately to use the same certificate.

Self Test

A Quick Answer Key follows the Self Test questions. For complete questions, answers, and explanations to the Self Test questions in this chapter as well as the other chapters in this book, see the Self Test Appendix.

1. One of the new reliability features in IIS 6.0 is the introduction of HTTP.Sys. HTTP.Sys is the new kernel mode driver for IIS 6.0. HTTP.Sys is engineered to increase the performance of IIS dramatically. You have been researching HTTP.Sys functionality. Your research indicates that one of the following about HTTP.Sys is true. What is HTTP.Sys is capable of?

    A. Create virtual directories for Web sites

    B. Implementing flexible caching

    C. Back up XML metabase

    D. Provides health detection data to IIS

2. You have been approached by the AllWebCustomers company to design the security structure for their new bookstore application. This application will run on Windows Server 2003 and IIS 6.0. The infrastructure architect has designed a Web farm with SQL cluster database connections. There is also an Active Directory available in the enterprise. You are contemplating the Windows logon authentication method for this application. Which of the following will be most suited to the Windows authentication method in Windows Server 2003?

    A. RADIUS authentication

    B. Digest authentication

    C. .NET cryptographic assembly authentication

    D. Anonymous login

3. You are contemplating using integrated Windows authentication or basic authentication for a shopping cart application. This application will be used by Internet Explorer, Netscape, and Opera browsers. There are more non-IE browsers than IE browsers. You are also implementing an SSL connection to secure the data transmission between the users and the IIS server. Which authentication model will suit this shopping cart application?

    A. Basic authentication because of the variety of browser types.

    B. Integrated Windows authentication because of the variety of browser types.

    C. Integrated Windows authentication because basic authentication will expose the credentials.

D. Basic authentication; however SSL, could be "overkill" for this application.

4. Your company network has recently implemented a wireless internal network. As the system administrator, you need to maintain this network, VPN, and Internet access to your company. You are currently using different usernames and passwords for each user on these three different networks. Therefore, a single user needs to remember three usernames and passwords to access the appropriate network. This is also an inconvenience for you as the systems administrator. You have heard of a RADIUS implementation in Windows Server 2003. You are currently deploying Windows Server 2003 in your company. What is the RADIUS implementation in Windows Server 2003?

   A. Advance Digest Authentication

   B. Internet Information Server 6.0

   C. Internet Authentication Service

   D. Internet Protocolv6

5. You have been instructed to install Windows Server 2003 on a Windows 2000 machine. The current Windows 2000 server is running under a FAT32 system. The Windows Server 2003 installation will permit you to upgrade or have clean installation. When you are performing the upgrade, you have an option between FAT32 and NTFS file systems. Which would you choose?

   A. FAT

   B. FAT32

   C. NTFS

   D. FAT64

6. You have installed IIS 6.0 successfully using the Configure Your Server Wizard. You want to experiment with the ASP.NET functionality in IIS 6.0. You have downloaded the QuickStart tutorials from Microsoft to try out ASP.NET scripts. You try to invoke one of the ASP.NET pages and get a 404 Not Found error. What could be the reason for this?

   A. IIS 6.0 does not support ASP.NET scripts.

   B. ASP.NET support has to be enabled through Web Services Extensions.

   C. ASP.NET support should be enabled through **Control Panel | Administrative tools**.

   D. IIS 6.0 only supports ASP.NET scripts inside ASP scripts.

7. You have created a commercial Web site with sensitive business information. Your senior architect has advised you to use Advance Digest Security to maximize security benefits on IIS 6.0. You have been doing research on Advance Digest Security. What is the incorrect piece of information you came across in your research?

   A. It uses the WinFX file system to store user credentials.

   B. It works with both HTTP 1.0 and HTTP 1.1 enabled browsers.

   C. It will work with Internet Explorer 5.0 with JavaScript 1.3 support.

   D. It only works with SSL support.

8. Phase One of the new IIS 6.0 features is implemented at the hardware level. The devices that implement this new feature can be described as Plug and Play devices. These devices implement an API called CryptoAPI and can be chosen from a list from IIS Manager. This new feature could be referred as:

   A. Server-gated Cryptography

   B. Selectable Cryptographic Service Provider

   C. Secure Sockets Layer support

   D. .NET System Cryptography library support

Self Test Quick Answer Key

For complete questions, answers, and explanations to the Self Test questions in this chapter as well as the other chapters in this book, see the Self Test Appendix.

1. **B**
2. **B**
3. **A**
4. **C**
5. **C**
6. **B**
7. **C**
8. **B**

Chapter 7

MCSE 70-298

Securing VPN and Extranet Communications

Exam Objectives in this Chapter:

3.5	Design security for communication between networks.
3.5.1	Select protocols for VPN access.
3.5.3	Design demand dial routing between internal networks.
3.5.2	Design VPN connectivity.
3.6	Design security for communication with external organizations.
3.6.1	Design an extranet infrastructure.
3.6.2	Design a strategy for cross-certification of Certificate Services.

- ☑ Summary of Exam Objectives
- ☑ Exam Objectives Fast Track
- ☑ Exam Objectives Frequently Asked Questions
- ☑ Self Test
- ☑ Self Test Quick Answer Key

Introduction

Just as Chapter 5, "Securing Network Services and Protocols," discussed new challenges in securing network transmissions for users in a LAN environment, the increasing prevalence of the Internet as a communications necessity has also made life both easier and harder for users who want to access network resources from a home office or other remote location. Even a scant half-decade ago, remote access for home users was primarily limited to dial-up modems connected directly to a LAN server, and satellite offices relied primarily on dedicated WAN links that merely extended the geography of the LAN—the bandwidth was not shared with other companies and only needed to be secured in the same manner as other LAN traffic. This provided good data security, but created great inconvenience and expense for remote users who were faced with long-distance telephone charges and costs of expensive dedicated links. Using the Internet as a communications medium, by contrast, allows individuals and businesses to leverage existing Internet connectivity (including the increasing number of broadband installations in residences) to access company resources. However, this ease of use comes at a price: without proper planning and implementation, network security could suffer significant losses from transmitting sensitive data over a public network like the Internet. This has led to the increasing popularity of virtual private network, or VPN, technology within the corporate enterprise.

Windows Server 2003 offers a number of remote connectivity services and applications that we discuss in this chapter. Depending on your connectivity needs, Windows Server 2003 can actually function as a basic router, acting as a "traffic cop" to direct network communications between geographically disparate locations. Windows uses two common, standards-based routing protocols to accomplish this: the Routing Information Protocol, or RIP, and the Open Shortest Path First, or OSPF, algorithm. We discuss both of these in detail.

The remainder (and indeed the bulk) of this chapter discusses the more common use of Windows Server 2003 as a VPN server. Windows Server 2003 offers a number of options to secure traffic between LANs, between routers, and for end users who want to connect to network resources. Within a corporate enterprise, network administrators can configure policies to ensure that all traffic is sufficiently encrypted, and to control the use of company resources for VPN usage. Remote access policies can control any aspect of the VPN connection process, accepting or rejecting connections based on user authentication, connection type, time of day, and the like. In this chapter, we focus on the best ways to design and deploy the Windows Server 2003 VPN technologies in a large environment, to provide remote access to those who need it without sacrificing the overall integrity of the corporate network data and resources.

EXAM 70-298 OBJECTIVE 3.5

Designing Security for Communication Between Networks

Many experts would agree that sharing information is the lifeblood of any company. Indeed, it is the need to share information that serves as the primary motivation for most corporations' computer networks. The majority of these networks are "traditional" in nature. That is, one or several servers are accessed by many clients, all of which are physically located in the same office. Indeed, most of the chapters in this book thus far have been aptly related to this kind of network and applicable security issues.

In recent years, however, more and more networks have to deal with "external" elements. These elements might include full-time telecommuters who need to access the corporate network from home or from the road, or they might include LAN-to-LAN links across vast geographical distances. For telecommuting road warriors, there are two choices. The user can connect directly to a company remote access server (usually by means of a dial-up modem), or the user can connect to the Internet and then connect to a company remote access server. One advantage of the latter method is that most Internet connections are made by accessing a local ISP, and can save companies large long distance bills. The other main advantage is that many users now have high-speed Internet access (thanks to the proliferation of cable and DSL modems), and are no longer limited to analog modems or ISDN connections.

Whether a user dials directly or uses a VPN to traverse the Internet to connect to the company LAN, Windows Server 2003 can play the role of the remote access server. As a matter of fact, using Routing and Remote Access Services (RRAS) allows Windows Server 2003 to be used as a local router or a so-called "perimeter" router, depending on how your network subnets are arranged. For a local router—one that connects two or more local subnets—the choice and implementation of routing protocols is probably the most important security consideration and we'll discuss it in detail shortly. The same goes for a perimeter router that interfaces with another perimeter router at a distant site with a dedicated connection.

When a routing and remote access solution includes demand dial or VPN connections, however, security considerations become more complex. Luckily, Windows Server 2003 comes with many new features and components such as Network Access Quarantine Control that are specifically designed to accommodate a wide variety of security needs when using RRAS. As we will see, connecting private networks together (especially across a public network) requires a great deal of thought and planning.

EXAM 70-298 OBJECTIVE 3.5.1

Using Windows Server 2003 as a Router

When they hear the word *router*, most people think of a dedicated hardware device. However, by using a computer running Windows Server 2003, it is possible to implement a secure and cost-effective routing solution across any internetwork. In the simplest of terms, a router segments networks into two or more sections. Perhaps the segments are in different geographical locations and are connected over a WAN link, or perhaps one segment has become too large and needs to be subdivided in order to efficiently control the routing of network messages. In either case, a multihomed computer (a system that has more than one network interface card, or NIC) running RRAS fits the bill nicely.

Exactly how a router works and why it might be beneficial to your network is beyond the scope of this book; however, to actually use Windows Server 2003 as one, you first need to configure RRAS.

EXAM WARNING

If you are not a domain administrator and are installing RRAS on a member server, you will need to have an administrator add the server's computer account to the RAS and IAS Servers security group before proceeding with RRAS configuration. Alternatively, the *netsh ras add registeredserver* command can be used—but only with administrative privileges.

In Exercise 7.01, we will configure RRAS to act as a simple router. Once the exercise is complete, you would need to add routes using one of the methods described in the next sections for the router to be functional.

EXERCISE 7.01

CONFIGURING ROUTING AND REMOTE ACCESS SERVICES

1. On a member server, click Start | Administrative Tools | Routing and Remote Access.
2. Right-click your server, and choose **Configure and Enable Routing and Remote Access** as shown in Figure 7.1.

Figure 7.1 Configuring Routing and Remote Access

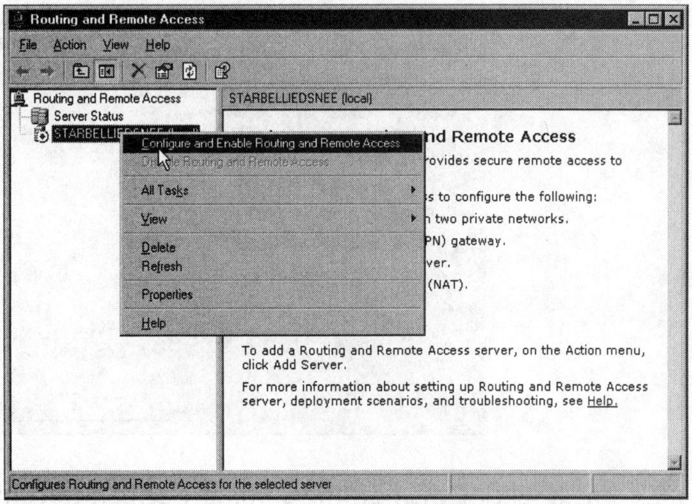

3. When the Routing and Remote Access Server Setup Wizard appears, click **Next** to get past the initial screen. On the Configuration screen, select **Custom Configuration** and click **Next**. See Figure 7.2.

Figure 7.2 Routing and Remote Access Server Setup Wizard

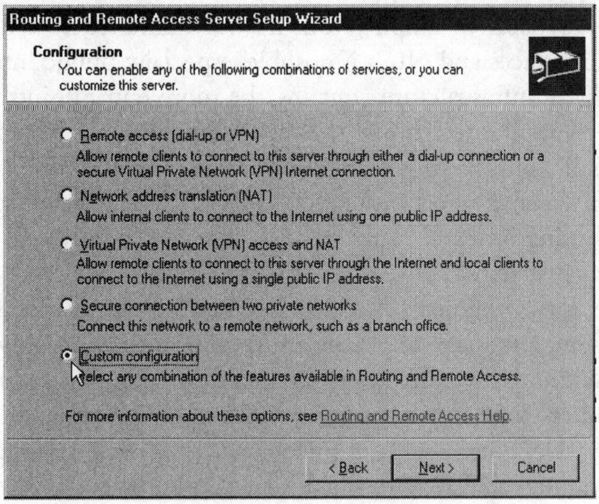

4. On the Custom Configuration screen, as in Figure 7.3, select **LAN routing** and click **Next**.

Figure 7.3 RRAS Custom Configuration Screen

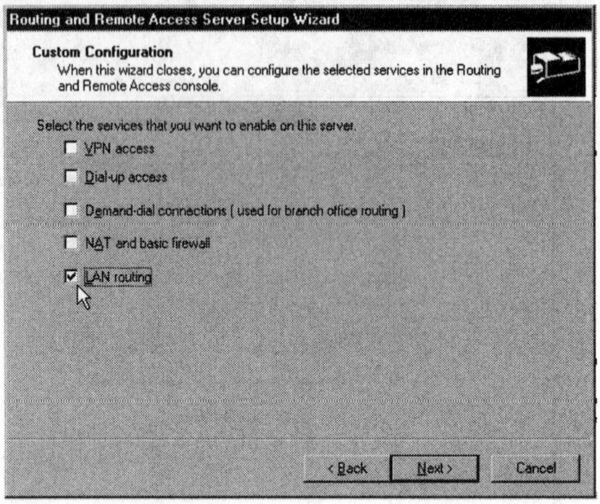

5. Finally, click **Finish** on the Summary screen to complete the task.

As far as security is concerned, the first line of defense is to secure the server running RRAS just as you would any other server using the principles you have already learned in this book. This might include physical security, as well as logical security pieces such as limiting administrator group membership and using strong authentication protocols.

It is also advisable to simplify your network infrastructure design. This can mean using fewer interfaces and NICs if possible, especially public interfaces. The more interfaces that an infrastructure contains, the more entry points an attacker has available to target—similar to a house that has a large number of windows and doors through which a burglar might choose to enter. Arguably the most important security consideration when dealing with a 2003 RRAS router, however, is the handling of routes and routing protocols. In a small network with only one router, the router by definition has first-hand knowledge of each network's address that is attached to it. For example, if two segments A and B are attached to a router and a host on B attempts to send a message to a host on A, the router will know how to reach the destination without any help. However, in a more complicated network with many segments, routers must rely on routing tables to assist them.

Routing tables contain entries (called *routes*) that help the router direct traffic. Think of a routing table as a crossroads sign. You know, the ones that say Paris is 500 miles this direction and Rome 450 miles that direction, and Berlin 800 miles in yet another direction. If you think about it, the information contained in such a table could be very valuable to an attacker. After all, it's a virtual roadmap to your entire infrastructure. Routing tables work like this. When a packet arrives at the router, the router consults its routing table, and forwards the packet appropriately. If a matching destination is not found, the router forwards the packet to its default route. Note that in the case where one router interface points to the Internet and another interface points to the local intranet, in order to prevent conflicts with the default route pointing to the Internet, you must not configure the default gateway on the intranet interface. As you can see, routing tables are critical to the implementation of RRAS as a router, and the security of these tables is certainly important. To understand some of the methods to protect the routes, we first need to understand how the tables are built.

Static Routes

One way to build a routing table is to have an administrator enter each route manually, using either the RRAS snap-in or the *netsh* utility. The problem is that the amount of administration is quite often prohibitive, especially on larger networks. After all, each and every router must have a table, and the larger your network, the more complex your routing tables are likely to be. Moreover, there is no fault tolerance for static routes. If a Windows Server 2003 router loses its static table, it must be rebuilt from scratch.

From a security standpoint, static routes are actually quite secure. Unless auto-static updates are used, routing information is not passed over the network. This makes it impossible to intercept such transmissions. When configuring static routes on a router, you can opt to use summarization routes. These routes encompass multiple subnets on the receiving router by shrinking the subnet mask, which makes implementation a bit easier but also lessens security slightly.

Head of the Class...

Summarization Routes

The concept of static routes is simple—an administrator programs each and every destination route into the routing table of the RRAS server. When a packet comes in to the server from one interface, the server checks its routing table to determine where the packet should be forwarded to. However, the more complex an infrastructure becomes, the more difficult it is to keep track of all the possible destination networks.

One possible answer is to use summarization routes, which are made possible through the mathematics of subnet masks. For an example, let's assume that you want to add destination routes of 192.168.15.0, 192.168.16.0, and 192.168.17.0 to your routing table. Let's further assume that each network has a subnet mask of 255.255.255.0, or 24 bits. Since each of the three networks has a common "root" network ID of 192.168, it is possible to insert just one entry to the routing table instead of three individual ones. The singular route of 192.168.0.0 with a 16-bit mask encompasses all three destinations, making the implementation and upkeep of routing tables much less work.

Continued

There is a possible price to be paid, however. In our example, any destination network that has the 192.168 root would be considered "reachable" by the server. This might include nonexistent networks that would slow down the server considerably (picture a mail carrier searching the block for a make-believe address), or it might include a real "rogue" network set up by an attacker. This type of network would be created deliberately for the purpose of intercepting traffic. However, this kind of attack would be extremely difficult to perpetrate—in part because it requires prior knowledge of not only the routing table, but the infrastructure as well. It would further require physical access to the network.

TEST DAY TIP

Auto-static updates are another method of populating a static routing table. A router interface that is configured in this way sends out a request asking for all of the routes on the other interfaces, similar to the RIP protocol. The auto-static request must be made by an administrator, however.

RIP

The Routing Information Protocol, or RIP, was designed to allow routers to build their routing tables dynamically, by periodically communicating with other dynamic routers. The largest advantage of such a design is that the route exchanges happen automatically without user intervention. RIP versions 1 and 2 are supported by Windows Server 2003's RRAS and are extremely easy to configure and use. However, RIP is not suitable for large networks for two reasons. First, networks that are more than 15 "hops" away are simply not reachable (a hop is a metric, which means that a router is traversed during transit). Second, the RIP protocols broadcast (version 1 or 2) or multicast (version 2 only) quite frequently. This can cause a deluge of network traffic when topology changes are implemented. RIP can be implemented by right-clicking **General** under **IP Routing** in the RRAS utility. This can be seen in Figure 7.4.

Figure 7.4 Setting Up a New Routing Protocol

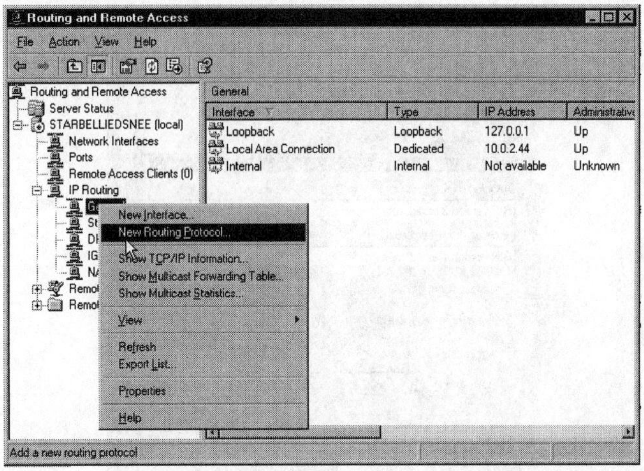

After selecting RIP Version 2 for Internet Protocol as in Figure 7.5, you will be able to configure it from the main screen.

Figure 7.5 Choosing RIP

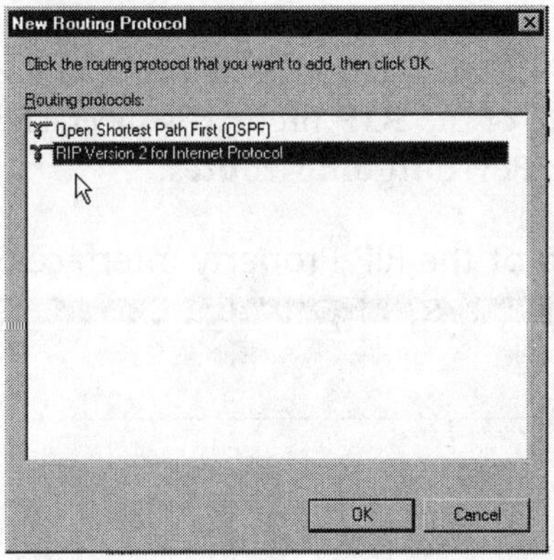

There are several security measures that you as an administrator can take to make RIP broadcasts less vulnerable to sniffing or other types of threats. If RIP version 2 is used, simple passwords can be set up such that any router receiving an RIP transmission checks to see if the password matches before accepting the announcement. Unfortunately, the simple passwords used are sent in plain text over the network, which provides no protection from network packet intercepting attacks. To enable passwords, select **RIP** from the **IP Routing** section of the RRAS snap-in. In the right-hand pane, right-click the interface that you want to enable passwords on. Click **Properties**, and on the **General** tab, check the **Activate authentication** check box. Finally, enter a password in the **Password** field as shown in Figure 7.6.

Figure 7.6 General Tab of the RIP Property Interface Sheet

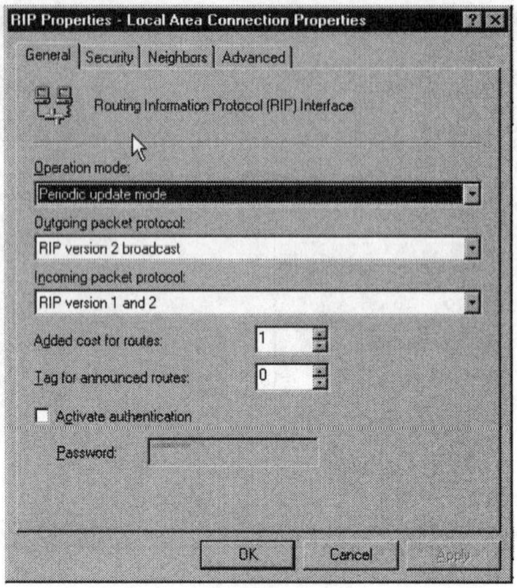

Another security measure is the use of route filters. Filters are used whenever a route is received and is being considered for "adoption" into the receiver's table. If the route is not potentially reachable on the internetwork (a 192.168.0.0 network, for example, would not be reachable from a 10.0.0.0 network, since both of these are private, nonroutable networks), it is discarded. Filters can be applied from the **Action** section of the **Security** tab of the **RIP** properties sheet, and you can select either **For incoming routes** or **For outgoing routes**.

Figure 7.7 Security Tab of the RIP Property Interface Sheet

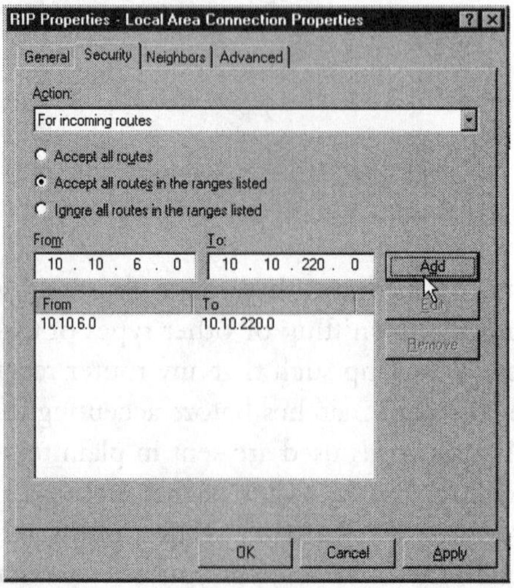

Finally, you can use peer limiting. Using peer limiting, you can specify that only immediate neighbors receive router announcements through a directed unicast packet rather than through broadcast or multicast. This is done on the **Neighbors** tab of the RIP Properties sheet—see Figure 7.8.

Figure 7.8 Neighbors Tab of the RIP Property Interface Sheet

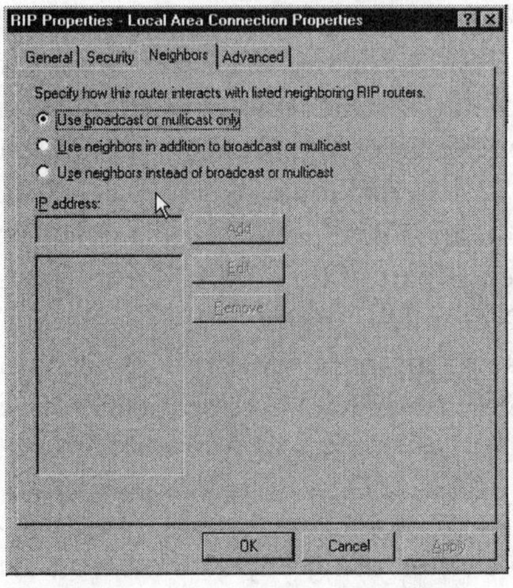

You can also add peer filters by means of the RIP Protocol's **Security** tab to specify by IP address which routers can send acceptable announcements. Note, however, that only immediate neighbors can be set for unicasting. All announcements received from routers not on the list will be discarded.

Open Shortest Path First

The final method used by routers to build their tables is the OSPF protocol. An extremely efficient model, OSPF is unfortunately rather difficult to set up and maintain properly. Most of this efficiency is a result of the concept of *areas* and *area border routers* (ABRs). Similar to how sites and bridgehead servers are used to control replication in Active Directory, areas and ABRs serve to lessen the amount of network traffic generated by topological changes while maintaining a high degree of accuracy and synchronicity.

Installing OSPF is similar to RIP as described in the last section, but OSPF is different from RIP because it does not simply use the number of hops to define the metric of a particular route. Instead, OSPF calculates the least-cost path to each segment of the network, and because the path is guaranteed to have the least cost, it is also guaranteed to not have any loops in the routing structure—something that RIP does not do. These least-cost paths are stored in the link-state database. Whenever changes to the database are received from another router, the database recalculates the routing table entries automatically.

Although the design of OSPF is quite complicated and beyond the scope of our discussion here, implementing security is not terribly difficult. An *autonomous system*, or AS, is the group of all the OSPF routers in the organization. Each router within the AS can advertise routes and they will be considered internal. However, external routes often need to be advertised as well, but by default only internal announcements are propagated as a security precaution. External routes can be static routes, RIP routes, or even SNMP routes. In order to have any of these routes announced through the AS, an OSPF router must be specially configured as an *AS boundary router*, or ASBR. Once a router is set as an ASBR, it imports and announces all routes that are defined as external. For added security, you would most likely want to limit the types or sources of external routes by setting up external route filters on all ASBRs.

All OSPF interfaces on an RRAS router have a default simple password of "12345678." It is presented as part of the OSPF "Hello" message, which is used to initiate announcements. Not only is the password simple, but it is sent in plain text. However, this password is not meant so much as a security measure, but more as a guard against corrupt OSPF data from a possibly unauthorized server.

TEST DAY TIP

OSPF is not available when using any of the 64-bit versions of the Windows Server 2003 family.

When all is said and done, whether your routing system uses static routes, RIP, or OSPF, the basic tenets of security are the same. Microsoft recommends that you implement physical security on the RRAS router, and that administrative rights only be given to those who are actually running RRAS—simple, but good advice indeed.

EXAM 70-298 OBJECTIVE 3.5.3

Designing Demand Dial Routing between Internal Networks

RRAS routers can be used in many situations. As we discussed earlier, one of the reasons for segmenting traffic might be the disparate geographical locations of your corporate offices. If you have a main office located near Washington, D.C. with two satellite offices in Salt Lake City and San Diego, it is fairly obvious that you want as little traffic as possible going across the WAN links. After all, even so-called high speed WAN links such as T1 and T3 carriers are slow when compared with most LAN connections like 100 Mbps Ethernet. Therefore, it makes sense to have each geographical location represented by at least one logically separate subnet. Furthermore, we need to understand that not all companies have the financial resources necessary to support the luxury of high-speed WAN communications, and it is to these ends that we introduce the topic of demand dial routing.

A demand dial interface works in this way: Let's assume that we have a user in Salt Lake City who is at IP address 10.10.220.3 and is attempting to connect to a resource located in Washington, D.C. at IP address 10.1.35.92 on a different subnet. The two cities are connected via routers with analog modems. The 10.10.220.3 computer sends packets to the local router, SLRouter1, which is configured with a demand dial interface. SLRouter1 determines that a demand dial interface exists to the 10.1.35.92 address by checking its routing table, and finds that the interface is in a disconnected state. At this point, SLRouter1 knows that it must use the modem, and does so.

On the other end, DCRouter1 answers the incoming call, and immediately demands authentication credentials from SLRouter1. SLRouter1 sends a username (such as demand_salt_lake) and password. If demand_salt_lake exists as a user account on DCRouter1 and the password checks out and demand_salt_lake has the required dial-in permission, then the connection is accepted. However, DCRouter1 needs to see if the incoming call is an individual user dialing in to RRAS, or if it is a demand dial connection from a remote router. If the username demand_salt_lake is found in DCRouter1's list of demand dial connections, then the status of demand_salt_lake is changed from "inactive or disconnected" to "connected." Finally, the packets can be delivered to 10.1.35.92.

Head of the Class...

Numbered and Unnumbered Connections

When an RRAS router initiates a demand dial connection to another RRAS router, it creates a *virtual interface*. After the creation takes place, the sending router asks the receiving router to assign its new interface a public or private IP address. The process is then reversed, and the receiving router creates its own virtual interface. Subsequently, the receiving router then asks the sending router for an IP address for the new interface. Once both interfaces have been assigned IP addresses from the other router, the logical interface connection is complete and communication can begin. This is known as a *numbered connection*.

The assignment of an IP to a virtual interface can be accomplished in a number of ways. The static addresses assigned to both routers' user accounts (via the Dial-in tab) can be used, as well as dynamic address taken from a static address pool, if such a pool is set up on the routers. Perhaps the most common way, however, is for DHCP to assign the addresses automatically. This requires that each subnet has a DHCP server. If no server is available, dynamic assignment is still made through Automatic Private IP Addressing (APIPA).

Continued

> Starting with Windows 2000 and continuing with Windows Server 2003, *unnumbered connections* can also be used with LAN-to-LAN communications. If an IP address is not available or is refused, a connection is still made—just without IP addresses. In this situation, static routes must be used because RIP and OSPF do not function over an unnumbered connection.

The security concerns of establishing a demand dial interface and connection are mainly focused on the authentication and authorization procedures. Eavesdropping and packet sniffing attacks are less likely on a demand dial connection than a LAN-to-LAN VPN connection (we'll discuss VPNs in the next section) because packets don't travel across public networks such as the Internet.

The strongest form of authentication that you can use for demand dial routing is certificate-based authentication that uses Extensible Authentication Protocol–Transport Level Security (EAP-TLS). According to Microsoft's TechNet Web site, the following steps are all required to implement such security:

1. Configure the calling and answering routers for demand dial routing.
2. Install a computer certificate on the main office router.
3. Configure the domain for Web-based certificate enrollment.
4. Create user accounts and export certificates.
5. Import the dial-out user certificate on the main office router.
6. Configure the main office router to support certificate-based authentication as a calling router and as an answering router.
7. Import the dial-in certificate on the branch office router.
8. Configure the branch office router to support certificate-based authentication as a calling router.
9. Connect to the main office and join the organization domain.

Certificates are covered extensively in Chapter 3, "Designing a Secure Public Key Infrastructure." If EAP-TLS is not appropriate for your security requirements, you can use MS-CHAP v2 with strong passwords to support a relatively secure environment. We will implement a demand dial connection as part of Exercise 7.02 when we set up a PPTP LAN-to-LAN VPN server.

The need for encrypting data can be met in two ways. If your concern is only to protect the data as it travels between the two routers, then Microsoft Point-to-Point Encryption (MPPE) at either 128-bit or 40-bit strength can be used if EAP-TLS or MS-CHAP authentication is in place. MPPE only encrypts packets between the routers, also known as *link encryption*. If a more complete encryption is required—

namely end-to-end—then IPSec can be used. IPSec encrypts data from the source host all the way to the destination host, not just between the routers. A more detailed discussion of IPSec can be found in Chapter 5, "Securing Network Services and Protocols."

EXAM 70-298 OBJECTIVE 3.5.2

Designing VPN Connectivity

So far in this chapter, we have discussed how to use Windows Server 2003 as a router between subnets in the same office, or between subnets in different geographical locations. You can also use Windows Server 2003 as a remote access server for end users to dial directly in to. Assuming you have the budget to pay for dedicated lines, these types of connectivity are superior both in terms of efficiency and security. However, with the proliferation of the Internet, companies have begun discovering the VPN as a way to cut costs from the bottom line.

The goal of the VPN is to provide a means for connecting corporate entities together by using the public Internet (or other public network) instead of costly telephone or digital leased lines. These entities can be end users telecommuting from home, an external business vendor who wants to connect to your network, or a branch office connecting to the main corporate office in another city. In any of these cases, either a remote access VPN or a LAN-to-LAN VPN can be established using RRAS, but the question is, how to secure such a configuration? To best understand the security needs of a VPN design, some knowledge about how a VPN works is necessary.

A VPN emulates a secure point-to-point connection, such as an employee who uses an analog modem to dial up the corporate remote access server. Even though the data might travel to any number of third-party locations during its sojourn on the public network, it ends up at the correct endpoint. This is accomplished by wrapping, or *encapsulating*, the data with enough information for the data to be routed properly to its destination. Once it is received at the destination, it is unpackaged so that the data inside can be read. To the end user, it looks like just another point-to-point connection. The security of a point-to-point link is emulated by encrypting the data that is to be sent. That way, even if packets are captured somewhere on the public network, they are still unusable to the attacker. This combination of encapsulation and encryption make the VPN an attractive alternative to an expensive point-to-point connection.

For a VPN design to be considered secure, it must exhibit proper user authentication, data encryption through the use of keys, and IP address assignment management. VPNs use tunnels and tunneling protocols to accomplish these tasks. Think of a VPN tunnel as you would a train tunnel through a mountain. Both before it enters and after it exits the tunnel, the train is visible and even vulnerable. Inside the tunnel, however, no outside source can see in the tunnel. Figure 7.9 shows how a VPN is used to connect two remote company sites:

Figure 7.9 Two Sites Connected via VPN Tunnel

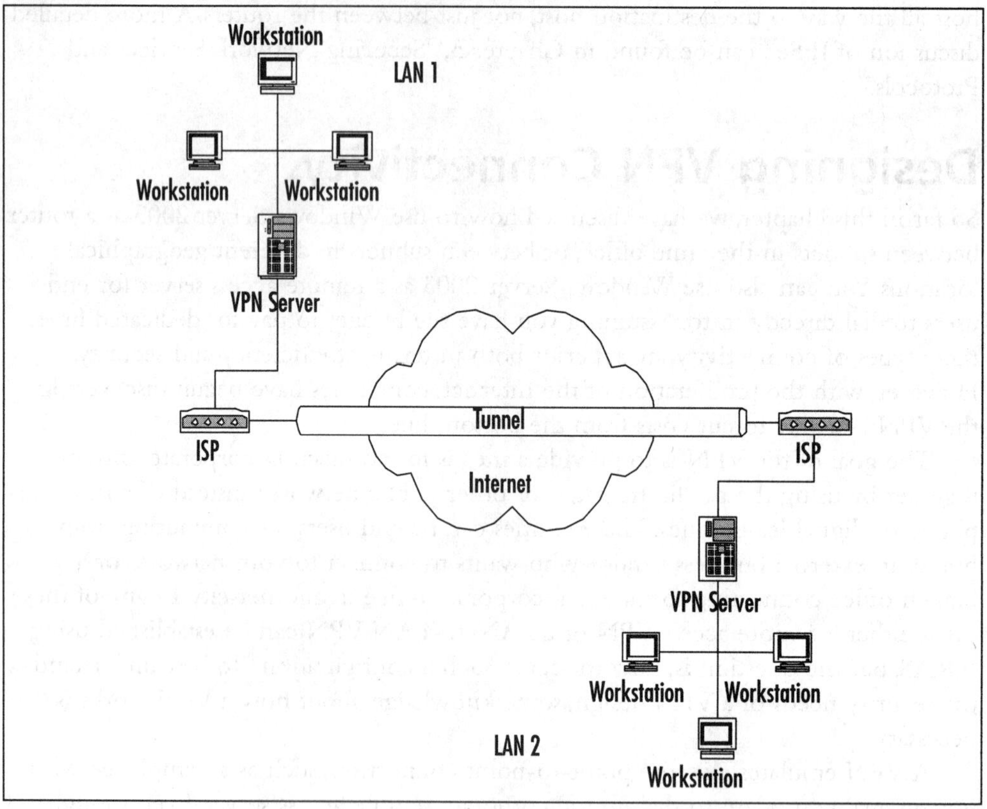

Notice that the satellite office router connects to a local ISP using either a dial-up or a dedicated connection. At headquarters, the VPN server is always connected to another local ISP in order to accept incoming connections. This way, all long-distance charges are saved. A similar situation is where a single user employs a client machine to connect to a local ISP and then to the corporate VPN server.

The key to all of this is the tunnel. It is the means by which data is made to traverse a "foreign" network. Consider an example in which you are trying to send an automobile from the city of Chicago in the United States to Osaka in Japan. Of course, the car can travel on highways from Chicago to, say, Los Angeles, but then what? Since the driver of the car has neither the specific knowledge of the ocean (after all, AAA doesn't make road maps of the Pacific) nor the ability to travel on it using only a car, he must rely on the "foreign" network of water instead of the familiar highway. The car can be loaded inside a cargo ship so it is protected from the wind and the waves, and assuming the ship has the appropriate navigational ability, it will arrive at a port in Japan some time later. Upon arrival, the car must be unloaded and then driven on a once-again familiar highway to its final destination.

Data travels across a VPN tunnel in much the same way. A packet originates on a computer and then travels as far as it can on the familiar network (the LAN). When it reaches the border of the Internet, it must be encapsulated and encrypted so that it can securely journey across the Internet to the destination site. Once there, it must be unwrapped and decrypted so that it can be delivered to the destination computer. In the next section, we discuss the protocols that make VPN tunnels possible.

Selecting Protocols for VPN Access

When designing a secure VPN solution, perhaps the most important choice to make is which tunneling protocol to use. Server 2003 supports both the Point-to-Point Tunneling Protocol (PPTP) and the Level 2 Tunneling Protocol (L2TP). Each has advantages and disadvantages, but the final decision on which to use might be limited by the design of your network infrastructure and your willingness to change that design. L2TP is widely regarded as more secure than PPTP, even by Microsoft, and should be the protocol of choice if strong security is a primary concern of your network design. PPTP, while less secure, requires less administrative effort to set up and maintain.

PPTP

PPTP is a standards-based protocol (RFC 2637) that can be used either in a LAN-to-LAN or a remote access VPN. It is based on the extremely popular Point-to-Point Protocol, or PPP. PPP has several features that make it a good base—in particular, user authentication, data compression, and dynamic address assignment. In fact, the PPTP packet that makes its way across the public network has, at its core, a PPP packet.

When using PPTP, a PPP packet is encapsulated by two headers—a Generic Routing Encapsulation (GRE) header and an IP header as shown in Figure 7.10. These headers allow the packet to be routed on the public network. Notice that the encrypted portion of the packet is only the PPP data itself.

Figure 7.10 Diagram of a PPTP Packet

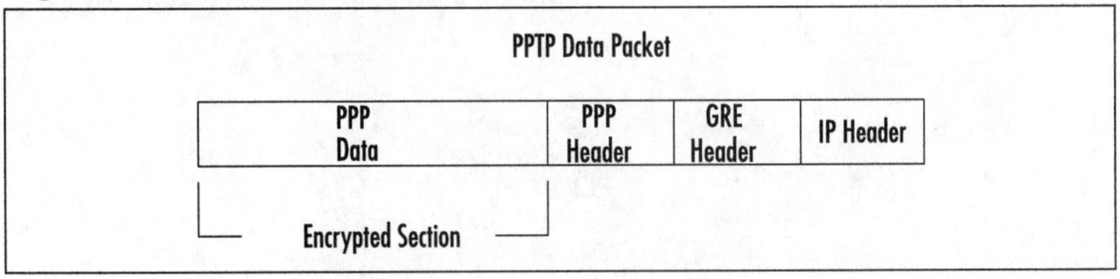

Before implementing PPTP, you need to be familiar with the authenticating protocols that PPP (and therefore PPTP) uses. Windows Server 2003's implementation of RRAS supports Password Authentication Protocol (PAP), Challenge-Handshake

Authentication Protocol (CHAP), Microsoft Challenge-Handshake Authentication Protocol (MS-CHAP), MS-CHAP version 2 (MS-CHAPv2), and Extensible Authentication Protocol (EAP). Among these, EAP is the strongest and should be used in a highly secure environment. MS-CHAPv2 is also considered secure but can only be used with Microsoft's more recent operating systems. MS-CHAPv2 provides mutual authentication (the client verifies the server and the server verifies the client) and allows for two encryption keys—one for sent data and the other for received data. If for any reason EAP cannot be used, MS-CHAPv2 is the next best thing. MS-CHAP, CHAP, and PAP (PAP uses vulnerable plain text) are not recommended unless absolutely necessary.

Implementing PPTP can be somewhat daunting. In Exercise 7.02, we'll take you step by step through the process of enabling RRAS in a router-to-router VPN scenario assuming a demand dial interface. As you will see, there are two major steps. First, we'll set up RRAS and then we'll set up the demand dial interface. This exercise assumes that you have *not* set up RRAS as an internal router as in Exercise 7.01. If you did, you can disable RRAS by right-clicking on the server name and disabling routing and remote access—you are then free to complete the following exercise.

EXERCISE 7.02

CONFIGURING A PPTP LAN-TO-LAN VPN

1. On the server that is to function as either the calling or the answering router, click **Start, Administrative Tools, Routing and Remote Access**.
2. Right-click your server, and choose Configure and Enable Routing and Remote Access.
3. On the Configuration screen, select **Remote access (dial-up or VPN)** and click **Next**. This is shown in Figure 7.11.

Figure 7.11 Configuration Screen of the Routing and Remote Access Setup Wizard

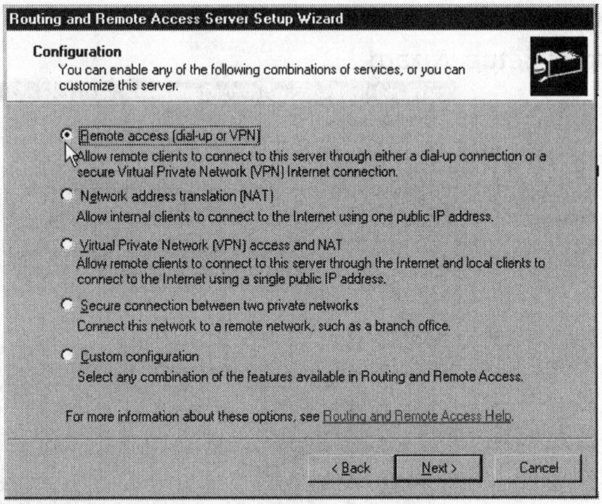

4. The next screen, Figure 7.12, gives you the choice of whether to accept VPN or dial-up clients. Choose **VPN** and click **Next**.

Figure 7.12 Remote Access Screen of the Routing and Remote Access Setup Wizard

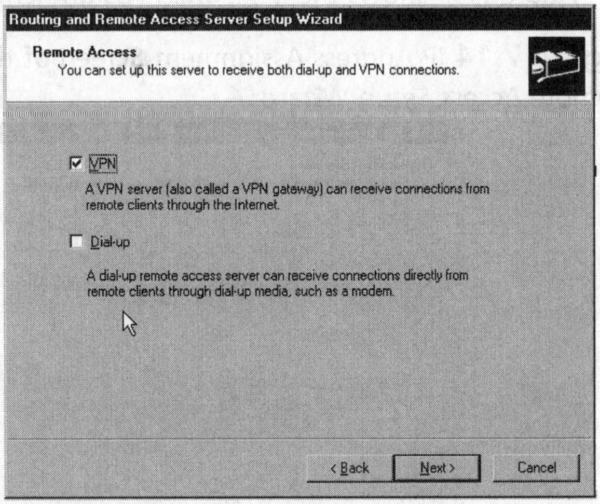

5. Figure 7.13 shows the VPN Connection screen. Here, select the interface that faces the Internet, and make certain that the **Enable security on the selected interface by setting up static packet filters** option is selected. This option allows VPN traffic

into the interface, but disallows all other types of traffic. Click **Next**.

Figure 7.13 VPN Connection Screen of the Routing and Remote Access Setup Wizard

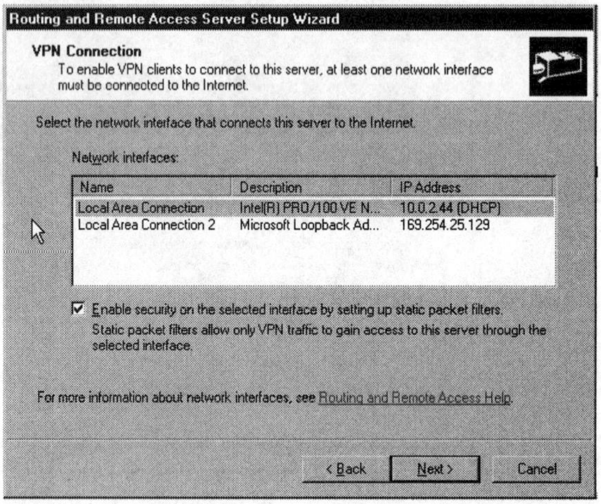

6. To assign an IP address to the remote client (or remote router in this case), you need to choose between DHCP and a static pool of addresses. For our purposes, select **Automatically** and click **Next**. Figure 7.14 shows the IP Address Assignment screen.

Figure 7.14 IP Address Assignment Screen of the Routing and Remote Access Setup Wizard

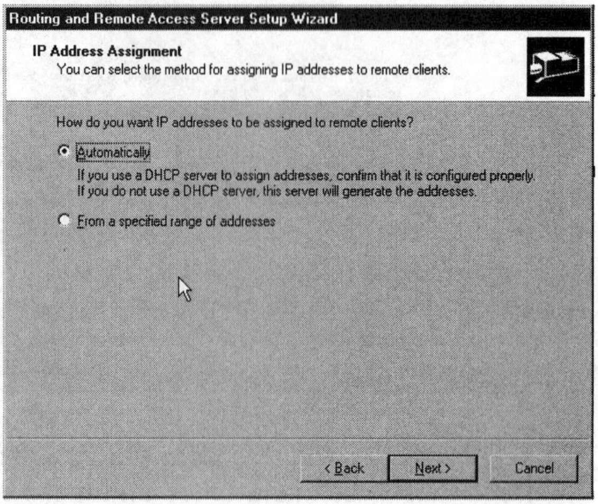

7. The Managing Multiple Remote Access Servers screen really does not apply in our scenario because we are only configuring two routers across a demand dial connection. Choose **No, use Routing and Remote Access to authenticate connection requests** and click **Next**.
8. Click **Finish** to complete the task. Figure 7.15 shows the dialog box that appears. It's a reminder to configure the DHCP Relay Agent to support relaying DHCP messages.

Figure 7.15 DHCP Relay Agent Reminder

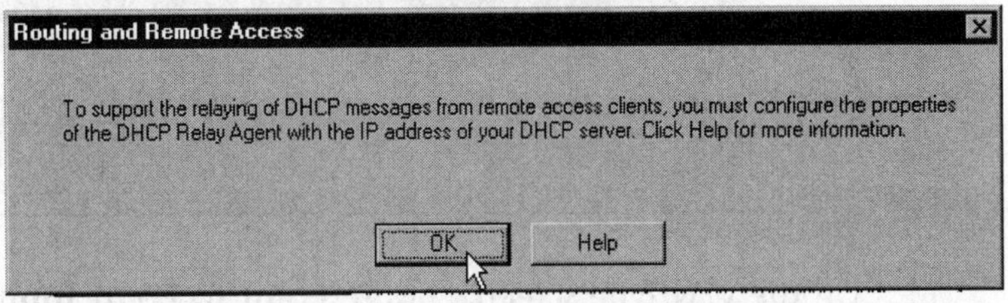

9. Now that RRAS has been configured, we will set up a demand dial interface. Right-click the **Network Interfaces** container on the main RRAS screen, and select **New Demand Dial Interface** as shown in Figure 7.16. Click **Next** to continue past the introductory screen.

Figure 7.16 Setting Up a Demand Dial Interface

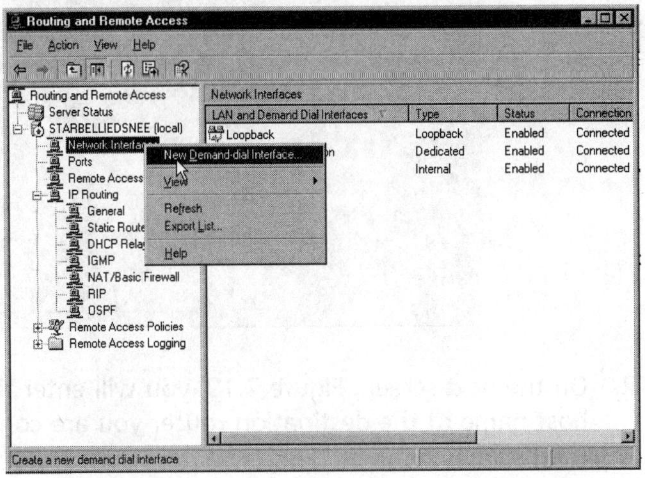

10. On the next screen, type a name for the demand dial interface—"Remote Router" will be sufficient. Click **Next** to proceed to the Connection Type screen, as seen in Figure 7.17. Select **Connect using virtual private networking (VPN)**, and click **Next**.

Figure 7.17 Connection Type Screen of the Demand Dial Wizard

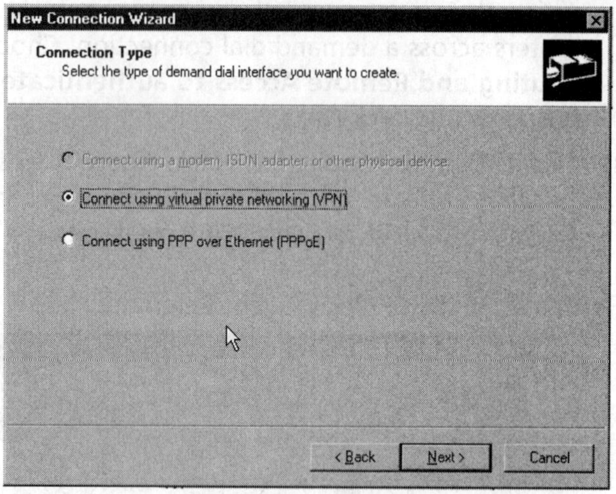

11. On the VPN Type screen, choose **Point to Point Tunneling Protocol (PPTP)**, and click **Next**. This is shown in Figure 7.18.

Figure 7.18 VPN Type Screen of the Demand Dial Wizard

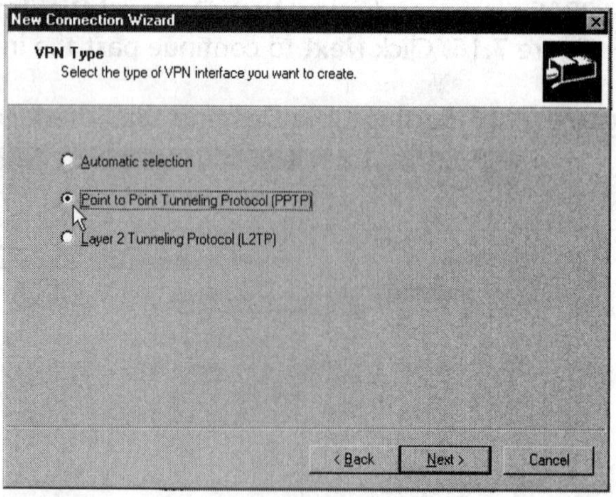

12. On the next screen, Figure 7.19, you will enter the IP address or host name of the destination router you are connecting to. Click **Next** when complete.

Figure 7.19 Destination Address Screen of the Demand Dial Wizard

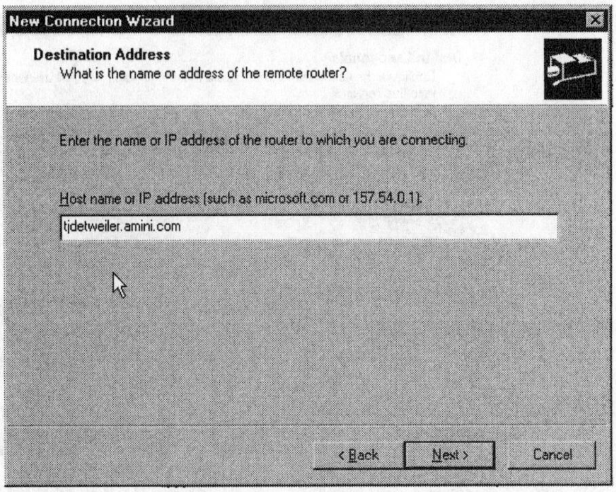

13. The Protocols and Security screen allows you to add a user account so a remote router can dial in. It also allows you to make certain that IP packets can be routed. Make sure both options are selected and click **Next**. See Figure 7.20.

Figure 7.20 Protocols and Security Screen of the Demand Dial Wizard

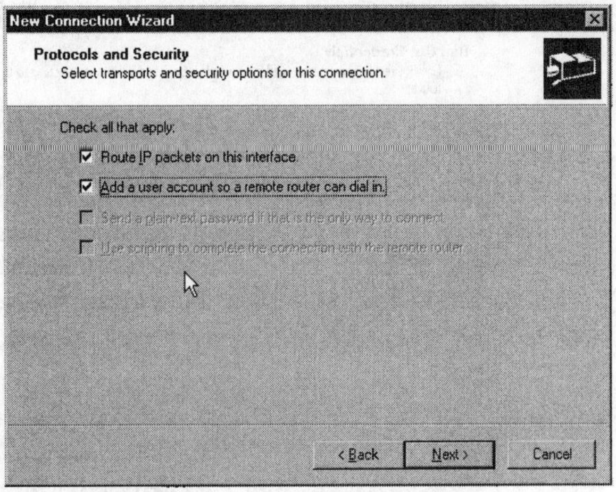

14. You need to enter a static route for the remote networks that you will connect to. After you do so, click **Next**. You are now presented with the Dial In Credentials screen as seen in Figure 7.21. Enter an appropriate password, confirm it, and click **Next**.

Figure 7.21 Dial In Credentials Screen of the Demand Dial Wizard

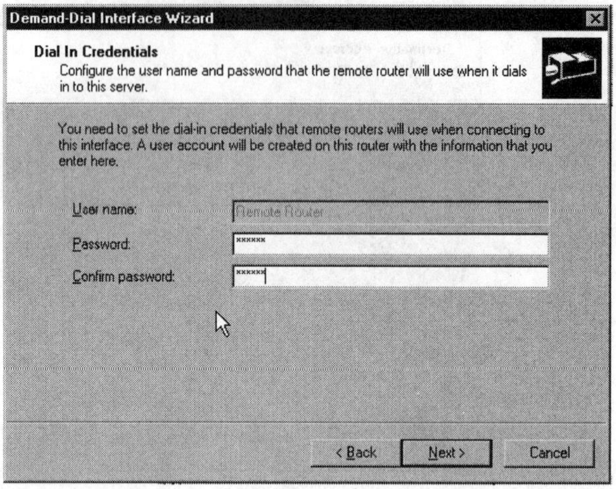

15. The Dial Out Credentials screen is similar, as you see in Figure 7.22. The difference lies in that you must enter a username (of the router) and a domain name. Enter values for these fields, click **Next**, and complete the wizard.

Figure 7.22 Dial Out Credentials Screen of the Demand Dial Wizard

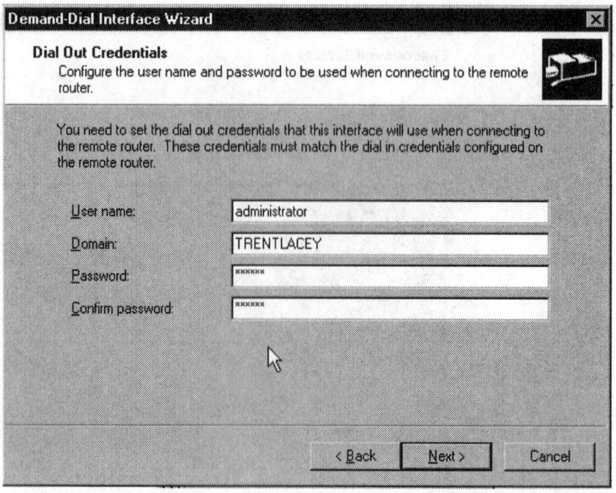

Implementing a PPTP remote access VPN is identical on the server end to the steps in the exercise we just completed, except that you would of course not need a demand dial interface. You would only need to configure the individual client.

In addition to user authentication, data encryption provides security that a VPN needs. Microsoft's implementation of PPTP uses the Microsoft Point-to-Point Encryption (MPPE) protocol for data encryption. MPPE uses automatically refreshing keys, and although the initial MPPE protocol was somewhat flawed, the version currently in use by PPTP is quite strong. It only encrypts the data, however, and does not encrypt the entire authentication process.

EXAM WARNING

Windows Server 2003 supports IPSec Network Address Translator (NAT) Traversal (NAT-T), but no other Microsoft operating system *natively* does. If you have a NAT server under Windows Server 2003, you can now use L2TP/IPSec as well as PPTP.

L2TP

L2TP is a protocol that was a new feature of Windows 2000. It is a combination of PPTP and Layer 2 Forwarding (L2F), which was put forth by Cisco Systems. L2TP can encapsulate PPP frames just as PPTP can, but in contrast can then be sent over IP, ATM, or Frame Relay. It is rather more complicated than PPTP, and it is more secure.

The IPSec Encapsulating Security Payload (ESP) protocol is used to encrypt L2TP traffic. As you can see in Figure 7.23, one advantage of IPSec is that it encrypts more than just the PPP data packet:

Figure 7.23 Diagram of an L2TP Packet

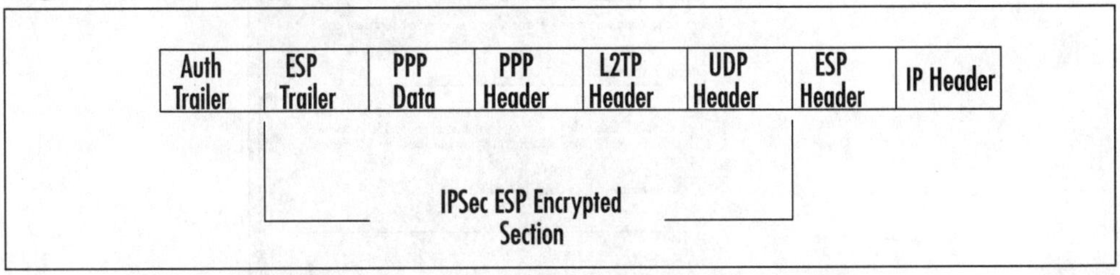

As to security, L2TP is extremely strong. In addition to requiring user authentication through PPP, L2TP requires machine authentication via certificates. Although certificates are covered in Chapter 3, you need to understand the following requirements for an L2TP implementation of a LAN-to-LAN VPN: First, a user certificate needs to be installed on the calling router, and a computer certificate needs to be installed on the answering router.

TEST DAY TIP

If the answering router is a member server in a domain, a computer certificate is required for L2TP. However, if the router is a domain controller (DC), a DC certificate is needed.

Next, the user certificate needs to be mapped to the answering router. Finally, to complete the answering router configuration, we turn to Exercise 7.03.

EXERCISE 7.03

CONFIGURING AN L2TP RRAS SERVER TO ACCEPT CERTIFICATES

1. Open the RRAS configuration utility, right-click the server, and choose **Properties**.
2. On the **Security** tab, click the **Authentication Methods** button as in Figure 7.24.

Figure 7.24 Security Tab of the Answering Router's Properties Sheet

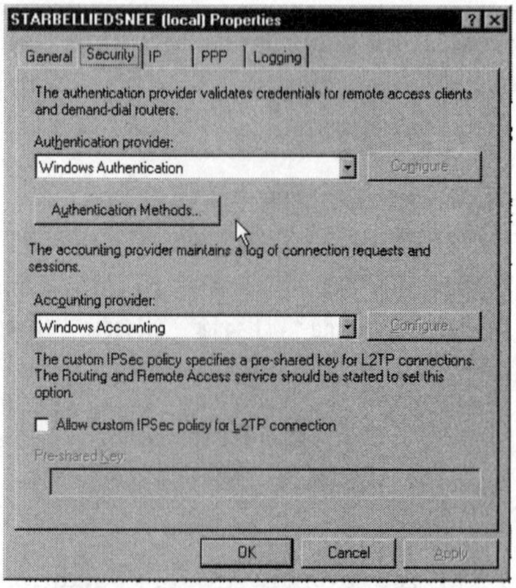

3. Make sure that the **Extensible authentication protocol (EAP)** and the **Microsoft encrypted authentication version 2 (MS-**

CHAP v2) are selected. If extra security is required, *clear* the Microsoft encrypted authentication (MS-CHAP) option.

Figure 7.25 Authentication Methods Screen

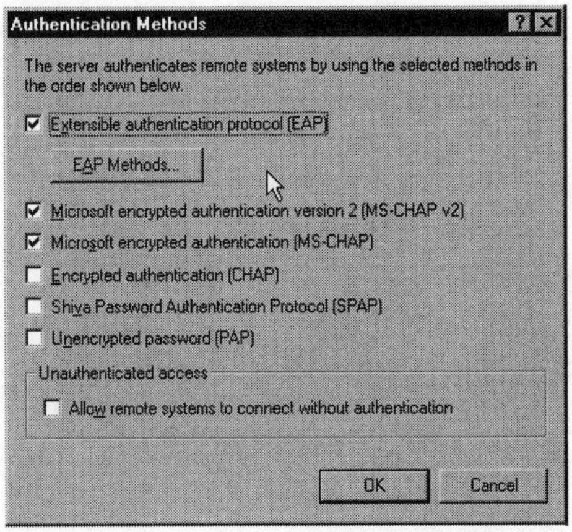

With the answering router thus set, we need to finish the configuration of the calling router. This involves making the enterprise root CA of the answering router trusted by the calling router. Finally, we need to configure the calling router's RRAS to use certificates—somewhat similar to Exercise 7.03, when we configured the answering router's RRAS to accept certificates.

The first step in this configuration is to right-click the appropriate interface from the **Network Interfaces** container (such as a demand dial interface) and select **Properties** as shown in Figure 7.26.

Figure 7.26 Choosing Properties of a Demand Dial Interface

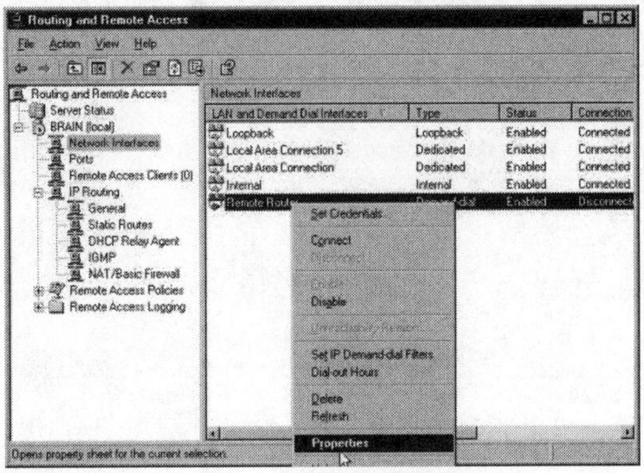

On the **Security** tab as in Figure 7.27, you would choose **Advanced (custom settings)** and then click the **Settings** button.

Figure 7.27 Security Tab of the Demand Dial Interface

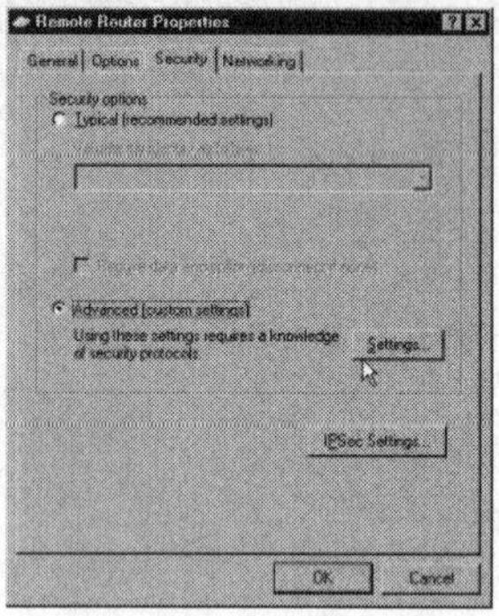

Next, you would choose **Use Extensible Authentication Protocol (EAP)**, and then click the **Properties** button. This is seen in Figure 7.28.

Figure 7.28 Advanced Security Settings Screen of the Security Tab

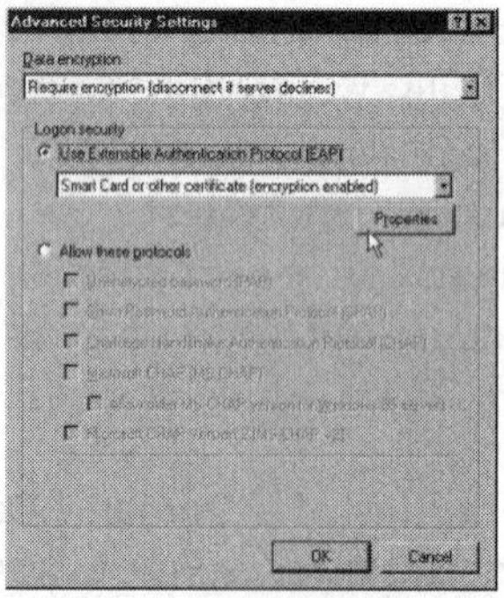

On the dialog box that appears, check the **Validate server certificate** box, and choose the trusted enterprise root CA that we spoke about earlier. Figure 7.29 illustrates this step.

Figure 7.29 Smart Card or Other Certificates Properties Screen

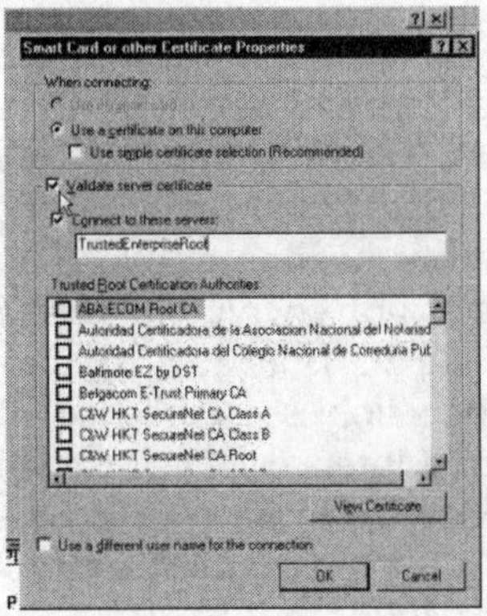

Finally, returning to the main RRAS window, you would again right-click the same interface and select **Set Credentials**, as shown in Figure 7.30.

Figure 7.30 Setting Credentials on the Demand Dial Interface

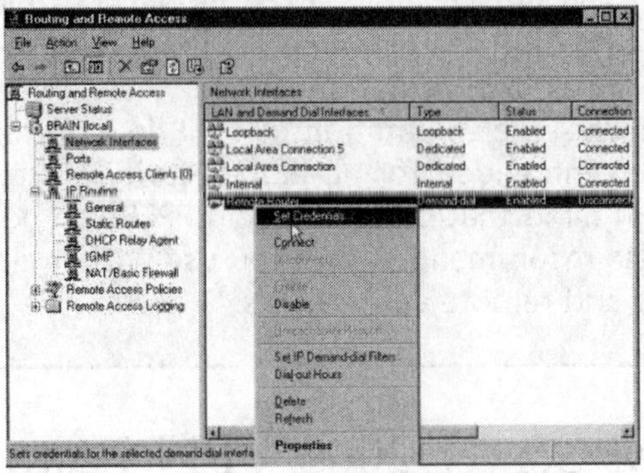

By setting the credential to the certificate that was mapped earlier, we will have completed the configurations on the calling router.

Designing & Planning...

PPTP versus L2TP

When choosing which layering protocol to use for a secure VPN, you should understand some of the differences between them. One of the largest differences between PPTP and L2TP is the method of encryption that each uses. PPTP uses MPPE, and L2TP uses IPSec ESP.

When PPTP negotiations happen between a client and the VPN server, the authentication phase is not encrypted, even when using the strongest form of MPPE (128-bit RSA RC4). IPSec encryption, however, is negotiated even before the L2TP connection is established. This allows the securing of both data and passwords. Moreover, IPSec can be configured to use Triple DES (3-DES). 3-DES is based on three separately generated 56-bit keys, for true 168-bit encryption. It is the strongest encryption method natively supported by Windows Server 2003.

Another consideration when choosing between L2TP and PPTP is how to implement packet filtering. In RRAS, packet filters can be implemented through the external interface's property sheet, located in the General IP Routing section. To allow only PPTP traffic through the VPN server requires the dropping of all traffic except TCP port 1723 and protocol ID number 47 on both the input and output filters. L2TP, however, is more complicated. It requires the dropping of all traffic except UDP port 500, UDP port 4500, and UDP port 1701.

Even though the implementation of L2TP is more administrative work than PPTP, it is recommended for all high-security environments. However, you should keep in mind that both L2TP and PPTP can be used on the same VPN server. It is also recommended that you use packet filtering and firewalls on all LAN-to-LAN and remote access VPNs.

New Windows Server 2003 VPN Features

In addition to providing general security (for example, limiting the membership of the Administrators group and physically securing the system) and choosing a tunneling protocol as described earlier, there are other security matters to be concerned with when designing a VPN strategy. We will discuss some of the key points, such as remote access policies and IP packet filtering, in a few moments. First, however, we will discuss two of Windows Server 2003's VPN components.

Connection Manager and *Connection Point Services* are billed by Microsoft as security points, but in reality they are more useful considered from an administrative view. The Connection Manager, or CM, is a combination of Connection Point Services (CPS), the Connection Manager Administration Kit (CMAK), and the CM client dialer software. The CMAK is a management tool that helps administrators design customized CM profiles (dialers). These profiles can boost security on the VPN client because when the user invokes them, they automatically configure the appropriate VPN connections, including security. CPS is used to create and distribute customized "phone books"—that is, collections of local phone numbers that users spread across a geographically disparate organization can use to dial local ISPs when starting the VPN connection process.

Network Access Quarantine Control is used to ensure that before a normal remote access connection is allowed to proceed, the connection is placed in a quarantined mode. The mode has very limited network access abilities, and is used until the remote system is checked for integrity and security. This check is performed by a script that is usually created by an administrator and implemented by policy on an Internet Authentication Server (IAS), and can be extremely useful in making certain that remote systems attempting to connect are "secure" themselves.

Using Remote Access Policies

One of the most important aspects of securing a remote access or VPN Windows Server 2003 system is the use of remote access policies and remote access profiles. Policies control such restrictions as what time of day and which groups have permission to connect, whereas profiles control such restrictions as maximum session time and idle timeout. In other words, think of a policy as defining *who* can access your remote access or VPN server, and a profile as *what* you can do once you get there.

After launching the RRAS utility, right-click on **Remote Access Policies** and select **New Remote Access Policy**. As you can see in Figure 7.31, you can add a number of policy conditions, such as authentication type and tunnel type matches. You can also control access by means of group membership—you simply specify the appropriate group membership as a policy condition. Authorization on an individual user basis can be done through the user object's property sheet on the Dial-in tab.

Figure 7.31 Remote Access Policy Settings Screen

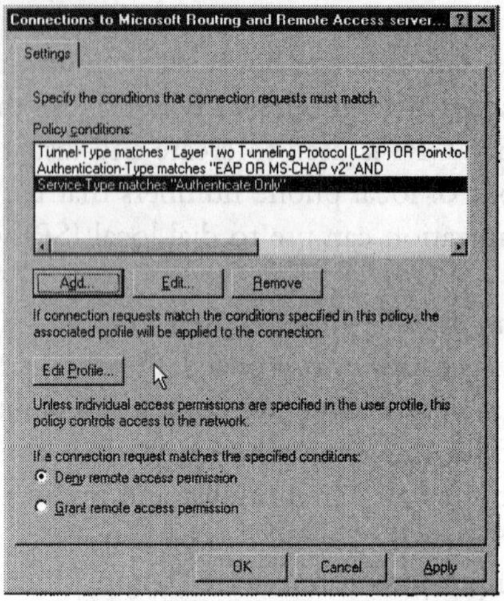

If any of the policy conditions don't match, access is denied or granted based on the option button choice made at the bottom of Figure 7.31. However, if all the conditions are met, the associated profile is then applied. Clicking the **Edit Profile** button gives us the screen shown in Figure 7.32. The Authentication tab allows you to choose which protocols are allowed for the connection. It is recommended that only EAP and MS-CHAP v2 be used in secure environments, and only under very controlled situations should you select unauthenticated access.

Figure 7.32 Authentication Tab of the Remote Access Profile Screen

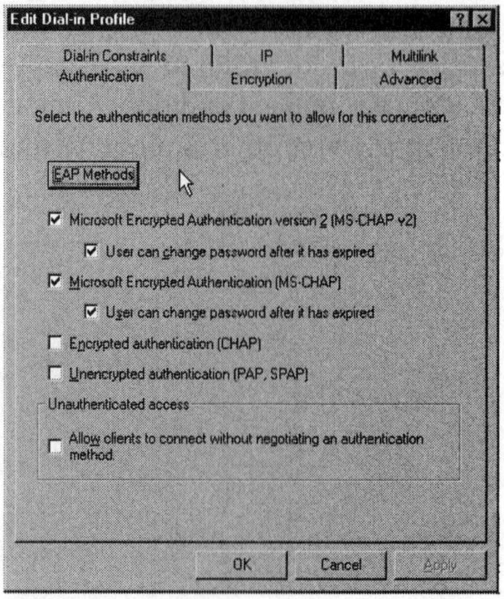

The Encryption tab, shown in Figure 7.33, gives you the choice of whether to use MPPE 40-bit basic level encryption, MPPE 56-bit strong level encryption, or MPPE 128-bit strongest level encryption.

Figure 7.33 Encryption Tab of the Remote Access Profile Screen

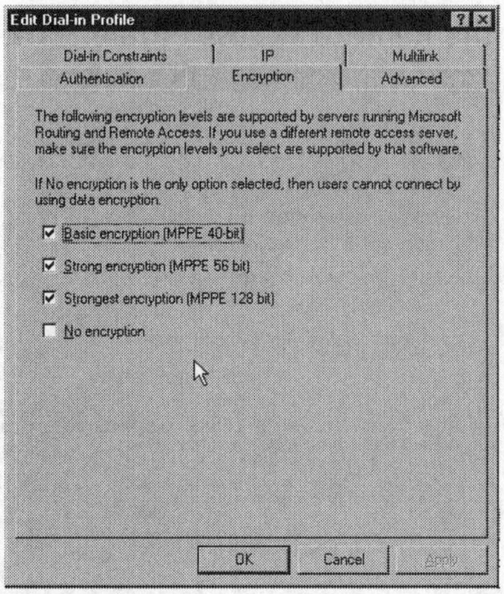

Once a client is connected to the remote access server, the Dial-in Constraints tab can be used to limit the amount of time the client can connect, set the amount of time the server can remain idle, or allow connections only during specified times set by the administrator. Figure 7.34 shows the details of this tab.

Figure 7.34 Dial-in Constraints Tab of the Remote Access Profile Screen

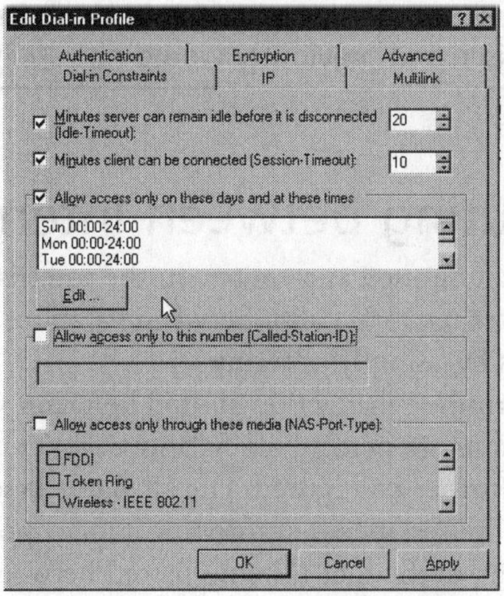

The tab that controls which packets can come and go is shown in Figure 7.35. The IP tab is used to set input filters and output filters. These filters define which packets the interface receives, based on type, and are perhaps the easiest and most effective component of remote access security that you can implement.

Figure 7.35 IP Tab of the Remote Access Profile Screen

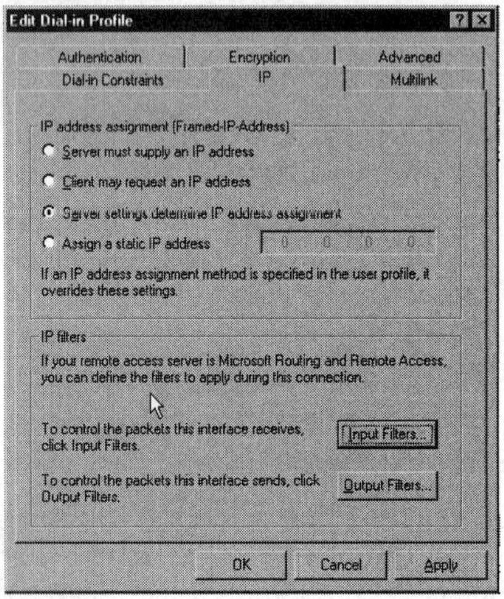

Test Day Tip

If multiple remote access servers are to be implemented in your network design, it is strongly recommended that you use IAS as a RADIUS server. This way, IAS can be used to centrally administer and control authentication for all the remote access servers in your organization. If this is the case, the policies and profiles discussed previously would not apply.

Designing Routing between Internal Networks

Windows Server 2003 can be used as a router on the internal network. As such, it can be used to secure internetwork traffic between locations and to control traffic between internal subnets by using IP filtering.

IP filtering can determine what action should be taken when IP traffic matches the IP filter criteria. Actions are permit, block, and negotiate. Negotiate allows the security measures to be further configured. The IP filters base their actions on source and/or destination IP addresses, specific protocols, and/or ports. This allows Windows Server 2003 to control the traffic that is being passed between internal networks.

EXAM 70-298 OBJECTIVE 3.6.1 3.6

Designing an Extranet Infrastructure

Most of the time, we think of using VPNs to connect remote users or branch offices to the local network. We can also use a VPN to create a link to another company such as a third-party vendor. In this case, we call the remote network an *extranet*. An extranet is a portion of the network that can be extended to business partners or vendors. It can make all or part of your network accessible to outside organizations. Since the network will be extended between the companies over a public network or Internet, security will always be a concern for both companies. Previous sections of this chapter have already covered the mechanisms required to design a secure VPN, and we now review some of those features that are used to create the extranet.

The extranet will require that you create a site-to-site (*router-to-router* or *LAN-to-LAN* are synonyms) VPN connection. In the extranet, the calling router initiates the VPN connection. The answering router listens for a connection request and then responds to create the connection. The calling router then authenticates itself to the answering router. The site-to-site VPN connection can be a persistent or a demand dial connection. Persistent connections are always connected. If the connection is lost, it is retried immediately. A persistent connection is created on the calling router by selecting **Persistent connection** on the **Options** tab on the VPN interface.

The answering router completes the persistent connection by going to the Dial-in Constraints tab on the site-to-site VPN connection's profile properties of the remote access policy. On the tab, clear the **Minutes server can remain idle before it is connected** and **Minutes client can be connected** check boxes. The demand dial connection for a site-to-site connection is only made to forward specific traffic across the VPN. The connection can be terminated if thresholds are reached for connection times or idle times. The answering router controls these times. To prevent the calling router from making unnecessary connection, demand dial filtering and dial-out hours can be set. Once the connection has been made, Remote Access Policy Profiles can control the traffic between the sites by implementing packet filtering. The profiles can specify the types of IP traffic, which VPN clients can send traffic, and which users are allowed to connect through the VPN. Remote access policies can also be used for authenticating and authorizing the traffic between sites.

One element that we have not yet discussed is the placement of the VPN server in relation to a firewall. Often, a VPN server will be placed outside the firewall to facilitate easy communication with potentially different extranets. In this case, however, traffic through the firewall can be limited to L2TP/IPSec and PPTP. If the VPN server is placed between two firewalls (a DMZ or "screened" subnet), traffic both to and from the server can be regulated. This is Microsoft's preferred method of VPN placement. Remember also, however, that the firewall will likely have to support other protocols such as HTTP on port 80 and SMTP on port 25. As a final note, ensuring that a firewall only permits traffic to pass that is *absolutely necessary* is a primary tenet of securing the network infrastructure.

EXAM 70-298 OBJECTIVE 3.6.2

Cross-Certification of Certificate Services

If you plan to use L2TP/IPSec connections or EAP-TLS authentication over the VPN, you will need to use cross-certification of certificate services. For the L2TP connections, a computer certificate will need to be installed on both the calling and answering VPN servers. This will provide the ability for both computers to provide the required authentication needed to create the session and enable the use of IPSec.

A computer certificate needs to be installed on the authenticating server, which can either be the answering VPN server or a RADIUS server (IAS) if EAP-TLS authentication will be used. A user certificate must then be installed on the calling VPN router.

Summary of Exam Objectives

This chapter was dedicated to those networks that rely on external communication of some nature. For some companies, the external partner might be a corporate LAN that is geographically distant from the main office (the typical branch office scenario). For other companies, the partner might be an individual user trying to connect to the network. Finally, the partner might be a separate company that needs to connect with your network for an alliance project. In any of these cases, the security risks of a normal network are increased.

When using Windows Server 2003 as a router that connects site to site, the choice of routing protocols will certainly impact your security design. Static routes, RIP, OSPF, and even Auto-Static routing can be used depending on your environment. Although static routes are secure, they frequently are difficult to administer and for non-demand dial connections, many turn to RIP or OSPF. These protocols can be made more secure by using password-based authorization, route filtering, and even peer limiting. Demand dial connections are frequently used in site-to-site communications if a persistent connection is unavailable. In this case, certificates or other strong authentication protocols such as MS-CHAP v2 can be used to heighten security. The data encryption needs of a site-to-site connection can be met by using MPPE or IPSec.

We next turned our attention to securing VPN servers when used for site-to-site or remote access scenarios. Frequently, the reason for establishing a VPN is to save a dollar, but since the data now passes over an insecure public network such as the Internet, security becomes top priority for most companies. One of the first choices that you must make in designing a VPN solution is which tunneling protocol to use. PPTP is a secure protocol that uses MPPE to encrypt traffic and is relatively easy to implement. For more demanding situations, L2TP with IPSec can be used. The IPSec ESP protocol uses a more impressive encryption standard than MPPE, and is considered to be unbreakable. However, to use L2TP you must have a certificate infrastructure so that user and computer certificates can be issued when necessary. The EAP-TLS protocol allows for certificate use, but while extremely secure, some might find the implementation of a PKI unnecessary.

The first line of defense for any VPN server is to demand authentication of entities that are attempting to connect. Remote access policies and profiles help accomplish the goal by limiting who is authorized to connect, and also by limiting how they connect and for how long. Network Access Quarantine Control and securing VPN traffic through an appropriate firewall can also be key points in the security design.

Windows Server 2003 has many features that are quite useful in creating a secure communication network with external partners. Some, like L2TP and EAP-TLS, are industry standards, and some, like MPPE and MS-CHAP v2, are Microsoft standards. Whichever combination you decide to use in your router and VPN implementations, however, you can be assured that attackers will be up against a formidable opponent if they attempt to siege your network.

Exam Objectives Fast Track

Designing Security for Communication between Networks

- ☑ RRAS is used to configure Windows Server 2003 as a router for internetwork communications. The route can be configured with either a dedicated connection or with a demand dial connection, and the design and implementation of a routing protocol is a key to good security.
- ☑ RIP version 2, OSPF, and static routes can be made secure if implemented properly. This can include using password-based router authentication, route filtering, and peer limiting.
- ☑ Demand dial connections can be kept secure by using certificates and router authentication for dial-in and dial-out events.

Designing VPN Connectivity

- ☑ VPN tunnels are created by either the PPTP or L2TP protocols. Both encrypt all data sent over the Internet—PPTP uses MPPE and L2TP uses IPSec ESP. L2TP is more secure because IPSec encrypts the authentication phase as well as the data.
- ☑ Remote access policies and profiles constrain who can connect to the network, and what they can do when they get there. Security considerations include authentication methods and time restrictions.
- ☑ Windows Server 2003 allows the administrator to use features like IP packet filtering, VPN/firewall placement, and Network Access Quarantine Control to secure VPN LAN-to-LAN and remote access connections.

Exam Objectives Frequently Asked Questions

The following Frequently Asked Questions, answered by the authors of this book, are designed to both measure your understanding of the Exam Objectives presented in this chapter, and to assist you with real-life implementation of these concepts. You will also gain access to thousands of other FAQs at ITFAQnet.com.

Q: Are VPN connections more secure than regular dial-up connections?

A: No. Regular dial-up connections do not transfer data over public networks. The capability of most attackers to intercept packets crossing the analog telephone network is small at best. With proper design, however, VPN connections can be made very secure.

Q: Do vendors besides Microsoft support RIP and OSPF?

A: Yes, but support for OSPF is more ubiquitous. OSPF is more complex than RIP, but is more efficient. Both protocols can be secured.

Q: Do demand dial routes use OSPF?

A: No. Static routes must be manually added for use with demand dial routes. Automatic static routes can be used, with slightly increased security risk.

Q: Can L2TP be used if my network uses Network Address Translation (NAT)?

A: Windows Server 2003 supports NAT Traversal (NAT-T), which means that L2TP packets can be forwarded across NAT. PPTP can cross a NAT server without the aid of NAT-T.

Q: If L2TP is more secure than PPTP, why would I want to use PPTP at all?

A: Using L2TP requires an existing public key infrastructure (PKI) in order to support certificate authentication. Implementing such an infrastructure can be needlessly complicated in a smaller network or one that does not require the highest security levels.

Q: Can my VPN be used behind a firewall?

A: Yes, but you will need to let through the appropriate tunneling traffic. This can mean allowing TCP port 1723 for PPTP, UDP port 500 and UDP Port 1701 among others for L2TP. If a firewall blocks everything but what is absolutely necessary, it is doing its job.

Self Test

A Quick Answer Key follows the Self Test questions. For complete questions, answers, and explanations to the Self Test questions in this chapter as well as the other chapters in this book, see the Self Test Appendix.

Designing Security for Communication between Networks

1. Your network consists of Windows Server 2003 domain controllers (DCs), Windows 2003 DNS servers, and Windows XP clients. You have recently added a firewall to the network to provide security for the network from attack from the Internet. You have placed your Web, e-mail, and DNS servers outside the firewall. Your company has established a written policy that allows only SMTP, HTTP, and DNS traffic to pass through the firewall. Which ports do you need to permit? (Choose all that apply.)

   A. TCP/UDP 21

   B. TCP/UDP 23

   C. TCP/UDP 25

   D. TCP/UDP 53

   E. TCP/UDP 80

   F. TCP/UDP 110

   G. TCP/UDP 443

2. You are designing a network implementation for your company and you want to have an Internet presence for your Web and e-mail servers. The Web server is called WebSvr1, and the e-mail server is named MailSvr1. Due to a recent bout of attacks, you need to implement a solution that will provide security and protection for your network. You are concerned about providing security for the Web and e-mail servers, yet you need to provide anonymous access to the Web server for the general public. You are worried that these anonymous users might use their access to investigate and attack the rest of your network as well. How do you design your network? (Select the best answer.)

   A. Install Windows 2003 Server to act as the host computer for the Web and e-mail servers. Implement access control authentication for the users accessing the Web server. Add the IUSR_WebSvr1 user account to the directories that contain the Web files. Grant the IUSR_WebSvr1 user account read-only access. Grant access permissions to the network users as necessary.

B. Implement a firewall solution to protect the network. Place the Web and e-mail servers outside of the firewall. Configure the firewall to block user access from the Internet.

C. Implement a firewall solution to protect the network. Place two firewalls between the Internet and the internal network. Place the Web and e-mail servers outside the firewalls. Configure the firewalls to block user access from the Internet. Add the IUSR_WebSvr1 user account to the directories that contain the Web files. Grant the IUSR_WebSvr1 user account read-only access. Grant access permissions to the network users as necessary. Configure both firewalls to allow internal users to have access to the Internet.

D. Implement a firewall solution. Configure two firewalls. Place the Web and e-mail servers between the two firewalls. Configure the first firewall to allow access to the Web and e-mail servers by anonymous users using the IUSR_WebSvr1 user account. Configure the second firewall to allow internal users to have access to the Internet. Configure the second firewall not to allow any external users to pass through the firewall.

E. Implement a firewall solution to protect the network. Place two firewalls between the Internet and the internal network. Place the Web and e-mail servers inside the firewalls. Configure the firewalls to block all user access from the Internet. Add the IUSR_WebSvr1 user account to the directories that contain the Web files. Grant the IUSR_WebSvr1 user account read-only access. Grant access permissions to the network users as necessary. Configure both firewalls to allow internal users to have access to the Internet.

3. You have a network that consists of four subnets. The networks IDs for the networks are 10.0.1.0/24, 10.0.2.0/24, 10.0.3.0/24, and 10.0.4.0/24. Each subnet has two Windows Server 2003 and 75 Windows XP clients. You are planning to add a VPN server to the network to provide connectivity for remote users. You need to summarize the internal network IDs on the VPN server. What is the minimum information needed to accomplish the desired result?

   A. An entry for each subnet is required in the static route table of the VPN server.

   B. An entry for each subnet is required in the static route table of the remote clients.

C. A route summarization entry, 10.0.0.0/16, can be added to the VPN server.

D. A route summarization entry, 10.0.0.0/16, can be added to the remote clients.

4. You are configuring routing on an RRAS server. The RRAS server's intranet interfaces are configured to be connected to the intranet with a manual TCP/IP configuration that will consist of the IP address, subnet mask, default gateway, and intranet DNS servers. You are now experiencing difficulties when users attempt to connect to the Internet. What must you do to resolve these conflicts?

   A. Configure the intranet interface to use the Internet DNS servers.

   B. Configure the intranet interface with a public IP address.

   C. Assign the IP address for the intranet interface to use DHCP.

   D. Delete the default gateway configuration on the intranet interface.

Designing VPN Connectivity

5. You are designing a VPN that will allow the company's sales force to travel to multiple cities around the Untied States. You are using an Internet service provider (ISP) that provides service across the United States and has local numbers in all major cities and many smaller cities as well. The ISP is constantly adding new telephone numbers as it expands its service area. The sales manager is concerned that his sales force will not know what the local access number will be in the cities where they will be traveling. He asks if there is a solution that will help the sales force to make the VPN connection so that they can pass confidential client information and sales orders back to corporate headquarters. What is the best solution to address this problem?

   A. There is nothing that can be done to help the sales force.

   B. You can configure an Access database that contains all of the telephone numbers for the ISP.

   C. You can configure a contact list in Exchange that lists the telephone numbers in all the cities that are supported by the ISP.

   D. Create a custom phone book using Connection Point Services.

6. You have designed a Windows Server 2003 VPN solution for your corporation. The solution has a Windows Server 2003 VPN server at headquarters. The VPN server has been placed behind the internal firewall protecting your network. You have created a DNS record on your Internet server in the DMZ so that you can perform name resolution to the VPN server. You have tested connectivity to

the VPN server from all of the client computers using the PING utility. The clients at the branch offices are running Windows 98 and Windows XP. The Windows 98 clients are configured to use PPTP to establish the VPN connections. The Windows XP clients are configured to use L2TP using IPSec. The Windows 98 clients are using MS-CHAP v 2 to authenticate themselves as users. The Windows XP clients are using user-level certificate authentication with EAP-TLS. The Windows XP clients are not experiencing any difficulties in connecting, but the Windows 98 clients are not able to connect to the VPN server. What should you check to resolve the connectivity issue for the Windows 98 clients?

A. Upgrade all of the Windows 98 computers to Windows 2000 or Windows XP.

B. Configure the firewall to allow PPTP traffic to pass.

C. Move the VPN server to outside the external firewall.

D. Change the default authentication protocol to use certificates.

7. You have just replaced many of your company's dial-in connections with VPN connections to reduce the costs of maintaining dial-in services. You have recently configured VPN access on a laptop for a user. You have specified the host name for the VPN server in the Host Name or IP Address box. Now the user is complaining that he is receiving the error message "Destination Host Unknown." What is the most likely cause for this error message?

   A. The DNS server has not been properly configured for the new VPN server.

   B. The laptop has not been authorized to connect to the VPN server.

   C. The VPN client has not been configured with the username with permission to access the VPN server.

   D. The Remote access policy has not been configured to allow access to the user.

8. You have just installed Routing and Remote Access on a Windows Server 2003 to function as a VPN server. Several remote users need to transmit confidential data to the company using the VPN server. The remote users are not members of your company's domain. The remote users are running Windows XP on the client computers, and they all have access to a local ISP to provide Internet connectivity. Data transmission security is critical to the company and to the remote users. All of the clients will be using L2TP to create the connection to the VPN server. Which secure authentication method should you use for these connections?

A. Configure L2TP to use MPPE 128-bit encryption.

B. Create a custom IPSec policy and select certificate-based 5 authentication. Apply the policy to the appropriate OU.

C. Configure L2TP to use MS-CHAP v2.

D. Use the certificate-based authentication method of the Routing and Remote Access custom IPSec policy for the L2TP connection.

Self Test Quick Answer Key

For complete questions, answers, and explanations to the Self Test questions in this chapter as well as the other chapters in this book, see the Self Test Appendix.

1. **C, D, E**
2. **D**
3. **C**
4. **D**
5. **D**
6. **B**
7. **A**
8. **D**

Chapter 8

MCSE 70-298

Securing Active Directory

Exam Objectives in this Chapter:

- 4.1 Design an access control strategy for directory services.
- 2.2.4 Establish account and password requirements for security.
- 4.1.2 Analyze auditing requirements.
- 4.1.1 Create a delegation strategy.
- 4.1.3 Design the appropriate group strategy for accessing resources.
- 4.1.4 Design a permission structure for directory service objects.

- ☑ Summary of Exam Objectives
- ☑ Exam Objectives Fast Track
- ☑ Exam Objectives Frequently Asked Questions
- ☑ Self Test
- ☑ Self Test Quick Answer Key

Introduction

All network access begins with one thing: a user account. You can grant network access to an individual user account, or to a group object that contains multiple accounts; whether it's a user or a group object, anything that you use to assign permissions is called a *security principal*. You will use security principals on your network to assign permissions to network resources such as file shares and folders, and rights assignments such as "Log on interactively" and "Backup files and folders." The total combination of rights and permissions assigned to a user account, along with any permissions assigned to groups that the user is a member of, defines what a user can and cannot do when working on a network.

Given the importance of user accounts, then, it stands to reason that securing the directory that houses your user database information should be one of the primary goals of your security design plan. Imagine, for example, that you've been asked to restrict access to a certain file to only your company's Senior Directors. What you're being asked to do here is twofold: to restrict who has access to the file, and to protect who has access to the accounts being used by the Senior Directors. If a Senior Director's username and password were compromised, then an unauthorized user would be able to access this confidential file. It is important to understand the potential risks to the Active Directory database, and to design your Active Directory user accounts in a secure fashion. In addition, we'll discuss the use of security countermeasures such as Account and Password policies to keep the Active Directory database safe. We'll also discuss the use of auditing to ensure that no unauthorized user activity or other potential security incidents are taking place.

We'll close this chapter with a discussion of some best practices in assigning user permissions to network resources and data. From your readings in preparing for the MCSE Core Four exams, you should be familiar with the acronym AGDLP, which describes the recommended way to assign permissions to a resource. In AGDLP, user accounts are added to global groups, and then global groups are added to Domain Local groups. Permissions or user rights assignments are finally assigned to the Domain Local group. In preparation for the 70-298 exam, we'll look at some scenarios where you'll determine how to create a group structure that will allow you to assign permissions and rights in a secure, efficient manner.

EXAM 70-298 OBJECTIVE 4.1

Designing an Access Control Strategy for Directory Services

A proper access control strategy begins with identifying the methods by which it will be enforced. There are several approaches you can take when designing security; your first step should be in identifying which one fits your organization's needs, and designing the strategy accordingly. Let's start by breaking down the access control strategy into two parts:

- **Access** This strategy calls for granting fairly open access to files and resources and then locking it down according to need. This philosophy has its advantages but seems to give priority to the idea of access over security. Needless to say, this can pose a larger security threat to your network.
- **Control** This strategy give priority to security and tends to start off by locking down resources to a maximum and then relaxing security gradually as the need arises. This approach ensures higher security but also makes it harder and more complicated to gain access.

So, which design strategy is right? There is no perfect answer for all situations; what you need is the perfect blend between access and control for your environment. You don't want to expose your resources unnecessarily, but you also don't want to lock down to the point where your design is unusable and impractical. Based on your company's nature and its approach to security, you should be able to formulate a good medium. However, because this guide is security oriented and the corresponding exam will be security focused, we recommend that you select the most restrictive access control (often referred to as "least permissions") and then relax those permissions as needed.

It is good to note, though, that based on the evolution of the Windows operating system and new out-of-the-box security enhancements, you will notice that Microsoft's strategy shifted from being access oriented with Windows 2000 and earlier, to being control oriented with Windows Server 2003. This change is mostly noticeable with the default settings that are given to NTFS and share permissions. With Windows 2000 and earlier, the Everyone group had full control by default on any new files or folders you created. Windows Server 2003 tightens this security by granting the Everyone group read and execute permission on NTFS files and folders, and restricting Everyone to only read permission on shared files and folders.

Access control lists (ACLs) are comprised of two layers of security: the NTFS permissions and the share permissions. Share permissions apply to users who are connecting across the network to a resource. NTFS permissions are applied on the actual files and folders. When requesting access to a resource, the most restrictive access of the combination of security between the NTFS and the share permissions is applied. Best practices call for leaving the share permissions at their default settings, and then using the NTFS permissions to restrict access. This is due to a number of disadvantages that share permissions have, including:

- Share permissions cannot be backed up; therefore, if you ever need to restore resources you will lose the permissions.
- Share permissions cannot propagate through the directory structure, so if you create files and folders under the main folder, the permissions can't be inherited.

- Share permissions aren't as flexible as NTFS permissions and are limited to read, change, and full control.
- Share permissions are lost if you decide to unshare the folder.
- Share permissions cannot be audited.

NTFS permissions, however, do not suffer from the preceding disadvantages and tend to support more complex file and folder structures, where you can drill down to subfolders and set proper permissions. Figure 8.1 shows the basic security that can be implemented using NTFS.

Figure 8.1 NTFS Permissions Configuration Window

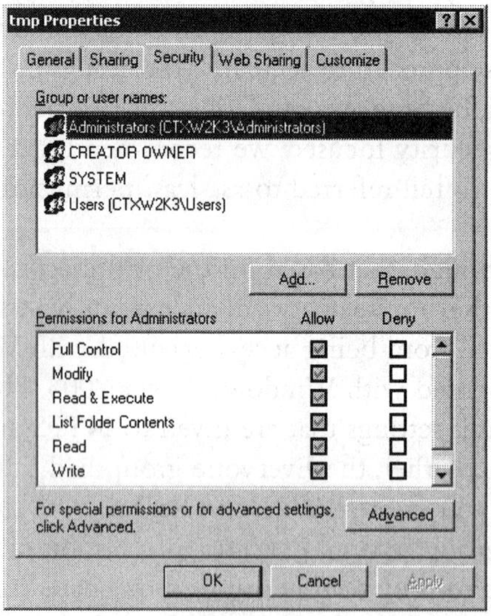

So, how does designing a proper ACL help increase security in your network? Before answering this question, we have to identify the "enemy"—who are you're attempting to secure your network *from*. Security can be breached on a network by either internal users or external users, and as such when designing security we should never neglect the task of securing our network against attack or misuse by internal users. Usually, we are focused on keeping external users out of our network, and this is mostly because of the media coverage and propaganda that hackers and virus makers get when they are able to breach security on networks. However, internal users can be as malicious and damaging (if not more so) in many instances.

ACLs are mostly used as a tool for securing against external attackers, but can also be used for protecting against internal users who are potentially in search of data theft or espionage, or just poking around out of simple curiosity. By not properly locking down files and folders at the NTFS security level, you expose these files and folders for data theft or deletion. Consider this scenario, one that reinforces the earlier point about finding a good medium for security on your network. A manager in your Human Resources department is working on a weekend where technical support is not available, and is trying to access files and folders that he or she should legitimately be able to access. Come Monday morning, this manager raises a complaint about how she commuted two hours into the office, only to be useless because she was unable to work. Let's say further that, as a result, you are asked to relax security on some network shares. Now it's several weeks later and you are getting swamped with calls about how important files are missing, or have been moved or modified. This demonstrates not only the importance of securing your files properly, but also of having appropriate levels of auditing enabled on your network. (We'll talk about auditing a bit later on.)

Now, if we switch our focus to external users, you will notice that the fight with external users begins at the firewall level or at the network perimeter, where you try to prevent them from ever gaining access to your network. They will try to find entry points to reach your data. So, for these types of users, the ACL would be considered your *second* line of defense, but still a necessary one in case an intruder managed to breach your firewall or perimeter network.

Analyzing Risks to Directory Services

Today's networks are so diversified and large that it is imperative to understand the vulnerabilities that an attacker can use to create risks within your directory services architecture. One thing you should always keep in mind is that, with user accounts, usernames are easy to guess because they are usually a predictable sequence like First Initial Last Name or some other similar combination. You can make this a bit harder to guess by appending the employee ID to the end of the username, for example, thus making it harder for an attacker to guess. Any additional information you add to the username that is unique to that user makes the username less vulnerable to being guessed. By doing this, if an attacker knows that a particular person works for this company, he or she will have to figure out the second ID appended to the username. Again, keep in mind you are trying to make it harder for a hacker to get any information that can help him or her compromise security on your network.

Now, if an attacker does figure out a legitimate username, this still leaves him or her with the dilemma of figuring out or "cracking" the password. In other words, the security to your entire network is one password away from broken. Weak passwords are something an attacker lives for. For this reason, your passwords should be complex and not easy to guess, especially passwords for administrative accounts.

Even though you can implement complex passwords for your network, if you do not obtain buy-in from your management staff you'll notice that they will resist these measures, and might ask you to relax the complexity requirements. This again leads us back to the strategy of "least permissions," in that you should always make sure that you don't give a user account more rights and permissions than the user needs access to in order to go about his or her daily job.

You should also be very vigilant about disabling and/or deleting accounts of users who have either left the company or have been on vacation for a long time. You want to make sure that you have a security policy in place where your Human Resources department always informs you about employee turnover, so that you don't allow a malicious user time to log in with his or her account and wreak havoc on the files and folders he or she has access to. This is especially critical when IT personnel are either fired or leave the company for any reason.

Assigning Rights and Permissions

Before you can assign rights and permissions, you need to know the distinction between the two. The terms seem to mean the same thing, but there is a world of difference between them:

- **Rights** allow a user to perform a specific task, such as the right to restart or shut down the system or maybe the right to change the time on the system.
- **Permissions** are assigned to an object, file, or folder and grant a user access to the resource such as the ability to change, delete, or read it.

The same way that you can grant rights and permissions, you can of course take away rights and deny permissions. For example, you can deny users from logging on locally to a domain controller (DC), or you could deny permissions to sensitive files and folders. User rights and permissions are assigned via group policy, and resource permissions can be applied manually by accessing the Properties tab of a file or folder.

Permissions can also be assigned using group policy, which can make this task easier to manage and maintain. To configure File and folder permissions using group policy, work through Exercise 8.01. (For the purposes of this example, we will edit the Default domain policy for a domain. You can also implement a group policy at the site or organizational unit (OU) level and follow the same steps.) In the following exercise, we'll go over the necessary steps to set permissions via group policy.

EXERCISE 8.01

SETTING PERMISSIONS USING GROUP POLICY

1. Open **Active Directory user and Computers**, and right-click the root of the domain, and click on **Properties**.
2. Edit the **Default Domain Policy**.
3. Browse to **Computer Configuration | Windows Settings | File System**.
4. Right-click **File System** and click **Add**.

5. Browse to the file or folder you want to set permissions on as shown in Figure 8.2 and click **OK**.

Figure 8.2 Setting Permissions on Folders via Group Policy

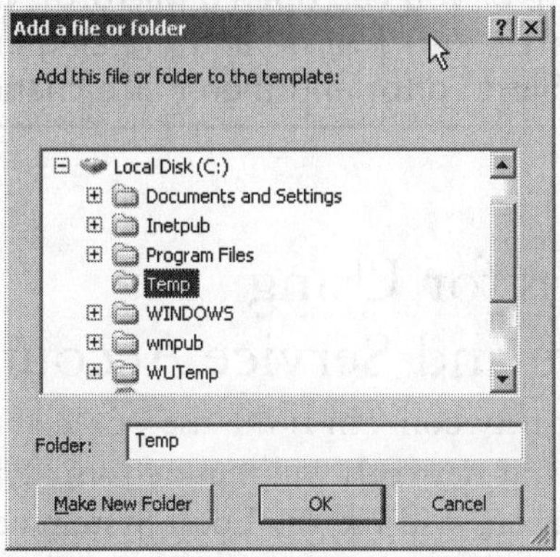

6. Set the proper permissions, specify the groups, and then click **OK**.
7. Select whether to inherit and propagate permissions to subfolders or to replace existing permissions and click **OK**.
8. Once you have added a file or folder, you can always right-click on it in the right control pane (see Figure 8.3) of the **File System** window and click on **Properties** and modify it.

Figure 8.3 Files and Folder Permissions Configured in Group Policy

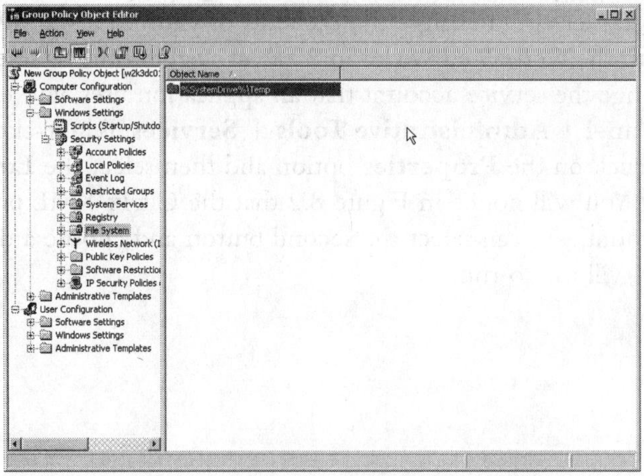

TEST DAY TIP

Keep in mind that there are several ways you can edit Group Policy in Windows 2000 and Windows Server 2003. You can use ADUC as in the examples shown, or you can open a Microsoft Management Console (MMC) by going to **Start | Run | MMC** and pressing **Enter**. You can then add the Group Policy Object Editor and then make changes to your policies.

Considerations for Using Administrative and Service Accounts

Another potential security concern is the use of *service accounts.* Many applications that are installed on your network will require some type of service accounts, and many of these applications will use the Local System account for that purpose. It is critical that you change this and create an account that has enough rights to perform everything the application needs to run properly. If a malicious user knows that a particular application is installed on your network and also knows that this application uses the default Local System account, this provides a tempting target to attempt to take over the security context of the Local System account to create denial-of-service (DoS) or elevation-of-privilege attacks. A good example of how this can be misused was the Blaster worm of 2003, which exploited a vulnerability in the RPC/DCOM service, caused DoS attacks and crashed the computers it infected by constantly rebooting them. This worm took advantage of the fact that the RPC service runs under the Local System account. Another example might be an IIS vulnerability where an attacker could change the contents of your Web site. (We've seen this happen with the Code Red worm in 2000, as well as other vulnerabilities.)

To change the service account that an application uses, you can go to **Start | Control Panel | Administrative Tools | Services**. Right-click the particular service; then click on the **Properties** option and then select the **Log On** tab (see Figure 8.4). You will notice in Figure 8.2 that the Citrix XML port is using the Local System account; you can select the second button and choose a different account that this service will use to run.

Figure 8.4 Changing the Account a Service Uses to Start

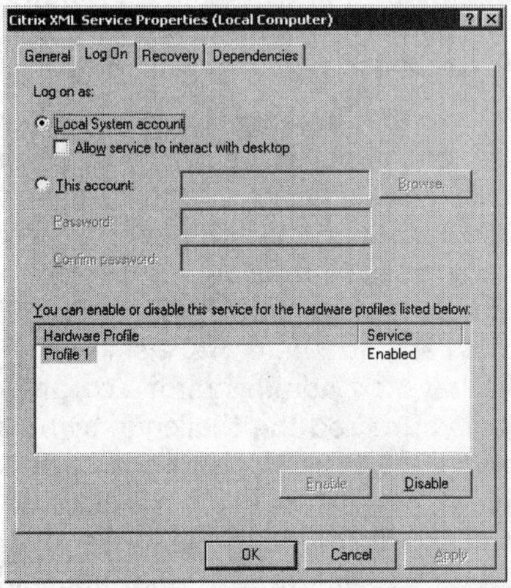

One thing you should try not to do is to use an Administrative account as a service account, because as we've already seen, attackers can exploit vulnerabilities in software that can allow them administrative access using this administrative server account. Another possibility would be if an attacker were a former IT employee (seeking revenge, for example). If that person is aware of the service account name, and the password hasn't been changed, he or she can use it to attack the network and leave no traces. For this reason, your service account passwords should be changed regularly and should only have enough rights to perform the action it is assigned to do.

However, you might sometimes run into a situation where an application will only run with administrative rights. If this happens, you can mitigate the risks to your network by giving the service account a long and complicated name and a complex password that is changed frequently.

Test Day Tip

When selecting an account to act as a service account, try to always make that account local to the server it is being used on rather than making it a domain account if possible. Using a local account can limit the scope of damage that an attacker can cause to the local machine only, whereas if you use a domain account with elevated privileges, the damage can quickly spread to other parts of the domain.

Configuring & Implementing...

A Decoy Administrative Account... Rename the Original but Keep a Fake

We are sure you are aware that best practices call for renaming the administrator account because that poses a direct security threat (since the attacker already knows 50 percent of what he or she needs to hack your account, which is the username). Renaming the administrator account is definitely recommended, but this still doesn't provide 100-percent security, because the administrator account has a unique Security Identifier (SID) that will identifies it regardless of what its name is. Therefore, a smart hacker, for example, will notice that you don't have an administrator account, and might be even more intrigued because you raised the challenge by renaming it. (Remember in Chapter 1, "Designing a Secure Network Framework," where we talked about external hackers who are motivated by the challenge of attacking a network? This is a prime example.) What the hacker might do at that point is run a utility like SID2USER to figure out what your administrator account name is using its unique SID.

Because of this, an additional step needs to be taken together with renaming the administrator account to harden security. After renaming the authentic administrator account, create a fake one and make sure the fake account has the exact same description as the original would have had. You can then set auditing on the "decoy" account, and even configure your system so that you are paged or e-mailed whenever anyone tries to access it.

As soon as this account is attacked, you should receive notification and should take immediate action because you know no one should be using this account, not even IT staff members.

Designing Effective Password Policies

All the security measures in the world will be of little use if your organization adopts a weak password policy, because one compromised password can expose your network to any number of attacks, starting from DoS attacks and ending in theft or destruction of your data. Using Windows Server 2003 Group Policy, you can design an effective password policy that can protect against users and even administrators who might otherwise use weak passwords.

Group Policy allows you to force all domain users to use complex passwords that consist of uppercase letters, lowercase letters, numbers, and special characters. You can also implement a password history, where once a password expires you cannot reuse it or any of a certain number of passwords that you previously used. You can also set a password expiration period, where which after a certain amount of time your users will be prompted to change their passwords.

EXAM 70-298 OBJECTIVE 2.2.4

Establishing Account Security Policies

Establishing a strong account security policy is crucial, because the user account is the single most important entity in Active Directory that links to all rights and permissions on the network. Windows 2000 and Windows Server 2003 allows us to implement security on accounts via Group Policy using the following steps:

1. Open an MMC console and add the Active Directory Users and Computers snap-in.
2. Right-click the root of the domain in the left control pane and click on **Properties**.
3. Click on the **Group Policy** tab, and then select the **Default Domain Policy** and click **Edit**.
4. Expand the Computer Configuration node and maneuver your way to **\Windows Settings\Account Policies**. You will notice it has three configurable policies under it: the Password policy, the Account Lockout policy and the Kerberos policy as shown in Figure 8.5.

Figure 8.5 Account Policies Window in Group Policy

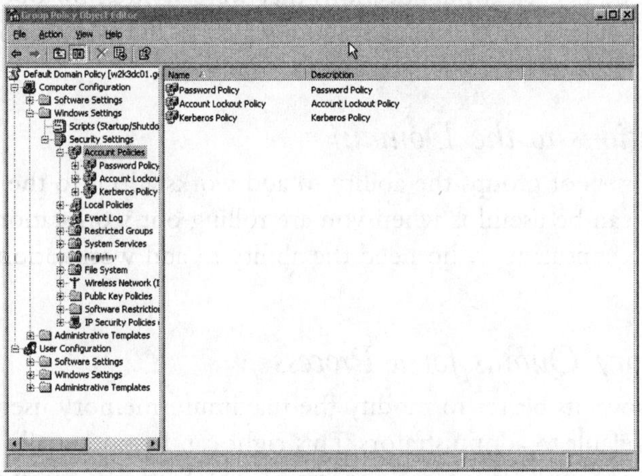

We will cover the Password policy later in this chapter and the Kerberos policy in the next few sections. Let's focus our attention on the Account Lockout policy, which has configurable options that are listed next.

User Rights Assignments

By configuring the different user rights, you can grant access to users to perform certain functions, or you can forbid users from completing a certain task. The configurable settings are detailed in the following sections.

TEST DAY TIP

Since this is a security-oriented exam, user rights assignment will most definitely come up. Make sure that you know what each right will allow an attacker to do so if it comes up in a scenario question you will be ready for it.

Access This Computer from the Network

This right specifies which users and/or groups can connect to a computer or server over the network. It is good to note here that Terminal Services is not affected by this setting, which means you don't have to enable this for TS users.

Act as Part of the Operating System

This right allows its bearer to imitate any user account without having to supply credentials for authentication to gain access. In other words, you can access any resources the account you're imitating has access to with the added advantage of not supplying credentials. This right is very dangerous and should not be used unless absolutely necessary. It is also worth noting here that the local system account already has this right. This right might be needed for applications that were written for operating systems prior to Windows Server 2003 (such as Windows 2000 and NT) for authentication purposes.

Add Workstations to the Domain

This right gives users or groups the ability to add workstations to the domain. A scenario where this can be useful is when you are rolling out workstations in your organization and have consultants who need the ability to add workstations to the domain.

Adjust Memory Quotas for a Process

This privilege allows its bearer to modify the maximum memory used by a process, and is given by default to administrators. This right can be potentially misused if given to the wrong user account, and can create a DoS attack against your network by setting the memory requirements for a certain process low enough to prevent it from running properly. An attacker can use this the other way around as well, by setting the memory utilization for a process very high so that it consumes all the available memory on a server or workstation.

Allow Log On Locally

This right allows a user or group to log on through the console of the machine by pressing **Ctrl + Alt + Del**. The terminology here is a bit tricky: logging in to the local machine usually means that you have a user account created on that machine, and when you go to log in you specify the local machine name in the domain drop-down box. This right allows the user or group to log on to a domain from the console of a machine. Basically, this right allows you to walk up to the console and log on, rather than accessing the computer across the network.

Allow Log On through Terminal Services

This right determines which users and groups can connect to a terminal server. This setting would need to be enabled if, for example, you have Citrix MetaFrame or other products that use the Terminal Services technology in Windows Server 2003.

Log On as a Batch Job

This right allows a user to be logged in as a batch job. The best way to illustrate what this setting does is to take the example of the Task Scheduler in Windows. When a user submits a task, the scheduler logs this user on as a batch job, rather than running the Scheduler interactively from the GUI. Logging the user as a batch means that the scheduled task will run at the specified time and date even if no user interactively logs on to the machine or server. This is helpful because without this right, the scheduler would not run the job until a user logged on through Ctrl + Alt + Del.

Back Up Files and Directories

This right enables its bearer to back up files and folders. Use caution when assigning this right, and only give it to trusted users since it can be misused to steal data or for espionage purposes. This right is equal to the following permissions given to a user or group: Read, List, Traverse Folder, and Read Extended Attributes.

Bypass Traverse Checking

This right overrides any permission set on directories and allows the user to traverse the directory. The user will not be able to list the contents of the directory, but will be able to navigate through it and through other subdirectories in it.

Change the System Time

Users or groups with this right can modify the internal system clock (time and date) on the local machine. This can have an effect on any files or folders created or modified, whereby the time and date stamp will reflect that of the local clock. Moreover, any events logged in the Event Viewer will bear the local timestamp. This can be used maliciously to attack the validity of system auditing, where you can't tell (or can't prove) that a certain action took place at a specific time.

Create a Pagefile

This privilege enables a user or group to create a pagefile by calling an API, or application programming interface. This functionality is used by the operating system, and is rarely given to users or groups.

Create a Token Object

This right enables a process to use the account with this privilege to create an access token and gain access to local system resources. This is usually an operating system function, and is rarely assigned to a user account. When the need arises for this functionality, you can use the Local System account, which has this right by default.

Create Global Objects

This right allows Terminal Server users to create global objects. By default, TS users have the right to create only session objects. In rare instances, you might need to grant this additional privilege to your TS users. It is worthwhile to note that this right was introduced in Windows 2000 SP4, and is still available in Windows Server 2003.

Create Permanent Shared Objects

This right enables an account to be used by a process to create a directory object in Windows 2000 Professional and Server, Windows XP, and Windows Server 2003 families. The process is a kernel-level process and as such is used by the operating system to extend namespace objects and to load .DLL files at boot time. Any process running in kernel mode already has this right and as such does not need to have it specifically assigned.

Debug Programs

This right is usually assigned to developers to allow them to debug the operating system or a third-party application; developers do not need this right if they are debugging applications they have written. This right is needed in cases where the developer needs to debug the kernel or an application new to him. Obviously, this right grants the developer a lot of power by revealing critical data, so use caution when granting this right.

Deny Access to This Computer from the Network

This right denies access to this computer from the network. This overrides the earlier right of Allow Access to this computer from the network. If a user has both rights applied to him or her, this one will take precedence and the user will be denied access.

Deny Log On as a Batch Job

This setting denies a user the ability to log on as a batch job. It supersedes the Log on as a Batch Job right, so if a user is subject to both policies, he or she will be denied this ability.

Deny Log On as a Service

This setting prohibits a user account from being registered as a service. This security right supersedes the Allow log on as a service, and as such, if a user is subject to both policies, this policy takes precedence.

Deny Log On Locally

This setting reverses the effect of the Allow log on locally security setting we discussed earlier, and prohibits users or groups from logging on to machines at the console.

Deny Log On through Terminal Services

This setting reverses the Allow Log On through Terminal Services, and as such, users and groups subject to this policy will be denied the ability to use their Terminal Services Client and access Terminal Server. If you have products such as Citrix MetaFrame in your environment, enabling this setting can disrupt the proper functionality of said application.

Enable Computer and User Accounts to be Trusted for Delegation

This right determines which users can configure the Trusted for delegation setting on user and computer accounts. Server processes and user accounts that are trusted for delegation can access resources on other computers. Use caution when assigning this right, as it can allow a malicious user to use a virus or a Trojan horse that impersonates users to wreak havoc on network resources.

Force Shutdown from a Remote System

This right allows its bearer to shut down a server or computer system remotely and potentially bring down critical servers and cause a great deal of damage. Use caution when assigning this right, and only do so for trusted users.

Generate Security Audits

This right allows a process to write an entry in the Security log of the Event Viewer. The Security log is used to monitor unauthorized access; the misuse of this right would allow an attacker to hide traces of a security breach.

Impersonate a Client After Authentication

This right allows a service or program to impersonate the user after logon, which means that the service or program can use the credentials that the user used to log in to perform an action, rather than the credentials the service or the program used to launch itself. This is a great security enforcer that was not available with Windows 2000 SP3 and earlier, but was introduced with SP4, and of course is available by default in Windows Server 2003. Prior to Windows 2000 SP4, any service or program could impersonate a user. This is how viruses and Trojan horses were able to exploit RPC vulnerabilities and attack home and business systems.

Increase Scheduling Priority

When this right is granted, a process can change the scheduling priority of another process through the Task Manager GUI, or graphical user interface.

Load and Unload Device Drivers

This right enables a process to load and unload device drivers into the kernel and can cause severe damage if misused. A user can use it to load harmful or dangerous code into the kernel and can take control of your system. Best practices calls for the use of the StartService() API instead. (The StartService() API is a tool used by developers that would allow them to start drivers or services.)

Lock Pages in Memory

This right allows a process to use an account with such rights to determine which data is kept in physical memory and not paged to virtual memory. This can cause severe system performance degradation because of lack of enough random access memory (RAM).

Log On as a Service

This right configures which user account a process can use as a service. In many cases, an application will require a user account to start one of its services on a server. Instead of using the administrator account for this task, which has more rights and can be misused by an attacker, you can create a specific account dedicated to this application and can configure this account with the Log on as Service right. This means that the account would be able to only log in for the purposes of starting the service to which it is assigned.

Manage Auditing and Security Log

This right empowers a user to create and edit an audit policy. It also allows a user to view and clear the Security log in Event Viewer.

Modify Firmware Environment Variables

This right grants users and/or groups the ability to modify firmware environment variables in nonvolatile RAM.

Perform Volume Maintenance Tasks

This privilege grants users and groups the ability to run administrative maintenance tasks such as defragmentation of the file system. Use caution when assigning this right, as it gives the user access to the entire file system.

Profile Single Process

This right allows users to use Performance Monitor on a system to monitor non-system resources.

Profile System Performance

This right allows users to use Performance Monitor on a system to monitor system resources.

Remove Computer from Docking Station

When this policy is enabled, a user can undock a laptop computer from its docking station without having to log on to the laptop first. When disabled, a user can obviously undock the machine with no problem.

Replace a Process Level Token

This setting allows a user to call the CreateProcessAsUser() API, which allows a service to start another service. A great example here is again the Task Scheduler, where you can use it to start another service at a given time.

Restore Files and Directories

This right determines which users or groups can overwrite file and folder security permission while performing a restore of files and folders. It also allows the bearer to set the owner of an object.

Shut Down the System

This setting specifies which users who are logged on locally through the console of the machine can use the *shutdown* command. Use caution when assigning this right, as the consequences can be a DoS for the downed machine.

Synchronize Directory Service Data

This right allows users or groups to synchronize Active Directory data between controllers in a domain or forest.

Take Ownership of Files or Other Objects

This right allows users to take ownership of resources, including files, folders, printers, and Registry keys. Needless to say, the harm this can cause is endless, since the owner of the object has virtually full control over that resource.

Using Restricted Groups

Restricted groups add another layer of security to sensitive user groups such as Domain Admins or Enterprise Admins or even Schema Admins. What this setting allows you to do is to control memberships to sensitive groups, where any users who you don't explicitly specify as members of that group will be removed from it the next time the policy is refreshed. In other words, let's say that John and Bob are the only two users who should be members of the Domain Admins group. However, you have a junior network administrator named Dave who wants to elevate his access, so he opens ADUC and adds himself to the Domain Admins group.

Without Restricted groups, you would need to manually audit the group in order to notice him and remove him from that group. In many cases, the damage is already done. By using Restricted groups, the group policy checks and notices that Dave isn't supposed to be a member of Domain Admins and removes him immediately. Now, group policies are refreshed every five minutes on DCs, so within five minutes Dave would be removed. Similarly, let's say that Dave not only adds himself to the Domain Admins group, but also revokes John and Bob's memberships. In this case, once the policy is refreshed, John and Bob will be restored and Dave will be removed.

Restricted groups can also be used to control the "Member Of" setting, where you can specify which groups are members of which other groups. Group Policy is responsible for ensuring that these group memberships are always configured properly.

In Exercise 8.02, we'll walk through the steps required to configure Restricted groups in Active Directory.

EXERCISE 8.02

CONFIGURING RESTRICTED GROUPS IN ACTIVE DIRECTORY

1. Launch an MMC console by clicking on **Start | Run**, type **MMC**, and press **Enter**.
2. Add the **Active Directory Users and Computers Snap-In** and click on **File | Add/Remove Snap-in**.
3. Click on **Add**, select **ADUC**, and click **Add**.
4. Expand **ADUC** and right-click at the root of the domain (configuring the policy at the root of the domain ensures it gets applied to all your domain users).

5. Click on **Properties**. Select the **Group Policy** tab, then select the **Default Domain Policy**, and click **Edit**.
6. Navigate to **\Computer Configuration\Windows Settings\Security Settings\Restricted Groups.**
7. Right-click **Restricted Groups** and click **Add Group**.
8. Click **Browse** and type the name of the group you want to configure; for the purposes of this example we will use **Domain Admins**. Click **OK**.
9. Next, you are presented with the window shown in Figure 8.6 where you can add the members of this group. In our example, we added the user **Eli**.
10. You can also add the **Member Of** group that Domain Admins should always be a part of, and for the purposes of our example, we used the **Administrators** group.
11. Click **OK**.

Figure 8.6 Configuring Restricted Groups in Group Policy

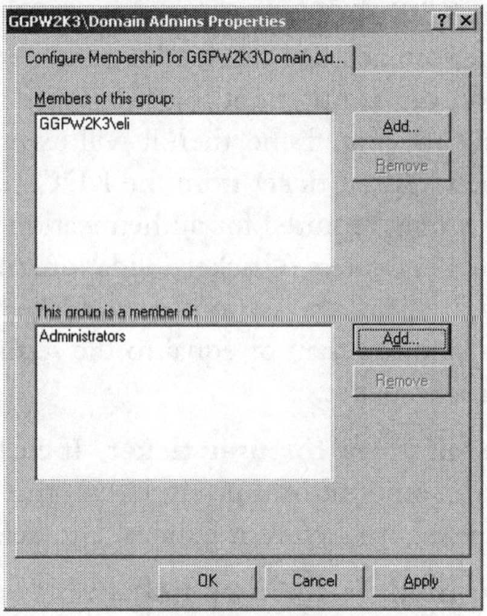

TEST DAY TIP

Make sure you are familiar with how to use Restricted groups. As a very effective method of controlling user memberships to sensitive groups, it is almost certain to be on the test in one form or another.

Creating a Kerberos Policy

Windows 2000 and Windows Server 2003 both offer support for Kerberos, which is a strong network authentication protocol that relies heavily on cryptography. Windows Server 2003 allows you to configure a Kerberos policy in Group Policy. In this section, we'll discuss some of the configurable settings:

- **Enforce user logon restrictions** If you enable this setting, you force every session to validate a ticket using the V5 Key Distribution Center, or KDC, against the User Rights policy of every user. This is disabled by default because of the extra resources it requires, and because it can potentially slow a system while it validates the ticket.
- **Maximum lifetime for service ticket** Defines the amount of time a session ticket can access a service (in minutes) before it expires. For example, you can configure it for 15 minutes. If you don't use a service ticket within this timeframe, then it will expire and you will need to request a new session ticket from the KDC. It is good to note that the session ticket is only required for authentication purposes; ongoing communication occurs regardless of ticket validation. After authentication, you can completely disregard the session ticket. The setting should be greater than 10 minutes, and less than or equal to the setting specified in the Maximum lifetime for user ticket.
- **Maximum lifetime for user ticket** If enabled, this setting determines the maximum amount of time (in hours) that a user's TGT, or Ticket-Granting Ticket, has before it expires. The default time is 10 hours.
- **Maximum lifetime for user ticket renewal** This setting determines the timeframe within which a user's TGT can be renewed. The time is in days and the default is seven days.
- **Maximum tolerance for computer clock synchronization** When this setting is configured, it regulates the time difference that Kerberos v5 will tolerate between the client and the DC that is providing the Kerberos authentication service. Kerberos v5 uses the time stamp as part of its protocol, and as such this policy regulates the difference in the clocks that will be permissible.

To create a Kerberos policy, follow these steps:

1. Launch an MMC console by clicking on **Start | Run**. Type **MMC** and press **Enter**.
2. Add the Active Directory Users and Computers Snap-in by clicking on **File | Add/Remove Snap-in**. Click on **Add**, select **ADUC**, and click **Add**.
3. Expand ADUC and right-click at the root of the domain (configuring the policy at the root of the domain ensures it gets applied to all of your domain users).
4. Click on **Properties**. Select the **Group Policy** tab, and then select the **Default Domain Policy** and click **Edit**.
5. Navigate **to \Computer Configuration\Windows Settings\Security Settings\Account Policies\Kerberos Policy**.
6. In the right control pane you can double-click on **Enforce user logon restriction** and enable the setting to force every session ticket to be validated.
7. Next, you can double-click on **Maximum lifetime for service ticket** and set the ticket expiration in minutes.
8. You can then double-click on **Maximum lifetime for user ticket** and set the appropriate time for the lifecycle of a ticket in hours.
9. Next, you can control how long a user has to renew an expired ticket before he or she would have to request a new session ticket. The value can be set in days. To do this, double-click **Maximum lifetime for user ticket renewal** and set the appropriate value.
10. You can control the time difference tolerance between the DC's clock and the connecting host's local clock by configuring the **Maximum tolerance for computer clock synchronization**.

Figure 8.7 Kerberos Policy Configuration

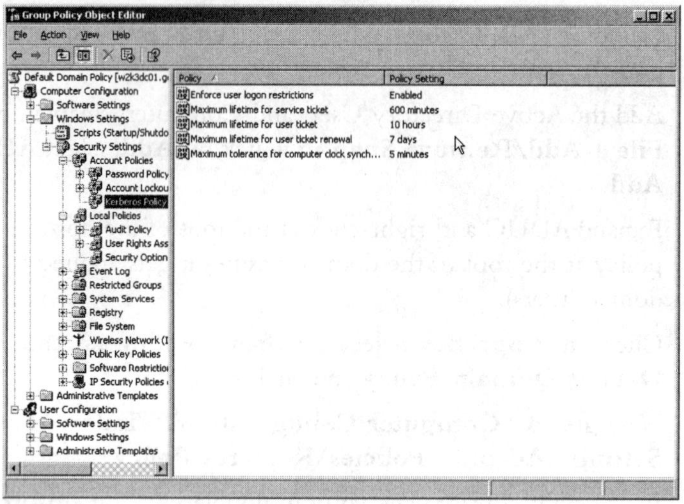

EXAM 70-298 OBJECTIVE 2.2.4

Establishing Password Security

Windows 2000 and Windows Server 2003 both offer settings enforced through Group Policy that allow you configure tightened password security within your organization. You can create these settings to take effect for all users by configuring the Password policy at the root of the domain. The Password policy has the following configurable settings:

- **Enforce password history** When enabled, this policy keeps a record of the passwords a user has used and will not allow a user to reuse an old password. The setting can be between 0 and 24. This is a good policy because it forces users to constantly generate a unique password and prohibits them from having a pool of passwords they rotate between every time their password expires.
- **Maximum password age** You can enable this setting to force a user to change his or her password after a certain number of days. Regular password change is a crucial security step. The range is between 1 and 999 days—as with all security settings, you should look for a happy medium. Best practice calls for a policy that requires the user to change passwords every 30 to 90 days. Experience might show that 30 days might be a bit too frequent, and your company's management might be more in favor of a 60-day expiration. Therefore, a good policy can be between 60 to 90 days for regular user accounts, and might be less for sensitive user accounts.
- **Minimum password age** This setting regulates how many days users should use their passwords before they are allowed to change it. In this case,

you can set the minimum age to 0, whereby users can change their passwords any time they want or anytime they feel they need to. The setting can be between 1 and 998. When using this setting, make sure the configured setting is less than that in the Maximum password age setting.

- **Minimum password length** This setting allows you to force the users to select a password that is of a certain length. The configurable settings are between 1 and 14. For example, if you set it to 8, then the user would have to select a password that is eight characters long at least or the system will refuse it. If you set the setting to 0, then no password length is in effect, which means your users can choose a blank password. This is a huge security concern, since at this point all an attacker would need is the username since the password is blank.
- **Password must meet complexity requirements** If this policy is enabled, it will force the user to select a password based on certain criteria:
  - The password cannot contain any part of the username.
  - The password should be at least six characters long; if the Maximum password length is more than six characters, then the user would have to meet that requirement.
  - The password must have at least one uppercase character between A–Z.
  - The password must have at least one lowercase character between a–z.
  - The password must a special character, such $, @, #, and so forth.
- **Store passwords using reversible encryption** If this setting is enabled, the system stores the user passwords in reversible encryption. This basically means it strips the password of the default levels of encryption offered by Active Directory. You should try to avoid enabling this policy for obvious reasons unless certain applications in your environment require it. For example, CHAP, or Challenge-Handshake Authentication Protocol, requires this setting to be enabled when authenticating via remote access or Internet Authentication Services (IAS). Another example that requires this policy to be enabled is Digest Authentication, which is used with Internet Information Services (IIS).

Exam Warning

When applications in your environment absolutely require **Store passwords using reversible encryption** setting enabled, you can enable this setting on specific user accounts that are required by the application to run properly instead of for all of your domain passwords. Open the **Properties** of any user account in Active Directory Users and Computers and select the **Account** tab. In the Account options window you will be able to enable this setting for this particular user account (see Figure 8.8).

Figure 8.8 Enabling Reversible Encryption on a Per-Account Basis

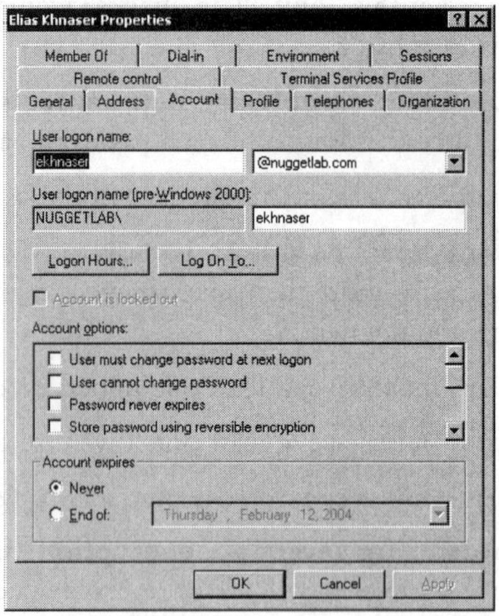

Designing & Planning…

Educating Users on Password Best Practices: User Password Tips

The best approach to protecting a user account is to educate the user on the principles of a password. Setting Password complexity requirements is an excellent idea that further encourages the user to follow your standards. However, if you fail to educate the user on the way he or she should create a secure and safe password, they will find a way to create an easy password that meets your complexity requirements, such as "JunkFood!" This password meets the complexity requirements you have set up, yet anyone who might know that this is your favorite type of food can easily guess your password and gain access to the network impersonating you.

Continued

Similarly, you will notice that no matter how great you think the Account lockout policy can be, a smart hacker can quickly start an attack intentionally providing wrong passwords and thus locking all of your users out of their accounts.

The bottom line is that there is no way around working with your user base (as frustrating as this can be at times) and educating them. A good idea is to create articles that can be published on your corporate intranet or portal that gives them tips on how to create strong passwords, including tips on what not to use. Something like this might be appropriate:

- Do not use common words or words that are spelled in a goofy way, such as P@as$w0rd for example.
- Do not add a numeral to the end of your expired password.
- Do not use passwords that can be guessed by looking at pictures in your cubicle, such as your wife's name, pet's name or favorite sports club.
- Use passwords that require you to use both hands so no one can guess it by watching you type it one letter at a time.
- Use uppercase, lowercase, numbers, and special characters in all your passwords.
- Use characters that require you to hold down the Alt key.

An article like this can greatly help guide your users in choosing strong passwords. Accompany this with a good Auditing policy and you should be well on your way to securing your user account information.

Setting Password Complexity Requirements

You might have noticed that there is a big emphasis on passwords in this section, and the reason is that the password remains an important factor in security. No matter what security precautions you take, if someone guesses your password then that person has complete access to your protected files and resources.

To set up a Password Complexity policy like the one we just discussed, follow these steps:

1. Launch an MMC console by clicking on **Start | Run**. Type **MMC** and press **Enter**.
2. Add the Active Directory Users and Computers Snap-in by clicking on **File | Add/Remove Snap-in**. Click **Add**, select **ADUC**, and click **Add**.

3. Expand **ADUC** and right-click at the root of the domain (configuring the policy at the root of the domain ensures it gets applied to all your domain users).
4. Click on **Properties**. Select the **Group Policy** tab, select the **Default Domain Policy**, and click **Edit**.
5. Navigate to **\Computer Configuration\Windows Settings\Security Settings\Account Policies\Password Policy**.
6. In the right control pane, double-click on **Password must meet complexity requirements**, check the box next to **Define this policy** setting, and select **Enabled** as shown in Figure 8.9.

Figure 8.9 Configuring Password Complexity

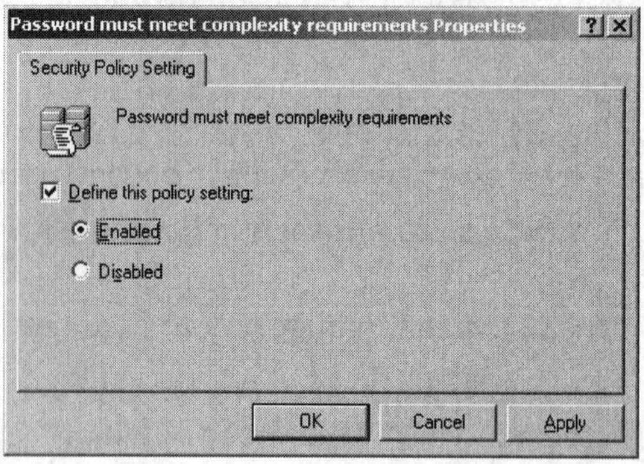

EXAM WARNING

Keep in mind that password policies are applied at the domain level only, which means if you create another policy with password or account lockout configurations, it will not override the Default Domain Policy even if the user accounts are in the OU where the policy is being defined. If you do configure an OU-based Password and Account lockout policy, it will only apply to the Local User Accounts of the servers or workstations in that OU. Be on the alert for trick questions or scenarios that might suggest otherwise.

Creating an Account Lockout Policy

An Account Lockout policy offers you an additional level of control and security by controlling how, when, and why an account can be locked out. The idea behind account lockout is to protect your network against someone trying to crack your passwords by continuously trying to guess them, or by running a password cracker against your account database. Account lockout settings can deter a hacker by locking the account and preventing any further attempts to guess passwords. However, sometimes the security measures we take can be used against us. For example, a hacker might purposely want to lock all of your users' accounts and create an uncomfortable situation for you and an effective DoS for your network. Even though security is not compromised in this situation, your users' productivity will still be halted for a period of time.

The Account lockout policy offers the following configurable settings:

- **Account lockout duration** This setting determines how long an account remains locked out. This setting works in conjunction with the Account lockout threshold setting. The available range is from 0 to 99,999. For example, let's say an attacker is trying a brute-force attack on a user account, is unsuccessful, and ends up locking the account. As a measure of security, the account will not be unlocked until after the duration you set here. If you set the lockout duration to 0, then an administrator would have to manually unlock the account.
- **Account lockout threshold** This setting regulates the number of unsuccessful logon attempts that will be allowed against a user account before the account is locked. This means if you set this setting to 3 and you try to log on unsuccessfully three times, your account will be locked out for your protection. The range is between 0–999. If you set it to 0, the account will never be locked out no matter how many bad password attempts it receives.
- **Reset account lockout counter after** This setting determines the amount of time in minutes that the lockout threshold remembers failed attempts during. For example, let's say you try to log on now and you fail. You come back after one hour and try again and fail. If you configure this setting to an hour, then the second attempt will be considered strike two. Now, based on how many failed attempts you have allowed in the Account lockout threshold, your account can be locked out accordingly. However, if you had configured this setting to 30 minutes and you tried again after an hour, then your unsuccessful logon would be considered your first attempt. The configurable settings are between 1 and 99,999.

To create an account lockout policy, follow these steps:

1. Launch an MMC console by clicking on **Start | Run**, type **MMC**, and press **Enter**.
2. Add the **Active Directory Users and Computers Snap-in** by clicking on **File | Add/Remove Snap-in.** Click on **Add**, then select **ADUC**, and click **Add**.

3. Expand **ADUC** and right-click at the root of the domain (configuring the policy at the root of the domain ensures it gets applied to all your domain users).
4. Click on **Properties**. Select the **Group Policy** tab and then select the **Default Domain Policy** and click **Edit**.
5. Navigate to **\Computer Configuration\Windows Settings\Security Settings\Account Policies\Account Lockout Policy**.
6. Double-click on **Account Lockout durations** and enable it by clicking the check box labeled "Define this policy setting." Enter the desired time in minutes; the default is 30.
7. Now, double-click on **Account Lockout Threshold** and define the setting. The default is five attempts. After five failed logon attempts, the account will be locked for a period of 30 minutes.
8. The last setting is **Reset account lockout counter after**; again, the default is 30 minutes, which means if a user waits 30 minutes between each logon attempt he or she can continue to have five attempts to authenticate without locking out the account.

Auditing User Account Activity

It is not enough for us to set up policies, regulations, and requirements. All of this is worthless if we don't have a way to monitor whether the policies and requirements that we created are being followed. Auditing is our way of making sure that our users and even administrators and engineers are abiding by and sticking to these policies. In addition, with auditing enabled, you will be able to gather information after a security incident occurs. You will be to tell which computers were compromised, which files were accessed, and other crucial information.

Auditing can also help prevent an attack before it occurs if it is configured properly and your response time is appropriate. Because you can configure auditing to e-mail or page you when specific events are logged, you might be able to stop a security breach before it happens or before it damages data on the network.

No security design is ever complete without using auditing. For this and other reasons, Windows 2000 and Windows Server 2003 offer us auditing capabilities through the use of group policy. The Auditing settings that are available to us are located in Group Policy under **\Computer Configuration\Windows Settings\Security Settings\Local Policies\Audit Policy** as follows:

- **Audit account logon events** This setting monitors the success or failure of users attempting to log on, and creates an entry in the Security log on the DC with the relevant information. You can set it to monitor all success logon events, all failed logon events, or both.

- **Audit account management** If you enable this setting, auditing on account management will be turned on and any events will be logged based on whether they succeeded or failed or both. Account management audits include any password changes, account creation or deletion, and so forth.
- **Audit directory service access** If this setting is configured, auditing will be enabled on Active Directory objects that have a system access control list (SACL) specified. What this means is when you right-click an object in Active Directory and click on the Security tab, you can assign security on that object. This setting monitors objects that have been configured with the SACL. It can monitor for success or failure or both, and writes an event to the Security log in the Event Viewer on a DC.
- **Audit logon events** If you enable this policy, you will be able to monitor logon events. Auditing can be set on successful logons or on failed attempts. The difference between this setting and the Audit account logon events setting is that, with the latter, events are only logged on the DC's Event Viewer when a user authenticates against Active Directory, whereas if you enable this setting, you will be able to monitor user access to resources that reside on servers like file and print servers, for example.
- **Audit object access** If enabled, this setting triggers auditing of user access to objects such as files, folders, Registry keys, and so forth. As with the other audit policies, you can either monitor the success or failure of these actions.
- **Audit policy change** If you enable this setting, you will be able to monitor any changes that are made to your Audit policies, User Rights Assignment policies, and your Kerberos policies.
- **Audit privilege use** This setting allows you to monitor a user based on his or her Rights assignments. Anytime users use any of their rights, an event is logged. Rights were assigned in the User Rights policies, which we covered earlier in this chapter.
- **Audit process tracking** If enabled this setting allows you to audit detailed information about a process, such as when a process exits or when duplicates exist of the same process.
- **Audit system events** This setting allows you to monitor system events, such as when a server is shut down or restarted, or when the Security log is being manipulated in any way.

Creating an Auditing Policy

You can enable an Audit policy either locally on the server or workstation or via Group Policy. Enabling it via Group Policy makes it a lot easier to manage and update later if the need arises. The following steps outline how to create an Audit policy using Group Policy:

1. Launch an MMC console by clicking on **Start | Run**, type **MMC**, and press **Enter**.
2. Add the **Active Directory Users and Computers Snap-in** by clicking on **File | Add/Remove Snap-in.** Click on **Add**, select **ADUC**, and click **Add**.
3. Expand **ADUC** and right-click at the root of the domain (configuring the policy at the root of the domain ensures it gets applied to all your domain users).
4. Click on **Properties**. Select the **Group Policy** tab, then select the **Default Domain Policy** and click **Edit**.
5. Navigate to **\Computer Configuration\Windows Settings\Security Settings\Local Policies\Audit Policy**.
6. In the right control pane, double-click on the desired settings from the ones we just discussed and configure whether you want to audit the success, failure, or both for any of these categories.

Auditing Logon Events

When you configure this policy, you will be able to track the success or failure of logon events. This policy allows you to track an intruder trying to crack the password on a user account, for example. With this policy, you will also be able to track user accounts that are trying to log on, and computer accounts that are trying to log on. As you know, Windows NT, 2000, XP, and Server 2003 have computer accounts that are objects in Active Directory. When you authenticate, your computer account also authenticates if the computer is part of the domain so that you get an extra layer of security.

NOTE

Windows 9x and Me do not have computer accounts, and as such, you will be unable to track computer accounts of users who are using these operating systems. Therefore, for these users, only the user account logon will be tracked.

There is one major difference that you should be aware of when dealing with logon events, and that is that the account logon event is recorded in the Security log of the server that authenticates that account. Logon events, however, are recorded in the Security log on the computer the user is actually logging in to.

Figure 8.10 Logon Events Registration Process

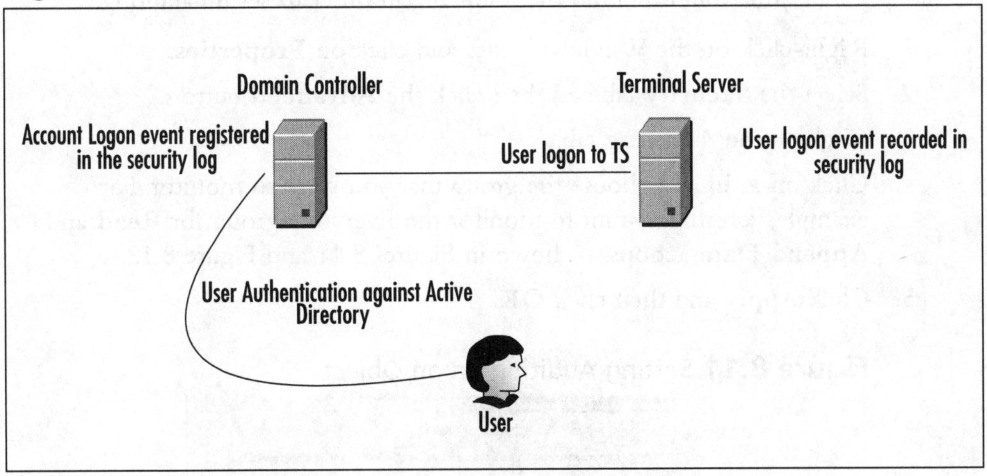

As an example, let's assume you have Terminal Services deployed in your organization where your users would need to log on through TS to get access to certain applications. In this scenario, when the user account is authenticated against Active Directory, an entry is recorded in the Event Viewer's Security log on the DC that authenticated the account. The Terminal server the user logged on to, however, registers an entry in its own Security log for the user logon (see Figure 8.10).

NOTE

When you apply a logon audit policy to servers that have Terminal Services enabled on them, you need to make sure you differentiate between console logons and Terminal Services client logons.

Best practices calls for always enabling success and failure logon attempts when configuring this kind of policy. The combination of success and failure audits will be useful to you later when conducting an investigation of how the security on your network was breached, for example. It might also be useful in preventing an intrusion if you are set up to be notified of frequent failure attempts on certain sensitive accounts such as Administrator accounts or service accounts.

Auditing Object Access

After enabling the Audit Object Access setting in Group Policy, you will then need to configure auditing for individual objects such as files and folders. Enabling the Audit policy is only one part of the process. For example, let's say you wanted to monitor file access and modifications on your c:\windows directory. After enabling the Auditing policy, you would then do the following in order to set up auditing:

1. Right-click on the Windows folder and click on **Properties**.
2. Select the **Security** tab and then click the **Advanced** button.
3. Click on the **Auditing** tab.
4. Click on **Add** and choose the group that you want to monitor. For example, you might want to monitor the Everyone group for **Read** and **Append Data** actions, as shown in Figures 8.11 and Figure 8.12.
5. Click **Apply** and then click **OK**.

Figure 8.11 Setting Auditing on an Object

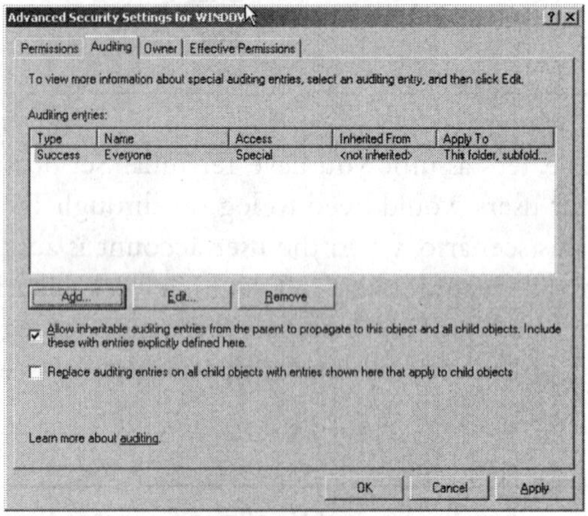

Figure 8.12 Advanced Auditing Settings

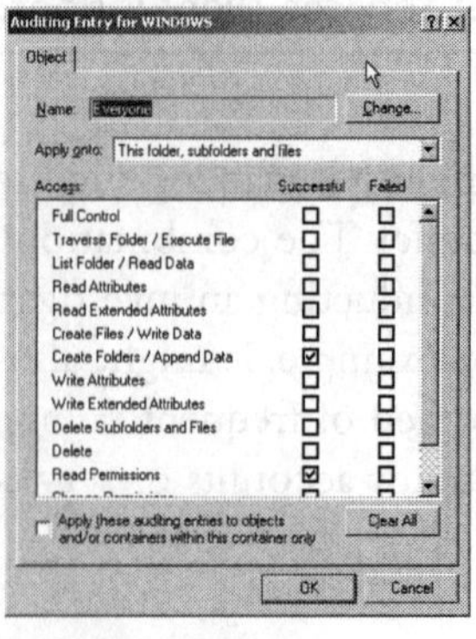

When auditing objects, you should have a clear understanding of what it is you are trying to audit and why. For example, a good Auditing policy would monitor Write and Append Data actions taken against executable files, since viruses, Trojan horses, and worms usually modify, change, or delete these particular types of files, and very few normal user activities would cause these actions to take place.

The reason why you should be careful when setting up auditing is that you can generate a lot of security events, such as if you enable auditing on .TXT files for all possible events. In this scenario, the system might generate numerous log entries each time the file is opened, edited, saved, and so on. This can quickly fill your Event log and create serious performance degradation on your overall system. Having a clear strategy about what to monitor and how much to monitor ensures that your Auditing policy does not affect system performance and overall business productivity.

Another example would be auditing a busy printer: just imagine the logging information that would be created if you monitored all successful print jobs. Your Event Viewer would quickly be full of fairly trivial informational logs that you will never sort through or care to know about.

NOTE

Antivirus software can also cause hundreds if not thousands of security logs if Full Control auditing is enabled. This would occur every time a system scan is initiated.

EXAM 70-298 OBJECTIVE 4.1.2

Analyzing Auditing Data

Once we've configured our auditing policy, we need to be able to analyze it and make sense of it all. Windows provides a central repository where auditing and other events are stored for later analysis and troubleshooting. This repository is the Event Viewer, which you can get to either by right-clicking **My Computer** and going to **Manage**, or simply by going to **Start | Run** and typing **Eventvwr**.

The Event Viewer has several different logs, based on what kinds of services are configured on the server you are trying to access. For example, on different servers you might find the Application log, the Security log, the System log, the DNS log, the File Replication log, and others. (All Windows Server 2003 servers will possess the first three; the rest are dependent on what kinds of services the machine is running.) What we are most interested in at this point is the Security log, where all our auditing settings and configuration will be stored. With the Event Viewer, you are able to:

- Sort events by type, time, and other parameters
- Filter events

- View advanced event information
- Sort events
- Export the log file to an .EVT, .TXT, or .CSV file
- Connect to a remote computer's Event Viewer

However, when you have more than a handful of servers in your environment, using the Event Viewer to browse through events can be very frustrating. There are other tools you can use that will query the Event logs on several servers and consolidate only the information you are interested in into files or databases. Consider these scripts that are available in the Windows 2000 Resource Kit and the Windows Server 2003 Resource Kit:

- **Eventlog.pl** is a Windows 2000 Resource Kit (Supplement 1) Perl script that allows you to manipulate the properties of the Event Viewer on remote machines. It allows you to do the following:
  - Modify the Event log properties
  - Clear all events in a log
  - Back up or export the event log
- **Eventquery.pl** is another Windows 2000 Resource Kit (Supplement 1) Perl script that allows you to display events from local and remote machines and offers many ways you can filter the data.
- **Dumpel.exe** is a very powerful tool that allows you to dump the events from remote servers into a tab-separated file, which can then be imported into Excel and sorted, filtered, and so forth in order to make sense of the data. Dumpel.exe is a command-line utility and stands for Dump Event Log. It can be downloaded from the Microsoft Web site.
- **EventcombMT.exe** is a Windows Server 2003 Resource Kit utility (also available from the Microsoft site) that allows you to query the Event logs of several servers at the same time. The advantage of EventcombMT is that you can specify the criteria you are looking for. For example, if you are interested in logon events only, this tool can query all the Event logs for just this event type and then collect the information for you, rather than just querying the Event logs as a whole like other tools do. You can filter it for any field in the Event log.

If you are interested in further automating these tasks or using a GUI instead, you can use tools from Microsoft such as Microsoft Operations Manager (MOM) or third-party utilities from other vendors such as Tivoli or HP.

EXAM 70-298 OBJECTIVE 4.1.1

Creating a Delegation Strategy

One of the best enhancements that was introduced in Windows 2000 and continues in Windows Server 2003 is the ability to delegate administration. What this means is that you can design an OU structure, place Active Directory Objects such as users and computers, and then give control of this OU to an administrator in your group. This allows you to have levels of security where administrators have access to only the Active Directory objects for which they are responsible. This is an added layer of security that was not available in the Windows NT days, where any administrator had to be a member of the domain Admins group or any other sensitive group before he or she could do any real work.

Delegation of authority can also be used to organize and isolate departmental or suborganizations in your environment. For example, your HR department might have its own IT staff that requires independent and sole access and management over their users, computers, group policies, and the like.

Service Administrators and Data Administrators

An organization usually delegates administration because of an operational need, an organizational need, or even a legal need. Once delegation is implemented, the delegated administrators can then administer service management and data management.

Delegated administrators fall into two main categories:

- **Service Administrators** (Service Management) This type of administrator is responsible for the design aspects of Active Directory, and have autonomy over DCs, directorywide configuration, and services maintenance and availability. Service Administrators can be Data Administrators, but Data Administrators are not typically Service Administrators.
- **Data Administrators** (Data Management) This type of administrator is responsible for the information saved in Active Directory, such as users, groups, and OU containers, but they don't have access over the directory-wide configuration and delivery of services. This type of administrator can be granted object level access and can be given control over certain sections of the directory.

Isolation and Autonomy

When designing your Active Directory delegation strategy, you have to first understand your organization's delegation requirements. These requirements will generally fall under the following two categories:

- **Isolation** Isolation allows for exclusive and independent access to data and services in a particular subset of the directory. This design allows administrators to isolate themselves and not share administrative rights with any other administrators in the forest. They have full and exclusive control over their portion of the directory tree.

- **Autonomy** Autonomy allows for shared administrative control over certain data and services. It allows administrators to independently manage all or parts of the services and data management that they are responsible to maintain. For example, a forest might have two domains, and each domain might be managed independently by a different group of administrators. In an autonomous model, however, they are still united by a single forest functioning as a security boundary. As such, Enterprise administrators will still have the ability to log in to and administer either domain.

Clearly, autonomy is less restrictive, and administrators working under this model understand and accept the need to share management responsibility with other equal or higher-level administrators who will be able to access and control their services and data. Administrators working in isolation, however, require sole administrative access to their resources and intentionally block other administrators from being able to access or manage their service and data. These are usually in sensitive areas like Legal or Human Resource departments in an organization.

The only way to implement an isolation strategy, whether it is for the purposes of data isolation or service isolation, is to create a separate forest for that portion of the directory. The forest is the only security boundary that will ensure that no other administrator in an organization can access or compromise any of your information.

However, autonomy can be achieved either by creating a separate domain or even by delegating control over an OU that has all the data and services you are responsible for managing.

EXAM WARNING

Isolation **and** ***autonomy*** **are new terms, and as such will likely be on the exam. Familiarize yourself with the definitions and concepts, as they will most likely appear in a delegation scenario question.**

Selecting a Delegation Structure

Any delegation structure is divided among forests, domains, and OUs. Based on the type of delegation an organization needs to apply, you can create delegated administration at any of these three container levels. The characteristics of each are as follows:

- **Forest** A forest is a collection of domains that share a common configuration and a single schema. Delegating authority at this level will ensure that the "forest administrators" (usually the Domain Admins group in the root domain of the forest) have full and isolated control across all domains in the forest.

- **Domain** A domain is a partition of the Active Directory forest, and the Domain Admins group in each domain will have full control over that domain. However, forestwide operations can still be performed by Enterprise Administrators, and Enterprise Admins can perform management functions within any individual domain within the forest.
- **OU** As you know, OUs are containers within a domain, in which objects, computers, and users can be placed. You can delegate autonomous control over one or more OUs manually using ACLs, or using the Delegation of Control Wizard. You can delegate full control of an OU, or a specific subset of tasks like the ability to create user objects or reset user passwords.

The higher in the directory structure you choose to delegate administration, the more isolation that a delegated administrator can have over services and data. Remember, however, that that comes at the price of a more complicated management model, and usually involves a higher cost of deployment and maintenance.

As we just mentioned, at the forest level, the Domain Administrators group of the root domain will have the ability to manage any aspect of the forest, including member domains. At the domain level, the Domain Admins group for that domain will have the ability to independently manage that domain. Finally, within a domain, you can create an OU and you can add workstations, servers, users, and other Active Directory objects into the OU, and then delegate administration of this OU to a user or group within your organization. For example, let's say you have a Citrix team within your IT department that requires the ability to manage their own servers and workstations, the ability to create test users within their OU, and other common administrative tasks. To delegate administration to this group, follow these steps:

1. Open Active Directory users and Computers by going to **Start | Run | MMC** and **add** the **ADUC snap-in**.
2. Create your OU; for the purposes of this example we will create the OU by right-clicking at the domain level and clicking on **New | Organization Unit**.
3. **Type** the name of the OU—in our case, Citrix—and click **OK**.
4. **Right-click** the Citrix OU and click **Delegate Control**.
5. The Delegation of Control Wizard Starts. Click **Next**.
6. Click **Add** and select the group that you want to manage the resources of this OU, click **OK**, and then click **Next**.

7. The next screen allows you to either delegate common tasks from a list as shown in Figure 8.13 or to create a custom task to delegate.
8. Selecting the second option presents you with a more detailed list of tasks to configure. Make the appropriate selection and click **Next**.
9. Click **Finish**.

Figure 8.13 Delegation of Control Wizard

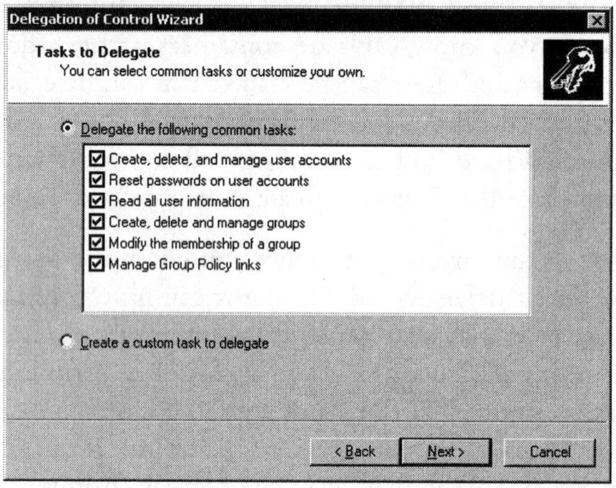

EXAM 70-298 OBJECTIVE 4.1.3

Designing the Appropriate Group Strategy for Accessing Resources

Just imagine if the concept of Active Directory groups did not exist. Managing your network resources would be an extremely complicated task, indeed. For example, imagine a folder that contained many subfolders where you had to manage a complex ACL with many different entries. Without groups, every time a user needed access to a subfolder, you would need to browse to that folder and add or remove the individual user. Take this one step further and imagine working with thousands of users and millions of files and folders—what a huge mess that would be!

Groups organize users, computers, and other objects and make them easier to manage, so that in the previous scenario you would add *groups* to the folder ACLs, rather than individual users. Since you'll have far less turnover in the names and types of groups on your network than you will with individual user objects, you can simply control membership to the groups to determine which user has access to what folder. When a new user needs to access a folder, he or she is added to a security group, and when access needs to be revoked, the user is removed. Rights and permissions can be assigned to groups, which will in turn apply these settings to all members of that group.

Three group scopes exist in Windows Server 2003 (these are identical to the group scopes that were introduced in Windows 2000):

- **Global groups** This type of group is used to group users or computers that are members of the same domain. When in Native mode, a Global group can contain other Global groups. It cannot contain users or groups in other domains. It can be used to regulate access to resources in any domain.
- **Domain Local groups** This type of group is used to secure resources that exist on servers that reside in the same domain as the group does. It cannot regulate permissions on resources that exist in domains outside the domain in which the group was created. Domain Local groups can contain users from any domain forest wide. It can contain other Local groups, Global groups, or Universal groups.
- **Universal groups** This type of group can contain any user or group from any domain in an entire forest. They can be used to regulate access to any resource on any domain. This combines the best of the Global and Domain Local groups. Its disadvantage, though, is that it writes every object into the Global Catalog (GC) server. Therefore, if you had a universal group with 1000 users, then these users would have to be written to the GC and then replicated to other GCs, which can place a heavy load on replication. This is workable for small to medium-sized networks, but you will find it highly uncommon and not recommended in large businesses because it will negatively affect network replication.

EXAM 70-298 OBJECTIVE 4.1.4

Designing a Permission Structure for Data

Designing a permission structure for data can be a challenging task and should be thought out carefully, because rectifying it later and making changes can be a complicated and very time-consuming task. For this reason, a well thought out design plan should rely on Microsoft recommended best practices for permission structure.

The Microsoft strategy for this kind of structure is known as the AGDLP, which is a strategy you should be familiar with from the core 4 requirements. The AGDLP calls for:

1. **A**dding domain users to **G**lobal groups
2. Adding global groups to **D**omain **L**ocal groups
3. Assign domain local groups **P**ermissions on resources

With the introduction of Universal groups in Windows 2000 and Windows Server 2003, you can now expand this best practice strategy to accommodate the new group type. The new strategy is known as the AGUDLP and calls for:

1. **A**dding domain users to **G**lobal groups
2. Adding global groups to **U**niversal groups
3. Adding universal groups to **D**omain **L**ocal groups
4. Assigning domain local groups **P**ermissions on resources

Using Global Groups

The first step in implementing the AGDLP is to assign users in every domain to Global groups in their domain. Users can only be added to a Global group in the same domain; therefore, Global groups cannot contain membership from users residing in a domain other than the one in which the group was created.

Using Domain Local Groups

The second step in the AGDLP strategy is to add Global or Universal groups to Domain Local groups. Domain Local groups are recommended for assigning permissions to resources in the most secure way. Domain Local groups can contain users and groups from any domain in the forest, but can only be assigned permissions on resources that reside in the domain where the group was created. For example, if you had a forest that has domains A, B, C, and D, you can create a Domain Local group in domain A and add users from any other domain. However, you can only assign permissions to resources (such as printers, files, and folders) located in domain A.

Using Universal Groups

In some instances, you might need to use Universal groups instead of Global groups. Universal groups are available in domains operating in at least Windows 2000 native mode, and are typically ideal when more than one domain exists, because Global groups are restricted in terms of user memberships to the domain in which they were created. Universal groups can accept user memberships from any domain. Universal groups can then be added to Domain Local groups, which in turn get assigned permissions over resources.

As appealing as Universal groups might seem, they do have a drawback. Each object in a Universal group is written in the GC and subsequently stored on all GC servers in your forest. In circumstances where there are thousands of Active Directory objects in Universal groups, replication traffic can quickly become an issue, especially when you have many DCs decentralized across a large WAN.

EXAM WARNING

The main difference between Universal groups and Domain Local groups is that Universal groups can be assigned permissions on any resource in any domain in the forest, whereas Domain Local groups are limited to the domain in which they were created.

Combining and Nesting Groups

When designed properly, nesting or combining groups can greatly reduce administrative overhead and reduce network traffic. However, like anything else, if configured without proper planning, it can be very complicated and hard to troubleshoot. Here are some tips you should keep in mind while designing a nesting strategy:

- Try to keep the number of nested groups to a maximum of two or three levels. This can keep it within a manageable scope for assigning permissions and troubleshooting any issues. It also minimizes the chances of adding groups that obtain excessive permissions through nesting and inheritance.
- Based on our discussion of group functions, design your nesting strategy so that you are using the most appropriate group for the task at hand. This would reduce the level of nesting required.
- Document every group's description and functionality. This would help you troubleshoot permission conflicts and other issues.

Domain Local groups can be nested in other Domain Local groups, but cannot be nested in Global or Universal groups. Global groups, however, can be nested within other Global groups, Domain Local groups, or Universal groups. Universal groups can be nested in other Universal groups and can *contain* Global groups but cannot be added to Global groups.

Consider this scenario for implementing AGDLP in an enterprise environment. EK Properties is a real estate company that specializes in acquiring shopping malls throughout the United States and in some parts of Europe. Currently, the company owns and operates 200 shopping malls spread out in every state. The company is headquartered in Chicago, Illinois, and has hired you to draw up the design plan for computerizing their current and future growth potential. The company also wants to deploy applications accessible only via Terminal servers that are located in HQ and want to give users access to these applications. All IT support staff will be located at the headquarters office with no technicians on site. The various malls will be connected to the headquarters office through WAN links of varying speeds, most of which will not be faster than 128K. Management is concerned about security at the mall locations because of the increased risk of employee turnover, and wants to place stricter security requirements on mall users in terms of passwords and account lockouts. How would you design the group structure to give access to users' data and printers, and how would you design the permissions structure for users who require access to application via Terminal servers?

Since the mall locations are separated by fairly slow links, your plan calls for a decentralized physical model in which you deploy a DC that also acts as a file and print server at every site to service the needs of the local users. User data and network printers will be configured on the local server. The DCs will be remotely administered via Remote Desktop since there will not be IT staff on location in the malls. Because of the differing security requirements, your design calls for one forest with two domains, one for the corporate headquarters and one for all the malls in the United States. User accounts should be created in the appropriate domain, either the headquarters domain or the mall users' domain. You create a separate OU for each mall location, and every mall should have a Global group that hosts all the users of that site. This Global group should then be placed in a Domain Local group and assigned permissions to local resources such as folders and printers.

Now, to allow users at all the malls access to applications running on the Terminal servers at HQ, you'll need to add users from the mall domain into a group in the HQ domain, and then assign that group right to access applications. To accomplish this, you'll use the Global groups you created for the mall users, and add those Global groups to a Domain Local group at HQ. You can then assign that the ability to access application via Terminal Services.

Domain and Forest Functional Levels

The concept of domain and forest level functional levels began with Windows 2000 to accommodate interoperability and backward compatibly with Windows NT. Windows 2000 offered two functional levels, Mixed mode and Native mode. Mixed mode had limited Active Directory features, and was backward compatible with Windows NT, which meant NT DCs could co-exist and function. Native mode enabled more Active Directory features such as Universal groups, but required that all DCs be running Windows 2000.

With the introduction of Windows Server 2003, Microsoft built on this idea and introduced new domain and forest functional levels. Each functional level has certain Active Directory feature limitations, with higher levels having the full features and power of Windows Server 2003. Let's look at the old and new functional levels that are available with Windows 2000 Server and now Server 2003:

- **Windows 2000 Mixed mode** This is the default functionality level in Windows 2000 and accepts DCs from Windows NT, Windows 2000, and Windows Server 2003 in the domain.

- **Windows 2000 Native mode** This level represents the highest level that was available in Windows 2000 and accepts only Windows 2000 and Windows Sever 2003 DCs.
- **Windows Server 2003 Interim** This domain functional level specifically allows co-existence between Windows NT DCs and Windows Server 2003 machines. Interim mode does not support Windows 2000 DCs.
- **Windows Server 2003** This type of domain functional level allows only Windows Server 2003 DCs. Once you raise the domain functional level to Windows Server 2003, you can no longer add any Windows 2000 or NT4 DCs to the domain. You will, however, enable the full features of Active Directory that were introduced with Windows Server 2003.

Similar to domain-level functionality, Windows Server 2003 also offers forest-level functionality that enables features across all the domains that are available in your forest. Windows Server 2003 offers three types of forest functionality:

- **Windows 2000** This is the default level at which the forest is set to, and this level accepts domains that have Windows NT ,Windows 2000, and Windows Server 2003 DCs.
- **Windows Server 2003 Interim** This type of forest-level functionality supports Windows NT4 and Windows Server 2003 DCs.
- **Windows Server 2003** This is the highest level of forest functionality and allows only Windows Server 2003 DCs.

The Interim level that is available in both the domain- and forest-level functionality is provided by Microsoft to those clients who skipped the Windows 2000 upgrade and want to upgrade from Windows NT directly to Windows Server 2003.

Once you raise the level of your forest to Windows Server 2003, you will no longer be able to add any DCs except Windows Server 2003 across all the domains in the forest.

Summary of Exam Objectives

An access control strategy is the building block on which you can start designing your directory services structure because it determines the overall strategy that you will follow in implementing security throughout the directory. There are two strategies that you will need to strike a balance between: access and control. Access means that you would build your directory security with easy accessibility in mind, focusing more on accommodating access than tightening security. Control implies that you grant the least permissions possible and would then move on to relaxing permissions as the need arises. This approach maintains system integrity and security as its top priority.

To implement a security strategy on files, folders, and directory objects, we need to enlist the help of ACLs or access control lists, which determine who has access to resources and how much access a given user has. ACLs are comprised of two layers of security, NTFS security and share security. NTFS security is implemented on the actual object, whereas share security is used when this resource is accessed over the network. When the NTFS and share permissions are not the same, the most restrictive permissions apply. NTFS permissions are the ideal place to set up your permissions because it has the ability to propagate its settings to subfolders, can be backed up, are more flexible, and can be audited, whereas shared permissions lack all of these.

When analyzing risks to your directory services, you should start by examining the methods by which your system can be compromised. The primary target is going to be user accounts and passwords; if an attacker can gain these credentials, then he or she can cause damage to the extent that the credentials will allow. Therefore, hardening your username and password strategy is a priority. To do this, you should avoid using known naming conventions for usernames, like first initial first name and complete last name or some other known configuration. Try to append this with an employee number or some other unique identifier.

This also brings us to password strategy. With Windows 2000 and Windows Server 2003, you can use Group Policy to enforce a strong password policy to protect your system. You can configure the password policy to force users to use a password with a certain character length. You can also enforce how often a password expires and should be changed. You can force your users not to use a password they have used before, and you can also enforce password complexity, which means the password would have to contain uppercase, lowercase, and special character letters before it is accepted by the system

User accounts have rights and permissions that can be assigned to them. On the one hand, this helps you regulate what they can do and what they can access on the network. This can also limit the scope of damage an attacker can do if he or she gains access to a user account, since the attacker will be limited by these rights and permissions. Rights allow a user to perform a task like shutting down the system or changing the system time, while permissions grant a user access to a resource such as a folder or a printer.

Many modern applications require what are known as service accounts, which are user accounts that are used solely by applications to start certain services and interact with users and the operating system. Service accounts can be common attack vectors for attackers looking for an easy entry point into your network. For this reason, it is important to grant service accounts just enough permission to complete its task. Many applications will use the Local System account by default to start its services. This account in particular has full control over the system, and if compromised can lead to denial-of-service (DoS) attacks by shutting down the system completely or stopping certain critical services. Whenever possible, service accounts should be local accounts on the system on which the application is running, so that if compromised, the extent of damage is limited to the system and not the domain.

Group Policy offers a great way to control user memberships to critical groups like Domain Admins and Enterprise Admins. Using Restricted groups, you can selectively choose which members are part of a group, and you can then enforce that membership. For example, if only Jim, Jack, and Jane are supposed to be Domain Admins, and Eli decides to add himself to the group, as soon as Group Policy refreshes, Eli will be removed since he is not included in the Restricted Group settings. In the same context, if Eli adds himself and removes all the other users, again as soon as Group Policy refreshes, Eli will be removed and the original users will be re-added.

Group Policy also allows you to implement Kerberos and Audit policies that can then be put into effect across an entire network. Kerberos is a strong network authentication protocol that can be configured in Group Policy under **\Computer Configuration\Windows Settings\Security Settings\Account Policies\Kerberos Policy**. Audit policies are imperative in any enterprise to monitor access to certain files, folders, and objects and can be set via Group Policy as well under **\Computer Configuration\Windows Settings\Security Settings\Local Policies\Audit Policy**.

When designing a delegation strategy, you should be aware that there are two types of administrators, Service Administrators and Data Administrators. Service Administrators are responsible for the overall integrity and availability of Active Directory; they maintain network services and functions for the entire user base. Data administrators are responsible for specific objects stored within Active Directory such as user and group accounts and the like. You should create your Active Directory design so that these two tasks can be separated and managed by two different people or job functions. When designing a delegation strategy, it's also imperative that you analyze your business needs for autonomy versus isolation. For example, your Human Resources department might require full and unshared control over their portion of the Active Directory and all of their network resources, with strict policies on security. In this case, the only way to give them this level of control is by creating a separate forest for them. Another department might be more willing to accept shared administration of their resources, in which case they would fall under the category of autonomy. At this point, you can create a separate domain or OU to subdivide their resources for them. Delegation of administration can be set the forest level, domain level, and OU level. The higher the level, the more isolated the administrative model. Conversely, the lower the level of delegation, the more it tends toward autonomous administration.

There are three types of groups that you can use to organize users within a forest: Domain Local groups, Global groups, and Universal groups. Domain Local groups are usually used to assign permissions on a resource. They can contain users and groups from any domain in the forest, but can only be assigned permissions on resources within their native domain. Global groups can contain users only from the domain in which they were created. Universal groups can contain users and groups from any domain in the forest and can be assigned permissions on any resource in the domain.

Microsoft best practices call for the use of AGDLP or AGUDLP when creating users and groups, with the intent of making permission assignments as flexible and easy to manage as possible. AGDLP calls for adding users to Global groups in their respective domains, adding the Global groups to Domain Local groups, and assigning permissions on resources to Domain Local groups. AGDULP uses a similar model, but Global groups would be added to Universal Groups, which would then be added to Domain Local groups and assigned permissions. You should carefully design any group nesting strategy so that you don't end up with more than two or three levels of nestings within a group to keep management simplified. You should also consider the best approach for the task at hand. Make sure you always document your group nestings and creation to account for disaster recovery and troubleshooting.

Finally, Windows 2000 and Windows Server 2003 have different functional levels for domains and forests. For domains, we have Windows 2000 mixed mode, which is the default for Windows 2000 and Windows Server 2003 domains. This allows for backward compatibility with Windows NT and Windows 2000. Windows 2000 native mode only allows for 2000 and 2003 DCs. You also have the option of using Windows Server 2003 interim mode, which will allow for backward compatibility with Windows NT4 DCs only. Finally, there is Windows Server 2003 mode, which will only allow Windows server 2003 DCs.

Likewise, there are three forest functional levels. Windows 2000 allows for Windows 2000, NT, and Windows Server 2003 DCs within all domains in the forest. Again, a Windows NT4 domain that is upgraded directly to Windows Server 2003 will be placed in Windows Server 2003 interim mode, which allows for Windows NT and Windows Server 2003 DCs. The final forest functional level is Windows Server 2003, which will only allow for Windows Server 2003 DCs in any domain in the forest. This unleashes the full potential and all the features of Windows Server 2003, since it does not need to be scaled back to accommodate older DCs that don't have the newest features and functionality.

Exam Objectives Fast Track

Designing an Access Control Strategy for Directory Services

- ☑ Access and control are the two methods you can choose from when implementing a strategy for directory services. Control is the favorite since it calls for least access and then relaxing permissions as needed.
- ☑ Group policy can be used to set permissions on files, folders, and resources.
- ☑ Restricted groups greatly enhances security because it gives you a mechanism by which to enforce user memberships to sensitive groups.
- ☑ A good password policy can ensure your system is not vulnerable to easy password attacks by hackers.

Designing the Appropriate Group Strategy for Accessing Resources

- ☑ There are three types of groups within a forest that you can create: Domain Local groups, Global groups, and Universal groups.
- ☑ Universal groups differ from Domain Local groups in that they can be assigned permissions on any resource in any domain in the forest, whereas Domain Local groups are limited to the domain in which they were created.
- ☑ There are four types of domain functional levels and three types of forest functional levels. Domain functional levels are Windows 2000 mixed, Windows 2000 native, Windows Server 2003 interim, and Windows Server 2003. The forest functional levels are Windows 2000, Windows Server 2003 interim, and Windows Server 2003.

Exam Objectives Frequently Asked Questions

The following Frequently Asked Questions, answered by the authors of this book, are designed to both measure your understanding of the Exam Objectives presented in this chapter, and to assist you with real-life implementation of these concepts. You will also gain access to thousands of other FAQs at ITFAQnet.com.

Q: What functions are available when I raise my domain functional level?

A.: The Windows Server 2003 domain functional level enables the following functions: domain rename tool, update logon timestamp, Universal groups for both security and distribution groups, full group nesting and converting, and the use of the SID history to migrate security principals between domains.

Q: Is there any way I can increase security in trusts between multiple forests?

A: When you create new users or computer objects in a domain, the domain SID is included in the security principal's SID to identify the domain where it was created. Outgoing external trusts use SID filtering to verify that incoming authentication requests only contain SIDs from security principals in the trusted domain. Windows does this using SID filtering, which compares the SIDs of the incoming security principal to the domain SID of the trusted domain.

Q: I have several existing Windows NT domains, with trust relationships between them that I don't want to redo. What's going to happen to these when I upgrade to Windows Server 2003?

A: When you upgrade a Windows NT domain to Windows Server 2003, all existing Windows NT trusts are preserved intact. Any trust relationships between Windows Server 2003 domains and Windows NT domains will be intransitive.

Q: I'd like to secure the file permissions my server's hard drive as much as possible. What are the minimum permissions I can set on a Windows Server 2003 server without affecting how the server functions on the network?

A: At a minimum, the Authenticated Users group needs to have Read, Read & Execute, and List Folder Contents permissions to the drive where Windows Server 2003 is installed. Otherwise, many necessary services won't be able to start.

Self Test

A Quick Answer Key follows the Self Test questions. For complete questions, answers, and explanations to the Self Test questions in this chapter as well as the other chapters in this book, see the Self Test Appendix.

1. Best Fit Inc is a clothing retailer that has been in business for over 25 years and grosses over 100 million dollars in annual sales. The company is experiencing tremendous growth and has added a Web store to reach customers in areas where it doesn't have a retail presence. This venture into the Web now poses a security issue for them. The company has asked the IT department to ensure proper procedure is in place so that they are informed anytime anyone attempts to access confidential data that's stored on the Web server. Which audit policy should you enable on the Web server? (Choose all that apply.)

   A. Audit success and failure of process tracking

   B. Audit success and failure of object access

   C. Audit success and failure of logon events

   D. Audit success and failure of directory service access

2. Elineken is a new brand of beer that is being produced by the Eli bottling company, which employs over 35,000 employees worldwide. The corporate headquarters is in San Francisco and the company has production facilities in Holland, Ireland, Germany, and Hong Kong. After finding great response to their brand of beer and getting numerous awards, the company is now expanding its market into the Middle East and has acquired a large production facility in Lebanon. This new facility will be home to some 2,000 employees who will service the needs of the area, and as such will require several file servers, Exchange servers, and DCs to be available on site for speedier authentication, mail delivery, and to avoid WAN reliability issues. The CIO is especially interested in the security procedures that will be in place to secure the local servers and has asked you to ensure the company is using best practices and that the servers will be as safe as possible. The CIO also has decided that the Lebanon facility will be incorporated into the existing domain model. How should you secure the new servers at the new Lebanon facility?

   A. Install the servers into a new OU and implement group policies at the site level.

   B. Install the servers into a new OU and implement group policies at the OU level.

C. Install the servers into their own Active Directory tree and implement group policies at the domain level.

D. Install the servers into the same Active Directory tree as stores and modify the schema.

3. Ground Up Properties is the third largest shopping mall owner and operator in the world with over 300 malls in the United States alone spread out across all states. The company currently has over 4000 employees and is headquartered in New York. Ground Up has been experiencing tremendous growth in its sector and is ready to acquire a major European real estate company that owns and operates 50 malls in Europe. The acquired European company does not have any network in place, and your integration team has decided to incorporate the newly acquired malls into the existing infrastructure and treat them as sites within the existing domain. This means that every site would need a DC that will also act as a file and print server and an exchange server. Because of time difference and language barriers, the company decides to hire a few local techs in the Paris regional office to accommodate the needs of the users in these malls. The CIO is requesting that the local helpdesk personnel be give enough access to manage the users and groups in the newly acquired facilities. Which strategy should you use to accommodate the newly acquired malls?

   A. Add the helpdesk employee to the Domain Admins group.

   B. Add the helpdesk employee to the Enterprise Admins group.

   C. Delegate authority at the domain level to the Paris helpdesk employees to manage users and groups.

   D. Delegate authority to the Paris helpdesk employees to modify accounts and groups in the European malls' OUs.

4. Didisoft is a technology company with products for the security industry. The company is a new startup based in San Francisco and employs 500 employees. The CIO is very aggressive about security and intrusion detection and has requested that the Windows Server 2003 architect implement all the tools and features the operating system offers in that direction so that it can be combined with the Didisoft Intrusion Squasher software that, in his opinion, would render the system impenetrable. The CIO wants to ensure that the sensitive administrative-level domain groups are not tampered with. What can you do to ensure only the appropriate users are members of domain Admins?

   A. Implement ACLs on the domain Admins group.

   B. Implement ACLs on the OU in which the domain Admins group resides.

   C. Use Restricted groups in Group Policy to enforce the membership.

D. Regularly check the domain Admins group membership to ensure no one has been modified.

5. Chocolate Chip is a chocolate-making company based in New Orleans. It employs 5000 employees. The company has recently experienced a security breach in which valuable information about the new chocolate flavor was stolen together with marketing strategy. The company had no security measures in place because the CIO claimed that security breaches are rare and overly exaggerated by the media and has assured management that no such thing would occur in the company. After the main competitor for Chocolate Chip released a product with a slightly different name and used the exact same marketing strategy that the Chocolate Chip company was planning to use, management found this a strange coincidence and started an investigation, only to be tipped off by an IT employee in the other company bragging about how easy it was to hack and steal from the Chocolate Chip network. The CIO immediately called a meeting of the IT staff and requested that auditing be enabled as a first step in a list of security measures that will follow. What should you include in an audit policy for the domain?

   A. Failure audit for account logon events
   Failure audit for directory service access
   Success and failure audit for policy change
   Success and failure audit for account management

   B. Failure audit for object access
   Failure audit for account logon events
   Failure audit for directory service access
   Success and failure audit for policy change

   C. Success and failure audit for object access
   Success and failure audit for policy change
   Success and failure audit for account logon events
   Success and failure audit for process tracking

   D. Success and failure audit for object access
   Success and failure audit for policy change
   Success and failure audit for account logon events
   Success and failure audit for directory service access

6. SV Corporation is a computer chip manufacturer based in San Francisco. The company employs 500 employees and is one of the leading computer chip manufacturers. The company recently avoided a security breach in which sensitive information could have been compromised or stolen by an international competitor. This incident immediately prompted the company to hire an external organization to attempt a penetration test and discover the possible vulnerabili-

ties that exist on the SV network. During the penetration test, the security consultants were able to penetrate the network and gain full access to it. The CIO gathers all the different teams within MIS to discuss this and requests that each group take immediate measures to ensure their systems are as secure as possible in accordance with industry best practices. Since you are responsible for the Windows environment at SV, which policies should you include in a security strategy for the domain? (Choose two.)

A. Enable account lockout

B. Disable password aging

C. Disable account lockout

D. Enforce strong passwords and password aging

7. Best Pix Inc. is the largest chain of photography studios in the world, with several locations in every country in Europe and several locations in almost all states in the United States. They currently employ over 20,000 employees. The company is undergoing a major migration from Windows NT to Windows Server 2003. Every location currently has a manager with several employees. As part of the company's marketing strategy, they are interested in offering their customers access to their photos with the ability to order reprints over the Web. Security is a large concern for Best Pix, and they want to ensure that the service they are offering does not compromise security for their network. This service is also posing a challenge to the IT department in terms of how customer accounts will be created and deleted. Because the company is so big and widespread, the IT team has decided to grant the office manager at each location some kind of delegation to assist with this task and to be able to respond to customer needs in a timely fashion. That office manager can also respond to security threats on customer accounts in a quick and time-effective fashion. Which task should you delegate to the office managers?

A. Modify the membership of a group

B. Manage Group Policy links

C. Create, delete, and manage customer accounts

D. Create, delete, and manage groups

8. Gourmet Distribution specializes in wholesale distribution of canned foods to supermarkets. The company has many distribution locations spread out across the United States. Every distribution site employs about 100 employees. The IT director has decided to place a DC, an Exchange server, and a file server at every location to meet each site's IT needs. An IT administrator will also be hired at every location to see to server maintenance. As part of the migration

from Windows NT to Windows Server 2003, you have decided to adopt a single domain model with separate OUs for every location. How should you grant the necessary permissions to the IT administrator at each distribution center?

A. Create a new administrator account for each distribution center's OU. Grant the necessary permissions to this account.

B. Create an administrator group for each distribution center's OU. Add an existing user designated as an administrator to this account. Grant the necessary permissions to this group.

C. Create a new administrator account for each distribution center's OU in the headquarters root. Grant the necessary permissions to each new administrator's account.

D. Create an administrator group for each OU at the headquarters root. Add an existing user designated as an administrator from each OU to this group. Grant the necessary permissions to this group.

Self Test Quick Answer Key

For complete questions, answers, and explanations to the Self Test questions in this chapter as well as the other chapters in this book, see the Self Test Appendix.

1. **B, C**
2. **B**
3. **D**
4. **C**
5. **D**
6. **A, D**
7. **C**
8. **B**

Chapter 9

MCSE 70-298

Securing Network Resources

Exam Objectives in this Chapter:

- 4.2 Design an access control strategy for files and folders.
- 4.2.4 Analyze auditing requirements.
- 4.3.2 Analyze auditing requirements.
- 4.3 Design an access control strategy for the registry.
- 4.3.1 Design a permission structure for registry objects.
- 4.2.1 Design a strategy for the encryption and decryption of files and folders.
- 4.2.3 Design security for a backup and recovery strategy.

- ☑ Summary of Exam Objectives
- ☑ Exam Objectives Fast Track
- ☑ Exam Objectives Frequently Asked Questions
- ☑ Self Test
- ☑ Self Test Quick Answer Key

Introduction

Now that you've secured the Active Directory database and created an efficient group structure for your organization in Chapter 8, "Securing Active Directory," the next step is to actually secure the files and folders themselves. Windows permissions are *discretionary*, which means that users with the Change Permissions or Full Control permissions or users who have ownership of a file or folder can change its permissions to their heart's content. With this in mind, you should design a permission scheme that will provide sufficient access for end users to do their jobs, but not unnecessary permissions that might affect the security of your overall network.

Windows Server 2003 establishes a default permission structure when you first install the operating system, but you might need to change these defaults to meet your needs. In this chapter, we examine some common risks that can affect your file shares, such as data corruption caused by viruses or security breaches arising from incorrectly assigned permissions. Then, we'll look at ways to design a permission structure for the files and folders in a large, multiserver environment, as well as best practices for securing the Windows Registry.

An advance in Windows 2000 gave users the ability to encrypt files on a hard drive using the Encrypted File System (EFS). EFS combines public key cryptography (using Certificate Services) with 3DES encryption to allow users and administrators to extend file security beyond NTFS permissions. This feature has been expanded and improved in Windows Server 2003, including the ability to encrypt files remotely, and to share encrypted files among multiple users. The proper use of EFS within an enterprise requires careful planning, both in terms of user education and technical implementations. For example, you need to implement a means to recover encrypted files if a user's private key is lost or damaged.

The last topic we'll talk about here is designing a secure backup and recovery strategy for your network resources. The disaster recovery process is really your last line of defense where security is concerned—if all else fails and your data has been compromised somehow, you can turn to your backup tapes to restore anything that has been lost or corrupted. However, what if your backups themselves create an avenue for attackers to compromise your network? We'll look at ways to secure the backup process itself, including physically securing backup media, and assigning rights and permissions to perform backups and restores in a secure manner.

EXAM 70-298 OBJECTIVE 4.2

Designing an Access Control Strategy for Files and Folders

One of the fundamental elements of data security is controlling access to information. The first step is authorizing users to gain access to the network. The second step is controlling what data those users can access via the use of access control mechanisms built into Windows Server 2003. Objects, including files and folders, can be managed via their access control lists (ACLs) that designate which users and groups can access the object (file, folder, printer, etc.) and in what manner. Managing network resources through access control adds a critical layer of security to a network. To use access control functions in Windows Server 2003, you need to format disk volumes with the NTFS file format, which provides the ability to control access to files at a very granular level and enables the ability to audit access to those files. The FAT or FAT32 file format does not provide this functionality and is therefore generally not suitable for a business environment. In this section, we'll take an in-depth look at designing and managing access control strategies for files and folders in Windows Server 2003.

Analyzing Risks to Data

One of the first steps in securing network resources is assessing the risks to your data. Every company is different and the risks will vary from one organization to another. However, there are common elements that should be reviewed and analyzed as part of a comprehensive security plan. These include:

- Physical loss of data
- Data corruption
- Data modification or corruption from viruses and other attacks
- Security breaches due to incorrectly configured permissions
- Auditing practices

Physical Loss of Data

Physical loss of data can occur for many reasons—from power outages to disk crashes to system failures. Physical loss of data is typically a result of events that cannot be easily anticipated, such as a power outage or even a bad sector on a hard disk. Routine maintenance can help spot trouble early, but often these events occur without warning and you must have a solid recovery plan in place. The risk of physical loss of data can be greatly reduced through the use of disk volumes such as striped sets with parity, mirrored volumes, and other dynamic disk configurations. These disk configurations reduce single points of failure, creating a more stable environment. Analyzing system volumes for errors and fragmentation is a good preventive course, and naturally, routine (and reliable) backups are essential. We'll discuss data recovery later in this chapter.

TEST DAY TIP

Make sure you've reviewed disk management concepts before the exam. These concepts include RAID-0 through RAID-5. RAID-0, RAID-1, and RAID-5 are supported in Windows Server 2003. RAID-0 is a stripe set without parity. Data is written across multiple disks without a parity stripe. This is a very fast configuration but provides no fault tolerance. If one disk fails, you must recover from a backup to restore the disk set.

RAID-1 is mirrored volumes (formerly called a mirrored set in Windows NT 4.0). A mirrored volume is an exact replica of another volume. If one drive fails, the mirrored volume can instantly be used because all data is identical to the failed volume's contents.

RAID-5 implements a striped set with parity. In a striped set with parity, data is written across several drives. A parity stripe contains information about the data stored in the set. If one drive fails, the parity stripe is used to recreate the data once the failed drive is replaced.

Another important point to remember is that RAID-5 is best used in an environment where data is more often read than written (written once, read many times). Conversely, RAID-1 is best suited to situations where data is constantly changing. It offers better performance than RAID-5 in those situations. With the cost of disk drives continuing to fall, RAID-0 is a more affordable solution than it was five years ago.

Data Corruption

Data corruption can happen for a number of reasons. Some corruption can happen due to bad sectors on the disk where the file was stored or unusual events that occur while working on the system that cause a file or folder to stop working. Data corruption can also occur as a result of viruses, worms, and other executables run on the system either intentionally or unintentionally. As with physical loss of data, these events can sometimes be random events that cannot be anticipated. However, checking the disk for errors, defragmenting when needed, and backing up critical data frequently is important for recovering from data corruption.

Viruses, Worms, and Other Software Attacks

Viruses, worms, and other software attacks can also corrupt or modify data. Configuring virus protection programs that monitor systems and e-mail programs for viruses as well as keeping the virus signature file up to date is crucial. In addition, the manner in which you manage access to the network can also mitigate virus risks. For example, ensuring that all user computers run the latest virus software and get regular signature file updates automatically will help reduce risk. Tightly controlling what can and cannot be downloaded from the Internet will also help reduce risk of virus attack. Managing noncorporate computer connections to your corporate network is also an element of mitigating risk, since laptops brought in by others outside your company can introduce viruses to the network if they are given access. Educating users is also important, since preventing attacks can be easier than protecting against them and recovering from them.

Security Breaches

Another risk to data is the risk of a security breach. Throughout this book, we've discussed various risks to security. One of the end goals of hackers is data (the other being system control). Security can be breached in a number of ways, but in this chapter, we're focusing on how to secure data. In Windows Server 2003, this is accomplished through managing users' ability to log on to the network and then through managing users' access to data once they've been authenticated. Strong authentication and access policies and procedures provide a strong line of defense against intentional attack. Access control is discussed in more detail in the next section and it's sure to be covered in the exam. Although a hacker might intentionally attack a system, the other type of security breach can occur when users are unintentionally given incorrect permissions. This typically happens due to simple administrative error, intentional administrative privilege abuse, or because the system of granting access is too complex and the inherited permissions did not behave as intended. In any case, developing a consistent method for managing user access will greatly enhance security by reducing error administrative work as well.

Auditing Practices

Finally, auditing practices can help keep data secure. Carefully defining auditing policies can improve security by monitoring access to various objects. If an object is being accessed inappropriately, the administrator can take steps to resolve the problem whether the cause is inadvertent access (wrong permissions) or intentional access (hacker). Auditing file access or use of privileges can provide clues to inappropriate network activity and provide you with valuable information to help uncover the problem and resolve it. We'll discuss auditing later in this chapter.

Reviewing Access Control and Access Control Lists

When designing a resource strategy, you must determine how to grant and manage appropriate access to users, groups, and computers. This entails designing a strategy that will provide a systematic way of applying and managing access to resources. In this section, we'll briefly review access control and resource authorization methods.

Access control defines which users, groups, and computers can access particular network resources. Once a user is authenticated, access settings determine what that user can do on the network. Access control is comprised of permissions, user rights, and object auditing.

Permissions

Permissions define the type of access given to a user, group, or computer. Permissions can be granted to any user, group, or computer. To use groups and manage permissions efficiently, administrators should use the practice often referred to as AGDLP. This acronym is used to remember how permissions should be granted. Add user *accounts* (A) to global *groups* (G), add global groups to *domain local* groups (DL), and then add domain local groups to the security properties of the resource for which you want to grant *permissions* (P). This AGDLP strategy provides flexibility while reducing the complexity and administrative burden of managing permissions across the enterprise.

Although it is not often a good idea to assign explicit access rights and permissions to individual user accounts, it can be done. It might be appropriate if there is a compelling reason to do so and if no other method provides a feasible alternative. For example, you might have several remote servers and you want only one person to have the ability to manage them. Rather than adding a group or creating a group for that person, you can simply add the user account to the appropriate ACL for the server. However, it's almost always easier to use the AGDLP method for managing permissions.

Permissions can be applied to any security objects, including Active Directory objects, files, folders, or Registry objects. The types of permissions available vary depending on the object. For example, there are different permissions available for Registry keys than there are for files or folders.

When an object is created, the creator is the owner and has full permission of that object by default. The owner can always change the permissions on the object, regardless of how the permissions on the object are set. The owner can grant other users and groups access to the object.

In addition, permissions can be assigned to special identities. Special identities include the creator owner, interactive, local system, network, and service, among others. The creator owner has full permissions on the object. The interactive group includes all accounts for users logged on locally or through Remote Desktop connections to a particular computer. The local system is an account used by the local operating system. As you might expect, the network group includes all users logged on via a network connection. The service group is a group that includes any security principals that have logged on as a service. This is an automated, behind-the-scenes function and access is controlled by the operating system.

Permissions can be inherited, and this is the primary way of managing permissions. The administrator can automatically cause objects within the container (for example, all files in a folder or all subfolders in a folder) to inherit all inheritable permissions of that container. Only permissions marked to be inherited will be inherited.

User Rights

User rights grant specific privileges and logon rights to users. Rights such as *Log on locally* or *Back up files and directory* are assigned by default to certain user groups. Users can be added to these groups to grant or deny permissions based on group membership. User rights can be assigned on a per-user basis, but this quickly becomes difficult to manage. The preferred solution is to add users to group and grant or deny permissions to that group (AGDLP). In this way, if users change positions or leave the company, permissions based on group membership are revoked when they are removed from the group. This is the preferred method for managing user rights both to ease administrative overhead and to maintain security on the network.

Object Auditing

You can use object auditing to view user's access to various objects. You should define auditing policies so that you frequently monitor sensitive resources and regularly monitor less sensitive resources. As an example, you might want to monitor access to the Registry more often than you want to monitor file access to commonly used files and folders.

Access Control Lists

Each resource has an ACL that controls the access to that resource. There are two types of ACLs: Discretionary (DACL) and System (SACL). The DACL is the part of the ACL that grants or denies permissions to specific users and groups. Only the owner of the resource can change the permissions—it is at the owner's discretion, thus the name. The SACL is the part of the object's description that specifies which events are to be audited per user or group. Auditing examples include access, logon attempts, or system shutdowns.

Access Control Entry

Each ACL is comprised of various *access control entries* (ACEs). An ACE is an entry in an ACL that contains the security ID (SID) for a user or group as well as an *access mask* that specifies which actions are granted, denied, or audited. An example of an ACL with ACEs for a document called *securedocument.txt* is shown in Figure 9.1. An example of an access mask is shown in Figure 9.2. In an ACE, various permissions are represented by one or more bits called an access mask. This functions in a manner similar to a subnet mask in networking. When access to an object is requested, the access request is compared to the mask. Bits that match are the permissions that are permitted. The example shown in Figure 9.2 is a simplified example of how a user's access token is compared with an object's access mask to determine what, if any, rights the user has. In this example, the user is granted generic read access for the object (leftmost bit is the only bit that matches).

Figure 9.1 Access Control List with Access Control Entries

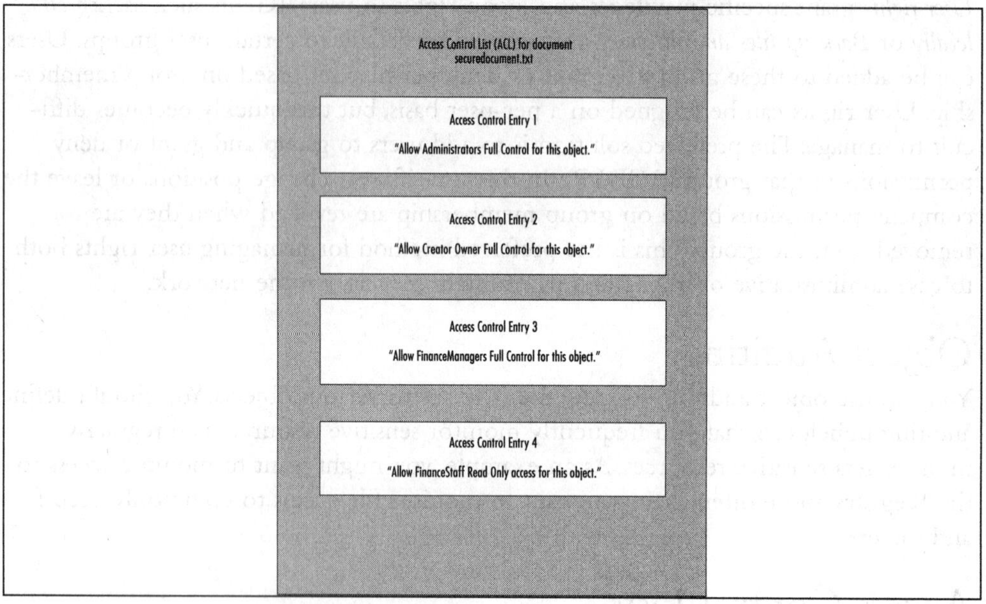

Figure 9.2 Access Mask Compared with Access Request

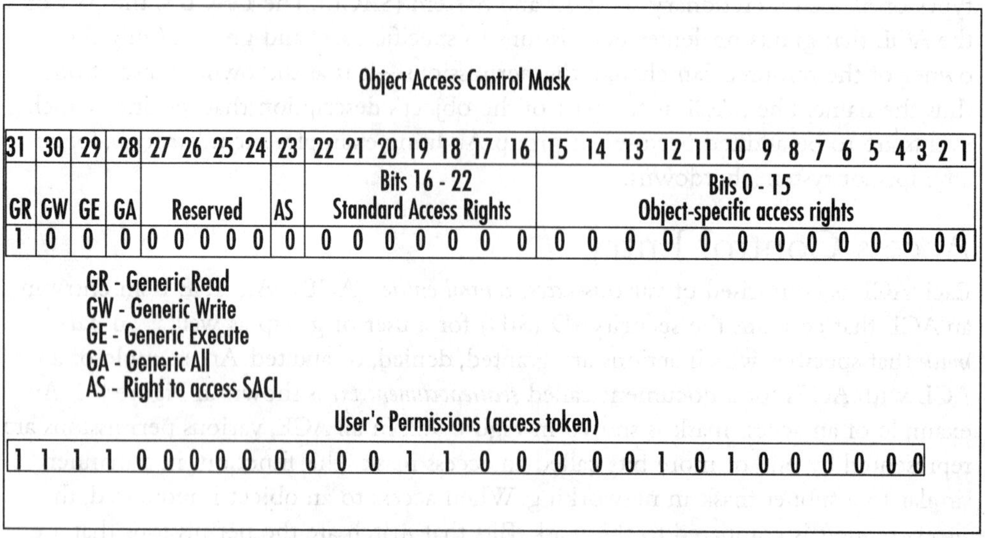

Groups

To fully understand access control, it's important to understand the definition of various groups. In Windows Server 2003, there are two types of groups available to you when using Active Directory. A *security group* is used to define, grant, or deny security settings including access control. These groups can be defined for a forest, domain, or local computer. A *distribution group* is used for a mailing list only and has no security function. Our discussion will be limited to security groups.

An *account group* is a security group whose members are user accounts or computer accounts that require the same permissions for a resource. For example, suppose your Finance department staff all require the same access to the Finance share on Server1. You would add users from the Finance department to an account group that you have created called FinanceUsers. FinanceUsers will all be given the same access to Finance resources on Server1. An account group is a security group that is not specifically associated with any particular object like a server or a file. Instead, it is used to group users who have similar access needs.

A *resource group* is a security group that has been added to the ACL of a resource and has been granted (or denied) specific permissions. Unlike an account group, a resource group is associated with a specific resource such as a server, file, or folder. Resource groups can be used to define specific sets of permissions for accessing an object. For example, support you have a file that contains sensitive information. You can create several resource groups for that object. You can create one group that has full control, one group that has read and write permissions only, and a third group that has read-only permissions. Then, you can add account groups to these resource groups. Using the same example, you might add the Executives account group to the full control resource group, you might add the FinanceManagers group to the read and write resource group, and you might add FinanceStaff group to the read-only resource group. In this way, you can closely manage permissions for the resource and add or delete account groups to these resource groups. This keeps the access for the resource well defined while allowing flexibility by being able to add or remove account groups rather than change the permissions for the resource.

Security Groups

Security groups are groups created to manage access and other security-related functions for ease of administration. Security groups contain user accounts, computer accounts, and other group accounts. Following best practices, permissions are granted or denied to security groups rather than individual accounts. Security groups can be organized by their scope, and the available groups in Windows Server 2003 are defined here. Although this chapter assumes a basic understanding of these groups and their scope, a brief review is included here to refresh your memory.

- **Local** Members of the local group can include groups and accounts from the domain, but permissions are restricted to the computer on which the group is defined.
- **Domain local** Members of domain local groups can include other groups and accounts from any Windows Server 2003, Windows 2000, or Windows NT 4.0 domain. Members of these groups can be assigned permissions only within the domain.
- **Global** Members of global groups can include other groups and accounts, but only from the domain in which the global group is defined. These global groups can be assigned permissions in any domain in the forest.
- **Universal** Members of universal groups can include other groups and accounts from any domain in the domain tree or forest. These universal groups can be assigned permissions in any domain in the domain tree or forest.

Some features, such as universal groups and group nesting, are available only on Active Directory domain controllers (DCs) and member servers.

TEST DAY TIP

Make sure you're comfortable with groups and permissions. Although a full discussion is outside the scope of this chapter, it's important that you're very comfortable with permissions because you'll find many questions that directly or indirectly test your understanding and ability to apply your understanding of permissions.

Access to Resources

In Windows Server 2003, there are essentially four methods for controlling access to resources: *User/ACL*, *Account group/ACL*, *Account group/resource group*, and *role-based authorization*. Each method provides benefits in certain settings and each comes with limitations that must be considered.

User/ACL

In this method, users are added directly to the ACL for the resource. Each user is then granted specific permissions for that resource. This is commonly used when someone wants to share access to a file or folder. Since the owner has a vested interest in the files and folders, he or she is likely to manage permissions to the resources effectively if only a small number of resources are involved. However, this method is generally not effective for an organization because it becomes unmanageable quickly. Table 9.1 summarizes the benefits and limitations of this method.

Table 9.1 Benefits and Limitations of User/ACL Method

Benefits	Limitations
Easy to implement.	Access to resources is inconsistent since it is set on a case-by-case basis.
Owner is likely to manage resources appropriately.	IT staff must deal with requests for permission changes to resources.
Might be appropriate for resources on which security must be very tightly controlled.	Difficult to manage access since it is at the resource level.
	Difficult to revoke permissions for staff who move or leave the company.
	In large organizations, poorly managed (or unmanaged) security descriptors can waste disk space.

Account Group/ACL (AG/ACL)

This method uses groups instead of individual accounts. A security group is created and users are added to the group. The group is then granted permission to the resource. When you want to change permissions for that resource, you simply change permissions for the security group or groups for that resource. This is a fairly scalable solution because you can use nested groups if you're running Windows 2000 or Windows Server 2003 in native mode. This is helpful if groups from multiple domains or forests require access to resources using identical permissions. In this case, they can be grouped together into one security group and assigned to the resource ACL. The downside of this method is that it requires more effort on the part of the resource owner, since each group has to be added to the ACL separately and permissions must be set for each group. Table 9.2 summaries the benefits and limitations of this approach.

Table 9.2 Benefits and Limitations of the Account Group/ACL Method

Benefits	Limitations
Scalable—security groups can be nested if the domain is running in Windows 2000 native mode or Windows Server 2003 functional level.	Can be more difficult to administer if different groups each require different permissions. For each different set of permissions, a different group must be added to the ACL.

Continued

Table 9.2 Benefits and Limitations of the Account Group/ACL Method

Benefits	Limitations
Easier to administer if groups require similar permissions.	If the domain is configured as a Windows 2000 mixed functional level, the resource owner has more administrative work, since group nesting is more limited. In this case, the best option is likely AG/RG, discussed next.
More secure—when users leave the organization, removing them from the domain security group removes their permissions for all objects to which that group had permissions.	
Useful if permissions require frequent changing.	

Account Group/Resource Group

You can manage access to resources by assigning users with similar access needs to account groups. Account groups can be added to resource groups, which are then added to resource ACLs. Permissions on the resource are then set on a resource group basis. This method is sometimes appropriate for larger companies with many shared resources. It's highly scalable and does not depend on the mode in which you're running Windows (native or mixed). It works with Windows 2000 in mixed mode and with Windows NT 4.0 domains. Table 9.3 summarizes the benefits and limitations of the AG/RG method. It takes more work initially to set it up, and if resources require frequent permission changes, it can be cumbersome.

Table 9.3 Benefits and Limitations of the AG/RG Method

Benefits	Limitations
Very scalable and maintainable at all domain functional levels.	Not recommended if resources require frequent changes to permissions.
Helpful if a group of related resources are being shared to multiple account groups.	More initial administrative overhead than other methods.
Easier to revoke or change permissions for users who move within the organization, leave or join the organization.	
Works in a mixed domain model.	

Role-Based Authorization

The fourth method of providing permissions is when users with similar roles are authorized to perform tasks based on scripts called *authorization rules*. You can finely control access in this method, but you must be running Windows Server 2003 and your applications must support this method. There are four domain functional levels available in Windows Server 2003, which are used to enable features of Active Directory depending on the domain's (or forest's) capabilities. The four levels are Windows 2000 mixed (default), Windows 2000 native, Windows Server 2003 interim, and Windows Server 2003. While a discussion of these is outside the scope of this chapter, it's important to understand these concepts. For this discussion, it's important to understand that role-based authorization can be used if the application supports it, and if you're running in the Windows Server 2003 domain functional mode. Table 9.4 summaries the benefits and limitations of the role-based authorization access control method.

Table 9.4 Benefit and Limitations of Role-Based Authorization Method

Benefits	Limitations
Allows very granular tuning of permissions.	Application must support role-based authorization.
	Must be using Windows Server 2003 domain functional level.

Selecting Domain Local Groups or Local Groups as Resource Groups

When designing security via the access control methods just described, you can use resource groups. These resource groups can be either domain local groups in the computer's domain or local groups on the computer that controls the resource. The decision as to which group type to use depends on a number of variables. When a user wants to share a resource and assign permissions, he or she is likely to simply use the local group. However, a network administrator assigning permissions to resources across the domain must look at the pros and cons of each model.

Domain Local Groups

From an administrative point of view, using domain local groups is an easier solution for managing access. Domain local groups can be managed anywhere in the domain and those groups are visible in Active Directory. If the group is named in such as way that it indicates the function of the group, administrative tasks can be greatly simplified using this approach.

However, there are several significant downside aspects that must be considered. If a file server has many shares and there are three resource groups that define three different sets of access permissions, the number of groups displayed in Active Directory will be the number of shares times the number of resource groups. If there were 200 shares, there would be 600 resource group listings in Active Directory. If there are 800 shares, there would be 2,400 groups listed. However, that's assuming there is only one computer with this number of shares. Suppose there are 10 or 50 or 100? As you can see, this can become a problem, both in terms of simply loading the list into the Active Directory Users and Computers snap-in and in terms of sifting through the groups looking for the specific one you want to work with. You can easily imagine that, in this scenario, an administrator might inadvertently modify the permissions on the wrong group, creating a security hole. If there are many shares on a computer, the better choice might be to use local groups as resource groups.

Another problem with using domain local groups as resource groups is that it is more difficult to retire a group. As resources are moved or changed, the resource groups associated with it must be managed.

Finally, there is another challenge in using domain local groups. As you know, when a user logs on, a security access token is created that is built from the security IDs (SIDs) of the groups to which the user belongs. If a user belongs to many groups, the token size might exceed the standard size. With the default settings in Windows Server 2003 and Windows XP, a user can belong to about 120 groups before the buffer for the token is exceeded. This buffer size can be resized, so if you choose to use domain local groups and users belong to perhaps hundreds of groups, you'll want to do this. For more information on resizing the security access token buffer, take a look at Microsoft Knowledge Base article 327825 "New Resolution Problems That Occur When Users Belong to Many Groups" http://support.microsoft.com/default.aspx?scid=kb;en-us;327825.

TEST DAY TIP

One of the results of a token size exceeding the buffer size is that the user will be unable to log on or gain access to network resources. Keep this in mind when working with problems that involve access or logon issues.

Local Groups

Local groups require the resource manager to create the groups on the computer where the resource resides. This is a disadvantage because it requires the resource manager to create groups on many different computers in order to manage access. Local groups are not going to display in Active Directory, which makes administration more difficult. The upside is that the resource manager is much more likely to properly manage permissions on a local computer than on a domain group via another administrator. If you are responsible for one server for your department, you are more likely to be actively involved with managing and more aware of the security needs for the data on that server. A remote administrator three states away is not as likely to be aware of the security needs for that server and the resources on that server. There is little danger of exceeding the token buffer size when using local groups as there is for domain local groups.

EXAM WARNING

You're definitely going to get a question or two that involves access to resources because access control is the foundation of security. Be very familiar with the four types of access control and the limitations of the various methods when you prepare for the exam.

Working with Security Groups

There are several critical elements you'll need to define in order to design secure access control for your network. Each of these elements is part of creating a sound, consistent policy for managing access to network resources. We'll look at each in more detail next.

- Defining security group creation policy.
- Defining a security group request process.
- Defining a security group naming policy.
- Defining a security group nesting policy.
- Defining a security group retirement policy.
- Delegating security group maintenance.
- Delegating resource group maintenance.

Defining Security Group Creation Policy

In many organizations, it's more efficient to delegate responsibility for various administrative tasks. To delegate security for network resources effectively, you should begin by defining your policy. By default, the following groups have permission to *Create Group Objects* and *Delete Group Objects*:

- Domain Admins
- Enterprise Admins
- Account Operators

If you would like to delegate permission to create and delete security groups to users who are not members of one of these three groups, you can create a separate security group and apply those permissions to that group. For example, you could create a group called Security Group Admins and add users to whom you want to delegate the ability to create and delete security groups.

Defining a Security Group Request Process

Now that you've defined who can create and delete groups, your next task is to determine how users will request the creation of security groups. This is an important step because it centralizes and standardizes group creation so that redundant or unnecessary groups are not created. A request for the creation of a security group should include the following information:

- Group owner
- Purpose and scope of group
- Proposed membership
- Relationship to other groups
- Expected lifetime of group

Ideally, these requests should be submitted in a manner that allows them to be stored in a database for later review and searching. This is particularly helpful in rooting out unused or obsolete groups, based on the expected lifetime information.

Defining a Security Group Naming Policy

The next step is to define a standard for naming security groups. It can be confusing and cause administrative errors when naming conventions are either not specified or not used. Errors are not just an inconvenience to users who might be accidentally moved or changed from a legitimate group. Errors can also place users in incorrect groups, granting them inappropriate access to sensitive information. If an unauthorized user gains legitimate access (via a group membership error) to payroll information or personal medical data, you not only have a security problem, you might also have a legal problem as well.

A sound naming policy should include these elements:

- Include the group's scope, purpose, and owner in its name and description.
- Conform to hierarchy structure beginning with the most general and ending with the most specific.
- Name and description combined should be less than 256 characters.

- Use abbreviations if practical. Only the first 20 characters are usually visible without resizing columns or scrolling. If you view the Properties dialog of the group, the first 50 characters are visible.

It's often helpful to use the business organization as the basis for the naming conventions. For example, some companies are organized by business units, others by geography, still others by function. A naming convention can use these or domain names or any other logical structure. A naming convention based on business unit might be Software (SW), Hardware (HW), Service (SVC), and Corporate (CP). Therefore, group names might begin with SW, HW, SVC, or CP. To drill down further, the name might next reflect the function within the units, so the names would develop in this manner: SWSALES, HWSALES, SVCSALES, and CPSALES. The next level might be a management level, so the names would continue: SWSALESMGMT, HWSALESMGMT, SVCSALESMGMT, and CPSALESMGT.

A naming convention based on geography might look something like this:

- WEST-SEA-Floor7-Laser
- WEST-SEA-Floor7-Inkjet
- WEST-SEA-Floor7-HiSpeed
- WEST-SEA-Floor8-Laser
- WEST-SF-Floor1-Inkjet
- EAST-NY-Floor38-Laser
- EAST-NY-Floor38-Inkjet
- EAST-NY-Floor38-HiSpeed

Another example is a naming structure based on the domain membership. If the domain is somecompany.com, you might have a naming structure that looks like this:

- Some-sales-mgmt
- Some-sales-staff
- Some-service-support-mgmt
- Some-service-support-users
- Some-service-parts-mgmt
- Some-service-parts-users

It's also important to note that there is no way to automatically enforce naming standards. Windows Server 2003 does not provide the ability to enforce standards, so clearly delineating standards, publishing standards, and educating users (especially those to whom you've given the permission to Create Group Objects) is important.

Defining a Security Group Nesting Policy

Nesting occurs when one security group is placed inside another security group. The nested group inherits all of the privileges and permissions granted to the parent group. As you learned earlier, unlimited nesting can cause problems with the user's security access token size. By default, a user should not belong to more than 120 groups to avoid the token buffer overflow issue. The buffer can be resized if group membership exceeding 120 groups cannot be avoided. Another challenge presented by nesting is that at some point, it becomes extremely difficult to determine what permissions are inherited by a group within a group many levels down. Clearly, then, defining a nesting policy will also help maintain a secure and logical structure.

Although you can create any framework that makes sense to you and your organization, one that follows a typical hierarchy structure will make it more logical and intuitive for all users that have the ability to create security groups. At the top, you might have the broadest group, ALL EMPLOYEES. Within that, you could create groups that represent different divisions of the company or different business units. From there, you can create addition groups within each division or business unit used for employees with different functions such as managers, supervisors, team members, and so forth.

With this type of structure, it's easy to see that when you hire a new employee as the sales assistant in the Keyboard division of the company, you simply add that employee to the team members' account group and he or she is granted appropriate permissions all the way through the organization.

If you choose to use the AG/RG model, you will have some level of nesting, but you have to use care not to allow nested groups to get out of hand. Figure 9.3 shows an example of a nested hierarchy.

Figure 9.3 Nested Group Hierarchy

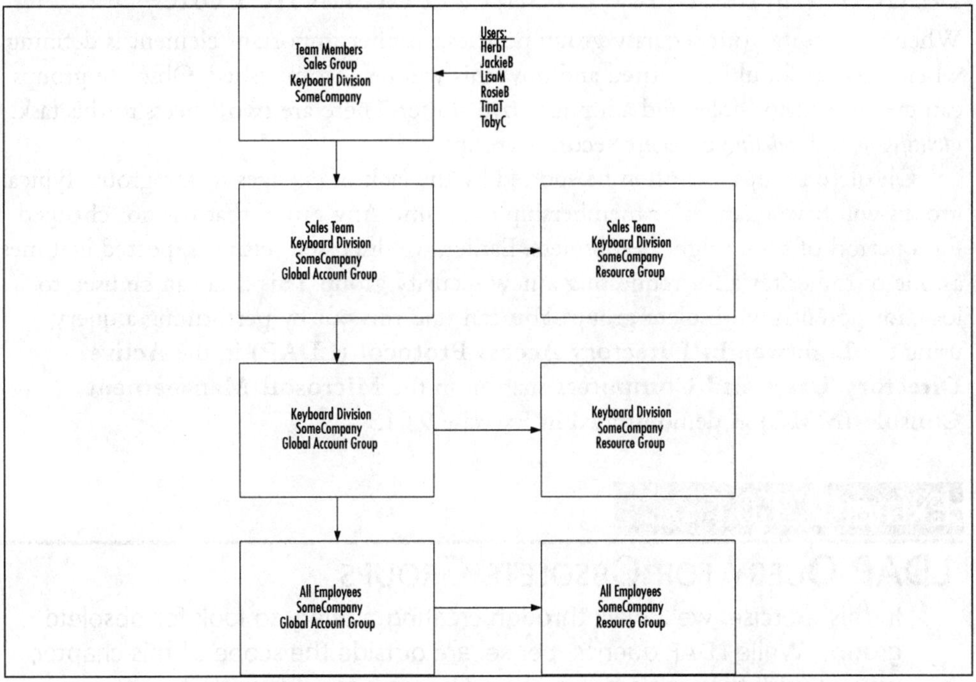

You can also modify the nesting to provide more global access to some users. For example, you might want division managers to have access to all resources in their divisions. This can be accomplished using a modified nesting hierarchy. Division managers' user accounts could be added to a Division Manager account group. This account group could be added to all account groups within the division. In a sense, this process is the reverse of the one outlined earlier. It can be useful for granting broader permissions for selected groups. The downside, though, should be considered. First, since those higher in the organization are often the targets of attacks, any breach of their accounts provides broad access within the organization. Second, this method causes the user to be a member of hundreds or thousands of groups. As we discussed earlier, this can cause the user's security ID token to become too large. Large tokens cause slow logons or the inability to log on or access resources. Although this strategy might be useful in your organization, you should consider these two issues before implementing this structure.

Defining a Security Group Retirement Policy

When you create your security group policies, another important element is defining when a group should be retired and how this will be accomplished. Obsolete groups can create security holes and administrative clutter. There are two aspects to this task: *identifying* and *deleting* obsolete security groups.

Obsolete groups can often be spotted by the lack of changes to the group. Typical groups will have changes to membership over time. Any group that has not changed for a period of time might be obsolete. Earlier, we discussed setting expected lifetimes as one of the criteria for requesting a new security group. This data can be used to look for potentially obsolete groups. You can find this out by performing a query using the **Lightweight Directory Access Protocol (LDAP)** in the **Active Directory Users and Computers** snap-in in the **Microsoft Management Console (MMC)** as demonstrated in Exercise 9.01.

Exercise 9.01

LDAP Query for Obsolete Groups

In this exercise, we'll walk through creating a query to look for obsolete groups. While LDAP queries, per se, are outside the scope of this chapter, we will walk through a query so you become familiar with it. For more information on LDAP and LDAP queries, you can search the Help and Support Center in Windows Server 2003.

1. Click **Start | Administrative Tools**, and then select **Active Directory Users and Computers**.
2. Click **Saved Queries** to select that node, click **Action**, and then select **New Query**. In the **New Query** dialog, type a name for the query such as *Obsolete Groups*. Type a description that will help you remember the purpose of the query, such as *Search for groups that have not changed since specific date*. Next, click the **Browse** button if the container for the query is not listed (should default to domain).
3. To search subcontainers, ensure the check box **Include subcontainers** is checked.
4. Click the **Define Query** button to define the LDAP query parameters.
5. In the **Find Common Queries** dialog box, click the drop-down arrow in the **Find** box. Select **Custom Search** from the list.
6. Click the **Advanced** tab to access the LDAP query function. In the text box labeled **Enter LDAP query**, type in the following string,

exactly as shown here (note: there are no spaces in this string). Figure 9.4 shows this step.

```
(&(objectCategory=group)(whenChanged<=20030630240000.0-5))
```

Figure 9.4 LDAP Query

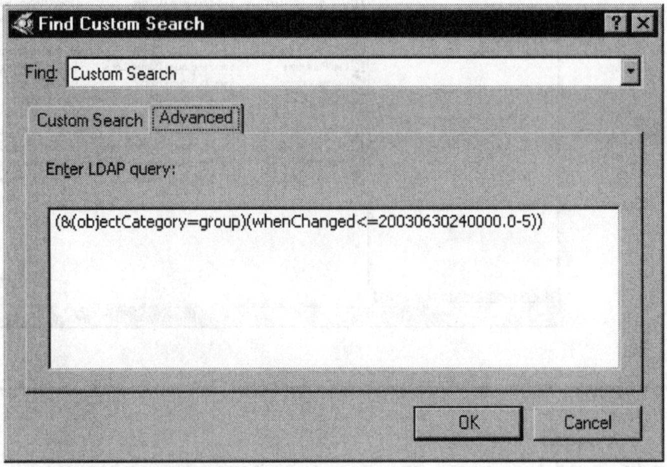

NOTE

The syntax of the LDAP query string includes the date in this format: YYYYMMDD followed immediately by the time in this format: HHMMSS. The final part of the string to the right of the period is .0Z. Z is the time zone as it relates to Greenwich Mean Time. For example, California is –8, New York is –5, meaning that the east and west coast of the United States are 5 and 8 hours behind (earlier than) Greenwich Mean Time. Thus, the string shown in this exercise is for June 30, 2003 at midnight (240000) in New York (or the east coast) at .0–5.

7. After you enter the string, click **OK** to return to the **New Query** dialog. Click **OK** to run the query.
8. The results are shown in Figure 9.5. Each group can now be examined to determine if it is obsolete.

Figure 9.5 Result of LDAP Query

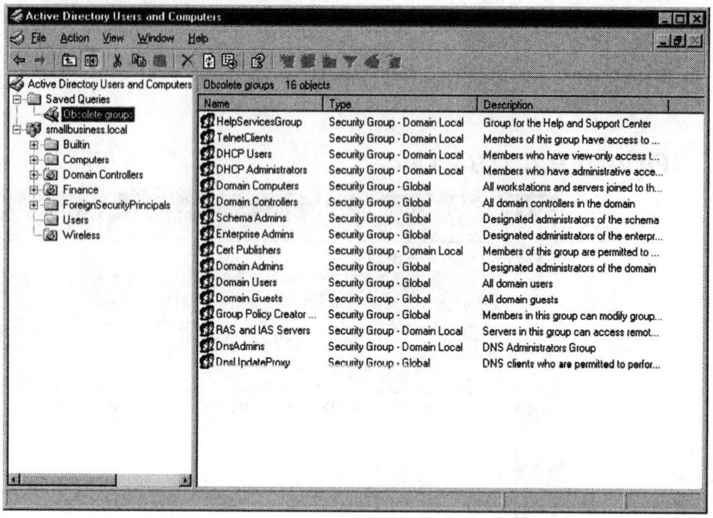

Keep in mind that some groups might have very stable membership, so you should closely examine any groups you believe to be obsolete before taking action. After you've identified obsolete groups, you can disable or delete them. However, keep in mind that group deletion is a one-way process; there is no "Undo" function. This is because when a group is created, it is given a unique SID. If a group is inadvertently deleted, it must be recreated and incorporated into the hierarchy.

Rather than deleting a group, you can choose to disable the group for a specified period of time in order to determine if the group truly is obsolete. This can be done by temporarily changing the group into a distribution group. This retains the group's unique SID as well as membership and other variables. If you audit changes in users' access permissions and do not receive any notifications that a user's access has changed, you can safely assume the group is no longer in use. You can change the group from a security to a distribution group by using the *dsmod.exe* command-line utility, which can be used to modify the attributes of an existing object in a specific type in the directory. In this case, you'd use the *dsmod group* command with the appropriate switches. The *–secgrp {yes | no}* sets the group as a security group (yes) or a distribution group (no). For more information on the *dsmod* utility, type **dsmod ?** at a command prompt. This type of modification cannot be done via the Active Directory Users and Computers snap-in.

Since deleting groups is a permanent step and recovering from an inadvertent removal of a group could be time consuming, your best bet is to limit the number of people with permission to delete groups and ensure they fully understand the implications of deleting a group.

TEST DAY TIP

You won't be tested on LDAP, but you will need to understand the concepts related to maintaining groups and group membership. Be familiar with these overall concepts and review them briefly before the exam. Outdated or unused groups create a security risk, so they'll likely appear in one or two questions someplace on the exam.

Delegating Security Group Maintenance

In small organizations, it might be possible for one or two administrators to manage the routine maintenance associated with security groups. In large organizations, however, this task is typically divided up and delegated to members of the organization who are not in the IT department. The added benefit of this is that those closest to the resource are most likely to keep it current. Delegation of these administrative tasks can be to anyone within a department or organization who is both trusted and familiar with personnel. An administrative assistant can be given the job of maintaining group membership for his or her department or area. Security groups in Windows Server 2003 can also be used in Microsoft Exchange 2000 mailing lists, so having an administrative assistant oversee this process can make even more sense.

Typically, it makes sense to have the resource owner manage the ACLs on the resource, whether that's a few files and folders on a member computer or a file server operator who maintains the company's file servers. The person responsible for the resource is generally the best person to manage the resource groups on that resource.

Delegating Account and Resource Group Maintenance

Account and resource group maintenance reduces the workload on the IT department but comes with its own set of challenges. Those to whom delegation is granted must be reliable and highly trusted employees since they are granted the power to add and remove users from various groups, granting access to corporate resources. Not only should these employees be highly trusted, they should also be given clear guidelines to help them maintain a secure environment. The security risk inside a company is often far greater than external security risks. A malicious person in this position could do damage to network resources. Also keep in mind that social engineering is the most common source of security breaches. Thus, if a trusted administrative assistant is given the authority to add or remove users from groups, he or she is more likely to be the target of such a maneuver. By educating these users as to the risks and benefits as well as the rules and guidelines, maintenance of these groups can be delegated while managing risk.

In addition, you must control and monitor who is a member of the group to whom you've delegated control. If you create a group such as *DivisionAdmins* to whom you delegate control for account group maintenance, you should monitor the membership in this group. This can be done centrally via the IT department or via security policy that enforces membership in groups such that any user added who is not in the policy will be removed the next time policy is refreshed. Depending on the size of your organization, you'll need to determine the most efficient and effective method for monitoring this group's membership.

Although resource group maintenance could be delegated to the admins listed earlier, *DivisionAdmins* in this example, it's possible that the requests for permissions to division wide resources might overwhelm the admin whose primary job is not maintaining network permissions. Therefore, it sometimes makes more sense to have resource owners manage resource group maintenance for that resource.

You can delegate administration for a wide variety of tasks. For example, you can delegate control of a domain, an organizational unit (OU), a server, or accounts. Delegation can be managed through the Delegation of Control Wizard, through the Authorization Manager snap-in in the MMC, or through the ACL Editor. We'll look at each of these tools briefly in case you're not already familiar with them. Let's begin with stepping through the Delegation of Control Wizard in Exercise 9.02.

EXERCISE 9.02

USING THE DELEGATION OF CONTROL WIZARD

The **Delegation of Control Wizard** is accessed through **Start | Administrative Tools | Active Directory Users and Computers**. This wizard is used to select groups or users to whom you want to delegate control and to select which tasks you want to delegate. This is a commonly used tool, so we'll step through this exercise to familiarize you with its functions and features.

1. Locate the object for which you want to delegate control. In this example, we've selected the Finance OU, shown in Figure 9.6. Select an object from the left pane that you want to use for this exercise.

Figure 9.6 Delegating Control of the Finance OU in Active Directory Users and Computers

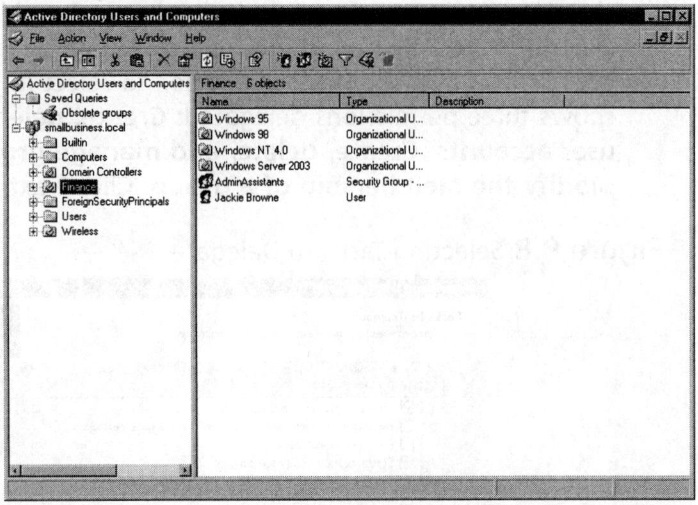

2. Right-click the object and select **Delegate Control**. The Delegation of Control Wizard launches the welcome screen. Click **Next** to continue.
3. Click **Add** to add users or groups (best practices suggest adding groups) to whom you want to delegate control. Type in the name and then click **Check Names** to verify the name selected. The verified names are added to the list, as shown in Figure 9.7. Click **OK** to accept the list and then click **Next** to select the **Tasks to Delegate**.

Figure 9.7 Adding Users to Delegate Control

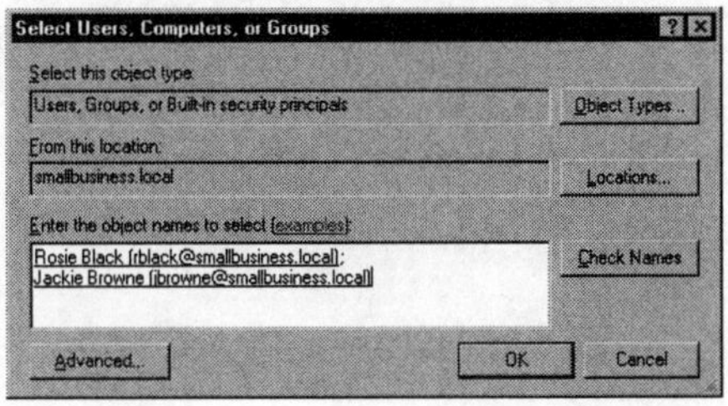

4. In the **Tasks to Delegate** screen, you can either choose from a pre-set list of tasks or you can create a custom set of tasks to delegate. If you choose from the pre-set list and then click **Next**, the final screen displays your selections so you can review them one

more time before accepting and applying them. If you choose the custom tasks, the pre-set list of tasks is disabled and you must click **Next** to begin selecting custom tasks. For this exercise, select **Delegate the following common tasks**, which is selected by default. To select a task, click the box to select it. Figure 9.8 shows three permissions delegated: **Create, delete, and manage user accounts, Create, delete, and manage groups**, and **Modify the membership of a group**. Click **Next** to continue.

Figure 9.8 Selecting Tasks to Delegate

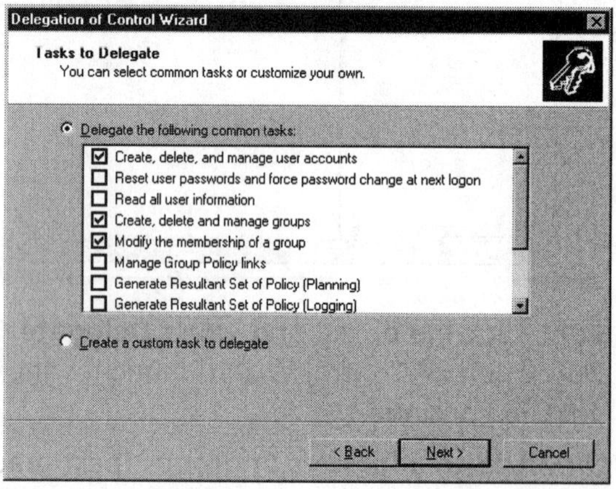

5. The **Completing the Delegation of Control Wizard** screen is displayed, showing the choices you've selected, including a) the object, b) the groups or users, and c) the tasks to be delegated. If you want to make any changes, click **Back**. If you want to exit without saving changes, click **Cancel**. Otherwise, click **Finish** to delegate control of the listed object, as shown in Figure 9.9.

Figure 9.9 Completion of Delegation of Control Wizard

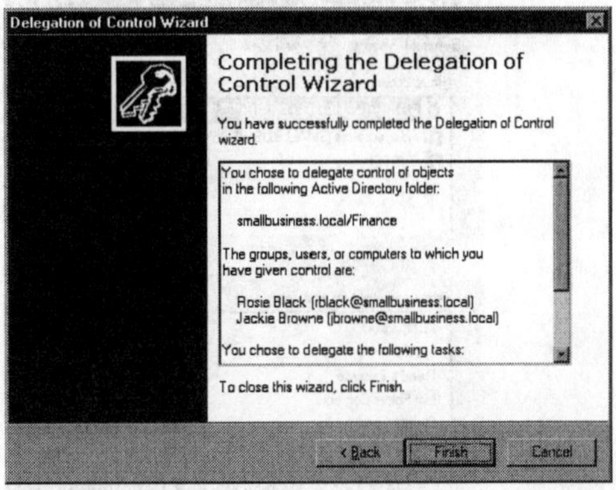

Using the Delegation of Control Wizard, you can easily delegate control of objects within the site, domain, or forest. Another way of managing delegation is through the Authorization Manager snap-in in the MMC. The Authorization Manager is a specific tool that can be used for role-based delegation with applications that support this method. We'll discuss role-based authorization and delegation later in this chapter. For now, it's important to understand that role-based administration is implemented to facilitate authorization and computer configuration. This is accomplished via the use of scripts. Typically, this is used when an application supports role-based authorization.

Finally, you can use the Access Control List Editor. For example, if you have a shared folder, you can right-click that folder and select **Sharing and Security**. In the Properties dialog for that folder, click the **Security** tab. The groups or users who have access are listed and the selected group or user's permissions are displayed in the box below that, as shown in Figure 9.10. You can access Advanced permissions by clicking the **Advanced** button. This gives you access to permissions, auditing, ownership, and effective permissions for the selected object. By editing the ACL in the object's properties, you can control access to the object at a very detailed level, if desired.

Figure 9.10 Shared Folder Permissions Access Control List

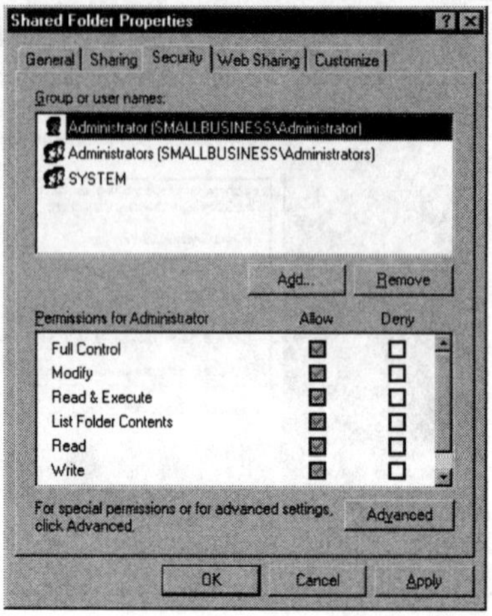

These three methods provide a variety of ways to delegate and manage access control in Windows Server 2003. The most commonly used tools are the Delegation of Control Wizard for efficiently managing delegation of administrative tasks and the direct editing of the ACL for objects over which you have control.

EXAM 70-298 OBJECTIVE 4.2.4 4.3.2

Analyzing Auditing Requirements

As part of designing network resource security, you should analyze your requirements for auditing to determine what level of auditing is appropriate for your organization. You can begin by identifying the types of attacks your system might be vulnerable to, and identify those audit events that would help determine if the system were successfully or unsuccessfully attacked. Remember, you can audit both successful and unsuccessful events, and determining which events are most meaningful is the key to defining auditing requirements that will protect your system.

It's important to create a list of events that are important. Auditing unimportant events will simply fill your event log with meaningless data and will create more work for you as you try to sort through a long list looking for the important events. If you choose to implement extensive auditing, you might want to use an additional tool, such as Microsoft Operations Manager (MOM), to help filter data to assist in identifying important events.

At first glance, you might think that unsuccessful attempts might be the only events worth looking at. Certainly, tracking unsuccessful events can help you see if someone is trying to gain access to resources to which he or she does not have permission. However, tracking successful events can also be useful if carefully chosen. Obviously, a majority of successful events indicate normal business activity (as do many unsuccessful events). However, a hacker who gains access will also log a successful event. If you regularly review events, you'll see patterns of usage that are normal, making it somewhat easier to spot irregularities. In addition, looking for a series of unsuccessful events followed by a successful event could indicate an unauthorized user has managed to get on to the network.

Knowing your business patterns will help you spot patterns in the audit events. If your business is typically a Monday through Friday 8 A.M. to 5 P.M. type of business, activity outside these hours could indicate a problem. Additionally, being aware of personnel changes can help you modify access as needed and can be used in combination with auditing. For example, many companies have a policy in place that requires the Human Resources department to immediately notify IT of any personnel actions such as suspension or termination. (This type of policy also helps when new employees are hired and need to be granted network access.)

There are a number of events that could be managed, but the following list is a good starting point:

- Logon events
- Account logon events
- Directory Service access events
- Privilege use events
- Object access events
- System events
- Process tracking events
- Policy change events

Logon Event

Logon events are generated when a user logs on to or off of a computer. Every time a user logs on or off, whether on a workstation or server, an event is generated. A variety of event IDs are associated with logon events. Table 9.5 shows a partial list of these event IDs. An explanation of how some of these IDs may be interpreted follows the table.

Table 9.5 Logon Event IDs and Descriptions

Logon Event ID	Description
528	A user successfully logged on to a computer.
529	Logon failure. A logon attempt was made with an unknown username or a known username with a bad password.

Continued

Table 9.5 Logon Event IDs and Descriptions

Logon Event ID	Description
530	Logon failure. A logon attempt was made with a user account outside of an allowed time.
531	Logon failure. A logon attempt was made using a disabled account.
532	Logon failure. A logon attempt was made using an expired account.
533	Logon failure. A logon attempt was made by a user who is not allowed to log on at this computer.
534	Logon failure. The user attempted to log on with a type that is not allowed.
535	Logon failure. The password for the specified account has expired.
536	Logon failure. The Net Logon service is not active.
537	Logon failure. The logon attempt failed for other reasons. (In some cases, the reason for the logon failure is unknown.)
538	A user logged off.
539	Logon failure. The account was locked out at the time the logon attempt was made.
540	A user successfully logged on.
541	Main mode Internet Key Exchange (IKE) authentication was completed between the local computer and the listed peer identity or quick mode has established a data channel.
542	A data channel was terminated.
543	Main mode was terminated. (This can occur when the security association time limit is expiring, when policy changes or either computer terminates the session.)
544	Main mode authentication failed because the peer did not provide a valid certificate or the signature was not validated.
545	Main mode authentication failed because of a Kerberos failure or because a password is not valid.
546	IKE security association (SA) failed because the peer sent an invalid proposal. A packet was received that contained invalid data.
547	A failure occurred during the IKE handshake.
548	Logon failure. The security ID from a trusted domain does not match the account domain SID of the client.

Continued

Table 9.5 Logon Event IDs and Descriptions

Logon Event ID	Description
549	Logon failure. All SIDs corresponding to untrusted namespaces were filtered out during an authentication across forests.
550	Notification that could indicate a denial-of-service (DoS) attack.
551	A user initiated the log off process.
552	A user successfully logged on to a computer using explicit credentials while already logged on as another user.
682	A user reconnected to a disconnected terminal server session.
683	A user disconnected a terminal server session without logging off.

Logon attempt failures can indicate a number of things. It could simply indicate that a user forgot a password or mistyped it. However, it could also indicate an attempt to attack the network. In a large environment, these events become numerous and difficult to interpret. If patterns emerge, repeat, or change, you should investigate, especially when the events fall outside of normal parameters. Events occurring outside of normal business hours or in greater-than-usual volume might indicate an attack.

Account misuse can be indicated by events 530, 531, 532, and 533. These events indicate the account name and password were correct but that other restrictions prevented the user from logging on such as time of day restrictions. These events should be investigated to determine if there is a problem or if the user simply needs changes to his or her access for legitimate business purposes.

Account lockouts occur when a set number of unsuccessful logon attempts have been made. These events can indicate an unauthorized user attempting to gain access to the network or it can indicate a legitimate user who forgot his or her password. To spot potential problems, look for earlier 529 events by the same user account and see if any pattern emerges.

Account Logon Event

An *account logon event* is generated on DCs for domain account activity, and on local computers for local account activity. Account logon events are created when a user's credentials are authenticated. When domain credentials are used, the account logon events are only generated in the DCs' event logs. If the credentials presented are local credentials (Security Accounts Manager (SAM) database), the account logon events are generated in the server's security log. You can choose to audit successful and unsuccessful logon events on critical servers. An important point to note is that because account logon events can be recorded by any valid DC in the user's domain, you'll need to consolidate event logs across the DCs in order to analyze all account logon events in the domain. You can consolidate event logs by using new features in Windows Server 2003. For example, System Monitor supports viewing data from multiple log files simultaneously and from data stored in a SQL database. Selected data from multiple log files can be saved as a separate file for later analysis. Windows Server 2003 supports log files greater than 1GB in size so performance data can be appended to an existing log file. In addition, you can log data directly to a SQL database using Open Database Connectivity (ODBC) connections.

Directory Service Access Event

Directory Service access events record when directory services were accessed. As you can imagine, directory service objects are successfully accessed on a regular basis, which generates a tremendous number of events. The attempted access generates an event ID 565. By looking at the event details, you can determine which object the event corresponds to. Due to the high volume and lack of specificity in the event, it's usually more helpful to audit unsuccessful directory service access to look for indicators of an attack.

Privilege Use Event

Privilege use events are logged every time a user uses any privileges. For example, you might want to monitor the use of the privilege "Create, delete, and manage user accounts" or "Create, delete, and manage groups." By monitoring the use of privileges, you can see when these privileges are used and by whom. For example, if Lisa has permission to create, delete, and manage user accounts and you notice that she has used this privilege about once per month on average, you'd suspect something was wrong if you suddenly saw Lisa using this privilege three or four times a week. As with directory service access, auditing successful events will generate large volumes of typically innocuous events. Therefore, it's more useful to audit successful use of privileges related to security such as changing user permissions or group membership, adding users to a group, and so forth. When you delegate various IT administrative tasks, you can audit the use of those privileges to ensure they're being used in an appropriate manner.

There are three specific event IDs that can be helpful to monitor the use of privileges, as shown in Table 9.6. Monitoring and interpreting this data can indicate users attempting to expand their privileges or cover their tracks.

Table 9.6 Privilege Use Event IDs

Privilege Use Event ID	Description
576	Specified privileges were added to a user's access token. (Generated when user logs on.)
577	User attempted to perform a privileged system service operation.
578	Privileges were used on an already open handle to a protected object.

The 577 and 578 events can indicate a user was attempting to gain elevated privileges by acting as part of the operating system. The GetAdmin attack attempts to add a user account to the Admin account using this method. The only entries for this event should be for the System account. Event IDs 577 and 578 can also be generated when a user attempts to change the system time in an attempt to cover his or her tracks and hide the actual time an event took place. These two IDs can also be generated when an attacker attempts to install or load a virus, worm, or Trojan horse by imitating a driver loading or unloading. Managing the audit logs, attempting to shutdown the system, and taking ownership of files or objects are also logged as event ID 577 or 578. Auditing changes to audit or event logs can be very helpful since attackers typically attempt to hide their activities by modifying the audit or event logs.

Object Access Event

Object access events record when any object with a system access control list (SACL) is accessed. Objects that can be accessed are essentially anything a user interacts with, such as files and folders, printers, and Registry keys. For all object access events you want to log, you must enable auditing for object access on the object and then define the SACL for each object. As with other types of events, auditing all object access events will slow system performance and generate volumes of information, making it difficult to distill the meaningful events from the long list of normal activity events. In general, it's helpful to audit access on targeted objects based on importance and sensitivity of the data. For example, you might want to audit all access to payroll files. An unusual pattern of access or reading and writing might indicate a problem.

System Events

System events are generated when the computer environment is changed in some significant way, either by a user or by a process. You should audit computer shutdown events for servers, although this function is enabled by default in Windows Server 2003. For earlier operating systems, logging shutdown events is important to know when servers are shut down and by whom. Other system events include when the system time is changed, when Windows is starting up or shutting down, or when the audit log is cleared, to name just a few.

Process Tracking Events

Auditing *process tracking events* monitors processes running on computers. There are so many processes running on computers throughout the course of even a single day that this typically is not a helpful auditing event. If you have a specific use for this or want to monitor a specific process, you will see event IDs 592, 593, 594, and 595. It's not common to audit for these events unless you have a specific need.

Policy Change Events

Auditing for *policy change events* allows you to see attempts to alter policy settings, including changes to audit policies. An attacker might attempt to change audit policy to stop auditing on the objects or in the areas of the intended attack. Event IDs 608 and 609 indicate that a user right was assigned (608) and a user right was removed (609). Auditing these events can help spot irregular policy change events. A number of attacks might be indicated by the 608 and 609 events, including:

- Attempt to act as part of the operating system
- Backup or restore files and directories
- Change system time
- Debug programs
- Force shutdown of local or remote system
- Load and unload device drivers
- Manage auditing and security log
- Take ownership of files or other objects

Although each of these events might be harmless, watching for patterns or unusual access patterns can tip you off to attempted intrusions. For example, changing user rights assignments might be harmless or it might indicate that a rogue user is trying to "upgrade" permissions for a user to gain unauthorized access. Changing the policy for backups or restores could be an attempt to gain access to the backup or restore process. Loading and unloading device drivers is typically a harmless event driven by dynamic processes on the system, but it can also be indication of a virus being loaded into the system area reserved for drivers. Changes to audit logging policies themselves can be an indication of a malicious user trying to stop logging of events while he or she does something to the system. Even changing the system time can be seen as an attempt to cover a malicious user's tracks to disguise the real time an intrusion occurred. Although most of these events are typically harmless, unusual patterns might indicate intrusion or attack.

TEST DAY TIP

Review the various events that can be audited and logged and think about scenarios involving patterns of events. The exam will not require you to memorize these event IDs, but you should understand what the events are and what kinds of attacks they might indicate when they appear in an audit log, especially when in groups or in particular patterns.

EXAM 70-298 OBJECTIVE 4.3

Design an Access Control Strategy for the Registry

The Registry is the heart of the Windows Server 2003 operating system and contains sensitive data about the files and folders, the applications, and the computer state. If a malicious user gains access to the Registry, he or she could do serious damage to the computer. Access to the Registry should be controlled and monitored to ensure the Registry is protected from intentional and unintentional harm.

The Registry is given a high level of security by default. The only users who are granted full access to the entire Registry are administrators. Other users are generally given full access to the keys related to their own user accounts located in HKEY_CURRENT_USER. They are also generally given read-only access to other areas of the Registry related to the computer and the software. Users are granted no access to other users' account data. If a user has permission to modify a key, that user can modify that key and any key beneath it in the hierarchy.

While permissions can be modified for the Registry using the Registry Editor (by using the *regedt32.exe* command at **Start | Run**), it makes sense in a larger organization to apply security to the Registry via group policy. Although this topic has been touched on earlier in this book, let's look again at the tools you have at your disposal for securing the Registry across the enterprise. We'll review the use of *regedt32.exe* and then we'll look at group policy.

When you launch the Registry Editor, you can view or modify any Registry keys to which you have access. As you're well aware, modifications to the Registry can cause a system to crash and can make recovery difficult and time consuming unless you've recently backed up the Registry. Use care when viewing or modifying the Registry and, if in doubt, always export a current copy of the Registry or make sure your Automated System Recovery (ASR) disk is up to date before making any changes. Exercise 9.03 steps through viewing Registry access permissions.

EXERCISE 9.03

VIEWING REGISTRY ACCESS PERMISSIONS

In this exercise, we'll step through reviewing Registry access permissions. We will not make any changes to the Registry settings, but you should still *use care*. You should also choose to **Cancel** out of screens or dialogs instead of clicking **OK**. If you were making changes that you wanted to keep (on the job), you would click **OK** instead. Most needed changes can be made without directly editing the Registry, and best practices dictate that any time you can avoid directly editing the Registry, you should do so.

NOTE

Any changes to the Registry, whether intentional or not, could cause your system to become unstable or unusable. Please do this exercise with care.

1. Click **Start | Run** and then type **regedt32** in the **Open** text box. Click **OK** to launch the **Registry Editor**.
2. Click **File** on the **Registry Editor** menu. Notice there is no **Save** or **Save As** function. This is because any changes you make in the various dialogs are applied immediately. Exiting closes the Registry Editor with whatever settings currently exist. There is no way to exit without saving changes. This is why it's critical to save the Registry before working on it, and use care when working in it.
3. In the Registry Editor, the left pane displays the nodes and the right pane displays any nodes or keys beneath the one selected on the left. Depending on the state of your Registry tree, you might only see one node, **My Computer**. If so, click the **+** to the left of **My Computer** to expand the tree. In most cases, you'll see My Computer listed with five nodes beneath it: HKEY_CLASSES_ROOT, HKEY_CURRENT_USER, HKEY_LOCAL_MACHINE, HKEY_USERS, and HKEY_CURRENT_CONFIG.
4. Click the **+** to the left of **HKEY_CURRENT_USER** to expand the tree. Notice the keys beneath HKEY_CURRENT_USER, including AppEvents, Control Panel, Printers, Software, and others.
5. Click **HKEY_CURRENT_USER** to select it. Right-click the selection or click **Edit** on the menu and select **Permissions**.

6. The Permissions dialog for HKEY_CURRENT_USER is displayed. In this dialog, you can add or remove users listed in the **Group or user names:** dialog. You can also edit permissions for the currently selected user or group. Figure 9.11 shows this dialog; notice that you can modify permissions for the Administrator group, which is currently selected in Figure 9.11.

Figure 9.11 Modifying Default Permissions on Registry Key

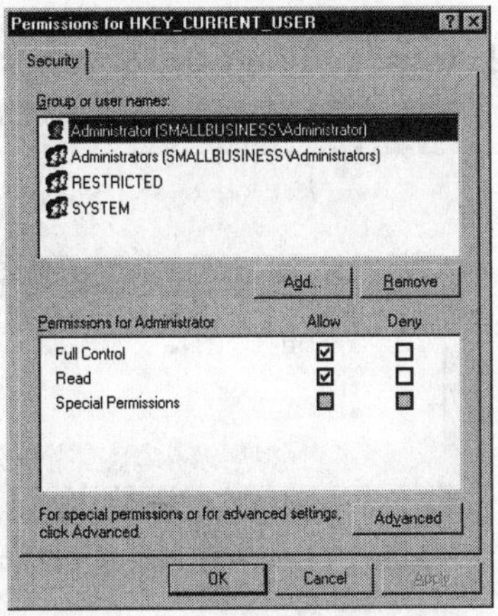

7. You can set special permissions and set advanced settings as well. Click the **Advanced** button to access this dialog.
8. The **Advanced Security Settings for HKEY_CURRENT_USER** dialog is shown in Figure 9.12. Notice several things in this dialog. First, you can view or modify permissions as well as set auditing, view or modify the owner, and view effective permissions. In addition, there are two important check boxes you should be familiar with.
9. The first check box is labeled **Allow inheritable permissions from the parent to propagate to this object and all child objects. Include these with entries explicitly defined here.** This box is checked by default. This will cause permissions to be inherited by all child objects. Removing this check box will cause permissions to be applied only to the object for which they are explicitly set. Understanding how permissions apply to child objects is important for understanding permissions throughout the network structure.

10. The second check box is **Replace permissions entries on all child objects with entries shown here that could apply to child objects.** This check box is not checked by default. Checking this box will cause all subfolders and files to have their permissions reset to those inheritable from the parent object. Once you select this, there is no Undo function and changes are permanent. If you want to modify permissions for child objects below the parent, you can use this to reset permissions but care should be used.

Figure 9.12 Advanced Registry Settings for HKEY_CURRENT_USER

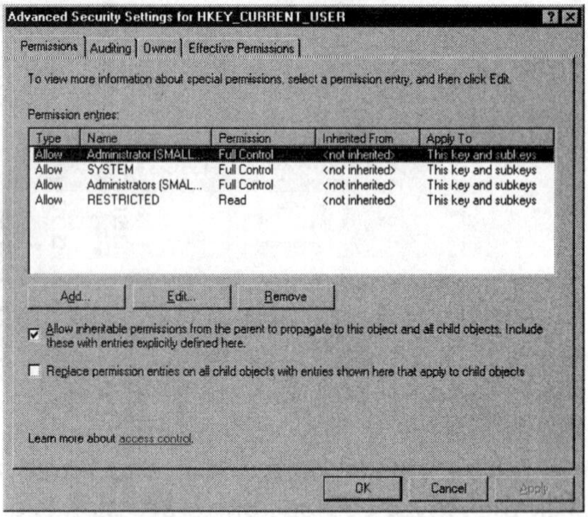

11. Click the **Auditing** tab. You can create, modify, or review auditing set for this object. Notice the same two check boxes regarding inheritance of permissions are located here as well, as shown in Figure 9.13.

Figure 9.13 Auditing Tab Options

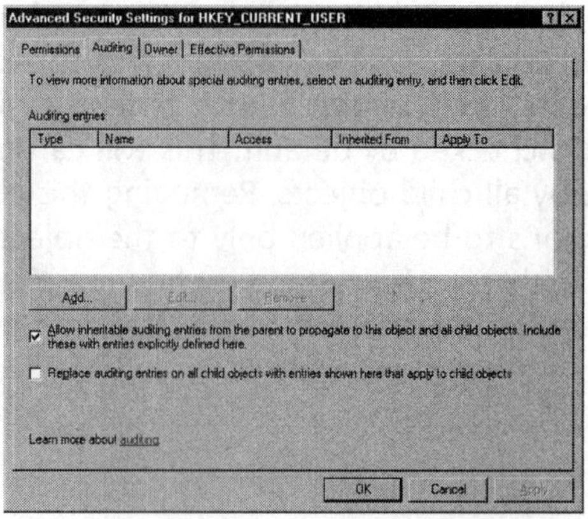

12. Click the **Owner** tab. On this tab, you can take or assign ownership of this object if you have the appropriate permissions to do so. You can also change ownership of subcontainers or child objects by selecting the check box labeled **Replace owner on subcontainers and objects.**
13. Click the **Effective Permissions** tab. On this tab, you can view the permissions that would be granted to the selected group or user based solely on the permissions granted directly through group membership, as shown in Figure 9.14. You begin by clicking the **Select** button, selecting the user or group, and then viewing effective permissions. This tool calculates the permissions granted to a specific user or group and takes into account group membership (for the user or group) and inherited permissions (from the parent object).

Figure 9.14 Effective Permissions Options

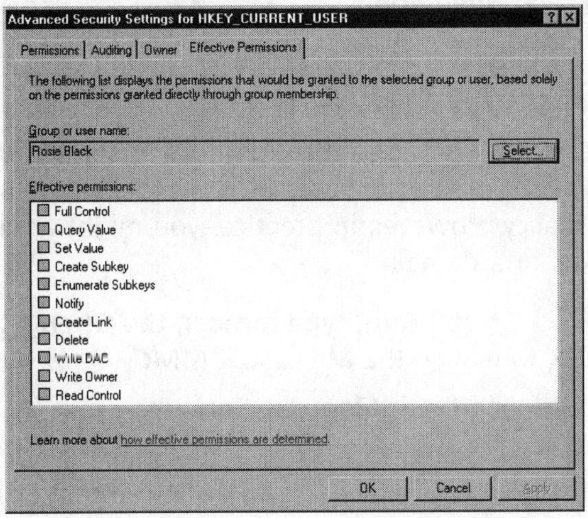

14. Click **Cancel** to exit the Advanced Security Settings for HKEY_CURRENT_USER dialog. Click **Cancel** to exit the Permissions for HKEY_CURRENT_USER dialog.
15. Click **File** on the **Registry Editor** menu, and select **Exit** to close the Registry Editor.

Now that we've looked at how to modify Registry settings via the Registry Editor, we'll look at a more global method of setting Registry settings. As you learned in Chapter 2, "Securing Servers based on Function," security templates can be used to set security across the enterprise in a consistent manner. There are also security settings that can be access via group policy. Using group policy to set Registry access is the recommended way for managing Registry access. It provides an efficient and reliable method for setting permissions, and ensures that settings are re-applied every time group policy is applied. This can help ensure that permissions are maintained as specified in the policy and avoids errors that might be made when directly editing the Registry. To use this method, the computer must be joined to a domain. Policy settings are refreshed every 90 minutes on workstations or member servers, and every 5 minutes on DCs by default (including every 16 hours if no changes have been detected). In Exercise 9.04, you'll step through setting Registry access permissions using the Group Policy Editor snap-in in the MMC.

EXERCISE 9.04

SETTING REGISTRY ACCESS PERMISSIONS VIA GROUP POLICY

In this exercise, we'll step through how to set Registry permissions via Group Policy. For the purposes of this exercise, we'll select the default domain policy. However, in practice, you might apply these settings to an OU, a site, or a domain.

1. Click **Start | Run**, type **mmc** in the **Open** text box, and then click **OK** to launch the **Microsoft MMC**.
2. Click **File | Add/Remove Snap-in**.
3. In the Add/Remove Snap-in dialog, click **Add**. Scroll through the list until you locate **Group Policy Object Editor**. Click to select then click **Add**.
4. The **Select Group Policy Object Wizard** will launch. The default Group Policy Object (GPO) selected is *Local Computer*. Click **Browse**.
5. In the **Browse for a Group Policy Object** dialog, locate **Default Domain Policy** on the Domains/OUs tab and then click **OK**.
6. Click **Finish** to close the **Select Group Policy Object Wizard**. Click **Close** to close the **Add Standalone Snap-in** dialog. Click **OK** to close the Add/Remove Snap-in dialog.

7. In the left pane of the MMC, click the + to the left of Default Domain Policy to expand the tree.
8. Click the + to the left of **Computer Configuration**. In the expanded tree, click the + to expand **Windows Settings**.
9. Click the + to expand the **Security Settings**. In the list under Security Settings, locate the **Registry** node. Click to select the Registry node. If there are no subnodes, the tree will not expand but the + will not be displayed, as shown in Figure 9.15.

Figure 9.15 Registry Node in Group Policy Object Editor Snap-In

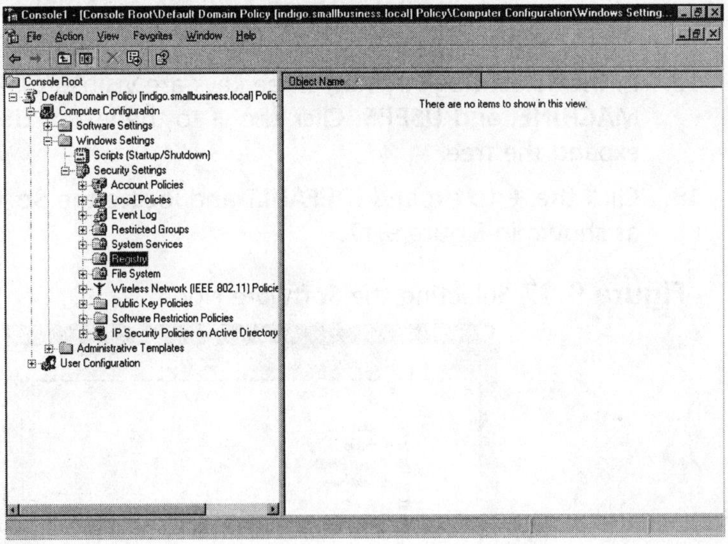

10. If any Registry policies exist, you can view or modify them here. If none exists, you can add a key.
11. For this exercise, let's assume you want to limit the ability to run the *Regedt32* command. Click **Registry,** and then on the menu, click **Action | Add Key**. The dialog, **Select Registry Key**, is displayed as shown in Figure 9.16.

Figure 9.16 Adding Key to Registry Access

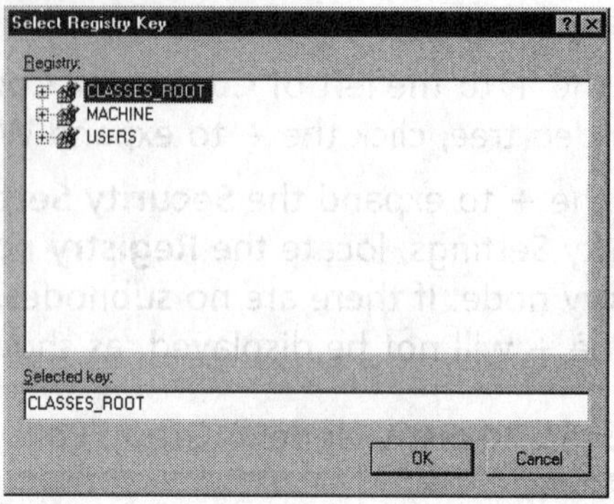

12. In the Select Registry Key, three keys are visible: **CLASSES_ROOT, MACHINE**, and **USERS**. Click the **+** to the left of **USERS** to expand the tree.
13. Click the **+** to expand **.DEFAULT** and locate the **Software** node, as shown in Figure 9.17.

Figure 9.17 Selecting the Software Node

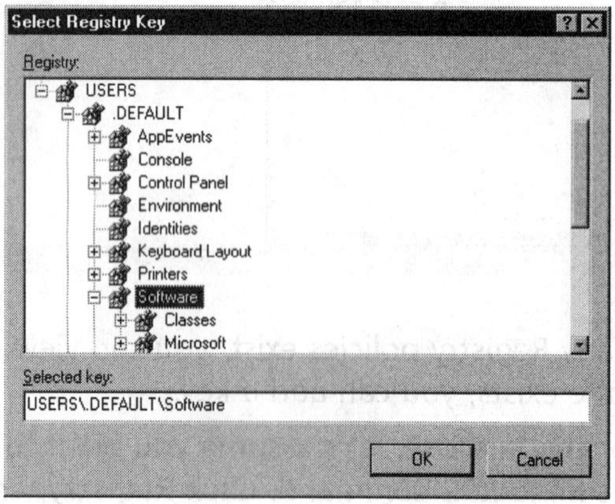

14. Expand the **Software** node, click the **+** to the left of the **Microsoft** node, and scroll down until you locate **RegEdt32**.
15. Click **RegEdt32** to select it and then click **OK**. The **Database Security for Users\.DEFAULT\Software\Microsoft\RegEdt32** dialog is displayed. You can now view or modify permissions for this key, as shown in Figure 9.18. The Administrators group is selected by default and has Full Control and Read permissions set to Allow by default.

Figure 9.18 View or Modify Permissions for Registry Key

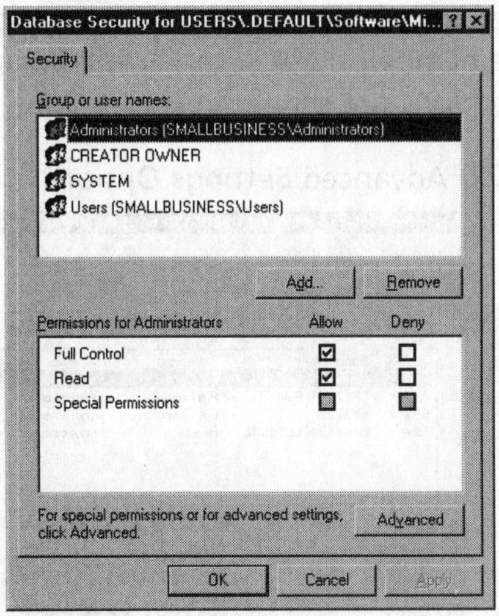

16. Click **Users** and notice that in the Default Domain Policy, Users permissions are set to allow **Read** only, shown in Figure 9.19.

Figure 9.19 Users Permissions Set to Read Only by Default

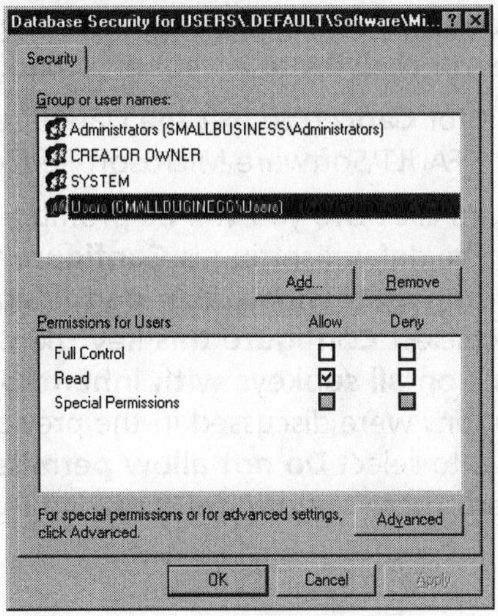

17. Users need to be able to read the Registry in order to perform normal system tasks, but they do not have the ability to modify the Registry in any way.

18. You can access **Advanced** settings to modify how permissions are inherited, to set auditing, or to change or delegate ownership as well. Remember, these settings will be applied via group policy. These options are shown in Figure 9.20.

Figure 9.20 Advanced Settings Options

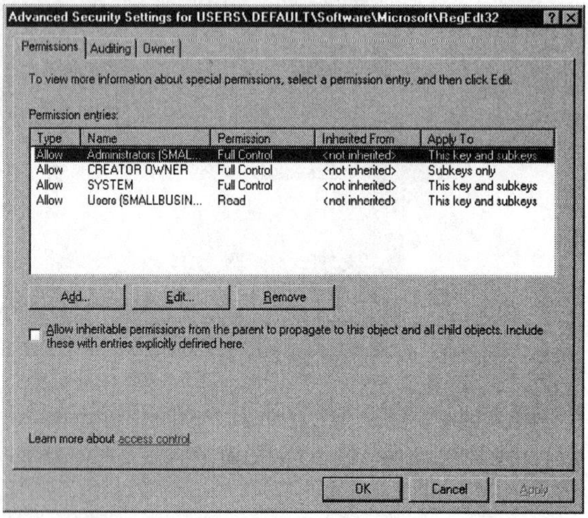

19. Click **Cancel** to exit the Advanced Settings dialog without saving changes, or click **OK** to accept any changes you've made.
20. Click **OK** (or **Cancel**) to exit the Database Security for Users\.DEFAULT\Software\Microsoft\RedEdt32b dialog.
21. When you click **OK**, you will be prompted by an Add Object dialog. The default setting is **Configure this key then...Propagate inheritable permissions to all subkeys**. You can also select **Configure this key then...Replace existing permissions on all subkeys with inheritable permissions**. These two options were discussed in the previous exercise. The third option is to select **Do not allow permissions on this key to be replaced**. These options are shown in Figure 9.21.

Figure 9.21 Modifying Permissions for the RegEdt32 Registry Key

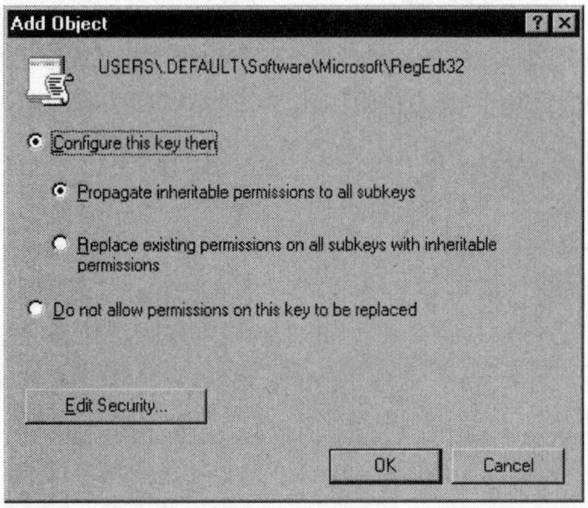

22. If you want to modify permissions, you can click the **Edit Security** button. Otherwise, click **OK**.
23. In the MMC, you now have an object listed in the right pane, which should reflect the Registry key we just added USER\DEFAULT\Software\Microsoft\RegEdt32, as shown in Figure 9.22.

Figure 9.22 Default Domain Policy with RegEdt32 Permissions Specified

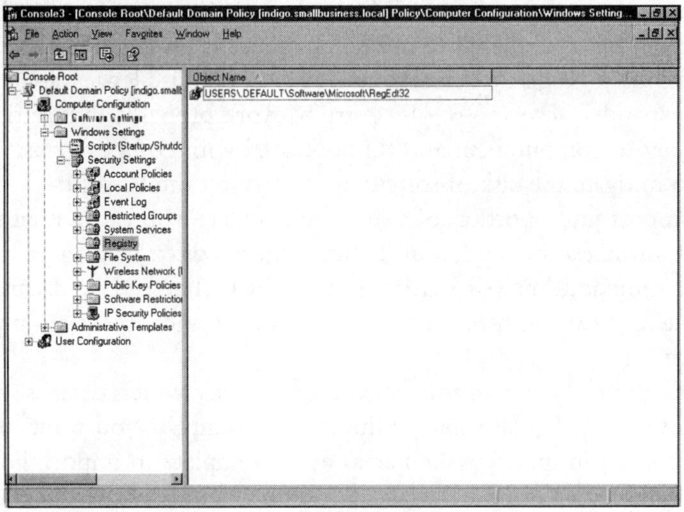

24. For the purposes of this exercise, we'll want to delete this key to leave the Default Domain Policy in its original state. Click the object, click the **red X** on the menu, or right-click and select **Delete**.

25. A Security Templates alert is displayed asking Are you sure you want to delete USERS\.DEFAULT\Software\Microsoft\RegEdt32? Click Yes to delete the key. Note that this does not delete the key from the Registry; it simply deletes the object from the policy.
26. Click **File | Exit** to exit the MMC. Click **No** when prompted to Save console settings.

EXAM 70-298 OBJECTIVE 4.3.1

Design a Permission Structure for Registry Objects

By default, when you install a clean version (not an upgrade) of Windows Server 2003, the Setup Security.inf security template is applied. This template sets up strong security for the computer on which it is installed, including setting appropriate Registry access permissions. This is also true for computers running Windows XP. However, this will not be the case on all computers, especially computers running Windows NT 4.0 or Windows 98.

Perhaps the easiest way to manage Registry settings is to use the settings provided in the predefined security templates in Windows Server 2003. Sections of the predefined templates can be imported and used to apply permissions to the Registry according to the computer's configuration. For example, suppose you want strong security on the Registry on DCs. The settings in securedc.inf, as they relate to the Registry, could be applied to all DCs in the domain even if you did not want to apply the entire securedc.inf template. The settings provided in the compatws.inf template loosen Registry permissions just a bit because legacy applications often require expanded access to the Registry to work properly. This setting could be propagated only to computers in an OU populated with computers using a legacy application to mitigate the risk of softening security on the Registry.

To import just a portion of a security template, you can use either the command-line tool, *secedit.exe*, or the Group Policy Object Editor snap-in or the Security Configuration and Analysis snap-in in the MMC. These were discussed in Chapter 2, but a brief review will help refresh your memory since this is an important concept for this exam.

Using the *secedit.exe* command, you can specify which database the settings will be imported into. You also specify the security template you want to import settings from, and you can specify which areas of the template to import. For example, you might only want to import the USER_RIGHTS area of the template. By default, if no area is specified, all areas are imported. By specifying the area or areas you want to import, you can select just a subset of settings to import and apply to the currently selected database (the security database into which you're importing settings). You can create a new database, import settings, and analyze them without applying them to the computer on which you're working. This is useful for testing configurations before implementing them.

An alternative to using the *secedit.exe* command line is the Group Policy Object Editor snap-in in the MMC. Using this tool, you can also import the security settings of a security template to apply to a GPO. For example, select the Local Computer as the GPO and expand the nodes in this manner to get to the Security Settings: **Local Computer Policy | Computer Configuration | Windows Settings | Security Settings**. If you right-click **Security Settings** you can select **Import Policy** or **Export Policy** from the menu. If you select **Import Policy**, you will be prompted to select a template from which to import policy.

Finally, you can use the **Security Configuration and Analysis snap-in**, also in the MMC, to open or create a database for use on a single computer, in an OU or across a domain. Once you have opened or created a database, you can import settings from security templates.

In most cases, the default Registry settings in the predefined security templates will provide the appropriate level of permissions for the Registry. In addition, you should use GPOs to modify Registry settings across the enterprise to avoid errors and to minimize the time and effort involved. If you have particular software packages that require special Registry settings, this too can be propagated across the domain via group policy. As always, you want to provide the least possible permissions to computers, applications, and users to maintain the most secure environment, while still allowing adequate access to required resources. If you look for every opportunity you have to simplify settings and provide the least privileges possible, your job will be much easier, things will run more smoothly, and security will be enhanced.

Designing the Encrypted File System

Windows Server 2003 includes an Encrypted File System (EFS) capability that enhances the earlier EFS capabilities of Windows 2000. In this section, we'll discuss EFS in Windows Server 2003, including how it works and how to best use EFS in the enterprise. This section assumes you're familiar with the basic elements of cryptography.

EFS can be used to encrypt files and folders on an NTFS formatted volume. EFS provides additional protection over that of NTFS. The NTFS format allows you to set permissions on files and folders on an NTFS formatted volume. This controls access to the files and folders based on user rights and permissions. EFS takes it one step further and encrypts files and folders. Thus, an unauthorized user will first be denied permission to access a file or folder based on NTFS permissions. If for some reason the permissions are incorrect or someone has found a way around the NTFS permissions, the file itself is encrypted and can only be decrypted by the owner of the file, a user to whom share privileges have been granted or by a recovery agent. One common way NTFS permissions are circumvented is when laptops are stolen. Thieves can remove the hard drive and install it in a system on which they have administrative privileges, effectively granting themselves full access to the data on the hard drive. If the data is encrypted, the thief will still be unable to access the data. As the popularity and need for mobile computers continues to increase, file encryption will be increasingly important in securing corporate data.

EFS is transparent to the user—files are encrypted and decrypted automatically in the background based on a process we'll review in a moment. However, as with all security measures, there is a trade-off between the use of encryption and system performance. EFS is notably slow the first time it is used because the encryption keys and certificates are being generated and checked. However, after the first instance, EFS is fairly fast and transparent, although it does take CPU cycles to encrypt and decrypt files and will have some impact on performance. Third-party programs are available that provide file encryption, but they are typically not as transparent to the user. These programs often require the user to encrypt and decrypt the files, requiring the user to remember to use the encryption program. This can create a security hole if users forget to encrypt important files. Every time security depends on a user taking a certain action, security is weakened. Automating security measures, such as using EFS, improves security by making the process transparent to the user rather than requiring the user to take action.

EFS uses keys for encrypting and decrypting data and can use certificate authority (CA)certificates, if available. However, one of the powerful features of EFS is that it does not require that a CA be available to use certificates. When one is not found, EFS will self-sign a certificate for use with file encryption. EFS can therefore be used on stand-alone systems as well as on members of a domain.

EFS uses the *CryptoAPI* (cryptography application programming interface) architecture to provide cryptographic functions. It encrypts files using a randomly generated key that is independent of a user's public/private key pair. This is the File Encryption Key (FEK), which is a *symmetric* encryption key used to encrypt the file. The FEK is then encrypted using *asymmetric* encryption for maximum security by using the public key from the user's certificate. (As you recall, a *symmetric* key uses the same key to encrypt and decrypt. An *asymmetric* key uses different keys, a public and private key set.) The encrypted FEK is stored along with the encrypted file and is a unique key for that file. To decrypt the file, the FEK must be decrypted, and this is done with the user's private key, which only the person that encrypted the file has. The combination of using a symmetric key to encrypt the file and an asymmetric key to encrypt the FEK provides an optimal balance between speed (symmetric) and security (asymmetric). The use of a symmetric key for file encryption/decryption speeds up processing time and is much faster than using an asymmetric key. The asymmetric key is used only for the FEK. Since the FEK protects the file, using an asymmetric key only for the FEK provides a good balance between performance and security.

There is another very important element of EFS called the *recovery agent*. Designated user accounts (typically domain Administrator accounts), called *recovery agent accounts*, are issued recovery agent certificates with public keys and private keys used for EFS data recovery operations. This is an important element because without the recovery agent function, a malicious user could encrypt files, denying others access to the data, or could encrypt files just before leaving the company, making important data inaccessible. With the EFS recovery agent accounts, encrypted files can be recovered. Recovery agent accounts are designated by EFS recovery policy and, by default, the recovery agent account is the highest-level Administrator account. EFS is designed so that only a system configured with one or more recovery agents can implement EFS, providing a failsafe method of data recovery. These credentials are called the Data Recovery Agent (DRA) certificates and private keys.

When a recovery agent certificate is issued, the certificate and keys are placed in the user profile of the user account that requested the certificate. The recovery agent credentials must be located on the computer on which the recovery action is to take place. The recovery agent certificate and private keys can be exported and stored in an archive or transferred to other user accounts and computers. In addition, there can be multiple recovery agent accounts for an EFS file, each with a different private key. If the recovery agent is used to recover a file, the data is unencrypted but the user's credentials are never exposed to the recovery agent. This maintains the security of the user's credentials while providing access to the encrypted data.

TEST DAY TIP

Be sure to understand the EFS encryption process for the exam. You won't likely be tested on the specific process of encryption and decryption, but you'll need to understand the mechanics to correctly answer at least a few questions on the exam.

EFS Behavior

When implementing EFS, it's important to understand how EFS works so you can design a system that is appropriate for your organization. Some of the behaviors might not be as expected, so it's good to be familiar with these traits before implementing EFS.

- EFS only works with the NTFS file system. It cannot be used with FAT or FAT32.
- You cannot encrypt system files or folders.
- EFS can be used to encrypt and decrypt files on a remote computer, but it does not encrypt data sent between computers (you'd implement IPSec for that function, if needed).

- You cannot encrypt compressed files and folders until you decompress them.
- EFS does not run if there is no recovery agent certificate.
- EFS will designate a recovery agent account by default and generate the certificate if you do not have a recovery agent certificate.
- If a folder is encrypted, temporary files in that folder will be encrypted (recommended).
- Copying a file into an encrypted folder will encrypt the file.
- Moving a file into an encrypted folder will leave the file in its original state—encrypted or unencrypted.
- Moving or copying EFS files to another file system removes the encryption.
- Backing up encrypted files preserves encryption.
- File permissions are not affected by encryption. A user can delete a file that is encrypted if that user has permission to do so, even if that user does not have permission to decrypt the file.
- Encryption is a file attribute and is listed with other attributes for that file.

EXAM WARNING

In Windows Server 2003, users are identified by their account names, including the server name. If a user encrypts a file while logged on to a domain account, that user can only access the file when logged in to that domain account. If that user logs on to a local account, the file will be inaccessible. This type of problem might be a common help desk issue on the job and might show up on the exam as well.

EFS Best Practices

EFS is a helpful business tool, especially with mobile users. However, certain practices help ensure the EFS is properly managed across the enterprise.

Encrypt Entire Folders Rather than Individual Files

- By encrypting folders, the files stored in those folders will be encrypted by default. This makes it easier to manage encrypted files. In addition, when a file is stored in an encrypted folder, the temporary files created during editing are also encrypted.

- By creating files in encrypted folders, the files are never written in plain-text. Plain-text copies of files, even if temporary, could be a security problem.
- Encrypting the My Documents folder is a useful practice when the user is connected to the same computer. Only encrypt the My Documents folder for roaming users if it is redirected to a shared network location.

Manage Private Keys to Maintain File Security

- Keep the number of designated recovery agents to a minimum. The fewer keys that exist, the fewer targets there are. Fewer recovery agents will be easier to manage and track, reducing the chance of inappropriate or unauthorized decryption by a recovery agent.
- Use Microsoft Certificate Services to manage EFS and DRA certificates and private keys.
- The designated recovery agent should export the data recovery certificate and private key to disk, secure them in a safe place, and then delete the data recovery private keys from the system. The only person who can recover the encrypted files on that system is the person who has physical access to the data recovery private key. This reduces the likelihood that someone could access and use the DRA keys if they gain access to the system without having the DRA credentials.
- If you use Certificate Services in Windows Server 2003 and a custom certificate template, do not select **Prompt the user during enrollment and require user input when the private key is used**. If selected, this will prevent private keys from being used for encryption and decryption, which reduces security for EFS.

Provide Security and Reliability of Data at All Times

- Encrypt sensitive data on all computers that are members of a domain to protect against offline cryptographic attacks. Even if a computer isn't mobile, disk drives can be removed from servers and other computers to gain unauthorized access to corporate data.
- Use IPSec to encrypt data as it travels the network, since encrypted files are transmitted in unencrypted form if IPSec is not used.
- Use Server Message Block (SMB) signing with EFS to ensure the transmission and reception of files across the network is secure.

- Regularly back up the entire server that stores server-based encrypted data. This ensures profiles with decryption keys can be restored. Selected backups might not preserve decryption keys in the event of a severe data loss caused by a disk crash or other problem.

Head of the Class...

New EFS Features in Windows Server 2003

Windows Server 2003 contains several improvements to EFS over those in Windows 2000. To provide improved security, Windows Server 2003 EFS provides *stronger encryption algorithms*, *sharing of encrypted files*, and *protection for locally cached files*. Let's take a quick look at these features.

- **EFS in Windows Server 2003 allows stronger encryption algorithms with larger keys.** EFS supports only Triple Data Encryption Standard (3DES) encryption algorithm for encrypting file data on NTFS formatted volumes. By default, EFS uses the Advanced Encryption Standard (AES) algorithm with a 256-bit key in Windows Server 2003. In Windows XP and Windows 2000, EFS uses Data Encryption Standard Extended (DESX), a variation of the standard Data Encryption Standard. DESX uses additional 64-bit *OR*ing for both encryption and decryption. This improves security against a brute force attack (an exhaustive key search attack), although it does not improve security against other more sophisticated attacks including differential and linear attacks (the discussion of which is outside the scope of this book). Windows Server 2003 improves the security of EFS by implementing 3DES, which does provide improved security over all types of attacks including differential and linear as well as brute force attacks.
- **Multiple users can be authorized to share encrypted files.** In previous versions of Windows Server, only one user could encrypt or decrypt a file, making file sharing of sensitive data impossible. EFS encryption keys are assigned on a per-domain-user basis to ensure each user's encryption keys are unique and secure. In Windows Server 2003, users can allow others to access encrypted files. In addition, the recovery agent mechanism provides a designated account (typically the Domain Admin account) the ability to recover encrypted files. This is done without the recovery agent having the user's private keys, increasing security at this level as well. Files that are decrypted using the recovery agent keys remain decrypted. This ensures that a rogue recovery agent does not decrypt files, read them, and re-encrypt them to cover his or her tracks. Users are added via the file's Properties dialog. We'll step through this process later in this chapter.

Continued

- **Offline files can be encrypted through EFS to protect locally cached documents.** Windows Server 2003 allows users to store local copies of offline files in EFS folders, unlike Windows 2000. This is a major enhancement since so many users download corporate data to laptops for mobile computing. Now, sensitive documents can be encrypted and stored safely on a local computer. Offline files allow users to keep locally cached copies of files from a file server. These are automatically synchronized with the file server when it's available to ensure users always have access to the most current version. A common database on the local machine is used to store all offline user files and to restrict access to those files by enforcing explicit ACLs. In previous versions of Windows, there was no way to protect these files.

  Windows Server 2003 preserves the caching and synchronization mechanisms used to store local copies of documents typically stored on the network. When offline files are encrypted, the entire database is encrypted using an EFS machine certificate. In this scenario, individual files and folders cannot be selectively decrypted. Therefore, the entire offline files database is protected from attacks using EFS. This process is transparent to the user and increases security on mobile computers.

- **Web folders and files can now be encrypted with EFS.** Windows Server 2003 provides the ability to encrypt Web folders and files. Although security could be applied in previous versions of Windows, the need for at least some public access of Web folders made security somewhat weak. Now, files stored in Web folders can be encrypted. Using the HTTP commands *GET* and *PUT*, raw encrypted files can be transmitted and used via the WebDAV function. *Web-based Distributed Authoring and Versioning (WebDAV)* is an extension of the HTTP protocol that allows users to collaboratively edit and manage files on a remote server. The Windows Server client maps a drive to a WebDAV server, and files encrypted on the local client are transmitted as raw encrypted files to the WebDAV server. Only public and private key pairs on the client are ever used in encrypting files, improving security while allowing Web files to be encrypted with EFS.

These improvements to the EFS function in Windows Server 2003 address several weak points in EFS and provide additional functionality and flexibility in securing folders and files, especially for mobile and Web-based users.

Implementing EFS in Windows Server 2003 is a relatively simple process. It's important you try this a few times to understand how it works and how encrypted files and folders are displayed in Windows Explorer. In Exercise 9.05, you'll create an encrypted folder and file and add users so you understand how this works and how transparent it is to users.

EXERCISE 9.05

IMPLEMENTING EFS ON THE LOCAL COMPUTER

In this exercise, we'll step through encrypting a folder and file on the local computer. You'll see this process is transparent to the user and is relatively fast. We'll also add other users to the file to share the encrypted file.

1. On your desktop, create a folder called **EFSTest**.
2. Right-click the folder and select **Properties**.
3. In the EFSTest Properties dialog, the **General** tab is selected by default. Click the **Advanced** button on the **General** tab.
4. The **Advanced Attributes** dialog is displayed, as shown in Figure 9.23.

Figure 9.23 Advanced Attributes for EFS Folder Encryption

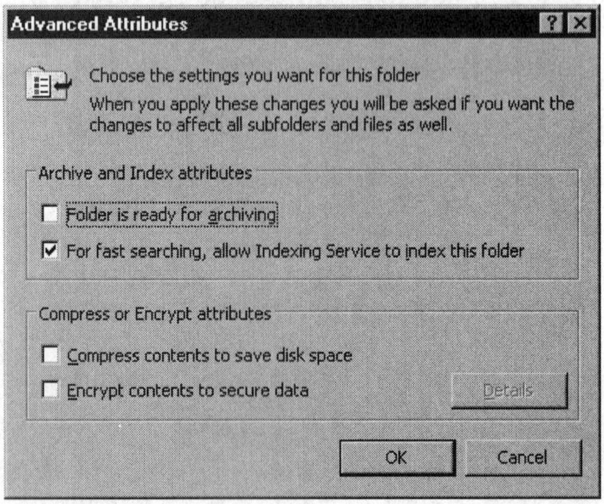

5. There are two sections in the Advanced Attributes dialog. In the second section labeled **Compress or Encrypt attributes** are two check boxes. The first check box, **Compress contents to save disk space**, will compress the contents of the folder. The second

check box, **Encrypt contents to secure data**, will enable encryption for the folder and all files in the folder. Notice that you cannot select both check boxes as the same time. You can select one or the other but not both (an unusual behavior for check boxes). This is because you must decompress a file before it can be encrypted, so you cannot use both simultaneously.

6. Click **Encrypt contents to secure data**, then click **OK**.
7. In the EFSTest Properties, click **OK** to close the dialog.
8. Right-click the **EFSTest** folder and then click **Explore**. In the left pane, click the **Desktop** node. In the right pane, the desktop items are listed, which should include the EFSTest folder. Notice that the EFSTest folder is listed in a different color and that the attribute is listed as AE. The "E" indicates the folder is encrypted.
9. Select the EFSTest folder in the left pane. Click **File | New** and select **Text Document**. A new document is created in the EFSTest folder called New Text Document.txt and it also has the AE attribute, as shown in Figure 9.24. Press **Enter** to access this new document name.

Figure 9.24 File Attribute Indicating Encryption

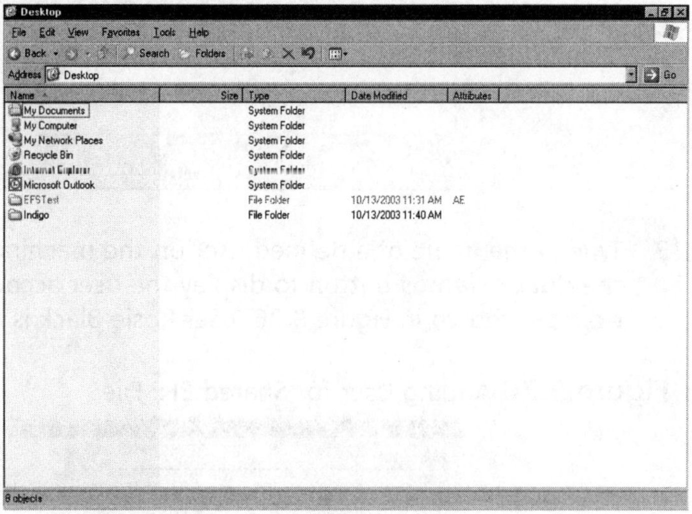

10. In the right-pane of Explorer, right-click the **New Text Document.txt** file and select **Properties**. Click the **Advanced** button on the **General** tab of the document's **Properties** dialog.

11. In the **Advanced Attributes** dialog, click the **Details** button to display the **Encryption Details for C:**. The path displayed will depend on the location of the file to be shared. This dialog, shown in Figure 9.25, provides the ability to add users who can access the file. However, any users to be added must have a valid certificate.
12. Click the **Add** button to display the **Select User** dialog. If you have additional users defined on the computer with certificates, they will be displayed. If the user is not displayed, you can click the **Find User** button.

Figure 9.25 EFS File Sharing Dialog

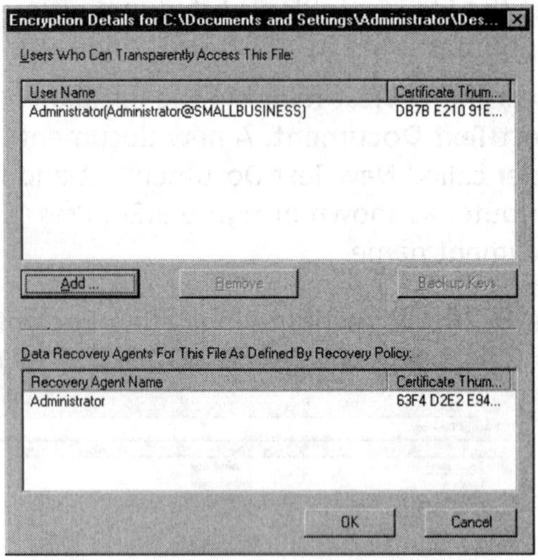

13. Type in the name of a defined user on the machine and then click the **Check Names** button to display the user account. In the example shown in Figure 9.26, user Rosie Black is added.

Figure 9.26 Adding User for Shared EFS File

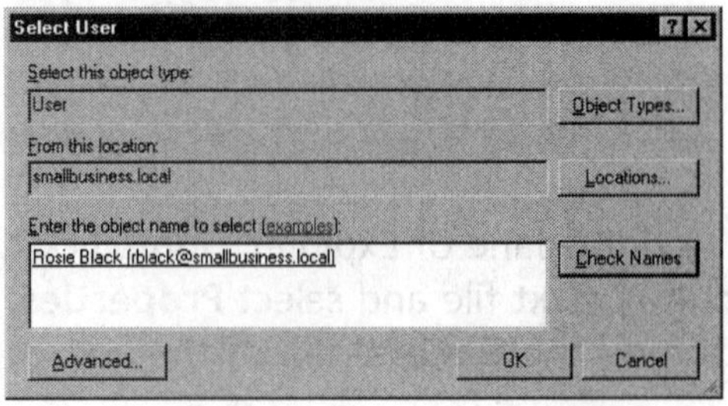

14. If the user you add does not have a certificate, you will see an alert indicating the selected user cannot be added because a certificate does not exist for that user, as shown in Figure 9.27.

Figure 9.27 No User Certificate Available

15. If you receive this alert, click **OK** to close the Select User Alert. Otherwise, if you do not receive this alert, the user has a valid certificate and is added to the Select User list. Click **OK** to accept or **Cancel** to reject changes and close the **Select User** dialog.
16. Click **OK** or **Cancel** to close the original **Select User** dialog.
17. In the **Encryption Details for** C:\... dialog, any users you've added are displayed in the upper portion of the dialog with **User Name** and **Certificate Thumbprint** displayed.
18. Click **OK** or **Cancel** to close the **Encryption Details** dialog. Click **OK** or **Cancel** to close the **Advanced Attributes** dialog. Finally, click **OK** or **Cancel** to close the **New Text Document.txt Properties** dialog.
19. If desired, drag the EFS Test folder to the Recycle Bin. If you do so, you can open the Recycle Bin and look in the EFS Test folder. The New Text Document.txt file is still encrypted, providing data security even when the file is deleted from the system.
20. Close Explorer by clicking the **X** in the upper-right corner or by clicking **File | Close**.

EFS can be implemented on the local computer or on a remote server. You can do this in one of several ways. You can set recovery policy via Group Policy on the local computer or for the domain via the MMC Group Policy Editor snap-in. You can also use a command line utility, *cipher.exe*, to display or alter encryption on folders and files. We'll discuss the *cipher.exe* command-line utility in just a moment.

Certificate Storage

User certificates that contain the public keys are stored in the Personal certificate store for the certificate owner's user account. A certificate provides assurance that the public key is bound or attached to a specific entity (typically a user or computer) that owns the private key. Certificates are stored in plain-text. Since they are public information and are digitally signed, they are protected from tampering. Private keys, however, must be kept secure so that only the owner of the private key has access to it.

Certificates are issued by CAs, which can be native to Windows or third-party CAs. EFS issues its own certificates if it cannot contact a CA. However, you can deploy Certificate Services to issue EFS certificates. Doing so provides several benefits, including:

- Centralized certificate management
- Certificate revocation lists
- Ability to issue alternate recovery agent certificates to designated user accounts

Each user's certificate store contains all certificates issued to that user. They are stored in the following location:

```
Systemroot\Documents and
Settings\<username>\ApplicationData\Microsoft\SystemCertificates\My\Certificates
```

Each time a user logs on, the person's certificates in the user's profile are written to the user's personal store in the system Registry. If a user has a roaming profile, the certificates are located on a DC so that the certificates are available regardless of where the user logs on. Certificates can be viewed and managed in the Certificates Snap-in in the MMC. A user might have more than one certificate related to EFS. In the Certificates snap-in, there is a column labeled Intended Purposes. If the entry in that column is Encrypting File System, the certificate is used with EFS.

Recovery certificates appear in the personal certificate store for the recovery agent account. In the column labeled Intended Purposes, the entry will be File Recovery instead of Encrypting File System.

Private keys are stored in the following path:

```
Systemroot\Documents and Settings\ApplicationData\Microsoft\Crypto\RSA
```

If a user has a roaming profile, the private keys will be stored on the DC in the RSA folder.

As mentioned earlier, private keys must be protected. Stolen or compromised private keys pose a serious security risk. All files in the RSA folder are automatically encrypted with a random, symmetric key called the *user's master key*. The user's master key is generated by the RC4 algorithm, which generates a 128-bit key for computers that support Enhanced CSP or a 56-bit key for computers that support Basic CSP. A CSP is a cryptographic service provider that is an independent software module providing actual cryptographic functions. The master key is generated automatically and is periodically renewed. Any file created in the RSA folder is automatically encrypted. Both EFS and CSPs look only in the RSA folder for private keys, which is why the RSA folder should never be moved or renamed.

As an additional security measure, certificates and private keys should be exported to a floppy disk or other removable media and stored securely. Private keys for recovery agents should be removed from the system. If the system crashes, the private key can be recovered. It also prevents recovery of the private key on a system that is stolen, as could be the case with a laptop.

Certificate Enrollment and Renewal

To encrypt files, EFS requires a certificate. EFS will use your current EFS certificate to encrypt files. If one is not available, EFS will search your personal store for an appropriate certificate. If one still cannot be located, EFS will enroll you for an EFS certificate with an online Windows Server 2003 CA that supports EFS templates. If EFS still cannot get a certificate for you, it will create a self-signed certificate. A self-signed certificate will also be used if you are logged in on an account that is not a domain account.

When a certificate expires, EFS performs a renewal by enrolling for a new certificate with a new key pair. EFS does not renew the current certificate, it enrolls your account for a new certificate. If you renew the EFS certificate and archive the old one (we'll discuss the importance of archiving certificates and private keys later in this chapter), EFS will continue to use the old certificate until its expiration date. When looking for a new certificate, EFS can grab a certificate that is different from the one you acquired through renewal if more than one EFS certificate exists in your personal store. After EFS begins using the new certificate, it can still be used to decrypt files encrypted with your previous certificate. EFS regenerates the metadata (file header) to use the new certificate.

Another note about EFS certificates is that EFS does not perform any revocation checking as is done with other types of certificates. This is one reason it is recommended you also use Certificate Services in Windows Server 2003, which does provide revocation checking. Revocation checking is an important security task that checks to see if the certificate is still valid. Typically, the authority that issues the certificate maintains a certificate revocation list (CRL). If a certificate is revoked and is on the revocation list, it is no longer valid. This can occur when the certificate's subject (user, computer, etc.) has a compromised (lost or stolen) private key, if it is discovered the certificate was obtained fraudulently, or when there is a change to the status of the certificate subject (such as an employee being terminated). Clearly, then, maintaining a CRL can be an important enhancement to security. Since EFS certificates are not checked for revocation, it's more secure to have EFS request and obtain a certificate from a CA that to maintain a revocation list. However, when this is not an option, EFS will use a self-signed certificate. This certificate will not be checked for revocation and could pose a security risk.

Using *cipher.exe*

cipher.exe is a command-line utility that can be used to display or alter encryption on folders and files in the NTFS file system. If it is used without any switches, the *cipher* command will display the encryption state of the current folder and all files within the folder. A number of switches can be used with the **cipher** command, as summarized in Table 9.7. We'll go through a few of the commands, including the */r* to generate a new recovery agent, which is used in a later exercise. The syntax for the *cipher* command is:

```
cipher [{/e|/d}][/s:Folder][/a][/i][/f][/q][/h][/k][/u [/n]][{PathName[…]] |
[/r:PathNameWithoutExtension | /w:PathName | /x:[PathName]
PathNameWithoutExtension}]
```

Table 9.7 *cipher.exe* Command-Line Switches

Cipher Switch and Parameters	Description and Use
/e	Encrypts specified folders. This will cause files added to the folder to be encrypted as well.
/d	Decrypts specified folders.
/s:*Folder*	Performs selected operation in the specified folder and all subfolders.
/a	Performs the operation for files and directories.
/i	Continues performing specified operation even after errors occur. By default, *cipher* stops when errors occur.
/f	Forces encryption or decryption of all specified objects. By default, *cipher* skips files that have been encrypted or decrypted already.
/q	Reports only the most essential information (quiet mode).
/h	Displays files with hidden or system attributes. By default, these files are not encrypted or decrypted.

Continued

Table 9.7 *cipher.exe* Command-Line Switches

Cipher Switch and Parameters	Description and Use
/k	Creates a new file encryption key for the user running *cipher*. If this option is used, all other options are disregarded.
/u	Updates the user's file encryption key or recovery agent's key to the current ones in all of the encrypted files on local drives. This option only works with */n*.
/n	This option only works with the */u* switch. It prevents keys from being updated and this option can be used to find all the encrypted files on local drives.
PathName	This variable specifies the pattern, file, or folder in the various switches.
/r:*PathNameWithoutExtensions*	If you use this option, all other options for the *cipher* command are ignored. This switch generates a new recovery agent certificate and private key and then writes them to a filename specified in the *PathNameWithoutExtensions*.
/w:*PathName*	If you use this option, all other options for the *cipher* command are ignored. This switch removes data on unused portions of a volume. The *PathName* option can be use to indicate any directory on the desired volume.
/x:*[PathName] PathNameWithoutExtension*	If you use this option, all other options for the *cipher* command are ignored. This switch identifies the certificates and private keys used by EFS for the currently logged on user and backs the certificates and private keys up to a file. If *PathName* is specified, the certificate and private key used to encrypt the file specified are backed up. Otherwise, the user's current EFS certificate and keys are backed up. Certificates and private keys are written to a file specified by the *PathNameWithoutExtension* parameter.
/?	Displays help at the command prompt.

Figures 9.28 and 9.29 show the command-line options and syntax (in two screens). One common use for the cipher command is to generate an EFS recovery agent key and certificate, using the */R* switch. The command to create a recovery agent key and certificate is:

```
cipher /R:salesdra
```

In this case, the file name is salesdra (Sales Data Recovery Agent), which might be used for all sales users, for example. The file will be written as salesdra.pfx, which contains both the certificate and the private key, and salesdra.cer, which contains only the certificate. An administrator can then add the contents of the .CER file to the EFS recovery policy to create the recovery agent for users. The administrator can also import the .PFX file (both key and certificate) to recover individual files. Figure 9.30 shows the process of creating a recovery agent via the *cipher.exe* command. Notice that you'll be prompted to create a password for the .PFX file.

Figure 9.28 *cipher.exe* **Commands, Part 1**

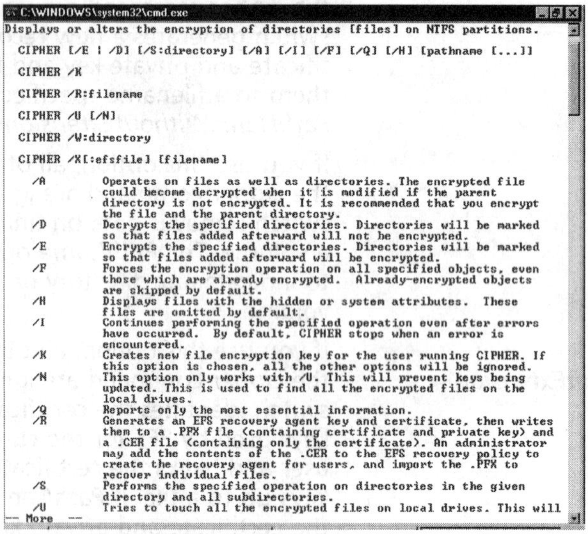

Figure 9.29 *cipher.exe* Commands, Part 2

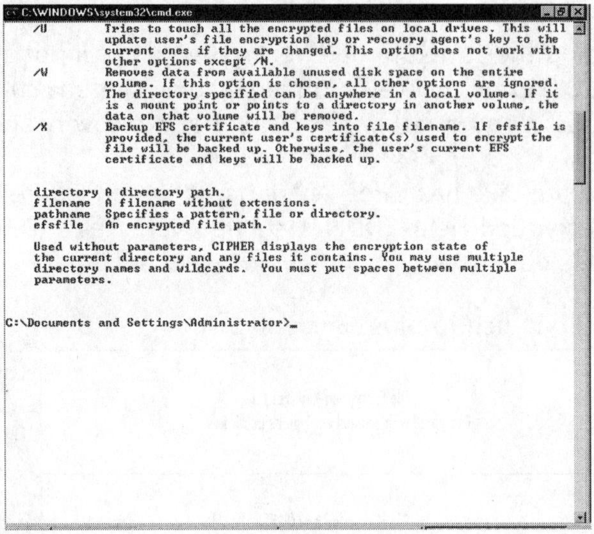

Figure 9.30 *cipher.exe /R* to Create Recovery Agent Key and Certificate

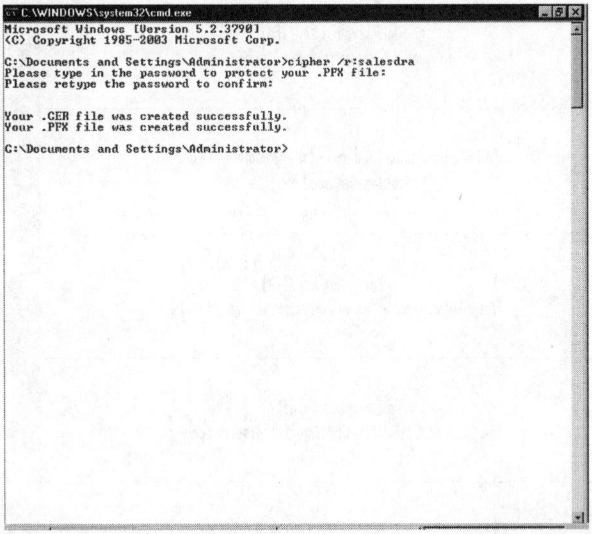

Once you've created the .PFX and .CER files, you can list the directory contents (*dir* command) and you should see salesdra.pfx and salesdra.cer in the directory.

Head of the Class...

Anatomy of an Encrypted File

Understanding the structure of an encrypted file will not specifically be covered on the exam. However, understanding this structure will help you when answering questions about EFS and recovery agents on the exam.

An encrypted file has three key parts, shown in Figure 9.31. These are the Data Decryption Fields (DDF), Data Recovery Fields (DRF), and the encrypted file data itself.

Figure 9.31 Structure of an Encrypted File

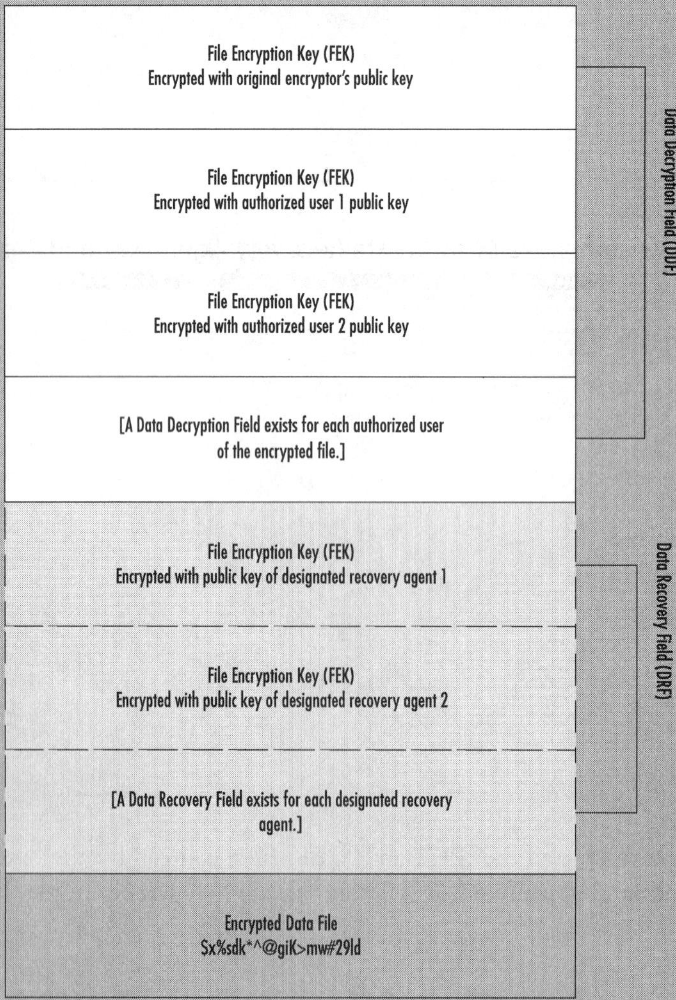

Continued

Earlier, we discussed sharing an encrypted file, and Exercise 9.04 stepped you through setting up additional users on an encrypted file. As you can see from the file structure, the encrypted file stores each authorized user's public key encrypted in the FEK in the Data Decryption Field (DDF). An encrypted file's header will contain a unique DDF for each authorized user. This is how multiple users can share an encrypted file in Windows Server 2003. The header will always contain at least one DDF when the owner encrypts the file.

The header also contains Data Recovery Fields (DRFs) if the computer's security policy designates one or more data recovery agents (DRAs). If so, copies of the FEK are encrypted for each DRA using the DRA's public key. There will be as many DRFs as there are DRAs for each encrypted file.

Looking at the structure of an encrypted file shows how multiple users can access a file and how the data recovery agent can recover a file since all of this data is stored in the header of each encrypted file. While it seems like a lot of work for each file, using both symmetric and asymmetric keys in the process, files can be encrypted and decrypted quickly and transparently for users.

EXAM 70-298 OBJECTIVE 4.2.1

Creating a Strategy for the Encryption and Decryption of Files and Folders

An encryption strategy for files and folders includes an assessment of vital data, an assessment of the environment, policies for using EFS, and procedures for recovering encrypted files. Obviously, not all files are sensitive enough to warrant encryption. In most cases, files protected with two layers of security—user authentication and ACLs—will be safe. However, files that contain sensitive data such as social security numbers, credit card data, medical or health data, or corporate trade secrets (to name just a few) should be protected with EFS.

Increasing User Awareness

There are two aspects to user awareness: identifying sensitive files and using EFS appropriately. As an IT administrator, there's a good chance you (or your department) are not fully aware of which files are most sensitive for various departments. Each department should identify which files or types of files are most sensitive. This is a good opportunity for you to educate users on what EFS is and what its capabilities are (and are not). Then, users can make intelligent decisions about which folders and files should be encrypted and how they can best manage EFS files. These steps are delineated here:

1. After sensitive data has been identified and encrypted folders have been created, sensitive files should be copied into the encrypted folders. Copying unencrypted files into encrypted folders will encrypt the files. The earlier unencrypted files should be deleted. New files should be created within the encrypted folder so they are encrypted by default.
2. Users should understand that files moved to a non-NTFS volume will be unencrypted.
3. Users might think that because they can read, modify, and save files that they are not encrypted. Explain to users that encryption is transparent to them, but that sensitive files should still be handled according to the guidelines established.
4. Users should also understand that although individual files can be encrypted and decrypted (via the file's Properties dialog), it is highly recommended that folders be encrypted and that sensitive files be created and stored in encrypted folders.
5. Users should clearly understand that encrypted files are not protected when transmitted across the network or Internet. Additional security such as SSL or IPSec should be used to transmit highly sensitive files. The IT administrator should work with users to determine how files are used and set up additional security for files that will travel across the network.
6. Users should export their EFS certificates and private keys to removable media and store the media securely. Private keys should not be removed from computers because users will be unable to decrypt any files without importing the private key. The most common problem with EFS is that users lose access to their private key in their user profile.
7. Encrypt user's My Documents folder. This is the default storage location for many user files (including Microsoft Office documents), and encrypting this folder will make sure that user files are properly encrypted without the user having to take any extraordinary steps.
8. For users of stand-alone computers, use password reset disks in Windows XP so that if they forget their passwords, they can reset their password and recover the master key for the stand-alone computer. Without it, the user might be unable to access the system to import their EFS certificate and/or private key.

TEST DAY TIP

Remember that EFS is not used to encrypt data traveling across the network, it does not authenticate users, it cannot be used to secure dial-in or VPN connections, and it cannot encrypt data on computers running other non-Windows operating systems.

There are additional steps you as the IT administrator should take to ensure EFS is security implemented within your organization. It's vital that you establish a safe, consistent, and methodical approach toward securing recovery agent certificates. Safely storing and archiving recovery agent credentials will ensure that you're always able to decrypt important files even after you've changed recovery agents. Files that might sit dormant for some time might need to be decrypted long after the file's owner leaves the company, so archiving is a critical step. The steps you should take to manage EFS throughout the organization are:

1. Export private keys for recovery accounts on secure media, stored in a safe place. Then, remove the private keys from the computers This prevents a user from using the recovery account to decrypt others' files. This is particularly important for stand-alone computers where the recovery account is typically the Administrator account. For a laptop, this makes sense because if the machine lost or stolen, the data cannot be recovered without the recovery account keys. If the private keys have been removed from the system, they will not be available as a potential security liability.
2. Only use the recovery agent account for file recovery. This keeps the credentials secure by limiting their use.
3. Work with users of stand-alone systems to make sure their systems remain safe. The requirements for stand-alone systems are slightly different than for computers joined to the domain. Stand-alone systems should create password reset disk and configure *Syskey* for startup key protection for the EFS users' private keys.
4. Change the default recovery agent account as soon as possible. By default, the Administrator of the first DC installed for the domain is the default recovery agent account. Set a password for each recovery agent account. Set auditing for the use of the recovery agent account to monitor use of this account.
5. Export each private key associated with recovery certificates into a .PFX file, protect it with a strong password, move it to secure removable media, and store it securely.

6. Do not destroy recovery certificates and private keys when recovery agent policy changes (or expires). Keep them archived until you are absolutely certain all files protected with them have been updated with new recovery agent credentials.
7. Create a recovery agent archive program to ensure files can be recovered via obsolete recovery keys. Export keys and store them in an access-controlled vault. Create a master and backup archive and store the backup archive securely offsite.
8. Designate two or more recovery agent accounts per OU. Designate one computer for each designated recovery agent account and grant appropriate permissions to the administrators to use the recovery agent accounts.
9. Never move or rename the RSA folder. The RSA folder is the only place EFS looks for private keys. (RSA stands for Rivest, Shamir, and Adelman, the inventors of a widely used encryption algorithm bearing the same name.)

In addition to implementing these practices both on users' computers and for the organization as a whole, you'll need to understand and manage recovery agents, since the most common problem with EFS is lost or inaccessible user credentials.

Configuring File Recovery Agents

Data recovery is important when employees leave the company or lose their private keys. If you ever lose your file encryption certificate and your private key through disk failure or some other reason, the designated recovery agent can recover the data. This is why it's critical to export, save, and archive recovery agent credentials. This also provides the ability for a company to recover an employee's data after he or she has left the company.

EFS recovery policy specifies the data recovery agent accounts to be within the scope of the policy (OU, domain, site, local computer). EFS requires an Encrypted Data Recovery Agent policy be defined before it can be used. If none has been chosen, EFS will use a default recovery agent account. Within the scope of a domain, only the Domain Admins group can designate an account as the recovery agent account. Where there is no domain, the local Administrator account is the default data recovery agent.

In Exercise 9.06, we'll step through adding a recovery agent for the local computer.

EXERCISE 9.06

ADD A RECOVERY AGENT FOR THE LOCAL COMPUTER

In this exercise, we'll add a recovery agent for the local computer.

1. Click **Start | Run,** type **mmc** in the Open: text box, and then click **OK.**
2. On the **File** menu, select **Add/Remove Snap-in,** and then click **Add.**
3. In the **Add Standalone Snap-in** dialog, scroll down until you locate **Group Policy Object Editor** and then click **Add**.
4. In the **Select Group Policy Object** screen, verify that **Local Computer** is the selected *Group Policy Object* and then click **Finish**.
5. Click **Close** to close the **Add Standalone Snap-in** dialog, then click **OK** to close the **Add/Remove Snap-in** dialog and return to the MMC.
6. In the left pane, click the + to expand the **Local Computer Policy** node.
7. Click to expand the following nodes, in order: **Computer Configuration | Windows Settings | Security Settings | Public Key Settings**.
8. Right-click **Encrypting File System** to select it and then select **Properties,** as shown in Figure 9.32.

Figure 9.32 Encrypting File System Properties Dialog

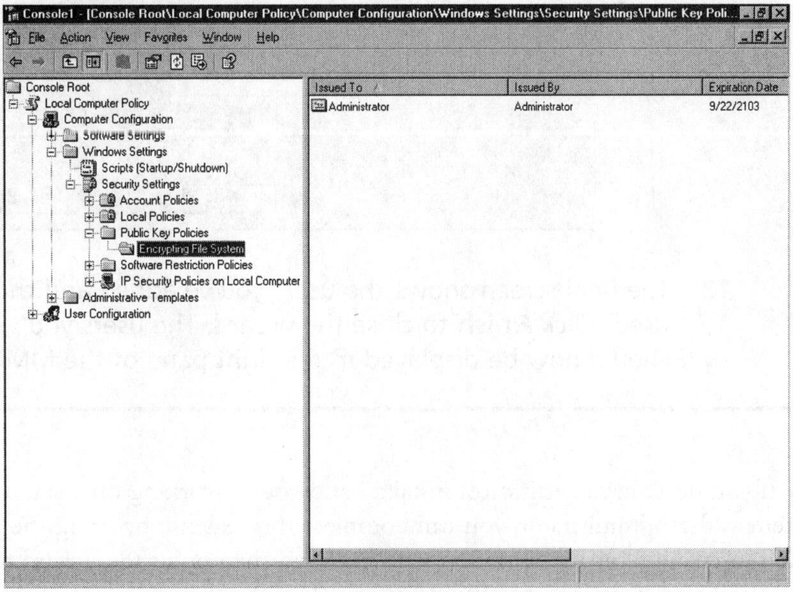

9. To disable EFS on this computer, clear the check box labeled **Allow users to encrypt files using Encrypting File System (EFS).** To enable EFS, this check box must be selected.
10. Click **OK** or **Cancel** to close the **Properties** dialog. Right-click the **Encrypting File System** node in the left pane and select **Add Data Recovery Agent**. This will launch the **Add Recovery Agent Wizard**. You'll need to provide the username for a user that has a published recovery certificate. You can also browse for .CER files that contain information about the recovery agent you're adding.
11. Click **Next** to access the **Select Recovery Agents** screen in the wizard. You can browse directories or folders, as shown in Figure 9.33. Once you've selected the users, click **Next**.

Figure 9.33 Select Recovery Agents Dialog

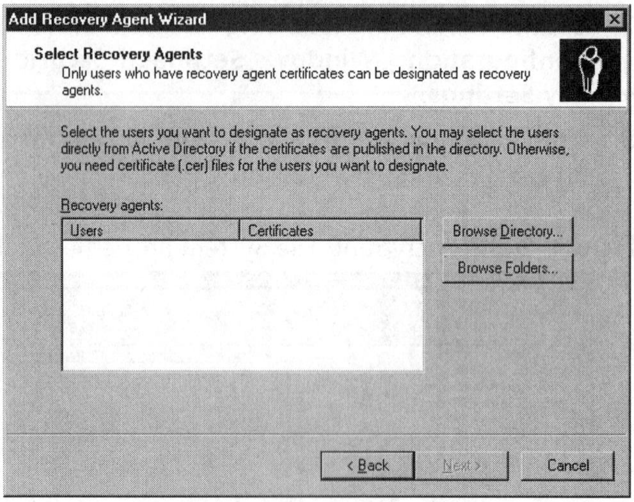

12. The final screen shows the users you've added and the certificates used. Click **Finish** to close the wizard. The users you've added should now be displayed in the right pane of the MMC.

If you don't have certificates installed and you're working on a stand-alone system as the Administrator, you can complete this exercise by using the *cipher* command to create a certificate and private keys and then point the wizard to these files. These steps are described briefly in Exercise 9.07.

Exercise 9.07

Using the *Cipher* Command to Add Data Recovery Agent

1. Click **Start | Run**, type **cmd**, and then click **OK**.
2. Type this command at the prompt and then press **Enter** to execute the command:

```
cipher /r:testdra
```

Note

If you do not specify a filename when using the *cipher /r:* command, files named .CER and .PFX will be created (essentially, no filename, just the extension). Instead, use a filename such as the testdra we used earlier. Once you've added the DRA to the EFS policy, you can right-click on the DRA and edit the properties, such as giving it a user-friendly name and a description.

3. When prompted, enter a password and then re-enter the password to verify the password. You'll be notified that the .PFX and .CER files have been created. Make a note of the folder in which they reside so you can easily browse to them. This was shown in Figure 9.30 earlier in this chapter.
4. Next, follow steps 1 through 11 in the previous exercise, Exercise 9.06, to access the Add Data Recovery Agent Wizard. When prompted to select recovery agents (Exercise 9.06, step 11), browse to the location of the .CER file. By default, this file resides in the path in which it was created. If you look at Figure 9.30, you'll see it should be located in C:\Documents and Settings\Administrator. If another path was selected, the .CER file resides in that alternate path. As shown in Figure 9.34, when you locate the .CER file, click to select it, and then click **Open**.

Figure 9.34 Importing Certificate for Recovery Agent

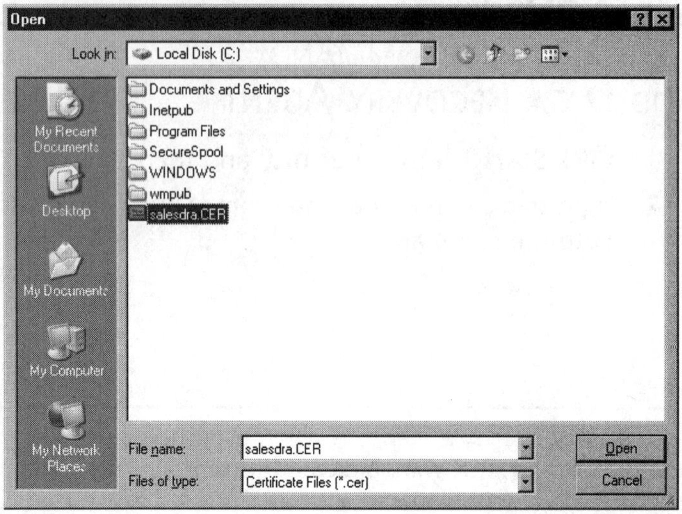

5. If the certificate was created by EFS, you will receive a notice that Windows cannot determine if the certificate has been revoked. (Recall that we discussed that EFS does not maintain certificate revocation lists.) This warning is shown in Figure 9.35. Click **Yes** to accept or **No** to reject. Click **Yes** to display the final screen of the wizard, which shows the user and certificate you've selected. Click **Finish** to close the **Add Recovery Agent Wizard** and return to the MMC.

Figure 9.35 Windows Warning Regarding Certificate Status

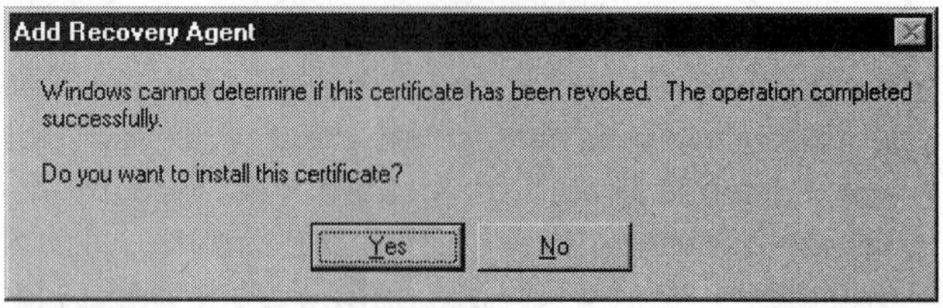

Adding recovery agents for the domain uses a similar process. Instead of selecting the Local Computer as the Group Policy Object (step 4 in the preceding exercise), you would select the GPO for which you want to establish the recovery agent (OU, domain, etc.). Figure 9.36 shows this node in the Default Domain Policy. Always back up recovery keys to floppy disk before making any changes. In a domain, the default recovery policy is implemented for the domain when the first controller is set up. The first domain administrator is issued a self-signed certificate used to designate the domain admin as the recovery agent. To change this default recovery policy for the domain, log on to the first DC as Administrator. If you want to add a recovery agent, you can use the steps outlined in the preceding exercise to Add Data Recovery Agents. However, the DC will contact a Windows Server 2003 CA to request a certificate. The certificate is based on the EFS Recovery Agent certificate template. If this template is not available or if you cannot obtain a certificate, you will receive an error and will be unable to add recovery agents.

Figure 9.36 Default Domain Policy Encrypting File System Node

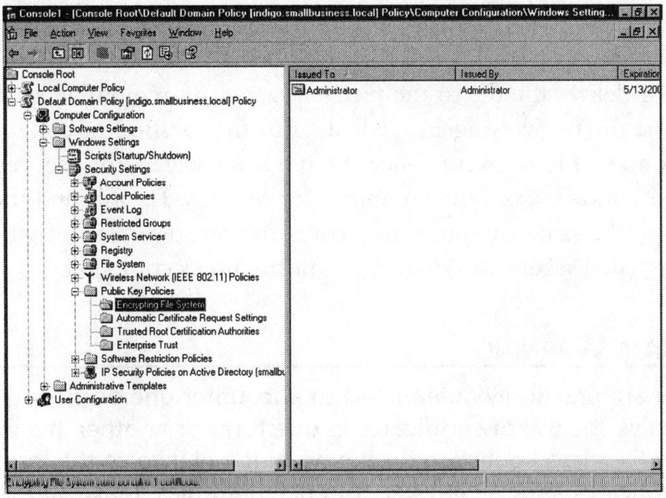

In addition to creating recovery agents, you can configure a GPO so that it does not require a recovery agent. You can configure this for any OUs, domains, or sites in the Active Directory forest to allow you to use EFS without a recovery agent. You will be unable to configure the GPO in this manner if you have an EFS policy defined. If so, you must delete the policy first. In the MMC with the Group Policy Object editor open, if you select **Encrypting File System** in the left pane, click **Action** on the menu, and select **All Tasks**, you'll have an additional option of **Do Not Require Data Recover Agents**. If this option is not available, you have not deleted the existing EFS policy.

Removing Recovery Agent Policy

It is possible that a company might implement a data recovery policy and later decide to remove or eliminate that policy. When a recovery policy is removed from a domain, it is no longer applied via group policy. In Windows 2000, once the group policy has been updated, no new files can be encrypted. In Windows XP and Windows Server 2003, computers will not be impacted. Encrypted files can still be opened, but they cannot be re-encrypted. Existing encrypted files remain encrypted until they are accessed or updated by a user who has a private key to decrypt those files.

Recovering Files

Files can be recovered in one of several ways. A file that has been saved via the Backup tool (or another backup utility) can be restored to the user's machine (or previous location), and the user's credentials can then decrypt the file. Files backed up using the Windows Backup tool will remain encrypted on the backup media and will remain encrypted when restored from the backups. If a user's certificate is lost or destroyed, the encrypted file can be sent to the designated recovery agent, and the recovery agent can decrypt the file and transfer it back to the desired location. Remember that the transmitted file will not be encrypted, so use a secure transfer method or deliver the file to the recovery agent on removable media. Conversely, you can import the recovery agent credentials to the location of the encrypted file for decryption and file recovery. Once the file is recovered, the recovery agent credentials should be removed from the computer for security. The file and the credentials must both be on the same computer to recover the file, regardless of whether this occurs on a designated secure workstation or on the user's computer.

EXAM WARNING

You are practically guaranteed to encounter one or more questions that involve the use of certificates in one form or another. It's likely that if you see an EFS-related question on the exam it will involve the loss of private keys or certificates and the recovery of encrypted files. Make sure you're comfortable with the concepts of EFS and data recovery for the exam.

Backing Up Keys

Certificates can be backed up with or without private keys. This is accomplished via the Certificates snap-in in the MMC. It's suggested you back up certificates with private keys to a floppy disk or other secure removable media and store this media in a secure location. For stand-alone computers or for mobile computers such as laptops, you should remove the private keys from the system and store them in a secure location. In the following exercise, we'll step through backing up certificates with private keys and you'll see how to remove the private key during this process.

EXERCISE 9.08

BACKING UP CERTIFICATES WITH PRIVATE KEYS

In this exercise, we'll use the Certificates snap-in in the MMC to export a certificate with private keys to a floppy disk. You'll also see how to remove private keys during the export process, if desired.

1. Click **Start | Run**, type **mmc** in the **Open** text box, and then click **OK.**
2. In the MMC, click **File | Add/Remove Snap-in**. Then, in the **Add/Remove Snap-in** dialog, click **Add**.
3. In the **Add Standalone Snap-in** dialog, scroll down to locate **Certificates**. Select Certificates and then click **Add**.
4. In the **Certificates Snap-in** dialog, select **My User Account** (selected by default) and then click **Finish.**
5. Click **Close** to close the **Add Standalone Snap-in** dialog. Then, click **OK** to close the **Add/Remove Snap-in** dialog and return to the MMC.
6. Click the + to the left of **Certificates** – **Current User** to expand the node. Click the + to expand the **Personal** node beneath. Click **Certificates** to select this node.
7. Click the certificate that displays the words **File Recovery**, as shown in Figure 9.37.
8. Right-click the certificate, select **All Tasks**, and then select **Export**. (Notice that you can also request and renew certificates here.)

Figure 9.37 Key Backup from Microsoft Management Console

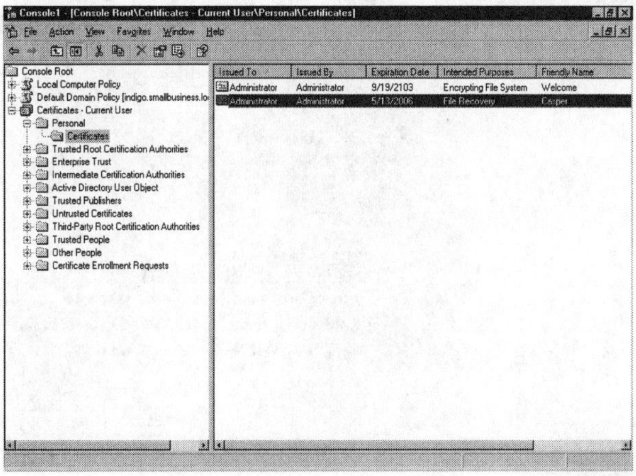

9. The Certificate Export Wizard is launched; click **Next**.
10. In the **Export Private Key** dialog, you can export the certificate with or without the private key. The private key is password protected, so if you select this option, you'll be prompted for a password in a subsequent screen. Select whichever option you want to use (in this example, we've selected **Yes, export the private key**) and then click **Next**.
11. The next screen **Export File Format** provides several options. If you selected **No** in the previous screen, this screen will enable the first set of options as shown in Figure 9.38. If you selected **Yes** in the previous screen, this screen will enable the second set of options, shown in Figure 9.39.

Figure 9.38 Export File Format for Certificate Only (Excludes Private Key)

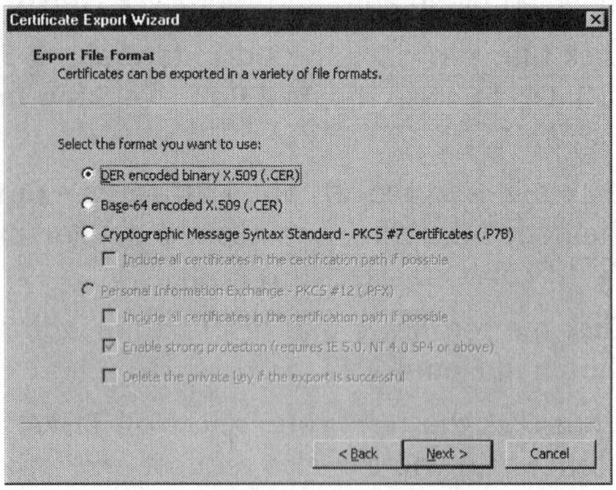

Figure 9.39 Export File Format Including Private Key with Certificate

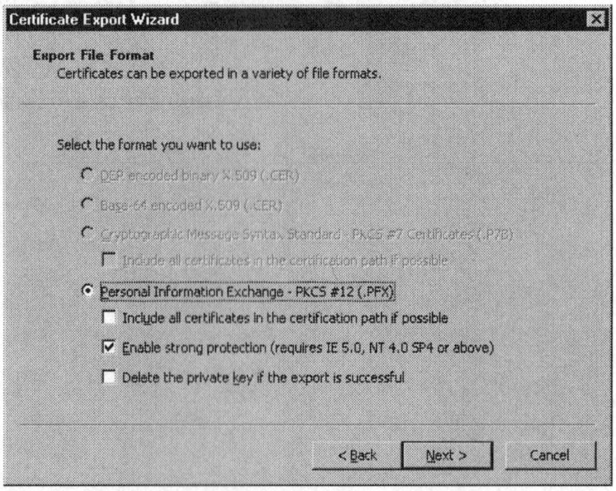

12. If you have more than one certificate in the path and want to export all certificates, select the check box labeled **Include all certificate in the certificate path if possible.**
13. The second check box in this section (shown in Figure 9.19), **Enable strong protection (requires IE 5.0, NT 4.0 SP4 or above)**, is selected by default. If you are using Windows NT 4.0 or earlier, you cannot use strong protection.
14. The third check box, **Delete the private key if the export is successful**, can be selected if you want to delete the private key. The key will only be deleted if the export is successful. Alternately, you can delete the key manually after verifying the successful export. Click **Next** to proceed.
15. The next screen requires a password if you chose to export the certificate with the private key. Enter your password twice and then click **Next**.
16. The next screen, **File to Export**, asks you to specify the file name or to **Browse** to a location to which you want to export. Often, this location is a floppy disk or other removable media. Click **Browse** and locate the removable media to which you want to export the certificate. (For this exercise, we called the file backupdra and exported to the local drive.) Click **Next** to continue.
17. The final screen in the wizard is the **Completing the Certificate Export Wizard** screen shown in Figure 9.40. This screen verifies the selections you've made and gives you the opportunity to make modifications if any of the settings are not as you want. To make modifications, click **Back**. If all settings meet your requirements, click **Finish**.

Figure 9.40 Certificate Export Wizard Successful Completion

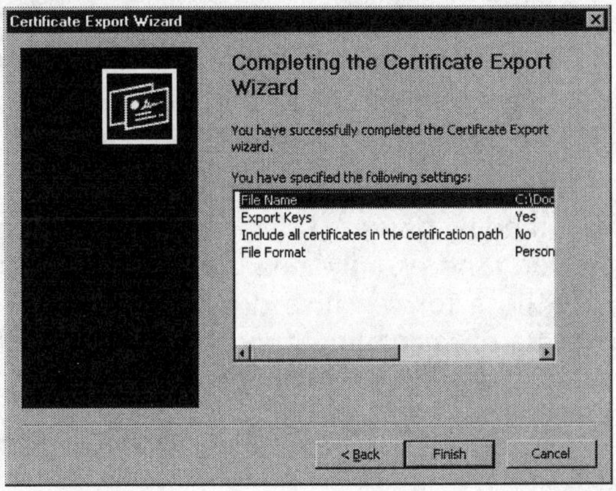

18. If the export is successful, you'll get a notification dialog, shown in Figure 9.41. This indicates the file was successfully exported to the location you specified with the settings you selected. If you selected the option to **Delete the private key if the export is successful**, your private key has also been deleted. The wizard will close and you'll return to the MMC.

Figure 9.41 Export Successful Notice

You can use the same steps to import a certificate. In the MMC Certificates snap-in, you would select **Personal | Certificates**, right-click on **Certificates** (or select **Certificates** and then click **Action** on the menu), and select **Import** and follow the instructions in the **Certificate Import Wizard**.

Designing & Planning...

Printing Encrypted Files

One of the places security can be weak is in the area of printing. When a file is encrypted with EFS, it is automatically and transparently decrypted and displayed on the user's monitor. That file can then be printed to a local or network printer. If the data is particularly sensitive, this can create a security hole. If your users will require the ability to print sensitive documents that are stored in an encrypted state, you should consider setting up a more secure printing environment.

When a user uses the Print function, the document is copied into a spool (.spl) file that resides on the local print provider (local computer or print server). By default, these spool files are stored in the following location:

`Systemroot\System32\Spool\Printers`

By default (and by design), that folder is unencrypted. This makes sense because you don't necessarily need every single print spool file to be encrypted, just those for sensitive documents. If you were to encrypt this folder, the process of encrypting and decrypting spool files would slow the printing process significantly and unnecessarily.

Continued

Instead, create a separate printer to be used for encrypted files. This defined printer ideally should be a local printer that is not shared to avoid the all-too-common "print and sprint" problem where users print to a shared printer and sprint down the hall to grab the document before someone sees the sensitive information. The defined printer can use the same hardware (same actual printer) as the regular printer, but the definition of this secure printer will be slightly different.

Once you've used the **Add a Printer Wizard** and added the appropriate printer and associated driver, right-click the printer and select **Properties**. You can click the **Advanced** tab and select the **Print directly to the printer** option button, as shown in Figure 9.42. You'll notice that most of the other options are disabled when you make this selection. By sending print jobs directly to the printer, a spool file is not created. This is one way you can improve security when printing EFS protected files. The downside to this method is that print jobs cannot be prioritized or scheduled.

Figure 9.42 Create Secure Printer

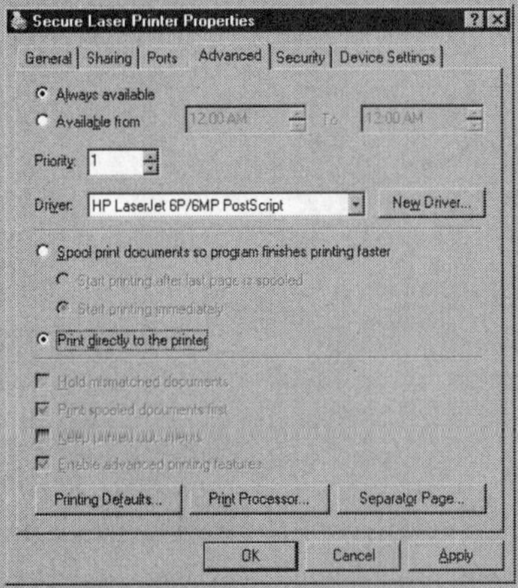

Alternately, you can create an encrypted folder and direct the print spool function for that printer to this encrypted folder. The result will be that all files spooled from the designated secure printer will be encrypted until printed. By default, spooled files are deleted after the print job is complete, so the temporary file will be encrypted and then deleted for maximum security.

To change the location of the spool folder for *a specific printer*, you must use the Registry Editor. As you know, editing the Registry directly can cause serious and unexpected consequences that render your system unstable or unusable. Be sure to update your Automated System Recovery set prior to making changes to the Registry. Assuming you've taken appropriate

Continued

safeguards, you can change the location of the print spool folder for a specific printer by taking the following steps:

1. Create a spool folder on the local computer.
2. Launch the Registry Editor by clicking **Start | Run** and then type **regedt32** in the **Open:** text box. Click **OK**.
3. Locate the following key:

`HKEY_LOCAL_MACHINE\SOFTWARE\Microsoft\WindowsNT\CurrentVersion\Print\Printers\`*<printername>*

4. Locate the **SpoolDirectory**, which has a data type of REG_SZ. This is shown in Figure 9.43.

Figure 9.43 SpoolDirectory in Registry

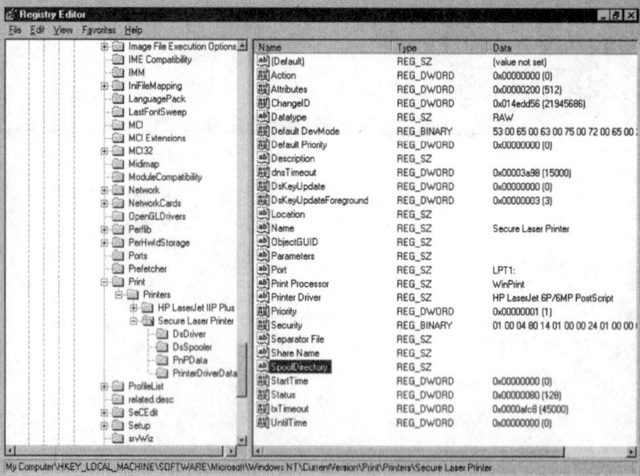

5. Double-click **SpoolDirectory** or right-click and choose **Modify**.
6. Change the Value: to the path to the new folder. For example, the path might be *c:\windows\secureprintspool.*
7. Close the Registry Editor and reboot to make the change go into effect.
8. The printer named in the Registry key should now send spool files to the desired folder.
9. Locate the new spool folder and enable encryption on the folder by right-clicking the folder, clicking the **Advanced** button, and selecting **Encrypt contents to secure data**. Click **OK** to close the **Advanced Attributes** dialog, and click **OK** to close the print spool folder **Properties** dialog.

Continued

> It's important to note that if you forget to create the new secure spool folder and you specify a path in the Registry **SpoolDirectory** entry for the specified printer, the files will spool to the default spool folder, which will not be encrypted and will not protect files during the print process. Also note that you can make changes to the location of the printer spool folder for all printers via the Server properties in Printers and Faxes Properties (on the Advanced tab of the Print Server Properties). This will affect all printers unless you have specifically created a new spool folder via the Registry, as we just did.
>
> By specifying a separate print spool folder, encrypting it, and sending secure documents to the secure printer, you can ensure that sensitive files that are encrypted by EFS will be secured during the printing process. Of course, securing the paper copy of the document is another challenge that's outside the scope of this chapter and often outside the control of the IT department.

Disabling EFS

You can disable EFS for a computer or for the entire domain via the EFS policy just discussed. If you want to disable it for the local computer, verify that **Local Computer** is selected as the GPO (step 4s and 9 in the preceding exercise). If you want to disable it for the domain, select the domain as the GPO and clear the check box (again, steps 4 and 9).

You can also disable EFS via the Registry. As always, it is recommended that you always try to use the user interface to make changes to the system rather than accessing the Registry directly. Incorrectly editing the Registry, as you know, can make a system unusable. As a best practice, it's always wise to update your Automated System Recovery (ASR) floppy disk before modifying the Registry.

However, if you choose this method, you can use these steps to modify the Registry to disable EFS on the local computer.

1. Click **Start | Run**, type **regedt32**, and then click **OK**.
2. Locate the following Registry key by expanding the nodes in the left pane:

   ```
   HKEY_LOCAL_MACHINE\SOFTWARE\Microsoft\WindowsNT\CurrentVersion\EFS
   ```

3. With the EFS node selected, click **Edit** on the menu, select **New**, and then select **DWORD Value**.
4. Type **efsconfiguration** in the **Value name** box and then press **Enter**.
5. Double-click the EfsConfiguration Registry key you just created and type the number **1** in the **Value Data** box.

6. Click **OK** to accept the change, and then close the Registry Editor by selecting **File | Close**.

Third-Party Encryption Options

You can use a third-party data encryption program, and within Windows Server 2003, you can use third-party certificates with EFS. There are numerous third-party data encryption software programs on the market that can be used instead of EFS. There are pros and cons to implementing third-party software, which you'll need to evaluate for your organization. For example, EFS works fine in a native Windows environment, but if you have a network of mixed operating systems, you might run into interoperability issues. There are operating system-independent solutions available as well, and these might make sense if you are running a mixed network. However, many third-party options use password-based recovery systems, which can leave them vulnerable to attack. EFS uses cryptography instead of password-based access, making it far more secure. Many third-party options also require user intervention—the user must take an action to cause a file to be encrypted or decrypted. This also creates a security hole when users don't want to take the time or don't understand exactly how to encrypt/decrypt files. If you choose to implement a third-party solution, you might use the option in Windows Server 2003 to disable EFS to avoid conflicts.

The benefits to using EFS in a Windows environment is that it is fully integrated into the operating system and can rely on the security structure already in place. It uses keys and certificates to keep data safe, which is a more secure solution that relying on passwords. It also is completely transparent to the user once an encrypted folder has been set up. The user simply opens, edits, and closes the file, and the encryption/decryption is handled automatically.

Although you can implement third-party solutions, make sure you've thoroughly researched the cost, the impact on users, and the relative security of the solution and compared it to the features of EFS.

Third-Party Certificates

Once EFS chooses a certificate, it cannot be modified via the user interface but can be modified in the Registry. Moreover, EFS dos not automatically switch certificates if another one becomes available. Such would be the case when EFS uses a self-signed certificate and later is able to connect to a CA. If you want to use a third-party certificate, you can install it via the Certificates snap-in in the MMC. The specified certificate can be used for a user account, service account, or computer account. Once the account is specified in the Certificates snap-in, you can import a third-party certificate.

EXAM 70-298 OBJECTIVE 4.2.3

Designing Security for a Backup and Recovery Strategy

We've probably all heard horror stories about companies (or individuals) that failed to back up their data and suffered the consequences. For many individuals, the loss of data is an inconvenience, although rarely a serious one. For companies whose businesses depend on the data stored on network computers, the consequences can be severe. Still, many companies, particularly smaller ones, have inadequate backup and recovery strategies. Backing server files up to tape and storing the tape in the desk drawer hardly constitutes a secure backup and recovery strategy, yet that's just what takes place in many companies.

Backing up and restoring data is your failsafe option—when all else fails, you rely on backups to restore your systems and network to their operational states. The task of backing up data can enhance security in an organization. If you think of security in broad terms such as "ensuring authorized users have access to needed data" and "protecting network data and services," you can easily see that the very act of backing up and restoring a system is a fundamental security task. In this section, we'll look at designing a secure strategy for backup and recovery. You'll find these kinds of questions on the exam and you'll certainly want to use this information on the job.

Securing the Backup and Restore Process

How many companies do you know of that perform regular backups and then store the media onsite? How many companies do you know of that perform regular backups but never test them? It's surprising how many companies do some, but not all, of the right tasks, leaving themselves exposed to potentially devastating data losses. The downtime for systems, loss of productivity for users, and the cost of recovering lost data (or worse, losing it entirely and being forced to recreate documents and information) is enormous when compared with relatively small time, effort, and cost of establishing a sound backup and recovery plan.

In this section, we'll look at the backup and restore process. We'll take a look at best practices and how to best secure the backup and restore process to ensure your systems. Backups and restores are essential elements in a security process since they represent the failsafe option—after data is lost, after a virus has hit, after an operating system has been disabled—that's when you need to be absolutely sure your data is secure via reliable backup and restore strategies. It's not a matter of *if* something will happen, it's a matter of how quickly and effectively you can respond *when* something does happen.

Currently, 60 to 70 percent of a company's data storage management efforts are associated with backup and recovery functions, according to Phil Goodwin, a senior program director at the Meta Group, an IT industry research and consulting firm. Most companies today use tape backup systems for both current backup and archival backups. A growing trend is the use of offsite storage locations. With the use of encryption and high-speed connections, a firm's data can be safely backed up to an offsite storage facility. This provides another layer of protection because the data is stored at a physically separate location and provides the ability to access the stored data at any time. The downside is that it is still not practical for a company with massive amounts of data to use this type of solution, and it introduces another security risk that must be managed.

Another growing trend is the use of disk-based systems. As the price of disk drives has come down, some companies have found using mirrored sets is a good solution. A mirrored disk contains an exact copy of the live disk at any given time. If one drive fails, the other can be placed in service immediately and often transparently. Disk clustering is another option that allows data to be stored across multiple drives. The downside of both these solutions is that the drives reside onsite. If there's a fire in the computer room or a theft of computers, the data is gone unless it has also been backed up. This sometimes entails using tape backup as a secondary recovery method.

Disk-based backups are becoming more common as declining disk costs drives the growth of disk-based backup appliances. A separate disk-based backup appliance can store network data and, because it is typically located away from servers on the network, can provide some additional security from the servers. However, if it is located onsite, it is still vulnerable to sitewide problems such as flooding or fire and it might be vulnerable to attack as well. It requires that disk data be transmitted across the network, so it might also require the use of additional security and data encryption, which could have a negative impact on network performance.

Some companies use co-location to have their data stored both on their site and mirrored at another site. This is often done for load-balancing purposes for Internet-accessible resources such as e-commerce sites that have servers around the country or globe in order to improve response times. In these configurations, data is replicated among these sites, often on a real-time basis. If one site fails due to site or connectivity issues, the other sites automatically pick up the slack. Once the failed site comes back online, the data is replicated to that site and it comes back into service.

The solution you select for your company will depend on a number of variables, including your company's size, relative importance of computers, data and the network in your business, your budget, and your company's risks relative to the costs of data loss. A solid backup and recovery plan is your best insurance against downtime and catastrophic data loss for the enterprise.

Remember, too, that disaster planning is part of the larger business continuity planning activity and should be incorporated into the corporate planning process. When IT disaster planning is viewed as a stand-alone departmental project, there might be serious gaps in the plan that could be addressed by a companywide disaster recovery planning process.

Table 9.8 outlines practices that will help ensure your data is safe regardless of any problem that might occur.

Table 9.8 Safeguarding Your Systems

Practice	Explanation
Best practices	Follow best practices for security, backups, and restores. Secure computers in access-controlled locations.
Specify what you want the computer to do if it stops unexpectedly.	In **Control Panel** under **System** on the **Advanced** tab, you can specify what you want the system to do during startup or recovery. Figure 9.44 shows these options found by clicking the **Settings** button in the **Startup and Recovery** section on the **Advanced** tab of System Properties in Control Panel.
Backups	Perform regular backups and follow best practices for backups to ensure security of data and backup media.
Create Automated System Recovery (ASR) backup set.	Use the ASR Wizard to create a backup of the system state and other critical configuration and system files.
Keep the installation CD accessible but safe from a malicious user.	You'll need the installation CD to recovery from a system failure using Recovery Console or the ASR set. Make sure the installation CD is accessible but secured. For example, leaving it in your desk drawer is not a good idea, but locking it in bank vault isn't a great idea either. Find a balance between accessibility and security.
Install the Recovery Console for x-86-based systems.	You might want to install the Recovery Console for x-86-based systems to assist with system failure recovery.
Review and test backup and recovery plans.	As you'll see in this section, good safeguards include creating backup and recovery plans and testing those plans on a regular, periodic basis to ensure each element of the plan works as expected.
Reduce single points of failure.	Finding and reducing single points of failure, especially related to disk devices, can reduce the likelihood of failure and improve recovery time after a failure.

Figure 9.44 Startup and Recovery Options for Local Computer via Control Panel

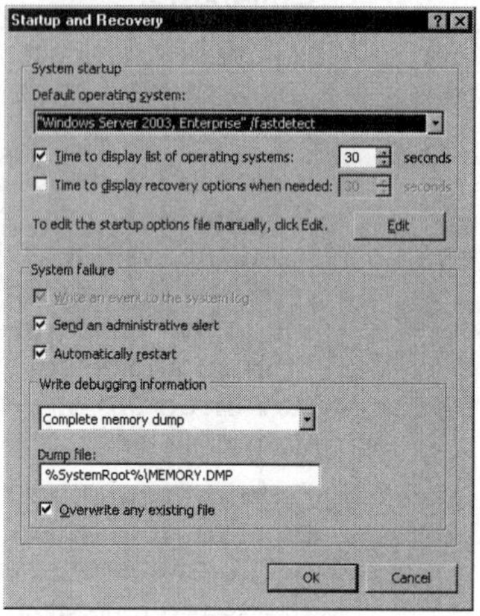

Designing a Secure Backup Process

A secure backup process includes planning the backup process, storing backup media, and assigning (and monitoring) backup and restore rights. The process of backing up files is an opportunity for a malicious user to make a copy of important data files and take them to a computer on which he or she has administrative rights and restore the data to his or her own computer. Therefore, the process of planning and implementing the backup process requires consideration of the security aspects along with everything else.

Planning the backup process requires that you think about where computers are located, where users store their data, and how often data should be backed up. Are servers located in one room, or across the state, country, or world? Are servers locally administered, or are servers administered remotely? How often does critical data change, and how often should you back up data files and system state data? Where are backup devices located and what's the best method for backing data up to these devices? Who's in charge of backing up the data? How will you know if it's been completed successfully? These and many other questions should be asked and answered during the planning phase to ensure that the data remains safe. A good security plan, while delineating possible attacks and desired defense methods, should also include how to recover *after* an attack or system device failure.

As a quick refresher, you probably remember that backups can be full, incremental, differential, copy, daily, or normal. Each is briefly described here:

- **Copy** Copies files but does not mark them as having been backed up.
- **Daily** Copies all selected files that have been modified on the day of the daily backup.

- **Differential** Copies all files that have been created or changed since the last normal or incremental backup was performed. Files are not marked as having been backed up.
- **Incremental** Copies all files that have been created or changed since the last normal or incremental backup was performed. Files are marked as having been backed up.
- **Normal** Copies all files you select and marks each as having been backed up.

Backing up files using incremental or differential backup methods can be faster, but requires the use of backup sets to fully restore a system. For example, if a system crashed, you would need the last normal backup set as well as every incremental (or differential) set created since the last normal backup was created. If you perform a normal backup every Sunday night and a system crashes on Saturday afternoon, you would need last Sunday's normal backup along with the incremental (or differential) backup from Monday, Tuesday, Wednesday, Thursday, and Friday. Although you save time each night during your backup process, you'll spend more time recovering. Conversely, if you perform a normal backup on a more frequent (or even daily) basis, you'll spend more time in the backup process but your recovery process will be fairly short. You'll need to review your company's situation to determine the best solution for you.

Another critical element of designing a secure backup process is giving thought to who should perform the backups. In highly secure environments, only members of the Administrators group should be given backup and restore rights. In medium- or low-risk environments, backup and restore rights can be assigned to different individuals. If one person has permission to back up but not the permissions to restore, the likelihood of malicious users gaining unauthorized access to data is reduced. While a malicious user could take the backups and restore them to a machine to which he or she has administrative rights, it is less dangerous than giving that person backup and restore permissions. Trusted staff can perform backups and restores and they should be fully trained in such procedures to ensure that they can perform their tasks unaided, if needed.

Finally, backup media must be secured. Using multiple sets allows for backups to be stored offsite. This can help in terms of safeguarding the media from fire or flooding, but makes the media less accessible in case there is the need to restore. For example, if you decide to store your media in a bank vault, you are out of luck if you need to restore from backup media in the middle of the night or on a Sunday when the bank is closed. As an alternative, you can use data storage companies—both offline and online. These carry their own risks, including placing your valuable data in someone else's hands. Some companies compromise and keep the latest backup onsite, and the second or third most recent backup in an offsite location. This way, if you need to restore, the worst case is that you'll have to restore from a backup that is a few days old that you retrieve from your offsite location. You must assess the pros and cons of such a plan and decide which is the best blend of security and convenience for your company given its unique risk profile.

Best Practices for Backups

A number of practices, when properly implemented, can create a secure method of backing up data. Table 9.9 summarizes these best practices.

Table 9.9 Best Practices for Backups

Backup Best Practice	Explanation
Develop backup and restore plans and test them.	Without a plan, it will be difficult to know if your all data is safe. Planning on when, where, and how backups are performed and data stored will help you recover more quickly if disaster does strike.
Train personnel on backup and restore procedures.	Depending on security needs, you can train staff (users who are not Administrators) to perform backups and restores. For minimum and medium security situations, train one person (or group) to perform backups and train a separate person (or group) to perform restores. Grant privileges for either backup or restore to separate these tasks to maintain some security. For high-security networks, only assign these permissions and tasks to members of the Administrator group. Train those with backup or restore rights thoroughly so these tasks are performed correctly.
Back up all data on system and boot volumes and the system state.	Backing up all data and the system state at the same time provides an accurate "snap shot" of the system, making restoring from backup easier in the event of a disk failure. The system state is not backed up along with disk data unless specifically selected. If the computer on which the backups are performed is a DC, the system state data will include the Active Directory database, SYSVOL directory. For all servers, system state data includes certificates. For servers and member computers, system state data includes the Registry, system files, boot files, and files under Windows File Protection.

Continued

Table 9.9 Best Practices for Backups

Backup Best Practice	Explanation
Create an Automated System Recovery (ASR) backup set.	Always create an Automated System Recovery (ASR) backup set whenever there are any changes to the system, including changes to the operating system, applications, hardware, drivers, or the application of patches and service packs. Having a current ASR can make recovering from a system failure much easier and faster.
Create a backup log.	Always opt to create a backup log, and then print and file the log. This will make it easier to find specific files later if the drive or system fails. The backup log is also helpful when restoring systems, especially if there are any problems during the recovery process such as failure of a backup medium.
Retain copies.	Some companies rotate between two backup sets, the one used yesterday and the one that will be used today. While this might be less confusing and more economical, it does not provide solid backup. Three sets should be the minimum, with one set stored offsite at a secure location.
Perform test restores.	Many companies do a great job backing up but never test their restore functions. The worst time to find out that your backups aren't working properly is when you're trying to restore after a disk failure. Periodically test your backups by restoring data with those backups. A test restore can also uncover hardware or software problems that might not appear when you simply verify the backup.
Use the default volume shadow copy backup.	A volume shadow copy is a duplicate copy of the original disk contents taken at the time the copy (backup) began. If you disable this feature, files that are open or are being used by the system will be skipped during the backup process, leaving you with an incomplete backup.

Continued

Table 9.9 Best Practices for Backups

Backup Best Practice	Explanation
Secure devices and media.	Both the storage device (tape drive, etc.) and the storage media (tapes, disks, etc.) should be secured. If someone gains access to backup devices and/or media, he or she could simply use the device and the backups on a computer on which he or she has administrative privileges.
Back up the server cluster effectively.	In the event of an application data or quorum loss, individual node or complete cluster failure, you should ensure you have: Performed ASR backup on each node in the cluster. Backed up the cluster disks from each node. Backed up each individual application running on the nodes.

Creating an Automated System Recovery Backup Set

To safeguard against catastrophic failure, you should create an *Automated System Recovery backup set*, and update the ASR every time a significant change occurs on the system. Significant changes include adding or removing applications or software, installing/removing or modifying drivers or hardware, or replacing components. You can use the Automated System Recovery Wizard, which will create two-part backups you can use to recover you system after other attempts have failed or after you've replaced a disk drive. ASR backs up the system state, including disk volumes, Active Directory, and other critical components. It also creates a startup disk that provides information about disk configuration, and how to perform the restore. We'll step through this process in Exercise 9.09.

Exercise 9.09

Creating an Automatic System Recovery Backup Set

In this exercise, you'll create an ASR backup set for your system. To perform this task, you must be a member of the Administrator group or Backup Operators group on the local computer, or you must have been delegated the proper authority. You will need a blank 1.44MB floppy disk, as well as media to hold your data files.

1. Click **Start | All Programs | Accessories | System Tools | Backup**.
2. Click **Next** on the Welcome screen of the **Backup or Restore Wizard**.
3. You can choose to either **Back up files and settings** or **Restore files and settings**. Back up files and settings is selected by default. Click **Next** to continue.
4. In the **What to Back Up** screen, you can select to back up **All information on this computer** or **Let me choose what to back up**. If you select **Let me choose what to back up**, the next screen will allow you to select which items you want from a list of all items on the computer. For this exercise, choose the default, **All information on this computer**.
5. The next screen is **Backup Type, Destination, and Name**. In this screen, you can select your backup type, choose the destination to which files should be saved, and give a unique name to the backup for easy identification later. Once you've specified these parameters, click **Next**.
6. The final screen of the Backup or Restore Wizard verifies the backup settings you've selected. If you want to modify these settings, click **Back**. If you want to access Advanced settings, click **Advanced**. Advanced settings include:
   - The ability to select Normal, Incremental, Differential, Copy, or Daily types of backups.
   - Whether to back up files that have migrated to Remote Storage.
   - Whether to use verification, compression, or disable volume shadow copy (discussed earlier).
   - Whether to overwrite data or append data and whether to restrict access to the data.
   - Whether you want to schedule the backup to occur now or at another time.
7. To begin backups, click **Finish**. If you do not want to start the backup, you can either select **Cancel** or click **Advanced** to schedule the backup for another time.
8. The backup file will be saved with the .BKF extension in the location you specified.

This backup will only back up files necessary to restore your system to a functional state; you'll need to back up data files separately. After you create the ASR set, perform a data backup and keep the ASR set and the backup media together and labeled as a set. To use the backup media, you'll need to use the floppy disk created as part of the ASR set. You cannot use a floppy belonging to an ASR set created at a different time. You must also have your Setup CD available at the time you perform Automated System Recovery (the recovery, not the backup).

If your system does not have a floppy disk, you can copy the asr.sif and asrpnp.sif files from the *%systemroot%*\repair directory to another computer, but you must then copy those files onto a floppy disk. Before you can restore a computer using ASR, you must install a floppy drive.

EXAM WARNING

You won't be specifically tested on the elements of best practices—you won't see questions asking which element is or is not a "best practice." Instead, you'll see questions in which the correct answer relies on best practices and the wrong answers do not. This can be subtle, so when looking for correct answers on the exam, consider whether the answer falls into best practices. If not, you know the answer is probably incorrect.

Disaster Recovery Best Practices

Disaster recovery includes creating backups, creating recovery options, and using repair and recovery tools. There are several practices that, if implemented, can significantly improve your disaster recovery preparedness and security. We all know that disks crash, viruses infect, and data corruption occurs due to intentional and unintentional acts. Trying to anticipate problems and planning for them is always the first step in any disaster recovery process. Table 9.10 summarizes these best practices.

Table 9.10 Disaster Recovery Best Practices

Best Practice	Description
Create a plan for performing regular backup operations.	Although we already covered best practices for backups, it bears repeating here. If you do backups occasionally, you'll lose significantly more time and data than if you perform regular backups. Depending on the nature of your company and its data, you might find that backups every few hours or twice a day are required to avoid significant data loss. For many businesses, daily backups are a good balance between the need to secure data and the actual process of performing the backups.
Keep the installation CD where you can quickly and easily find it.	In some cases, you can recover a system by using the installation CD and the Recovery Console or Automated System Recovery. We'll discuss each of these later in this chapter. However, some people mistakenly think that securing the installation CD offsite or in an access-controlled location to which they do not have free access is a good idea. Always make sure the installation CD is readily available, although keeping it in a secure location onsite is certainly advisable.
Use Emergency Management Services, if applicable.	This is a new feature in Windows Server 2003. With Emergency Management Services, you can remotely manage a server in emergency situations that would normally require local access to keyboard, mouse, and monitor, such as when the network is unavailable or the server is not working properly. There are specific hardware requirements for Emergency Management Services, and it can be used only for Windows Server 2003 computers. We'll discuss this later in the chapter.
Install (and secure) the Recovery Console as a startup option.	If you are running a computer based on the Intel x-86 chip, you can install the Recovery Console in the event you are unable to restart Windows. You cannot install the Recovery Console on an Itanium-based computer. We'll look at this in this later in this section.

Continued

Table 9.10 Disaster Recovery Best Practices

Best Practice	Description
Specify startup and recovery options.	You can configure the computer to take specific actions if the computer stops unexpectedly. For example, you can configure it so that your computer restarts automatically and generates a log file. We'll look at this later in this section as well.

A disaster recovery plan should also include an assessment of the most likely risks to your business and its data. For example, if you live in an area where flooding is common, you should think about the impact of a flood on your business and how you might recover if your building were to be flooded. What impact would a fire in the building have on the network and computers? Thinking of possible scenarios and creating plans for these "what if" scenarios will help you create thorough disaster recovery plans. In a moment, we'll look at some of the features in Windows Server 2003 that you can use for disaster recovery. First, though, it's important to understand the terms *in-band* and *out-of-band*, since they are important in recovery scenarios in Windows Server 2003.

Head of the Class...

In-Band and Out-of-Band Management

In the next section, as well as in other discussions of server management, you might hear or read about in-band management and out-of-band management. Let's take a look at these briefly.

In-band refers to two computers that can connect using normal network services. It relies on a standard network such as the LAN or the Internet. You can use standard management tools such as Remote Desktop or Telnet to manage the computer because it is online and working properly. You are able to communicate in a normal fashion with this remote computer via the established connection. This is called *in-band management* or an *in-band connection*.

In-band connections are available only when the computer is fully initialized and functioning properly. The typical in-band remote management hardware device is the network adapter, although an Integrated Services Digital Network (ISDN) or analog modem can be used as the in-band remote management hardware device. Some of the tools available in Windows Server 2003 to manage in-band connections are the MMC, Systems Management Server, Telnet, Terminal Services Remote Desktop for Administration, and the Windows Management Instrumentation

Continued

(WMI). There are also numerous non-Microsoft in-band management tools available on the market.

Out-of-band refers to a connection that can be made when a remote computer is not working properly. When you are unable to manage the server via an in-band connection, the ideal alternative is to be able to manage the server through a reliable alternate connection called an out-of-band connection. An out-of-band connection does not rely on network drivers to function properly as an in-band connection does. Using special hardware or firmware, you can manage a remote server that is disabled or not functioning using an out-of-band connection.

Out-of-band connections can be useful if:

- The computer is turned off.
- The server is not functioning properly because of a Stop message event,.
- The BIOS power-on self test (POST) test is running.
- The server is low on resources.
- The network stack is malfunctioning.
- An operating system component has failed (including failure of the Recovery Console, discussed later in this section).
- The server is not yet fully initialized.

As you can see, having a reliable out-of-band method of managing a remote server can be very useful in many different scenarios.

For out-of-band connections, the hardware device is most commonly the serial port for several reasons. First, most x-86 servers have at least one serial port. Second, serial ports are simple, reliable ports that provide a flexible solution since serial port communication standards are well established and supported across all operating systems.

Now that you understand the in-band and out-of-band management systems for Windows Server 2003, let's take a look at Emergency Management Services, which relies on out-of-band connections.

Securing Emergency Management Services

Emergency Management Services is a new feature in Windows Server 2003, and provides native support for server operation and management that can be performed remotely without a local keyboard, mouse, or monitor. It can be used on x-86 and Itanium-based systems.

Emergency Management Services uses a terminal text mode rather than a graphical user interface (GUI). This provides the ability to manage computers that are not fully functional or not fully initialized. It also provides interoperability with other platforms, including UNIX. Emergency Management Services are typically available during all phases of computer startup, including when the computer is turned on, when firmware is initializing, when the operating system is loading, and when other elements (GUI, for example) are loading or when any of these elements runs into problems.

There are three key features in Emergency Management Services that we'll discuss here:

- Console redirection
- Special Administration Console (SAC) environment
- !Special Administration Console (!SAC) environment

Console Redirection

Console redirection is the process whereby a computer receives keyboard input from a remote computer and responds with output to the remote computer's monitor using an in-band or out-of-band connection. A computer can be controlled by both in-band and out-of-band connections at the same time. Emergency Management Services output is available using a terminal emulator. If a computer is configured with Emergency Management Services, the following computer services will redirect their output to the out-of-band management port and to the video card, if one is present:

- Setup loader
- Text-mode Setup
- Recovery Console
- Remote Installation Services
- Stop error messages
- Loader

Console redirection uses a text display mode for compatibility. Character mode (rather than a graphical user interface) is more compatible with serial ports and slower connections. Character mode is what you use when you open a command prompt in Windows Server 2003 by clicking **Start | Run | cmd**. In addition to hardware compatibility, character mode is also a more flexible option across software platforms. Character mode is a basic mode and is supported by Windows as well as by non-Microsoft operating systems, including UNIX.

There are essentially three ways console redirection can occur under Windows Server 2003. The computer for which console redirection is desired can have specialized firmware or hardware install that support console redirection, or it can use Windows components such as *Ntldr* via Emergency Management Services.

Firmware Console Redirection

System *firmware* that supports console redirection can be used with Windows Server 2003 and with Emergency Management Services. For x-86-based systems, the Basic Input Output System (BIOS) can support console redirection. On Itanium-based systems, the extensible firmware interface (EFI) supports console redirection. The EFI on Itanium-based systems supports console redirection by default, but you might need a firmware upgrade for x-86-based systems before console redirection can be implemented. Once available, console redirection can be used in four specific ways, summarized in Table 9.11.

Table 9.11 Firmware Console Redirection

Management Task	Description
Remotely view startup process.	You can monitor the progress of the Power On Self Test (POST), disk error messages, and other messages displayed by the firmware during the startup process. A computer using firmware console redirection typically can complete the POST process without an attached keyboard, mouse, or monitor.
Remotely view and edit firmware settings.	You can remotely access the configuration program via the firmware to make changes such as changing the boot order or disabling an integrated hardware device. Without this firmware functionality, you would have to make these changes at the local computer.
Remotely view and respond to Pre-Boot eXecution Environment (PXE) prompts.	If the firmware supports the PXE standard, you can remotely view and respond to the F12 network boot prompt.
Remotely view and respond to the boot from CD prompt.	With the firmware console redirection capability, you can remotely respond to the prompt Press Any Key to Boot From CD when starting the server from the Windows Server operating system CD.

Service Processor Console Redirection

A server that contains specialized hardware can also support console redirection. This component is called a *service processor and* supports a range of activities, including console redirection. Since a service processor is a hardware component, you should consult the service processor documentation to understand the features of the particular hardware component installed. Service processors are typically integrated into the motherboard or into a PCI adapter. Since Emergency Management Services requires that the Windows loader or kernel be at least somewhat functional, a service processor that can respond when the remote computer is completely unresponsive might be useful in some scenarios. In cases where the Windows loader or kernel is completely disabled, a service processor can still respond because it operates independently of the computer's processor(s) and the operating system. Service processors contain their own firmware and can respond with console redirection and other functions even when the operating system is disabled. Most service processors use the serial port or RJ-45 Ethernet port for out-of-band connections. If the out-of-band connection used is a serial port, you can only use one tool at a time. This means that you can either use the service processor *or* the Emergency Management Services, but not both at the same time.

Windows Console Redirection

Windows contains services that support console redirection as well. The *Ntldr* component of Windows supports console redirection and can be used with Emergency Management Services. If Emergency Management Services is enabled when Windows Server 2003 initializes, the operating system takes over the responsibility for console redirection from the firmware. The ability to redirect console output is built into several Windows components, summarized in Table 9.12.

Table 9.12 Windows Components that Support Console Redirection

Windows Component	Description
Windows loader for x-86-based systems (*Ntldr*)	When *Ntldr* is running, you can remotely view or select the Recovery Console. On x-86-based systems with a multiboot option, you can select which operating system to boot.
Windows kernel (*Ntoskrnl.exe*)	The *kernel* is the core of the Windows operating system. Code that runs as part of the kernel can directly access hardware devices and system data. As a result, the Windows kernel can redirect console output so you can remotely view normal system operations or view Stop message text when a problem occurs.

Continued

Table 9.12 Windows Components that Support Console Redirection

Windows Component	Description
Recovery console	The Recovery Console is a command-line utility that allows you to perform advanced troubleshooting and maintenance, such as disabling a device or driver you suspect is causing problems during the boot process.
Command prompt (*cmd.exe*)	A character mode user interface for running commands and applications.
Text-mode Setup (including the CD-ROM Setup loader)	Early in the Windows installation process, the system is in text mode when files are being copied from the distribution source to the local hard drive.
Startrom.com at 9600 baud for x-86-based computers	Starts the x-86-based Remote Installation Services (RIS) process. The startrom.com file is downloaded and run by the RIS client to initiate operating system installation. Special versions of the startrom.com program that use 9600 baud are required to support Emergency Management Services console redirection.

Special Administration Console Environment

The *Special Administration Console (SAC)* is the primary Emergency Management Services command-line environment. As a kernel mode component, SAC provides out-of-band management functionality when Windows runs in GUI mode. You can use SAC to manage the server during normal operations, in safe mode, and in the GUI phase of Windows Server 2003 startup. Once you've enabled Emergency Management Services, SAC is always available as long as the kernel is functional. Using SAC during an operating system upgrade or installation, though, might cause the upgrade or installation to become unstable or fail.

SAC is not secured by password and logon requirements. As such, physical access to computers running Emergency Management Services must be restricted. We'll discuss securing Emergency Management Services in a moment.

SAC provides a number of commands that you can use to perform remote management tasks, including:

- Restarting or shutting down the computer.
- Viewing a list of processes that are currently active.
- Ending processes.
- Setting or viewing the IP address of the computer.

- Generating a STOP error to create a memory dump file.
- Starting and accessing command prompts.

!Special Administration Console Environment

The *!Special Administration Console (!SAC)* is an abbreviated version of the SAC. !SAC accepts input from and directs output to an out-of-band connection. !SAC is a separate function from SAC and from the command prompt (*cmd.exe*). You cannot access !SAC directly as you can with SAC. Instead, if a particular point of failure occurs, Emergency Management Services transitions from SAC to !SAC automatically. For example, if the graphics driver fails or you are attempting to start in safe mode via SAC and safe mode fails to start, the Emergency Management Services will automatically revert to !SAC. Since SAC runs during normal mode, safe mode, and the GUI phase of startup, if errors or failures occur in any of these operating modes, !SAC is invoked. !SAC has a more limited set of functionality than does SAC. !SAC can:

- Remotely view STOP message text.
- Restart the computer.
- View an abbreviated log of loaded drivers and some kernel events.
- Obtain computer identification information.

Enabling Emergency Management Services

If you want to have the capability to manage a computer remotely, you would install Emergency Management Services onto that remote computer. Before you begin a CD-based Windows Server 2003 operating system setup, you must enable the computer's firmware to support console redirection (discussed in a moment). Emergency Management Services configures itself during a bootable CD installation by reading the Serial Port Console Redirection (SPCR) table. If Emergency Management Services is enabled, you are prompted at the end of text-mode Setup to allow setup to automatically configure your system without user input. You must choose this option. Otherwise, the next part of the setup, known as the GUI-mode Setup, completes only if you provide input through a local monitor and keyboard. If the computer's firmware does not support the SPCR table, you must fully automate setup.

To enable Emergency Management Services after Windows Server 2003 has been installed, you must edit the Boot.ini file to enable Windows loader console redirection and Special Administration Console. The Boot.ini file controls the system startup and is located on the system partition root. The Boot.ini file can be edited via the *Bootcfg.exe* command-line utility.

Headless Servers

A *headless server* is a computer than is configured to run without a local keyboard, mouse, or display device (typically a monitor). Emergency Management Services, with support of hardware or firmware console redirection, makes it possible to configure headless servers running Windows Server 2003. Since a computer running Emergency Management Services can use both in-band and out-of-band connections, you can manage a headless server without any local input or output devices.

Terminal Concentrators

Terminal concentrators provide remote access to multiple servers via out-of-band connections. The servers connect to serial ports on the terminal concentrators via null modem cables. A null modem cable crosses the Clear to Send (CTS) and Ready to Send (RTS) signals, emulating the process of modems communicating with one another. This type of cable is often used for direct connections on serial ports between two devices in a local connection configuration. The remote management computer establishes a connection to the terminal concentrator via its network port. Most often, you'll use Telnet or a Web interface to manage servers connected via a terminal concentrator. This provides the ability to manage several remote servers via the terminal concentrator, and allows multiple administrators to simultaneous view or manage servers remotely.

Many terminal concentrators come with built-in security functions, such as enabling the use of passwords and/or encryption. Some support Secure Shell (SSH), a secure command-line utility that is comparable to the nonsecure Telnet function. SSH provides strong in-band security, including authentication, encryption, and protection against some network-level attacks. SSH is independent of the operating system and is therefore suitable for use in a mixed operating system environment. However, not all terminal concentrators provide built-in security functions, so you'll need to consult with the vendor's documentation to see what, if any, security is provided. If the terminal concentrator provides no support for authentication and encryption, you have several options for securing out-of-band traffic, including:

- Use a router to secure the network traffic.
- Use SSH (if supported) rather than Telnet.
- Use a secondary management network that you can access via direct-dial remote access or via a VPN connection.

Uninterruptible Power Supplies

Emergency Management Services works with intelligent *uninterruptible power supplies* (UPS) if firmware-based console redirection is supported. Many companies use the UPS capability to maintain consistent power to critical computers during times of electrical instability or failure. Electrical service can become unstable during lightning storms, for example, or during peak load times when power cycles and lights dim in response to heavy loads. A UPS can provide power in the event of a total power failure, although for most companies it is typically used for the orderly shutdown of computers rather than as a method of keeping computers running after power is off.

Some UPS units, known as *intelligent UPSs*, provide the ability to remotely cycle the power on a computer. By itself, this capability is limited, but it can be used in conjunction with Emergency Management Services. For Emergency Management Services systems with firmware console redirection enabled, an intelligent UPS system can extend Emergency Management Services by responding to commands sent to it. To use an intelligent UPS with Emergency Management Services, the UPS must be able to passively monitor traffic on the serial port and respond to key sequences related to UPS functions.

Securing the Remote Management Process

Although remote management is outside the scope of this chapter, it's important to understand that remote management can create a security risk. Before managing computers remotely, especially using out-of-band tools, it's important to develop a remote management plan that will ensure you use the most appropriate (and secure) remote management tools and configurations for your organization. The plan should include server configuration, server location, and server roles, as well as availability requirements and designated administrators for servers you plan to manage remotely. Addressing these elements will ensure you do not inadvertently create a security hole via remote management capabilities.

Out-of-Band Security

We've seen how Emergency Management Services works when the computer is in various stages of startup, setup, and operation. These capabilities are an important part of disaster planning and recovery. Remote server management creates its own unique set of challenges related to security. When you manage servers remotely, information that would not normally cross the network is sent as part of the remote management function. This information might include server identification, configuration information, or other sensitive data, including usernames and passwords. If someone is sniffing or eavesdropping on the network, you must be sure this remote management data is secure. Moreover, when using out-of-band connections via serial ports, null modem connections between servers and management computers (or terminal concentrators) provide no logical security at all.

A secure remote management strategy includes setting up the following constraints:

- Servers that allow administrative commands only from an authenticated computer.

- Servers that accept administrative commands only from an authenticated administrator.
- Confidential information such as usernames, passwords, and server information cannot be intercepted, read, or changed.
- Log files are viewed by using a secure method.

While configuring security for remote management is outside the scope of this chapter, you should consider strong authentication and encryption of data, and consider implementing IPSec for traffic between the remote management server and the remote server to secure sensitive data such as server identification information and passwords as they traverse the network. It's also very important to limit physical access to both remote management servers and the remote servers. A headless remote server provides some element of security if it does not employ the use of a keyboard, mouse, or monitor. However, because the connection is typically by serial port (or sometimes a commonly used RJ-45 Ethernet connection), the physical connections should be secured and the best way to do that is to put the servers in access-controlled areas. In addition to secure areas, keeping cable lengths short prevents them from being extended outside the secured area to another computer. Finally, using terminal concentrators or intelligent UPSs to consolidate access to servers and keeping these components in access-secured areas also helps.

For logical security, ensure that you properly assign rights and permissions for computers that will be used to remotely manage other servers. Best practices suggest providing the fewest permissions to the fewest people in order to adequately perform the necessary tasks.

Best Practices for Securing Emergency Management Services

Table 9.13 summarizes best practices related to securing Emergency Management Services and out-of-band connections. Typically, in-band connections are secured via normal network security, so our focus is on out-of-band connections.

Table 9.13 Securing Emergency Management Services Out-of-Band Connections

Action	Description
Limit physical access to the server(s).	Place servers running Emergency Management Services in access-controlled locations.
User a terminal concentrator with security features.	If you use a terminal concentrator for accessing servers via out-of-band connections, choose one that provides security when you connect through the network.

Continued

Table 9.13 Securing Emergency Management Services Out-of-Band Connections

Action	Description
Use service processors with well-designed security.	If you decide to use service processors in your implementation, select ones that have well-designed security. Service processors provide additional access, which creates a security risk. Ensure the service processors you use have strong security that secures the access to the server via the service processor.
If needed, set up a second network for remote management.	In some cases, it might make sense to set up a separate remote management network for all management traffic, including Emergency Management Services traffic. A separate network used with a router or firewall can add a layer of security. Only allow secure management workstations and authenticated users. Do not allow any connections to the Internet.

EXAM WARNING

Emergency Management Services is a new feature in Windows Server 2003, so expect to see at least a question or two that involves using this feature. Using Emergency Management Services or the Recovery Console introduces security risks that must be addressed, so expect to see questions along that line in the exam.

Securing the Recovery Console

If safe mode and other startup options fail, you can use the Recovery Console to enable and disable services, format drives, read and write data, and perform other administrative tasks. You must use the built-in Administrator account to use the Recovery Console. There are two ways to start the Recovery Console—from the Setup CD or from the Recovery Console *boot.ini* option. You cannot install the Recovery Console on an Itanium-based computer. If you install the Recovery Console on a computer, it will be an available option during the boot sequence. If you have a dual-boot or multiboot machine, you'll need to choose which installation you want to log in to, and you will need to password for the built-in Administrator account for that installation. You can invoke the Recovery Console via the Setup command-line tool, *winnt32.exe*, using the */cmdcons* switch (*winnt32 /cmdcons*). You cannot run Winnt32.exe on an Itanium-based computer, and therefore the */cmdcons* command that invokes the Recovery Console is unavailable.

The Recovery Console provides commands that you can use to do simple operations such as changing or viewing directories, as well as more complex operations such as repairing the boot sector. Typing **help** at the Recovery Console command prompt accesses available Help commands.

Since installing the Recovery Console essentially provides an alternate means of logging on to a computer, it creates a security risk because it bypasses many of the built-in security mechanisms in Windows Server 2003. It's important to assess and understand the security risks involved with the installation of the Recovery Console before installing it. Ideally, the computer should be in an access-controlled area to prevent unauthorized access. Basic security is enforced by requiring the use of the built-in Administrator account username (if different than the default) and password. If you enter the incorrect password three times, Recovery Console will close and the computer will restart. Recovery Console also prevents access to Program Files, Document and Settings, and other installations of the operating system. If you have alternate installations of the operating system, they will be displayed in the initial Recovery Console screen and you can select the installation that you want to work on. Otherwise, by default, you cannot access data files and other installations through Recovery Console.

There are two Group Policy options that can be used in conjunction with the Recovery Console. If you have installed the Recovery Console option, you can enable or disable these two policies:

- **Recovery console** Allow automatic administrative logon.
- **Recover console** Allow floppy copy and access to all drives and all folders.

These are accessed via the Group Policy snap-in or the Security Configuration and Analysis snap-in for the Local Computer in the MMC. After loading the snap-in, select the following path by expanding nodes in the left pane: **Local Computer Policy | Computer Configuration | Windows Settings | Security Settings | Local Policies | Security Options**

The **Recovery console: Allow automatic administrative logon** option determines if a password for the local built-in Administrator account must be given before access to the system is granted. Clearly, if you enable this, you allow anyone to access the system via the Recovery Console. While there might be appropriate uses for this in your organization, it is important to understand that this creates a very easy way to access a system. Even if the computer is in an access-controlled location, you should not enable this unless you have a compelling reason to do so. It is disabled by default and this option is not available unless you have installed the Recovery Console. If you have not, the policy shows in Security Options but both the Enable and Disable functions are disabled (grayed out).

The **Recovery console: Allow floppy copy and access to all drivers and all folders** option enables the Recovery Console SET command, which allows you to set the Recovery Console environment variables listed in Table 9.14.

Table 9.14 Recovery Console Environment Variables

Environment Variables	Description
AllowWildCards	Enables wildcard (*) support for some commands that support wildcards, such as the *DEL* command.
AllowAllPaths	Allow access to all files and folders on the computer.
AllowRemovableMedia	Allow files to be copies to removable media including floppy disk.
NoCopyPrompt	Do not prompt when overwriting an existing file.

As you can see, the environment variables you can set using the **Recovery console: Allow floppy copy and access to all drives and all folders** policy reads like a hacker's wish list. This option is disabled by default. Even if you have opted to **Allow automatic administrative logon** (bypassing the need for a password), the Administrator (or other user) would still be limited in his or her access to the system. By default, Recovery Console limits access to Program Files, and Documents and Settings, among others. However, when you enable the **Allow floppy copy and access to all drives and all folders** policy, you enable access to all files, all folders, allow the use of wildcards, and allow files to be copied to removable media.

Clearly, the security risk of enabling these policies must be evaluated against whatever organizational need you believe justifies enabling them. If you believe the risk outweighs the benefits, you should not enable these options. If you believe the benefit outweighs the risk and you're confident that you understand your organization's risk profile, then you can elect to enable these via the Security Policy options.

Specifying Startup Options for Computers

You can specify what actions a computer should take if it does stop unexpectedly. This is set in the computer's System properties in Control Panel. Exercise 9.10 steps you through the process of specifying startup and recovery options on the local computer.

Exercise 9.10

Configuring System for Startup and Recovery Options

In this exercise, we'll step through configuring startup recovery options for the local computer.

1. Click **Start | Control Panel | System**.
2. In the System Properties dialog, click the **Advanced** tab.
3. In the **Startup and Recovery** section, click **Settings**.
4. In the **System startup** section, select **Time to display recovery options when needed**. Set the time, in seconds, to the length of time you want recovery options to be displayed.
5. In the **System failure** section, notice that **Write an event to the system log** is selected but disabled, as shown in Figure 9.45. This is selected by default for Windows Server 2003 and cannot be de-selected. This option is available in Windows XP and can be enabled or disabled.

Figure 9.45 Startup and Recovery Options

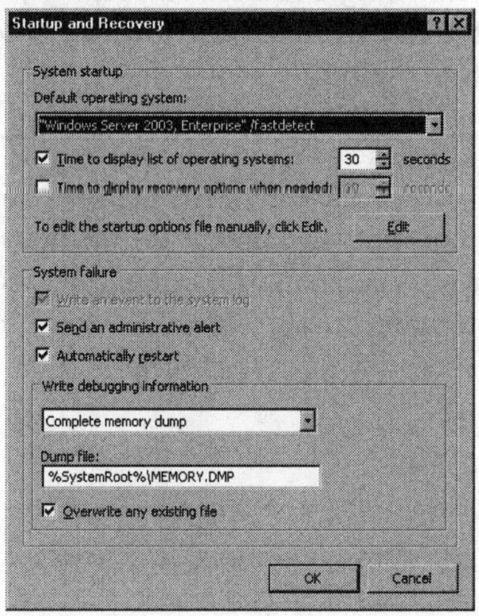

6. In the **System failure** section, you can also select **Send an administrative alert** and **Automatically restart**, which are selected by default. Selecting **Send an administrative alert** causes the system to send an alert to the system administrator when a Stop error occurs. Windows uses the *net send* command

to send the alert over the network to the system administrator. If **Automatically restart** is selected, the computer will restart after sending the alert.

7. In the **Write debugging information,** you can select **None, Small memory dump (64K), Kernel memory dump**, or **Complete memory dump**. **Complete memory dump** is selected by default. A small memory dump will provide basic information about an unexpected stop. A kernel memory dump only records kernel memory information. It is larger than a small memory dump and will take a bit more time but is faster than a complete memory dump. A complete memory dump is not available on computers with more than 2GB of RAM. If you select this option, you must have a paging file on the boot volume that is the size of the physical system RAM plus 11MB.
8. You can specify the name and location of the dump file, which defaults to **%systemroot%\memory.dmp**. In addition, by default, the check box is selected to **Overwrite any existing file**. If you choose not to overwrite the existing file, you should occasionally delete old files so you do not take up disk space with unneeded dump files.
9. After confirming the desired settings, click **OK** to accept changes or **Cancel** to exit. Click **OK** or **Cancel** to exit the **System Properties** dialog.

Since a dump file contains the contents of memory at a particular point in time, it might contain sensitive data. Dump files should be secured in the same manner you secure other sensitive data, including with EFS on the local drive and with IPSec when transmitting the data across the network.

Summary of Exam Objectives

Along with designing security to keep the network safe from intrusion, it's equally important to provide security for the files and folders on the network. Creating a robust security plan entails securing network resources at each access point. In this case, after users are authenticated (or in the event that a malicious user gains network access), files and folders can be secured via access control, encryption, and through backup and recovery activities. Protecting sensitive and valuable corporate data is the ultimate goal of all security activities, and in this chapter, we looked at the specific activities included in designing effective access control strategies, implementing and managing the Encrypting File System (EFS), and designing and testing backup and recovery strategies.

Securing data on the network is one of several elements in an overall security plan. Controlling access to files, folders, and other resources is the second line of defense after a strong user authentication strategy. Once users gain access to the network, access control strategies provide another layer of security by controlling and monitoring access to system objects at a very granular level. Through the use of access control lists (ACLs), users can be granted access via groups (typically) to needed resources. Following best practices, users are added to groups and groups are added to ACLs to gain specific privileges using the AGDLP method.

User access can be managed via one of several different frameworks, including user/ACL, account group/ACL, account group/resource group, and role-based permissions. Each method has pros and cons and should be reviewed to determine which method is best suited to your organization.

Auditing events provides an additional measure of security and visibility. Auditing activities can include monitoring logon, account use, privilege user, object access, and more. Determining appropriate auditing events and reviewing auditing logs can improve security by showing patterns of access as well as potential intrusion or abuse of privileges.

Registry access is controlled via group policy as well as via security templates (which are applied via group policy). The ability to manage access to the Registry adds a layer of security since the Registry is the heart of any Windows-based computer (since Windows 95).

The Encrypted File System (EFS) is a built-in feature in Windows Server 2003 that includes several enhancements over the Windows 2000 capabilities. EFS protects files and folders with encryption. If a malicious user manages to gain access to network resources, he or she will be unable to read an encrypted file. This is especially helpful on mobile computers such as laptops that can easily be stolen and hard drives removed to systems on which the thief has administrative privileges. In this case, the files remain encrypted and will be useless to the thief. EFS is also a good tool for securing sensitive corporate files. It adds an additional layer of security after user authentication and access control. Even if these are both breached, an encrypted file will still be unusable for an unauthorized person.

With EFS, folders and files can be encrypted in a manner completely transparent to the user. Following best practices, folders should be encrypted so that all files within the folder are automatically encrypted as are any temporary files related to the encrypted file. When EFS is implemented, it will use the user's certificate if one exists or will request on from a certificate authority (CA), if available. If neither is available, EFS will self-generate a certificate for file and folder encryption. A file is stored with both the user's encrypted certificate information and the recovery agent certificate information in the header. This ensures that any file encrypted by any user can be decrypted by the user or the recovery agent in the event the user loses his or her credentials or the user leaves the firm. Through recovery policy, you can designate any number of recovery agents that are authorized to recover encrypted files. If the recovery agent's credentials are used to recover the file, the file remains decrypted. It cannot be re-encrypted by the recovery agent to prevent a rogue recovery agent from viewing files without discovery. If a rogue recovery agent opens a file for viewing, it remains decrypted, leaving evidence of tampering.

The *cipher.exe* command can be used to encrypt and decrypt individual files and folders as well as to create recovery agents and other activities related to file and folder encryption. This command-line utility works in conjunction with EFS, which relies on the CryptoAPI, to manage folder and file encryption.

The last line of defense on any system is typically the backup and recovery capabilities. If systems fail due to hardware failure or sabotage, if systems are compromised through intentional attack or viruses, or if a natural disaster such as flooding or fire occurs, backup and recovery procedures can bring a network back online and return the network or system to full functionality.

The key in disaster recovery planning is that it be integrated with corporate business continuity planning so that all strategic business elements are included. IT disaster planning alone might leave gaps in capabilities that are not discovered until the firm is in a recovery phase, which is far too late. Planning includes assessing the data, data types, frequency of data modification, location of data, and more. Once all corporate data has been assessed, creating backup plans includes frequency of backup, type of back up (normal, incremental, differential), backup media (tape, disk, clusters), and location (onsite tape backup, onsite backup appliances, disk sets, offsite tape, offsite disk mirroring).

Recovery plans include not only how and where backups are created and stored, but how to best recover from a system failure. Reducing single points of failure is an important part of reducing the likelihood of needing to recover. Beyond that, a sound recovery plan also includes regular backups, testing backups and restore capabilities, training users (or admins) on backup and restore procedures, as well as using Windows Server 2003 tools such as Emergency Management Services, Automated System Recovery backup sets, and the Recovery Console.

Backup and recovery must also be performed in a secure manner, including securing backup media in secure, access-controlled locations, making multiple backup sets and storing one set offsite, splitting permissions for backup and restore between trusted users or groups to prevent one user from having permission to both backup and restore data, and monitoring all backup and restore activities.

Exam Objectives Fast Track

Designing an Access Control Strategy for Files and Folders

☑ System objects, including files and folders, have access control lists (ACLs) comprised of access control entries (ACE) that grant or deny users or groups specific permissions.

☑ Users can be added directly to ACLs, although this is not a scalable solution and should typically not be used except in specific scenarios where you want to severely limit access (by adding a single user rather than an entire group).

☑ User account groups can be added to ACLs, and this method affords the ability to manage permissions through group membership.

☑ User account groups can be added to resource groups, which are groups on the resource itself (such as a file, folder, or printer). Account groups can be added to resource groups, which are then added to ACLs and assigned specific permissions. This is highly scalable, appropriate for large organizations, but is not recommended if permissions change frequently.

☑ Role-based access requires the use of Windows Server 2003 and applications must support this framework. This method provides very granular setting of permissions based on defined roles within an application.

☑ Auditing allows you to monitor access to files, folders, accounts, and objects. You can also audit the use of privileges to ensure that accounts and permissions are being used as intended.

☑ You can restrict Registry access by using group policy, security templates, or editing the Registry.

Designing an Encrypted File System Strategy

- ☑ Files and folders can be encrypted and decrypted on a folder or file basis using EFS in Windows Server 2003.
- ☑ EFS relies on the CryptoAPI for encryption services.
- ☑ Files that are encrypted can only be decrypted by the original encryptor, users who have been granted permission to access the encrypted file, or the recovery agent.
- ☑ Sharing encrypted files is a new feature of Windows Server 2003 EFS as is the ability to encrypt Web-based files, also a new feature in Windows Server 2003.
- ☑ EFS uses a user's certificate, requests a certificate from a CA, or generates a certificate for use with the encrypted file.
- ☑ A recovery agent is used to recover an encrypted file in the event a user's credentials are lost or a user leaves the company.
- ☑ Additional recovery agents and other recovery settings can be configured via recovery policy in the Group Policy Editor snap-in in the Microsoft Management Console (MMC).
- ☑ The *cipher.exe* command-line utility can be used to encrypt and decrypt files and folders as well as to perform other EFS-related functions such as creating a recovery agent.
- ☑ It's important that a recovery agent's credentials and the user's private key be removed from the system for security purposes. These can be restored to a system to decrypt a file if needed.
- ☑ Importing and exporting certificates and keys can be done via the Certificate snap-in to the MMC.

Designing Security for a Backup and Recovery Strategy

- ☑ Backup and recovery planning are essential elements of security.
- ☑ If a system fails or is compromised in some manner, it must be restored using current backups.
- ☑ Backups should be well planned to provide adequate security for data. Depending on the frequency of data modification, backups can be scheduled in real-time, hourly, daily, or weekly.

- ☑ Backups can be daily, copy, normal, incremental, or differential.
- ☑ Backups can be to local resources or offsite resources, and media typically is either tape or disk.
- ☑ Backup media should be secured since it contains a copy of all corporate data.
- ☑ Backup sets should be created and at least one set should always be kept offsite in the event of a problem with the site itself such as flooding or fire.
- ☑ Recovery plans must include all aspects of bringing the system back online, including restoring the system itself and restoring data to the system.
- ☑ Windows Server 2003 includes several built-in tools that can be used, including Emergency Management Services, the Recovery Console, Automated System Recovery backup sets, and the ability to specify what a system will do in the event of an error or Stop.

Exam Objectives Frequently Asked Questions

The following Frequently Asked Questions, answered by the authors of this book, are designed to both measure your understanding of the Exam Objectives presented in this chapter, and to assist you with real-life implementation of these concepts. You will also gain access to thousands of other FAQs at ITFAQnet.com.

Q: What exactly is the difference between DACLs and SACLs?

A: A discretionary access control list (ACL) defines which users can access an object and with what level of privileges and is often referred to simply as the ACL. The system access control list (SACL) is the part of the object's description that specifies which events are to be audited per user or group. Auditing examples include access, logon attempts, or system shutdowns.

Q: What is the difference between an account group and a resource group?

A: An account group contains users or other groups that are granted permissions to objects via ACLs. A resource group is associated specifically with a resource. Resource groups are granted a specific set of permissions on that resource. Account groups are added to resource groups to grant those specific permissions to those account groups. A resource might have four different resource groups defining four different sets of permissions. Account groups are added to the appropriate resource group to assign those different permissions.

Q: What's the best way to determine an auditing policy?

A: There is always a trade-off between auditing events and system performance. If you audit too many events, the log files become huge and filled with often useless or meaningless data. Conversely, if you do not audit events appropriately, you might miss trends that indicate possible intrusion or attack. Determining which resources are most critical and most vulnerable to what types of attacks will help define an audit policy that is both manageable and meaningful.

Q: What is the difference between using EFS and using a third-party encryption program? What are the pros and cons of each?

A: EFS is built in to Windows Server 2003 and provides encryption of files and folders in a manner transparent to users. It does not require user intervention and works seamlessly with Windows Server 2003. Third-party programs might require user intervention, which weakens security. They might also use password-based recovery agents that are vulnerable to relatively simple password attacks. EFS uses certificates and encryption to protect files, providing the highest level of protection. Third-party programs might not use such strong protection and might create system vulnerabilities. Third-party programs can be helpful in mixed operating system environments where EFS is not available.

Q: Our company doesn't use certificates; can we still use EFS?

A: Yes, EFS will self-generate certificates for use with EFS and file recovery, if no other source of certificates is available. This is especially useful on stand-alone computers that might not have access to network certificate services.

Q: Can I still back up EFS encrypted files or do I need a special tool for this?

A: The Backup program in Windows Server 2003 as well as most third-party backup utilities support copying encrypted files for backup. In Windows Server 2003, those files will remain encrypted when backed up to other media and will remain encrypted when restored from backup media.

Q: We use RAID and mirrored sets, so we don't need additional backups, do we?

A: Both provide redundancy, which helps eliminate single points of failure and reduces the likelihood of data loss through device failure. However, since all your data is still in one location or at one site, it is still vulnerable to other issues such as virus infection, malicious data corruption, or even a natural disaster that can damage or destroy a site. Creating backups and storing them safely offsite will help you recover if any of these events occur.

Q: What is the difference between ASR, Emergency Management Console, and Recovery Console?

A: The Automated System Recovery is made when a backup set is made and allows you to recover system data. This provides the capability to restore a system because the ASR, matched to a backup set, will re-establish system variables and system states, while backups restore data files. The Emergency Management Console can be installed on a system. When installed, it allows an administrator to connect to it via an out-of-band connection such as a serial port or RJ-45 Ethernet port, to issue commands that can manage a disabled system remotely. Emergency Management Console uses console redirection to send and receive simple commands for managing a system. The Recovery Console can be installed on a system and used as a recovery option in the event a system shuts down or fails unexpectedly. The Recovery Console, when enabled, is an option at startup that can be used if safe mode and other start up options fail.

Self Test

A Quick Answer Key follows the Self Test questions. For complete questions, answers, and explanations to the Self Test questions in this chapter as well as the other chapters in this book, see the Self Test Appendix.

Designing an Access Control Strategy for Files and Folders

1. You have been asked to design an access control strategy for your firm and it must be done as soon as possible. The company currently has about 85 employees, each of whom has a desktop or laptop computer. There are four servers functioning in various roles. The departments are Finance, Administration, Customer Service, Trucking, Warehouse Operations, Purchasing, and IT. Your company plans to expand operations in the next one to two years, adding about 28 new employees in that period of time. There is fairly high turnover in the Trucking and Purchasing departments. Seasonal help comes in during the holidays to assist with warehouse operations, and some seasonal staff have computer access. There are a number of staff that change from one department to another based on external business drivers and internal staffing skills. There have never been any attacks on the network and most users have fairly basic computer skills. All systems are Windows Server 2003, Windows 2000 native mode, and Windows XP. Most users have the ability to use e-mail, word processing, and spreadsheet programs. About 10 employees, including those in

the IT department, have advanced skills, and the IT department is comprised of five people, three of whom have advanced programming skills. Based on this information, which access control model is best suited to your organization?

A. Role-based

B. Access group/ resource group

C. Access group/ACL

D. User/ACL

2. You've been looking at users and groups on your network and have decided there are a lot of groups that are probably no longer used. Several key projects have wrapped up and there were several groups created just for those projects. After examining these groups, you decide they're no longer in use and you delete them. During the next hour, you receive phone calls complaining that users can no longer access network resources. What is your best course of action in this situation?

A. Use the *Undo* command to undo the action and restore the deleted groups.

B. Use the *Restore* command to undo the action and restore the deleted groups.

C. Recreate the deleted groups using the same names. The groups will inherit the same permissions as the deleted groups if Active Directory has not been replicated in between deleting the groups and recreating the groups.

D. Recreate the deleted groups and assign users and permissions to restore access to users.

3. Your company is upgrading to Windows Server 2003 and Windows XP across the board. You're using Active Directory in all domains. Your current structure consists of three domains: somecompany.com, admin.somecompany.com, and sales.somecompany.com. In the sales.somecompany.com domain, there are four domain local groups called Managers, Sales, Service, and Tech. Members of the Managers group should have the same permissions as the Executive global group in the admin.somecompany.com domain. What is the best way to give Managers the same privileges as Executives?

A. Add the Managers group to the Executive group.

B. Add the Executive group to the Managers group.

C. Create a universal group named ExecMgr and add both the Executive and Manager groups.

D. Create a nested group under Executives called ExecMgr and add members of the Managers group to this new group.

4. You look in Event Viewer and notice an odd series of events that were logged last night beginning at 11:36 P.M. The events are as listed. Your company runs Monday through Friday, 7 A.M. to 7 P.M., but there are a number of managers who sometimes work late to monitor Web orders and other end-commerce functions. These managers sometimes log in from home and have no restrictions on time-of-day access. Other users have time-of-day restrictions and can only log on between 6:30 A.M. and 7:30 P.M. Four employees are currently on vacation, and two other employees were recently terminated. Based on these events, what is the most likely explanation for what's happening?

```
11:36pm    531: Logon failure. A logon attempt was made using a disabled
                account.
11:37pm    540: A user successfully logged on.
11:37pm    531: Logon failure. A logon attempt was made using a disabled
                account.
11:37pm    531: Logon failure. A logon attempt was made using a disabled
                account.
11:39pm    529: Logon failure. A logon attempt was made with an unknown user
                name or a known user name with a bad password.
11:43pm   540: A user successfully logged on.
11:43pm   529: Logon failure. A logon attempt was made with an unknown user
               name or a known user name with a bad password.
11:44pm   551: A user initiated the log off process.
11:44pm   529: Logon failure. A logon attempt was made with an unknown user
               name or a known user name with a bad password.
11:47pm   551: A user initiated the log off process.
11:47pm   539: Logon failure. The account was locked out at the time the
               logon attempt was made.
```

A. It appears that one of the managers was attempting to log in and mistyped his or her password or username.

B. Someone is attempting a brute force attack.

C. One of the former employees gained unauthorized access to the system.

D. Two attacks might be in progress: one by a former employee and one by an outsider.

Designing an Encrypted File System Strategy

5. Your company recently sent out an e-mail to an employee distribution list that consisted of all managers and all members of the Research department. The e-mail requested that all employees receiving the e-mail immediately begin encrypting all files related to a particular high-profile client. The e-mail suggested that there had been recent attempts to compromise the network and gain access to these sensitive files. The e-mail outlined steps for using EFS to encrypt these sensitive files. Lisa is a corporate executive who works with this high-profile client. She was on a business trip visiting this client when she received the e-mail. While she was waiting for her flight at the airport, she followed the instructions in the e-mail to encrypt sensitive files. Based on this information, what type of encryption certificate does Lisa have?

   A. An EFS self-signed certificate.

   B. An EFS certificate based on cached login credentials.

   C. A certificate issued by the corporate CA.

   D. A temporary EFS certificate to be used until a more reliable certificate is obtained.

6. You use execute the following command in a command prompt window: **cipher /r:financedra** and then you open the MMC, add the Group Policy Editor snap-in, and add to the FinanceOU policy. You expand the nodes until you locate the Encrypting File System node. You click **Add Data Recovery Agent** and specify *financedra.cer*. What have you just accomplished?

   A. You have imported a recovery agent that can be used for all computers and users in the FinanceOU.

   B. You have imported a recovery agent for the local computer that is part of the FinanceOU.

   C. You cannot import this file via the Group Policy Editor snap-in into the Encrypting File System policy. Instead, use the **Certificates snap-in** and import the *financedra.cer* file.

   D. Although you used the *cipher* command, the */r* switch will only create the recovery agent. You must create the private keys and certificate using additional parameters in the *cipher* command.

Design Security for a Backup and Recovery Strategy

7. Your company has four critical servers located in one server room. The first server holds various data files, including all users' files stored on the network. The second server is a proxy server. The third and fourth servers provide critical network functions, including DC and DNS server. You have standard (default) installations of Windows Server 2003 on all servers. You perform incremental backups each night and a full backup on Sundays at 11:30 P.M. for each server. On Monday morning around 9:40 A.M., a brand new virus attacks the proxy server and disables the computer. You're able to download a just-released update for your virus signature file and install it on the proxy server to remove the virus. However, the system is not operational and it appears much of the data has been corrupted. Users cannot reach the Internet and the help desk is suddenly flooded with calls and e-mails. You send out a global e-mail in response and let people know that you expect to have the system up by 11 A.M. What recovery method will best restore the system to a functional state?

   A. Reformat the hard drive on the proxy server, reinstall the operating system, and restore the data files.

   B. Use the Automated System Recovery set generated with the backups to restore both system state and data files.

   C. Use the Emergency Management Services to redirect the console to a remote machine, view the kernel log, and then restore the parts of the system affected by the virus.

   D. Use the Recovery Console option to restore the system to its original state, and then use the backups to restore data files.

8. You have previously installed Windows Server 2003 on seven servers. On four of these servers you've enabled Emergency Management Services. One of these servers experiences a Stop message. You are not sure what's causing the problem, but you notice that the prompt is shown as !SAC. You assumed that you would be able to use the Special Administration Console (SAC) for monitoring, reviewing, and repairing a wide range of problems, but it is not available. The system won't boot in safe mode and you are unable to determine the nature of the problem. What is the most likely cause of the SAC not being available?

   A. !SAC is always available before SAC. Once you've determined the nature of the problem via !SAC commands, you can resolve the problem and use SAC to restore the system to its functional state.

   B. Stop messages typically invoke SAC. In this case, however, because the system cannot start in Safe mode, !SAC was called by the Recovery Console.

C. SAC is not available because some system component failed causing the Stop message.

D. If the server is stopped and restarted via Emergency Management Services using console redirection on an out-of-band connection, it will restart in the !SAC mode by default.

Self Test Quick Answer Key

For complete questions, answers, and explanations to the Self Test questions in this chapter as well as the other chapters in this book, see the Self Test Appendix.

1. **C**
2. **D**
3. **C**
4. **D**
5. **A**
6. **A**
7. **B**
8. **C**

Chapter 10

MCSE 70-298

Securing Network Clients

Exam Objectives in this Chapter:

- 5.3 Design a strategy for securing client computers. Considerations include desktop and portable computers.
- 5.3.1 Design a strategy for hardening client operating systems.
- 5.3.2 Design a strategy for restricting user access to operating system features.
- 5.1 Design a client authentication strategy.
- 5.1.1 Analyze authentication requirements.
- 5.1.2 Establish account and security requirements.
- 5.2 Design a security strategy for client remote access.
- 5.2.1 Design remote access policies.
- 5.2.2 Design access to internal resources.
- 5.2.3 Design an authentication provider and accounting strategy for remote network access by using Internet Authentication Service (IAS).

Introduction

In our final chapter, we discuss a topic that sometimes has a tendency to be overlooked: client security. It's easy to get so wrapped up in securing our servers and infrastructure that we forget how important the client desktop can be to an organization's security. After all, you can secure and patch your servers all you want, but if a single end user copies a file from a floppy disk that infects his workstation with a Trojan horse, your entire network will be affected (often severely) by this vulnerability. Because of this, we'll spend some time examining the ways to maintain the overall security of the workstations on your network, including ways to secure the client operating system and maintain and enforce virus protection and patch management for all your users.

Another critical issue is that of client authentication. You obviously want your clients to use the strongest level of authentication available, but that is sometimes not practical in a heterogeneous environment. We'll talk about ways to improve the security of your user accounts, and how to select the best authentication protocols to fit the needs of your enterprise. This can include Kerberos, NTLM authentication, Certificate-based authentication, or even a combination of all three. Once you've created your user authentication scheme, we'll go over ways to enforce that choice throughout your network through tools such as Group Policy.

Finally, we'll talk about creating a secure remote access plan for your end users. We've discussed virtual private network (VPN) technologies from an infrastructure standpoint earlier in this guide; here we'll examine how remote access choices will affect your end users. This includes your choice of remote access medium: dial-up or VPN, your choice of remote access protocols, and the creation of remote access policies to control the use of your network resources. We'll close with a discussion of Internet Authentication Service, or IAS, which is Windows Server 2003's RADIUS implementation that can be used for large-scale or heterogeneous remote access deployments.

EXAM 70-298 OBJECTIVE 5.3

Securing Client Computers

While the MCSE Core Four exams focus a great deal of attention on securing the server operating system, services, and processes, most network administrators will tell you that securing end-user desktops can present a far greater challenge in a real-world network. Servers exist in a tightly secured environment: software is (hopefully) installed and updated only under well-controlled conditions, and only after thorough testing. Moreover, security patches and updates for server services often receive more visibility and attention from vendors and security watchdogs alike. However, securing network clients is a critical process, if for no other reason than that your network clients outnumber your servers 10, 100, or even 1000 to 1. Staying abreast of any new vulnerabilities for your client computers and patching those vulnerabilities in a timely and efficient manner can mean the difference between a well-secured network and a Code Red infestation waiting to happen. In this section, we'll discuss some of the important concepts in hardening client computers, including the importance of antivirus software and patch management.

EXAM 70-298 OBJECTIVE 5.3.1

Hardening Client Operating Systems

When you receive a new workstation from a major manufacturer, you'll often find that the operating system has been installed in an insecure fashion. Often, a vendor will create a default operating system installation designed to make a new computer easy to use and navigate for an inexperienced user; however, this can have major ramifications in terms of the security of a newly installed computer. You'll often find new operating systems installed with any number of development tools and utilities, or automatic access to a poorly secured Administrator account. Although this type of behavior can be beneficial to a new user, it also provides potential back-door access to an organization's systems.

Hardening client operating systems is a critical first step in safeguarding your client operating systems from internal or external intrusion and attackers. At a minimum, this involves the removal of any nonessential tools, utilities, or other administrative options that could be exploited by an attacker to gain access to your systems. The hardening process will also ensure that all necessary security features have been activated and configured correctly for any administrative or nonadministrative user accounts used to gain access to the client system, rather than simply providing easy access to an Administrator account.

Minimizing Attack Vectors

A term that you'll hear quite often when dealing with computer and information security is the notion of an *attack vector*. Put simply, an attack vector is the exploit that a malicious user uses to gain access to a system, whether it's through guessing weak passwords or using a buffer overflow attack against an unpatched system. When designing secure systems, one of your goals should be to minimize the potential avenues of attack that a hacker can use to gain access to your company's systems. You can think of this as a castle with a drawbridge that's surrounded by a moat: since there's usually only one way into and out of the castle, the people defending that castle can concentrate on defending the main gate and the drawbridge. This makes securing a castle much simpler than a building with many easily reached doors and windows that can all provide a means of access to gain entry. (To further the analogy, it's still necessary to defend other parts of the castle, since a determined attacker could probably find a way to cross the moat and scale the castle walls, given enough time and resources.)

So, what does this mean for securing computing systems? It means that, when configuring and installing clients within your secure network design, you should only install the software and services that are necessary for your clients to perform their job duties effectively. For example, there have been one or more software vulnerabilities attached to the Microsoft Windows Media Player, but if your client computers did not have Windows Media Player installed to begin with, then this vulnerability would have no chance of affecting the security of your systems. Likewise, most modern Windows client operating systems are capable of running a stripped-down version of IIS called Personal Web Server (PWS) from a client desktop; if this option isn't necessary for your clients to function, then it should be disabled as well. (The Code Red and Nimda worms exploited many Windows desktops where the users didn't even realize that they'd had this desktop version of IIS installed to begin with.) Any steps that you can take to minimize or eliminate any unnecessary software or services running on your desktop computers will go a long way in preventing attackers from finding these different (and often superfluous) vulnerabilities to exploit.

Creating an Antivirus Protection Scheme

In Chapter 1, "Designing a Secure Network Framework," we discussed the threat posed to a modern network by malicious attackers using viruses, Trojans, and worms to affect the confidentiality, integrity, and availability of the data on a corporate network. It's not enough to provide virus protection at the server level; each client on your network needs to have antivirus software installed and updated with the latest virus definitions in order to provide the best defense for your systems and data. Viruses can often enter a corporate network through a single end user either opening an infected e-mail attachment or browsing to a Web site that contains malicious code. Because of this, you need to design virus protection for all systems on your network that interact with the Internet and the rest of the world at large. Are you running an e-mail server? Be sure that you are scanning incoming and outgoing e-mail messages for virus infections. Do your end users have Internet access from their desktops? Be sure that each network-connected workstation has anti-virus software that provides real-time antivirus scanning. You can also install antivirus software at other points on your network, including at the firewall or proxy server that will scan *all* incoming network traffic for virus infections. While there are any number of commercial and freeware options available for virus protection, it's critical that a secure network design make allowances for its installation, use, and management.

TEST DAY TIP

Real-time protection refers to anti-virus software's ability to scan files as they are created or accessed, thus providing instant notification if a downloaded file contains a virus or other form of malicious code. Most commercial anti-virus software packages provide this feature.

Enabling Patch Management

While Microsoft's focus on security is evident in Windows Server 2003, the fact remains that the discovery of new security vulnerabilities (and attacks that exploit them) is often simply a fact of life. As an administrator, you need to be able to determine which patches and updates are required by your enterprise computing systems, and the best way to deploy those updates as quickly and efficiently as possible. Creating an effective patch management scheme will reduce downtime and costs on your network associated with system outages or data corruption, and increase the overall security and integrity of your company's assets and intellectual property.

As a part of the Trusted Computing Initiative, Microsoft has attempted to streamline the patch management and installation process using both built-in functionality within Windows Server 2003 and freely available services and add-ons. The first step in effective patch management is obviously the ability to know that a patch is necessary and available. The Security Bulletin Notification Service provides e-mail bulletins whenever a security vulnerability for a Microsoft product has been reported and confirmed, usually along with information on how to obtain necessary patches or otherwise reconfigure vulnerable systems. The notification service classifies security vulnerabilities into one of four categories, as shown in Table 10.1. By remaining alert to the presence of security updates and patches, you can then define processes to distribute the necessary software updates to all of your network clients.

Table 10.1 The Microsoft Security Bulletin Classification System

Rating	Definition
Critical	A vulnerability of this severity could allow an Internet worm or virus to spread without user action, or even awareness.
Important	A vulnerability of this level can compromise the confidentiality, integrity, or availability of a user or company's data, or the availability of other network resources.
Moderate	The risk of this type of vulnerability is often greatly mitigated by factors such as the default configuration of the operating system, auditing, or difficulty of exploitation.
Low	A vulnerability whose exploitation is extremely difficult or whose impact is minimal.

Group Policy

One of the most powerful tools for installing software updates is actually freely available for download from the Microsoft Web site, and integrates right into the Windows Server 2003 operating system. By using the Software Installation settings within Group Policy, you can automatically distribute security updates to an entire domain, site, or organizational unit (OU), or even to a single user or computer, from one centralized location. (For more information on configuring Software Installations in Group Policy, see *MCSA/MCSE Exam 70-290: Managing and Maintaining a Windows Server 2003 Environment* (ISBN: 193226660-7) from Syngress Publishing.) Unfortunately, there are a few drawbacks to relying solely on Group Policy. Remember that Software Installation settings do not apply when a client is logging on to Active Directory over a slow link (anything slower than 56Kbps.) This means that if you have a remote office that connects to a corporate LAN via a dial-up modem, no software installation settings will be propagated to the remote systems; if Group Policy is your only means of distributing patches, then these systems will remain unprotected. Group Policy also requires you to manually create and distribute software installation patches. However, the freely available Software Update Services (which we'll discuss next) goes a long way toward improving this process for a corporate LAN.

Software Update Services

Microsoft Software Update Services (SUS) was designed to simplify the process of keeping your Windows client and server systems updated with the latest critical updates. SUS will enable you to quickly and efficiently deploy critical updates to your Windows 2000 and Windows Server 2003 systems, and any client systems running Windows 2000 Professional or Windows XP Professional. You can use SUS to deploy critical updates, security patches, and Windows service packs for all supported operating systems (with SUS SP1 or later). The SUS service relies on two major components:

- **Microsoft Software Update Services** This is the server component that you'll install on a computer running Windows 2000 Server or Windows Server 2003 that's located inside your corporate firewall. The server component synchronizes with the Microsoft Windows Update site to download all critical updates and service packs for Windows 2000, Windows Server 2003, and Windows XP. This synchronization process can be configured to occur automatically, or you can perform the process manually. Once you've downloaded any updates, you can then test them within your environment and then *approve* updates for installation throughout your organization.
- **Automatic Updates** This is the component that actually installs all approved updates on your client machines. The Automatic Update component is included by default on Windows 2000 Service Pack 3 (SP3) and

later, Windows XP SP1 and later, and Windows Server 2003. Any of your clients who are running Windows 2000 Service Pack 2 or earlier can install the Automatic Update component manually if they cannot be upgraded to the latest service pack level. Automatic Update allows your servers and client computers to connect to your internal SUS server and receive any updates. You can control which SUS server each Windows client should connect to, and schedule when the client should perform all installations of critical updates. This configuration is something you can perform manually for one or two machines, or through Group Policy settings for a large environment. You can configure the automatic updates to come from an internal SUS server, or directly from the Microsoft Windows Update site.

EXAM WARNING

The most recent word from Microsoft is that SUS cannot be used to apply security updates to clients running Windows NT 4 or earlier operating systems, and it can only be used for critical updates and service packs. Updates for applications such as MS Office will need to be deployed using another means. For real-world use, check the most recent SUS release to see if this has changed.

Third-Party Tools

If you find that Group Policy and SUS don't fully meet your patch management requirements (you're supporting a number of down-level clients, for example), any number of third-party alternatives can assist you in deploying security patches in an efficient manner. A common option in this case is Microsoft Systems Management Server (SMS), which is a fully functional network management solution that will allow you to monitor and control many aspects of your network, not just the patch management process. The key differences between SUS and SMS are outlined in Table 10.2. Other third-party tools include HFNetCHK Pro from Shavlik Technologies, LANDesk from Intel, and many others. The 70-298 exam will not expect you to be able to select a specific third-party solution; however, you should be able to recognize a scenario where one would be required.

Table 10.2 Key Differences between SUS and SMS

Installation and Distribution Features	SUS	SMS
Content	Built-in synchronization service can automatically download the latest critical updates from Microsoft.	Automatic downloading of necessary updates.
Targeting	Basic targeting in which machines receive all applicable patches from the SUS server that they are assigned to.	Granular targeting based on criteria such as inventory, groups/OUs, and subnets.
Geographical Distribution	SUS can be scheduled to automatically synchronize content with the list of approved updates from other SUS servers or a distribution point within your network.	Site-site distribution that can be scheduled and is sensitive to WAN links.
Installation	Manual or simple scheduling based on group policy. Downloads are fault tolerant based on bandwidth, and can be scheduled.	Manual or advanced scheduling based on the targeting criteria listed.
Status	Status reported via Internet Information Services IIS logs.	Built-in filters and reports.

Securing Laptop Computers

The increasing prevalence of laptop computers in a corporate network has created new challenges for providing network security. Securing mobile computers involves using technical measures, and increasing user awareness of the role that they play in keeping their computers and data secure. (We talked about the importance of user awareness in Chapter 1.) The first layer of security for laptop and mobile computers is securing the physical hardware itself, using hardware locks to prevent the computer from being stolen if it's left unattended. You can also enable a setup or boot password in the system BIOS to prevent the laptop from powering on if the correct password isn't provided.

Perhaps the best way to secure a mobile computer, however, is through the use of the Syskey utility. Most password-cracking software used in attacking computer systems will target the SAM database or the Windows directory services to access user accounts. The Syskey utility (located in the %systemroom%\system32 directory) will encrypt password information stored either on a local computer or in the Active

Directory, thus providing an extra line of defense against would-be attackers. To use this utility on a workstation or member server, you need to be a member of the local Administrators group on the machine in question. (If the machine is a member of a domain, remember that the Domain Admins group is added to the local Administrators group by default.) On a domain controller (DC), you need to be a member of the Domain Admins or Enterprise Admins group.

TEST DAY TIP

On workstations and member servers, password information is stored within the computer's Registry. DCs integrate password information into the directory services database that is replicated between controllers.

In the following exercise, we'll go through the steps in enabling the System Key Utility on a Windows Server 2003 server.

EXERCISE 10.01

USING THE SYSKEY UTILITY

1. From the Windows desktop, click **Start | Run**, then type **syskey** and click **OK**. You'll see the screen shown in Figure 10.1.

Figure 10.1 Enabling Syskey Encryption

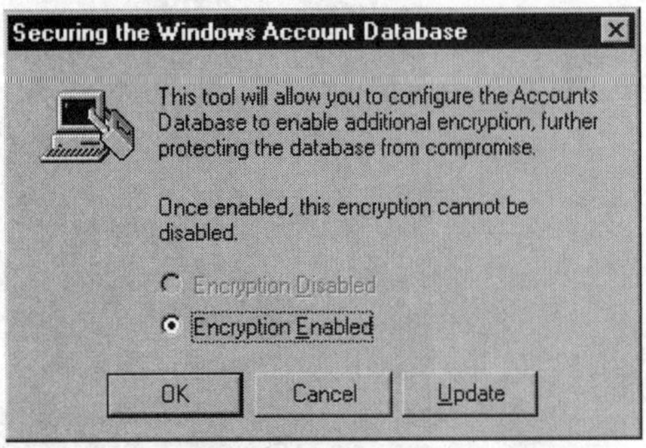

2. Click **Encryption Enabled**, and then click **Update**.
3. Choose from the security options shown in Figure 10.2. The different options available to you are as follows:

- **System Generated Password, Store Startup Key Locally** This encrypts the SAM or directory services information using a random key that's stored on the local computer. You can reboot the machine without being prompted for a password or a floppy disk; however, if the physical machine is compromised, the System Key can be modified or destroyed. Of the three possible options when using Syskey, this is the least secure method.

- **Password Startup, Administrator-Generated Password** Like the first option, this will encrypt the account password information and store the associated key on the local computer. In this case, however, you will select a password that will be used to further protect the key. You'll need to enter this password during the computer's boot-up sequence. This is a more secure option than storing the startup key locally, since the password used to secure the system key isn't stored anywhere on the local computer.
- **System Generated Password, Store Startup Key on Floppy Disk** This option stores the system key on a separate floppy disk, which must be inserted during the system startup. This is the most secure of the three possible options, since the system key itself is not stored anywhere on the local computer, and the machine will not be able to boot without the floppy disk containing the system key.

Figure 10.2 Selecting Syskey Encryption Options

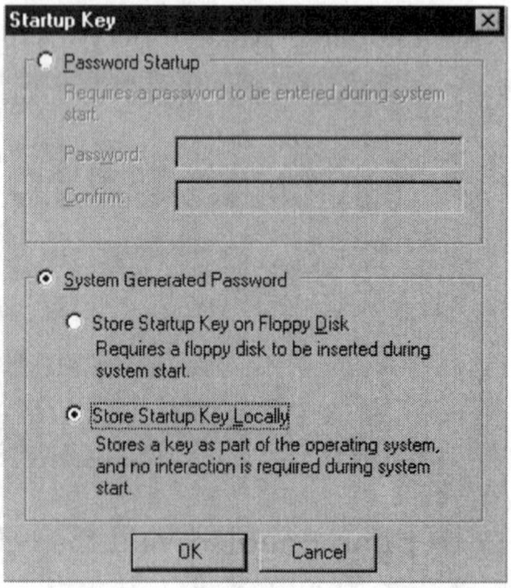

Exam Warning

If you lose the floppy disk or forget the password that you created when you ran Syskey, you won't be able to boot the computer in question without restoring the Registry or the Active Directory database from a point before you implemented Syskey.

4. Once you have selected the option that you want, click **OK** to finish encrypting the account information. You'll see the confirmation message shown in Figure 10.3.

Figure 10.3 Confirmation of Syskey Success

EXAM 70-298 OBJECTIVE 5.3.2

Restricting User Access to Operating System Features

As we mentioned previously when talking about hardening client operating systems, sometimes the default installation of an operating system gives the users more control over their desktop than you, the administrator, would really like. Windows Server 2003 makes it a relatively simple matter to "lock down" operating system features using Group Policy Objects (GPOs). You can restrict access to items such as the command prompt, the run line, and Control Panel. You can prevent users from mapping or disconnecting network drives, adding or deleting network printers, and any number of other levels of granular control over the end-user experience. As with all GPO settings, these restrictions can be applied at the domain, site, or OU level, and you can set multiple policies and/or restrict how policies are inherited from a parent OU to any child OUs. (However, as you'll see, some security policies can only be set at the domain level.)

Here are some of the common operating system features that you can restrict through the use of group policies:

- Hide all icons on desktop
- Don't save settings at exit

- Hide specified drives in My Computer
- Remove the Run option from the Start menu
- Prohibit user from using the Display icon in Control Panel
- Disable and remove links to Windows Update
- Disable changes to taskbar and Start menu settings
- Disable/Remove the Shut Down command
- Hide the My Network Places icon
- Remove the Map Network Drive and Disconnect Network Drive
- Disable Internet Options in Internet Explorer

When you are using GPOs to restrict this type of user access in a complex environment, keep the following points in mind:

- If a user or computer has multiple GPOs that can be applied at the same level in the Active Directory structure, any conflict resolution will apply to individual GPO settings, not to the entire GPO. Therefore, you can have a single setting in a GPO encounter a conflict that needs to be resolved, while other settings in the same GPO are applied without issue.
- Child OUs inherit Group Policy settings from parent OUs by default, but child *domains* do not inherit Group Policy settings from their parent domains.
- Certain Group Policy settings can only be applied at the domain level, particularly password policies and account lockout policies.
- The Enforce setting will force a GPO to apply to all Active Directory objects within a given site, domain, or OU regardless of what settings might be applied later. If multiple GPOs are applied with the Enforce option, the setting that is enforced *first* will win. This is the *reverse* of the usual GPO processing rules.
- Block Inheritance applies to an entire site, domain, or OU, and prevents any GPO settings from being applied unless the GPO has the Enforce setting enabled.
- Be aware of Enforce and Block Inheritance settings, since they will cause the usual inheritance and processing rules to no longer apply.

EXAM 70-298 OBJECTIVE 5.1

Designing a Client Authentication Strategy

Any network security design needs a client logon strategy that addresses the following three topics: authentication, authorization, and accounting (you'll sometimes see the last one referred to as "Auditing"). This "AAA Model" is an Internet standard for controlling various types of network access by end users. Put simply, authentication is concerned with determining that a user is *who* he or she claims to be. Authorization focuses on *what* a user is permitted to do once he or she has passed the authentication stage, and accounting or auditing tracks *who did what* to a network file, service, or other resource. Windows Server 2003 addresses all three facets of this security standard with the use of the user authentication strategies that we'll discuss in this chapter.

Regardless of which protocol or technical mechanism is used, all authentication schemes need to meet the same basic requirement of verifying that a user or network is actually who or what it claims to be. This can include verifying a digital signature on a file or an entire hard drive, or verifying the identity of a user or computer that is attempting to access network resources such as a file share. Windows Server 2003 offers several protocols and mechanisms to perform this verification process, including (but not limited to) the following:

- Kerberos
- NTLM
- SSL/TLS
- Digest authentication
- Smart cards
- Virtual Private Networking (VPN) and Remote Access Services (RAS)

User authentication is a necessary first step within any network security infrastructure, because it establishes the identity of the user. Without this key piece of information, Windows Server 2003 access control and auditing capabilities would not be able to function. Once you understand how the various Windows authentication schemes and protocols work, you'll be able to create an effective user authentication strategy for your network. The location of your users, whether they are connected to the LAN via a high-speed network connection or a simple dial-up line, and the client and server operating systems in use throughout your organization will dictate the best authentication strategy to implement within your security design. Keep in mind that a real-world authentication strategy will almost certainly involve a combination of the strategies and protocols described in this chapter, since a single solution will not meet the needs of an enterprise organization. Your goal as a network administrator is to create an authentication strategy that provides the optimum security for your users, while allowing you to administer the network as efficiently as possible. In the following sections, we'll describe the particulars of each authentication mechanism available with Windows Server 2003, and how you can use each to improve your network security design.

EXAM 70-298 OBJECTIVE 5.1.1 5.1.2

Analyzing Authentication Requirements

The most common authentication mechanism, one that goes back as far as the days of mainframe computing, is the use of *password authentication*. In this model, the user supplies a password to a server or host computer, and the server compares the supplied password with the information that it has stored in association with the username in question. If the two items match, the system permits the user to log on. Simple password authentication is not in heavy use anymore because of concerns that user passwords were being transmitted via clear-text over a network connection, thus allowing anyone monitoring network communications to steal the password. This concern is so great that many modern password authentication schemes such as NTLM and Kerberos never actually transmit the user password over the network at all.

Another concern with password authentication that is perhaps even more difficult to address is that of user education. Even after continually reminding users to choose strong passwords and to avoid sharing their login credentials, many still use their children's names as passwords or share their passwords with coworkers or assistants. In an enterprise network that is connected to the Internet, the importance of creating strong password policies as part of your network's security plan simply cannot be overstated. To assist in this, Windows Server 2003 allows you to establish password policies to mandate the use of strong, complex passwords. You can also mandate that your users log in using smart cards, a topic that we'll cover in depth in a later section.

A key feature of Windows Server 2003 is its support for Single Sign-on, an authentication feature that allows domain users to authenticate against any computer in a domain, while only needing to provide their login credentials one time, usually when they log on to their local workstation. This mechanism will allow you to manage a single account for each user on your network, rather than face the administrative load of establishing and maintaining multiple user accounts across different servers or domains. This greatly enhances convenience for users as well as administrators, since accessing the network is simplified by only needing to maintain a single password or smart card. However, whether your authentication scheme uses single sign-on or not, any authentication process will involve two major steps. First, the user must perform an *Interactive Logon* to access the local computer. After users have authenticated themselves to their local workstations, *Network Authentication* will allow users to access other resources located elsewhere on the network. In this section, we'll examine both of these processes in detail.

Network users perform an *interactive logon* when they present their network credentials to the operating system of the computer that they are attempting to log on to. (This is usually their desktop workstation.) The logon name and password can either be a user account stored in the local computer's account database, or a domain account stored on a DC. When logging on using a local computer account, the user presents credentials that are stored in the Security Account Manager (SAM) database on the local machine. While any workstation or member server can store the SAM, the accounts within the local SAM can only be used for access to that specific computer. When using a domain account, the user's domain information is forwarded to the Active Directory database. This allows the user to gain access, not only to the local workstation, but to the Windows Server 2003 domain itself. In this case, the user's domain account bypasses the workstation's SAM database entirely, authenticating to the local workstation using the information stored in Active Directory. Figure 10.4 provides a comparison of these two processes.

Figure 10.4 Interactive Logons Using Local vs. Domain Accounts

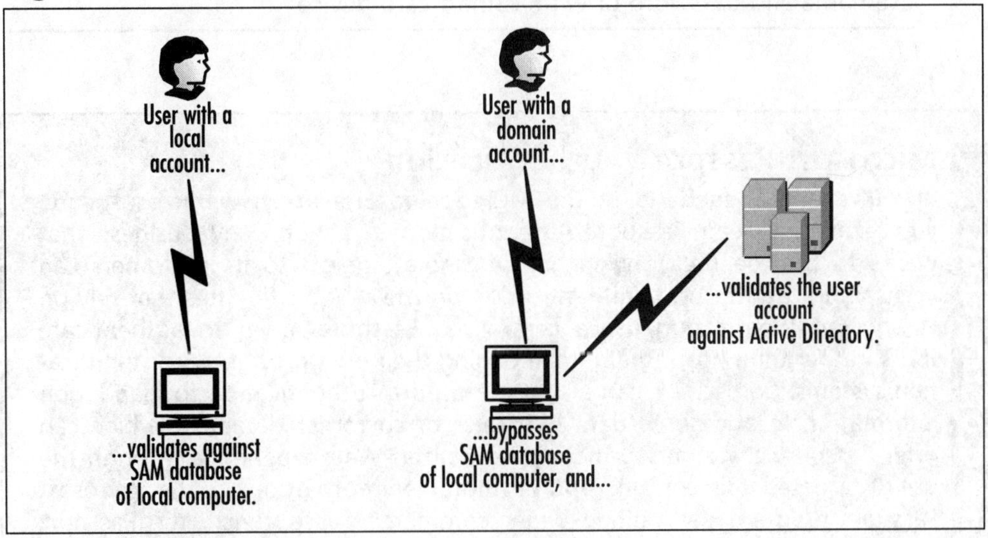

Network Authentication

Once users have gained access to a physical workstation, it's almost a given that they will require access to resources stored on other machines on the local or wide area network. *Network authentication* is the mechanism that will confirm the users' identity to whatever network resource they attempt to access. Windows Server 2003 provides several mechanisms to enable this type of authentication, including Kerberos, Secure Socket Layer/Transport Layer Security (SSL/TLS), and NTLM to provide backward compatibility with Windows NT 4.0 systems.

Users who log on using a local computer account must provide logon credentials every time they attempt to access a network resource, since the local computer account only exists within the individual workstation or member server's SAM database rather than a centrally managed directory service like Active Directory. (Refer to the description of the Interactive Logon process in the previous section to see how this works.) If users are logged on to the network using a domain account, however, their logon credentials will be automatically submitted to any network services they need to access. Because of this, the network authentication process is transparent to users in an Active Directory environment; the network operating system handles everything behind the scenes without the users even being aware of it. This feature provides for single sign-on in a Windows Server 2003 environment by allowing users to easily access resources in their own domain, as well as other trusted domains.

TEST DAY TIP

Network authentication using a domain account can be accomplished via a username and password or with a smart card device.

Head of the Class...

Microsoft Passport Authentication

If you've ever logged on to the MCP Secure Site at www.microsoft.com, you've already seen Passport Authentication in action. Any business that wants to provide the convenience of Single Sign-on to its customers can license and use Passport Authentication on their Web site. Sites that rely on Passport Authentication use a centralized Passport server to authenticate users, rather than hosting and maintaining their own proprietary authentication systems. Companies can also use Passport Authentication to map logon information to additional data in a sales or customer database, which can offer Passport customers a more personalized Web experience through the use of targeted ads, content, and promotional information. As the Microsoft Passport program has gained wider commercial acceptance, the Passport Sign-on logo (shown in Figures 10.5 and 10.6) has begun to appear on more and more corporate and e-commerce Web sites.

Continued

Figure 10.5 Passport Sign-On through www.ebay.com

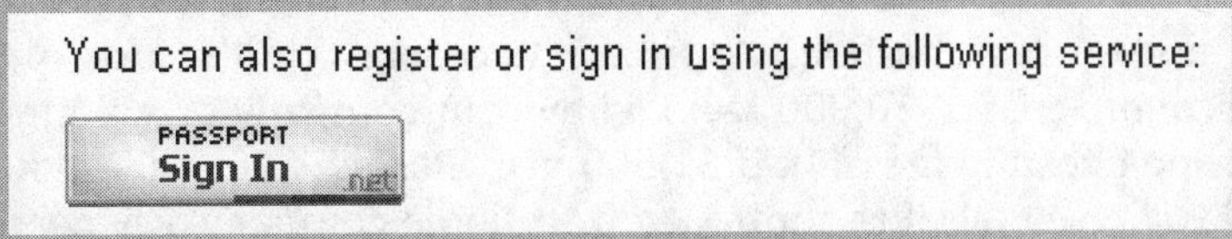

Figure 10.6 Passport on www.expedia.com

From a technical perspective, Passport Authentication relies on standards-based Web technologies including SSL encryption, HTTP redirects, cookies, and symmetric key encryption. Because the technology used by Passport Authentication is not proprietary, it is compatible with both Microsoft Internet Explorer and Netscape Navigator, and some flavors of UNIX systems and browsers. The single sign-on service is similar to forms-based authentication that is common throughout the Internet; it simply extends the functionality of the sign-on features to work across a distributed set of participating sites.

Microsoft introduced the .NET Passport service in 1999, and since then, Passport Authentication has authenticated more than 200 million accounts for businesses such as McAfee, eBay, NASDAQ, Starbucks, and many others. If you are considering integrating Passport Authentication into your user authentication strategy, here are some of the advantages that will be available for Web authentication:

- **Single sign-in** allows your users to sign on to the Passport site once to access information from any participating Web site. This alleviates the frustration of registering at dozens of different sites and maintaining any number of different sets of logon credentials. The Passport service will allow the over 200 million Passport users quick and easy access to your site.
- The **Kids Passport** service provides tools that will help your business comply with the legal provisions of the U.S. Children's Online Privacy Protection Act (COPPA). Your company can use this service to conform to the legal aspects of collecting and using children's personal information, and to customize your Web site to provide age-appropriate content.
- **Maintain control of your data** Since the Passport service is simply an authentication service, your customer information and

Continued

data will still be controlled inhouse, and is not shared with the Passport servers unless you configure your Web site to do so.

At the time of writing, there are two fees for the use of Passport Authentication: a USD$10,000 fee paid by your company on an annual basis, and a periodic testing fee of USD $1,500 per URL. The $10,000 is not URL specific and will cover all URLs controlled by a single company. Payment of these fees will entitle your company to unlimited use of the Passport Authentication service for as many URLs as you have registered for periodic testing.

Microsoft has created several key features within Passport Authentication to ensure that the security and privacy of your customers and users can be maintained at the highest possible level. Some of the security features employed by Passport Authentication include:

- The Web pages used to control the sign-in, sign-out, and registration functions are centrally hosted, rather than relying on the security mechanisms of each individual member site.
- All centrally hosted pages that are used to exchange usernames, passwords, or other credential information always use SSL encryption to transmit information.
- Passport Authentication-enabled sites use encrypted cookies to allow customers to access several different sites without retyping their login information. However, an individual site can still opt to require users to return to the Passport sign-in screen when accessing their site for the first time.
- All cookie files related to Passport Authentication use strong encryption: when you set up your site to use Passport, you will receive a unique encryption key to ensure the privacy of your users' personal information.
- The central Passport servers will transmit sign-in and profile information to your site in an encrypted fashion. You can then use this information to create local cookies, avoiding any further client redirection to the Passport servers.
- A Web site that participates in Passport Authentication will never actually receive a member's password. Authentication information is transmitted via a cookie that contains encrypted timestamps that are created when the member first signs on to Passport. The Microsoft Passport sign-out function allows users to delete any Passport-related cookies that were created on their local machine during the time that they were logged on to Microsoft Passport.

Continued

- A participating Web site will only communicate directly with the central Passport server to retrieve configuration files, which are then cached locally by the individual member server. All information that is exchanged between clients and the Passport servers takes places using HTTP redirects, cookies, and encrypted queries.

Securing User Accounts

So, now that you've seen how Windows user accounts factor into the authentication process, what's the best way to go about securing them? There are any number of security settings within Group Policy that you can configure for an entire Windows Server 2003 domain, as we've already discussed in Chapter 8, "Securing Active Directory," and these security settings will carry over to your local workstations. Most of the best practices for securing user accounts center around the use (and controlling the potential *misuse*) of administrative accounts. Some key factors to keep in mind, especially when securing your end-user workstations, include:

- **Restrict administrator accounts to log on to specific computers only.** You can use the Account Properties tab within Active Directory Users and Computers to restrict the members of the Domain Admins group to only log on to servers and specific administrative workstations. This can obviously create some administrative headaches if you need to use administrative rights on a disallowed workstation, but it might be appropriate for extremely high-security environments.
- **Require multifactor authentication.** You can install smart card readers on your servers and/or workstations, and require administrators to use smart cards to authenticate when logging on with an administrative account. You can extend this to include Terminal Services authentication.
- **Control membership in Administrative groups.** You should only add a new user to the Domain Admins, Enterprise Admins, or Schema Admins group if that user has a legitimate need to perform the kinds of duties associated with those security groups. You might be faced with a technical support call for a third-party application that is malfunctioning and be told to "Add the user to the local administrators group, since that fixes the problem." This type of shortcut is one that you should avoid at all costs, since it makes for lazy security standards and potential vulnerabilities for your entire network. In most circumstances, you would not want regular end users to have administrative access to their workstations, since any virus or worm that they encounter would be able to function in the security

context of an administrative user, creating the potential for even more damage resulting from any sort of malicious code or attack.

- **Require administrators to use a "non-administrative" account for day-to-day activities.** There is no good reason for a system administrator to log on to a machine using administrative access if all she is doing is checking e-mail or doing Internet research. While this practice is difficult to enforce from a technical standpoint, promote security awareness among your network administrators to encourage the use of the RunAs function to use administrative access only when necessary.

Securing Account Naming Conventions

Even the names you select for your network user accounts can either improve or hinder your overall network security. Sound paranoid? Try this on for size: An internal employee notices that all network accounts use the convention of first initial-last name, so that Joanna Smith is jsmith, Bryan Hopkins is bhopkins, and so forth. Let's say that this person wants to try to look at secured files that only the CFO has access to. If he knows that the CFO's name is Evan Lansing, then he can easily deduce that the user account whose password he needs to figure out is elansing. To look at another example, many automated hacking tools that are available for download from the Internet attempt to break in to "well-known" user account names like Administrator, backup, SQLAgent, Supervisor, and so on. If even one of these well-known accounts is in use on your network and possesses a weak password, a so-called "script kiddie" could gain access to your network without too much difficulty. Depending on the security requirements of your organization, you can lower the risk of these kinds of attacks by varying the account naming conventions to include random numbers or letters, and certainly avoid using commonly known account names like Administrator. Remember that when dealing with password-based authentication schemes, the logon process is a puzzle containing two pieces: the username and the password. If attackers can determine a username to attempt to undermine, then they're already halfway to breaking into your network.

Choosing Authentication Protocols

Windows Server 2003 offers several different authentication methods to meet the needs of even the largest heterogeneous corporate network. The default authentication protocol for a pure Windows Server 2003 environment is Kerberos version 5. This protocol relies on a system of tickets to verify the identity of network users, services, and devices. For Web applications and users, you can rely on the standards-based encryption offered by the SSL/TLS security protocols, as well as Microsoft Digest. In addition, to provide backward compatibility for earlier versions of Microsoft operating systems, Windows Server 2003 still provides support for the

NTLM protocol as well. In this section, we'll examine the various authentication options available to you as you create your network design.

Kerberos

As we just mentioned, the primary authentication protocol in a Windows Server 2003 Active Directory domain is Kerberos version 5. Kerberos provides comprehensive authentication by verifying the identity of network users, and the validity of the network services that users are attempting to access. This latter feature was designed to prevent users from attaching to "dummy" services created by malicious network attackers to trick users into revealing their passwords or other sensitive information. Verifying both the user *and* the service that the user is attempting to use is referred to as *mutual authentication*. Kerberos authentication can only be used by network clients and servers running Windows 2000, Windows Server 2003, or Windows XP Professional; any Windows 9*x* or NT clients that attempt to access a Kerberos-secured resource will use NTLM authentication instead. (We'll discuss NTLM more fully in the next section.) All 2000/2003/XP Professional machines that belong to a Windows Server 2003 or Windows 2000 domain will use the Kerberos protocol as the default mechanism for network authentication for domain resources.

Kerberos authentication relies on a Key Distribution Center (KDC) to issue *tickets* to enable client access to specific network resources. Each DC in a Windows Server 2003 domain functions as a KDC, which creates fault tolerance in the event that a DC becomes unavailable. Network clients will use Domain Name Service (DNS) to locate the nearest available KDC; once they've located the KDC they will provide a pass phrase in order to acquire a *ticket*. Kerberos tickets contain an encrypted password that confirms the user's identity to the requested service. These tickets will remain active on a client computer system for a configurable amount of time, usually 8 or 10 hours. The longevity of these tickets allows Kerberos to provide single sign-on capabilities, where the authentication process as a whole becomes transparent to the users once they've initially entered their logon credentials.

EXAM WARNING

The obvious downside to this is that the ticket will remain active on the client workstation even if the user leaves the machine unattended: if someone else gains physical access to the workstation while the Kerberos ticket is still active, he or she will be able to access resources using that ticket. Shortening the ticket lifespan will reduce the risk of this, but will force users to re-enter their pass phrase more often.

When users enter their network credentials on a Kerberos-enabled system, the following steps take place to process the authentication and authorization request.

These steps occur completely behind the scenes; the users are only aware that they've entered their password or PIN number as part of a normal logon process.

1. Using a smart card or a username/password combination, a user authenticates to the KDC. The KDC issues a *ticket-granting ticket* (TGT) to the client system. The client retains this TGT in memory until needed.
2. When the client attempts to access a network resource, it presents its TGT to the *ticket-granting service* (TGS) on the nearest available Windows Server 2003 KDC.
3. If the user is authorized to access the service that it is requesting, the TGS issues a *service ticket* to the client.
4. The client presents the service ticket to the requested network service. Through *mutual authentication*, the service ticket will prove the identity of the user and the identity of the service.

Exam Warning

Kerberos authentication relies on timestamps to function properly. As such, all clients that are running the Kerberos client must synchronize their time settings with a common time server. If the time on a network client is more than five minutes slow or fast compared to the KDC, Kerberos authentication will fail.

The Windows Server 2003 Kerberos authentication system can also interact with non-Microsoft Kerberos implementations such as MIT and UNIX-based Kerberos systems. This new "realm trust" feature, covered in Chapter 4, "Securing the Network Management Process," will allow a UNIX client in a Kerberos realm to access resources in an Active Directory domain, and vice versa. This interoperability will allow Windows Server 2003 DCs to provide authentication for client systems running UNIX/MIT Kerberos, including clients that might be running operating systems other than Windows XP Professional or Windows 2000. Conversely, it will also allow Windows-based clients to access resources within a UNIX-based Kerberos realm. (We discussed this interoperability more fully in Chapter 1.)

NTLM Authentication

Instead of Kerberos, Windows operating systems prior Windows 2000 use NT LAN Manager (NTLM) to provide network authentication. In a Windows Server 2003 environment, NTLM will be used to communicate between two computers when one or both of them is running NT4 or earlier, as well as communications between computers that are not part of an Active Directory domain. For example, NTLM authentication would be used in the following situations:

- Workstations or stand-alone servers that are part of a peer-to-peer workgroup, rather than a domain, will use NTLM authentication.
- Windows 2000 or Windows XP Professional computers logging on to an NT 4.0 primary domain controller (PDC) or backup domain controller (BDC).
- A Windows NT 4.0 Workstation client authenticating to an NT4.0, Windows 2000, or Windows Server 2003 DC.
- Users in a Windows NT 4.0 domain that has a trust relationship with a Windows 2000 or Windows Server 2003 domain or forest.

NTLM encrypts user logon information by applying a mathematical function (or *hash*) to the user's password. The NT4.0 SAM database doesn't store the user's password, but rather the value of the hash that is created when NTLM encrypts the password. Using simple numbers for the sake of an example, let's say that the NTLM hash takes the value of the password and multiplies it by 3. Let's say further that user LHunter has a password of "4." The conversation between LHunter, LHunter's workstation, and the DC will go something like this:

LHunter: "My password is '2''"

LHunter's workstation: "Hey, Domain Controller! LHunter wants to log in."

DC: "Send me the hash value of LHunter's password."

LHunter's workstation: "The hash value of her password is '6'."

DC: "That's not the hash value that I have stored for LHunter. Care to try again?"

LHunter's workstation: "Hey, LHunter. That password was incorrect. Sure you typed it in right?"

LHunter: "Sorry. My password is '4'."

LHunter's workstation: "The has value of LHunter's password is '12'."

DC: "Okay, the number '12' matches the value that I have stored in the SAM database for the hash of LHunter's password. I'll let her log in."

To further improve security, the client machine actually applies the hash to the user's password *before* transmitting it to the DC, which means that the user's password is never actually transmitted across the network. (And the transmission of the hash value itself is transmitted in an encrypted form, increasing the protocol's security even further.)

Digest Authentication

Microsoft uses Digest Authentication as a means of providing authentication for Web applications running on IIS. Digest Authentication uses the *Digest Access Protocol*, a challenge-response mechanism for applications that are using HTTP or Simple Authentication Security Layer (SASL)-based communications. When a user logs on to a Web application using Digest Authentication, IIS creates a *session key* that is stored on the Web server and used to authenticate subsequent authentication requests without needing to contact a DC for each individual authentication request. Similar to NTLM, Digest authentication sends user credentials across the network as an encrypted hash. Digest Authentication requires the following:

- Clients using Digest Authentication need to be using Internet Explorer 5 or later.
- The user attempting to log on to the IIS server, as well as the IIS server itself, need to be members of the same domain or belong to another domain that is connected via a trust relationship.
- The authenticating users need a valid account stored in Active Directory on the DC.
- The domain that the IIS server belongs to must contain a DC running Windows 2000 or Windows Server 2003. The Web server itself also needs to be running Windows 2000 or later.
- Digest Authentication requires user passwords to be stored in a reversibly encrypted (clear-text) format within Active Directory. You can establish this from the Account tab of a user's Properties sheet in Active Directory Users and Computers, or use a group policy to enable this feature for a large number of users. After changing this setting, your users will need to change their passwords so that a reversibly encrypted hash can be created: the process is not retroactive.

SSL/TLS

Anytime you visit a Web site that uses an https:// prefix instead of http://, you're seeing SSL encryption in action. SSL provides three major functions in encrypting Web-based traffic:

- **Server authentication** allows a user to confirm that an Internet server is really the machine that it is claiming to be. This is another example of mutual authentication, similar to that provided by the Kerberos protocol. For example, server authentication assures the users that they're looking at a legitimate site and not a duplicate created by a hacker to capture their credit card and other personal information.
- **Client authentication** to allow a server to confirm a client's identity. This would be important for a bank that needed to transmit sensitive financial information to a server belonging to a subsidiary office, for example.
- **Encrypted connections** allow all data that is sent between a client and server to be encrypted and decrypted, allowing for a great deal of confidentiality. This function also allows both parties to confirm that the data was not altered during transmission.

The next generation of SSL is the *Transport Layer Security* (TLS) protocol, which is currently under development by the Internet Engineering Task Force (IETF). It will eventually replace SSL as a standard for securing Internet traffic, while remaining backward compatible with earlier versions of SSL. RFC 2712 describes the way to add Kerberos functionality to the TLS suite, which will potentially allow Microsoft and other vendors to extend the usefulness of Kerberos beyond LAN/WAN authentication and allow it to be used throughout the Internet as a whole.

EXAM 70-298 OBJECTIVE 5.2

Designing a Secure Remote Access Plan

When designing a network, most modern corporations will need to include some means of remote access for traveling and telecommuting members of their workforce. One could almost say that the prevalence of the Internet has destroyed the time-honored tradition of the snow day, where a blizzard left you free to sit on the couch and watch movies—the increasing prevalence of laptops and broadband Internet connections has made it much simpler (and therefore expected) to be able to access corporate resources from remote locations. As a network administrator, you need to be concerned not only with providing this type of access, but also with ensuring that allowing remote access will not compromise the confidentiality, integrity, or availability of your company's data and resources. The design decisions that you make will need to strike a balance between creating convenience for your users and not sacrificing the security of your corporate network. In this section, we'll examine common remote access technologies and protocols, and look at the relative security merits of each. Having a firm grasp of this information will assist you in preparing for the 70-298 exam, and designing a secure remote access for a real-world network.

Choosing a Remote Access Method

There are two general options that you can choose from when designing a remote access solution for your network. The first option is to use a direct-dial remote access server that's running the Routing and Remote Access service with a modem, bank of modems, or dedicated WAN connection physically attached to the server. You should already be aware of the cost implications of this solution: using a direct-dial number can become prohibitively expensive if you're dealing with users who are dialing in from around the country or the world—whether the expense is borne by the users themselves making long-distance connections, or by the company supporting a toll-free access number.

From a security standpoint, direct-dialed access can be quite attractive, since network access will be restricted to the corporate network itself and will not be traversing the Internet or other shared networks. However, keep in mind that dial-up remote access is not a panacea—it will not absolutely safeguard you from attackers. For example, dial-up remote access is vulnerable to attack when end users store their passwords with their connection information—if a traveling user's laptop is stolen and she has stored her password with her RAS connection, the person who stole her laptop will be able to access the corporate network using that saved password information. You might also encounter situations where malicious users will attempt to attack a toll-free 800 number itself, either running up phone charges for the sake of mischief, or attempting to use the toll-free access to make other unauthorized phone connections once the RAS connection has been established. (Some companies that have been victim to this type of attack only became aware of it when their telephone bill showed up in a box instead of an envelope!) While telephone and PBX security is beyond the scope of the 70-298 exam, it's a real-world consideration that you should definitely be aware of when designing a network.

If you want to avoid the cost considerations of supporting a dial-up RAS server, you can opt instead to allow VPN connections to your internal network. RAS and VPN were covered in detail in Chapter 7, "Securing VPN and Extranet Communications," but as a refresher, you should recall that your VPN design should call for the most secure encryption that your RAS clients will be able to support. (We'll discuss RAS and VPN protocols in the next section.) Since VPN traffic is traversing the Internet, you need to mandate the strongest level of encryption possible to ensure the confidentiality and integrity of your data and your users' account and password information.

Selecting a Remote Access Protocol

For each remote access method, there are a number of different protocols that you can select for your client workstations to connect with. While you obviously want to use the best encryption possible, you need to keep in mind any technical constraints created by your network clients, since not all operating systems can support all protocols.

- **Dial-up remote access protocols**
  - **Password Authentication Protocol (PAP)/Shiva Password Authentication Protocol (SPAP)** Both of these protocols are supported by Windows Server 2003 for backward compatibility only. PAP sends user credentials to the remote access server in *cleartext*, and SPAP uses a primitive encoding method that isn't much better. If possible, connections using these protocols should not be allowed by any secure remote access server.
  - **Challenge Handshake Authentication Protocol (CHAP)** This protocol encrypts a RAS user's credentials (username and password) using the *MD5* encryption algorithm. While this is an improvement over PAP and SPAP, only the user's credentials are encrypted: any *data* transmitted during the RAS connection is sent in clear-text. Additionally, CHAP requires that user passwords in Active Directory be stored using reversible encryption, which makes Active Directory DCs subject to additional types of network attacks. CHAP should only be used if your network is supporting remote access users who are running the Macintosh or UNIX platform.
  - **Microsoft Challenge Handshake Authentication Protocol(MS-CHAP)** This is a Microsoft-specific implementation of CHAP that improves somewhat on the encryption used by CHAP. It does not require passwords to be stored using reversible encryption. You should only allow MS-CHAP connections if you are supporting legacy RAS clients that are running Windows 95 or older Microsoft operating systems.
  - **MS-CHAP version 2** This improvement on MS-CHAP introduces *mutual authentication*, where both the client and the server verify their identity to one another. MS-CHAP uses a much stronger encryption algorithm, and uses separate encryption keys for sending and receiving data. MS-CHAPv2 is supported by Windows 98 and Windows NT 4.0, allowing you to use a stronger encryption method than MS-CHAP unless you are supporting very old RAS clients.
  - **Extensible Authentication Protocol (EAP)** As the name implies, EAP allows developers to extend remote access authentication to include a number of advanced features, including two-factor authentication using smart cards or biometric devices (such as retina scanners or thumbprint recorders). EAP-TLS uses public key certificate-based authentication for remote access, and is the strongest RAS authentication method available under Windows Server 2003. However, EAP-TLS can only be used by clients that are running Windows 2000, Windows XP, or Windows Server 2003.

If you will be using VPN technologies to enable remote access, you have two main choices of protocols that you can enable. Your choice of protocol will be largely dependent on the client operating systems and network hardware that you need to support.

- **Virtual private networking protocols**
  - **Point-to-Point Tunneling Protocol (PPTP)** PPTP is a VPN tunneling protocol that is supported by all Microsoft clients since Windows NT 4.0. PPTP can encrypt data using a 40-bit, 56-bit, or 128-bit encryption key. Unless you have a specific reason not to, you should mandate 128-bit encryption when using PPTP, since the 40-bit and 56-bit keys have been broken and are therefore vulnerable to decoding.
  - **Layer Two Tunneling Protocol (L2TP)** This is a stronger form of encryption that's supported natively by Windows 2000 and Windows XP, and by Windows 98, Me, and NT 4.0 with the installation of an add-on client. L2TP does not provide its own data encryption, but instead relies on IPSec to encrypt data using either a 56-bit DES key, or three 56-bit DES keys using 3DES encryption. Before the release of Windows Server 2003, PPTP was necessary if you were using Network Address Translation (NAT) devices, since L2TP and IPSec could not *traverse* NAT devices. However, Windows Server 2003 supports NAT traversal natively, and Microsoft has released an update for Windows XP and Windows 2000 that will allow their L2TP/IPSec clients to do so, as well.

No matter which authentication and encryption protocols you choose, you should mandate their use by your remote access clients by configuring remote access policies, which we'll discuss next.

EXAM 70-298 OBJECTIVE 5.2.1

Designing Remote Access Policies

You can use remote access policies to verify any number of settings both before and after a RAS client is allowed to connect to your corporate network. For example, you can use remote access policies to either allow or reject connection attempts based on group memberships, time of day, day of the week, and the like. You can further require a specific authentication method and encryption strength, and even limit the amount of time a RAS client can remain connected to your network. When planning your remote access policy strategy, you can use one of the following three approaches:

- **Common policy** You can create a single common policy that creates a universal connection template for anyone connecting using a particular access method—you can create a policy to handle all VPN clients, one to configure all wireless clients, and so forth.

- **Default policy** If you're not concerned with restricting remote access usage based on connection methods, group membership, and the like, you can use one of the default policies that are installed with the Routing and Remote Access service. These default policies will grant remote access to any user with a valid Active Directory account.
- **Custom policy** This will allow you to specify a more detailed configuration for a particular access method. This will be necessary if you want to manage connection attempts at an extremely granular level. We'll look at each possible connection setting that you can control through a custom policy in the next section.

Understanding the Elements of a Remote Access Policy

Remote access policies consist of the following elements: conditions, permissions, and profiles. We'll discuss each of these elements in turn, and list how each can be used to control remote access attempts by your network clients.

Remote Access Conditions

Remote access conditions consist of one or more attributes that can be compared against a connection attempt by a remote user. A remote access policy can specify one or more of these attributes that should be checked before allowing access. If a policy specifies multiple conditions, then *all* of the conditions need to match in order for the policy to find a match. For example, let's say that a remote access policy will only allow VPN connections on Saturdays and Sundays, and only from members of the SalesVP group. If a member of the SalesVP group attempts to establish a VPN connection on a Friday, the connection attempt would be rejected, since both conditions were not met. Table 10.3 lists the various attributes that you can set as part of a remote access policy.

Table 10.3 Remote Access Conditions

Attribute Name	Description
Authentication Type	The type of authentication that is being used by the access client. Authentication types include CHAP, EAP, MS-CHAP, and MS-CHAP v2.
Called Station ID	The phone number that the client is dialing in to.
Calling Station ID	The phone number that the caller is dialing in *from*.

Continued

Table 10.3 Remote Access Conditions

Attribute Name	Description
Client Friendly Name	The name of the RADIUS client that is requesting authentication. This name is configured in Friendly name on the Settings tab in the properties of a RADIUS client in IAS. This attribute is a character string. This attribute is used by IAS, which we'll discuss in a late section.
Client IP Address	The IP address of the client.
Client Vendor	The vendor of the network access server (NAS) that is requesting authentication—this is most often used in a site-to-site VPN like the ones discussed in Chapter 7. You can use this attribute to configure separate policies for different NAS manufacturers who are connecting via IAS.
Day and Time Restrictions	The day of the week and the time of day of the connection attempt. The day and time is relative to the day and time of the server providing the authorization.
Framed Protocol	The type of framing for incoming packets, such as PPP, SLIP, Frame Relay, and X.25.
NAS Identifier	The name of the NAS. This attribute is a character string. You can use pattern-matching syntax to specify multiple NASs.
NAS IP Address	The IP address of the NAS (the RADIUS client) that sent the message.
NAS Port Type	The type of media that is used by the access client, such as a plain old telephone line, ISDN, wireless, or VPN connection.
Service Type	The type of service that is being requested. Examples include framed (such as PPP connections) and login (such as Telnet connections).
Tunnel Type	The type of tunnel that the client is requesting—either PPTP or L2TP, as we discussed earlier.
Windows Groups	The names of the groups to which the user or computer account that is attempting the connection belongs. You don't need to have a separate remote access policy for each group. Instead, you can use multiple groups or nested groups to consolidate and delegate the administration of group membership.

Remote Access Permissions

If all of the conditions set by a remote access policy are met, then permission to access the network will be either granted or denied. The best way to set remote access permissions for your users is to configure your accounts to **Control Access through Remote Access Policy**, rather than granting or denying permissions to each individual account.

Exam Warning

The remote access permission specified on a user's account Properties page overrides any permissions set through a remote access policy. Therefore, if a user account has been manually configured to Grant Remote Access, that user will be able to make a RAS connection no matter what remote access policies are in place. This is why using the **Control Access through Remote Access Policy** option is a best practice in a large enterprise environment.

Remote Access Profiles

A remote access profile is a set of conditions that are applied to a connection *after* it has been authorized, either through the user's account Properties, or through a remote access policy. Once a user has been granted a remote access connection, you can fine-tune the connection by setting any of the following profile conditions:

- **Dial-in constraints can include any of the following:**
  - **# of minutes a client can remain idle before it is disconnected.** By default, this property is not set.
  - **# of minutes a client can remain connected.** This specifies the maximum amount of time that a client can remain connected, after which the connection is disconnected by the access server after the maximum session length. By default, this property is not set, which means that there is no maximum session limit.
  - **Allow access only on specific days and times.** The days of the week and hours of each day that a connection is allowed. If the day and time do not match the configured profile, the connection will be disconnected. However, if a client makes a connection during an allowed time, the session will not be disconnected if the client remains connected past the allowed day/time restrictions.
  - **Allow access to this number only.** The specific phone number that a caller must call in order for a connection to be allowed. If the dial-in number of the connection attempt does not match the configured dial-

in number, the connection attempt is rejected. By default, this property is not set so that all dial-in numbers are allowed.

- **Allow access only through these media.** The specific types of media, such as modem, ISDN, VPN, or wireless that a caller must use for a connection to be allowed. If the dial-in medium of the connection attempt does not match the configured dial-in media, the connection attempt is rejected. By default, this property is not set and all media types are allowed.

- **Possible IP profile constraints include the following:**
  - The access server must supply an IP address.
  - The access client can request an IP address.
  - IP address assignment is determined by the access server (this is the default setting).
  - A static IP address is assigned. A static IP address assigned to the user account overrides this setting. The IP address assigned is typically used to accommodate vendor-specific attributes for IP addresses.

TEST DAY TIP

You can also use the IP profile constraints to configure IP traffic filters that apply to remote access connections. You can configure either input or output filters on an *exception basis*. This means that all traffic is allowed *except* for the traffic specified in the filters, or all traffic is *blocked* except for traffic that is specifically allowed.

- You can use **Multilink** profile settings to configure the maximum number of ports that can be taken up by a Multilink connection. You can also configure the Bandwidth Allocation Protocol so that extra multilink ports can be freed up if they are not being actively used.
- **Authentication profiles** will mandate what type of authentication a client must use to connect. By default, MS-CHAP and MS-CHAPv2 are enabled. You can add or remove other authentication methods as needed, including EAP, or lower forms of authentication if required.
- **Encryption** properties will specify one of the following encryption strengths:

- **No encryption** will allow a client to connect to your RAS server using no encryption at all. To require encryption, it's important to clear this option.
- **Basic encryption** requires a 40-bit key for PPTP connections, or a 56-bit DES connection with L2TP connections. Since both of these encryption levels are fairly weak, do not allow this option unless it's absolutely necessary.
- **Strong encryption** enables a 56-bit connection for PPTP, or a 56-bit DES connection for L2TP.
- **Strongest encryption** mandates a 128-bit connection for PPTP or a 3DES connection for L2TP. This is the best encryption method possible, and should be mandated by your remote access configuration if possible.

Your goal as an administrator is to create remote access policies that reflect the usage needs of your company or clients. If your remote access capabilities are limited to three dial-up modem connections, for example, you might want to restrict the use of these modems during the day to those users who have a specific need for it. You might have a small number of regional sales directors who work from various locations and need to access reporting data during the day, and you do not want to have their connection attempts refused because non-mission-critical RAS connections are tying up the available connections. In the following exercise, we'll create a remote access policy that limits remote access connections on your network to members of the SalesVP group between the hours of 8 A.M. and 5 P.M., Monday through Friday. Creating this policy will allow your company's sales vice presidents to access the information they need rather than allowing extraneous remote access connections to tie up your limited resources.

Exercise 10.02

Creating a Remote Access Policy

1. Open the Routing and Remote Access MMC by clicking on **Start | Programs | Administrative Tools | Routing and Remote Access**.
2. Right-click on **Remote Access Policies** and select **New Remote Access Policy**. Click **Next** to bypass the initial screen in the wizard. You'll see the screen shown in Figure 10.7. Click **Use the wizard to set up a typical policy for a common scenario**, enter a name to describe the policy, and then click **Next**.

Figure 10.7 Creating a Remote Access Policy

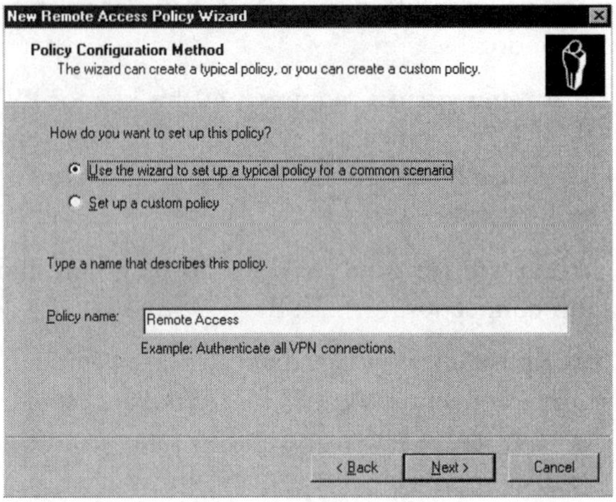

3. From the **Access method** screen, select the access method that this policy will apply to. You can select one of the following methods:
   - VPN access
   - Dial-up access
   - Wireless access
   - Ethernet
4. For the purpose of this example, select **Dial-Up Access**, and then click **Next**.
5. Decide whether to grant remote access permission on a user or group level. Using groups will provide easier and more efficient administration since you can group users with common remote access needs and add or remove users from the group as needed. Select **Group**, and add the SalesVP group. Click **Next** to continue.
6. In the screen shown in Figure 10.8, select the authentication method that this remote access policy will use. If your clients are using software that can handle the higher encryption levels, you can disable weaker encryption schemes like CHAP to prevent users from connecting with a lower level of encryption.

Figure 10.8 Remote Access Authentication Methods

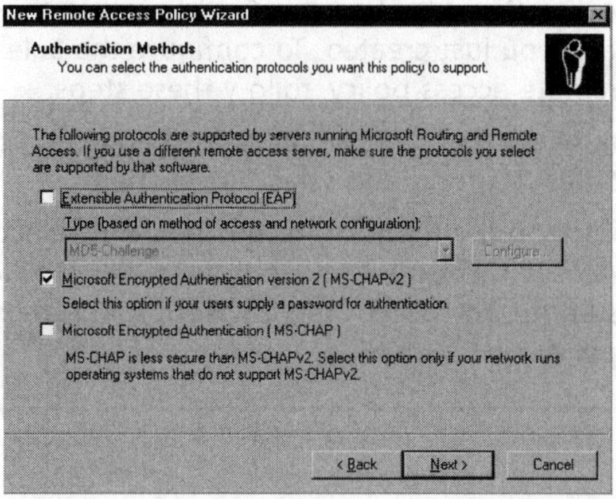

7. Click **Next** to continue. On the next screen, select the levels of encryption that your users can employ to connect to the IAS server. You can select an encryption level of 40-, 56-, or 128-bit encryption, or choose not to mandate encryption at all. Click **Next** and then click **Finish** to set these standard policy settings.
8. Next, you'll want to further modify the remote policy so that users can only connect to your dial-up modems between 8 A.M. and 5 P.M., Monday through Friday. Right-click on the **Remote Access Policy** that you just created, and select **Properties**.
9. Click **Add** to include another condition to this policy, adding new conditions one at a time. Figure 10.9 illustrates the various conditions that you can use to grant or deny remote access to your clients.

Figure 10.9 Remote Access Policy Conditions

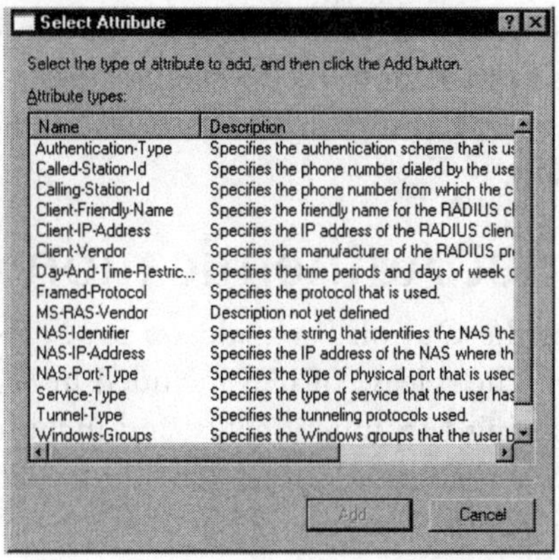

The final step in enabling remote access is to configure your Active Directory Users or Groups to use the remote access policy that you just created. To configure the SalesVP group to use the remote access policy, follow these steps:

10. In Active Directory Users and Computers, right-click on the **SalesVP** group and select **Properties**.
11. Click on the **Remote Access** tab, and select **Click on Control Access through Remote Access Policy**. Click **OK**, repeating this step for any other users or groups who require the remote access policy.

EXAM 70-298 OBJECTIVE 5.2.2

Providing Access to Internal Network Resources

Once you've granted access to your network through any of the remote access methods we've discussed, you'll need to provide your users the ability to connect to the actual resources and data contained within your network. (Otherwise, the entire exercise of planning and deploying remote access technology wouldn't be very useful, now, would it?) It is not enough to simply grant remote access permissions via a policy or a user's account properties in Active Directory Users & Computers; you'll need to create the appropriate NTFS permissions to actual file and application shares within your internal network.

Perhaps the most convenient feature of remote access in Windows Server 2003 is that your clients, once granted access, will use standard tools and interfaces to connect to internal network resources. Any services that are available to a user connected via the LAN will be made available to RAS clients by way of the RAS authentication and logon process. From Windows 2000 or XP Professional workstations, remote access users can create network drive mappings or access files and printers using the familiar Windows Explorer or My Network Places interface. Windows Server 2003 fully supports the use of drive letter mappings and Universal Naming Convention (UNC) connections from remote access clients. Because of this, most Microsoft and third-party applications will function over a RAS connection just as though the user were connected locally.

EXAM 70-298 OBJECTIVE 5.2.3

Using Internet Authentication Service

Beginning as early as the Option Pack add-on for NT 4.0, Microsoft has offered IAS as a RADIUS server. The release of IAS included in Windows Server 2003 expands and improves the existing IAS functionality, and includes connection options for wireless clients, as well as authenticating network switches and the ability to relay requests to remote RADIUS servers. IAS is available in the Standard, Enterprise, and

Datacenter Editions of Windows Server 2003, but not the Web Edition. Since it functions with a wide range of wireless, remote access, and VPN equipment, IAS can be used for everything from the smallest corporate remote access solution to managing the user base of a major Internet service provider (ISP). IAS is capable of managing the entire user login process: managing the user authentication process, then verifying that a user is authorized to access various network resources, and finally creating an audit trail to provide accountability for each user's activities.

EXAM WARNING

Windows Server 2003, Standard Edition, can only support a maximum of 50 RADIUS clients and 2 RADIUS server groupings. The Enterprise and Datacenter Editions of Windows Server 2003 will allow you to configure an unlimited number of RADIUS clients and server groups.

Authentication Protocols Supported by IAS

IAS supports a variety of authentication methods that can meet the needs of most client platforms. In addition, you can create custom authentication methods to meet any specialized requirements of your network security policy. The default authentication methods supported by IAS are password-based PPP and EAP, which we've already discussed. By default, IAS supports two EAP protocols: EAP-MD5 and EAP-TLS. Other supported PPP protocols include:

- Password Authentication Protocol (PAP)
- Challenge Handshake Authentication Protocol (CHAP)
- Microsoft Challenge Handshake Authentication Protocol (MS-CHAP)
- MS-CHAP version 2

Once a user has been authenticated using one of these protocols, IAS is able to use a number of methods to verify the authenticated user's authorization to access various services or resources. Just as with authentication methods, you can either use a default authorization scheme or use the Software Development Kit (SDK) to create custom methods to meet your company's needs. IAS supports the following authorization methods "out of the box," with no need for custom codes or scripting:

- **Dialed Number Identification Service (DNIS)** bases its authorization decision on the phone number that the caller is using. As a cost-saving measure, for example, you can authorize only users within a local calling area to use a particular number.

- **Automatic Number Identification/Calling Line Identification (ANI/CLI)** is the opposite of DNIS; it authorizes access based on the number that a user is calling *from*.
- **Guest Authorization** allows access to an access point or dial-up number without a username and password. This is becoming more common in airplane terminals, coffee shops, and the like, where businesses provide a wireless access point as a convenience for their clientele. To protect the access point in question, users connecting with Guest Authorization will typically have a severely curtailed set of actions that they can perform: they might be limited to Web browsing only without access to the My Network Places browser, for example.
- **Remote access policies** are the most effective way to determine authorization for Active Directory user accounts. As we've already discussed, remote access policies can authorize network access based on any number of conditions such as group membership, time of day, the telephone access number being used, and so forth. Once a user has been authorized, you can also use remote access policies to mandate the level of encryption that remote access clients need to be using in order to connect to your network resources, and set any maximum time limits for a remote connection or inactivity timeout values. Packet filters can also control exactly which IP addresses, hosts, and/or port numbers a remote user is permitted to access while connected to your network.

Designing & Planning...

New Features in Internet Authentication Service

While IAS has been around in one form or another since Windows NT 4.0, several new features have been introduced with Windows Server 2003 that make IAS an ideal solution for securing enterprise environments. Some of these new features include:

- **RADIUS proxy** In addition to providing its own RADIUS authentication services, you can configure an IAS server to forward authentication requests to one or more *external* RADIUS servers. The external RADIUS server does not need to be another Microsoft IAS server; as long as it is running an RFC-compliant RADIUS installation, the external server can be running any type of platform and operating system. IAS can forward these requests according to username, IP address of the target RADIUS server, as well as other conditions. In a large, heterogeneous environment, IAS can be configured to differentiate between the RADIUS

Continued

requests that it should handle by itself, and those that should be forwarded to external servers for processing.

- **Remote RADIUS-to-Windows-User Mapping** Allows you to further segregate the authentication and authorization processes between two separate servers. For example, a user from another company can be authenticated on the RADIUS server belonging to his or her separate company, while receiving authorization to access your network through this policy setting on your IAS server.
- Support for **Wireless Access Points** to allow authentication and authorization for users with IEEE 802.1x-compliant wireless network hardware. IAS can authenticate wireless users through the Protected Extensible Authentication Protocol (PEAP), which offers security improvements over EAP.
- IAS can log auditing information to a **SQL database** for better collection and reporting of security information.

Using IAS for Dial-Up and VPN

The RADIUS support provided by the IAS service is a popular way to administer remote user access to an enterprise network. For example, you can instruct your users to dial a local telephone number for a regional ISP, and then authenticate against your IAS server using a VPN client. Or, if the remote user is in the same local calling area as your corporate network, you can integrate IAS with the familiar Routing & Remote Access feature to allow them to dial directly in to a modem attached to the IAS server. IAS will then use RADIUS to forward the authentication and authorization request to the appropriate Active Directory domain, thus providing the same level of security regardless of where the user is connecting from. In Exercise 10.03, we'll cover the necessary steps to install and configure IAS on a DC in your Windows Server 2003 domain.

EXAM WARNING

Microsoft recommends that you configure at least two IAS servers within your Active Directory environment. If you have only one server configured and the machine hosting IAS becomes unavailable, dial-up and VPN clients will be denied access to network resources until you bring the IAS server back online. By using two servers, you can configure your remote access clients with the information for both, allowing them to automatically fail over to the secondary IAS server if the primary one fails. This way, your remote users will be able to have continuous access to your internal resources without sacrificing the security provided by IAS.

EXERCISE 10.03

CONFIGURING IAS ON A DOMAIN CONTROLLER

1. From the Windows Server 2003 desktop, open the Control Panel by clicking on **Start | Programs | Control Panel**. Double-click on **Add/Remove Programs.**
2. Click **Add/Remove Windows Components**. When the **Windows Components Wizard** appears, click **Networking Services,** and then **Details**. You'll see the screen shown in Figure 10.10.

Figure 10.10 Installing the Internet Authorization Service

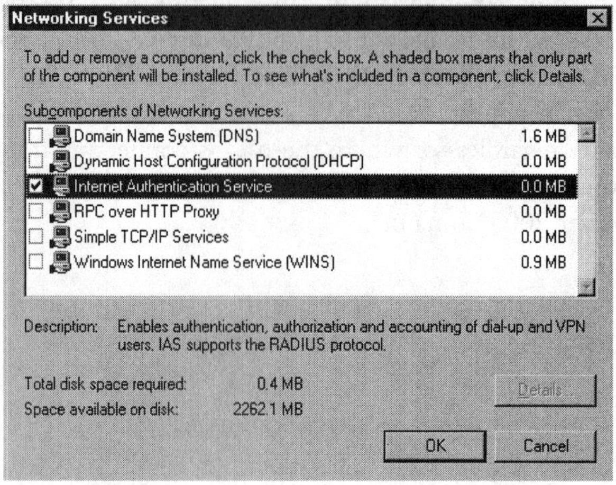

3. Place a check mark next to **Internet Authentication Service** and then click **OK**.

4. Click **Next** to begin the installation. Insert the Windows Server 2003 CD if prompted. Click **Finish** and **Close** when the installation is complete.

   Now that you've installed IAS, you need to register the IAS server within Active Directory. (This is similar to authorizing a newly created DHCP server.) Registering the IAS server will allow it to access the user accounts within the Active Directory domain.

5. Click on **Start | Programs | Administrative Tools | Internet Authentication Service**. You'll see the screen shown in Figure 10.11.

Figure 10.11 The IAS Administrative Console

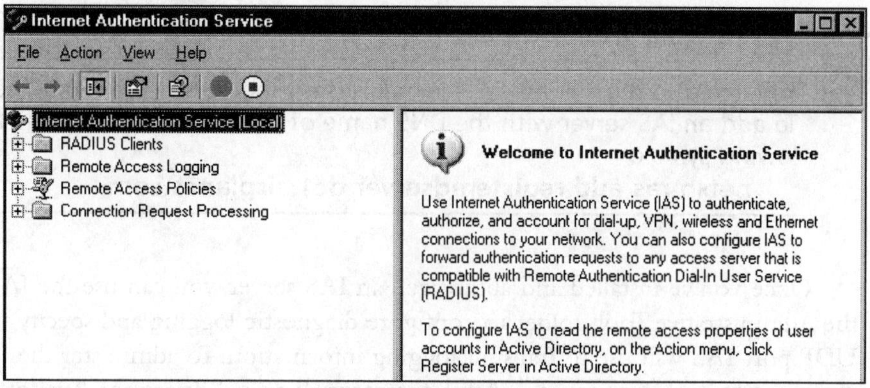

6. Right-click on the **Internet Authentication Service** icon and click on **Register Server in Active Directory**.
7. Click **OK** at the next screen, shown in Figure 10.12. This will allow IAS to read the dial-in properties for the users in your domain, thus allowing the IAS server to authenticate users within Active Directory.

Figure 10.12 Configuring Permissions for IAS

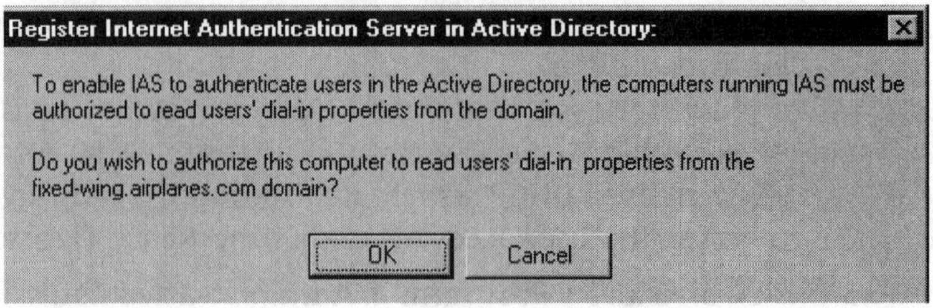

TEST DAY TIP

You can also register an IAS server by using the *netsh* command-line utility. To add an IAS server with the DNS name of dc1.airplanes.com, use the following syntax:

netsh ras add registeredserver dc1.airplanes.com

Once you've installed and authorized an IAS server, you can use the IAS icon in the Administrative Tools folder to configure diagnostic logging and specify which UDP port IAS will use to transmit logging information. To administer the IAS server, click on **Start | Programs | Administrative Tools | Internet Authentication Service**. Once you've configured IAS, you'll need to create remote access policies to enable your Active Directory users to access your network through the IAS server, similar to the policies we've already discussed in this chapter and elsewhere in this guide. You can use IAS in many different situations to provide various types of remote access for your network users. Besides the uses we've already covered, you can also configure IAS to handle the following:

- **Authenticating switches** You can use remote access policies to allow IAS to act as a RADIUS server for Ethernet switches that have the ability to authenticate to a central server. You can enforce this type of authentication to ensure that no "rogue" or unauthorized switches are brought online within your network infrastructure, or to ensure that only authorized personnel can plug in to a switch that supports authentication.
- **Outsourcing remote access connections** IAS allows an organization to outsource its remote access infrastructure to a third-party ISP. In this situation, users connect to an ISP's dial-up, but their login credentials are forwarded to your corporate IAS server for processing. Therefore, your end users will be able to dial in to the corporate network using local ISP dial-

up numbers, but your internal IAS server will also handle all logging and usage tracking for your remote users. This can provide a great deal of cost savings for your organization, allowing you to use an ISP's existing network infrastructure rather than creating its own network of routers, access points, and WAN links. IAS can also provide a similar service for outsourcing wireless access, where a third-party vendor's Wireless Access Point (WAP) forwards the user's authentication information to your IAS server for processing.

Using IAS for Wireless Access

As we discussed earlier, Windows Server 2003 has made it a relatively straightforward matter to enable a WAP to interact with the wired LAN. Furthermore, wireless clients can authenticate against an IAS server using a smart card, a digital certificate, or a username and password. The actual sequence of events when a wireless device requests access to your wired network occurs as follows:

1. When a wireless client comes within range of a WAP, the WAP will request authentication information from the client.
2. The client sends its authentication information to the WAP, which forwards the login request to the RADIUS server (in this case, IAS).
3. If the login information is valid, IAS will transmit an encrypted authentication key to the WAP.
4. The WAP will use this encrypted key to establish an authenticated session with the wireless client.

To allow wireless clients to access your network, you'll need to perform two steps: create a remote access policy that allows wireless connectivity, and add your WAPs as RADIUS clients on the IAS server so that they can forward login information to IAS for processing. (You'll configure your WAP as a RADIUS client according to the instructions provided by the WAP manufacturer.) A remote access policy for wireless users should contain the following information:

- **Access method** Wireless access
- **User or Group** Group, specifying the WirelessUsers group, for example
- **Authentication methods** Smart card or other certificate
- **Policy encryption level** Strongest Encryption, disable all other possible encryption levels
- **Permission** Grant remote access permission

Using Network Access Quarantine Control

One of the most exciting new features in Windows Server 2003 is Network Access Quarantine Control, which allows you to delay remote access clients from accessing your network resources until you've examined and validated their computer configuration, including making sure that they are running anti-virus software and are not vulnerable to any known security vulnerabilities. This prevents situations that were quite common in the past where a legitimate user's remote workstation was virus-infected; when the user was permitted access to the remote access server, the virus infection spread to machines on the internal network via the remote user's connection. Network Access Quarantine Control helps to eliminate this risk to your corporate network.

When a remote computer attempts to make a connection with a RAS server, the user is authenticated and the remote access computer is assigned an IP address. However, the connection is initially placed into *quarantine mode*, where network access is severely curtailed. While the machine is in this quarantined state, a script created by the network administrator is launched on the remote computer. This script is the component that checks for specific configuration details like anti-virus definitions, service pack level, and so forth. If the script completes successfully, it notifies the RAS server that the quarantined computer complies with network security standards. Only at this point is the remote user is granted normal access to the corporate network.

Remote Access Account Lockout

Another new feature in Windows Server 2003 is the ability to specify how many times a remote access connection can provide an incorrect password or other logon credential before the connection attempt is denied remote access. This is especially critical for VPN connections, since malicious users on the Internet can try to access your network's resources by perpetrating a password attack against a remote user account. With remote access account lockout enabled, such an attack would be stopped after a certain number of failed logon attempts.

EXAM WARNING

Be sure not to confuse this feature with the Account lockout settings in the Default Domain Group Policy Object. This setting applies only to remote access connection attempts.

Summary of Exam Objectives

To wrap up our preparations for the 70-298 exam, we closed with an overview of improving the security of client workstations. Because client workstations often prove to be the point of entry for many attacks and attackers, whether it's through a weak password, a laptop, or desktop session that's left unattended, or through a user opening an infected e-mail attachment, planning for client security is a critical piece of any network security design. Patching and updating servers and services is clearly only one piece of the security puzzle; including workstation security concerns in your security design will be crucial to its overall success. To help you in this, we examined various ways to improve or maintain the overall security of the workstations on your network, including ways to secure the client operating system and enforce anti-virus protection for all of your users. We also looked at patch management, which has become a hot topic for security-conscious administrators everywhere.

Another issue to consider when securing your network clients is that of authentication protocols. While we'd obviously all like to mandate strongest level of authentication available across the board, that wish can be less than feasible in a large environment supporting many different flavors of client operating systems. We looked at the various authentication protocols available for your use, and talked about how to choose the best one to fit the needs of your enterprise, whether that choice was Kerberos, NTLM authentication, Digest authentication for Web applications, or a combination of all three. We also discussed ways to improve the overall security of your user accounts, including the use of the Syskey utility to lock down the authentication process to a degree not previously available.

Finally, we closed with a discussion of remote access, and how to secure this process for your end users. While we already covered VPN technologies earlier in the 70-298 guide, here we talked about the ways that your remote access choices ultimately affect your end users. This extends to your choice of remote access medium, remote access protocols, and the use of remote access policies to restrict and secure remote access attempts. We closed with a discussion of Internet Authentication Service, or IAS, which is Windows Server 2003's RADIUS implementation for large-scale or heterogeneous remote access deployments, as well as some new features in Windows Server 2003 that greatly improve your ability to administer and secure the remote access process.

Exam Objectives Fast Track

Securing Client Computers

- ☑ *Hardening* a desktop machine refers to the process of securing the default operating system installation to make the system more resilient against malicious or unintentional damage by end users or network attackers.
- ☑ You can reduce the likelihood that your network clients will be targeted by attackers if you reduce the number of services that they are running; for example, disable the workstation version of IIS on any client computers that don't have a need to be running it.
- ☑ With the proliferation of viruses and worms showing no signs of stopping, a client security strategy needs to include measures for consistent anti-virus protection, as well as a patch management strategy to keep all of your network clients up to date with critical software updates.

Designing a Client Authentication Strategy

- ☑ Windows 2000, XP, and Server 2003 machines operating in an Active Directory domain will use Kerberos version 5 as their default authentication protocol. Down-level clients and servers, or machines functioning in a workgroup environment, will use NTLM version 2.
- ☑ You can use Group Policy Objects (GPOs) to mandate the authentication protocol in use on your network.
- ☑ Digest Authentication will allow you to use Active Directory credentials for Web authentication, but password information needs to be stored using reversible encryption, which means that DCs need to be subject to tight physical security controls.

Designing a Secure Remote Access Plan

- ☑ Remote access policies can be used to restrict RAS connections based on any number of factors, including Windows group memberships, day and time restrictions, connection type, and encryption strength.
- ☑ Windows Server 2003 has improved L2TP/IPSec so that it can now perform NAT traversal natively for Server 2003, and with a free software update for Windows 2000 and XP machines.

☑ Two new features that will help secure the remote access process are Network Access Quarantine Control and the Remote Access Lockout feature. Network Access Quarantine will restrict remote user connectivity until their computer configuration can be verified as secure and virus free, while Remote Access Lockout will prevent a malicious user from using RAS resources to perform a dictionary attack against Active Directory accounts.

Exam Objectives Frequently Asked Questions

The following Frequently Asked Questions, answered by the authors of this book, are designed to both measure your understanding of the Exam Objectives presented in this chapter, and to assist you with real-life implementation of these concepts. You will also gain access to thousands of other FAQs at ITFAQnet.com.

Q: Are there any technical limitations restricting how Internet users can connect to Web sites that use Passport Authentication?

A: Passport authentication supports both the Internet Explorer and Netscape Navigator browsers. However, both need to be at version 4 or later in order to access sites that are using Passport.

Q: Does the Kerberos authentication protocol possess any major weaknesses?

A: The largest concern to be aware of when using Kerberos authentication centers on the physical security of your Key Distribution Centers (KDCs), as well as your local workstations. Since Kerberos attempts to provide single sign-on capabilities for your users, an attacker who gains access to your workstation console will be able to access the same resources that you yourself are able to. Kerberos also does not protect against stolen passwords; if a malicious user obtains a legitimate password, he or she will be able to impersonate a legitimate user on your network.

Q: I have deployed a SUS server within my corporate LAN. We have a home-grown application that needs to be updated on several hundred clients Can I use SUS to push out this update?

A: Unfortunately, no. SUS can only deploy the compatible updates that it receives from the Microsoft Windows Update site. To deploy an update for a third-party or internal application, you will need to rely on logon scripts, or another utility such as SMS.

Q: Are there any restrictions on what kind of machine I can use to host a SUS server?

A: In its original release, you could not run SUS on a DC or Small Business Server. SUS Service Pack 1 has removed this restriction, although you should be careful to stress-test any existing server that you want to use for SUS to ensure that it can handle the additional network, memory, and processor requirements. In terms of hardware, you need to have a machine that is a PIII 700 or better, with a minimum of 512MB of RAM and 6GB of free disk space to store downloaded updates.

Q: We have had some recent issues with remote access clients infecting our internal network because their anti-virus software has not been up to date. How can I quickly get up and running with the Network Access Quarantine Control function on my network?

A: The best place to start is the NAQC white paper available for free download from the online Windows Server 2003 resource center from www.microsoft.com/windowsserver2003/techinfo/overview/quarantine.mspx. This paper will give you a quick but thorough introduction to how Quarantine functions, and a sample Quarantine script to get you started.

Q: I've seen several references to ISA on the Microsoft Web site. Is this the same thing as IAS?

A: No. Internet Authentication Service, or IAS, is the Microsoft implementation of RADIUS authentication that allows for central authentication of remote access clients. ISA server is the Internet Security & Acceleration server, which is the Microsoft firewall and proxy server solution for securing Internet access for a corporate LAN and WAN. While both technologies can be used to secure your network environment, they are entirely different entities. Further, detailed knowledge of ISA server is not required to pass the 70-298 exam, although being aware of its existence and its basic functionality certainly won't hurt.

Self Test

A Quick Answer Key follows the Self Test questions. For complete questions, answers, and explanations to the Self Test questions in this chapter as well as the other chapters in this book, see the Self Test Appendix.

Securing Client Computers

1. You are the network administrator for the Blue Sky, LTD, airplane manufacturer. The vice president of the Finance department has reported that some technically savvy users within the department have been attempting to access confidential information by browsing the available network shares from the Network Connections desktop icon. He has requested that users within subdepartments of the Finance area not be able to map network drives or browse network shares that they have not been explicitly granted access to. However, you have assigned a word processing application to the entire organization using a default GPO, and you do not want to reconfigure this portion of the Active Directory structure. In response to the VP's request, you have configured your Active Directory environment as shown in Figure 10.13. (Please note that, in the illustration, "Enforce" means that the "Enforce settings" property has been applied to the GPO in question.) Which setting(s) will be applied to a workstation in the Collections OU? (Choose all that apply.)

Figure 10.13 Question 1 Illustration

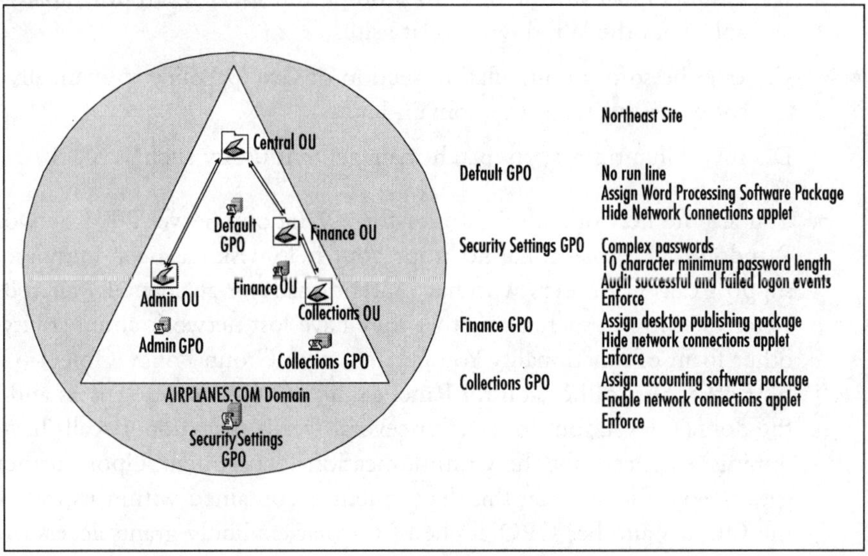

A. The desktop publishing package will be assigned.

B. The Network Connections applet will be hidden.

C. The Network Connections applet will be visible.

D. The Run line will be hidden.

2. You are the administrator for a Windows Server 2003 domain. Your network consists of five locations connected by high-speed Internet connections. Your network servers are running solely Windows Server 2003, but you are supporting network clients that are a mixture of Windows XP Professional, Windows 2000, and Windows NT 4.0 Workstation. Because of the recent spate of critical security updates that have been released by Microsoft, you need to design a strategy to apply security updates to all of your workstations in a quick and efficient manner. Given the current environment, what option can you use to roll out updates for all of your network clients?

   A. Install an internal SUS server and use Group Policy to configure clients to download approved updates from the SUS server.

   B. Configure all workstations to prompt end users when downloads are available from the Windows Update site.

   C. Use the software installation section of Group Policy to manually deploy software updates at the domain level.

   D. Invest in a third-party patch management utility such as SMS.

3. You are the network administrator for a Windows Server 2003 network with Windows XP Professional desktops. Your help desk has been inundated with support calls from users who have intentionally or accidentally altered their system settings in such a way that they have lost network connectivity or some other form of functionality. You create a new Group Policy Object (GPO) that restricts access to the Control Panel for all of your network users and link it to the domain level. You notice after several weeks that support calls have greatly diminished except for the Communications department. Upon further investigation, you discover that this department is contained within its own OU, and the OU has another GPO applied to it that explicitly grants access to the Control Panel, along with several other settings that the department manager insists are critical for his employees to perform their job functions. How can you enforce the Control Panel lockout without otherwise adversely affecting the Communications department?

   A. Delete the GPO that is linked to the Communications OU.

   B. Configure the "Control Panel lockout" GPO with the Enforce setting.

C. Configure the Communications OU to Block Inheritance so that the existing GPO will no longer be applied to it.

D. Merge the Communications OU GPO settings into the default domain GPO.

Design a Client Authentication Strategy

4. You are the network administrator for a medical research facility running Windows Server 2003. Your firm is beginning a joint research operation with a major university, and many of your users will need to access files and folders on the university's network. The university that you are collaborating with is operating using a UNIX Kerberos environment with UNIX clients at each desktop. Your company's resources should also be accessible by the university staff. How can you accomplish this with the least administrative effort?

   A. Create a realm trust between your network and the UNIX network, and create account mappings in Active Directory for the UNIX clients.

   B. Create separate accounts for the clients on the UNIX network.

   C. Mandate the use of NTLMv2 authentication on the Windows network.

   D. Mandate the use of MS-CHAP from the UNIX clients.

5. You are the network administrator for a large e-commerce site. Your Web developers have created a Web application to share information on the company intranet; this application relies on Digest Authentication to allow users to log on. For some reason, employees seem to be unable to access the new application. You check the account properties of one of the user accounts and see the screen shown in Figure 10.14. What is the most likely reason why your users cannot authenticate?

Figure 10.14 Administrator Properties Sheet

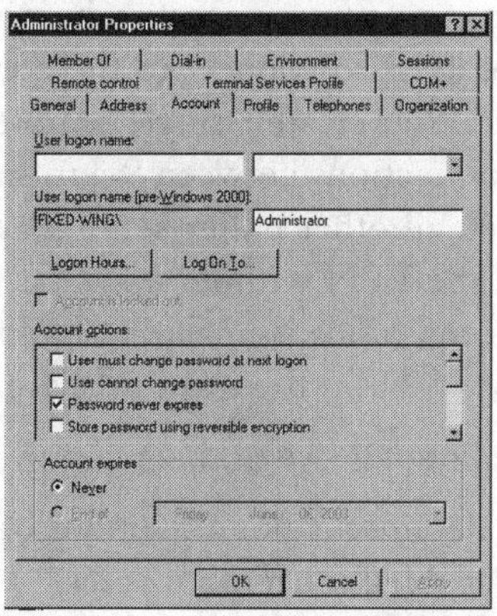

A. When logging on using Digest Authentication, the Windows username is case sensitive.

B. To use Digest Authentication, users must be running Internet Explorer version 6.

C. Your users' passwords are set to expire every 60 days, which is causing Digest Authentication to fail.

D. You must enforce the **Store passwords using reversible encryption** setting for all users who need to authenticate using Digest Authentication.

Designing a Secure Remote Access Plan

6. You are a local administrator within a large, multinational corporation. You would like to offer remote access capabilities for the users on your Windows Server 2003 domain. However, your corporation's security policies dictate that all remote access authentication needs to be processed by several UNIX-based RADIUS servers located at various points within the company's global infrastructure. How can you establish remote access authentication for your users that adheres to the corporation's security policies?

   A. Use IAS as a RADIUS proxy to forward user authentication requests to the corporate RADIUS servers.

   B. Create a realm trust between your Windows Server 2003 domain and the UNIX domain containing the RADIUS servers.

   C. Ask the administrator of the corporate RADIUS servers to enable the Guest account on the RADIUS server.

   D. Enable Digest Authentication for your domain users.

7. You are the network administrator for Blue Collar, Inc. clothing manufacturers. You have just installed a high-speed Internet connection at the corporate office, and you are designing a remote access scheme that will allow your branch offices and remote users to connect to the corporate LAN to access file shares and other resources. You create a single remote access policy that allows incoming VPN connections between 9 a.m. and 9 p.m., Monday through Friday. You have left all other policy settings at their default values. Most users are connecting to the VPN without issue, but your graphics designer who works from her home office is unable to connect to the VPN using her Macintosh desktop. What is the most likely reason why this is occurring?

   A. You need to allow CHAP authentication within the remote access policy.

   B. The graphics designer is not a member of the appropriate Active Directory group that is enabled for remote access.

C. The RAS server needs to have the AppleTalk protocol installed.

D. The clock setting on the graphics designer's computer is inaccurate.

8. You are the network administrator for a multisite Active Directory-based network. Your current network infrastructure consists of the following server machines:

- MAX-DC1
  - Windows Server 2003 DC
  - Dual Pentium III 733MHz processors
  - 1GB RAM
  - 20GB free disk space on a RAID-5 disk array
- MAX-DC2
  - Windows Server 2003 DC
  - Dual Pentium 4 1.0GHz processors
  - 1GB RAM
  - 20GB free disk space on a RAID-5 disk array
- MAX-FPS1
  - Windows Server 2003 member server
  - Pentium 4 2.04GHz processor
  - 512MB RAM
  - 25GB free disk space on a RAID-5 disk array
- MAX-FPS2
  - Windows NT 4 member server
  - Pentium III 600MHz processor
  - 512MB RAM
  - 50GB free disk space on a single disk
- MAX-APP1
  - Windows 2000 Advanced Server member server
  - Pentium III 833MHz processor
  - 256MB RAM
  - 50GB free disk space on a RAID-5 array

Your network contains over 1,000 users on Windows 2000 and XP Professional workstations belonging to a single Windows Server 2003 domain. The load on the DCs is fairly high, with processor utilization spiking to over 90 percent at several points during the day, especially first thing in the morning and close to 5 P.M. MAX-APP1 is a dedicated application development server that receives similar processor-heavy requests from your department of application developers. With the recent spate of software vulnerabilities, you would like to implement a patch management solution for the clients and servers on your network. Because of some sensitive development environments and documents on your network, you want to be able to test any updates before you apply them to your network servers and clients. You do not have any available budget for new hardware upgrades or purchases. What would be your best course of action in this scenario? (Choose all that apply.)

A. Install SUS on MAX-FPS1.

B. Install SUS on MAX-APP1.

C. Install SUS on MAX-DC2.

D. Configure a GPO to point your clients to the internal SUS server.

E. Create a logon script to modify client Registry entries to point to the internal SUS server.

F. Configure a GPO to point your clients to the Windows Update site.

Self Test Quick Answer Key

For complete questions, answers, and explanations to the Self Test questions in this chapter as well as the other chapters in this book, see the Self Test Appendix.

1. **A, B, D**
2. **D**
3. **B**
4. **A**
5. **D**
6. **A**
7. **A**
8. **A, D**

Appendix A

MCSE 70-298

Self Test Questions, Answers, and Explanations

This appendix provides complete Self Test Questions, Answers, and Explanations for each Chapter.

Chapter 1: Designing a Secure Network Framework

1. In performing a risk analysis of your network, you determine that your company lost approximately $100,000 last year from losses relating to laptops being stolen from unattended offices. Your company's CEO and CFO agree that they want to implement some type of safeguard that will reduce that number to a maximum of $50,000. You have been presented with three options to reduce losses. Option 1: A fully staffed reception desk that will sign visitors in and out of the building and examine all outgoing equipment to ensure that it is not leaving the premises illegally. It is expected that this will reduce losses due to equipment theft by 80 percent. The total annual cost for this measure, including equipment and personnel, will be $60,000. Option 2: A card-swipe system will be installed on all entrances that will ensure that only employees carrying legitimate access cards will be able to enter company premises. It is expected that this measure will reduce losses due to equipment theft by 65 percent. The total annual cost for this measure, including equipment and installation, will be $15,000. Option 3: A user-awareness campaign will be launched to make users more cognizant of the risks inherent in leaving their laptops and other equipment unattended. Certain employees will be designated as "Loss Prevention Monitors" to keep an eye out for potentially hazardous situations such as laptops being left unattended, and inform management so that the offending employee can be reminded of the importance of securing his or her equipment. It is expected that this measure will reduce losses due to equipment theft by 25 percent. The total annual cost for this measure, including personnel time, will be $10,000. Which of these measures is the most cost-effective way to meet the request of your CEO and CFO?

   A. Implement Option 1.

   B. Implement Option 2.

   C. Implement Option 3.

   D. None of these solutions is cost-effective.

   ☑ **B**. When you are assessing the cost-effectiveness of a security measure, you need to take the amount of money that it is expected to save, and subtract from that the actual cost of the safeguard itself. In Option 2, the cost related to equipment losses will be reduced by $65,000 (65 percent of 100,000). You then need to subtract the cost of the safeguard itself, so the total savings to the company will be $65,000 – $15,000 = $50,000. This meets the requirements put forth by the company CEO and CFO.

☒ Answer **A** is incorrect, because the cost savings from Option 1 will be $80,000 (80 percent of $100,000) minus the cost of the safeguard. Therefore, the total savings to the company will be $80,000 – $60,000 = $20,000. This does not meet the requirements put forth by the CEO and CFO. Answer **C** is incorrect because the cost savings will be $25,000 (25 percent of $100,000). You then subtract the cost of the safeguard itself for a total cost savings of $25,000 – $10,000 = $15,000. This does not meet the requirements put forth by the company CEO and CFO. Answer **D** is incorrect because Option 2 is a cost-effective solution that meets the requirements set forth by company management.

2. You are creating a security design for the Blue Sky LTD Corporation. The company CEO knows that many people on the network currently use information like their pets' or children's names for their network passwords; she is extremely concerned about hackers attempting to guess these passwords and gain access to corporate network resources. She has requested that password security be made more stringent in the new design, with a minimum of a 24-character password for all systems. What would you tell her is a potential drawback of requiring user passwords to be this long?

   A. Users will be more likely to write down a password that is so difficult to remember.

   B. User passwords should be at least 30 characters long to guard against brute-force password attacks.

   C. There are no drawbacks; this creates network passwords that will be impossible for an unauthorized user to penetrate.

   D. Windows 2003 will not allow a password of more than eight characters.

   ☑ **A.** Even if you could set a minimum password requirement of 25 characters (the maximum for this setting is 14 characters), a 25-character password would be unreasonably long, and would prompt your users to write it down on their monitors or in their wallets. This creates another avenue of attack that can easily render such a strong password meaningless.

   ☒ Answer **B** is incorrect, because a password length of 8 to 14 characters is usually sufficient to guard against most brute-force attacks. Answer **C** is incorrect because a 25-character password will create the issues described in Answer **A.** Answer **D** is incorrect because Windows passwords can be up to 255 characters in length.

3. You are a security analyst for the Widgets Corporation, which uses Windows Server 2003 servers to store data regarding several patent-pending products that they are developing. Because of the sensitive nature of this information, both

successful and failed attempts to access product-related data on the file server is logged to the Windows Security log, and the information can only be accessed from within the Widgets headquarters—there is no current means of using VPN or other forms of remote access. While you are looking over the security logs one week, you notice that one of the Widgets product managers, Ethan Hopkins, accessed files for a number of different projects on a day when you know that he was out of the office for several days. When you question Ethan about it, he verifies that he was out of the office on that day and has no idea what could have happened. However, you discover in a passing conversation with your help desk manager that someone claiming to be Mr. Hopkins called the help desk that day demanding to have his password reset, since he had been called in for an important sales presentation and couldn't wait. What kind of attack has occurred here?

A. Password guessing

B. Spoofing

C. Network sniffing

D. Social engineering

☑ **D**. Social engineering attacks take advantages of unsuspecting users and weaknesses in administrative security policies to gain access to a user account or password. This type of attack can be addressed through security awareness and a stringent adherence to security policies for administrators, help desk associates, and end users of all levels.

☒ Answer **A** is incorrect because in this case, the attacker did not need to guess the user's password—it was given to him by the help desk as a result of his social engineering. Answer **B** is incorrect because spoofing is a technical attack in which one machine is made to look like another. Answer **C** is incorrect because network sniffing is a technical attack in which network packets are physically intercepted and analyzed by someone running a copy of Network Monitor or some other packet sniffer.

4. You are the network administrator for a large Windows Server 2003 network, supporting 40 servers and over 1000 Windows 2000 Professional and Windows XP Professional clients. You have received a call from a user who is complaining that his computer will no longer boot correctly. Upon investigating, you discover that the machine will only get halfway through the logon sequence before displaying the Blue Screen of Death. When you ask the user if he noticed anything unusual before the computer began misbehaving, he reports that he had just downloaded a game from a URL that a friend had sent him via e-mail. The machine seemed to run fine after the game was installed, but as soon as the user rebooted the machine, it no longer powered on correctly. What is the most likely reason why the user's machine is no longer booting correctly?

A. The downloaded game is not compatible with Windows XP Professional.

B. The workstation has suffered a hardware failure.

C. The downloaded game was actually malicious code containing a Trojan horse.

D. The workstation is undergoing a DoS attack.

☑ **C.** Trojan horses are pieces of malicious code embedded in an otherwise harmless-looking program such as a game or a screensaver. These attacks most often infect end-user workstations via files downloaded from the Internet or from an e-mail attachment. Based on the description of the problem, this is the most likely reason why the user's workstation is not booting correctly.

☒ Answers **A**, **B**, and **D**, while all possibilities, are far less likely reasons for the workstation failure than the likelihood that the downloaded game contained malicious code such as a Trojan horse.

5. You are performing a security audit of a Windows Server 2003 network for the branch office of a bank. You have detected an unauthorized computer that is capturing network traffic being sent between your head teller's workstation and the server used to settle account information at the end of the day. You suspect that this computer has changed some of the network data that has been transmitted between these two computers to alter the financial records coming from the teller workstation. What type of attack is most likely taking place in this scenario?

A. DoS

B. Man-in-the-middle

C. Password guessing

D. IP Spoofing

☑ **B.** When an attacker intercepts network traffic between two parties and alters the data before the transmission is completed, this is called a MITM attack. When this occurs, both parties believe that they are only communicating with one another, when in fact the attacker is intercepting the entire conversation.

☒ Answer **A** is incorrect because a DoS attack is designed to overwhelm a vulnerable computer so that it cannot provide resources and access to legitimate users. Answer **C** is incorrect because a password-guessing attack cannot alter network data, but simply attempts to brute-force its way into guessing a legitimate user's password. Answer **D** is incorrect because a spoofing attack is one where an attacker disguises his or her attack so that it appears that it is coming from another location, or else impersonates a trusted computer to trick unsuspecting users into giving the attacker their information.

6. You are performing a Risk Analysis for Blue Sky, LTD., a charter plane service running a Windows Server 2003 network. Since Blue Sky receives a significant portion of its client referrals from the blueskyltd.com Web site, the CFO has decided that any losses due to a Web server outage would pose an extreme financial risk to the company. Because of this, you have decided to outsource the hosting of your Web site to a third party. You will pay this hosting service a monthly fee, in return for which they will guarantee 99.999-percent uptime and availability of the Blue Sky Web site for your customers. Which principle of Risk Management have you employed by taking this measure?

   A. Risk Avoidance

   B. Risk Mitigation

   C. Risk Transference

   D. Risk Acceptance

   ☑ **C.** When you transfer the responsibilities associated with a particular risk to a third party, you have transferred that risk. A similar tactic would be performing risk transference by taking out an insurance policy against the theft of an automobile.

   ☒ Answer **A** is incorrect because hosting your Web site externally does not remove the possibility that losses associated with downtime will occur. An example of Risk Avoidance would be to avoid risks associated with Web server downtime by removing your company's Web presence altogether. Answer **B** is incorrect because Risk Mitigation refers to taking steps to lessen the likelihood that a risk will occur. Placing a Web server behind a firewall and proactively installing security patches would be a method of Risk Mitigation. Answer **D** is incorrect because Risk Acceptance means that you are taking no further measures to alleviate any risks to your network, either because the value of the asset is too little, or because the risk cannot be reduced any further in a cost-effective manner.

7. You are working as the network administrator responsible for monitoring and maintaining 25 Windows Server 2003 servers and 500 Windows XP Professional workstations. You are checking the Network Monitor that is running on your Web server and notice a sudden influx of TCP SYN (Synchronization) packet requests with no subsequent completion of the TCP handshake. What is this type of activity most likely an indicator of?

A. Your network is beginning to sustain a DoS attack.

B. Someone is attempting to guess passwords of user accounts on your network.

C. This is normal activity and not something that you should worry about.

D. Your company's Internet connection has failed and you should contact your Internet service provider (ISP).

☑ **A.** A common way to begin a DoS attack is to send a stream of TCP SYN, or Synchronization, packets to a server and never complete the rest of the TCP connection. Because most servers will leave these "half-open" connections waiting to be completed, they can overwhelm a server to the point that it cannot respond to legitimate user requests.

☒ Answer **B** is incorrect because a password-guessing attack would not use the TCP SYN flooding that is common with DoS attacks. In a password attack, you would be more likely to see a series of failed logon attempts in the Security Log of the Event Viewer. Answer **C** is incorrect because TCP SYN flooding is not a normal network condition, and therefore one that you should investigate as a potential security incident. Answer **D** is incorrect because a lost Internet connection would manifest itself by an inability to reach hosts on the Internet, transmit e-mail and the like; it does not typically create a SYN flood against a specific server.

8. You have been hired as a consultant by the Widgets, Inc. manufacturing company to design security for their company headquarters. The current network consists of several Windows NT4 application and file servers; users connect to the servers via NT4 workstations located throughout the floor of the manufacturing plant. Because of a specialized interface between the manufacturing equipment and the mission-critical software that controls it, user workstations cannot be upgraded away from NT4 until the Widgets developers are able to port the application to a new version of the desktop operating system. Because of a concern regarding the security of user passwords and logon information, the Widget's CTO wants all network communications to be encrypted. What is the highest level of encryption that you would recommend in this scenario?

A. LM

B. NTLM

C. NTLMv2

D. Kerberos

☑ **C.** If the Windows NT 4 workstations cannot be upgraded to a more recent version of the operating system, the highest encryption level that this network can currently support is NTLM, version 2. Windows NT 4 Workstation does not support the use of Kerberos for LAN communications.

☒ Answer **A** is incorrect, because LM authentication is a legacy authentication method that predates even Windows NT4 and was used primarily for the Windows 9*x* family of operating systems. LM authentication is fairly insecure with several well-known vulnerabilities that can allow passwords and other information to be obtained by anyone running a network sniffer. Answer **B** is incorrect, because while NTLM authentication is an improvement over LM, the updated NTLMv2 resolves several vulnerabilities and provides greater encryption than its predecessor. Answer **D** is incorrect because the Windows NT4 operating system does not support Kerberos; this is only supported in Windows 2000 or later.

9. You have been contracted to create an Internet-based VPN solution for an organization with a large traveling sales force. The organization has standardized on Windows Server 2003 servers. Sixty percent of the sales force has been issued a new laptop running the Windows 2000 Professional operating system within the past year. As part of the VPN deployment, the remainder of the sales force will receive laptops that are running Windows XP Professional. The CEO and CTO both agree that the VPN solution should use the best security possible. Which protocol should you recommend when designing a VPN solution in this scenario?

A. SPAP

B. IPSEC/L2TP

C. PPTP

D. MS-CHAPv2

☑ **B**. When designing a VPN solution, the IPSec/L2TP will provide the best security if all clients can support it. IPSec/L2TP is supported natively by Windows 2000 and XP Professional, and support for it can be added to Windows NT4.

☒ Answer **A** is incorrect because SPAP is a legacy protocol used for dial-up accounts that uses minimal encryption and can easily be sniffed. Answer **C** is incorrect, because while PPTP was the standard VPN protocol for use with NT4 and previous operating systems, the more modern OSs specified in this scenario will allow you to use IPSec/L2TP. Answer **D** is incorrect because MS-CHAPv2 is used for negotiating basic dial-up modem connectivity, not for securing VPN traffic.

10. You are the network administrator for a network whose infrastructure is made up of a combination of Windows Server 2003 and UNIX servers. Currently, your company's DNS servers all exist on DNS servers using BIND version 8.1.2. You would like to transition the DNS service to Windows Server 2003 in order to take advantage of secure updates. Your CTO is concerned that the transition needs to be seamless, and has asked you to bring a single Windows Server 2003 DNS server online and configure it to coexist with the existing BIND servers to ensure that client name resolution will not be interrupted. What should you be concerned with when configuring a Windows Server 2003 DNS server to coexist with a BIND DNS server? (Choose all that apply.)

    A. Securing the zone transfer process.

    B. Securing WINS lookups from the BIND DNS servers.

    C. Configuring the BIND servers to use NTLMv2 authentication.

    D. Securing the record update process.

    ☑ **A, D**. When you are configuring a Windows Server 2003 DNS server to coexist with a UNIX-based DNS server, you need to ensure that the zone transfer process has been secured. In a homogeneous Windows environment, you can control which servers can and cannot retrieve zone transfer information through the Windows GUI. If you will be requesting zone transfers from a UNIX server, these same kinds of controls need to be created. Therefore, Answer **A** is correct. Second, you need to ensure that the process of sending record updates to the UNIX DNS server is encrypted so that your company's DNS information cannot be intercepted by a curious or malicious user running a packet sniffer. Therefore, Answer **D** is correct.

    ☒ Answer **B** is incorrect because only BIND DNS servers do not integrate with the Windows Server 2003 WINS service when performing DNS lookups. Answer **C** is incorrect because NTLM is a Windows-specific authentication mechanism—you will need to find a secure alternative when configuring authentication to a UNIX DNS server.

Chapter 2: Securing Servers Based on Function

1. You are the network administrator for a small network that has 40 computers on a network. You have two Windows Server 2003 computers, one of which is a DC and the other is providing remote access to users who travel throughout the United States. The computer running the remote access services also runs DHCP, DNS, and WINS for your firm. There are two file and application

servers running Windows 2000, and you have client computers running Windows XP, Windows 2000, and Windows 98. Your applications are all the latest versions, although one was originally written for Windows 95 and another was developed in-house about six years ago. Based on this information, applying which predefined template might cause disruptions on the network?

A. Secure*.inf

B. Hisec*.inf

C. Compat*.inf

D. Setup security.inf

☑ **B.** The Hisec*.inf security settings are not compatible with down-level clients, including Windows 98. Since you have clients running this operating system, you would need to review and modify the settings in the hisec*.inf template or install the Directory Service client for the Windows 98 computers. The hisec*.inf template rejects the LAN Manager authentication protocol. Client computers are required to respond with NTLM v2 if they do not support other more advanced authentication. Windows 98 cannot respond with NTLM v2 without installing the Directory Service. Otherwise, Windows 98 computers might not be able to connect to needed resources, including WINS and DHCP as well as other domain services.

☒ Answer **A** is incorrect because the secure*.inf template requests the use of stronger security functions but does not require them. For example, it will use NTLM v2 if the client supports it but it will accept a response from a client that cannot use NTLM v2. Therefore, this answer is not the best answer. Answer **C** is incorrect. The Compat*.inf template is used to provide access to certain system and registry areas needed by older applications. You might need to use this template in this scenario because of the two older applications you're running. This template would not cause disruption, but it might create security holes that should be monitored closely. Answer **D** is incorrect. The Setup security.inf template is the default template applied to all computers that have Windows Server 2003 installed as a clean installation. These security settings, by default, are much tighter than previous versions of the operating system, but should not cause problems with down-level clients.

2. In the MMC snap-in Security Configuration and Analysis, you open a new database you call Test1. You select the securedc.inf template and click OK. At this point, what is the state of the security on the computer you're working on?

A. The settings from the computer and the securedc.inf template have been merged.

B. The settings from the securedc.inf template have been applied.

C. The settings from the database, including the imported securedc.inf template, have been applied.

D. The settings on the local computer have not changed.

☑ **D.** The settings on the local computer have not changed. The Security Configuration and Analysis snap-in allows you to test (configure and analyze) security settings before applying them. This snap-in is used to test various scenarios and analyze settings compared to local computer settings, but settings are not applied unless you select the Configure Computer Now option in the snap-in.

☒ Answer **A** is incorrect. The security settings are typically merged when a template is applied to a system. However, the Security Configuration and Analysis snap-in allows you to test configurations in a virtual manner without applying them to your local computer. Since you opened a new database, the template settings were the only settings present. Answer **B** is incorrect. The settings from securedc.inf have been imported and will be used only if Configure Computer Now is selected. Answer **C** is incorrect. The settings from the database, Test1, and the securedc.inf template will be merged if applied to the local computer. However, the Test1 database is a blank database with no settings; therefore, if applied, the settings would be the default securedc.inf settings along with the local computers existing security settings.

3. You have opened the securedc.inf template via the MMC snap-in Security Templates. You expand the nodes in the left pane until you find the Account Policies. You select Kerberos Policy and notice that all the policies are "Not Defined." What step do you need to take in order to define any one of those policies?

   A. None. If a policy is not defined in a predefined security template, you cannot modify it.

   B. None. You should never modify the settings in a predefined security template.

   C. Double-click the policy, modify the settings, check the box to "Define this policy setting in the template," and click OK.

   D. Right-click the policy, check the box to "Define this policy setting in the template," and click OK.

   ☑ **D.** You must check the box "Define this policy setting in the template" before you can actually modify any policy settings that are "Not Defined." When you click the check box, the policy setting options are enabled (no longer grayed out) and you can set the options. Even if you choose to disable an option, you must define it before you can assign it a value.

☒ Answer **A** is incorrect. Predefined security templates are simply a way to manage a wide range of security settings across the enterprise. Predefined settings can be modified via the Security Templates snap-in to the MMC. Answer **B** is incorrect. It is true that you should not modify the predefined security templates. However, to use the settings provided in a predefined security template as a baseline and make modifications from that point, you can make the modifications and then right-click the predefined security template node in the left pane and select Save As to save the predefined template with a custom name so that you preserve the original template files. Answer **C** is incorrect. One way to access the policy settings dialog is to right-click; another is to double-click the policy. However, you will be unable to modify the settings until you select "Define this policy setting in the template." If the policy setting is already defined, you can simply double-click the policy and modify the settings.

4. After upgrading a computer from Windows 2000 to Windows Server 2003, you notice that some of the settings in the USER_RIGHTS area of security are not exactly as you'd like them. You'd like to use the settings for USER_RIGHTS found in the secure*.inf template. What is the best way to apply the settings for USER_RIGHTS from the secure*.inf template to the local computer?

   A. Use the *secedit.exe /configure* command using the */cfg* switch to specify the securews.inf template, the */overwrite* switch to clear the existing database settings, and the */area* switch to specify USER_RIGHTS.

   B. Use the *secedit.exe /analyze* command to analyze the difference between the USER_RIGHTS on the local computer and the USER_RIGHTS settings in the securews.inf template.

   C. Use the *secedit.exe /cfg /USER_RIGHTS* command to configure the USER_RIGHTS area of the current security template.

   D. Use the *secedit.exe /analyze* command with the */db* switch to specify which database should be analyzed. You do not need the */cfg* switch to analyze the settings in the configuration stored in the current database.

   ☑ **A.** The task here is to set the USER_RIGHTS security settings according to the USER_RIGHTS settings area of the secure*.inf template. The recommended method is via the *secedit.exe* command-line tool. In this case, you want to configure current database settings with the USER_RIGHTS settings. This command would use the following syntax: *secedit /configure /db oldsecurews.dbs /cfg securews.inf /overwrite /USER_RIGHTS /log oldsecurews.log*

☒ Answer **B** is incorrect. Analyzing the difference in USER_RIGHTS in the current configuration, and the securews.inf template is certainly a good step to take to understand the difference in the settings. However, you've already determined that the settings are not as you want them. Therefore, the next step is not to analyze the difference, but to import the settings from this one security area of a predefined template, secure*.inf. Answer **C** is also incorrect. The */cfg* switch in the *secedit* command-line tool is a switch that defines which security template you will use. However, you must first specify which action you want to take. In this case, you want to configure, so you would need to specify the */configure* action before using the */cfg* switch. You must also specify which template to use, and you cannot use the */cfg* switch without a filename. Answer **D** is incorrect. You need to configure, not analyze, your settings, so using the */analyze* command will not accomplish your task. In addition, you must specify both the database you want to configure (required parameter) and which security template settings (/cfg filename parameter) you want to use.

5. You've just completed a security audit and determined that you should tighten up password security settings on one of your Active Directory sites. Currently, the minimum password length is not defined, meaning that users could elect to use a blank password. To rectify this situation, you assign the task of modifying this to one of the junior network administrators. He implements the policy for the site through Active Directory Sites and Services, but the policy does not take effect. When he comes back to you to report the problem, what can you tell him about this problem?

   A. A local policy might be overwriting this new policy. Check local policy settings.

   B. Active Directory Sites and Services does not support applying security policies.

   C. You must use the *gpupdate* command-line tool to refresh the policy in order to see the policy in place.

   D. Password and account policies are applied at the domain level.

   ☑ **D**. Password and account policies are always applied and managed at the domain level. Setting them at the site level will have no effect. The domain policies will take precedence over site settings for password and account policies.

   ☒ Answer **A** is incorrect. In some cases, local policy can overwrite other policies since policies are applied in this priority: OU, domain then local computer. Domain password account policies will always take precedence. Answer **B** is incorrect. You can apply security policies via the Active

Directory Sites and Services interface. By selecting the properties for the selected site, you can link to group policies and review or edit security settings via the Group Policy and Security tabs, respectively. Answer **C** is incorrect. If the policy has not yet updated, using the *gpudate* command will force a refresh. However, in this case, the problem is not the refresh interval but the fact that password and account policies are applied at the domain level, not the site level.

6. You've performed an analysis of your server's current security configuration as the first step in identifying the security settings you want to use for your application servers throughout the domain. The analysis results are as shown in Figure 2.22. (Results of the analysis that are typically listed under the Database Setting and Computer Setting have intentionally been removed.) Based on the data in this screenshot, what statements can you make about the results?

Figure 2.22 Security Analysis Results

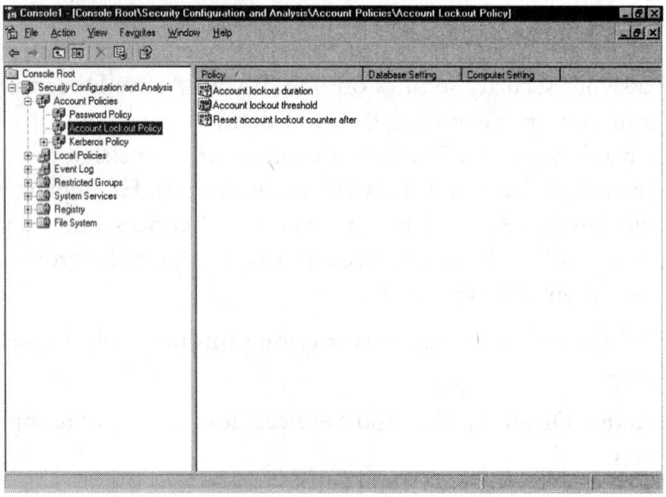

A. The **Account lockout duration** and **Reset account lockout counter after** were not analyzed because they did not exist on the local system.

B. The **Account lockout duration** and **Reset account lockout counter after** were not analyzed because they did not exist in the analysis database.

C. The **Account lockout duration** and **Reset account lockout counter after** were analyzed but the database settings did not match the local computer settings.

D. The **Account lockout duration** and **Reset account lockout counter after** were analyzed but the database did not contain definitions for these settings.

☑ **B**. The policy with the icon containing the question mark indicates that the setting was not defined in the analysis database and was not analyzed.

☒ Answer **A** is incorrect. The icon with the question mark does indicate the setting was not analyzed, but because it was not defined in the database, not the local system. If the setting were not analyzed because it did not exist on the local computer, you would have seen an exclamation point icon. Answer **C** is incorrect. The question mark icon denotes the setting on the local computer was not analyzed. If the settings were analyzed and did not match, the icon would include the red X as shown with the Account lockout threshold policy shown in Figure 2.22. Answer **D** is incorrect. If the database did not contain certain settings, those settings could not be analyzed. If the settings were not analyzed, the icon might have had no flag or a question mark

7. You've recently been tasked with upgrading several Windows 2000-based file and print servers to Windows Server 2003. You've already installed Windows Server 2003 on four other servers in the organization, two of which are located in another city connected by a high-speed Internet-based connection. What can you do to ensure that all Windows Server 2003-based file and print servers have exactly the same default settings on their drives?

   A. Apply the Setup security.inf template to all servers to set a baseline.

   B. Apply the DC secure.inf template to all servers to set a baseline.

   C. Apply the rootsec.inf template to all servers to set a baseline.

   D. Apply the securedc.inf template to all servers to set a baseline.

☑ **C**. To establish default settings for the root of the system drive, you would apply the rootsec.inf template. This template defines permissions for the root of the drive and can be used to reset values to defaults or to ensure drives all have the same default baseline settings.

☒ Answer **A** is incorrect. The Setup security.inf template is used to set all security settings for a system. Although it might be appropriate to use this template to establish baseline settings for upgraded systems, the question specifically asked about drive settings. This is not the best answer for this scenario. Answer **B** is incorrect. The DC security.inf template is created when a server is promoted to a DC. It does set file, Registry, and system service defaults. However, these computers are not being promoted to DCs, but are being used as file and print servers. Therefore, this template is not applicable. Answer **D** is incorrect. The secure*.inf template—in this case the securedc.inf template—would be applied to DCs on which you want to establish tighter security. This template would not establish a baseline because templates are applied and their settings are cumulative. In addition, this template would not be used for file and print servers that were not also DCs.

8. You work at a software company that sells an accounting software package to large institutions, including governmental organizations and school systems. The software package requires the use of SQL Server, and the company has found over the course of several years that this requirement has made selling the product more difficult. In a recent meeting, you suggest running the SQL Server-based application on the company's servers and providing access to the software package to client via Terminal Server. In talking with clients, you've discovered that most of them are running Windows 95, Windows 98, or Windows XP clients. The VP of Client Services asks you about security, knowing that governmental agencies and school districts might be quite averse to transmitting financial data across the Internet to your company. You tell the VP you've devised a security plan to address just those questions. What elements does your plan include for the highest possible security?

    A. The Terminal Server computer will run only the application for clients. It will use NTFS on the file system and will use Full Security. Clients will be able to access the application only via a secure connection. The computer will be in a controlled-access location and you'll disable drive redirection. You also require Client Compatible encryption and limit the number of user logon attempts and connection times.

    B. The Terminal Server computer will run only the application for clients. It will use NTFS on the file system and will have the Notssid.inf template applied to remove unnecessary Terminal Server SIDs. Strong passwords will be required. The computer will be in a controlled-access location, and CD and floppy drive access will be restricted to the Remote Desktop Users group.

    C. The Terminal Server computer will use NTFS on the file system, and additional security will be placed on the file system and Registry via the hisecws.inf template. Auditing the Remote Desktop Users group for unsuccessful logons will ensure only authorized users can make a connection. Strong passwords will be required. You will disable drive redirection and require encryption.

    D. The Terminal Server computer will use NTFS on the file system. It will be placed in a secure location, and CD and floppy drive access will be restricted to Administrators. You limit the number of user logons and restrict connection times. You also set the encryption requirement to High so that data to and from the Terminal server is encrypted using 128-bit encryption.

☑ **A**. By configuring Terminal Server to host only the application users need, you reduce the number of people who will be accessing the server, thereby increasing security. Formatting the system drive with NTFS secures the data on the drive. Setting Terminal Server to use Full Security will provide set security defaults to the highest possible settings while still allowing normal Terminal Server functions to occur. Older applications often cannot run in the Full Security mode because they must be written to run in the context of an ordinary user. However, because your firm is the developer of the application, you can make any modifications needed to ensure the application runs in the Full Security mode. Physically securing the system is always a good security measure when you are concerned about internal security. Disabling drive redirection will prevent users from redirecting data on the Terminal server to their own computer. Although using Client Compatible encryption will not provide the strongest encryption possible, it will allow legacy users to connect. Although not discussed in this scenario, a better security solution (not necessarily better for your firm's clients) is to require users to run Terminal Server clients that can use the High 128-bit encryption, or upgrade clients to enable the use of FIPS Compliant encryption, which meets government standards. Limiting user connections and connection times can also help prevent unauthorized connections and usage. Although there are other steps that can be taken to secure Terminal Server, these steps are a good starting point.

☒ Answer **B** is incorrect. Running only the client application, using NTFS, using strong passwords, and controlling access to the server are all good security measures. Restricting access to CDs and floppy drives to the Remote Desktop Users group would be an unusual setting, since the Remote Desktop Users group is empty by default and the answer does not address group membership. However, applying the Notssid.inf template does not improve security. This template is used to remove Terminal Server SIDs and is typically used on computers that will not be running as Terminal servers. Answer **C** is incorrect. Using the NTFS format is a good way to secure data on the hard drive. However, using the hisecws.inf template places restrictions on a number of security areas, not just the file system and Registry, and will likely cause problems with users and connectivity, especially because you have legacy clients. Auditing the Remote Desktop Users group for unsuccessful logons will not improve security. That group is empty by default and the answer does not discuss group membership. Using strong passwords, disabling drive redirection, and requiring encryption can all help in creating a secure environment. Answer **D** is incorrect. Using NTFS as the file system format is an important security element, as is placing the server in a secure location and restricting access to CDs and floppy drives. These protect the data on the Terminal server. Limiting the number of user logons and connection times can also help protect against unauthorized use. However, when you require High encryption, only clients that can handle 128-bit encryption will be able to connect. If you believe that security needs to be heightened, you would first need to work with your customers to upgrade their clients to enable 128-bit encryption.

9. Your network consists of four OUs located in three separate cities. Some clients require the use of WINS, so you've set up four WINS servers, two with static IP addresses. In two particular locations, computer names change frequently. Since replication takes place across a WAN and you're concerned with security, you've implemented the requirement to secure all replication data using IPSec. Based on this information, what is the most likely result?

   A. Using IPSec will cause a significant problem with the WINS replication process, because IPSec cannot be used to secure WINS data across a WAN.

   B. Name changes will be replicated across the WAN only during off-peak hours. Other WINS data will not be replicated unless there are changes made to the WINS database.

   C. If you implement IPSec to encrypt the WINS replication data, logging of all WINS events is enabled by default, which can decrease network performance.

   D. The replication time might be significantly increased and users might complain both of slower network connection times across the WAN and the inability to reach resources.

   ☑ **D**. Microsoft recommends encrypting WINS replication traffic that travels across a public network. In this scenario, the data is traveling across a WAN and therefore should be secured. However, implementing the IPSec protocol requires more system resources for encrypting and decrypting data, and this can affect performance, especially across slower WAN links. In addition, replication across WAN links is usually performed less often than replication across faster connections to avoid further degradation of performance. As a result, if computer names change frequently, users in other locations might not be able to locate resources until replication has occurred. This could result in users reporting they are often unable to locate resources in other locations.

   ☒ Answer **A** is incorrect. IPSec might cause replication problems across the WAN but not because it is not supported. In fact, IPSec is frequently used across WANs because it encrypts data from one end to the other. Answer **B** is incorrect. When and how frequently WINS database changes are replicated are a function of the WINS server settings. Although both of these might be ideal settings for this scenario, this would not be "the most likely result" of using IPSec to secure WINS replication data. Answer **C** is incorrect. Logging of WINS events is not enabled by default. In fact, WINS logging should only be used during troubleshooting because the logging activities are very resource intensive and the logged events could quickly exceed your system event log limits.

10. You have configured one of your servers to provide streaming media services to internal users. However, you want to make sure the data on the server is secure. You've formatted the server drive with NTFS to be able to manage file and folder permissions on the system. You also want to apply additional file system security to the server. You've previously created a security template based on the secure*.inf template, named securesv.inf, and you want to apply the permissions from that template to this server. The server's current security database is named winmedia.sdb. What is the easiest way to accomplish this task?

    A. *secedit.exe /import /db securesv.inf /cfg winmedia.sdb /FILESYSTEM /quiet*

    B. *secedit /db winmedia.sdb /cfg securesv.inf /overwrite /FILESYSTEM*

    C. *secedit /configure /db winmedia.sdb /cfg securesv.inf /overwrite /FILESTORE*

    D. *secedit /import /db winmedia.sdb /cfg securesv.inf /FILESTORE /quiet*

    ☑ **C.** The *secedit* command used with the */configure* switch will use a database or configuration file to configure settings on the local computer. In this case, we specified the configuration file, securesv.inf, the security template created earlier based on the secure*.inf template. By specifying the area to be configured, the changed values were limited to those in the FILESTORE section of the template. These apply only to file system permissions on the local file storage system. The */overwrite* switch is used to ensure that all settings in the FILESTORE area of the current database are overwritten with those in the securesv.inf file, which is what the scenario specified as the desired result.

    ☒ Answer **A** is incorrect. The *secedit* command's filename is secedit.exe, but it does not require the use of the extension to run properly. The */import* switch is used to import settings that can be used to configure or analyze the security settings. However, the database file uses the .sdb extension, and the configuration file uses the .inf extension. Answer **B** is incorrect. This *secedit* command is missing the primary parameter telling secedit what action to take. This command requires the */configure* parameter to be specified before it will run properly. Answer **D** is incorrect. The */import* switch will pull in settings from the specified configuration file. However, without the */overwrite* switch, the settings will be merged, leaving you with unspecified security settings. To ensure the settings are exactly as configured in the securesv.inf FILESTORE section, you should use the */overwrite* option.

Chapter 3: Designing a Secure Public Key Infrastructure

1. NoMoreHackers Inc. is implementing a PKI implementation. You have been asked to work as a consultant to design the PKI blueprint for the company. You have met with the CIO and the senior management to gather the requirements. You are confident of creating a sophisticated PKI architecture for the company. What will be your first step in the process?

   A. Determine the location of the CAs.

   B. Design the root CA.

   C. Determine which CA trust hierarchy we will use.

   D. Design the head office CA first, and then proceed to the regional offices.

   ☑ **B**. The first step of designing the PKI implementation is to structure your root CA. The root CA will manage and delegate the rest of the CAs of the enterprise.

   ☒ Answer **A** is incorrect. The locations of the CAs should be taken into account at the design phase. However, the choice of the root CA might dictate the location for the subordinate CAs (the subordinate CAs can also be based close the root CA to reduce network and data transmission costs). Answer **C** is incorrect. The CA hierarchy is controlled by the root CA. The hierarchy can be modified to suit a location or an organizational structure. However, the root CA will remain as the authority. The root CA does not need to reside in the head office of the enterprise; it could easily be accommodated in one of the IT departments. Therefore, we do not need to design the security implications for the head office and proceed to the regional offices; hence, Answer **D** is incorrect.

2. IronCladSecurity Ltd's organization structure has several components. The majority of IT needs of the enterprise are met by the IronCladSecurity staff. This includes manufacturing, accounting, and sales divisions of the company. They also subcontract to other IT companies to provide IT services. The proposed PKI security structure should support all these business activities. What do you recommend to implement at IronCladSecurity under Windows Server 2003?

   A. Have one root CA and one intermediary CA.

   B. Have one root CA for internal use and one intermediary for external use.

   C. Have one root CA and two intermediaries for internal and external use.

   D. Have two root CAs for internal and external use.

☑ **C.** There can be only one root CA in a Windows Server 2003 PKI architecture. There are clear internal and external activities at this company. The best practice is to have an intermediary CA for internal use and an external CA for external use.

☒ Answer **A** is incorrect. To have one root CA is correct. However, we need at least two intermediaries to delineate the internal and the external users. The root CA will be for both internal and external use; therefore, Answer **B** is incorrect. You cannot have two root CAs in a Windows Server 2003 environment; hence, Answer **D** is incorrect.

3. You are contemplating the hierarchy of the CA servers at IronCladSecurity. IronCladSecurity has 40 offices in the United States, Germany, and Singapore. They have both contractors and permanent employees working for them, and have multiple IT departments. However, there is no Active Directory implementation for the enterprise. IronCladSecurity prefers to have independent entries as subsidiaries. Therefore, they do not prefer to link the three IT systems to accommodate a global IT system. What trust hierarchies can IronCladSecurity support?

   A. Geographical and network

   B. Network and organizational structure

   C. Geographical and organizational structure

   D. Organizational structure and network

   ☑ **C.** IronCladSecurity can easily accommodate geographical and organizational trust CA hierarchies. We need to have a global directory (such as Active Directory) to support network CA hierarchy.

   ☒ Answer **A** is incorrect because we cannot implement a network hierarchy without Active Directory at IronCladSecurity. We can easily accommodate a geographical hierarchy, not a network hierarchy. Answer **B** is also incorrect. We can accommodate an organizational structure hierarchy, not a network hierarchy. Answer **D** is also incorrect. We can implement an organizational structure, not a network hierarchy.

4. You are reviewing a previous PKI implementation of a company called NoMoreHackers. It has come to your attention that all of the CA servers are connected to the network. The root CA, intermediary, and issuing CAs are connected to the same domain. You believe this a severe security risk and have instructed the company to take the servers offline. What step will not assist you to make the CA servers offline?

   A. Shut down the CA computer.

   B. Shut down the CA service.

C. Shut down the CSP service.

D. Configure CA as a Windows Server 2003 stand-alone server that is not connected to the domain.

☑ **C**. The question is about CAs, not CSPs. The CSPs (cryptographic server providers) store the key information in memory or on hardware devices. Therefore, shutting down the CSP service will not have an impact on taking the CA offline.

☒ Answer **A** is incorrect. Shutting down the CA computer will make the CA offline. The CA could be taken offline by shutting down the CA service also. Therefore, Answer **B** is incorrect. We can also take the CA offline by configuring it as a Windows 2003 stand-alone server that is not connected to a domain. It will be difficult for the hackers to find the CA even if they hack into the domain; hence, Answer **D** is also incorrect.

5. You are proposing a new PKI implementation for NoMoreHackers to replace the existing security structure. You have proposed a three-tier CA server structure with online and offline CAs to protect the CAs from intruders. You will have root CA, policy CAs, and issuing CAs in your implementation. Which CAs will be set as offline CAs?

A. Only the root CA; the issuing and policy CAs can be online.

B. The root CAs and policy CAs; the issuing CAs will be online.

C. Only the policy CAs; the root CA and issuing CAs can be online.

D. The policy and issuing CAs will be offline; the root CA will be online.

☑ **B**. The root CA and the policy CAs should be protected and should be offline to the users. The issuing CAs need to be online to provide the certificates to the end users.

☒ Answer **A** is incorrect. The policy CAs need to be offline also. The policy CAs have sensitive information of the enterprise, and therefore need to be protected. The root CA must be offline; hence, Answer **C** is incorrect. Answer **D** is also incorrect. The root CA should never be online.

6. You are about to install a CA on Windows Server 2003. You have a choice of two machines. One is a single processor machine with 1GB of memory with an existing Windows Server 2003 on a FAT file system. The other system is a twin processor with 512MB of memory on an NTFS file system. Which one would you choose to host the CA?

A. Use the first CA with 1GB of memory. The CA needs a lot of memory.

B. Use the first option because of the FAT file system.

C. Use the second option because Windows Server 2003 works best on a single-server system.

D. Use the second system because of the NTFS system.

☑ **D**. The CA implementation on Windows Server 2003 should be installed on an NTFS file system. This will enable the CA to communicate with Active Directory and share Windows account information.

☒ Answer **A** is incorrect. Windows Server 2003 does not require a lot of memory. There is not much difference between 1GB and .5 GB of memory. Answer **B** is also incorrect. We should not install a CA on a FAT file system. Windows 2003 CA is not optimized to run on single servers; therefore, Answer **C** is also incorrect.

7. We are going through the wizards to install a CA on a Windows Server 2003 server. We have selected the type as a stand-alone root CA. We have also selected the MS Strong Cryptographic Provider as the CSP. Now we need to select a hashing algorithm for the private and public key pair. What is a Windows 2003 hashing algorithm that comes with default CA installation?

A. Asymmetric

B. .NET Crypto API

C. Triple DES

D. SHA-1

☑ **D**. SHA-1 is a hashing algorithm that comes with the Windows Server 2003 CA Service.

☒ Answer **A** is incorrect. Asymmetric algorithms have key pairs that are not identical. The PKI process generates asymmetric keys; it is not a hashing algorithm. Answer **B** is also incorrect. .NET Cryptographic libraries are used to encrypt data communication in .NET assemblies. Triple DES is also an encryption mechanism to protect data communication; hence, Answer **C** is also incorrect.

8. Our management has asked us to install a CA to issue certificates to the employees and the business partners of our company. We are contemplating either Windows 2000 Server or Windows Server 2003 as our CA implementation. You have read that there are several new features in the Windows Server 2003 CA architecture that support a better implementation for the company. What are the new features?

A. Certificate templates

B. Auto-enrollment and Active Directory support

C. Web enrollment support interface and Active Directory support

D. Auto-enrollment and Web enrollment support interface

☑ **D**. The new features are auto-enrollment and Web support CA interface.

☒ Answer **A** is incorrect. Certificate templates are available in Windows 2000 servers. The requirement for certificate templates is an Active Directory, not Windows 2000. Active Directory support is also available in Windows 2000. It does not integrate as smoothly as Windows Server 2003 does; however, it is present. Therefore, Answer **B** is incorrect. The same applies for Answer **C**.

9. You are been appointed as the new CA administrator of one of the subordinate CA servers. You will administer the CA through the MMC Certification Authority application. You are experimenting with the different functionalities of the CA console. What is not available to you modify in the CA MMC console?

   A. Revoke certificates

   B. Issue certificates from the pending queue

   C. View certificate details

   D. Change certificate's hash algorithm

   ☑ **D**. You will not be able to change the certificate's hash algorithm through the CA MMC console. The algorithm is determined when the user requests a certificate. The administrator will not be able to change this. The certificate will be invalid if the algorithm is altered.

   ☒ Answer **A** is incorrect. You can choose to revoke certificates from the CA console. Answer **B** is also incorrect. The administrators can also issue certificates form the pending queue. We can also view the certificate data by double-clicking on the certificate in the CA console; hence, Answer **C** is also incorrect.

10. Several of your company resources are behaving strangely. You have noticed that some of the printer queues were deleted using an administrator account. All of these printers are protected using the PKI certificates of the company. You suspect that someone has obtained the CA keys and is impersonating the administrator account to delete the print queue. How will you solve this puzzle?

    A. Monitor the CA auditing logs and renew the CA keys.

    B. Disable auditing to save space for larger new key pairs.

    C. Monitor the CA auditing logs; however, stick with the old key pairs.

    D. Disable auditing and generate a new public key; however, use the same private key.

☑ **A.** We need to monitor auditing on a CA server to track intruder access. When we find the intruder, we need to disable his or her access. In addition, we need to create a new private and public key pair for the enterprise to avoid future hackings.

☒ Answer **B** is incorrect. Disable auditing is not the correct step to take. It also does not save a lot of space for large key pairs. Using the old key pairs is not safe for the enterprise. The hacker might have passed the key to others or published it on a Web site. This will trigger future attacks. Therefore, the keys need to be regenerated. Hence, Answer **C** is incorrect. Answer **D** is also incorrect. We cannot disable the auditing, and we need to replace both private and public keys.

Chapter 4: Securing the Network Management Process

1. Your forest is structured according to the illustration in Figure 4.15. You have a group of developers in the east.fixed-wing.airplanes.com domain who need to access files in the development.central.biplanes.airplanes.com domain on a regular basis. The users are complaining that accessing the files in the development domain is taking an unacceptably long time. What can you do to improve their response time?

Figure 4.15 Figure for Question 1

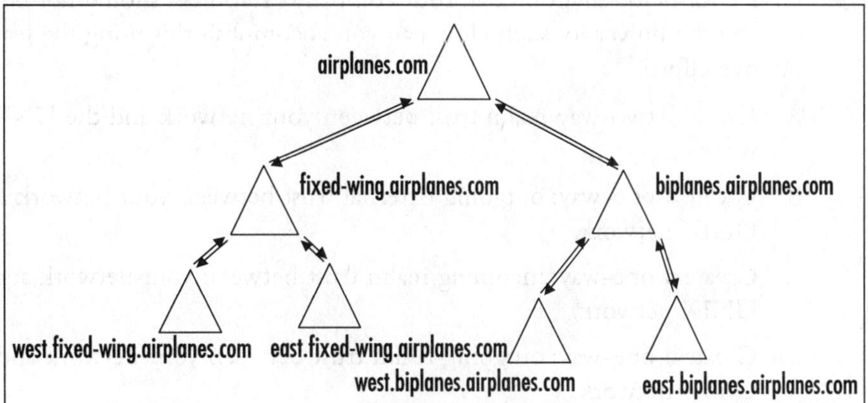

A. Create a domain local group in the development domain and add the developers' user accounts to it.

B. Create a shortcut trust between the east.fixed-wing.airplanes.com domain and the development.central.biplanes.airplanes.com domain.

C. Place the resources in the development domain into an OU. Use the Delegation of Control Wizard to grant the users in the east.fixed-wing.airplanes.com domain the appropriate permissions.

D. Create an external trust between the fixed-wing.airplanes.com domain and the biplanes.airplanes.com domain.

☑ **B.** A shortcut trust will allow logon and resource requests to process more quickly by bypassing the usual traversal of domain trusts.

☒ Answer **A** is incorrect because creating a domain local group will not speed the logon request process. Answer **C** is incorrect because grouping the resources into a separate OU will not improve logon requests from other domains in the network. Answer **D** is incorrect because an external trust is used to establish a trust relationship between a Windows Server 2003 Active Directory forest and a Windows NT4 or 2000 domain. In this case, the two domains in question are part of the same Windows Server 2003 forest.

2. You are the network administrator for a medical research facility running Windows Server 2003. Your firm is beginning a joint research operation with a major university, and many of your users will need to access files and folders on the university's network. The university that you are partnering with uses a UNIX Kerberos environment. Your company's resources should not be accessible by the university staff. How can you accomplish this using the least administrative effort?

A. Create a two-way realm trust between your network and the UNIX network.

B. Create a one-way: outgoing external trust between your network and the UNIX network.

C. Create a one-way: incoming realm trust between your network and the UNIX network.

D. Create a one-way: outgoing realm trust between your network and the UNIX network.

☑ **C.** A one-way, incoming realm trust will allow users from your network to access files on the UNIX Kerberos network while not allowing the UNIX users to browse any of your network resources.

☒ Answer **A** is incorrect because it will allow users on the UNIX network to access your network resources. Answer **B** is incorrect because an external trust is used to establish a trust relationship with a Windows NT or 2000 forest, not a UNIX Kerberos realm. Answer **D** will create the trust in the incorrect direction; the UNIX users would be able to access information on your network, but your users would not be able to browse resources in the Kerberos realm.

3. You have a critical software update that needs to be installed for the Payroll OU of your Windows Server 2003 domain. You create a new GPO and assign the MSI package to the Computer Configuration section and then link the new GPO to the Payroll OU with the appropriate security filtering permissions. You send an e-mail to the members of the payroll department instructing them to log off their workstations and log back in to prompt the software installation to begin. You run the MBSA utility to verify installation of the patch, but you discover that it has not been installed, even after you ask the payroll users to log off and onto their workstations several times. What is the most likely reason that the software update has not been installed?

   A. The workstations in the payroll department need to be rebooted before the software update will be installed.

   B. Software installation packages can only be assigned at the domain level.

   C. The software can be installed using the Add New Programs section of the Add/Remove Programs Control Panel applet.

   D. Logon scripts are running asynchronously; they must be reconfigured to run synchronously.

   ☑ **A.** When a software installation package is assigned through the Computer Configuration section of a GPO, it will only be installed when the computer starts up. The logoff/logon process is not sufficient to launch the installation process.

   ☒ Answer **B** is incorrect because software installation packages can be published or assigned at the site, domain, or OU. Answer **C** is incorrect because only *published* software packages are available through Add/Remove Programs; this package was *assigned*. Answer **D** is incorrect because the software will be installed at startup, not logon.

4. Hope Pharmaceuticals is a large organization that is headquartered in Chicago, Illinois. The company has six other locations in North America and Europe. In North America, the company has locations in Chicago, New York, and Arizona. In Europe, it has locations in Paris, London, and Rome. The Active Directory infrastructure consists of two forests: one for North America and one for

Europe. Recently, the Chicago location and the Paris location have been working together closely on deals and possible mergers. Users have started to complain of slow response times in authenticating and accessing resources in either domain. What would be the best way to improve authentication performance between Chicago and Paris?

A. Create a shortcut trust between the Chicago office and the Paris office.

B. Create a realm trust between the Chicago and Paris offices.

C. There is nothing you can do to improve performance.

D. Move the Paris domain into the North America forest.

☑ **A.** A shortcut trust is the ideal trust for this scenario. To improve performance and to avoid having authentication travel across thee entire domain trees before it authenticates against the correct domain, a shortcut trust allows the Chicago domain users and the Paris domain users to authenticate directly against the Chicago and Paris domains.

☒ Answer **B** is incorrect because realm trusts are used to connect Windows-based domains with a different realm or technology such as UNIX. Answer **C** is incorrect because you can use a shortcut trust to improve performance for your network users. Answer **D** is technically correct, but it is not the best solution, since reorganizing your forest and domain structure should be done only as a last resort.

5. You are the IT manager for an organization with three locations in Fresno, San Francisco, and La Jolla, running Windows Server 2003 on the server side and Windows XP Professional on the client side. To cut down on Internet bandwidth usage from the Windows Update client, you have installed an SUS server in each of the three locations. The SUS server is configured as the master SUS server, and Fresno and La Jolla's servers are configured as child servers. Microsoft releases a critical security update, and a few hours later you learn that a hacker group from Eastern Europe has already released an Internet worm to take advantage of any unpatched machines. You quickly download the new patch to your SUS server in San Francisco and approve the patch for distribution. Your CEO asks if your network is protected from this new threat, and you assure him that your patch management solution is up to the task. Unfortunately, you receive several calls toward the end of the day from users in Fresno who report that their machines are rebooting without warning and that network response time is almost nonexistent. On further investigation, you discover that the machines in Fresno and La Jolla were not updated with the new Microsoft patch and became victims of this new Internet worm. Your workstations and servers in the San Francisco office have received the patch. Why did SUS fail to update the machines in your two remote locations?

A. You did not install the SUS client on your client workstations.

B. The Internet connection between the Fresno and La Jolla offices did not permit the SUS traffic to pass.

C. The SUS servers in Fresno and La Jolla had not received the new update yet.

D. The security update was incompatible with your client workstations.

☑ **C**. Child SUS servers synchronize with master servers on a set schedule. Most administrators configure this synchronization to take place during off-hours, when bandwidth utilization will be affected as little as possible. In this scenario, the most likely explanation for your remote offices not getting patched is that their SUS servers had not yet received the update from the master SUS server.

☒ Answer **A** is incorrect because Windows XP Professional has the SUS client installed by default; it only needs to be configured via Group Policy. Answer **B** is incorrect because there is nothing in the scenario to suggest that you are filtering any type of Internet traffic that would prevent SUS from functioning. Answer **D** is incorrect because the SUS administrative page will allow you to download patches appropriate to each operating system, and the SUS client will automatically download the appropriate patch to the client workstation.

6. Your network is experiencing massive Internet bandwidth consumption from external sources. On investigating, you discover that a new Internet worm has been created that exploits a newly discovered vulnerability in Microsoft's Internet Information Service. You have seven IIS servers in your organization that are colocated in various cities across the United States to provide load balancing for your Web applications. Within Active Directory, all your Web servers are contained within a single OU. What is the quickest way to efficiently patch all your company's IIS servers against this new vulnerability while minimizing downtime for your Web server applications?

   A. Force the SUS server to immediately update all machines in the domain.

   B. Manually install the patch on each Web server.

   C. Create a GPO within the Computer Configuration | Software Installation settings. Link it to the Web Server OU. Reboot each Web server in turn so that the update can be applied.

   D. Create a GPO within the User Configuration | Software Installation settings. Link it to the Web Server OU. Perform a logout/login on each Web server so that the update can be applied.

☑ **D**. Software Settings applied to the User Configuration section of a Group Policy Object will take effect when a user logs in. By applying the GPO to the User Configuration instead of the Computer Configuration, you will not need to reboot the Web servers for the update to be applied.

☒ Answer **A** is incorrect because there is no way to manually force SUS to update any clients; it is designed to take place in the background. Answer **B** is incorrect because it would not be an efficient way to patch your servers, especially since they are located in various parts of the country, where you might or might not have an administrator on site. Answer **C** is incorrect because assigning the Software Installation to the Computer Configuration will require the machine to reboot before the installation takes effect. While the presence of seven servers in a load-balancing configuration will minimize the effects of these reboots, this solution will still create unnecessary downtime for your Web servers.

7. You have 12 servers at various locations that you want to manage remotely. You have read about Emergency Management Services and believe this is a good solution for your environment. You review the hardware for each of the servers in question and determine that the firmware on all of them supports console redirection. Your servers are already running Windows Server 2003 and are x86-based systems. What is your next step in implementing EMS for these servers?

   A. Use the EMS Special Administration Console to install EMS for the remote computer. Configure console redirection via the server firmware after EMS is installed.

   B. Reinstall Windows Server 2003 from the installation CD. EMS configures itself during a bootable CD installation if the computer supports firmware console redirection and the Serial Port Console Redirection (SPCR) table.

   C. Reboot the computer into Safe mode. Install EMS from the Run line, and then reboot to enable EMS.

   D. Use Bootcfg.exe to edit the Boot.ini file located on the system partition root to enable Windows loader console redirection and the SAC.

   ☑ **D**. If Windows Server 2003 is already installed, you can configure EMS by editing the Boot.ini file. The Bootcfg.exe utility is used to edit the Boot.ini file. This will allow you to instruct Windows loader (Ntldr) to redirect the console output to an out-of-band connection and will enable the Special Administration Console.

   ☒ Answer **A** is incorrect because the Special Administration Console is available only after you've enabled EMS. Once you've installed EMS, SAC and !SAC become available. Answer **B** is incorrect because you do not need to reinstall Windows Server 2003 in order to implement EMS after the operating system has already been installed. Instead, you can edit the Boot.ini file using the Bootcfg.exe utility. However, if you were installing a fresh installation of Windows Server 2003, the statements are all true. Installing from the bootable CD will configure EMS if the computer's firmware supports console redirection and the Serial Port Console Redirection (SPCR) table. Answer **C** is incorrect because you do not need to run in Safe mode nor can you install Emergency Management Services from the Run line.

8. You are the network administrator for a large, multinational corporation. Your Active Directory tree is configured with one domain for North America, one for Europe, and one for Asia. Each office on each continent has been configured with its own OU, and an administrative assistant in each office has been delegated the authority to reset user passwords within each OU. You have a single global group in each domain that contains the user accounts for the central help desk for each domain. To assist the local administrators with troubleshooting issues, you have distributed instructions concerning the use of the Remote Assistance feature in Windows XP and Windows Server 2003. After a server outage in the Dresden office, you discover that a local administrator was having a network issue and sent a Remote Assistance request to a friend of hers, who uploaded a virus-infected executable to the Dresden network, thinking that it was a diagnostic utility. What is the most efficient way to prevent this situation from recurring on your network? (Choose all that apply.)

   A. Use Group Policy to restrict to whom your users can send Remote Assistance requests.

   B. Use PGP encryption to encrypt the Remote Assistance e mail request.

   C. Disable Remote Assistance on all client workstations. Manually re-enable it as needed.

   D. Create a network security policy forbidding Remote Assistance requests to any users other than central IT staff.

   ☑ **A, D**. Using Group Policy, you can configure your network clients so that they can send Remote Assistance requests to only specific users or groups, in this case the central IT staff. Therefore, Answer **A** is correct. In combination with this step, you should explain the importance of this policy to your distributed staff so that they understand why it is critical to the security of the corporate network. Therefore, Answer **D** is correct.

   ☒ Answer **B** is incorrect because although PGP encryption will secure the contents of an RA e-mail message, it will do nothing to prevent to *whom* those messages are sent. Answer **C** is incorrect because it would be an inefficient solution, especially in a large enterprise.

Chapter 5: Securing Network Services and Protocols

1. A recent task force in your company defined several threats to the network that need to be addressed. As the head of that task force, you have been assigned the job of mitigating these threats with the least restriction to users and network availability. The top threat was identified as password attacks. Which solution would best address this threat while still meeting the criteria set forth?

   A. Implement strong password policies on all OUs and monitor network traffic to determine if data modification is taking place.

   B. Implement strong password policies at the domain level, and apply account lockout policies.

   C. Implement IPSec for all communication between clients and domain infrastructure servers.

   D. Limit user logon hours to normal working hours and implement account lockout policies. Monitor all logons attempted outside of specified logon hours.

   ☑ **B**. Strong passwords help protect user accounts from password attacks such as dictionary or brute force attacks. Strong passwords include requiring minimum length, age, and complexity. Account lockout policies can be set to lock out accounts after a set number of failed logon attempts. This helps prevent password attacks that continually try to "guess" the correct password, whether manually (by someone typing on the keyboard) or automatically (by an automated software program).

   ☒ Answer **A** is incorrect. Strong password policies will help prevent password attacks, but password policies are implemented at the domain level, not the OU level. Although monitoring network traffic can help determine if data modification is taking place, the primary threat was that of password attacks, so monitoring other things such as successful and failed logon attempts would yield better clues as to the source of the problem. Answer **C** is incorrect. IPSec communication can protect data between clients, but unless it's implemented along with strong authentication methods such as certificates or smart cards, the password attack will still be a threat. Answer **D** is incorrect. Limiting logon hours might help reduce some threats, but a password attack can occur at any time, including during allowed logon hours. Account lockout policies will help protect against password-based attacks, but **A** is a better answer because it has less impact on users and network usability, per the stated requirements.

2. Your firm has 12 Windows XP Professional SP1 computers used in a manufacturing environment that are located on the shop floor where about 200 employees work. These computers are used by a variety of staff, and in any given work day, there might be 20 or 30 people that log on to the various computers. Recently, you've noticed some odd IP traffic on the computers early in the morning, just before the start of the first shift. You had previously applied IPSec policy to the computers in this group via an OU that contains these 12 computers. What else could you do that might protect these computers and the network based on this information?

   A. Apply persistent policies to the 12 computers in the OU so that the computer is protected during startup and shutdown.

   B. Use smart cards for user authentication to prevent unauthorized access before and after working hours.

   C. Modify the IPSec policy to filter all IP traffic prior to start of shift.

   D. Check to see if the odd IP traffic is related to power fluctuations that might occur as other equipment on the shop floor is powered up at start of shift.

   ☑ **A**. Persistent policy can be used to protect computers during startup and shutdown. Typically, a computer must start up, connect to the network, and then have group policies applied. To better protect some computers, you can implement persistent policies, which are stored in the computer's local Registry and are implemented at startup.

   ☒ Answer **B** is incorrect. Smart cards do provide stronger user authentication than do password-based solutions. However, the problem is only occurring early in the day and you have not positively identified the source of the problem. If you suspected an intentional intruder, you might expect to see the problem at other times as well. Regardless, applying persistent policy to protect these computers during startup is a solution that is far easier (and less expensive) to implement than smart cards. Answer **C** is incorrect. IPSec policies are applied via group policy and remain in effect for the computer until they are a) modified, b) removed, or c) the IPSec Services is manually stopped. You would typically filter all traffic all the time, not just at certain times of day This is not the best answer. Answer **D** is incorrect. Although power fluctuations could possibly impact the computers on the shop floor, it would not show up as odd IP traffic. You might see the computer screen flicker or the system halt or shut down.

3. You're checking the configuration of several computers that are connected directly to the Internet. One of the computers recently suffered a denial-of-service (DoS) attack, but the other three were fine. You notice that the computers that were not attacked had IPSec policies applied as shown in Figure 5.22. These settings are not the same as on the computer that was attacked. Which setting(s) are the most likely reason why these computers were not attacked or not successfully attacked?

Figure 5.22 IPSec Settings

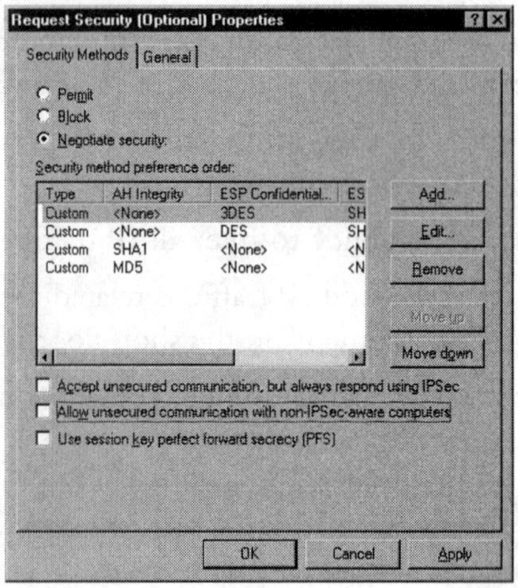

A. The computers that were not successfully attacked did not have the check box selected for **Accept unsecured communication, but always respond using IPSec**.

B. The computer that was successfully attacked did not have the check box **Allow unsecured communication with non-IPSec-aware computers** selected.

C. The computers that were not attacked did not have the **Use session key perfect forward secrecy (PFS)** selected.

D. The computers that were not successfully attacked had the check box **Allow unsecured communication with non-IPSec-aware computers** selected.

☑ **A.** The computers that were not successfully attacked did not have the check box selected for **Accept unsecured communication, but always respond using IPSec**. When this box is selected, computers can be intentionally overloaded with non-IPSec requests, forcing the computer to respond with IPSec and causing a DoS. This option not being selected on the computer that was attacked is the most likely cause of the problem.

☒ Answer **B** is incorrect. The computer that experienced the DoS attack might or might not have had this check box selected. However, what this does is allow unsecured communications with down-level clients. If an intruder configures his or her system to not use IPSec, it would appear as a down-level client. However, the DoS attack was successfully launched because the computer was set to always respond with IPSec, which takes more overhead and is likely to cause a DoS if flooded with request. Therefore, this is not the best answer. Answer **C** is incorrect. The computers that were not attacked did not have the PFS box selected, that is true. However, this is not the reason why they were immune from the DoS attack. The **Use session key perfect forward secrecy (PFS)** option is used to guarantee that no keying material will be reused. The attack did not involve compromised keys *and* this option was *not* selected on the computers that were not attacked. Therefore, this setting on the computer that *was* attacked is irrelevant to this question. Answer **D** is incorrect. because, as you can see in Figure 5.22, **Allow unsecured communication with non-IPSec-aware computers** was not selected.

4. Your network consists of three servers running Windows NT 4.0 SP6a, two servers running Windows 2000, and one server configured as a domain controller (DC) running Windows 2000. The client computers are a mix of Windows 95, Windows 98, and Windows XP. You decide to upgrade the network to improve security. You retire two of the computers running Windows NT 4.0 and replace them with two computers on which you will configure Windows Server 2003. You install Windows Server 2003 on the first computer and configure it as a DC and DHCP server. You install Windows Server 2003 on the second computer and configure it as a DC and DNS server. You configure secondary DHCP and DNS server services on one of the Windows 2000 computers, which is configured as a member server. After you complete this, you find that none of the Windows 95 computers can connect to the domain and only some of the Windows 98 computers can. What is the most likely cause of this problem?

   A. The Windows 95 and Windows 98 computers are still trying to be authenticated by the two Windows NT 4.0 servers that were replaced. Reconfigure all clients to use the Windows Server 2003 computers instead.

   B. Windows Server 2003 DCs require SMB message block signing and cannot communicate with Windows 95 computers in a domain. Upgrade the Windows 95 computers. Upgrade the Windows 98 computers to Windows XP.

   C. Windows Server 2003 DCs require SMB message block signing. Windows 95 and Windows 98 support this only with the Active Directory client installed. Install the Active Directory client service or upgrade the operating system to Windows XP.

D. The Windows Server 2003 DCs require SMB message block signing and as a result, the remaining NT 4.0 server and the Windows Server 2003 computers are not communicating. Upgrade the Windows NT 4.0 server to Windows 2000 or Windows Server 2003.

☑ **C.** Windows Server 2003 DCs are configured to require SMB message block signing, by default. Although this can be disabled, it is not recommended. Instead, the best solution is to upgrade legacy clients or, where possible, install the Active Directory client service. The Active Directory client service is available for Windows 95 and 98 computers as well as for Windows NT 4.0 (via SP4 or higher). Windows XP supports SMB message block signing and has it enabled by default. Therefore, when a Windows Server 2003 DC requires SMB message block signing, Windows XP clients will respond with SMB message block signing. The default setting in Windows XP is to respond with SMB when the server requests it.

☒ Answer **A** is incorrect. It is possible the Windows 95 and Windows 98 computers are trying to connect to domain services (DHCP, for example) on one of the Windows NT computers, if they were using static settings for the DHCP service. However, there is no information as to the configuration of the NT servers or the Windows 95 and 98 clients that would give you enough information to make this assumption. In addition, only some of the Windows 98 computers are not connecting to the network now, so you would look for what the difference was between the Windows 98 computers that were connecting and those that were not. SMB message block signing is not supported in older operating systems without add-on software and it is required, by default, on Windows Server 2003 DCs. Therefore, this is a possible answer but not the best answer. Answer **B** is incorrect. Windows Server 2003 DCs have SMB message block signing enabled by default. It can be disabled, which would allow the Windows 95 computers to connect to the DC, so the statement that Windows 95 computers cannot connect to Windows Server 2003 computers is not completely correct. In addition, although it is recommended you upgrade your Windows 95 computers to Windows XP to take advantage of a number of new security features, including SMB message block signing, this answer does not address the problem with some of the Windows 98 computers. Answer **D** is incorrect. If the remaining Windows NT 4.0 server were not running the latest service pack, it might be true that the Windows NT 4.0 computer and the Windows Server 2003 computer were not able to communicate since Windows NT 4.0 requires at least SP4 to use SMB message block signing. Therefore, this is not the correct answer.

5. You've just been hired as the IT manager for a small company. The company's IT infrastructure consists of one domain, three segments, a handful of servers, and about 95 client computers, most of which are running Windows XP. Internet access is provided through a firewall and proxy server via an Internet service provider (ISP). The corporate Web site is hosted externally by a third party, and employees connect to the Web site just as they would to any other Web site. The company has recently expanded and there are two groups of employees who regularly share files among themselves using Windows XP-based laptops. You've been tasked with finding a solution that will provide these two groups with connectivity in two different areas to enable file sharing. As always, the company is on a tight budget and wants this done quickly on a small budget. What's the best solution?

   A. Configure the two groups that require file sharing to use ad hoc wireless networking.

   B. Configure the two groups to use shorter DHCP IP lease times by applying wireless policies to them.

   C. Install wireless access points. Determine if PKI and RADIUS are implemented, and if not, implement them to provide security.

   D. Issue smart cards to the members of the two groups to provide strong authentication for the wireless users and provide wireless access via WAPs throughout the building.

   ☑ **A**. Of the solutions given, this is the best immediate solution given the parameters. The two groups regularly share files. Ad hoc wireless networking does not connect the users to the wired infrastructure, only to each other in a peer-to-peer mode. This solution would be fast to implement since Windows XP supports ad hoc wireless networking and the wireless components for laptops are relatively inexpensive. If you later implement an infrastructure-based wireless solution, you might be able to use the same wireless components (if compatible).

   ☒ Answer **B** is incorrect. It is true that wireless clients should use DHCP IP lease times that are shorter than the default, and this can be configured via DHCP scope settings. However, this does not address the first step, which is connecting the laptops together. Answer **C** is incorrect. This is certainly one solution but does not meet the needs outlined for a fast, inexpensive solution. If you already have PKI and RADIUS/IAS implemented, you would still need to ensure it was configured for wireless networking and install wireless access points. This is not the best solution for this scenario. Answer **D** is incorrect. Smart cards rely on PKI and RADIUS/IAS. As in Answer **C**, it is not clear whether the company has implemented these, but based on the size of the company and the overall IT infrastructure described, it is not likely that they have a PKI/RADIUS infrastructure. Therefore, this is neither the fastest nor the least expensive option.

6. Your firm has three wireless network defined via Wireless Network (IEEE 802.1X) Policies. One network is configured to use Network authentication (Shared mode). The two other wireless networks use Data encryption (WEP enabled). Based on this information, what steps can you take immediately to improve security across the board?

   A. Enable *Network authentication (Shared mode)* on the two wireless networks currently using *Data encryption (WEP enabled).*

   B. Edit the properties for the one network configured to use *Network authentication (Shared mode)* and set it to use WEP or, preferably, 802.1X. In addition, on the RADIUS server or wireless access points, force re-authentication every 10 minutes by changing the WEP key refresh option.

   C. Edit the WEP properties on the wireless network and configure the *Data encryption (WEP enabled)* setting to use both PEAP with EAP-TLS and EAP-TLS.

   D. Delete the network that is using *Network authentication (Shared mode)* and create a new network using the *Data encryption (WEP enabled)* setting.

   ☑ **B**. Network authentication (Shared mode) is not a secure option for wireless networking because it shares a key with all WAPs and wireless clients. This makes it vulnerable to attack. Setting this network to use WEP will improve security on that one network. Next, set the key refresh options on the WAPs or RADIUS server (wherever it's implemented in the network) to be 10 minutes or less. While this does create more overhead, it makes the likelihood of the WEP key being cracked much lower.

   ☒ Answer **A** is incorrect. This is just the opposite of the correct solution. Enabling Network authentication (Shared mode) on all wireless networks would expose the wireless networks a higher likelihood of the shared key being cracked. Answer **C** is incorrect. Although the use of PEAP with EAP-TLS or simply EAP-TLS will improve security, they should not be implemented together. Using the same authentication method with and without PEAP creates a security hole. Answer **D** is incorrect. Although you do want to enable WEP instead of Network authentication, you do not need to delete the network and create a new one. The existing network can be edited via the Wireless Network (IEEE 802.1X) Policies settings.

7. You are implementing a wireless network in portions of your large warehouse facility. There are a number of computers used by different users throughout the day for pulling or verifying orders. Users log on with smart cards to verify their

identity so that orders are tied to user logon for verifying inventory, order accuracy, and other business metrics. You implement PEAP with EAP-TLS for strong authentication since users have smart cards. Throughout the day, some of these computers are used and some are idle and the pattern of usage varies depending on the day, time, and volume of business. You typically manage these computers remotely so that you can do things like update virus definition files or install software upgrades. You configure the settings as shown in Figure 5.23. Based on this information, what is the most likely result?

Figure 5.23 Network Configuration

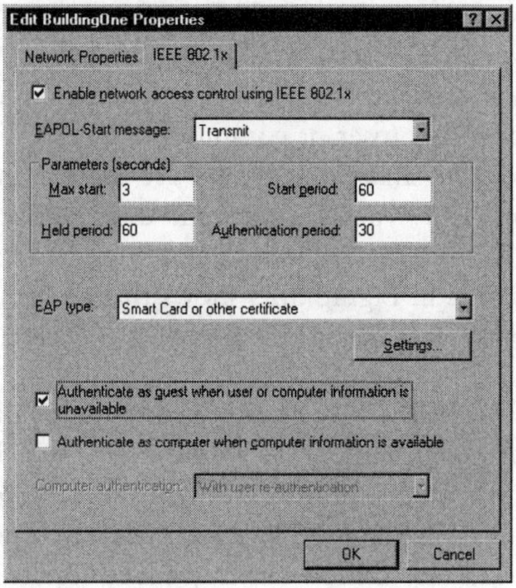

A. You will improve security by requiring authentication as guest when user or computer information is unavailable.

B. You will have to provide smart cards for any Guest users who need to access the network.

C. You will not be able to authenticate users via smart cards.

D. You will be unable to remotely manage the computers on the wireless network.

☑ **D.** The computer must be set to use computer authentication if you want to remotely manage the computer when no users are logged on. This box is checked by default to allow computer authentication to occur when users log off. Thus, user or computer authentication is in effect at all times. Computer authentication allows the computer to be connected to the wireless network in a secure manner even when no users are logged on.

☒ Answer **A** is incorrect. You essentially remove security when you select the option to **Authenticate as guest when user or computer information is unavailable**. This setting is most commonly used to provide public wireless access to the Internet when the wireless network is completely isolated from the corporate network. Otherwise, any user can gain access to the corporate network, essentially bypassing any security you might have implemented in other settings. Answer **B** is incorrect. Smart cards are typically only issued to authorized employees of the company. There might be some instances when you provide smart cards to nonemployees, such as a contractor working on a long-term basis who might need access to the network. However, there is nothing in this scenario that suggests you have authorized Guest users. In addition, the setting you selected does not require any credential because it will allow a Guest to authenticate if no other credentials (user or computer) are used. Thus, even authorized employees *with* smart cards could use these computers *without* using their smart cards and bypass security and desired business practices, including accuracy and work load assignment tracking. Answer **C** is incorrect. This setting shown in Figure 5.23 shows that the EAP type is set to use *Smart Card or other certificate*, so this answer is incorrect.

8. Your network infrastructure already makes use of PKI technologies to create a secure network environment. The infrastructure included a remote access server, and most servers are running Windows Server 2003, although there are still a handful running Windows 2000. All clients have been upgraded over the past 18 months to Windows XP. You recently added IAS to your infrastructure and configured the remote access server as a RADIUS client. You have implemented several wireless networks in your building. You've installed numerous wireless access points throughout the building and coverage is quite good throughout the building where wireless users roam. There is an area of the building that is not configured with WAPs because the area is a secure area that requires strong authentication just to physically access the area. You have not implemented wireless security in this area but are concerned about rogue WLANs being installed by employees in this highly secure area. What is the best solution to this situation?

   A. Implement a WLAN in the highly secure area using 802.1X using PEAP with EAP-TLS. Establish the WAPs as RADIUS clients and use the RADIUS server to authenticate computers and users.

   B. Regularly inspect user computers in the highly secure area for signs of wireless components. Set up a filter to prevent any IP packets with the IP address of the highly secure network segment to get into the rest of the network.

C. Implement a WLAN with limited range in the highly secure area. This way, users outside of the highly secure area cannot freeload.

D. Implement a WLAN in the highly secure area that is not connected to the wired network. Require strong authentication and data encryption using PEAP-EAP-MS-CHAPv2 since some of the servers are running Windows 2000.

☑ **A**. If you believe there is enough need for a WLAN in the highly secure area that users will create rogue WLANs on their own, you could implement a secure WLAN by using 802.1X with PEAP with EAP-TLS to use smart cards or certificates for strong authentication and TLS for data security. This protects against rogue WLANs because clients (can be configured for both computers and users) must be authenticated by the RADIUS server. By setting up the WAPs as RADIUS clients, users and computers will be authenticated via the RADIUS server (IAS) and data will be encrypted between wireless clients and WAPs.

☒ Answer **B** is incorrect. Regular inspection of the highly secure area might be warranted, but this is not the best solution. If rogue WLANs are being installed, there might be a legitimate business need that the IT structure is not addressing (this assumes you don't have a personnel problem within the highly secured area that is intentionally trying to compromise the security and the company's policies). You can set up IPSec filtering to set requirements for data security on computers within the highly secure area, but this is a separate issue from whether or not rogue WLANs are being installed. Answer **C** is incorrect. Although you can control range to some limited degree, this is not the best solution. If you implement wireless components that have a range of 300 feet, it's difficult (if not impossible) to control the "shape" of that 300 feet except by pointing wireless antennae in different directions. However, this is not really the crux of the problem. The problem is rogue WLANs within the highly secure area. If implemented with 802.1X features including strong authentication and data encryption, users outside the highly secure area whose wireless-enabled computers can find a signal will be unable to connect because access policies will prevent them from doing so. Answer **D** is incorrect. Implementing a WLAN that does not access the corporate network defeats the purpose of the WLAN and will not discourage rogue WLANs from being installed. PEAP with MS-CHAPv2 is used for password-based systems, which are not needed since users have smart cards. Windows 2000 does not support PEAP but does support MS-CHAPv2. Although this is not an issue with the highly secure WLAN, it is an incorrect statement that you would use PEAP with EAP-MS-CHAPv2 because you have Windows 2000-based computers.

Chapter 6: Securing Internet Information Services

1. One of the new reliability features in IIS 6.0 is the introduction of HTTP.Sys. HTTP.Sys is the new kernel mode driver for IIS 6.0. HTTP.Sys is engineered to increase the performance of IIS dramatically. You have been researching HTTP.Sys functionality. Your research indicates that one of the following about HTTP.Sys is true. What is HTTP.Sys is capable of?

   A. Create virtual directories for Web sites

   B. Implementing flexible caching

   C. Back up XML metabase

   D. Provides health detection data to IIS

   ☑ **B**. HTTP.Sys does implement flexible caching. IIS 6.0 will enable caching at the kernel level. This is referred to as flexible caching.

   ☒ Answer **A** is incorrect. Virtual directories are not created by HTTP.Sys. They are done by using the inetinfo.exe process. XML metabase backups are not done by HTTP.Sys. Therefore, Answer **C** is also incorrect. HTTP.Sys does not provide health detection data to IIS. HTTP.Sys is primarily responsible for analyzing the incoming Web requests. Therefore, Answer **D** is also incorrect.

2. You have been approached by the AllWebCustomers company to design the security structure for their new bookstore application. This application will run on Windows Server 2003 and IIS 6.0. The infrastructure architect has designed a Web farm with SQL cluster database connections. There is also an Active Directory available in the enterprise. You are contemplating the Windows logon authentication method for this application. Which of the following will be most suited to the Windows authentication method in Windows Server 2003?

   A. RADIUS authentication

   B. Digest authentication

   C. .NET cryptographic assembly authentication

   D. Anonymous login

   ☑ **B**. Digest authentication is an IIS 6.0 authentication option. It will authenticate users with the help of the Active Directory.

   ☒ Answer **A** is incorrect. RADIUS authentication enables multiple remote mechanisms to use a "single sign- on" method. There are no remote VPN or dial-up Internet networks mentioned here. Answer **C** is incorrect. .NET cryptographic library authentication is not available in IIS 6.0. This is only used in .NET managed code (C#, VB.NET, and so forth) execution. Anonymous login is the least secure of the IIS 6.0 login mechanisms. We will not be using the Active Directory if we implement anonymous login. Therefore, Answer **D** is also incorrect.

3. You are contemplating using integrated Windows authentication or basic authentication for a shopping cart application. This application will be used by Internet Explorer, Netscape, and Opera browsers. There are more non-IE browsers than IE browsers. You are also implementing an SSL connection to secure the data transmission between the users and the IIS server. Which authentication model will suit this shopping cart application?

   A. Basic authentication because of the variety of browser types.

   B. Integrated Windows authentication because of the variety of browser types.

   C. Integrated Windows authentication because basic authentication will expose the credentials.

   D. Basic authentication; however SSL, could be "overkill" for this application.

   ☑ **A**. Basic authentication is the most supported authentication mechanism. We have myriad browsers to support in our architecture. The non-IE browser numbers will exceed the IE browser numbers. Therefore, we should implement basic authentication to support many types of browsers.

   ☒ Answer **B** is incorrect. Integrated Windows authentication is tightly coupled into the Windows architecture. Therefore, non-IE browser base will need substantial effort to implement a secure implementation of the application. Basic authentication will expose the credentials as clear text. However, SSL will provide a secure channel to transfer data between the client and the server. Therefore, Answer **C** is incorrect. Answer **D** is also incorrect. We do need SSL if we implement a basic authentication model. Therefore, it is not "over kill" for the application (it is not optional; it is a necessity).

4. Your company network has recently implemented a wireless internal network. As the system administrator, you need to maintain this network, VPN, and Internet access to your company. You are currently using different usernames and passwords for each user on these three different networks. Therefore, a single user needs to remember three usernames and passwords to access the appropriate network. This is also an inconvenience for you as the systems administrator. You have heard of a RADIUS implementation in Windows Server 2003. You are currently deploying Windows Server 2003 in your company. What is the RADIUS implementation in Windows Server 2003?

A. Advance Digest Authentication

B. Internet Information Server 6.0

C. Internet Authentication Service

D. Internet Protocol v6

☑ **C.** The RADIUS protocol implementation in Windows Server 2003 is called Internet Authentication Services.

☒ Answer **A** is incorrect. Advance Digest Authentication is an authentication mechanism to authenticate users to IIS 6.0. Answer **B** is also incorrect. Internet Information Server (IIS) 6.0 is the Web server in Windows Server 2003. It does not implement RADIUS authentication. Internet Protocol (IP) V6 is a transport protocol; therefore, Answer **D** is also incorrect.

5. You have been instructed to install Windows Server 2003 on a Windows 2000 machine. The current Windows 2000 server is running under a FAT32 system. The Windows Server 2003 installation will permit you to upgrade or have clean installation. When you are performing the upgrade, you have an option between FAT32 and NTFS file systems. Which would you choose?

   A. FAT

   B. FAT32

   C. NTFS

   D. FAT64

   ☑ **C.** The preferred file system is NTFS. IIS 6.0 and other servers rely on NTFS security permissions to authenticate users.

   ☒ Answer **A** is incorrect. File Allocation Table (FAT) is an old DOS version of a file system. This was superceded by FAT32 version. FAT32 was a 32-bit file allocation system; therefore, Answer **B** is also incorrect. The FAT64 system was a proposed 64-bit file allocation system that follows the FAT format. This option is not implemented yet; hence, Answer **D** is incorrect.

6. You have installed IIS 6.0 successfully using the Configure Your Server Wizard. You want to experiment with the ASP.NET functionality in IIS 6.0. You have downloaded the QuickStart tutorials from Microsoft to try out ASP.NET scripts. You try to invoke one of the ASP.NET pages and get a 404 Not Found error. What could be the reason for this?

   A. IIS 6.0 does not support ASP.NET scripts.

   B. ASP.NET support has to be enabled through Web Services Extensions.

C. ASP.NET support should be enabled through **Control Panel | Administrative tools**.

D. IIS 6.0 only supports ASP.NET scripts inside ASP scripts.

☑ **B**. ASP.NET is not enabled by default after the IIS installation. You need to manually enable the support through Web Service Extensions.

☒ Answer **A** is incorrect. IIS 6.0 does support ASP.NET. Answer **C** is incorrect because the Web Server Extension can be found in the **IIS Manager**, not in **Control Panel | Administrative Tools**. Answer **D** is also incorrect. We can run ASP scripts inside ASP.NET applications, not vice versa.

7. You have created a commercial Web site with sensitive business information. Your senior architect has advised you to use Advance Digest Security to maximize security benefits on IIS 6.0. You have been doing research on Advance Digest Security. What is the incorrect piece of information you came across in your research?

A. It uses the WinFX file system to store user credentials.

B. It works with both HTTP 1.0 and HTTP 1.1 enabled browsers.

C. It will work with Internet Explorer 5.0 with JavaScript 1.3 support.

D. It only works with SSL support.

☑ **C**. Advance Digest Security only works with HTTP 1.1 enabled browsers. The HTTP 1.1 support was enabled after Internet Explorer version 5.0. The JavaScript 1.3 support is irrelevant.

☒ Answer **A** is incorrect. The WinFX file system is not available in Windows Server 2003; it is a "longhorn" feature. Advance Digest Security can only be implemented on HTTP 1.1 browsers. Therefore, Answer **B** is incorrect. Answer **D** is also incorrect. We do not need SSL support to implement an Advance Digest Security on IIS 6.0.

8. Phase One of the new IIS 6.0 features is implemented at the hardware level. The devices that implement this new feature can be described as Plug and Play devices. These devices implement an API called CryptoAPI and can be chosen from a list from IIS Manager. This new feature could be referred as:

A. Server-gated Cryptography

B. Selectable Cryptographic Service Provider

C. Secure Sockets Layer support

D. .NET System Cryptography library support

☑ **B**. Selectable Cryptography Server provider will let you select a device from an IIS list that implements Crypto API.

☒ Server-gated Cryptography is a software feature that extends SSL support. Therefore, Answer **A** is incorrect. Answer **C** is also incorrect. Secure Sockets Layer support is not new and has been around for a long while. The System Cryptography .NET library is a set of libraries available for .NET code (C#, VB.NET) to implement cryptography in scripts. This is a software implementation, not a hardware implementation. Therefore, Answer **D** is incorrect

Chapter 7: Securing VPN and Extranet Communications

1. Your network consists of Windows Server 2003 domain controllers (DCs), Windows 2003 DNS servers, and Windows XP clients. You have recently added a firewall to the network to provide security for the network from attack from the Internet. You have placed your Web, e-mail, and DNS servers outside the firewall. Your company has established a written policy that allows only SMTP, HTTP, and DNS traffic to pass through the firewall. Which ports do you need to permit? (Choose all that apply.)

   A. TCP/UDP 21

   B. TCP/UDP 23

   C. TCP/UDP 25

   D. TCP/UDP 53

   E. TCP/UDP 80

   F. TCP/UDP 110

   G. TCP/UDP 443

   ☑ **C**, **D**, **E**. SMTP corresponds to TCP/UDP port 25, DNS is TCP/UDP port 53, and HTTP is TCP/UDP port 80. These are the ports that need to be open based on the scenario.

   ☒ Answers **A**, **B**, **F**, and **G** are incorrect. TCP/UDP port 21 is FTP, TCP/UDP port 23 is Telnet, TCP/UDP port 110 is POP3, and TCP/UDP port 443 is HTTPS.

2. You are designing a network implementation for your company and you want to have an Internet presence for your Web and e-mail servers. The Web server is called WebSvr1, and the e-mail server is named MailSvr1. Due to a recent bout

of attacks, you need to implement a solution that will provide security and protection for your network. You are concerned about providing security for the Web and e-mail servers, yet you need to provide anonymous access to the Web server for the general public. You are worried that these anonymous users might use their access to investigate and attack the rest of your network as well. How do you design your network? (Select the best answer.)

A. Install Windows 2003 Server to act as the host computer for the Web and e-mail servers. Implement access control authentication for the users accessing the Web server. Add the IUSR_WebSvr1 user account to the directories that contain the Web files. Grant the IUSR_WebSvr1 user account read-only access. Grant access permissions to the network users as necessary.

B. Implement a firewall solution to protect the network. Place the Web and e-mail servers outside of the firewall. Configure the firewall to block user access from the Internet.

C. Implement a firewall solution to protect the network. Place two firewalls between the Internet and the internal network. Place the Web and e-mail servers outside the firewalls. Configure the firewalls to block user access from the Internet. Add the IUSR_WebSvr1 user account to the directories that contain the Web files. Grant the IUSR_WebSvr1 user account read-only access. Grant access permissions to the network users as necessary. Configure both firewalls to allow internal users to have access to the Internet.

D. Implement a firewall solution. Configure two firewalls. Place the Web and e-mail servers between the two firewalls. Configure the first firewall to allow access to the Web and e-mail servers by anonymous users using the IUSR_WebSvr1 user account. Configure the second firewall to allow internal users to have access to the Internet. Configure the second firewall not to allow any external users to pass through the firewall.

E. Implement a firewall solution to protect the network. Place two firewalls between the Internet and the internal network. Place the Web and e-mail servers inside the firewalls. Configure the firewalls to block all user access from the Internet. Add the IUSR_WebSvr1 user account to the directories that contain the Web files. Grant the IUSR_WebSvr1 user account read-only access. Grant access permissions to the network users as necessary. Configure both firewalls to allow internal users to have access to the Internet.

☑ **D.** This solution creates a DMZ to protect your network. Anonymous users will have access to the Web and e-mail servers. Internal users will have access to the Internet. The firewalls will block unnecessary traffic that could be used to allow hackers to gain access to the network.

☒ Answer **A** is incorrect because anonymous users will still be able to attempt to exploit the network through any open ports. There is nothing in place to isolate the network from the Internet. Answers **B** and **C** are incorrect because the Web and e-mails servers are vulnerable to attack from the Internet. Answer **E** is incorrect because this will block anonymous users from the Web server.

3. You have a network that consists of four subnets. The networks IDs for the networks are 10.0.1.0/24, 10.0.2.0/24, 10.0.3.0/24, and 10.0.4.0/24. Each subnet has two Windows Server 2003 and 75 Windows XP clients. You are planning to add a VPN server to the network to provide connectivity for remote users. You need to summarize the internal network IDs on the VPN server. What is the minimum information needed to accomplish the desired result?

   A. An entry for each subnet is required in the static route table of the VPN server.

   B. An entry for each subnet is required in the static route table of the remote clients.

   C. A route summarization entry, 10.0.0.0/16, can be added to the VPN server.

   D. A route summarization entry, 10.0.0.0/16, can be added to the remote clients.

   ☑ **C.** You can add a route summarization entry for the internal subnets on the VPN server. This will be the easiest solution.

   ☒ Although you could add an individual entry for each subnet, it would be easier to provide a route summarization for this task, so Answer **A** is incorrect. You do need to provide any routing information on the remote clients, so Answers **B** and **D** are incorrect.

4. You are configuring routing on an RRAS server. The RRAS server's intranet interfaces are configured to be connected to the intranet with a manual TCP/IP configuration that will consist of the IP address, subnet mask, default gateway, and intranet DNS servers. You are now experiencing difficulties when users attempt to connect to the Internet. What must you do to resolve these conflicts?

   A. Configure the intranet interface to use the Internet DNS servers.

   B. Configure the intranet interface with a public IP address.

   C. Assign the IP address for the intranet interface to use DHCP.

   D. Delete the default gateway configuration on the intranet interface.

☑ **D**. To prevent default route conflicts with the default route pointing to the Internet, you must not configure the default gateway on the intranet interface.

☒ By setting the intranet interface to use the DNS servers on the Internet, you will not be able to perform internal network name resolution. This makes Answer **A** incorrect. Answer **B** is incorrect because it will prevent any of the clients from being able to connect to the router providing Internet access. It is preferable to statically assign IP addresses on an interface that will be used for routing. In addition, DHCP typically will assign default gateway information to all of the DHCP clients so that the DHCP clients can connect to the Internet. This will cause default gateway conflicts. This makes Answer **C** incorrect.

5. You are designing a VPN that will allow the company's sales force to travel to multiple cities around the Untied States. You are using an Internet service provider (ISP) that provides service across the United States and has local numbers in all major cities and many smaller cities as well. The ISP is constantly adding new telephone numbers as it expands its service area. The sales manager is concerned that his sales force will not know what the local access number will be in the cities where they will be traveling. He asks if there is a solution that will help the sales force to make the VPN connection so that they can pass confidential client information and sales orders back to corporate headquarters. What is the best solution to address this problem?

   A. There is nothing that can be done to help the sales force.

   B. You can configure an Access database that contains all of the telephone numbers for the ISP.

   C. You can configure a contact list in Exchange that lists the telephone numbers in all the cities that are supported by the ISP.

   D. Create a custom phone book using Connection Point Services.

   ☑ **D**. Connection Point Services allows you to automatically update and distribute phone books that contain multiple Points of Presence for the ISP. The phone book will give the sales force complete information so that when they travel they can connect to the different local access numbers provided by the ISP.

   ☒ **A** is incorrect because you can create a phone book using Connection Point Services. Answers **B** and **C** are incorrect because the Access database and Exchange will not automatically distribute its information to the sales force. The ability of the Connection Point Services to automatically distribute itself to the desired users makes it the best solution.

6. You have designed a Windows Server 2003 VPN solution for your corporation. The solution has a Windows Server 2003 VPN server at headquarters. The VPN server has been placed behind the internal firewall protecting your network. You have created a DNS record on your Internet server in the DMZ so that you can perform name resolution to the VPN server. You have tested connectivity to the VPN server from all of the client computers using the PING utility. The clients at the branch offices are running Windows 98 and Windows XP. The Windows 98 clients are configured to use PPTP to establish the VPN connections. The Windows XP clients are configured to use L2TP using IPSec. The Windows 98 clients are using MS-CHAP v 2 to authenticate themselves as users. The Windows XP clients are using user-level certificate authentication with EAP-TLS. The Windows XP clients are not experiencing any difficulties in connecting, but the Windows 98 clients are not able to connect to the VPN server. What should you check to resolve the connectivity issue for the Windows 98 clients?

   A. Upgrade all of the Windows 98 computers to Windows 2000 or Windows XP.

   B. Configure the firewall to allow PPTP traffic to pass.

   C. Move the VPN server to outside the external firewall.

   D. Change the default authentication protocol to use certificates.

   ☑ **B.** The most probable reason why the Windows 98 clients are not able to connect to the VPN server is that the firewall is configured to allow L2TP traffic and to block the PPTP traffic. By allowing the PPTP traffic to pass, you should resolve this issue.

   ☒ Answer **A** is incorrect because upgrading the Windows 98 clients to Windows 2000 or Windows XP will not solve the problem that the PPTP clients are being blocked at the firewall. Answer **C** would allow all of the clients to connect to the VPN server; however, you would also increase the security risk to the VPN server so this is not an optimal solution. Answer **D** is incorrect because the issue at hand is that PPTP is being blocked at the firewall. The Windows 98 users will be able to authenticate themselves using MS-CHAP v2. Although more secure, certificate authentication is not required in this situation.

7. You have just replaced many of your company's dial-in connections with VPN connections to reduce the costs of maintaining dial-in services. You have recently configured VPN access on a laptop for a user. You have specified the host name for the VPN server in the Host Name or IP Address box. Now the user is complaining that he is receiving the error message "Destination Host Unknown." What is the most likely cause for this error message?

A. The DNS server has not been properly configured for the new VPN server.

B. The laptop has not been authorized to connect to the VPN server.

C. The VPN client has not been configured with the username with permission to access the VPN server.

D. The Remote access policy has not been configured to allow access to the user.

☑ **A.** The DNS server must be configured with an appropriate entry for the VPN server. Without the DNS entry the VPN server will be unreachable.

☒ Answer **B** is incorrect because the error message would be denied access if the remote computer was not authorized to connect to the VPN server. Answer **C** is incorrect because if it had been an authentication problem, the message would tell you that the authentication was incorrect. Answer **D** is incorrect because if it had been a remote policy access issue, "access denied" would have been the message.

8. You have just installed Routing and Remote Access on a Windows Server 2003 to function as a VPN server. Several remote users need to transmit confidential data to the company using the VPN server. The remote users are not members of your company's domain. The remote users are running Windows XP on the client computers, and they all have access to a local ISP to provide Internet connectivity. Data transmission security is critical to the company and to the remote users. All of the clients will be using L2TP to create the connection to the VPN server. Which secure authentication method should you use for these connections?

   A. Configure L2TP to use MPPE 128-bit encryption.

   B. Create a custom IPSec policy and select certificate-based 5 authentication. Apply the policy to the appropriate OU.

   C. Configure L2TP to use MS-CHAP v2.

   D. Use the certificate-based authentication method of the Routing and Remote Access custom IPSec policy for the L2TP connection.

   ☑ **D.** Routing and Remote Access allows you to create custom IPSec policies for the VPN connections. This policy will be applied to all connections made to the VPN server. Since the users are not members of your company's domain, a policy applied to a GPO will not affect them. A policy applied to the connection itself will enforce that the desire authentication method will be used.

   ☒ Answer **A** is incorrect because MPPE is used with PPTP connections. In addition, the question asks about the authentication method, not the data encryption scheme. Answer **B** is incorrect since the remote users are not members of the domain, and any policy applied to an OU will not have the desired effect. You will need to create a policy that is applied whenever a connection is established. Answer **C** is incorrect because certificate-based authentication is the highest form of security available under Server 2003, not MS-CHAP v2.

Chapter 8: Securing Active Directory

1. Best Fit Inc is a clothing retailer that has been in business for over 25 years and grosses over 100 million dollars in annual sales. The company is experiencing tremendous growth and has added a Web store to reach customers in areas where it doesn't have a retail presence. This venture into the Web now poses a security issue for them. The company has asked the IT department to ensure proper procedure is in place so that they are informed anytime anyone attempts to access confidential data that's stored on the Web server. Which audit policy should you enable on the Web server? (Choose all that apply.)

   A. Audit success and failure of process tracking

   B. Audit success and failure of object access

   C. Audit success and failure of logon events

   D. Audit success and failure of directory service access

   ☑ B, C. Audit success and failure of object access, and Audit success and failure of logon events, are correct. Auditing object access would allow you to monitor any changes that are made to objects, including files, printers and the Registry, while auditing logon events would help to determine if unauthorized users are attempting to access logon-restricted areas of the company Web server.

   ☒ Answer A would not be appropriate in this case because you are asked to monitor changes to data, whereas auditing process tracking would monitor an application, when that application exists or duplicates, and so forth. Answer D is also incorrect because it is auditing access to objects in Active Directory, not on the Web server's file system.

2. Elineken is a new brand of beer that is being produced by the Eli bottling company, which employs over 35,000 employees worldwide. The corporate headquarters is in San Francisco and the company has production facilities in Holland, Ireland, Germany, and Hong Kong. After finding great response to their brand of beer and getting numerous awards, the company is now

expanding its market into the Middle East and has acquired a large production facility in Lebanon. This new facility will be home to some 2000 employees who will service the needs of the area, and as such will require several file servers, Exchange servers, and DCs to be available on site for speedier authentication, mail delivery, and to avoid WAN reliability issues. The CIO is especially interested in the security procedures that will be in place to secure the local servers and has asked you to ensure the company is using best practices and that the servers will be as safe as possible. The CIO also has decided that the Lebanon facility will be incorporated into the existing domain model. How should you secure the new servers at the new Lebanon facility?

A. Install the servers into a new OU and implement group policies at the site level.

B. Install the servers into a new OU and implement group policies at the OU level.

C. Install the servers into their own Active Directory tree and implement group policies at the domain level.

D. Install the servers into the same Active Directory tree as stores and modify the schema.

☑ **B**. Best practices calls for placing resources in an OU and implementing group policy at the OU level.

☒ Answer **A** is incorrect because sites are typically used for separating traffic on the basis of geography and WAN connectivity—you might decide to open another office in the same site that will require different security or delegation settings, and that would require you to completely overhaul your policy implementation. Answer **C** is incorrect because the CIO already made it clear that the Lebanon facility will be in the current domain. Answer **D** incorrect because you do not need to modify the Active Directory schema in order to secure resources.

3. Ground Up Properties is the third largest shopping mall owner and operator in the world with over 300 malls in the United States alone spread out across all states. The company currently has over 4000 employees and is headquartered in New York. Ground Up has been experiencing tremendous growth in its sector and is ready to acquire a major European real estate company that owns and operates 50 malls in Europe. The acquired European company does not have any network in place, and your integration team has decided to incorporate the newly acquired malls into the existing infrastructure and treat them as sites within the existing domain. This means that every site would need a DC that will also act as a file and print server and an exchange server. Because of time difference and language barriers, the company decides to hire a few local techs

in the Paris regional office to accommodate the needs of the users in these malls. The CIO is requesting that the local helpdesk personnel be give enough access to manage the users and groups in the newly acquired facilities. Which strategy should you use to accommodate the newly acquired malls?

A. Add the helpdesk employee to the Domain Admins group.

B. Add the helpdesk employee to the Enterprise Admins group.

C. Delegate authority at the domain level to the Paris helpdesk employees to manage users and groups.

D. Delegate authority to the Paris helpdesk employees to modify accounts and groups in the European malls' OUs.

☑ **D.** The best answer is to delegate authority to the Paris helpdesk employees to modify accounts and groups in the European malls' OUs, thus limiting their scope to the users they are supposed to be accommodating.

☒ Answer **A** is technically correct but gives them excessive rights that they should not have access to. Answer **B** also is technically correct but gives the local helpdesk the ability to make major changes domain and enterprise wide and should be seen as an example of what never to do. Answer **C** also grants the helpdesk group more authority and rights than are needed to go about their daily tasks.

4. Didisoft is a technology company with products for the security industry. The company is a new startup based in San Francisco and employs 500 employees. The CIO is very aggressive about security and intrusion detection and has requested that the Windows Server 2003 architect implement all the tools and features the operating system offers in that direction so that it can be combined with the Didisoft Intrusion Squasher software that, in his opinion, would render the system impenetrable. The CIO wants to ensure that the sensitive administrative-level domain groups are not tampered with. What can you do to ensure only the appropriate users are members of domain Admins?

A. Implement ACLs on the domain Admins group.

B. Implement ACLs on the OU in which the domain Admins group resides.

C. Use Restricted groups in Group Policy to enforce the membership.

D. Regularly check the domain Admins group membership to ensure no one has been modified.

☑ **C.** The use of Restricted groups is the ideal method by which you can enforce which users are members of a group. Using this method every time Group Policy refreshes, it checks to see if any of the authentic users are members of the group. If they have been removed, Group Policy adds them back; if a new user was added to the group using a method other than Group Policy, it removes him or her from that group. It is the ideal and automatic way to monitor sensitive administrative groups.

☒ Answer **A** is incorrect because if attackers or malicious users gain domain Admin level that would allow them to add themselves to the Admin group, they can modify the ACL and deny you access to it. Answer **B** is incorrect because security on the OU might be compromised, and as such the attacker can then prevent you from accessing the OU. Answer **D** is incorrect because it is not an effective and quick method of enforcing your policies.

5. Chocolate Chip is a chocolate-making company based in New Orleans. It employs 5000 employees. The company has recently experienced a security breach in which valuable information about the new chocolate flavor was stolen together with marketing strategy. The company had no security measures in place because the CIO claimed that security breaches are rare and overly exaggerated by the media and has assured management that no such thing would occur in the company. After the main competitor for Chocolate Chip released a product with a slightly different name and used the exact same marketing strategy that the Chocolate Chip company was planning to use, management found this a strange coincidence and started an investigation, only to be tipped off by an IT employee in the other company bragging about how easy it was to hack and steal from the Chocolate Chip network. The CIO immediately called a meeting of the IT staff and requested that auditing be enabled as a first step in a list of security measures that will follow. What should you include in an audit policy for the domain?

   A. Failure audit for account logon events
   Failure audit for directory service access
   Success and failure audit for policy change
   Success and failure audit for account management

   B. Failure audit for object access
   Failure audit for account logon events
   Failure audit for directory service access
   Success and failure audit for policy change

   C. Success and failure audit for object access
   Success and failure audit for policy change
   Success and failure audit for account logon events
   Success and failure audit for process tracking

   D. Success and failure audit for object access
   Success and failure audit for policy change

Success and failure audit for account logon events
Success and failure audit for directory service access

☑ **D**. This choice configures an audit policy for success and failure on object access so that if someone is trying to manipulate or even read the recipes files, that person can be detected, or at least you can have a trail of evidence. Auditing success and failure of policy ensures no one is modifying the policy to disable some settings so that he or she doesn't leave a trail when stealing information, such as disabling auditing on object access to hide the evidence of it. Account logon audits are great as a means of intrusion detection for user accounts and can be used to stop an attack if you get the information in a timely manner. Success and failure audits on directory service access means any changes to the auditing that you have in place on objects in Active Directory is logged and thus a trail is left if any Active Directory objects are modified.

☒ Answer **A** is incorrect because it is monitoring only failure or success in some instances, where best practices always calls for monitoring success and failure attempts so that if someone successfully logs in you can at least figure out how it happened. Answer **B** again is only monitoring a limited subset of the information that should be included in a comprehensive auditing plan. Answer **C** is monitoring success and failure, but if you closely examine the last choice, you will find that auditing success and failure for process tracking is not the most appropriate in this case. Process tracking monitors applications and is more appropriate in detecting viruses or Trojan horses.

6. SV Corporation is a computer chip manufacturer based in San Francisco. The company employs 500 employees and is one of the leading computer chip manufacturers. The company recently avoided a security breach in which sensitive information could have been compromised or stolen by an international competitor. This incident immediately prompted the company to hire an external organization to attempt a penetration test and discover the possible vulnerabilities that exist on the SV network. During the penetration test, the security consultants were able to penetrate the network and gain full access to it. The CIO gathers all the different teams within MIS to discuss this and requests that each group take immediate measures to ensure their systems are as secure as possible in accordance with industry best practices. Since you are responsible for the Windows environment at SV, which policies should you include in a security strategy for the domain? (Choose two.)

A. Enable account lockout

B. Disable password aging

C. Disable account lockout

D. Enforce strong passwords and password aging

☑ **A, D**. Enable account lockout ensures that after a specified number of attacks are made against an account to crack its password, the account should be disabled. Answer **D** is also correct because strong passwords should be implemented with password complexity so that users don't choose easily crackable passwords that would create an opportunity for attackers to gain access to the network by guessing a weak password. Password aging is also much recommended so that users cannot use a password they used the last three, four, or five times they changed their passwords.

☒ Answer **B** is incorrect because it disables password aging, which would allow the user to keep selecting one or two passwords. This is a security hole and should be viewed as an example of what not to do. Answer **C** is incorrect because this particular scenario has an emphasis on stopping hackers who have intent to steal data. In this case, account lockout is good because as soon as the hacker sees there is no way he or she is getting access to these accounts, the hacker will most likely walk away. If we were concerted with hackers who just want to disrupt productivity, then this might have been a good answer because hackers can sometimes use your policies against you; in this case, hit all the user accounts until they get locked out and users can't log in.

7. Best Pix Inc. is the largest chain of photography studios in the world, with several locations in every country in Europe and several locations in almost all states in the United States. They currently employ over 20,000 employees. The company is undergoing a major migration from Windows NT to Windows Server 2003. Every location currently has a manager with several employees. As part of the company's marketing strategy, they are interested in offering their customers access to their photos with the ability to order reprints over the Web. Security is a large concern for Best Pix, and they want to ensure that the service they are offering does not compromise security for their network. This service is also posing a challenge to the IT department in terms of how customer accounts will be created and deleted. Because the company is so big and widespread, the IT team has decided to grant the office manager at each location some kind of delegation to assist with this task and to be able to respond to customer needs in a timely fashion. That office manager can also respond to security threats on customer accounts in a quick and time-effective fashion. Which task should you delegate to the office managers?

   A. Modify the membership of a group

   B. Manage Group Policy links

   C. Create, delete, and manage customer accounts

   D. Create, delete, and manage groups

☑ **C.** The office manager should be able to create, delete, and manage customer accounts, which is necessary to run the office and provide the service set forth by the company to its customers.

☒ Answer **A** is incorrect because the office manager has no business modifying group memberships; as part of the branch office setup you should also set up the appropriate groups and those groups should only be modified by you. Group creation is also not a task that would stop or even delay customers gaining access to their data, especially after the initial setup. Answer **B** is not relevant to the manager's job function; he or she does not need to manage GP links to get customers an account to view their pictures. Answer **D** is incorrect because an office manager does not need to create groups. It does not affect their ability to service their customers, and as such any such changes should come from the central IT department.

8. Gourmet Distribution specializes in wholesale distribution of canned foods to supermarkets. The company has many distribution locations spread out across the United States. Every distribution site employs about 100 employees. The IT director has decided to place a DC, an Exchange server, and a file server at every location to meet each site's IT needs. An IT administrator will also be hired at every location to see to server maintenance. As part of the migration from Windows NT to Windows Server 2003, you have decided to adopt a single domain model with separate OUs for every location. How should you grant the necessary permissions to the IT administrator at each distribution center?

   A. Create a new administrator account for each distribution center's OU. Grant the necessary permissions to this account.

   B. Create an administrator group for each distribution center's OU. Add an existing user designated as an administrator to this account. Grant the necessary permissions to this group.

   C. Create a new administrator account for each distribution center's OU in the headquarters root. Grant the necessary permissions to each new administrator's account.

   D. Create an administrator group for each OU at the headquarters root. Add an existing user designated as an administrator from each OU to this group. Grant the necessary permissions to this group.

☑ **B.** Answer **B** is correct and adheres to best practices; an administrative account should be placed inside a group and then given permission on the appropriate OU.

☒ Answer **A** is technically correct but does not adhere to best practices because the administration of user accounts on an individual becomes a nightmare, especially if you have to set permissions on resources and so on. It becomes more complicated if the IT administrator leaves and a new one is hired, since you would need to redo security on all the resources, whereas if you had created a group, added the user to the group, and then set security on the group, you would only need to add the new user to the appropriate group. Answer **C** is incorrect because it is granting excessive rights to the IT administrators of every distribution center. Answer **D** is incorrect because it does not adhere to the best practices suggested by Microsoft for delegation of authority using group objects.

Chapter 9: Securing Network Resources

1. You have been asked to design an access control strategy for your firm and it must be done as soon as possible. The company currently has about 85 employees, each of whom has a desktop or laptop computer. There are four servers functioning in various roles. The departments are Finance, Administration, Customer Service, Trucking, Warehouse Operations, Purchasing, and IT. Your company plans to expand operations in the next one to two years, adding about 28 new employees in that period of time. There is fairly high turnover in the Trucking and Purchasing departments. Seasonal help comes in during the holidays to assist with warehouse operations, and some seasonal staff have computer access. There are a number of staff that change from one department to another based on external business drivers and internal staffing skills. There have never been any attacks on the network and most users have fairly basic computer skills. All systems are Windows Server 2003, Windows 2000 native mode, and Windows XP. Most users have the ability to use e-mail, word processing, and spreadsheet programs. About 10 employees, including those in the IT department, have advanced skills, and the IT department is comprised of five people, three of whom have advanced programming skills. Based on this information, which access control model is best suited to your organization?

   A. Role-based

   B. Access group/ resource group

   C. Access group/ACL

   D. User/ACL

   ☑ **C.** The Access group/ACL model appears to be most suited to the organization based on the given parameters. From the information, we know that there are 85 employees and will be 113 total in two years. However, there is a fair amount of change both in terms of group membership and changing permissions. Since employees move around, it mighty be difficult to manage access control using other methods. Adding users to access groups and adding those groups to ACLs is the easiest method to implement and manage in this small-to-medium-sized business. The access group/ACL model is scalable and easier to administer if groups require similar permissions. It's useful if permissions require frequent changing.

☒ Answer **A** is incorrect. Role-based access control is only supported in Windows Server 2003 and must be supported by the applications running it. This is a specialized model that would not be appropriate in this scenario because no data was presented that supports this. Answer **B** is incorrect. The access group/resource group is a good solution for large organizations, but it requires more administrative overhead initially. It does not work well when permissions change frequently, as it appears they do in the organization. Moreover, although it can be used in native mode, the AG/RG model is suitable for a mixed environment. These indicate that although you could implement the AG/RG model, it's not the best solution for your organization. Answer **D** is incorrect. Although you can add users to the ACL for various objects, this is not the most efficient or secure solution. If a user moves into a new department or leaves the company, you must locate all the objects to which the user has permissions and change them. Using an account group method (AG/ACL or AG/RG) allows you to remove the user from the group and the user no longer has permission to access resources. From a security and administrative standpoint, the User/ACL method is limited and is not the best answer for this situation.

2. You've been looking at users and groups on your network and have decided there are a lot of groups that are probably no longer used. Several key projects have wrapped up and there were several groups created just for those projects. After examining these groups, you decide they're no longer in use and you delete them. During the next hour, you receive phone calls complaining that users can no longer access network resources. What is your best course of action in this situation?

   A. Use the *Undo* command to undo the action and restore the deleted groups.

   B. Use the *Restore* command to undo the action and restore the deleted groups.

   C. Recreate the deleted groups using the same names. The groups will inherit the same permissions as the deleted groups if Active Directory has not been replicated in between deleting the groups and recreating the groups.

   D. Recreate the deleted groups and assign users and permissions to restore access to users.

☑ **D.** The only way to recover when you've deleted groups is to recreate the groups, add users to those groups, and assign whatever permissions to the group needed to restore user access to its prior state. A deleted group cannot be recovered.

☒ Answer **A** is incorrect. There is no *Undo* command available. Once a group is deleted, it cannot be recovered. Answer **B** is incorrect. There is no *Restore* command to recover a deleted group. You can perform a system restore if you recently performed a backup, assuming the backup included system state data such as Active Directory data and not just data files. However, to restore these groups means that you'll lose whatever data was on changed between the time of the last backup and the restore, which is likely not a reasonable solution. However, there is no *Restore* command, per se. Answer **C** is incorrect. You can recreate the deleted groups using the same names. However, permissions will not be inherited. They must be recreated based on group membership.

3. Your company is upgrading to Windows Server 2003 and Windows XP across the board. You're using Active Directory in all domains. Your current structure consists of three domains: somecompany.com, admin.somecompany.com, and sales.somecompany.com. In the sales.somecompany.com domain, there are four domain local groups called Managers, Sales, Service, and Tech. Members of the Managers group should have the same permissions as the Executive global group in the admin.somecompany.com domain. What is the best way to give Managers the same privileges as Executives?

   A. Add the Managers group to the Executive group.

   B. Add the Executive group to the Managers group.

   C. Create a universal group named ExecMgr and add both the Executive and Manager groups.

   D. Create a nested group under Executives called ExecMgr and add members of the Managers group to this new group.

☑ **C.** A universal group can include groups and accounts from any domain in the domain tree or forest. These universal groups can be assigned permissions in any domain. To grant Managers from one domain the same permissions as Executives in another domain, you would have to use a universal group.

☒ Answer **A** is incorrect. Managers is a domain local group in the sales.somecompany.com domain. Executives is a global group in the admin.somecompany.com domain. You cannot add groups from other domains to a global group. Answer **B** is incorrect. It would not serve any purpose to add the global group Executive to the domain local group Managers. The problem is how to grant Managers the same privileges as the Executive group, not how to give the Executive group the privileges granted to the Managers group. Answer **D** is incorrect. Even as a nested group, the Executive group can only contain groups or members from the same domain; therefore, this is basically the same answer as A and is incorrect.

4. You look in Event Viewer and notice an odd series of events that were logged last night beginning at 11:36 p.m. The events are as listed. Your company runs Monday through Friday, 7 a.m. to 7 p.m., but there are a number of managers who sometimes work late to monitor Web orders and other end-commerce functions. These managers sometimes log in from home and have no restrictions on time-of-day access. Other users have time-of-day restrictions and can only log on between 6:30 a.m. and 7:30 p.m. Four employees are currently on vacation, and two other employees were recently terminated. Based on these events, what is the most likely explanation for what's happening?

```
11:36pm   531: Logon failure. A logon attempt was made using a disabled
               account.
11:37pm   540: A user successfully logged on.
11:37pm   531: Logon failure. A logon attempt was made using a disabled
               account.
11:37pm   531: Logon failure. A logon attempt was made using a disabled
               account.
11:39pm   529: Logon failure. A logon attempt was made with an unknown
               user name or a known user name with a bad password.
11:43pm  540: A user successfully logged on.
11:43pm  529: Logon failure. A logon attempt was made with an unknown
              user name or a known user name with a bad password.
11:44pm  551: A user initiated the log off process.
11:44pm  529: Logon failure. A logon attempt was made with an unknown
              user name or a known user name with a bad password.
11:47pm  551: A user initiated the log off process.
11:47pm  539: Logon failure. The account was locked out at the time the
              logon attempt was made.
```

A. It appears that one of the managers was attempting to log in and mistyped his or her password or username.

B. Someone is attempting a brute force attack.

C. One of the former employees gained unauthorized access to the system.

D. Two attacks might be in progress: one by a former employee and one by an outsider.

☑ **D**. The pattern here suggests possibly two different attacks. The first event is someone attempting to log in to a disabled account. This could be one of the recently terminated employees or one of the employees on vacation (whose account you temporarily disabled for security purposes) attempting to log in. It's not clear based only on the first event. The next event indicates a successful logon. Since a user will not be able to log in to a disabled account, this success event indicates use of a different account. Without additional information or evidence, it would be reasonable to assume that this might have been a legitimate access by one of the managers. The next two events indicate someone was trying to access a disabled account. Again, this could be a terminated employee (attack) or an employee on vacation (benign event). However, the next event, 529, indicates someone attempted to log on with the wrong username or password. If this were an employee on vacation, this event would likely not occur. If a former employee was trying to gain access, this might be evidence of an attack. The next event, 540, indicates a successful logon. This could indicate another manager successfully logged on or that the attacker was successful at guessing a username/password combination to gain access to the network. The next event is another 529 logon failure. It would indicate that the prior successful logon might have been a legitimate user and the attacker is still trying different combinations. The 551 event indicates a user logged off, probably one of the managers who had successfully gained access. The next event, another 529 failure, indicates a possible attack. The 551 indicates a user logged off, which could be associated with the one of the successful logons. Finally, the 539 event indicates that the account was locked out and someone tried to access it. This could indicate an attacker who guessed wrong three times and was locked out. Although this could be an employee on vacation (not understanding his or her account would be disabled during vacation), it could also be an outsider trying to guess at usernames and passwords. Therefore, there is the possibility of two attacks occurring here: one by a former employee and one by an outside attacker.

☒ Answer **A** is incorrect. A manager might have accidentally mistyped his or her username and password, but it is unlikely that it would occur four times and cause the account to be locked out. This is not the most likely cause of this string of events, although you would need to look at the details of the events to be absolutely sure this was not the case. Answer **B** is incorrect. A brute force attack occurs when someone is attempting to guess passwords through repeated attempts. This might be the case evidenced by the series of 529 logon failure events. However, this is probably not all that is going on since someone also attempted to use a disabled account. It is unlikely that an attacker would successfully guess the username on a disabled account. Although this is part of what might be occurring, it is not the best explanation for all events listed. Answer **C** is incorrect. As with Answer **B**, this is probably only one part of the explanation. The attempts to log in to a disabled account indicate that either an employee on vacation or a recently terminated employee is trying to gain access to the network. Without knowing the company's policy on terminated employees (are accounts disabled immediately and deleted later or simply deleted immediately?), it is impossible to tell. However, there are two different types of access being attempted: indicating possibly two different attacks.

5. Your company recently sent out an e-mail to an employee distribution list that consisted of all managers and all members of the Research department. The e-mail requested that all employees receiving the e-mail immediately begin encrypting all files related to a particular high-profile client. The e-mail suggested that there had been recent attempts to compromise the network and gain access to these sensitive files. The e-mail outlined steps for using EFS to encrypt these sensitive files. Lisa is a corporate executive who works with this high-profile client. She was on a business trip visiting this client when she received the e-mail. While she was waiting for her flight at the airport, she followed the instructions in the e-mail to encrypt sensitive files. Based on this information, what type of encryption certificate does Lisa have?

   A. An EFS self-signed certificate.

   B. An EFS certificate based on cached login credentials.

   C. A certificate issued by the corporate CA.

   D. A temporary EFS certificate to be used until a more reliable certificate is obtained.

   ☑ **A**. Since the question gave no indication that the company already uses certificates for other security functions, and since Lisa is not connected to the corporate network, she must have a self-signed EFS certificate. When no CA exists, EFS will create a certificate for file encryption.

   ☒ Answer **B** is incorrect. EFS will not use cached credentials, per se. EFS will generate a certificate for the user. If the user logged on to the laptop using cached credentials, those cached credentials will be used to create a security access ID token for the user. EFS will generate a certificate based on a legitimate user, but the certificate is not specifically linked to cached credentials. Even if the user were logged on to a network and no CA were available, EFS would generate a self-signed certificate for the authenticated user. Answer **C** is incorrect. EFS will look for a CA when first enabled. In this case, one was not available and EFS created a self-signed certificate. Answer **D** is incorrect. EFS will not create a temporary certificate; it will generate a self-signed certificate. This self-signed certificate will have an expiration date, as do other certificates, but it will not be any shorter than the normal duration. It is not considered "temporary."

6. You use execute the following command in a command prompt window: **cipher /r:financedra** and then you open the MMC, add the Group Policy Editor snap-in, and add to the FinanceOU policy. You expand the nodes until you locate the Encrypting File System node. You click **Add Data Recovery Agent** and specify *financedra.cer*. What have you just accomplished?

   A. You have imported a recovery agent that can be used for all computers and users in the FinanceOU.

   B. You have imported a recovery agent for the local computer that is part of the FinanceOU.

   C. You cannot import this file via the Group Policy Editor snap-in into the Encrypting File System policy. Instead, use the **Certificates snap-in** and import the *financedra.cer* file.

   D. Although you used the *cipher* command, the */r* switch will only create the recovery agent. You must create the private keys and certificate using additional parameters in the *cipher* command.

   ☑ **A**. Using these steps, you've added a recovery agent via the Group Policy Editor snap-in. This will be applied to whatever object you've chosen—local computer, domain, OU, and so forth. In this case, you've selected a policy for the FinanceOU. By Adding Data Recovery Agent and importing the .CER file, you create a data recovery agent that can be used to decrypt files for the FinanceOU.

   ☒ Answer **B** is incorrect. You have imported the .CER file and created a data recovery agent. However, it is not just for use on the local computer; it is for use within the FinanceOU. If the computer is part of the FinanceOU, then the DRA will be available. Answer **C** is incorrect. You can use this method to import the financedra.cer file for the local computer or for your account (default). However, this will not create a Data Recovery Agent for the FinanceOU. Answer **D** is incorrect. The */r* switch for the recovery agent creates two files, the .PFX file and the .CER file. The .PFX file contains the private keys and the certificate, and the .CER file contains only the certificate data. Once you use the **cipher** */r:filename* command, you create both the *filename*.PFX and *filename*.CER files.

7. Your company has four critical servers located in one server room. The first server holds various data files, including all users' files stored on the network. The second server is a proxy server. The third and fourth servers provide critical

network functions, including DC and DNS server. You have standard (default) installations of Windows Server 2003 on all servers. You perform incremental backups each night and a full backup on Sundays at 11:30 p.m. for each server. On Monday morning around 9:40 a.m., a brand new virus attacks the proxy server and disables the computer. You're able to download a just-released update for your virus signature file and install it on the proxy server to remove the virus. However, the system is not operational and it appears much of the data has been corrupted. Users cannot reach the Internet and the help desk is suddenly flooded with calls and e-mails. You send out a global e-mail in response and let people know that you expect to have the system up by 11 a.m. What recovery method will best restore the system to a functional state?

A. Reformat the hard drive on the proxy server, reinstall the operating system, and restore the data files.

B. Use the Automated System Recovery set generated with the backups to restore both system state and data files.

C. Use the Emergency Management Services to redirect the console to a remote machine, view the kernel log, and then restore the parts of the system affected by the virus.

D. Use the Recovery Console option to restore the system to its original state, and then use the backups to restore data files.

☑ **B**. If you generate an Automated System Recovery set with your backups, you will save system state data, including Active Directory database (if applicable), the Registry, and other system information. ASR does not restore data files, so it is used in conjunction with backups. These are sets that capture the system in a given state, and the ASR set must be used with its associated backup set.

☒ Answer **A** is incorrect. You might need to restore the operating system, but reformatting the hard drive is a drastic step that should not be taken unless it is clear there is an issue with drive formatting. While this might be the appropriate step if evidence points to a deep problem on the hard drive caused by the virus that cannot be resolved in any other manner, this is not the best answer. Answer **C** is incorrect. There might be no need for remote management capabilities since the server is in a server room in one building and the company is not very large (based on the fact it has only four critical servers). If you have not installed any additional services, you have not implemented Emergency Management Services. Therefore, this will not be an option. Answer **D** is incorrect. As with Answer **C**, if you have not installed the Recovery Console, it is not an available option for you. By default, Emergency Management Services and Recovery Console are not installed or implemented. The Recover Console can be launched from the installation media, but the Recovery Console is most useful if you need to copy a file from floppy or CD-ROM to the hard disk or if you need to reconfigure a service that is causing problems. Since data was corrupted, your best option is to restore from a backup.

8. You have previously installed Windows Server 2003 on seven servers. On four of these servers you've enabled Emergency Management Services. One of these servers experiences a Stop message. You are not sure what's causing the problem, but you notice that the prompt is shown as !SAC. You assumed that you would be able to use the Special Administration Console (SAC) for monitoring, reviewing, and repairing a wide range of problems, but it is not available. The system won't boot in safe mode and you are unable to determine the nature of the problem. What is the most likely cause of the SAC not being available?

   A. !SAC is always available before SAC. Once you've determined the nature of the problem via !SAC commands, you can resolve the problem and use SAC to restore the system to its functional state.

   B. Stop messages typically invoke SAC. In this case, however, because the system cannot start in Safe mode, !SAC was called by the Recovery Console.

   C. SAC is not available because some system component failed causing the Stop message.

   D. If the server is stopped and restarted via Emergency Management Services using console redirection on an out-of-band connection, it will restart in the !SAC mode by default.

   ☑ **C**. If there is a serious problem and system components are compromised, the system might not be able to boot in safe mode. After a specific failure point is reached, Emergency Management Services components shift from SAC to !SAC. !SAC becomes available automatically if SAC fails to load or is not functioning. In this case, you received a Stop message, the most likely cause for SAC not being available.

   ☒ Answer **A** is incorrect. Just the opposite is true—SAC is always available after Emergency Management Services is installed. If SAC is unavailable, it is because one of the components that supports SAC has failed. When this occurs, !SAC is invoked. !SAC is a subset of SAC functionality that can be used to view Stop messages or to restart the computer. Answer **B** is incorrect. Stop messages typically disable SAC and cause the system to use !SAC. When the system cannot start in Safe mode, !SAC is typically called by the system so you can restart the system or view a Stop message. !SAC is never invoked by the Recovery Console. You can enable Emergency Management Services console redirection via the Recovery Console. !SAC is only invoked when SAC fails. Answer **D** is incorrect. If the server is stopped and restarted via Emergency Management Services, it is done either via SAC (when possible) of !SAC, if SAC is unavailable due to system component failures. !SAC is not a default mode for Emergency Management Services; it is a failsafe option if SAC fails.

Chapter 10: Securing Network Clients

1. You are the network administrator for the Blue Sky, LTD, airplane manufacturer. The vice president of the Finance department has reported that some technically savvy users within the department have been attempting to access confidential information by browsing the available network shares from the Network Connections desktop icon. He has requested that users within subdepartments of the Finance area not be able to map network drives or browse network shares that they have not been explicitly granted access to. However, you have assigned a word processing application to the entire organization using a default GPO, and you do not want to reconfigure this portion of the Active Directory structure. In response to the VP's request, you have configured your Active Directory environment as shown in Figure 10.13. (Please note that, in the illustration, "Enforce" means that the "Enforce settings" property has been applied to the GPO in question.) Which setting(s) will be applied to a workstation in the Collections OU? (Choose all that apply.)

Figure 10.13 Question 1 Illustration

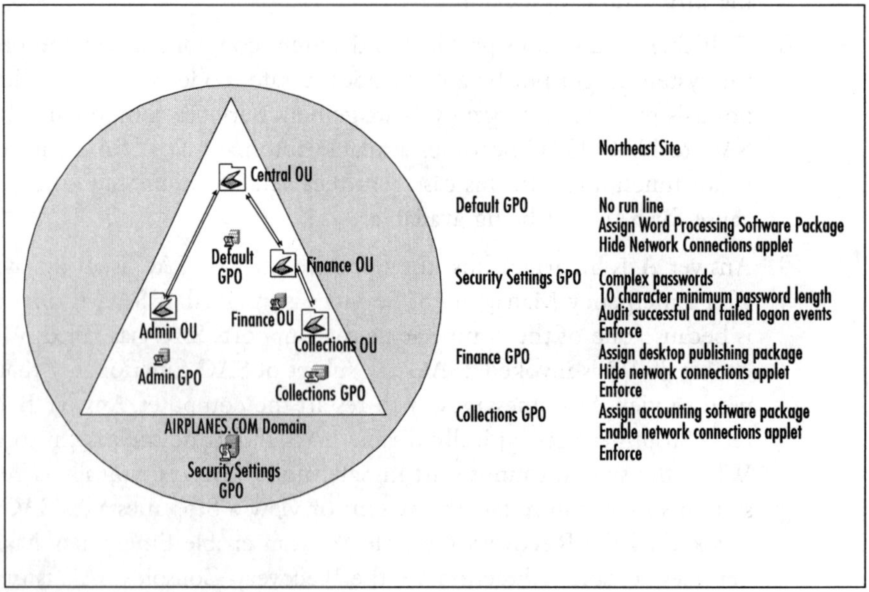

A. The desktop publishing package will be assigned.

B. The Network Connections applet will be hidden.

C. The Network Connections applet will be visible.

D. The Run line will be hidden.

☑ **A**, **B**, **D**. Since the Collections GPO does not have the Block Inheritance property set, it will inherit the desktop publishing package installation from the Finance GPO. Therefore, Answer **A** is correct. Although the Collections GPO has the Enforce property set, the Finance GPO (which exists at a higher level in the OU hierarchy) *also* has the Enforce property set. In the case of conflicting enforced settings, the setting that occurs *higher* in the hierarchy takes precedence. This is the reverse of the usual GPO inheritance rules. Therefore, Answer **B** is correct. The Marketing OU will also inherit the "No Run Line" property from the Default GPO. Therefore, Answer **D** is correct.

☒ Answer **C** is incorrect because even though the Marketing GPO has enabled the Network Connections applet enabled along with the Enforce property, it is overridden by the Enforce property in the Finance GPO.

2. You are the administrator for a Windows Server 2003 domain. Your network consists of five locations connected by high-speed Internet connections. Your network servers are running solely Windows Server 2003, but you are supporting network clients that are a mixture of Windows XP Professional, Windows 2000, and Windows NT 4.0 Workstation. Because of the recent spate of critical security updates that have been released by Microsoft, you need to design a strategy to apply security updates to all of your workstations in a quick and efficient manner. Given the current environment, what option can you use to roll out updates for all of your network clients?

A. Install an internal SUS server and use group policy to configure clients to download approved updates from the SUS server.

B. Configure all workstations to prompt end users when downloads are available from the Windows Update site.

C. Use the software installation section of Group Policy to manually deploy software updates at the domain level.

D. Invest in a third-party patch management utility such as SMS.

☑ **D**. Given the need to support down-level clients in this scenario, SUS and Group Policy will not be sufficient to deploy security updates to all of your network clients. In this case, a third-party solution is required.

☒ Answer **A** is incorrect because SUS can only be used to deploy updates to Windows 2000, Windows XP, and Windows Server 2003 machines. Answer **B** is incorrect because security updates should be tested before being deployed in a production environment in case they interfere with any production services or applications. Answer **C** is incorrect because Windows NT 4 clients cannot use the software installation settings available through Group Policy.

3. You are the network administrator for a Windows Server 2003 network with Windows XP Professional desktops. Your help desk has been inundated with support calls from users who have intentionally or accidentally altered their system settings in such a way that they have lost network connectivity or some other form of functionality. You create a new Group Policy Object (GPO) that restricts access to the Control Panel for all of your network users and link it to the domain level. You notice after several weeks that support calls have greatly diminished except for the Communications department. Upon further investigation, you discover that this department is contained within its own OU, and the OU has another GPO applied to it that explicitly grants access to the Control Panel, along with several other settings that the department manager insists are critical for his employees to perform their job functions. How can you enforce the Control Panel lockout without otherwise adversely affecting the Communications department?

   A. Delete the GPO that is linked to the Communications OU.

   B. Configure the "Control Panel lockout" GPO with the Enforce setting.

   C. Configure the Communications OU to Block Inheritance so that the existing GPO will no longer be applied to it.

   D. Merge the Communications OU GPO settings into the default domain GPO.

   ☑ **B**. Using the Enforce setting will ensure that all users in your domain will have access to the operating system features in the Control Panel restricted.

   ☒ Answer **A** is incorrect because this will remove any other settings in the Communications OU GPO, which would adversely affect the Communications department's ability to work. Answer **C** is incorrect because the Block Inheritance setting will only ensure that GPOs applied at a higher level in the Active Directory structure will not be applied to the Communications OU. Answer **D** is incorrect because that would cause the Communications GPO settings to be applied to the entire Active Directory structure, rather than to the single OU.

4. You are the network administrator for a medical research facility running Windows Server 2003. Your firm is beginning a joint research operation with a major university, and many of your users will need to access files and folders on the university's network. The university that you are collaborating with is operating using a UNIX Kerberos environment with UNIX clients at each desktop. Your company's resources should also be accessible by the university staff. How can you accomplish this with the least administrative effort?

   A. Create a realm trust between your network and the UNIX network, and create account mappings in Active Directory for the UNIX clients.

   B. Create separate accounts for the clients on the UNIX network.

   C. Mandate the use of NTLMv2 authentication on the Windows network.

   D. Mandate the use of MS-CHAP from the UNIX clients.

   ☑ **A.** A realm trust will allow users from UNIX clients to be able to connect to your network resources.

   ☒ Answer **B** is incorrect because a realm trust will enable UNIX clients to access your network without the extra administrative effort. Answer **C** is incorrect because NTLMv2 can only be used by Microsoft clients; it isn't supported by UNIX. Answer **D** is incorrect because MS-CHAP is an authentication protocol used for remote access authentication from Microsoft clients, not for LAN access by UNIX clients.

5. You are the network administrator for a large e-commerce site. Your Web developers have created a Web application to share information on the company intranet; this application relies on Digest Authentication to allow users to log on. For some reason, employees seem to be unable to access the new application. You check the account properties of one of the user accounts and see the screen shown in Figure 10.14. What is the most likely reason why your users cannot authenticate?

Figure 10.14 Administrator Properties Sheet

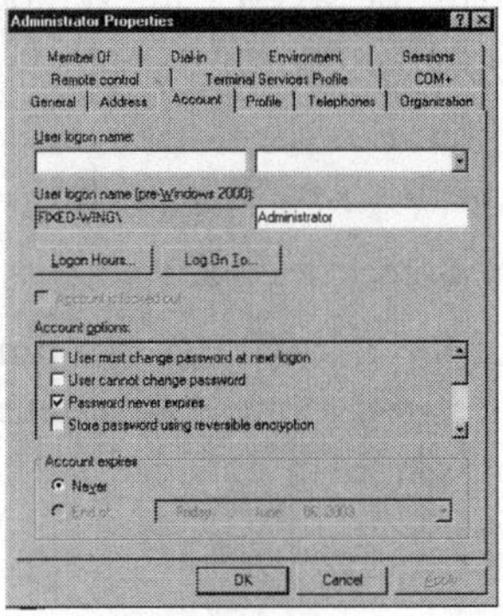

A. When logging on using Digest Authentication, the Windows username is case sensitive.

B. To use Digest Authentication, users must be running Internet Explorer version 6.

C. Your users' passwords are set to expire every 60 days, which is causing Digest Authentication to fail.

D. You must enforce the **Store passwords using reversible encryption** setting for all users who need to authenticate using Digest Authentication.

☑ **D**. For Digest Authentication to function properly, you must select this option for the user accounts that need to use Digest Authentication, either manually or through a policy. Once you've enabled this setting, the users in question will need to change their passwords so that the reversibly encrypted value can be recorded in Active Directory.

☒ Answer **A** is incorrect because a user's password is case sensitive when accessing any Windows application, but not the username. Answer **B** is incorrect because Digest Authentication will function under Internet Explorer version 5.0 or later. Answer **C** is incorrect because Digest Authentication will not fail simply because a user changes his or her Active Directory password.

6. You are a local administrator within a large, multinational corporation. You would like to offer remote access capabilities for the users on your Windows Server 2003 domain. However, your corporation's security policies dictate that all remote access authentication needs to be processed by several UNIX-based RADIUS servers located at various points within the company's global infrastructure. How can you establish remote access authentication for your users that adheres to the corporation's security policies?

A. Use IAS as a RADIUS proxy to forward user authentication requests to the corporate RADIUS servers.

B. Create a realm trust between your Windows Server 2003 domain and the UNIX domain containing the RADIUS servers.

C. Ask the administrator of the corporate RADIUS servers to enable the Guest account on the RADIUS server.

D. Enable Digest Authentication for your domain users.

☑ **A**. In Windows Server 2003, IAS can function as a RADIUS proxy, forwarding authentication requests to a central RADIUS server regardless of the target server's platform or location.

☒ Answer **B** is incorrect because realm trusts are used to create trust relationships between a Windows Server 2003 domain and a UNIX-based Kerberos 5 domain; they are not related to remote access authentication. Answer **C** is incorrect because enabling the Guest account on a production server such as a corporate RADIUS server creates a glaring security flaw. Answer **D** is incorrect because Digest Authentication is used to provide authentication for Web applications, not for remote access purposes.

7. You are the network administrator for Blue Collar, Inc. clothing manufacturers. You have just installed a high-speed Internet connection at the corporate office, and you are designing a remote access scheme that will allow your branch offices and remote users to connect to the corporate LAN to access file shares and other resources. You create a single remote access policy that allows incoming VPN connections between 9 a.m. and 9 p.m., Monday through Friday. You have left all other policy settings at their default values. Most users are connecting to the VPN without issue, but your graphics designer who works from her home office is unable to connect to the VPN using her Macintosh desktop. What is the most likely reason why this is occurring?

   A. You need to allow CHAP authentication within the remote access policy.

   B. The graphics designer is not a member of the appropriate Active Directory group that is enabled for remote access.

   C. The RAS server needs to have the AppleTalk protocol installed.

   D. The clock setting on the graphics designer's computer is inaccurate.

   ☑ **A.** The CHAP authentication protocol is the strongest protocol that Macintosh and UNIX remote access clients can support. By default, a remote access policy will only enable MS-CHAP and MS-CHAPv2. For the graphics designer to connect to the VPN using her Macintosh desktop, you need to manually add CHAP to the list of allowable authentication protocols.

   ☒ Answer **B** is incorrect because you have not restricted remote access based on group membership in this scenario, only time of day/week. Answer **C** is incorrect because the RAS server does not necessarily require the AppleTalk protocol to communicate with a Macintosh client—as long as both the client and the server have TCP/IP installed, they will be able to communicate. Answer **D** is incorrect because the time-of-day restriction is based on the time according to the RAS server, not the incoming client.

8. You are the network administrator for a multisite Active Directory-based network. Your current network infrastructure consists of the following server machines:

- MAX-DC1
  - Windows Server 2003 DC
  - Dual Pentium III 733MHz processors
  - 1GB RAM
  - 20GB free disk space on a RAID-5 disk array
- MAX-DC2
  - Windows Server 2003 DC
  - Dual Pentium 4 1.0GHz processors
  - 1GB RAM
  - 20GB free disk space on a RAID-5 disk array
- MAX-FPS1
  - Windows Server 2003 member server
  - Pentium 4 2.04GHz processor
  - 512MB RAM
  - 25GB free disk space on a RAID-5 disk array
- MAX-FPS2
  - Windows NT 4 member server
  - Pentium III 600MHz processor
  - 512MB RAM
  - 50GB free disk space on a single disk
- MAX-APP1
  - Windows 2000 Advanced Server member server
  - Pentium III 833MHz processor
  - 256MB RAM
  - 50GB free disk space on a RAID-5 array

Your network contains over 1,000 users on Windows 2000 and XP Professional workstations belonging to a single Windows Server 2003 domain. The load on the DCs is fairly high, with processor utilization spiking to over 90 percent at several points during the day, especially first thing in the morning and close to 5 P.M. MAX-APP1 is a dedicated application development server that receives similar processor-heavy requests from your department of application developers. With the recent spate of software vulnerabilities, you would like to implement a patch management solution for the clients and servers on your network. Because of some sensitive development environments and documents on your network, you want to be able to test any updates before you apply them to your network servers and clients. You do not have any available budget for new hardware upgrades or purchases. What would be your best course of action in this scenario? (Choose all that apply.)

A. Install SUS on MAX-FPS1.

B. Install SUS on MAX-APP1.

C. Install SUS on MAX-DC2.

D. Configure a GPO to point your clients to the internal SUS server.

E. Create a logon script to modify client Registry entries to point to the internal SUS server.

F. Configure a GPO to point your clients to the Windows Update site.

☑ **A, D**. Answer **A** is correct because MAX-FPS1 is the best choice of the machines available to host an SUS server. It possesses the necessary hardware requirements, and is not already at the limits of its capacity to service network requests. Answer **D** is correct because, in a Windows 2000/XP client environment, you can use a GPO to automatically configure your clients to point to an update site. Pointing your clients to an internal SUS server will allow you to test any updates before deploying them in a production environment.

☒ Answer **B** is incorrect because MAX-APP1 does not meet the minimum hardware requirement of 512MB of RAM. It is also heavily taxed already by the application developers in your environment. Answer **C** is incorrect because, while MAX-DC2 meets the minimum hardware requirements for a SUS server, it is already heavily taxed by servicing user logon requests. Adding a SUS installation to this server would negatively affect server performance and user productivity. Answer **E** is incorrect because Windows 2000 and XP clients can be configured automatically with a GPO, rather than manually scripting the necessary registry entries. Answer **F** is incorrect because you need to test all updates before deploying them to your network, which makes using the internal SUS server an appropriate choice for hosting client updates.

Index

128-bit encryption, 206
3DES. *see* Triple Date Encryption Standard
40-bit DES, 253
503 errors, 398, 402

A

AAA (authentication, authorization, accounting) Model, 639
ABR (area border routers), 419
Acceptable Use Policy (AUP), 4–5
access
  anonymous, 109–110
  default IIS options, 377
  Deny Access to This Computer from the Network right, 466
  group strategy for accessing resources, 490–495
  Network Access Quarantine Control and, 670
  registry, securing, 615
  removable media, 108
  user, securing, 615
  wireless using IAS, 669
access control. *see also* data access control
  audit requirement analysis, 534–541
  domain local groups and, 520
  files/folders design strategy, 617
  registry access control, 541–553
access control entries (ACEs), 513–514
Access Control List Editor, 533
Access Control Lists (ACLs)
  NTFS/share permissions, 455–457, 496
  data access and, 509
  overview of, 513
access control strategy
  account security policies, 463–474
  administrative and service accounts, 460–462
  auditing user account activity, 480–486
  delegation strategy, 487–490
  for directory services, designing, 454–457, 499
  important points about, 496
  password policies, designing, 462
  password security, 474–480
  rights/permissions, assigning, 458–460
  risks to directory services, 457–458
access design strategy, 455
access mask, 514
access request, 514
Access This Computer from the Network right, 464
accidental network access, 317, 343
account group, 515
Account Group/ACL (AG/ACL), 517–518, 621–622
Account Group/Resource Group (AG/RG), 518
account groups, 619
Account lockout duration setting, 479
Account Lockout policy
  creating, 478–480
  duration, 68
  password security and, 477
  Restricted groups, 470–472
  scenario, 503–504
  user rights assignments, 463–470
Account lockout threshold setting, 479
account logon event, 537–538
account management, 481
account policies, 67–69, 145
account security policies
  implementing via Group Policy, 463
  Kerberos policy, creating, 472–474
  Restricted groups, 470–472
  user rights assignments, 463–470
accounts
  administrator, 645
  local system, 512
  naming conventions, securing, 646
  user, securing, 645–646
ACEs (access control entries), 513–514
ACL. *see* Access Control Lists
Act as Part of the Operating System right, 464
Active Directory (AD)
  certificate temples and, 188
  DNS RR in, 302–303
  domains, 133
  IAS servers and, 666
  IPSec policy stored in, 273–274
  for network infrastructure security, 246
  role-based delegation with, 198
  WLAN network infrastructure requirement, 322
Active Directory Client Services extensions, 74–75
Active Directory security
  access control strategy for directory services, 454–457
  account security policies, 463–474
  administrative and service accounts, 460–462
  auditing user account activity, 480–486
  delegation strategy, 487–490
  group strategy for accessing resources, 490–495
  overview of, 454
  password policies, designing, 462
  password security, 474–480
  rights/permissions, assigning, 458–460
  risks to directory services, 457–458
Active Directory Users and Computers Snap-in
  Account Lockout policy creation with, 479–480
  Audit policy creation with, 482
  setting Password Complexity policy with, 477–478
Active Directory-Integrated zones, 300–301
ad hoc wireless network
  described, 315
  scenario, 347
  when to use, 343
Add Workstations to the Domain right, 464
Adjust Memory Quotas for a Process right, 464
administration delegation strategy, 487–490
Administrative account, 461–462
administrative credentials, 283
administrative policies, 4
administrator accounts, 645, 646
administrators
  authority delegation for, 197–199
  credentials restriction of, 195–196, 231
  delegation strategy, 487–490
  securing tools for, 197–199
  security policies for administrators/IT personnel, 197
advanced digest authentication, 385–386
Advanced Digest Security, 407
AG/ACL (Account Group/ACL), 517–518, 621–622
AG/RG (Account Group/Resource Group), 518
AGDLP
  defined, 454
  described, 491, 498, 512
  nesting groups, 493–494
  user rights and, 513
AGUDLP strategy, 491–492, 498
AH. *see* Authentication Header
AIA (Authority Information Access) 168-169. *see* Authentication Header
All ICMP Traffic filter list, 269
All IP Traffic filter list, 269
Allow automatic administrative logon, 611, 612
Allow floppy copy and access to all drivers and all folders, 612
Allow Log On Locally right, 464–465
Allow Log On through Terminal Services right, 465
/analyze, 90–91
anonymous access restriction, 109–110
anonymous authentication, 362–364
anti-virus protection, 630
anti-virus software, 485
APIPA (Automatic Private IP Addressing), 421

Application log, 396
Application server mode, Terminal Services, 202
application servers, 129, 131
application sharing security, 250–251
application-layer attack, 248
Apply Group Policy permissions, 215
area border routers (ABR), 419
/areas, 89
AS boundary router (ASBR), 420
ASP.NET
 404 errors and, 406
 IIS 6 authorization options, 388–389
 IIS hardening and, 382
ASR. *see* Automated System Recovery
assets risk analysis, 23
asymmetric encryption, 153–154. *see also* public key cryptography
asymmetric keys, 304
ATM (Automatic Teller Machine), 153
attack vectors, 629–630
attacks. *see also* specific type of attack
 analysis of, 623
 combating network, 18
 external, motivations for, 22
 network infrastructure security and, 247–249
 nontechnical, 20
 overview of, 39
 recognizing indicators of, 27
 risk analysis and, 510–511
 threat to wireless networks, 317–318
Audit account logon events setting, 480
Audit account management setting, 481
Audit directory service access setting, 481
audit events, domain controller, 108
Audit logon events policy, 482–483
Audit logon events setting, 481
Audit object access setting, 481, 484–485
Audit policy
 creating, 482
 Group Policy for, 497
 Manage Auditing and Security Log right, 468
 on Web server, 501
 what to include in, 503
Audit policy change setting, 481
Audit privilege use setting, 481
Audit process tracking setting, 481
audit requirement analysis, 534–541
Audit system events setting, 481
auditing
 of account logon events, 537–538
 attack indicators and, 27
 of Directory Service access events, 538
 enabling in IIS, 392–396
 enabling on CA server, 181–183, 187
 of logon events, 535–537
 of object access events, 539
 overview of, 615
 of policy change events, 540
 policy for, 620
 practices for data security, 511
 of privilege use events, 538–539
 of process tracking events, 540
 requirements analysis, 534–535
 of system events, 539
auditing data analysis, 485–486
auditing user account activity
 analyzing auditing data, 485–486
 Audit policy, creating, 482
 Auditing settings, 480–481
 logon events, 482–484
 object access, 484–485
AUP (Acceptable Use Policy), 4–5
authentication
 anonymous, 362–364
 basic, 364–365
 client design strategy, 639–640
 client requirements analysis, 640–641
 digest, 366–367
 DLL for IIS security incident detection, 399
 with EAP, 316
 IEEE 802.1x, 347–348
 IIS 6.0, 401
 IIS certificate, 362–369, 400
 IIS hardening and, 382
 IIS RADIUS, 369–375
 IIS user, 353–356
 IIS Windows logon, 362–369
 logical authentication strategy, designing, 165–167, 186–187
 multifactor, 645
 mutual, 647
 network, 641–645
 protocols for client access, 646–651
 protocols overview, 671
 protocols supported by IAS, 663–665
 remotely managing wireless network, 348
 selecting scope for users in trusts, 223–224
 strategy for clients, 672
 strong, 127
 via SSL/TLS, 304, 305
 for wireless networks, 328–336, 340
authentication data header, 261
Authentication Data, ESP authentication trailer, 263
authentication firewall, 224
Authentication Header (AH)
 with ESP, 343
 ESP *vs.*, 259
 function of, 339
 IPSec modes and, 256–257, 260–261
 IPSec packet protection with, 257–258
 no confidentiality with, 263
authentication methods, 118, 254–255
authentication profiles, 658
authentication traffic digital signatures, 110–112
Author Mode, MMC, 201
authority delegation, 197–199
Authority Information Access (AIA), 168–169
authorization framework, IIS 6.0, 388–389
Authorization Manager snap-in, 533
authorization rules, role-based, 519
authorization, role-based, 519
auto-enrollment, CA, 181
Automated System Recovery (ASR)
 vs. Emergency Management Console/Recovery Console, 621
 when to use, 625
 backup set, creating, 596–598
 backup set, described, 595
automatic mode, IPSec driver, 279
Automatic Private IP Addressing (APIPA), 421
Automatic Teller Machine (ATM), 153
Automatic Updates, SUS, 632–633
autonomous system (AS), 420
autonomy, 488, 497–498
auto-static updates, 416

B

Back Up Files and Directories right, 465
backup
 designing security for, 589
 of encrypted files, 620
 of IIS audit logs, 393
 of keys, 580–584
 log, 595
 media, securing, 593
 overview of, 616–617
 process, designing secure, 592–593
 process, securing, 589–601
 security strategy design, 618–619
backup events, domain controller, 108
bandwidth
 CA implementation and, 161
 network trust hierarchy and, 165
 security and, 33–34
baseline security template, 143–146
basic authentication
 e-commerce and, 405–406
 HTTP W3C and, 403
 NNTP security and, 384
 overview of, 364–365
 SMTP and, 385
batch job, 465, 467
best practices
 for backups, 594–596
 for disaster recovery, 598–600
 for Encrypted File System (EFS), 556–560
 for securing EMS, 609–610
BIND. *see* UNIX Berkeley Internet Name Domain (BIND) DNS implementation
Blaster worm, 460
blended threats, 21
block mode, 279, 280
Bluetooth, 314
/boot, 95

Boot.ini, 606
boundaries, 243–244, 292–293
breach, security, 511
brute force attack, 247–248
business requirements analysis
existing policies/procedures, 3–6
hardware loss and, 42–43
overview of, 40
requirements for securing data, 6–8
security practices analysis, 8–13
Bypass Traverse Checking right, 465

C

CA administrator
approving certificates by, 179–180
request certificate from Web Enrollment Support, 177–179
revoking certificates by, 180–181
CA MMC console, 191
CA Web Enrollment Support
install/uninstall, 176
request certificate from, 177–179, 187
cache, DNS Server Service, 298
cell phones, 314
central processing unit (CPU), 305
certificate authority (CA). *see also* enterprise CAs
defined, 320
design factors to consider, 158–162
EFS and, 554, 616
enrollment and distribution, 177–179
exclude from certificate request, 283
geographical hierarchy, 162–163
installing on Windows Server 2003, 172–176
network trust hierarchy, 164–165
organizational hierarchy, 163–164
in PKI architecture, 156
in PKI process, 154–155
certificate authority (CA) servers
enabling auditing on, 181–183
securing enterprise hierarchy, 169–170
securing stand-alone CA, 170–171
threats against, 167–169
factors to consider, 161
trust hierarchies for, 162–165
certificate distribution
approving certificates by CA administrators, 179–180
enrollment and distribution, 177–179
installing CA on Windows Server 2003, 172–176
questions about, 190–191
renewal and auditing, 181–184
revoking certificates by CA administrators, 180–181
certificate policy and practice statements, 157
certificate repositories, PKI, 157
certificate request, 283
Certificate Revocation List (CRL)
EFS and, 565
function of, 320
offline CAs and, 168–169
defined, 157
Certificate Services
common threats against, 167–169
designing PKI that uses, 186
function of, 320
functionality of, 152
installing on Windows Server 2003, 172–176
on VPNs, 444
certificate template, 188
Certificate Trust List (CTL), 157
certificate, authentication, IIS, 399
certificate-based authentication, 422
certificates
approving certificates by CA administrators, 179–180
authentication, IIS, 356–362, 401
configuring L2TP RRAS to accept, 434–438
cross-certification of, 444
described, 254
EFS and, 580, 620, 624
EFS and third-party, 588
enrollment, 565–566
enterprise/stand-along CAs and, 160
function of, 319
PKI scalability and, 161
with private keys, backing up, 580–584
recovery agent, 554–555
renewal of, 565–566
request from CA Web Enrollment Support, 177–179
revoking certificates by CA administrators, 180–181
root CAs/subordinate CAs and, 159
RRAS and, 451–452
SGC, 387
storage, EFS and, 564–565
for wireless access authentication, 337
certutil.exe, 184, 185
Challenge Handshake Authentication Protocol (CHAP), 653, 678–679. *see also* Microsoft Challenge Handshake Authentication Protocol
Change the System Time right, 465
CIA triad, 6–8
cipher.exe, 566–569, 577–579, 616
Clear This Database check box, 137
Client (Respond Only) policy, 265, 284
client authentication, 308
client authentication settings, 60–61
client setting, SMB signing, 310–312
clients
authentication protocols, choosing, 646–651
authentication requirements analysis, 640–646
authentication strategy design, 639–640
DNS, securing, 303
down-level, configuring, 74–75
identifying non-current, 215–217
internal resource access for, 662
Network Access Quarantine Control and, 670
OS features, restricting access to, 637–639
OS hardening for, 629–637, 672
protocol selection for, 652–654
remote access account lockout and, 670
remote access plan overview, 651–652
remote access policy for, 654–662
security overview, 628–629, 671
using IAS for, 662–669
CM (Connection Manager), 438–439
CMAK (Connection Manager Administration Kit), 439
co-location, backup, 590
command-line tools
cipher.exe, 566–569
dsmod.exe, 528
GPUpdate command, 94–95
Hfnetchk.exe, 51–52
netsh, 668
secedit.exe, 51, 88–95, 140
common policy, remote access, 654
compat*.inf template
down-level clients and, 75
overview of, 57
server roles and, 131
compromised key attack, 248
computer account management plan, 165
computer forensics, 30
computer startup mode, IPSec driver, 278–279
computer-based authentication, Wi-Fi, 334–335
computers. *see* clients; laptop computers; servers
conditions, remote access, 655–656
confidential data, 26
confidentiality, ESP, 263
/configure, 88–90
Configure Your Server Wizard
described, 141
for IIS, 113
using, 103–106
Connection Manager (CM), 438–439
Connection Manager Administration Kit (CMAK), 439
Connection Point Services (CPS), 438–439
connections
encrypted, SSL/TLS and. *see* Secure Socket Layer/Transport Layer Security
numbered/unnumbered, 421–422
persistent in extranets, 443
console redirection
EMS and, 602–603
service processor, 604
Windows, 604–605
content, 399, 404
Content Management Server (CMS), 399, 404
contexts, *netsh.exe* command, 272–273

control design strategy, 455
copy backup, 592
corruption, data, 510
CPS (Connection Point Services), 438–439
CPU (central processing unit), 305
Create a Pagefile right, 466
Create a Token Object right, 466
Create Global Objects right, 466
Create Permanent Shared Objects right, 466
CreateProcessAsUser, 469
credentials, basic authentication, 364
critical security updates, 41
CRL. *see* Certificate Revocation List
cross certificate, 164–165
CryptoAPI (cryptography application programming interface), 554
Cryptographic API (Crypto API), 387
cryptographic service provider (CSP)
  described, 565
  installing CA and, 174
  securing stand-alone CA, 170–171
  shut down, 189
cryptography, 386–388
CSP. *see* cryptographic service provider
CTL (Certificate Trust List), 157
custom policy, remote access, 655

D

DACL. *see* Discretionary Access Control Lists
daily backup, 592
data
  analysis for different types of, 25–26
  EFS encryption and, 557–558
  identifying valuable information, 245
  permission structure for, 491–495
  practices for safeguarding, 591
data access control
  groups, working with, 521–534
  overview of, 508–509
  resource access, 516–521
  reviewing access/ACLs, 511–516
  risk analysis, 509–511
Data Administrators, 487, 497
Data Encryption Standard (DES), 253
Data Encryption Standard Extended (DESX), 558
data modification
  as attack type, 247
  DNS servers and, 121
  threat to DNS, 294
  threat to wireless networks, 317
Data Recovery Agent (DRA)
  adding for local computer, 574–577
  adding with cipher.exe, 577–579
  configuring, 574
  described, 555
  policy, removing, 579–580
data storage, 589–590
data transmission security
  port authentication for switches, 312
  S/MIME, 309
  segmented networks, 313
  SMB signing, 309–312
  SSL/TLS, 303–309
database settings, CA installation, 175–176
DC. *see* domain controllers
DC Security.inf template
  overview of, 56–57
  DC/DHCP servers, 143
  domain controllers and, 130
Debug Programs right, 466
decentralized management model, 200
decryption. *see* Encrypted File System
default exemptions, 281
default IPSec policies
  IP packet filtering, 272
  IPSec rules, 264
  list chart, 265–266
  netsh commands, 272–273
  predefined filter actions, 270–272
  predefined filter lists, 269–270
  view Server (Request Security), 267–269
default lease period, Wi-Fi, 327
Default Locked down status, 388
default policy, remote access, 655
default security settings, 56
default security template, 55–56
default trust relationship, 222
defense in depth, 198
delegated administrators, 487
delegated namespace, DNS, 295
delegation, 197–199. *see also* groups
Delegation of Control Wizard, 530–534
delegation strategy
  delegation structure, selecting, 488–490
  example of, 502
  important points about, 497–498
  isolation/autonomy, 487–488
  scenario, 504
  Service/Data administrators, 487
delegation structure, 488–490
Delta Certification Revoke List (Delta CRL), 157
demand dial routing
  described, 446
  between internal networks, 420–423
  OSPF and, 447
denial-of-service (DoS)
  DNS servers and, 121
  defined, 248
  overview of, 15–16
  STRIDE and, 14
  TCP SYN packet requests and, 45
  threat to DNS, 294
  threat to wireless networks, 317
Deny Access to This Computer from the Network right, 466
Deny Log On as a Batch Job right, 467
Deny Log On as a Service right, 467
Deny Log On Locally right, 467
Deny Log On through Terminal Services right, 467
DESX (Data Encryption Standard Extended), 558
device drivers, 468
DHCP. *see* Dynamic Host Configuration Protocol
diagnostic mode, IPSec driver, 278, 280
dial-up connection
  security *vs.* VPNs, 447
  IAS and, 665
differential backup, 593
Diffie-Hellman encryption. *see also* public key cryptography
Diffie, Whitman, 253
Diffie-Hellman (DH) group 1 (low), 282
Diffie-Hellman (DH) groups, 255–256, 281
Diffie-Hellman encryption, 253
digest authentication
  MD5 hash and, 403
  overview of, 366–367, 650, 672
  WebDAV and, 386, 404
  Windows logon with, 405
Digest Security, 385–386
digital certificates, 153–158
digital encryption, 110–111
direct-dial remote access, 652
directory object, 466
Directory Service access event auditing, 538
Directory Services (DS)
  access control strategy for, 454–457
  auditing setting for, 481
  mapping, 356
  risks to, 457–458, 496
directory traversal vulnerability, 20
disabled mode, IPSec driver, 279
disaster recovery
  best practices for, 598–600
  corporate business continuity and, 616
  overview of, 616–617
discretionary access control list (DACL)
  in Active Directory-Integrated zones, 300–301
  described, 513
  securing DNS Server Service and, 299
  vs. SACL, 619
disk
  based backup, 590
  management, 510
  volumes, data loss and, 509
Distributed Denial-of-Service, 16–18
distribution group, 515
DLL, authentication, 399
DNS. *see* Domain Name Service
DNS Resource Records, 302–303
DNS Server Service, 297–300
DNS zones, 300–302
Domain Admins group, 470, 489
Domain Controller Default security template, 56–57
domain controllers (DCs)

anonymous access restriction, 109–110
authentication traffic digital signatures, 110–112
common threats to, 107–108
configuration overview, 106–107
configuring IAS on, 666–669
DC security.inf and, 56–57
L2TP and, 434
removable media access restriction, 108
summary of services for, 129
template application on, 80–82
template for, 130
DC Security.inf template and, 143
securing DNS Server Service, 299
domain delegation structure, 489
domain functional levels
described, 498
Server 2003, 227–230
with Windows Server 2000/2003, 494–495
Windows Server 2003 domain functional level, 500
domain local groups
described, 516
function of, 491
nesting, 493
overview of, 519–520
in permission structure, 492, 493, 498
Domain Name Service (DNS)
clients, 303
DNS Server Service, 297–300
namespace, 295–296
resource records, 302–303
securing, 293–295
security, 250
server log, 395
for wireless network infrastructure, 327
WLAN network infrastructure requirement, 322
zones, 300–302
Domain Naming System (DNS) servers
DNS clients, securing, 303
threats to, 294–295
configuring, 120–122
summary of services for, 129
domain-based IPSec policy, 275–276
domains
adding recovery agents for, 578–579
functionality of, 229–230
models for trust relationships, 221–226
templates application with Group Policy Editor, 77–80
trust relationships and, 217–221
DoS. *see* Denial-of-Service
down-level clients, 74–75, 226–228
DRA. *see* Data Recovery Agent
DS. *see* Directory Services
dsmod.exe, 528
dump files, 614
Dumpel.exe, 486
<Dynamic> Default Response rule
in all IPSec policies, 264
disabling, 269–270
removing, 293
Dynamic Host Configuration Protocol (DHCP)
RRAS and, 450
security, 249–250
for WLAN network infrastructure, 326–327
WLAN network infrastructure requirement, 322
Dynamic Host Configuration Protocol (DHCP) servers
configuring, 120
DC Security.inf template and, 143
summary of services for, 129
VPNs and, 451

E

EAP. *see* Extensible Authentication Protocol (EAP)
EAP-TLS. *see* Extensible Authentication Protocol-Transport Level Security
eavesdropping, 247, 317
e-commerce, 152–155, 308
Edit Rule Properties dialog, 288
EFS. *see* Encrypted File System
elevation of privilege, 14
e-mail, 154–155, 308
Emergency Management Console, 621
Emergency Management Services (EMS)
for disaster recovery, 599
securing, 601–610
designing security for, 208–210
implementing, 238
Enable Computer and User Accounts to be Trusted for Delegation right, 467
Encapsulated Security Payload (ESP)
with AH, 343
encryption with, 339
IPSec modes and, 256–257
IPSec packet protection with, 258–259
L2TP and, 433
Encrypted File System (EFS)
adding Data Recovery Agent with cipher.exe, 577–579
backing up keys, 580–584
behavior, 555–556
best practices for, 556–560
certificate enrollment/renewal, 565–566
certificate storage and, 564–565
certificates and, 624
design strategy, 618
disabling, 587–588
encryption/decryption strategy, 571–576
implementing on local computers, 560–563
overview of, 553–555, 570–571, 615–616
printing encrypted files, 584–587
recovering files and, 580
Recovery Agent policy, removing, 579–580
Server 2003 and, 508
vs. third-party encryption, 620
third-party encryption options with, 588
using cipher.exe, 566–569
encryption
demand dial routing and, 422–423
with ESP, 261
IPSec algorithms, 252–253, 256
Password policy setting for, 475–476
remote access and, 658–659
SSL/TLS, 304–305
symmetric/asymmetric, 153–154
WEP for wireless networks, 329
WEP vulnerability, 335–336
Enforce password history setting, 474
Enforce user logon restrictions, 472
enrollment
auto-enrollment for CAs, 181
of EFS certificates, 565–566
request certificate from Web Enrollment Support, 177–179
enterprise CAs
Active Directory and, 186
defining, 158
function of, 160, 185
root CA and, 168
securing, 169–170
security for, 166–171
enterprise, security application across, 132–137
ESP. *see* Encapsulated Security Payload
Ethernet port type, 312
event auditing, 534–541
event log monitoring, 395–396
Event Log node, 71–72
Event Logs, 42
Event Viewer, 485–486
EventCombMT, 42
EventcombMT.exe, 486
Eventlog.pl, 486
Eventquery.pl, 486
Exchange Server 2003, 309
expiration dates, PKI certificate, 166
Export Policies command, 277
/export secedit.exe switch, 92–93
Extensible Authentication Protocol (EAP)
for authentication, 316
authentication methods using, 329–330
dial-up remote access and, 653
for VPNs, 426
Extensible Authentication Protocol-Transport Level Security (EAP-TLS)
demand dial routing and, 422
switch access authentication via, 312
wireless network authentication with, 330
extensions

Active Directory Client Services, 74–75
security to Group Policy, 51, 138–139
external attacks, 22
external CA, 161
external queries, 296
external routes, 420
external trusts, 222–223
extranets
IIS security for, 375–376
infrastructure design, 443

F

fallback to clear, 270–271
FAT file system, 172, 190
Federal Information Processing Standard (FIPS), 124, 206
file authorization, ASP.NET, 389
File Encryption Key (FEK), 554
file permissions, Server 2003, 500
file recovery agent. *see* Data Recovery Agent
file servers, 123, 129, 131–132
file sharing, 250–251
file structure, 382
File System node, 74
File Transfer Protocol (FTP)
anonymous access and, 403
certificate authentication and, 404
IIS, securing, 383–384
files. *see also* data access control
EFS encryption of, 556–557
encrypted, overview of, 570–571
offline, encrypting, 559
recovering with EFS, 580
FILESTORE, 89
filter actions
configuring IPSec policy, 285
IPSec, predefined, 264–265
predefined, 270–272
recommendations, 289–290
filter lists
configuring IPSec policy, 285
IPSec, predefined, 264–265
in IPSec process, 274–275
predefined, 269–270
recommendations, 289–290
filtering
IP packet, 272, 438
IP, designing, 289–292
stateful filtering during startup, 282
filters
IPSec filters update IP configurations, 281
peer, RIP and, 419
route, RIP and, 418
FIPS. *see* Federal Information Processing Standard
firewalls. *see also* Internet Connection Firewall
authentication, 224
configuration, 292–293
for POP3 servers, 117–118
PPTP and, 450–451
for secure boundaries, 243–244
SSL/TLS and, 309
VPN servers placement and, 443
VPNs and, 447
Web servers and, 448–449
firmware console redirection, 603
firmware environment variables, 469
flexible caching, 355, 405
floppy drives, 598
footprinting, 121, 294
Force Shutdown from a Remote System right, 467
forensics, computer, 30
forest functional levels
described, 498
with Windows Server 2000/2003, 494, 495
forests
delegation structure at, 488–489, 498
functionality of, 229–230
models for trust relationships, 221–226
security in trusts between, 500
trust relationships and, 217–221
framework for security implementation
corporate network risks, addressing, 23–25
data types, security analysis for, 25–26
external attack motivations, 22
overview of, 13, 40
predicting network threats, 13–15
recognizing external threats, 15–21
risk analysis implementation, 23
free-loading, 317
FTP. *see* File Transfer Protocol

G

Generate Security Audits right, 467
/generaterollback, 93–94
geographical hierarchy, 162–163, 189
GINA (graphical identification and authentication), 202
Global Catalog (GC) server, 491
Global groups
described, 516
function of, 491
nesting, 493, 494
in permission structure, 492, 498
global objects, 466
GPO. *see* Group Policy Objects
GPUpdate command, 94–96
graphical identification and authentication, 202
Gravity Storm Software Service Pack Manager 2000, 216–217
Group Policy
account security policies in, 463
applying security templates via, 133–137
Audit policy creation with, 482
auditing settings in, 480–481
client/server authentication settings, 60–61
configuring Restricted groups in, 470–471
deploying security settings with, 76–80
for domains, 80–82
group security with, 497
IPSec policies and, 342–343
Kerberos policy creation in, 472–474
for password policy design, 462
patch management and, 632
Recovery Console options, 611
setting permissions via, 458–460
setting registry access permissions via, 546–552
tunnels configured via, 260
for WLAN network infrastructure, 322–326
Group Policy Editor snap-in, 310
Group Policy Management Console (GPMC), 97–98
Group Policy Object Editor snap-in, 331–334
Group Policy Objects (GPOs)
assigning IPSec policy and, 277–278
assigning IPSec policy to, 285–286
IPSec policy assignment and, 275
RSoP and, 9
AD configuration and, 675–676
for administrator security, 197
for deployment of software updates, 213–215, 232
OS access restriction and, 637–638, 672, 676–677
for patching IIS servers, 237
recovery agents and, 579
group policy settings, 802.1x, 331–334
group scopes, 491
group strategy for accessing resources
group scopes, 491
important points about, 499
permission structure for data, 491–495
uses for groups, 490
GROUP_MGMT, 89
groups
account *vs.* resource, 619
account, maintenance delegation, 529–530
Administrative, 645–646
combining/nesting, 493–494
default for DNS RRs in Active Directory, 302–303
default for DNS Server Service, 299
default in AD-Integrated zones, 300–301
deleted, troubleshooting, 622
interactive, 512
local as resource groups, 519–521
obsolete, LDAP query for, 526–529
overview of, 515
privileges and, 622
resource, maintenance delegation, 529–530
Restricted groups, 470–472
security, 515–516
groups, security
creation policy defining, 521–522
Delegation of Control Wizard, 530–534

described, 515
maintenance, delegating, 529
naming policy, defining, 522–523
nesting policy, defining, 524–525
request process, defining, 522
retirement policy, defining, 526–529
described, 528

H

hackers
Account Lockout policy and, 478–479
Administrative account and, 462
common types of attacks, 247–249
threats to DNS, 294
handshake layer, 304
hardening
client OSs, 629–637, 672
IIS, 381–383
hardware CSPs, 171, 185, 186
hardware, network infrastructure, 243
hash, 649–650
hashing algorithm
default with CA installation, 190
for digital certificate, 153
IPSec, 253–254, 256
in PKI process, 154–155, 185
for SSL/TLS, 304
headless servers, 607
health detection, 392–396
Health Insurance Portability and Accountability Act (HIPAA), 5, 318
heart beat, 397, 398
Hellman, Martin, 253
Hfnetchk.exe, 51–52, 140
high security policies, 246, 284
Highly Secure template, 59–62
HIPAA (Health Insurance Portability and Accountability Act), 5, 318
hisec*.inf template, 59–62, 144
SMB signing required in, 309
hisecdc.inf template, 130
HP OpenView, 216
HTTP.Sys
described, 401
flexible caching and, 405
IIS logging and, 390
IIS user authentication and, 353–354, 355–356
HyperText Transfer Protocol (HTTP)
HTTP 1.1, 367
server-gated cryptography and, 386

I

IAS. *see* Internet Authentication Server
ICANN. *see* Internet Corporation for Assigned Names and Numbers
ICF. *see* Internet Connection Firewall
identity spoofing, 247
identity, worker process, 388
IEEE 802.11a, 315–316
IEEE 802.11b, 315
IEEE 802.11g, 316
IEEE 802.15, 314
IEEE 802.11
development of/specifications, 315–316
identity verification/authentication, 328
WEP encryption, 329
WLAN defined by, 314
IEEE 802.1x
authentication for wireless networks, 329, 347–348
EAP and, 329–330
group policy settings, 331–334
IAS support for, 331
IETF. *see* Internet Engineering Task Force
IIS. *see* Internet Information Server
IIS Lockdown Wizard, 130
IISLockdown, 114–116
IKE. *see* Internet Key Exchange
Impersonate a Client After Authentication right, 468
implementation. *see* framework for security implementation
/import, 91–92
import IPSec policy, 276, 277
in-band connections, 600–601
in-band management, 209
inbound passthrough, 270, 271
Incident Response plan, 28–30
Increase Scheduling Priority right, 468
incremental backup, 593
incremental policies, 102
inetinfo.exe, 353, 396–397
information disclosure, 14
infrastructure capabilities analysis, 32
infrastructure servers template, 131
infrastructure-based wireless network, 315
installations, IIS, 376–381
Institute of Electrical and Electronic Engineers (IEEE), 315, 316
integrated Windows authentication
NNTP security and, 384
overview of, 367–369
SMTP and, 385
interactive group, 512
interactive logon, 641
interfaces, DNS Server Service, 297
intermediary CAs
in CA hierarchy, 159
in geographical hierarchy, 162–163
in organizational hierarchy, 163–164
in PKI architecture, 187
root CA and, 186
internal CA, 161
internal namespace, DNS, 295–296
internal networks, 442
Internet
filter actions and, 271
firewall and, 292, 293
IPSec best practices for, 283
Internet Authentication Server (IAS)
overview of, 674
RADIUS and, 369–370, 406, 678
as RADIUS server, 442
security issues with, 374
Server 2000/2003 and, 404
support for 802.1x authentication, 331
using, 370–373, 662–670
Network Access Quarantine Control and, 439
Internet Connection Firewall (ICF), 292, 378–381
Internet Corporation for Assigned Names and Numbers (ICANN), 295
Internet Engineering Task Force (IETF), 155
Internet Engineering Task Force (IETF) Request for Comments (RFCs) 2401-2409, 251
Internet Information Server (IIS)
5.0 sub-authentication, 364
6.0 template for, 130–131
6.0, summary of services for, 129
certificate authentication, 356–362
FTP, securing, 383–384
installations, securing, 376–381
monitoring strategy for, 389–399
NNTP, securing, 384
RADIUS authentication, 369–375
security design overview, 375–376, 402–403
security overview, 352
servers, risks to/hardening, 381–383
SMTP, securing, 385
SSL security access information and, 404
updating, content management strategy for, 399
user authentication design overview, 353–356, 401–402
version 6.0, security features in, 385–389
Windows logon authentication, 362–369
basic security for, 114
Configure Your Server to set up, 113
configuring to use SSL, 306–308
security, 250
security overview, 112–113
on Server 2003, 142
using URLScan/IISLockdown, 114–116
Internet Key Exchange (IKE)
filtering traffic, 293
in IPSec policy application, 274–275
process, 252–256
Internet Protocol Security (IPSec)
filters for network infrastructure servers, 119
filters for POP3 servers, 117–118
for IIS, 114
spoofing, 294
WINS servers and, 146–147

demand dial routing and, 422–423
ESP on L2TP, 438
firewall configuration, 292–293
IAS access and, 374
modes, 256–257
for network infrastructure security, 244
for network services security, 250–251
overview, 251
overview of, 242
persistent policies, 345
PKI and, 156
policies, applying, 273–284
policies, default, 264–273
policies, designing, 284–289
policies, group policies and, 342–343
policies, rules, 246
policy settings, 345–346
process, 263–264
protocols, 257–263
security associations, 252–256
summary of, 339

Internet Protocol Security (IPSec) policies
applying, 273–284
best practices for, 282, 283
default, 264–273
designing, 284–289
in IPSec process, 263–264

Internet Security & Acceleration server, 674
Internet Security Association and Key Management Protocol (ISAKMP)/Oakley, 252–256
Internet Server Application Programming Interface (ISAPI), 353
interoperability
constraints analysis, 34–38
designing security for, 226–228
overview of, 39

interoperability constraints analysis
and MIT Kerberos, 35–37
overview of, 34–35
UNIX DNS with Server 2003, 37–38

intranet, 375–376
IP address
DNS clients, securing, 303
DNS security and, 293–294
DNS Server Service security and, 297
IPSec modes and, 256–257
NNTP security and, 384
SMTP security and, 385
spoofing, 247

IP filtering, 272, 289–292
IP forwarding, 293
IP packet
with AH in IPSec modes, 260–261
with ESP, 261–262
IPSec process, 263–264
protection with IPSec protocols, 257–259

IP protocol 50. *see* Authentication Header
IP protocol 51. *see* Encapsulating Security Payload
IP Routing. *see* Routing Information Protocol
IP Security Monitor snap-in, 282
IP Security Policy Management
to configure IPSec policy, 285
for exporting/importing IPSec policy, 276
tunnels configured via, 260

IP Security Policy Management snap-in, 286–289
IPSec. *see* Internet Protocol Security
IPSec context, *netsh.exe*, 273
IPSec deployment plan, 282
IPSec driver
modes, 278–282
packet secured with, 263
policy application with, 274–275

IPSec Policy Agent Service, 263, 274
IPSec Policy Management console, 283
IPSec polling interval, 277
IPSEC/L2TP, 46
ISAKMP (Internet Security Association and Key Management Protocol), 252–256
ISAPI (Internet Server Application Programming Interface), 353
isolation mode, worker process, 354–355
isolation, delegation requirement, 487–488
issuing CAs, 162–164
IT personnel, 197
Itanium-based systems, 603
IUSR_ComputerName account, 401, 403. *see also* anonymous authentication

K

KDC (Key Distribution Center), 35, 647, 648
Kerberos
account policies and, 68
Group Policy for, 497
IIS Windows authentication and, 369
liabilities of, 673
vs. NTLM, 367–368
policy, 472–474
Server 2003 and, 646–647

Kerberos Realms, 224–225
Kerberos v5, 255, 283
kernel, 604
Key Distribution Center (KDC), 35, 647, 648
Key Exchange Security methods, 287–288
Key Exchange Security Methods dialog, 268
key retrieval/recovery, 157
keyed-hashing for Message Authentication Code (HMAC), 304
keys
backing up with certificates, 580–584
IPSec security associations and, 252–256
private, 557

Kids Passport, 643

L

LAN Manager, 57–59, 61–62
laptop computers, 634–637
Layer 2 Tunneling Protocol (L2TP)
in Virtual Private Networks (VPNs), 425
configuring to accept certificates, 434–438
NAT and, 447
vs. PPTP, 438, 447
in Virtual Private Networks (VPNs), 433–434
VPNs and, 654

lease, DHCP, 326–327
Length header, 261
Lightweight Directory Access Protocol (LDAP), 526–529
link encryption, 422
Load and Unload Device Drivers right, 468
local authentication strategy, 165–167
local computer policy, 278
local groups, 516, 520–521
local IPSec policy, 277–278
local policies security templates, 69–71
Local System account
Create a Token Object right and, 466
described, 512
security of, 460
service accounts and, 497

Lock Pages in Memory right, 468
lockdown, 271
lockout. *see* Remote Access Account Lockout
/log filename, 89
Log On as a Batch Job right, 465
Log On as a Service right, 468
logging diagnostic mode, 280
logging in IAS, 375
logic bomb, 22
logical authentication strategy, 186–187
/logoff GPUpdate parameter, 95
logon
auditing settings for, 480, 481
interactive, 641
user rights assignments, 464–465, 467

logon authentication, 362–369
logon event auditing, 482–483, 535–537
logs, event, 395–396
logs, IIS, 389–392

M

MAC (Message Authentication Code), 304
mail servers. *see* POP3 mail servers
maintenance, 529
Manage Auditing and Security Log right, 468
management. *see also* network management process, securing
man-in-the-middle (MITM) attacks, 14, 45, 248, 309
manual mode, IPSec driver, 279
many-to-one mapping, 359–362
many-to-many mapping, 359, 400, 401
mapping
  described, 400
  Directory Service, 356
  many-to-one, 359–362
  one-to-one, 357–359
  Windows login accounts and, 404
Master Key Perfect Forward Secrecy (PFS), 268
Maximum lifetime for service ticket setting, 472
Maximum lifetime for user ticket renewal setting, 472
Maximum lifetime for user ticket setting, 472
Maximum password age setting, 474
Maximum tolerance for computer clock synchronization setting, 472
MBSA. *see* Microsoft Baseline Security Analyzer
MD5. *see* Message Digest
media, backup, 593, 596
"Member Of" setting, 470
member servers, 123, 131–132
memory, 464, 468
Message Authentication Code (MAC), 304
message digest, 153–154
Message Digest (MD5), 253–254, 304
Message Digest (MD5) hash
  advanced digest authentication and, 385–386
  digest authentication and, 366–367, 403
Microsoft Baseline Security Analyzer (MBSA)
  described, 140
  Hfnetchk.exe and, 51–52
  for non-current client identification, 215–216, 232
Microsoft Challenge Handshake Authentication Protocol (MS-CHAP), 127, 653
Microsoft Challenge Handshake Authentication Protocol (MS-CHAP) v2
  demand dial routing and, 422
  dial-up remote access and, 653
  for VPNs, 426
Microsoft Exchange Server 2003, 117
Microsoft Management Console (MMC). *see also* consoles
  network security management and, 201
  view Server (Request Security) policy with, 267–269
Microsoft Operations Manager (MOM), 534
Microsoft Passport Authentication, 642–645, 673
Microsoft Point-to-Point Encryption (MPPE), 422
Microsoft Security Bulletin Classification System, 631
Microsoft Site Server 4.0, 399
Microsoft strong cryptographic provider algorithm, 154
minimal security, 245
minimal security policies, 284
Minimum password age setting, 474–475
Minimum password length setting, 475
mirrored disk, 590
mirrored volume. *see* RAID-1
MIT Kerberos, 35–37
Mixed mode, 494
Modify Firmware Environment Variables right, 469
MOM (Microsoft Operations Manager), 534
monitoring, IIS, 389–399
MPPE (Microsoft Point-to-Point Encryption), 422
MS-CHAP (Microsoft Challenge Handshake Authentication Protocol), 127, 653
MS-CHAP (Microsoft Challenge Handshake Authentication Protocol) version 2
  demand dial routing and, 422
  dial-up remote access and, 653
  for VPNs, 426
multifactor authentication, 645
Multilink, 658
mutual authentication, 647

N

name, CA, 174–175
namespace, DNS, 295–296
naming conventions, 522–523, 646
NAT. *see* Network Address Translation
Native mode, 494, 495
NAT-T (Network Address Translation traversal), 281
Negotiate security, 276
nesting groups, 493–494, 524–525
NetIQ Security Manager, 216
Netscape Communications Corporation, 304
netsh command-line utility, 668
netsh ipsec dynamic mode, 273
netsh ipsec static importpolicy command, 277
netsh ipsec static mode, 273
netsh ras add registeredserver command, 412
netsh.exe command
  to configure IPSec policy, 285
  has IPSec contect, 281
  IPSec context, 272–273
  for IPSec driver, 280
  for IPSec driver state, 279
  for IPSec policy, 276
network "audit" tools, 315
Network Access Quarantine Control
  getting started with, 674
  overview of, 673
  remote access and, 670
  Server 2003, 439
Network Address Translation (NAT)
  L2TP and, 447
  Server 2003 and, 447
Network Address Translation traversal (NAT-T), 281
network baseline, 27
network communications. *see* Virtual Private Networks
network framework
  business requirements analysis, 3–13
  design overview, 2
  security incidents, responding to, 26–31
  technical constraints, analyzing, 31–38
  threat prediction, 13–26
network infrastructure security
  attacks, types of, 247–249
  data transmission security, designing, 303–313
  DNS clients, 303
  DNS namespace, 295–296
  DNS resource records, 302–303
  DNS, securing, 293–295
  DNS Server Service, 297–300
  DNS zones, 300–302
  elements of, 243
  important points for, 340–341
  IP filtering, designing, 289–293
  IPSec modes, 256–257
  IPSec overview, 251
  IPSec policies, applying, 273–284
  IPSec policies, default, 264–273
  IPSec policies, designing, 284–289
  IPSec process, 263–264
  IPSec protocols, 257–263
  IPSec security associations, 252–256
  overview of, 242
  physical security, 342
  PKI and RADIUS/IAS, 319–321
  risk for network services, assessing, 249–251
  steps for, 243–247
  wireless access infrastructure, 336–338
  wireless networks, authentication for, 328–336
  wireless networks security, designing, 313–316
  wireless networks, threats to, 317–318
  WLAN network infrastructure, 321–328

of WLAN, designing, 321–328
network infrastructure servers, 118–119
Network Interface Card (NIC), 414
network management process
administrative tools, securing, 200–208
administrators and, 195–200
EMS, designing security for, 208–210
overview of, 194–195, 231
security update infrastructure, 210–217
trust relationships, 217–230
Network Monitor, 42
Network News Transfer Protocol (NNTP), 384
network services
post-attack recovery, 31
risk assessment, 249–251
securing. *see* network infrastructure security
network switches, 312
network traffic security, RAS, 126
network trust hierarchy
for CAs, 164–165, 189
root CA and, 188
networks
addressing risks to, 23–25
authentication, 641–645
communication security overview, 411
extranets, 443
policy management of, 200
resources, providing access to, 662
routing between internal, 442
segmented networks, 313
Next Header, 261, 262
NIC (Network Interface Card), 414
Nimda worm, 21
NNTP (Network News Transfer Protocol), 384
No Terminal Server User SID template, 63
nonrepudiation, 153
nontechnical attacks, 20
nontransitive trust, 221
normal backup, 593
notssid.inf template, 63
NT Lan Manager (NTLM) authentication, 57–59, 367–368, 648–650, 672
NT Lan Manager (NTLM) v2, 46, 74
NTFS file system
access control and, 509
for CA, 190
on DNS servers, 300
EFS and, 553
on file/print/member servers, 123
on IIS, 116
Server 2003 upgrades and, 406
NTFS permissions
access control lists and, 496
access control security with, 455, 456
Ntldr, 604
NTLM. *see* NT Lan Manager
Ntoskrnl.exe, 604
numbered connections, 421–422

O

object access auditing, 481, 484–485, 513, 538–539
objects, 512
offline CAs, 167–169, 185, 189–190
one-to-one mapping, 357–359
one-way trust, 217–219, 235
Open Shortest Path First (OSPF), 419–420, 447
open system authentication, 328
Operating Systems (OSs)
hardening for clients, 629–637
restricting access to, 637–639
multiple, GPMC and, 97–98
operational mode, 278, 279–280
operators, 384, 385
organizational hierarchy, 163–164, 189
Organizational Units (OUs)
assigning domain-based IPSec policy, 275–276
assigning IPSec policy to, 285
assigning OU-based IPSec policy, 277
creating, 198–199
delegation structure at, 489
IPSec policy design and, 284
for security, 198
OSPF. *see* Open Shortest Path First
OU-based IPSec policy, 277
out-of-band connections, 601
out-of-band management, 208–209
out-of-band security, 608–610
outsourcing, network management, 200
/overwrite, 89
owner, object, 512

P

packet filtering, IP. *see* IP packet filtering
packet filtering, L2TP/PPTP, 438
Padding field, 262
Padding Length, 262
pagefile, 466
Passport. *see* Microsoft Passport Authentication
password authentication, 640
Password Authentication Protocol (PAP), 653
Password Complexity policy, 477–478
Password must meet complexity requirements setting, 475
password policies
for authentication strategy, 166
configuration of, 496
designing, 462
settings, 474–476
password security, 474–480
account lockout policy, creating, 478–480
important points about, 496
password complexity requirements, 477–478
Password policy settings, 474–476
user password tips, 476–477
password-based attack, 247, 344
passwords
AD and, 145
random password generators, 398
RIP and, 417–418
security and, 43–44
security of, 457
for service accounts, 461
storage locations, 635
Store passwords using reversible encryption setting, 677–678
strong, requirements of, 68
Syskey and, 635–637
patch management. *see also* Software Update Services
Group Policy and, 632
overview of, 631
Software Update Services and, 632–633
third-party tools for, 633–634, 676
update testing and, 679–680
PEAP with EAP-MS-CHAPv2, 330
PEAP with EAP-TLS, 330
peer limiting, 419
Perform Volume Maintenance Tasks right, 469
performance
EFS and, 554
IAS server, 375
SSL/TLS and, 387
Performance Monitor, 469
permission structure for data
AGUDLP strategy, 491–492
combining/nesting groups, 493–494
Domain Local groups, 492
domain/forest functional levels, 494–495
Global groups, 492
Universal groups, 492–493
permissions
assigning, 458–460
default, for DNS Server Service, 299
default, in AD-Integrated zones, 300–301
discretionary, 508
for DNS RRs in Active Directory, 302–303
groups and, 516
overview of, 512
registry objects and, 552–553
remote access, 657
scenario, 504–505
for service accounts, 497
for user accounts, 496
Permit filter action, 270
permit mode, 279
persistent connections, 443
persistent IPSec policy, 282, 345
persistent policies, 278
personal identification number (PIN), 153
PFS (Master Key Perfect Forward Secrecy), 268
Phase I Security Association
authentication methods, 254–255

Diffie-Hellman groups, 255–256
IPSec encryption algorithms, 252–253
IPSec hash algorithms, 253–254
Phase II Security Association, 252, 256
physical policies, 4
physical security, 171, 342
Ping of Death, 15
PKI. *see* public key infrastructure
Point-to-Point Tunneling Protocol (PPTP)
firewalls and, 450–451
vs. L2TP, 438, 447
VPNs and, 425–433, 654
policies
acceptable use, 4–5
account, Security Templates and, 67–69
audit, enabling on local machine, 394–395
auditing, 620
local, Security Templates and, 69–71
nesting, for security groups, 524–525
network management, 200
overview of, 39
password/account, 145
physical/technical/administrative, 4
Recovery Agent, removing, 579–580
remote access, 654–662
Resultant Set of, 9
retirement, for security groups, 526
for security groups creation, 521–522
settings, results review, 82–85
Terminal Services single-session, 206
policy CAs, 185. *see also* intermediary CAs
policy change auditing setting, 481
policy change events, 540
policy negotiation, 252–256
POP3 mail servers
authentication methods, 118
security levels, 117–118
security overview, 116–117
summary of services for, 129
template for, 131
port authentication, 312
ports
configuring for two-way trusts, 233
IIS hardening and, 382
network communications and, 447
PPTP/L2TP and, 448
Terminal Services, changing, 202–204
Power On Self Test (POST), 603
PPTP. *see* Point-to-Point Tunneling Protocol
Pre-Boot eXecution Environment (PXE), 603
predefined filter actions, 270–272
predefined filter lists, 269–270
predefined IPSec policies. *see* default IPSec policies
predefined security templates. *see* security templates
Preferred Networks tab, 324–325
pre-shared keys, 255, 282
print servers
configuring, 123
summary of services for, 129
template for, 131–132
printing, 580–587
privacy, 4–5, 261–263
private data, 25
private key pair, 181–184
private keys
file security and, 557
installing CA and, 174
key retrieval/recovery, 157
in PKI process, 154
in public key cryptography, 153
security of, 564–565
privilege use, 481, 538–539
process tracking, 481, 540
Profile Single Process right, 469
Profile System Performance right, 469
profiles, remote access, 657–659
protocols
authentication, 671
Digest Authentication, 650
Kerberos, 646–648
L2TP for VPN access, 433–438
NTLM authentication, 648–650
PPTP for VPNs, 425–433
selecting for clients, 646–647, 652–654
Server 2003 user authentication, 639
SSL/TLS, 650–651
supported by IAS, 663–665
proxy servers, 244, 309
public data, 25
public key
digital certificates hold, 156
installing CA and, 174
in public key cryptography, 153
public key cryptography
described, 153
for digital certificates, 153–154
public key infrastructure (PKI)
architecture of, 155–158, 187–188
basic concepts of, 152–155
certificate distribution, designing, 172–184
with Certificate Services, designing, 186
certification authority implementation, designing, 158–165
design questions, 188–190
designing security for CA servers, 167–171
logical authentication strategy, designing, 165–167
overview of, 152
review of, 319–320
viability of, 344
for wireless network infrastructure, 327
WLAN network infrastructure requirement, 322
public key infrastructure X.509 (PKIX), 155
public key pair, 181–184
Publishing Points ACL, 128
PXE (Pre-Boot eXecution Environment), 603

Q

qualitative loss, 3
quantitative loss, 3
/quiet, 89, 92–93

R

radio frequency (RF), 314, 315–316
RADIUS. *see* Remote Authentication Dial-In User Service
RAID-1, 510
RAID-5, 510
random password generators, 398
rapid-fail protection, 388, 398
RAS. *see* Remote Access Servers
RC4 stream cipher, 329
RDA. *see* Remote Desktop for Administration
RDU (Remote Desktop Users) group, 206
Read permissions, 215
realm trusts, 224–225
real-time protection, 630
record layer, 304
recovery. *see* disaster recovery
recovery agent. *see also* Data Recovery Agent
importing, 624
overview of, 554–555
policy, removing, 579–580
Recovery Console
vs. Automated System Recovery/Emergency Management Console, 621
described, 605
for disaster recovery, 599
overview of, 610
securing, 610–612
recursion, 298
redirection, 121, 294
redundancy, 620
/refreshpolicy, 94
registry
access control strategy overview, 541
access permissions via Group Policy, 546–552
modifications for IAS server performance, 375
objects, permission structure for, 552–553
viewing access permissions, 542–546
Registry Policy, 73
REGKEYS, 89
remote access
conditions, 655–656
of internal resources for clients, 662

overview of, 671, 672–673
permissions, 657
plan overview, 651
policy design, 654–662
profiles, 657–659
selecting method for, 652
selecting protocol for, 652–654
SSL/TLS for, 308
Remote Access Account Lockout, 670, 673
Remote Access Policies, 439–442, 445
Remote Access Servers (RAS)
template for, 132
configuration overview, 125–126
network traffic security, 126
server security, 126
strong authentication, 127
Remote Assistance, 207–208, 238
Remote Authentication Dial-In User Service and Internet Authentication Service (RADIUS/IAS)
authentication process, 320–321
support for 802.1x authentication, 331
for wireless network infrastructure, 328
WLAN network infrastructure requirement, 322
Remote Authentication Dial-In User Service (RADIUS)
authentication, 369–375
described, 400
viability of, 344
IAS and, 662–663, 678
networks switches and, 312
for RAS, 127
Remote Desktop for Administration (RDA)
network security management and, 205–206
Terminal Services and, 202
for terminal servers, 123–124
Remote Desktop Users (RDU) group, 206
Remote Desktop Web Connection, 125
remote management process, 608
removable media, 108
Remove Computer from Docking Station right, 469
renewal of keys, 183–184
renewal, EFS certificates, 565–566
Replace a Process Level Token right, 469
repudiation, 14
request process, security group, 522
Request Security (Optional) filter action, 270–271
Require Security filter action, 271–272
Reset account lockout counter after setting, 479
resource groups, 515, 619
Resource Records, DNS, 302–303
resources
access to, 516–521
group strategy for accessing, 490–495
network, providing access to, 662
restore events, 108
Restore Files and Directories right, 469
restores, 595. *see also* backup
Restricted groups
configuring in Active Directory, 470–472
example of use of, 497, 502
overview of, 69–71
using, 470
Restricted Groups node, 72
Resultant Set of Policies (RSoP)
for IPSec, 281
using, 9–12
reviewing result of, 82–85
retirement, policies, 526
reversible encryption, 475–476
RF (radio frequency), 314, 315–316
rights
assigning, 458–460
for user accounts, 496
user rights assignments, 463–470
RIP. *see* Routing Information Protocol
risk analysis
for data, 509–511
disaster recovery and, 600
implementing, 23
risk management, administrator, 195–196
risks
acceptance, 24–25
assessment for network infrastructure security, 245
define security policies based on, 245–246
to directory services, 457–458
of IIS, 381–383
rogue wireless networks, 317
role-based authorization, 519
roles. *see* server roles
root CA
arrangement of, 159
design considerations, 158, 186
in geographical hierarchy, 162–163
issuing certificates, 187
network trust hierarchy and, 164, 165, 188
in organizational hierarchy, 163–164
PKI design and, 188–189
security for, 167–169
in three-tier CA, 185
root hints, 298
rootsec.inf template, 62–63, 145–146
route filters, 418
router, Server 2003, 411–423
routes, 415–416, 449–450
Routing and Remote Access Services (RRAS)
security, 250
certificate-based authentication and, 451–452
configuring, 412–415
demand dial routing and, 420–423
described, 446
DHCP and, 450
routing design between internal networks, 442
Routing Information Protocol (RIP), 416–419, 447
routing tables, 414–415
routing, demand dial, 420–423
RRAS. *see* Routing and Remote Access Services
RSA, 154
RSoP. *see* Resultant Set of Policies
rules
configuring IPSec policy, 285
filters for, 272
IPSec, 264–265
RunAs function, 223

S

S/MIME, Secure/Multipurpose Internet Mail Extensions
SA (Security Association), 252–256, 286
SAC (Special Administration Console) environment, 605–606, 625
SACL. *see* system access control list
safeguards, 8, 25
SAM (Security Account Manager), 641
scalability, Windows Server 2003 PKI, 161
scheduling priority, 468
scopes, DHCP, 326
scripts, 95–96
SEA (Spokesman Election Algorithm), 315
secedit.exe
described, 51, 140
registry objects permissions and, 552–553
overview of, 138–139
in scripts, 95–96
for settings reset, 139
streaming media servers and, 148
USER_RIGHTS and, 144–145
using, 88–95
secret data, 26
secure boundaries, 243–244
Secure cache against pollution option, 298
secure dynamic updates, 300
Secure Hash Algorithm 1 (SHA1), 190, 253, 254, 304
secure mode, IPSec driver, 279
Secure Shell (SSH), 607
Secure Sockets Layer (SSL)
security certificates, 404
configuring IIS to use, 306–308
in IIS, 356
NNTP security and, 384
Secure Sockets Layer/Transport Layer Security (SSL/TLS)
configuring, 305–308
described, 303–304
firewalls and, 309
pros/cons of, 305

server-gated cryptography and, 386–387
overview of, 650–651
secure templates, 57–59
secure*.inf template
hisec*.inf comparison, 62
IIS 6.0 and, 130–131
modifying, 142
overview of, 57–59
server roles and, 131
SMB signing required in, 309
Secure/Multipurpose Internet Mail Extensions (S/MIME)
for e-mail security, 308, 309
PKI and, 156
securedc.inf template
for domain controllers, 107, 130
Kerberos and, 144
registry objects permissions and, 552
security. *see also* Active Directory security; network infrastructure security
best practices, 8–9, 140
for CA servers, 166–171, 185
deployment with scripts, 95–96
for interoperability, 226–228
logical authentication strategy, 165–167
vs. privacy, 4–5
update infrastructure, designing, 210–217
vs. usability, 6, 141
security access token buffer, 520
Security Account Manager (SAM), 641
Security Association (SA), 252–256, 286
security awareness, 12–13
security boundary, 221
Security Configuration and Analysis snap-in
adding, 64–66
described, 140
function of, 142–143
overview of, 51, 138
registry objects permissions and, 552–553
for review of settings, 85–88
secure*.inf and, 144
Windows NT 4.0 and, 143
Security Configuration Manager. *see* Security Configuration Tool Set
Security Configuration Tool Set
described, 140
overview of, 51–52, 138
Security Configuration Manager and, 142
Security Extensions to Group Policy
described, 140
overview of, 51, 138–139
security groups. *see* groups, security
security incidents, responding to
attack indicators, recognizing, 27
network services, recovering, 31
overview of, 26
response plan, creating, 28–30
Security log
event types, 396–397
Generate Security Audits right and, 467
logon events in, 483
security negotiation, 270–271
Security Parameter Index (SPI), 261, 262
security policies, 245–246. *see also* policies
Security Policy Editor, 205
security principal, 454
Security Template snap-in, 310
adding, 64–66
overview of, 138
secure*.inf template and, 142
security templates
application on domain controllers, 80–82
applying, 141
best practices for, 52–53
configuring, 66–74
and console, saving, 67
defining baseline, 50–52
deployment overview, 75–76
described, 140
incremental, 102
modifying baseline according to server roles, 129–137
overview of, 139
predefined, 140, 141
recommended for server roles, 130–132
secure, overview of, 57–59
SMB signing and, 309–310
security templates, deploying
overview of, 75–76
using Group Policy, 76–80
on DCs, 80–82
result of, 82
using RSoP MMC snap-in, 83–85
using secedit.exe, 88–95
using Security Configuration and Analysis, 85–88
security threats
predicting network, 13–15
recognizing external, 15–21
recognizing internal, 12–13
security updates, 41. *see also* Software Update Services
security*.inf, 55–57
SECURITYPOLICY, 89
segmented namespace, DNS, 296
segmented networks, 313
Selectable Cryptographic Service Provider, 387–388, 407
Selective Authentication, 224, 233
Sequence Number, 261, 262
Server (Request Security) policy
described, 265–266
as high security default policy, 284
properties of, 287, 288
as standard security policy, 284
viewing, 267–269
Server (Require Security) policy, 266
server authentication settings, 60–61
server certificates, 400, 404
Server Message Block (SMB)
signing, 309–312, 346
EFS and, 557
secure*.inf and, 59
server roles
common, 100–101
defining/implementing/securing, 101–102
described, 141
overview of, 99–100
server security, function based
best practices for, 102–106, 141
default settings, reapplying, 56–66
DHCP servers, 120
DNS servers, 120–122
domain controllers configuration, 106–112
down-level clients, configuring, 74–75
file/print/member servers, 123
high-profile servers, 141
IIS role, 112–116
modifying baseline templates according to role, 129–132
multiple OSs and GPMC, 97–98
network infrastructure servers, 118–119
overview of, 50
policy settings, reviewing result of, 82–85
POP3 mail servers configuration, 116–118
RAS servers, 125–127
security application across enterprise, 132–137
security deployment with scripts, 95–96
security settings review, 85–88
Server 2003 templates, 53–56
server roles, 99–102
streaming media servers, 128
template application on domain controllers, 80–82
template deployment overview, 75–76
templates, best practices for, 52–53
templates, configuring, 66–74
templates, defining baseline, 50–52
terminal servers, 123–125
using Group Policy to deploy settings, 76–80
using secedit.exe, 88–95
WINS servers, 122–123
server setting, SMB signing, 310–312
Server-Gated Cryptography (SGC), 386–387
servers
headless, 607
IIS, risks to/hardening, 381–383
security of, 501–502
SUS, 213–214
service accounts, 460–461, 497
Service Administrators, 487, 497
service processor, 604, 610
service ticket, 472
SERVICES, 89
services, clients, 629–630, 672
session ticket, 472
settings, security

deploying with Group Policy, 76–80
reapplying default, 56–66
review of, 85–88
Setup security.inf template
described, 140
IIS 6.0 and, 130
overview of, 55–56, 139
server roles and, 131
SGC (Server-Gated Cryptography), 386–387
SHA1. *see* Secure Hash Algorithm 1
share permissions, 455–456, 496
shared key authentication, 328
Shiva Password Authentication Protocol (SPAP), 653
shortcut trusts, 225–226, 234–235, 236
Shut Down the System right, 469
shut down, CA server, 168
shutdown, 467
signature algorithm, 154
Simple Mail Transport Protocol (SMTP), 116, 385
single namespace, 295
single-session policy, 206
Single Sign-on, 640, 643
smart cards
for CA authentication strategy, 166
for CA security, 171, 185
enterprise CAs and, 160
wireless network authentication and, 348
SMB. *see* Server Message Block
SMS (Systems Management Server), 216, 633–634
SMTP (Simple Mail Transport Protocol), 116, 385
sniffer attack, 248
social engineering attacks, 20, 43–44, 196, 248–249
software
GPOs for deployment of, 213–215
of network infrastructure, 243
restriction policies for Terminal Services, 206
for security updates, 211–213
vulnerabilities, network security threats and, 19–20
Software Update Services (SUS)
application updates and, 673
design overview, 210–211, 232
identifying non-current clients, 215–217
for patch management, 632–633
rebooting and, 236
server requirements, 674
vs. SMS, 634
for software, 211–213
for software, using GPOs for deployment, 213–215
Solicited Remote Assistance, 207
SPAP (Shiva Password Authentication Protocol), 653
Special Administration Console (SAC) environment, 605–606, 625
special identities, 512
SPI (Security Parameter Index), 261, 262
Spokesman Election Algorithm (SEA), 315
spoofing
identity described, 14
recognizing indicators of, 41
threat to wireless networks, 317
SQL access, 308
SSH (Secure Shell), 607
SSL. *see* Secure Sockets Layer
SSL/TLS. *see* Secure Socket Layer/Transport Layer Security
stand-alone CAs
certificate template in, 188
certificates and, 160
issue certificates, 186
as root CA, 168
scalability of, 161
securing, 170–171
defining, 158
standard security policies
based on risk, 245–246
when to use, 284
startrom.com, 605
startup and recovery options
disaster recovery and, 600
for safeguarding data, 591, 592
startup options, 612–614
stateful filtering, 282
stateful mode, 279
static routes, 415–416
Store passwords using reversible encryption setting, 475–476
Streaming Media servers
configuring, 128
and internal users, 148
summary of services for, 129
template for, 132
STRIDE, 14–15
striped set with parity. *see* RAID-5
strong authentication, RAS, 127
sub-authentication component, 364, 404
subordinate CA, 159
summarization routes, 415–416, 449–450
SUS. *see* Software Update Services (SUS)
switches, 312
symmetric encryption, 153
symmetric keys, 304
SYN flood, 15
/sync, 95
Synchronize Directory Service Data right, 469
Syskey utility, 634–637
system access control list (SACL)
described, 513
auditing setting for, 481
vs. DACL, 619
object access events and, 539
system clock, 465, 472
system events auditing, 481, 539
System log, 396
System Management Server (SMS), 216, 633–634
system root security template, 62–63
System Services Policies, 72
system state, 594

T

tables, routing, 414–415
Take Ownership of Files or Other Objects right, 470
tampering with data, 14
Task Scheduler, 465
TCP ports, 290–291
technical constraints analysis
existing infrastructure capabilities, 32–34
overview of, 31–32, 40–41
technology limitations, identifying, 34
technical policies, 4
technology limitations, 34
Telnet, 208
templates, baseline, 129–132
templates, security. *see* security templates
terminal concentrators, 607
Terminal Servers
configuring, 123–125
network security management and, 201–204
to remotely manage IPSec, 283
securing, 147
summary of services for, 129
template for, 132
Terminal Services (TS)
IAS access and, 374
Audit logon events policy and, 483
user rights assignments and, 464, 465, 467
text-mode setup, 605
third-party encryption, 588, 620
third-party tools for patch management, 216–217, 633–634, 676
threat prediction, 13–26
threats
against CA servers, 167–169, 185
common types of attacks, 247–249
to DNS servers, 294–295
to domain controllers, 107–108
password-based attack, 344
to wireless networks, 317–318
three-tier CA model
described, 185
described/examples of, 162–165
securing enterprise hierarchy, 169–170
tickets, Kerberos, 647–648
time limit, account usage, 166
timestamps, 648
token object, 466
tokens, access, 466, 520, 525
tools. *see also* command-line tools
administrative, securing, 200, 231
MMC, 201
for patch management, 216–217
Remote Assistance, 207–208
Remote Desktop for Administration, 205–206

for securing administrators, 197–199
Syskey utility, 634–635
Telnet, 208
Terminal Server, 201–204
third-party for patch management, 633–634, 676
traffic, authentication, 110–111
transference, risk, 24, 45
transitive trust, 217, 219–222
Transport Layer Security (TLS). *see also* Secure Sockets Layer/Transport Layer Security
PKI and, 156
uses HMAC, 304
transport mode
with Authentication Header, 257
described, 256
with ESP, 258
ESP in, 261
IP packet with AH in, 260
Triple Data Encryption Standard (3DES)
described, 253
EFS and, 558
L2TP and, 438
trojan horses, 18–19, 44
trust hierarchies
geographical, 162–163
network, 164–165
organizational, 163–164
three-tier CA, 162
trust relationships
designing, 232–233
digest authentication and, 367
between domains/forests, overview of, 217–221
forest/domain functionality, 229–230
forest/domain models for, 221–226
security for interoperability in, 226–228
Trusted for delegation setting, 467
trusts
PKI system dependent, 152
security of, 500
Windows Server 2003 upgrade and, 500
TS. *see* Terminal Servers
tunnel mode
with Authentication Header, 258
described, 256–257
with ESP, 259
ESP in, 261, 262
IP packet with AH in, 261
tunnels, 423–425, 446
two-way trust, 219–221

U

U.S. Privacy Act of 1974, 5
UDP ports, 290–292
Uninterruptible Power Supply (UPS), 607–608
Universal groups
described, 516
function of, 491
nesting, 493
in permission structure, 491–492, 493, 498
UNIX, 677
UNIX Berkeley Internet Name Domain (BIND) DNS implementation, 37–38
UNIX Berkeley Internet Name Domain (BIND) servers, 47
UNIX DNS, 37–38
unnumbered connections, 421–422
unsecured communication, 283
updates. *see also* Software Update Services; patch management
auto-static for routing tables, 416
critical security, 41
IIS and, 399
UPS Uninterruptible Power Supply (UPS), 607–608
URL authorization, ASP.NET, 389
URLScan, 114–116
usability
network security and, 244–247
vs. security, 6, 141
Use Add Wizard, 288
user accounts
account security policies, 463–474
auditing user account activity, 480–486
management plan, 165
rights/permissions, 496
risks to, 457–458
security of, 454
user password tips, 476–477
user rights assignments, 463–470
user authentication. *see* authentication
user rights, 463–470, 513
user ticket, 472
User/ACL, 516–517
USER_RIGHTS, 89, 144–145
user-based authentication, Wi-Fi, 334
username, 457
users. *see also* clients
accounts, securing, 645–646
default for DNS RRs in Active Directory, 302–303
default for DNS Server Service, 299
default in AD-Integrated zones, 300–301
EFS and, 571–574
restricting access to OS features, 637–639
securing access for, 615

V

Vadasz, Les, 318
/validate, 93
vectors, attack, 629–630
VeriSign
certificates, 152
overview of, 356
as reputable CA, 154
Victim computer, 16–17
virtual interface, 421
virtual local area network (VLAN), 312
Virtual Private Networks (VPNs)
NT 4.0 and, 34
connections costs, 652
connectivity design overview, 423–425
connectivity overview, 446
DNS and, 451
extranet infrastructure design, 443
IAS and, 665
L2TP in, 433–438
PPTP in, 425–433
protocols overview, 425
Remote Access Policies and, 439–442
remote access with, 445
routing design between internal networks, 442
securing, overview of, 410
security *vs.* dial-up, 447
Server 2003 features, 438–439
tunnels, 446
viruses
clients and, 630, 672
Network Access Quarantine Control and, 670
overview of, 18–19
risk analysis and, 510–511
VLAN (virtual local area network), 312
volume shadow copy, 595

W

W3C log file, 390–391
/wait:, 95
WAPs. *see* wireless access points
wardriving, 315
Web Distributed Authoring and Versioning (WebDAV), 386
Web Enrollment Support System, 166
Web Folders. *see* Web Distributed Authoring and Versioning
Web Server Certificate Wizard, 305
Web servers, patching, 237
Web Service Extensions, 377
Web sites
for Gravity Storm Software Service Pack Manager 2000, 216–217
for HP OpenView, 216
IANA list of TCP/UDP ports, 290
IEEE, 316
for incremental policies, 102
for NetIQ Security Manager, 216
for Network Access Quarantine Control, 674
Passport Authentication and, 642–645
for security access token buffer, 520
for Server 2003 snap-ins, 65
for URLScan/IISLockdown, 114
WEP. *see* Wired Equivalent Privacy
Wi-Fi Protected Access (WPA), 316
Windows, 604–605
Windows 2000
domain/forest functional levels, 494–495
Mixed mode, 494
Native mode, 495
Windows 2000 templates, 54

Windows Components Wizard, 172–176
Windows Internet Naming Service (WINS), 250
Windows Internet Naming Service (WINS) servers
  configuring, 122–123
  IPSec and, 146–147
  summary of services for, 129
Windows logon authentication
  basic, 364–365
  described, 400
  digest, 366–367
  integrated Windows authentication, 367–369
  overview of, 362–364
Windows Media servers, 128
Windows NT 4.0, 57–58, 107
  logon security and, 34
  VPNs and, 34
  Windows Server 2003 upgrade and trusts, 500
  Security Configuration and Analysis snap-in and, 143
  SUS and, 212, 633
  trust relationships and, 226, 234
Windows Server 2003
  anonymous access in, 109–110
  control strategy of, 455
  DNS and BIND servers, 47
  domain/forest functional levels, 229–230, 494–495
  domain functional levels, 227–228, 495, 500
  EFS features of, 558–560
  file encryption and, 556
  hardware requirements for, 32–33
  implementing EFS on, 560–563
  improvements to network security in, 339
  installing CA on, 172–176
  integrating UNIX DNS with, 37–38
  IPSec changes in, 280–283
  as KDC for MIT Kerberos, 35–37
  Kerberos and, 646–648
  NAT traversal and, 654
  new CA features of, 190
  RADIUS clients/servers and, 663
  remote access and, 672
  remote connectivity with, 410
  role-based administration in, 195
  as router, 411–423
  routing protocols and, 445
  security templates, 53–56
  server roles, 139–140, 141
  Terminal Services and, 205
  UNIX and, 677
  VPN protocols and, 433
  VPNs and, 438–439
Windows Server 2003 Interim level, 495
Windows Server 2003 Resource Kit, 486
Winnt32.exe, 610
WINS. *see* Windows Internet Naming Service
Wired Equivalent Privacy (WEP)
  encryption for wireless networks, 329
  flaws/threat/countermeasures, 335–336
  reasons to use, 343–344
  security provided by, 316
  in wireless network policy creation, 325
wireless access, 669
wireless access infrastructure, 336–338
wireless access points (WAPs)
  IAS and, 669
  wireless network authentication and, 331
  for WLAN, 314
wireless access policies, 337
wireless local area networks (WLANs)
  described, 314
  wireless networks, authentication for, 328–336
  network infrastructure, designing, 321–328
  security, 349
  threats to, 317–318
  for wireless access infrastructure, 337–338
wireless metropolitan area networks (WMANs), 314
wireless network infrastructure, 347
wireless network policy, 322–326
wireless networks
  accidental connection to, 343
  authentication for, 328–336
  PKI and RADIUS/IAS, 319–321
  security, designing, 313, 341–342, 347–348
  security of, 242
  summary of, 339–340
  threats to, 317–318
  types of, 314
  wireless access infrastructure, 336–338
  wireless history, 315–316
  WLAN network infrastructure, 321–328
wireless personal area networks (WPANs), 314
wireless wide area networks (WWANs), 314
WLANs. *see* wireless local area networks
WMANs (wireless metropolitan area networks), 314
worker process
  vs. IIS 5.0 isolation mode, 354–355
  IIS 6.0, 353, 388, 401
workstations. *see also* clients
  Add Workstations to the Domain right, 464
  templates application with Group Policy Editor, 77–80
World Wide Web (WWW), 559
worms
  clients and, 630, 672
  overview of, 18–19
  risk analysis and, 510–511
WPA (Wi-Fi Protected Access), 316

X

x-86-based systems, 603

Z

Zombie computer, 16–17
zone delegation, 302
zone transfers, 301
zones, DNS, 300–302, 327